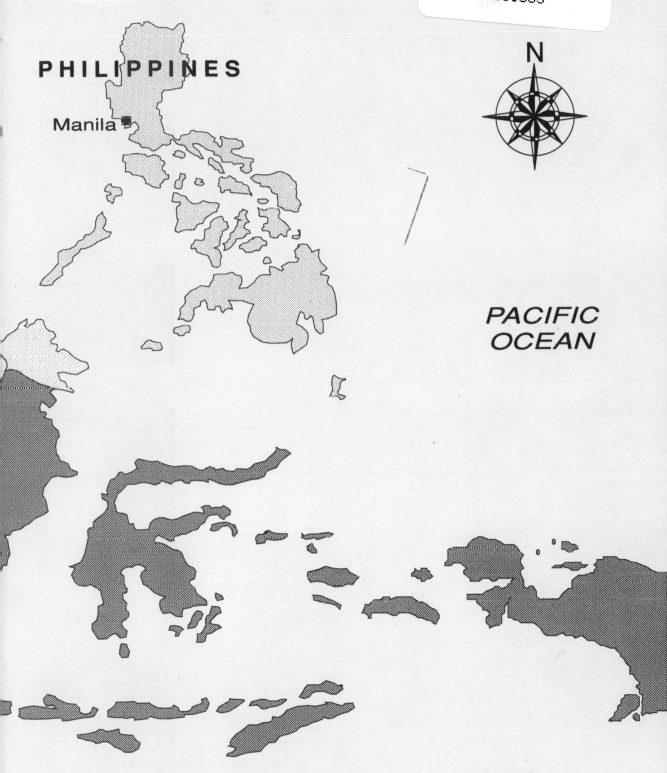

PHILIPPINES

Manila

N

*PACIFIC
OCEAN*

, and Thailand.

AUSTRALIA

THE
ASEAN READER

THE
ASEAN READER

compiled by
K.S. Sandhu, Sharon Siddique,
Chandran Jeshurun, Ananda Rajah,
Joseph L.H. Tan, Pushpa Thambipillai

 Institute of Southeast Asian Studies

Front Cover. The flags of each of the six ASEAN member countries are shown on the cover. From the top left-hand corner, clockwise, are the flags of Indonesia, the Philippines, Thailand, Singapore, Malaysia, and Brunei Darussalam.

Published in Singapore in 1992 by
Institute of Southeast Asian Studies
30 Heng Mui Keng Terrace
Pasir Panjang
Singapore 119614
Internet e-mail: publish@iseas.edu.sg
World Wide Web: http://bookshop.iseas.edu.sg

Cataloguing in Publication Data

The ASEAN reader/compiled by K.S. Sandhu, Sharon Siddique . . . [et al.].
   1. ASEAN.
   2. Regionalism—Asia, Southeastern.
   3. ASEAN countries—Politics and government.
   4. ASEAN countries—Economic integration.
   5. ASEAN countries—Social conditions.
   I.   Sandhu, Kernial Singh.
   II. Siddique, Sharon.
JX1979 A854   1992   sls92-91464

ISBN 981-3016-41-8 (soft cover)
ISBN 981-3016-42-6 (hard cover)

The responsibility for facts and opinions expressed in this publication
rests exclusively with the authors and their interpretations do not
necessarily reflect the views or the policy of the Institute or its supporters.

Typeset by The Fototype Business
Printed in Singapore by Markono Digital Solutions Pte Ltd.

CONTENTS

SECTION III: THE POLITICS OF ASEAN

SECTION IV: SOCIAL AND CULTURAL ISSUES IN ASEAN

SECTION V: ECONOMIC CO-OPERATION: STOCKTAKING, ISSUES, AND TRENDS

SECTION VI: INTRA-ASEAN ECONOMIC CO-OPERATION

SECTION VII: ASEAN EXTERNAL ECONOMIC RELATIONS

SECTION VIII: DEFENCE AND SECURITY

PREFACE TO THE REPRINT EDITION

This volume was originally compiled to commemorate the first twenty-five years of ASEAN. Nineteen ninety-two was an upbeat year, and this volume reflects this optimism. The ASEAN Six (Brunei Darussalam, Indonesia, Malaysia, Philippines, Singapore, Thailand) were continuing to enjoy positive annual growth rates, trade expansion, and a relatively smooth economic restructuring process. AFTA had just been launched, and the decision had been taken to strengthen the ASEAN Secretariat.

With the sweeping events in the past decade (1992–2002) — ASEAN expansion, the establishment of the ARF, the stunning emergence of China as a major power, and the impact of 9/11 and more recently, SARS — one can be forgiven for concluding that the only constant appears to have been change. And yet, this assumption needs to be examined carefully. Re-reading the selections in this volume, one is forcefully reminded that there have been continuities as well.

The late Professor K. S. Sandhu, who penned the original Preface, was prescient indeed when he wrote: "ASEAN was not founded to promote economic co-operation or political integration ... but rather to promote *stability* and *security*." This volume allows students of the twenty-first century to appreciate the constants underpinning ASEAN as an organization, and as a vision for the future of the region. Thus, even though the events described in this Reader have been consigned to history, the lessons which can be drawn from a critical analysis of them will prove invaluable cues to future actors on the ASEAN stage.

To further assist in promoting knowledge of ASEAN as a region, ISEAS will be publishing *The Second ASEAN Reader*. This second volume will focus primarily on the past decade of change (1992–2002), and include a comprehensive analysis of the stages of ASEAN's expansion from six to ten members (with the inclusion of Cambodia, Laos, Myanmar, and Vietnam), the 1997 Asian economic crisis, and ASEAN's revamped bilateral and multilateral relationships with the rest of the world. To again quote the late Professor K. S. Sandhu, "If past experience is anything to go by, then the ASEAN countries ... have weathered uncertainties and international shocks better than many other parts of the world". How true!

October 2003

PREFACE

The Association of Southeast Asian Nations, or ASEAN for short, consisting of Brunei Darussalam, Indonesia, Malaysia, the Philippines, Singapore and Thailand, celebrated its 25th anniversary in 1992, having been formally inaugurated on 8 August 1967 with the signing of the Bangkok Declaration. Despite the fact that it has been around this long — that is, only ten years less than the EC — ASEAN's progress and performance to date continue to evoke quite different reactions amongst different peoples. Thus, to some, ASEAN still does not amount to anything much more than rhetoric — a mere talking shop; to others, ASEAN is the veritable panacea to the region's problems — the magic wand that will bring abundance and good cheer to all. Needless to say, the reality lies somewhere in between such extremes. Some aspects of this reality are becoming fairly clear. For instance, that ASEAN is going to be around for quite some time is no longer in doubt. Likewise, the benefits that ASEAN can provide through regional co-operation are no more issues of debate. After all, ASEAN is about the size of India in area, is the home of about the same number of people as inhabit the whole of Western Europe, and is a world leader in the production of a number of tropical products like rubber, copra, and palm oil, as well as substantial quantities of minerals and manufactures, particularly electronics and computer parts and peripherals. Moreover, for all their failings and weaknesses, the various ruling power groups in the region — as distinct from any particular cabinets of the day — are firmly in control of their respective countries, and the pace of development in the area is such as to make ASEAN one of the fastest growing parts of the world in the 1990s.

Nevertheless, one may be tempted to say that all this sounds well and good, but in reality what has ASEAN, *as an organization*, achieved in terms of, for example, encouraging economic co-operation and integration amongst its members? Its record here is hardly inspiring, bearing in mind that intra-ASEAN trade has generally failed to reach 20 per cent of the total overall regional trade over the last two and a half decades. The promotion of national interests has continued to be the order of the day. Indeed, it is not too long ago when civil servants were rumoured to be spending considerable energies in devising "the giving away" of tariff concessions on imaginary regional trade items like snowploughs and samurai swords.

However, to judge the achievements and performance of ASEAN on such criteria as the foregoing is largely to misunderstand the objectives and goals of the Association. Why? Because ASEAN was not founded to promote economic co-operation or political integration *à la* European Community, or any other similar organization, but rather to promote *stability* and *security*. And this it has done remarkably well, despite its member countries being politically relatively young, intensely nationalistic, and until recently mutually suspicious of, if not actually antagonistic towards, one another. Can we think of any other group of five or six Third World countries that have not fired a shot in anger across their borders at each other over a quarter of a century? (The five founder members of ASEAN in 1967 did not include Brunei Darussalam which joined the Association only in January 1984 when it gained independence.)

This relative peace and quiet has allowed political leaders, civil servants, and business executives to come to know and interact with one another on a close, first-name basis, in the process fostering a uniquely ASEAN non-legalistic, consensual, low-key, pragmatic, approach to problems and settling issues. In other words, over the years, there has developed a philosophy and *modus operandi* that is both practical and eclectic, long-term based yet rooted in prevailing realities, and finally one that seeks to build upon existing structures and strengths rather than inventing new ones. Equally, if not most importantly, the resulting stability and security has allowed market forces to operate and these, together with generally outward-looking and development-oriented economic policies, have seen the region grow by leaps and bounds. Indeed, the region's economic and social dynamism is almost palpable, with whole societies and peoples on the move — a situation often likened to the proverbial Rip Van Winkle waking up from a hundred-year-long sleep, and wanting to make up in 10–20 years what it normally takes nations 100–200 years to achieve. In the process, enormous energies are being released; ambitions are being multiplied overnight. This startling pace of change reverberates even more when combined with developments in neighbouring places like China, Hong Kong, Taiwan, Korea, and elsewhere in Asia. Thus, within the next 10 to 20 years the combined GDPs of ASEAN, the Asian NIEs,

and Japan are expected to equal and eventually surpass those of Europe and the Americas, setting ASEAN well on the road to becoming both a gateway to, and a hub in, a grid of vibrant economies and trading networks.

Striking though these quantitative transformations are, their qualitative nuances are even more profound. For instance, the structure of Indonesia's exports has altered beyond recognition in less than ten years, in that compared to 1982/83 when oil comprised about 80 per cent of the country's export earnings, some two-thirds of such earnings today come from non-oil items, with manufactured goods accounting for almost 80 per cent of these! The move up the economic ladder in several of the other ASEAN countries is even more astounding: rather than being satisfied with being assembly lines for MNC operations, they are becoming innovators and state-of-the art producers of sophisticated goods in their own right. Looking ahead, they are seeking to become fully computerized societies. Towards this end, an information technology plan envisions that within fifteen years Singapore, for example, will be an "intelligent island", with every home, office, school, and factory connected via computers that hook into telephones and television sets.

Paralleling such developments is a massive revamping and upgrading of education and human skills, together with the growth and the spread of a "business" culture right across ASEAN societies. Concepts and notions of financial management, productivity, value for money, accountability, and so on, are becoming part and parcel of everyday household vocabularies and practices. This in turn is reflected, among other things, in the ASEAN societies today being amongst the world's largest savers — averaging gross domestic savings rates of some 30 per cent, compared to the approximately 16 and 20 per cent in the United States and Europe respectively. This has given the ASEAN countries an estimated investment capital base of some US$300 billion, quite apart from making it an attractive world-class market for a growing number of products and economic activities. Opportunities in the construction industry alone are presently estimated to be worth US$350 billion. If these are extended to include China, the NIEs and Japan, the estimated figure reaches a staggering US$2 to US$3 trillion.

ASEAN's growing wealth and economic buoyancy quite naturally are generating greater confidence in the region and amongst its peoples. This is also leading to a re-assessment of the potentialities of intra-ASEAN economic co-operation, particularly as the impulses for such co-operation are now being driven not so much by diplomatic niceties or political considerations, but more by market forces and intra- and inter-firm commercial requirements. These trends are not only witnessing a mushrooming of business across borders in geographically contiguous areas, as for example, in the Growth Triangle linking Johor (Malaysia), Riau (Indonesia) and Singapore, but in January 1992 actually saw ASEAN taking the decision to create an ASEAN Free Trade Area, or AFTA, within fifteen years.

To facilitate this new realism and integration, moves are afoot to restructure the ASEAN administrative machinery, as well as to create an *ASEAN-minded* body of regular or permanent officials, to replace the current practice of nationals being assigned for ASEAN duties on a temporary basis. These moves towards greater economic co-operation and a strengthening of the ASEAN bureaucracy and decision-making processes will not, of course, overnight result in ASEAN producing its own versions of Jean Monets or Jacques Delores or an "ASEAN Single Market" along the lines of Europe, but they are nevertheless significant steps — certainly initiatives which would have been unthinkable a few years ago.

The growing camaraderie among the ASEAN nations, together with the increasing convergence of interests, has also seen ASEAN assuming a larger and more important role in regional and international political and security affairs. Thus, having successfully withstood and

weathered the Vietnamese invasion of Cambodia and its aftermath, including totally reversing the so-called "falling dominoes theory", ASEAN rapidly moved to convert its Post-Ministerial Conference with its Dialogue Partners into a forum for the discussion of not merely the usual bilateral matters, but of larger security concerns as well, with perhaps a benchmark being reached in July 1992 when ASEAN issued a joint statement calling upon China to show restraint in pressing its claims over the Spratly Islands. If any further indication of ASEAN's growing political and economic stature was needed then this was amply supplied by the fact that not only was the region chosen as the site for the Asia-Pacific Economic Cooperation, or APEC, Secretariat, to be based in Singapore, but the Association is also being actively courted by countries ranging from India and Vietnam to Chile and Mexico. There is even talk of a formal linkage between NAFTA, or the North American Free Trade Agreement, and AFTA.

In short, ASEAN's potentialities and prospects are numerous and compelling. True, they could be upset if, for instance, a major catastrophe were to shake up the international economic system, or if ASEAN's main trading partners like Japan, the United States and the EC were unable to come out of their present doldrums, or if the GATT talks were to collapse, or on account of some other similar major catastrophe. Although such imponderables and dangers are real, they nevertheless have to be set in context. If past experience is anything to go by, then the ASEAN countries, like their East Asian cohorts, have weathered uncertainties and international shocks better than many other parts of the world. Indeed, they have time and again confounded their critics by their resilience and ability to adapt rapidly to changing demands, even to the extent of often turning adversity to advantage.

The development of ISEAS has in a way paralleled that of ASEAN, in that over the years the Institute has steadily consolidated its gains and constantly fine-tuned its research activities to encompass the whole of Southeast Asia, as well as all its principal international linkages, including the United States, Japan, and Europe, which interact with and impact on the region and its long-term well-being.

THE ASEAN READER is a selection of research material on ASEAN carefully culled and arranged by a multi-disciplinary team of ISEAS researchers from the thousands of pieces of scholarly research which have been published in ASEAN over the past 25 years. As ISEAS itself has been a leader in the promotion of research and publications as well as in the development of significant library resources on ASEAN, it was quite natural that substantial portion of the entries contained in THE ASEAN READER have been drawn from ISEAS' own extensive publications.

THE ASEAN READER is divided into ten sections. Sections 1 and 10 provide an overview of the past and speculations on the future. Section 2 is devoted to the origins and organizational structure of ASEAN. Four of the sections (3, 7 and 9) deal with politics, international relations, defence and security issues, while another three (5, 6 and 7) concentrate on economic themes. Section 4 sets out ASEAN social and cultural issues.

Each of the foregoing is preceded by a short introduction, written by the compiler of that section. Every effort has been made to ensure a balance between the disciplinary and thematic aspects of the life and times of ASEAN; likewise, in terms of the right mix of Asian and Western presentations. In doing so, while every care has been taken to include all the leading scholars of ASEAN studies, it has, of course, not been possible to accommodate each and every one of those who have over the years written on ASEAN.

As the materials contained in the READER have come from a variety of publications, incorporating a wide range of styles and formats, editorial control has been particularly taxing as, among other tasks, superscripts and notes have had to be renumbered. We have diligently sought to avoid the introduction of new errors, and to reproduce the published originals accurately. Similarly, Addenda notes have only been added when considered absolutely essential.

The compilers have also put together a bibliography that in itself will serve as a useful reference tool. It does not, nevertheless, pretend to be exhaustive. It comprises all references cited in the various sections, as well as significant research completed during the past few years. Complementing the bibliography are brief biographical notes on the contributors.

We are indeed grateful that two of the original signatories to the 1967 ASEAN Declaration — senior statesmen Mr Thanat Khoman and Mr S. Rajaratnam (then Foreign Ministers of Thailand and Singapore, respectively) — graciously accepted our invitation to write a foreword each for this volume. In fact, these serve more than a mere foreword: they are both insightful, reflective pieces from unique perspectives.

Last but not least, we would like to thank the Konrad Adenauer Foundation for the generous grant which made this publication possible.

K.S. Sandhu
Director
Institute of Southeast Asian Studies

ASEAN
Conception and Evolution

THANAT KHOMAN

On 8 August 1967 the "Bangkok Declaration" gave birth to ASEAN, the Association of Southeast Asian Nations, an organization that would unite five countries in a joint effort to promote economic co-operation and the welfare of their peoples.

After repeated unsuccessful attempts in the past, this event was a unique achievement, ending the separation and aloofness of the countries of this region that had resulted from colonial times when they were forced by the colonial masters to live in *cloisons etanches*, shunning contact with the neighbouring countries.

In effect this historical event represented the culmination of the decolonization process that had started after World War II. Following their victory in the war, the colonial powers tried their best to maintain the status quo. However, since they had not even been able to ensure the protection of their territories against the Japanese invasion, how could they justify their claim to control them again. In their defeat, the Japanese had effectively undermined colonial rule by granting some form of autonomy or even independence to the territories they had earlier invaded, thus sowing the seeds of freedom from the colonial masters. The process of decolonization, inside and outside the United Nations, then advanced at a fast pace and led to the emergence of a number of independent and sovereign nations.

This created an entirely novel situation which necessitated new measures and structures. Thailand, as the only nation which had been spared the plight of colonial subjection thanks to the wisdom and political skill of its Monarchs, felt it a duty to deal with the new contingencies. Pridi Panomyong, a former Prime Minister and statesman, tried to promote new relationships and co-operation within the region. I, myself, posted as the first Thai diplomat in the newly independent India, wrote a few articles advocating some form of regional co-operation in Southeast Asia. But the time was not yet propitious. The world was then divided by the Cold War into two rival camps vying for domination over the other, leading the newly emerging states to adopt a non-aligned stance.

When, as Foreign Minister, I was entrusted with the responsibility of Thailand's foreign relations, I paid visits to neighbouring countries to forge co-operative relationships in Southeast Asia. The results were, however, depressingly negative. Only an embryonic organization, ASA or the Association of Southeast Asia, grouping Malaysia, the Philippines, and Thailand could be set up. This took place in 1961. It was, nevertheless, the first organization for regional co-operation in Southeast Asia.

But why did this region need an organization for co-operation?

The reasons were numerous. The most important of them was the fact that, with the withdrawal of the colonial powers, there would have been a power vacuum which could have attracted outsiders to step in for political gains. As the colonial masters had discouraged any form of intra-regional contact, the idea of neighbours working together in a joint effort was thus to be encouraged.

Secondly, as many of us knew from experience, especially with the Southeast Asia Treaty Organization or SEATO, co-operation among disparate members located in distant lands could be ineffective. We had therefore to strive to build co-operation among those who lived close to one another and shared common interests.

Thirdly, the need to join forces became imperative for the Southeast Asian countries in order to be heard and to be effective. This was the truth that we sadly had to learn. The motivation for our efforts to band together was thus to strengthen our position and protect ourselves against Big Power rivalry.

Finally, it is common knowledge that co-operation and ultimately integration serve the interests of all — something that individual efforts can never achieve.

However, co-operation is easier said than done.

Soon after its establishment in 1961, ASA or the Association of Southeast Asia, the mini organization comprising only three members, ran into a snag. A territorial dispute, relating to a colonial legacy, erupted between the Philippines and Indonesia on the one hand and Malaysia on the other. The dispute centred on the fact that the British Administration, upon withdrawal from North Borneo (Sabah), had attributed jurisdiction of the territory to Malaysia. The *konfrontasi*, as the Indonesians called it, threatened to boil over into an international conflict as Malaysia asked its ally, Great Britain, to come to its support and British warships began to cruise along the coast of Sumatra. That unexpected turn of events caused the collapse of the fledgling ASA.

While ASA was paralysed by the dispute on Sabah, efforts continued to be made in Bangkok for the creation of another organization.

Thus in 1966 a larger grouping, with East Asian nations like Japan and South Korea as well as Malaysia, the Philippines, Australia, Taiwan, New Zealand, South Vietnam and Thailand, was established and known as ASPAC or the Asian and Pacific Council.

However, once again, calamity struck. ASPAC was afflicted by the vagaries of international politics. The admission of the People's Republic of China and the eviction of the Republic of China or Taiwan made it impossible for some of the Council's members to sit at the same conference table. ASPAC consequently folded up in 1975, marking another failure in regional co-operation.

With this new misfortune, Thailand, which had remained neutral in the Sabah dispute, turned its attention to the problem brewing to its south and took on a conciliatory role in the dispute. At the time, I had to ply between Jakarta, Manila, and Kuala Lumpur. After many attempts, our efforts paid off. Preferring Bangkok to Tokyo, the antagonists came to our capital city to effect their reconciliation.

At the banquet marking the reconciliation between the three disputants, I broached the idea of forming another organization for regional co-operation with Adam Malik, then Deputy Prime Minister and Foreign Minister of Indonesia, the largest country of Southeast Asia. Malik agreed without hesitation but asked for time to talk with the powerful military circle of his government and also to normalize relations with Malaysia now that the confrontation was over. Meanwhile, the Thai Foreign Office prepared a draft charter of the new institution. Within a few months, everything was ready. I therefore invited the two former ASA members, Malaysia and the Philippines, and Indonesia, a key member, to a meeting in Bangkok. In addition, Singapore sent S. Rajaratnam, then Foreign Minister, to see me about joining the new set-up. Although the new organization was planned to comprise only the former ASA members plus Indonesia, Singapore's request was favourably considered.

The first formal meeting of representatives

from the five countries — Indonesia, Malaysia, the Philippines, Singapore, and Thailand — was held in the Thai Ministry of Foreign Affairs. The group then retired to the seaside resort of Bangsaen (Pattaya did not exist at that time) where, combining work with leisure — golf to be more exact — the ASEAN charter was worked out. After a couple of days, using the Foreign Office draft as the basis, the Charter was ready. The participants returned to Bangkok for final approval of the draft, and on 8 August 1967, the Bangkok Declaration gave birth to ASEAN — the Association of Southeast Asian Nations. (ASEAN owes its name to Adam Malik, master in coining acronyms.)

The formation of ASEAN, the first successful attempt at forging regional co-operation, was actually inspired and guided by past events in many areas of the world including Southeast Asia itself. The fact that the Western powers, France and Britain, reneged on their pacts with Poland and Czechoslovakia promising protection against external aggression, was instrumental in drawing the attention of many countries to the credibility of assurances advanced by larger powers to smaller partners. The lesson drawn from such events encouraged weak nations to rely more on neighbourly mutual support than on stronger states that serve their own national interests rather than those of smaller partners. For Thailand, in particular, its disappointing experience with SEATO taught it the lesson that it was useless and even dangerous to hitch its destiny to distant powers who may cut loose at any moment their ties and obligations with lesser and distant allies.

Another principle to which we anchored our faith was that our co-operation should deal with non-military matters. Attempts were made by some to launch us on the path of forming a military alliance. We resisted; wisely and correctly we stuck to our resolve to exclude military entanglement and remain safely on economic ground.

It should be put on record that, for many of us and for me in particular, our model has been and still is, the European Community, not because I was trained there, but because it is the most suitable form for us living in this part of the world — in spite of our parallel economies which are quite different from the European ones.

However, although we had clearly defined our aims and aspirations, international realities forced ASEAN to deviate from its original path. Several developments began to preoccupy ASEAN: the defeat and withdrawal of the United States from Vietnam and even from the mainland of Asia; the growing Vietnamese ambitions nurtured by the heady wine of victory; and the threat of Ho Chi Minh's testament enjoining generations of Vietnamese to take over the rest of French Indochina in addition to the northeastern provinces of Thailand. Such developments forced ASEAN to turn its attention to more critical issues, like Cambodia, with the result that economic matters were almost entirely neglected and set aside.

Although not the original plan or intention of the founders of ASEAN, the effective and successful opposition to the implementation of Vietnam's Grand Design, using only diplomatic and political means, won a great deal of plaudits and international credit, lifting it from an insignificant grouping of small countries to a much courted organization with which more important states now seek to have contact and dialogue. This has not been a negligible result. Indeed, ASEAN has greatly benefited from its deviated performance. ASEAN has now become a well established international fixture.

While applauding the successes of the Association, it is not my intention to pass over its weaknesses and shortcomings.

In the first place, the partnership spirit is not fully developed. Some parties seek to take more than to give even if in choosing the latter course, they may be able to take much more later on. Indeed, some of them do not hesitate to reduce their allotted share in projects, which, in their opinion, would not immediately bring the highest return, and thus they leave the burden to other members. In fact, it is common practice at many meetings, to jockey for selfish gains and advantages, not bearing in mind the general interest.

Nevertheless, the most serious shortcoming of the present system resides in the lack of political will as well as the lack of trust and sincerity towards one another. Yet each and everyone in their heart realizes that the advantages of ASEAN accrue to them all, and no one is thinking of leaving it.

Be that as it may, there is no readiness to admit to these shortcomings. That is why they put the blame for these deficiencies on the Secretariat which was set up by the governments themselves. Indeed, they distrust their subordinate officials to the point that they have not been willing, until recently, to appoint a Secretary-General of ASEAN, but only a Secretary-General in charge of the Secretariat.

Whatever problems exist at present, it is not my intention to dwell on them. They should, however, be resolved as expeditiously and effectively as possible. Personally, I prefer to look ahead and chart out a course that will lead to the objectives originally set out, so as to meet the expectations of our peoples.

The question we should ask is: ASEAN, *quo vadis*? Where do we go from here?

To this, I would reply that, first of all, we must set ourselves on the economic track we designed for the Association. This is necessary, even imperative, now more than ever as the world is being carved into powerful trade zones that deal with one another instead of with individual nations. At present, many countries outside our region are prodding us to integrate so that a single or more unified market will simplify and facilitate trade. That stands to reason and yet it was only in 1992 when all partners were convinced of the veracity of the proposition, when the then Thai Prime Minister, Anand Panyarachun, officially put the idea of an ASEAN Free Trade Area for discussion at the ASEAN Summit at Singapore. This meaningful move was logical since ASEAN was born in Thailand. However, it may take some fifteen years — as requested by some

members — before a rudimentary single, integrated market comes into being.

For the months and years to come, gradual economic integration should be the credo for ASEAN if we want our enterprise to remain viable and continue to progress. Otherwise, it may become stagnant, unable to keep up with the pace of global activity. In spite of the Maastricht setback where the Danes voted against ratifying the Treaty on European Union, the European Community will most probably witness sustained expansion with the addition of former EFTA members as well as a number of Central and East European countries waiting to join. Meanwhile, NAFTA — the North American Free Trade Area — is coming into being, parallel to another one further south of the American continent. Likewise, on the southeast wing of Europe, Turkey is busy organizing some form of co-operation with the Islamic states of the Black Sea region of the defunct Soviet Union. All these activities should be sufficient indication that there is an urgent need for ASEAN to scrutinize itself, to update its role, and to implement wider and more serious organizational reforms — measures that are more meaningful than simply revamping the Secretariat.

On the non-technical side, political will and the spirit of partnership greatly need to be strengthened. In the future, competition will be severe. Political and economic pressure through the use of unilateral measures and threats will be resorted to without mercy by those who believe in brute force rather than civilized negotiations, a method which I call "crowbar" diplomacy proudly proposed by the "Amazon Warrior" before the legislative authorities of her country. Without appropriate adjustments and improvements, ASEAN may lose in the race for survival. And time is of the essence. ASEAN, in my opinion, does not have much leeway to idle or doodle. We should realize that two or three years are all we really have to implement urgent reforms.

While the pursuit of economic aims, as originally assigned, is essential, it does not mean the Association should abandon the considerable political gains it has made. On the contrary, ASEAN should continue to build upon the prestige and recognition that the outside world has accorded it. The results of ASEAN's past performance especially in the resistance against Vietnamese military conquests and territorial expansionism, as well as the unqualified success in preserving peace and stability against all odds, are evident. Without doubt, ASEAN must strive to consolidate these assets which will complement its efforts on the economic side. In other words, the arduous task ahead for the Association will be a double- or triple- track endeavour which can be crowned with success provided that the weaknesses mentioned earlier are remedied and all the members, for their own good and that of their people, decide to carry out their duties and obligations with determination and a sense of purpose.

On the other hand, we should foresee that, in time to come, not only will ASEAN have to face the difficult task of creating and maintaining harmony among its members who have different views, different interests, and are of different stages of development — factors that in the past have made the adoption of needed reforms so uneasy — but ASEAN will also have to cope with the extremely complicated problems of dealing with hard-nosed opponents and interlocutors among the developed countries.

Finally, as with all organizations and entities, ASEAN will have to realize that it will not be nor can it be the ultimate creation. In truth, it should be only a stepping stone, a preliminary or intermediate stage in the process of international development. As the world progresses, so will ASEAN. At this juncture, everyone within the Association is aware of this reality. It should be prepared to move on to the next stage and raise its sights towards wider horizons. Some nascent possibilities like PECC (the Pacific Economic Co-operation Council) and APEC (the Asia Pacific Economic Co-operation forum) are already in existence and more or less ready to bloom into something more stable and viable. So far, ASEAN members have not been willing to merge with the new entities, for various reasons, the most important of which may be a lack of conviction in the latters' viability. Perhaps correctly, ASEAN members prefer to wait for more convincing indications assuring them of their capacity to survive. They continue to insist that ASEAN remains the nucleus from which peripheral relationships might radiate. This is not an unwise approach, apparently dictated by realism and caution in view of the audacity and increasing arrogance of certain major powers. A precipitous decision may result in undesirable entanglement or worse strangulation. Nevertheless, it may be wise for ASEAN not to lose sight of two important countries further to the south of Asia — Australia and New Zealand. If and when, they should express a clear willingness and desire to play a genuine partnership role, they should be welcome to join in any common endeavour. Their contribution will undoubtedly increase the strength and capacity of our existing and future co-operative undertakings, thus enabling us to meet with every chance of success in future encounters and negotiations with similar entities of other continents.

Lately, ASEAN has taken up a new assignment by engaging in discussions on security matters, more precisely on the Spratly Islands which are claimed by a number of nations, including Vietnam and the People's Republic of China. The dispute threatened to erupt into an armed conflict after concessions for oil exploration were granted by the People's Republic of China to some American oil companies. If one or more contestants resort to violence the dispute may degenerate into an ugly conflict thereby disrupting the peace and stability of the region. For that reason, Indonesia has already been moved to organize "workshop" discussions to explore the possibility of an acceptable solution.

In the light of the Spratly problem, the ASEAN members prepared a draft "Code of International Behaviour" which rules out any resort to violence. This draft was tabled at the Manila Ministerial Meeting in 1992 which approved it, as did the PRC and Vietnam, a dialogue partner and a signatory of the ASEAN Treaty on Amity and Co-operation respectively. This was what ASEAN could do, although it was only a moral gesture. Obviously, it could not obtain from the main parties to the dispute, a categorical pledge not to resort to violence. It may not be much. It was nevertheless better than nothing and certainly better than to bury one's head in the sand. It is hoped that in this, as in any other case, wisdom and restraint will prevail.

What will ultimately be the fate of ASEAN?

To this question, I am ready to offer a candid reply, forgetting my role as a co-founder of the Association. My faith in the usefulness and "serviceability" of ASEAN cannot and will not diminish. If anything, members will find it beneficial to strengthen it. This is the rationale. In the post Cold War world, the Western countries find it fit to assert with little restraint or moderation their ascendancy and dominance, and some even seek to establish their hegemony over the entire world by claiming undisputed leadership in a so-called New World Order framework because of the absence of Soviet challenge and rivalry. The ultimate result would be that other nations will, *ipso facto*, become nothing but mere pawns of different size. The smaller ones will shrink still further and become even smaller and less significant. In fact, they will count less on the world scene than before the advent of the New World Order. Therefore, if they do not combine their minuscule strength, they will lose all meaning. Now the only place where they can do something with a measure of success is none other than the ASEAN forum. Therefore, for our own interests, we cannot afford to be oblivious of this plain truth and fail to act accordingly.

Bangkok
1 September 1992

ASEAN
The Way Ahead

S. RAJARATNAM

If the last decade of the 20th century, to whose final death throes we are now the unhappy witnesses, can be termed the Age of Nationalism, then the 21st century, whose pale dawn is visible over the horizon, can be aptly described as the Coming Age of Regionalism.

This Foreword focuses on regionalism rather than on ASEAN because the latter is no more than a local manifestation of a global political, economic and cultural development which will shape the history of the next century.

Should regionalism collapse, then ASEAN too will go the way of earlier regional attempts like SEATO, ASA and MAPHILINDO. All that remains today of these earlier experiments are their bleached bones. Should the new regional efforts collapse, then globalism, the final stage of historical development, will also fall apart. Then we will inevitably enter another Dark Ages and World War III, fought this time not with gun-powder, but with nuclear weapons far more devastating than those exploded in Hiroshima and Nagasaki.

Modern technology and science are pushing the world simultaneously in the direction of regionalism and globalism. What is responsible for today's economic disintegration, disorder and violence is the resistance offered by nationalism to the irresistible counter-pressures of regionalism and globalism.

As of today, there are only two functioning and highly respected regional organizations in the world. They are, in order of their importance and seniority, the European Community (EC) and the Association of Southeast Asian Nations (ASEAN). The first came into being in 1957 and the second in 1967. A mere ten years separates the two. The population of the European Community as at 1990 was 350 million, and that of ASEAN an estimated 323 million. In terms of population, they are not all that unequal. In terms of political and economic dynamism, though, the gap is qualitatively wider. The economic dynamism and the proven political cohesion of ASEAN is nevertheless slowly but steadily narrowing the gap between the European Community and ASEAN. To compare ASEAN with the so-called Little Dragons of Asia is to compare unrelated political species. The Little Dragons are lone wolves hunting separately. They lack collective strength or awareness. With them it is a case of each wolf for itself. In the case of ASEAN, as integration proceeds, its strength will be the cohesiveness of over 300 million people with far greater resources than any of the lone baby dragons.

The most remarkable feature about the two regional organizations is their continuity and coherence despite the persistence and often unmanageable turbulence and tensions that have and still characterize the post-war world. There have been some 100 international, civil, racial and religious conflicts. Far from abating, these are growing in number. By comparison the European Community and ASEAN are the still centres in the eye of the storm. There is apprehension that chaos, not order, is the draft of world politics and economies today. For many, the expectation is that tomorrow will be worse than yesterday and that history has been a descent from the Golden Age to the Dark Ages. To quote the poet Yeats, though the world is seemingly intact: "Things fall apart, the centre cannot hold."

Yet the two multi-racial and multi-cultural regional organizations I have mentioned continue to grow in maturity, cohesiveness, and confidence. They believe that regionalism can survive the buffeting winds and storms.

The European Community, unlike ASEAN, has had far more experience with regional organization because its founding members, in particular Britain, France, Holland, Belgium and even Germany participated in the creation and management of far-flung complex global empires. Their scientific and technological cultures were many light years ahead of all preceding cultures and civilizations. However eminent and admirable pre-European traditional civilizations were, the 19th and 20th century culture created by the West cannot be surpassed or displaced by invoking ancient creeds. Only Japan has so far demonstrated that the gap between medieval and modern cultures can be narrowed and possibly over taken. Moreover, only Western nations and Japan have demonstrated a capacity for constructing massive modern empires, though unfortunately, they demonstrated this by their ability to organize and unleash modern wars. No Asian nation, however, has fought, let alone won, wars of comparable magnitude. Saddam Hussein's chest-thumping has the resonance of hollow drums.

Western Europeans have over a period of 500 years built a chain of multi-racial and multi-national empires that at their peak stretched from Portugal and Spain to the Pacific shores of Russia, and parts of Asia and Africa. So reconstituting a West European regional community should be child's play for them.

But creating and managing, within a brief period of only 25 years, an ASEAN community of six economically and industrially under-developed peoples who had no experience of administering a modern, complex multi-racial regional organization verges, in my view, on the miraculous.

The reach of the ancient empires of Greece, Rome, China, India, Persia and Babylon, ruled by allegedly Divine emperors, was ludicrously short and their claims of being rulers of world empires were fanciful exaggerations. The effective extent of their empires did not go beyond the palace and surrounding villages.

Modern nationalism, regionalism and globalism are of a different order politically, economically and even psychologically. Nationalism is a 19th century concept. Earlier forms of nationalism were, in fact, imperialism. It united petty principalities, states and clans into nations. These have now outlived their usefulness.

But regionalism is based on concepts and aspirations of a higher order. Asian regionalism was first launched on 25 April 1955 at Bandung. It was initially a comprehensive Afro-Asian Conference presided over by Heads of Government. It included legendary figures like Sukarno, Nehru, Zhou Enlai, Kotalawela of what was then Ceylon, Sihanouk and Mohammed Ali, the Prime Minister of Pakistan. However, this regional effort did not last long. Asian and African nationalisms which helped speed up the collapse of Western, and later Japanese imperialisms, did not last long.

Within a few years after its founding, not only Afro-Asian solidarity but also the solidarity of individual Asian and African nation states was in disarray. The destruction of nationalism is today being brought about, not by Western imperialism, which had already grown weary, thanks to two world wars, of holding sway over palm and pine, but by Third World nationalism. The economic and political underpinnings of European nationalisms were in fact, even before the start of the 20th century, beginning to crack. In fact, Lord Acton, towards the end of the 19th century, predicted the inevitable collapse of nationalism. I quote his judgement-"Nationality does not aim either at liberty or prosperity, both of which it sacrifices to the imperative necessity of making the nation the mould and measure of the state. It will be marked by material and moral ruin." This prophecy is as accurate today as it was when Lord Acton made it in 1862. So was Karl Marx's prophecy about the inevitable collapse of nationalism but for different reasons. He predicted the overthrow of nationalism and capitalism by an international proletariat. So did Lenin and so did Mao with their clarion call of: "Workers of the World unite."

Internationalism has a long history. Chinese, Christians, Greeks, Romans and Muslims were never tired of announcing themselves as "World Rulers". However, after World War II, empires went out of fashion. It is today being gradually replaced by a more rational form of political and economic organization.

The early years of the 20th century witnessed, for example, experiments with a novel form of regionalism — continental regionalism. It was formed by simply prefixing the word "Pan" to the continents of Europe, Asia and America — Pan-Europa, Pan-America and Pan-Asia, of which Japan, after having in 1905 defeated the Russian fleet in one of the most decisive naval battles ever fought in the Tsushima Straits, became Asia's most persistent publicist. After World War II, Pan-African and Pan-Arab movements were added to the list. However, these early "Pan" movements have since then either collapsed totally or are in the process of violent disintegration because of dissension on grounds of race, religion, language or nation.

However, the word "Pan" has recently been revived in East Europe. It is called "Pan-Slavism" and is today being revived with bloody vengeance. The multi-racial and multi-cultural Yugoslav nation that President Tito created during World War II and which is today being torn apart is a grim warning of what can happen to nations possessed by racial and religious demons.

The new regionalism that is now emerging out of the ruins of post-World War II nationalism appears to have learnt from the errors of the past. A more sophisticated and realistic form of regionalism is being constructed, not as an end in itself but as the means towards a higher level of political, social and economic organization.

I propose to do no more than list the names of some of the new regionalisms now taking shape. Basic to this approach is that there is not going to be any sudden great leap forward from regionalism to globalism. However, none of the new regionalisms now taking shape are as bold as either the European Community or ASEAN. The latter two are more rationally focussed regionalism. But a word of caution is necessary. We must know how to handle these new regionalisms intelligently. They could be steps towards global peace, progress and cultural development or they could be fuel for World War III.

Foremost among the new regional approaches is the North American Free Trade Area (NAFTA) and the Asia-Pacific Economic Co-operation forum. Among the many other regional concepts waiting in the wings are: the Organisation of Economic Co-operation and Development (OECD); the Group of Seven (G7); East Asian Economic Caucus (EAEC); Pacific Economic Co-operation Conference (PECC); the amiable Little Dragons of South Korea, Singapore, Hong Kong and Taiwan for which no acronym has yet been announced. There are also the distant rumbles of the possible emergence of Big Dragons but as a Chinese saying goes: "There is a lot of noise in the stairways, but nobody has so far entered the room." One fervently hopes that when a Big Dragon turns up, it would be an amiable Great Dragon and one which would know its way around the Spratly and Paracel Islands but without being a Dragon in a China shop. World War II started, it must be remembered, simply because the German and Japanese Dragons got their maps all wrong.

Real regionalism requires a world-view if it

is not to lose its way in the global world of modern technology and science. It must also have a rational and deep understanding of the new history which is being shaped not by heroic individuals, but through the co-operative interaction of some 5 billion people who today live in a vastly shrunken planet and who, thanks to growing literacy and fast-as-light electronic communication, are better informed about the world we live in than earlier generations.

Nobody, not even super-computers can predict what will happen when each day the flow of history is cumulatively determined by individual decisions made by 5 billion human beings who are asserting their right to a decent and just society. Fewer and fewer people today believe that oppression, hunger and injustice is God's will to which they must meekly submit. People today know the difference between "Let us pray" and "Let us prey".

The end of the Cold War and the collapse of communism has, in no way, made for a more peaceful world. Wars have ended in the Western world but not so elsewhere. World War III, should it ever be unleashed, would be the last war mankind will ever fight.

As a student of history, I believe that it is not common ideals but common fears that generally hold groups and nations together. The moment the common fear disappears, the brotherhood becomes an arena for dissension, conflict and even bloodshed. Two world wars and what is going on in Africa, Asia and Central Europe provide ample proof that we live in dangerous times today.

However, I believe there is evidence suggesting that ASEAN is an exception to the rule. ASEAN was born on 8 August 1967 out of fear rather than idealistic convictions about regionalism. As one of the two still surviving founder members of ASEAN (the other being Dr Thanat Khoman) I can attest to the triumph of fear over ideals.

The anticipated military withdrawal of the Americans from Vietnam in the eighties raised the spectre of falling non-communist dominoes in Southeast Asia. It appeared then that both the East and West winds of communism had joined forces to sweep over Southeast Asia.

Fortunately, Adam Smith's Invisible Hand came to ASEAN's rescue. The Sino-Soviet split started. The East and West communist winds were suddenly blowing in contrary directions.

The second outburst of ASEAN fear was in December-January 1980 when Vietnam with the backing of the Soviet Union proclaimed the liberation of not only its Indochina Empire but also of the whole of Southeast Asia.

Fortunately for the first time in the history of an Asian regionalism, ASEAN, instead of trembling with fear, dug its toes in and decided to stand up against a Vietnam that had never ceased to boast that it had defeated two great Western powers in Vietnam — first the French and then the Americans.

So in the case of Vietnam, it was not belief in regionalism but resolution, born out of common fear, that eventually brought about the collapse of communist Vietnam.

Today a new fear haunts ASEAN and which, I believe, now makes inevitable the emergence of ASEAN regional solidarity, and, no less important, the actualization of the ASEAN Free Trade Area or AFTA. I also believe this solidarity will manifest itself politically and militarily so long as a common fear persists.

Singapore
1 September 1992

Member States
of
ASEAN
(Association of Southeast Asian Nations)

- BRUNEI DARUSSALAM
- INDONESIA
- MALAYSIA
- PHILIPPINES
- SINGAPORE
- THAILAND

The historic meeting in Bangkok in 1967 which marked the signing of the ASEAN Declaration. Seated from left to right are Foreign Ministers Mr Narciso Ramos of the Philippines, Mr Adam Malik of Indonesia, Mr Thanat Khoman of Thailand, Tun Abdul Razak of Malaysia, and Mr S. Rajaratnam of Singapore.

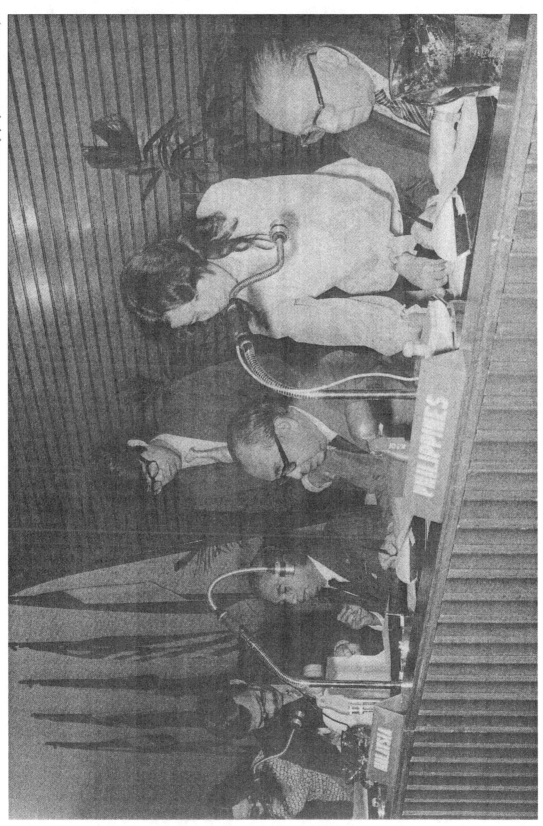

The signing of the Kuala Lumpur Declaration of 1971,
also known as the ZOPFAN (Zone of Peace, Freedom and Neutrality) Declaration.

The ASEAN Heads of Government signing the Treaty of Amity and Co-operation in Southeast Asia at the First ASEAN Summit in Bali in 1976.

Official opening of the Fourth ASEAN Summit held in Singapore in 1992.

Section *I*

HISTORY OF REGIONALISM IN SOUTHEAST ASIA

Introduction

Sharon Siddique

Section I is a rather presumptuous, but an altogether necessary, Southeast Asian preamble which all readers are encouraged to peruse prior to immersing themselves in the ASEAN events of the last twenty-five years, which are narrated and analysed in the remaining sections of this volume.

The Section is presumptuous because it presumes to condense the essence of some flavours of "Southeast Asia", from prehistory through protohistory, and, with ever more detailed descriptions, through colonialism and decolonization to the nascent attempts at "region-building" prior to the formation of ASEAN, the Association of Southeast Asian Nations. While the rest of the book concentrates on a twenty-five year period, this Section catapults the reader through millennia.

The Section is necessary precisely because it serves to place ASEAN in the historical development of the region — a region with an intensely interesting and complex past.

Most students of contemporary Southeast Asia know little about the history of the region, and certainly the selections in this short section are not meant to fill this gap. But it is stimulating and somewhat humbling to be reminded by O.W. Wolters that "...by the beginning of the Christian era a patchwork of small settlement networks of great antiquity stretched across the map of Southeast Asia". As prehistorians continue to put together the

pieces of their puzzle, it is fascinating for the non-historian to follow them into their hypotheses concerning what is indigenous to the region.

As this book is about regionalism, it is justifiable to spend some effort in exploring this question of "regional identity", and this is what Donald G. McCloud accomplishes when he grapples with the question of whether or not "Southeast Asia" is — or ever was — a "viable global unit". McCloud reminds us that prior to the colonial period the region was certainly recognized by Chinese, Arabic, Egyptian and even Greek and Roman writers. In the 1990s it is possible to see with increasing clarity just how disruptive the colonial imposition of artificial boundaries was, and how this has affected the recovery of the region's image of itself.

The first stage in this regional rediscovery took place in the immediate post-World War II period, which was of course marked by the emergence of independent nation states. When John Bastin and Harry J. Benda describe just how cataclysmic this period really was, we are forcefully reminded that the twenty-five years of ASEAN peace and progress are indeed a fragile heritage.

Indeed, it can be argued that a re-emerging sense of Southeast Asian regionalism was an integral part of the decolonization process. Although Russell H. Fifield correctly cautions against overemphasizing the importance of the American Southeast Asia Command to the re-emergence of Southeast Asia as a concept, it is certainly important to record the regional approach taken by the British and Americans during the war, and in the immediate post-war period. Peter Lyon rather bluntly notes that the period until the second half of the 1950s "...was shaped and characterized mostly by the dominance of the United States and Britain in deciding what of regional associations in and for Southeast Asia there should be".

Finally, the string of ASEAN's immediate regional precursors should be mentioned as a sobering reminder of just how precarious a process regionalizing Southeast Asia can be. SEATO (Southeast Asia Treaty Organization), ASA (Association of Southeast Asia), Maphilindo (an acronym formed from MAlaysia, PHILippines and INDOnesia) and ASPAC (Asian and Pacific Council) each have there individual instructive lessons, as summarized by Norman D. Palmer.

One hopes that the reader will emerge from the historical encounters represented in these selections with a more vivid appreciation for the evolution of Southeast Asia as a region. Certainly if there is a single lesson to be learned, then it must be that the twenty-five year history of ASEAN — which has emerged out of, and is woven into, the complex historical fabric of the region — is nothing short of miraculous. Thus wherever ASEAN proceeds from here, it has already unequivocally earned its place as a milestone in the history of the region.

1.

EARLY SOUTHEAST ASIAN POLITICAL SYSTEMS

O.W. WOLTERS

A remarkable development in Southeast Asian studies since the Second World War has been the steadily improving knowledge of the region's prehistory.[1] The best known discoveries, made possible by scientifically conducted excavations and the tools of carbon dating, thermoluminescence, and palaeobotany, are signs of bronze-working and domesticated agriculture at certain sites in northeastern Thailand attributable to the fourth millennium BC. Iron-working, too, seems to have been under way at one of these sites by about 1500 BC. Moreover, by the second half of the second millennium BC at the latest, metallurgy had become the most recent stage in a local cultural process over a sufficiently wide area in northern Vietnam to permit Vietnamese archaeologists to broach sophisticated sociological enquiries.

For my purpose, the important consequence of current prehistoric research is that an outline of the ancient settlement map is beginning to be disclosed. The map seems to comprise numerous networks of relatively isolated but continuously occupied dwelling sites, where residential stability was achieved by exploiting local environmental resources to sustain what is sometimes called continually expanding "broad spectrum" subsistence economies. The inhabitants' original skills were those of "forest efficiency", or horticulture, although during the second millennium BC domesticated modes of wet-rice agriculture were probably appearing in the mainland alluvial plains.[2]

These tendencies in prehistoric research provide helpful perspectives for historians of the early Southeast Asian political systems, for they are now being encouraged to suppose that by the beginning of the Christian era a patchwork of small settlement networks of great antiquity stretched across the map of Southeast Asia. For example, no less than about three hundred settlements, datable by their artifacts as belonging to the seventh and eighth centuries AD, have been identified in Thailand alone by means of aerial photography.[3] Seen from the air, they remind one of craters scattered across the moon's surface. The seventh-century inscriptions of Cambodia mention as many as thirteen toponyms sufficiently prominent to be known by Sanskritic names. The multiplicity of Khmer centres, for there were surely more than thirteen, contradicts the impression provided by Chinese records of protohistoric Cambodia that there was only a single and enduring "kingdom of Funan".[4] "Funan" should not, I shall suggest below, be invoked as the earliest model of an "Indianized state" in Southeast Asia.

Excerpted from O.W. Wolters, *History, Culture, and Region in Southeast Asian Perspectives* (Singapore: Institute of Southeast Asian Studies, 1982), by permission of the author and the publisher.

The historian, studying the dawn of recorded Southeast Asian history, can now suppose with reasonable confidence that the region was demographically fragmented. The ethnic identity and remotest origins of these peoples are questions that I shall eschew. Before the Second World War, prehistorians framed hypotheses based on tool typology to argue that culturally significant migrations into the region took place from the second half of the second millennium BC. These hypotheses have now been overtaken by the disclosing chronology of much earlier technological innovation established by means of prehistoric archaeology. Rather than assuming migrations from outside the region, we can be guided by Donn Bayard's view that prehistoric Southeast Asia was a "continually shifting mosaic of small cultural groups, resembling in its complexity the distribution of the modern hill tribes".[5] The focus of attention must be on what some of these groups could do inside the region and what they became.

The ancient inhabitants of Southeast Asia were living in fairly isolated groups, separated by thick forests, and would have had powerful attachments to their respective localities. I shall have occasion later to discuss the continuation of the prehistoric settlement pattern in historical times, and I shall content myself here by noting that in Java, for example, local scripts[6] and local sung poems[7] survived through the centuries. Or again, Malyāng, a small principality in north-western Cambodia during the seventh century, disappears from the records after the late eighth century but reappears in the late twelfth century as a rebellious area when Angkor was sacked by the Chams in 1177.[8] The modern names of villages and subregions are also often identifiable in early written records.

The multiplicity of settlement areas, each of which could go its own way, means that the historian should be cautious before he decides that any part of the region once occupied only a peripheral status in the general picture. Everything depends on what the historian is looking at in particular times in the past. For example, one still knows very little of the early history of the Philippines, but one should not conclude that these islands remained on the fringe of early Southeast Asia. Their inhabitants did not perceive their map in such a way. They are more likely to have looked outward to what is the Vietnamese coast today or to southern China for the more distant world that mattered to them. Every centre was a centre in its own right as far as its inhabitants were concerned, and it was surrounded by its own group of neighbours.

The ancient pattern of scattered and isolated settlements at the beginning of the Christian era would seem to suggest little prospect that the settlements would generate more extensive contact between themselves. The tempo of communication was probably slow even though linguists have been able to delineate major and overarching language families. The languages of the archipelago can be conveniently defined as belonging to the "Austronesian" language family. The language map of mainland Southeast Asia is much more complicated. In early times, the Mon-Khmer, or "Austroasiatic", family of languages stretched from Burma to northern Vietnam and southern China. The Tai and Burman languages were wedges thrust into the Mon-Khmer language zone. But the reality everywhere in Southeast Asia is likely to have been that the major language families were represented by numerous local and isolated speech variations. Only in later times did some variations take on the characteristics of neighbouring speeches, a development that gradually led to a more widely used standardized speech. Linguistic similarities were not in themselves cultural bridges. When, therefore, we enquire how these scattered settlements were able to reduce their isolation, we have to consider other cultural features with greater possibilities for creating more extensive relationships within the region.

There are, in fact, several such features, though we must bear in mind that not all societies can be attributed with identical features.

Exceptions can always be found. Moreover, similar cultural features did not in themselves guarantee that extensive relationships would develop across localities as a matter of course, even if their inhabitants came to recognize that they had something in common.

One well-represented feature of social organization within the lowlands in the region today is what anthropologists refer to as "cognatic kinship",[9] and we can suppose that this feature was present throughout historical times. In simple terms, the expression means that descent is reckoned equally through males and females and that both males and females are able to enjoy equal inheritance rights.[10] The comparable status of the sexes in Southeast Asia may explain why an Indonesian art historian has noted the unisex appearance of gods and goddesses in Javanese iconography, whereas sexual differences are unambiguously portrayed in Indian iconography.[11]

A notable feature of cognatic kinship is the downgrading of the importance of lineage based on claims to status through descent from a particular male or female. This does not mean that early settlements were egalitarian societies; prehistoric graves with sumptuary goods and status symbols reveal hierarchical distinctions evolving from before the beginning of the Christian era. Moreover, the principle of cognatic kinship by no means implies that kinship ties are unimportant. The contrary is the case. Kinship ties are the idiom of social organization in the region and part of its history. For example, when the Khmers founded or endowed religious cult centres, their commemorative inscriptions mention a variety of male and female kinship relationships over several generations. Nevertheless, the forebears, members of the devotees' kin (*kula*), are not presented as a lineage. Certain forebears are signalled out for their personal accomplishments, but the focus of the inscriptions is always on those who are performing and commemorating their own acts of devotion. One inscription explicitly excludes the devotee's parents from enjoying the fruits of his devotion.[12]

The relative unimportance of lineage means that we have to look elsewhere for cultural factors which promote leadership and initiative beyond a particular locality, and I suggest that leadership in inter-personal relations was associated with what anthropologists sometimes refer to in other parts of the world as the phenomenon of "big men". Here is a cultural trait in early Southeast Asia that seems to offer a helpful perspective for understanding much of what lay behind intra-regional relations in later times.

The leadership of "big men", or, to use the term I prefer, "men of prowess", would depend on their being attributed with an abnormal amount of personal and innate "soul stuff", which explained and distinguished their performance from that of others in their generation and especially among their own kinsmen. In the Southeast Asian languages, the terms for "soul stuff" vary from society to society, and the belief is always associated with other beliefs. The distinctions between "soul stuff" and the associated beliefs are so precise and essential that they can be defined only in the language of each society.[13] Nevertheless, a person's spiritual identity and capacity for leadership were established when his fellows could recognize his superior endowment and knew that being close to him was to their advantage not only because his entourage could expect to enjoy material rewards but also, I believe, because their own spiritual substance, for everyone possessed it in some measure, would participate in his, thereby leading to *rapport* and personal satisfaction. We are dealing with the led as well as the leaders.

Difficulties are bound to arise in studying continuities in early Southeast Asian experiences when one thinks of "states", as I have done for too long.[14] Even prehistorians, when they are correcting earlier misapprehensions about what happened during the several millennia before the beginning of the Christian era, may tend to reinforce earlier dogma about the appearance of "states" during protohistory. Prehistorians are interested in "incipient state formation and political centralization" prior to Indian influence, but, while they can now show that Indian influence did not move into a vacuum when it brought a "state" like Funan into being,[15] they still cannot rid themselves of an awareness of discontinuity between prehistory and protohistory. The reason is that they take "Funan" as their model of the first fully-fledged state and attribute to it such features as "the ruler's strategy of monumental self-validation" and "time-tested Indian strategies of temple-founding, inscription-raising, and support for brahmanical royal cults".[16] A state, according to this line of thought which owes much to Van Leur's ideas in the 1930s, must be distinguished from anything else in prehistory. The effect is that a new lease of life is given to the significance of Indian influence.

I suggest that a gap persists between prehistory and protohistory represented by "Funan" because different terminologies are used when discussing each period. An outline of "incipient state formation" depends on such Western terms as "fairly extensive trade relations", wet-rice, iron technology, and "probably increasing population density and political centralization in some of the alluvial plains of the mainland".[17] These terms, taken by themselves, signify economic developments that would be accompanied by the appearance of more complex political systems. Nevertheless, prehistorians have to deny prehistory the achievement of "statehood" by indigenous processes because of what they believe is known of the fully-fledged "state of Funan". The elaboration of the features of a "Funanese" typology, however, depends on an altogether different set of signifiers that owe their origin to Chinese documents and are therefore influenced by Chinese preconceptions of a "state". The Chinese supposed, for example, that any state should be associated with rules of dynastic succession and be described by fixed boundaries. No such polity existed anywhere in earlier Southeast Asian history except, as we shall see below, in Vietnam. Yet the Chinese were unable to conceptualize "Funan" as being anything other

than a "state", albeit an unstable one, and, because of this Chinese perspective, "Funan" has become the earliest Southeast Asian example of what sociologists refer to as a "patrimonial bureaucracy", a model that does not seem to fit the prehistoric evidence.[18]

The two sets of signifiers — Western and Chinese — have precise meaning only in cultural contexts outside Southeast Asia, and the result of linguistic confusion is that the passage of the region from prehistory to protohistory reads in language that is bound to give the impression that the Southeast Asian peoples could graduate to statehood only with the assistance of Indian influence. The same reading may even lead scholars to postulate a lag in the process of state formation in some parts of the region, exemplified by the "impermanence" of certain polities,[19] or to assume that particular geographical circumstances influenced the pace of the graduation to statehood.

In other words, the criteria for incipient and fully-fledged states are established by an arbitrary vocabulary drawn from an archaeology with an economic bias and from Chinese conventions transferred to a part of the world which was virtually unknown to them. The result is that one is in danger of looking for what could never be there in either prehistoric or protohistoric times. If, however, we think simply of "political systems" — a neutral expression — the way is open for considering other cultural phenomena such as religious and social behaviour that can be expected to affect political and economic activities in both prehistory and protohistory. No evidence at present exists for supposing that unprecedented religious and social changes were under way in the protohistoric period that sharply distinguish it from late prehistory. For example, there is no evidence to suppose that a chief's small-scale entourage in late prehistory was different in kind from the large-scale entourages of the historical period that supplied rulers with practical means of exercising political influence. In both periods, services are likely to have been rewarded with gifts of honour, posts of responsibility, and produce from the land.[20] All these gifts would be valued because the recipients knew that they participated in the donor's spiritual authority.

The territorial scale of a political system is certainly not the correct measurement for describing and defining it. Instead, we should think of sets of socially-definable loyalties that could be mobilized for common enterprises. This was the case in protohistoric times, and it would be surprising if these loyalties did not have their origin in prehistory. In late Balinese prehistory, for example, persons were buried according to their rank on earth,[21] which indicates some kind of hierarchy, with one person in the neighbourhood perceived as the point of reference for distinguishing ranks. This prehistoric background may be reflected in a Sanskrit inscription from western Java in the fifth or sixth century. The inscription has been translated as referring to a ruler's "allies",[22] but the term used is *bhakta* ("worshippers" or "princes devoted [to him]"). Khmer chiefs in the seventh century also frequently referred to themselves as *bhaktas* and ven-

erated their overlord because of his spiritual relationship with Śiva which brought spiritual rewards to those who served him. The Javanese inscription may refer to a chief's entourage with "prehistoric" features but described in the Sanskrit language.

The peoples of protohistoric Southeast Asia retained, I suggest, much more than vestiges of earlier behaviour, though their behaviour would not have been identical in every locality. But their cultures are unlikely to be entirely illuminated by artifacts recovered from graves or by Chinese evidence of commercial exchanges in the protohistoric period. Tools and trade represent only fractions of a social system.

I have dwelt on definitions partly because I believe that the time is now promising for a re-examination of the passage of Southeast Asia from prehistory to protohistory in terms of continuities rather than of discontinuities. But I am especially anxious to indicate the origins of the early political systems that furnish the appropriate background to later tendencies in Southeast Asian intra-regional relations.

NOTES

1. For recent surveys of current prehistoric research, see I.W. Mabbett, "The 'Indianization' of Southeast Asia: Reflections on Prehistoric Sources", *Journal of Southeast Asian Studies* (hereafter cited as *JSEAS*) 8, no. 1 (1977): 1–14; the "Introduction" in R.B. Smith and W.Watson, eds. *Early South East Asia. Essays in Archaeology, History and Historical Geography* (hereafter cited as *Early South East Asia*), pp. 3–14; Donn Bayard, "The Roots of Indochinese Civilisation", *Pacific Affairs* 51, no. 1 (1980): 89–114; Nguyên Phuc Long, "Les nouvelles recherches archéologiques au Vietnam . . .", *Arts Asiatiques*, Numéro special, 31 (1975); Jeremy H.C.S. Davidson, "Archaeology in Northern Viet-Nam since 1954", in *Early South East Asia*, pp. 98–124; and Hà Văn Tân, "Nouvelles recherches préhistoriques et protohistoriques au Vietnam", *Bulletin de l'École Francaise d'Extrême-Orient* (hereafter cited as *BEFEO*) 68 (1980): 113–54.

2. See Donn Bayard, op. cit., p. 105, for an evaluation of the evidence of rice-cultivation techniques.

3. I am grateful to Srisakra Vallibhotama for this information.

4. Claude Jacques," 'Funan'. 'Zhenla.' The Reality concealed by these Chinese Views of Indochina", in *Early South East Asia*, p. 378; O.W. Wolters, "North-western Cambodia in the seventh century", *Bulletin of the School of Oriental and African Studies* (hereafter cited as *BSOAS*) 37, no. 2 (1974): 378–79; and "Khmer 'Hinduism' in the Seventh Century", in *Early South East Asia*, p. 429.

5. Donn Bayard, op. cit., p. 92. Recent excavations at Ban Chiang in northeastern Thailand have suggested a movement of people into the alluvial plains in the millennium after the transition to wet-rice cultivation at Ban Chiang; ibid., p. 105.

6. J.G. de Casparis, *Indonesian Palaeography. A History of Writing in Indonesia from the beginning to c. A.D. 1500*, p. 72.

7. Martin F. Hatch, "Lagu, Laras, Layang. Rethinking melody in Javanese music", pp. 38–50. Old Javanese inscriptions show that those who called themselves "Mahārāja" retained the words "Raka of ..." in their titles to indicate their home territory; see F.H. van Naerssen, *The Economic and Administrative History of Early Indonesia*, pp. 46–55.

8. Wolters, "North-western Cambodia in the seventh century", p. 358.

9. This generalization does not include important groups such as the Chams and Minangkabau. I am referring, for example, to the Burmans, Thai, Khmers Malays, Javanese, and Tagalogs. I follow Keesing's definition of "cognatic" as meaning: (a) a mode of descent reckoning where all descendants of an apical ancestor/ancestress through any combinations of male or female links are included; (b) bilateral kinship, where kinship is traced to relations through both father and mother. See Roger M. Keesing, *Kin Groups and Social Structure*, chapter 6 and the glossary. Sometimes examples are found of nuclear families and neolocal residence. The *Sui-shu*, referring to Cambodia in about AD 600 states: "When a man's marriage ceremonies are completed, he takes a share of his parents' property and leaves them in order to live elsewhere". See O.W. Wolters, "Khmer 'Hinduism' ..." p. 430. Excavations in Bali indicate burials of nuclear families; see R.P. Soejono, "The Significance of the Excavation at Gilimanuk (Bali)", in *Early South East Asia*, p 195.

10. The nuclear family was the typical family in the Lê legal code, and both husbands and wives enjoyed property rights, see Insun Yu, "Law and family in seventeenth and eighteenth century Vietnam". The Chinese census statistics in Vietnam during the early centuries of the Christian era purport to reveal an increase in the number of households rather than in the total population, and one would expect this evidence in a society practising bilateral kinship. I am grateful to Keith Taylor for the information.

11. I owe this observation to Satyawati Suleiman. For a discussion of female property rights and the appearance of women in negotiations with royal representatives, see J.G. de Casparis, "Pour une histoire sociale de l'ancienne Java principalement au Xème s", *Archipel 21* (1981): 147.

12. A. Barth and A. Bergaigne, *Inscriptions sanscrites du Cambodge et Champa* (hereafter cited as *ISCC*), p. 20, v. 34.

13. Anthropological studies about "soul stuff" in a regional context do not seem available at the present time. Indeed, James Boon remarks in respect of Indonesia that "the ultimate comparativist accomplishment would be to plot the various soul-power terms — *semangat, roh*, and so on — against each other across Indonesian and Malay societies"; see James A. Boon, *The Anthropological Romance of Bali 1597–1972*, p. 240, n. 7. See Appendix A: Miscellaneous notes on "soul stuff" and "prowess".

14. Virginia Matheson, writing about the inhabitants of the Riau-Lingga archipelago as they are described in the *Tuhfat al-Nafis*, addresses this matter of terminology: ". ... I can find in the *Tuhfat* no evidence for the existence of the state as a concept, an abstract ideal above and beyond the ruler, which was to be sustained and protected. What does seem to have existed was a complex system of personal loyalties, which it was in the ruler's interest to maintain": see Virginia Matheson, "Concepts of state in the *Tuhfat al-Nafis* [The Precious Gift]" in *Pre-Colonial State Systems in Southeast Asia*, p. 21.

15. Donn Bayard, op. cit., p. 106.

16. Bennet Bronson, "The Late Prehistory and Early History of Central Thailand with special reference to Chansen," in *Early South East Asia*, p. 316.

17. Donn Bayard, op. cit., p. 106.

18. *Ibid.*, p. 107. Karl Hutterer, studying how far the lowland societies of the Philippines had reached urban and state formation on the eve of the Spanish intervention, observes that "there is no evidence whatsoever for the formation of bureaucratic structure that would have been interjected between the chief and the daily affairs of politics, commerce and religion, as is usually found in state societies"; see Karl L. Hutterer, "Prehistoric Trade and the Evolution of Philippine Societies: a Reconsideration", *Economic and Social Interaction in Southeast Asia: Perspectives from Prehistory, History, and Ethnology*, p. 191.

19. See for example, B. Bronson, "Exchange at the Upstream and Downstream Ends: Notes Toward a Functional Model of the coastal State in Southeast Asia", *Economic and Social Interaction in Southeast Asia*, p. 51; and Bennet Bronson and Jan Wisseman, "Palembang as Srivijaya: The lateness of early cities in southern Southeast Asia", *Asian Perspectives* 19, no. 2 (1978): 234.

20. Van Naerssen suggests that the origin of the Javanese *raka* can be explained in ecological terms. The *raka* was responsible for the equitable distribution of water over a number of agrarian communities (*wanua*), and he therefore had the right to dispose of the produce and labour of his subjects; see F.H. van Naerssen, *The Economic and Administrative History of Early Indonesia*, pp. 37–38.

21. R.P. Soejono, op. cit., p. 198.

22. B. Ch. Chhabra, *Expansion of Indo-Aryan Culture*, p. 94.

2.

SOUTHEAST ASIA AS A REGIONAL UNIT

DONALD G. McCLOUD

Although the region has been recognized for centuries in political and geographic terms by kings, writers, merchants, and travelers, the term *Southeast Asia* (also South East Asia and South-East Asia) is relatively new in Western political thought. Occasionally used by European, especially German, writers in the late nineteenth century, it was first brought to general prominence with the establishment of a Southeast Asia military command by the British during World War II — one of the first attempts to bring together the previously fragmented colonial perspectives of the British, Dutch, French, and Americans.[1]

The ethnocentric views of Southeast Asia as well as the political and economic divisions, established during the colonial era and perpetuated ever since, have made it very difficult for Westerners to perceive or accept Southeast Asia as a viable global unit. The acceptance of the concept of a regional unit has been made more difficult by the social and cultural complexities of the region and by the paucity of available data for historical analysis. In recent years the regional concept has been further obscured by Western scholars, particularly international relations theorists bent on applying culturally biased models and theories of regional systems models to their analyses of the contemporary realities of Southeast Asia.[2] One concerned scholar has been prompted to note that "*Southeast Asia*, as a conventional term, has become increasing the property of university area specialists," thus possibly limiting and obscuring intellectual "horizons through an over-obsession with a geographical convention."[3]

Yet prior to the colonial period, the region was historically recognized with some clarity by Chinese, Arabic, Egyptian, and even Greek and Roman writers. Such clearly functional recognition was based primarily on the role played by Southeast Asian states in the international trading systems. The Chinese provided for Southeast Asians, as for other barbarians in the theoretical world view of the Middle Kingdom, by dividing the outlying regions according to the points of the compass and in terms of distance. They used the generic terms *Nanyang* to refer to the region of the Southern Seas and, by the third century B.C., employed the term *K'un lun* as a referent for islands or states in the Southern Seas. The latter term designated volcanic lands "endowed with marvelous and potent powers" and also denoted ocean-going peoples engaged in international trade.[4] The Chinese later divided the region into Burma, Laos, and Annam while

Excerpted from Donald G. McCloud, *System and Process in Southeast Asia: The Evolution of a Region* (Boulder, Col.: Westview Press, 1986), by permission of the author.

maintaining a "separate and distinct set of relationships" for the rest of Southeast Asia.[5] The Japanese, using a term with a similar meaning, referred to Southeast Asia as *Nan yo*.[6] The early Arabic term *qumr*, used as a reference for Southeast Asia, was later replaced by *Waq-Waq*,[7] which evolved to mean all of the little-known area from Madagascar to Japan.[8] The term *Zabag* was used by the Arabs to refer to Southeast Asia, and the Indians called the region *Suvarnadvipa*.[9]

By the end of the seventh century A.D., Arab navigators were sailing with some regularity to Southeast Asia[10] in search of spices and medicines.[11] The region was also known to the Greeks and Romans. International trade by sea is known to have been frequent by the end of the second century A.D.,[12] although the sea routes through Southeast Asia may have been active as early as the middle of the third century B.C., when the land routes across Central Asia and India were blocked.[13] Southeast Asia was recognized, although its geographic limits and location were obscure, as a mysterious region that produced spices and other exotic products and that was peopled by skilled and courageous seafarers.

Implicit in this latter point is that the Southeast Asians themselves were active in the transshipment of cargo in the early centuries A.D. As already noted, they traveled as far west as Madagascar in such numbers and with such frequency that early geographers and navigators often thought of Madagascar as part of Southeast Asia. Thus, from the earliest times, Southeast Asia was an integral part of the evolving world trading system, providing valuable commodities and fulfilling vital functions in linking the Asian and Middle Eastern segments of the system.[14]

Southeast Asia's close association with, if not dependence on, international trade has continued to the modern era. Historically, when overland caravan routes from China through Central Asia to Europe were open the sea route and concurrently the welfare of Southeast Asia declined; conversely, when the caravan routes were closed, Southeast Asia flourished economically and politically. The Europeans recognized the importance of Southeast Asia when they sought, through colonial expansion, to monopolize international trade by controlling Southeast Asia directly.

The domination by the colonial powers of writing and intellectual thought over a period of three hundred years, as much as the political domination of the region, fragmented the integrity of Southeast Asia as a cultural, political, and economic unit. Although colonial administrators and European businessmen emasculated the indigenous political and economic systems, the national perceptions of British, Dutch, and French writers ensured that the regional history would be perceived as an appendage of European history and that little comparative study on a regional basis (across colonial boundaries) would be undertaken. Ironically, however, it was also during the colonial period that the details of Southeast Asia's cultural richness became known to the world. The rediscovery and repair of the great religious monuments at places like Angkor in Cambodia and Prambanan and Borobudur in Indonesia, the beginnings of records of the sociology of peasant society, and reports of linguistic and cultural aspects of Southeast Asian societies by early European scholars provided the foundations for a contemporary understanding of Southeast Asia.

In recent decades following World War II, Southeast Asia has been viewed by the scholarly community with varying degrees of uncertainty. The debate concerning the validity of Southeast Asia as an "independent" region has been weighed down by the mass of Chinese and Indian cultural imprints. Nevertheless, as bits of history have been uncovered, the concept of Southeast Asia as an entity unique in its regional and global contexts has been strengthened. The process has been evolutionary. Some have argued that, in fact, Southeast Asia existed only culturally as a colonial annex of India.[15] There remains, for example, an organization called the All-India Kamboj Association, which claims that Indians founded the "overseas"

Kamboja and that "fraternal relations have existed between the Kamboja or India and the Cambodians since the time of the Mahabharata when Rana Sudarshan Kamboj and his followers had established 'blood bonds' between the two countries."[16] These views have been re-stated as a theory of cultural extension and adaptation in which Southeast Asia developed a civilization of its own, though of Indian parentage.[17] According to J.C. van Leur,[18] this indigenous culture, strengthened by selective borrowings from India and China, provided the impetus for the growth of a *Southeast Asian history*, which is still progressing.[19]

NOTES

1. See D.G.E. Hall, "The Integrity of Southeast Asian History," *Journal of Southeast Asian Studies* 4 (September 1973); and Hugh Tinker, "The Search for the History of Southeast Asia," *Journal of Southeast Asian Studies* 11 (September 1980).

2. Morton Kaplan, *System and Process in International Relations* (New York: John Wiley & Sons, 1957). Among regional integration theorists, see Philip E. Jacob and James V. Toscano, eds., *The Integration of Political Communities* (New York: J. B. Lippincott, 1964); Joseph S. Nye, Jr., ed., International Regionalism (Boston: Little, Brown, 1968); and Louis J. Cantor and Steven L. Spiegel, *The International Politics of Regions* (Englewood Cliffs, N.J.: Prentice Hall, 1970).

3. Michael Leifer, "Trends in Regional Association in Southeast Asia," *Asian Studies* 2 (August 1964), p. 198.

4. Keith Taylor, "Madagascar in the Ancient Malayo-Polynesian Myths," *in Explorations in Early Southeast Asian History: The Origins of Southeast Asian Statecraft*, edited by Kenneth R. Hall and John K. Whitmore (Ann Arbor: Michigan Papers on South and Southeast Asia, 1976), p. 33, and Gabriel Ferrand cited within.

5. Wang Gungwu, "China and South-East Asia, 1402–1424," in *Studies in the Social History of China and South-East Asia: Essays in Memory of Victor Purcell*, edited by Jerome Ch'en and Nicolas Tarling (Cambridge: Cambridge University Press 1970), p. 389.

6. Fisher, *South-East Asia*, p. 7, fn. 9.

7. Taylor, "Madagascar in the Ancient Malayo-Polynesian Myths," pp. 33–38.

8. J.V. Mills, "Arabic and Chinese Navigators in Malaysian Waters in About A.D. 1500," *Journal of the Malaysian Branch of the Royal Asiatic Society* 47 (December 1974). The confusion of Madagascar with the islands of Southeast Asia may be related to the fact that Malay sailors frequently traveled there, leaving a cultural imprint that masked the geographic distance in the very early centuries of the Christian era.

9. Tate, *The Making of South-East Asia*, vol. 1, p. 8. See also W.J. van der Meulen, "Suvaradvipa and the Chryse Chersonesos," *Indonesia*, no. 18 (October 1974), pp. 1–40.

10. G.R. Tibbetts, *Arab Navigation in the Indian Ocean Before the Coming of the Portuguese* (London: Royal Asiatic Society of Great Britain and Ireland, 1971), pp. 472–503.

11. G.R. Tibbetts, *A Study of the Arabic Texts Containing Materials on South-East Asia* (Leiden: 1979), p. 3.

12. Tibbetts, *A Study of Arabic Texts*; and C.G.F. Simkin, *The Traditional Trade of Asia* (London: Oxford University Press, 1968).

13. Joseph Desomogyi, *History of Oriental Trade* (Hildesheim, FRG: Georg Olms Verlagsbuch-handlung, 1968), p. 24.

14. For an analysis of the major components of this historical system, see Adda B. Boseman, *Politics and Culture in International History* (Princeton, N.J.: Princeton University Press, 1960); Jeremy A. Sabloff and C.C. Lamber-Karlovsky, *Ancient Civilization and Trade* (Albuquerque: University of New Mexico Press, 1975); K.N. Chaudhuri, *Trade and Civilisation in the Indian Ocean: An Economic History from the Rise of Islam to 1750* (Cambridge: Cambridge University Press, 1985); and Immanuel Wallerstein, *The Modern World System: Capitalist Agriculture and the Origins of the European World Economy in the Sixteenth Century* (New York: Academic Press, 1974).

15. K.M. Panikker, R. Mookeriji, and R. C. Majumbar were among the protagonists of this view. See Hall, *A History of South-East Asia*, p. 16.
16. B.R. Chatterji, "A Current Tradition Among the Kamboja or North India Relating to the Khmers of Cambodia," *Artibus Asiae* 24 (1961), pp. 253–254.
17. See George Coedes, *Les Etats Hindouises d'Indochine et d'Indonesia* (Paris: E. de Boccard, 1948) or the English translation entitled *The Indianized States of Southeast Asia* (Honolulu: East-West Center Press, 1968).
18. J.C. van Leur, *Indonesian Trade and Society* (The Hague: W. van Hoeve, 1955).
19. For two summary reviews of the progression of thought on Southeast Asian history, see Hall, "The Integrity of Southeast Asian History," and Tinker, "The Search for the History of Southeast Asia." See also Donald K. Emmerson, "Southeast Asia: What's in a Name?" *Journal of Southeast Asian Studies* 15 (March 1984), pp. 1–21.

3. POST-COLONIAL SOUTHEAST ASIA

JOHN BASTIN and HARRY J. BENDA

Only twenty-odd years have elapsed since Japan's sudden surrender to the Allied powers dramatically inaugurated the most recent chapter in Southeast Asian history. The decolonization process has, historically speaking, barely begun, and it is therefore difficult to know what on the swiftly changing scene is ephemeral and what destined to perdure. In such countries as Burma, Indonesia, and Vietnam, postwar changes have, moreover, borne many of the hallmarks of political and incipient social revolutions; and these almost certainly have not yet run their full course. What has up to now emerged may, then, be no more than surface phenomena shrouding hidden factors and forces that may still emerge.

Postwar developments in Southeast Asia are, however, only one facet of the new power relationships in Asia as a whole, just as the area's incorporation into the Atlantic state system had been part of a larger historical process. The rise of the West in Asia had culminated in the subjugation of the Indian subcontinent by Britain in the late eighteenth century, followed by the virtual disintegration of the Chinese empire in the second half of the nineteenth. Though the great powers continued to pay lip service to her "territorial integrity," China

ceased to be a truly independent country. Moreover, Japan, at that time Asia's only modernizing state, had become a partner in the Atlantic system from about the turn of the twentieth century: she owed this spectacular ascendancy to her victories over China in 1894–95 and over Tsarist Russia in 1904–5, as well as to her participation in World War I on the side of the victorious Allies.

Japan's contracting out of the Atlantic system by making war on the Western colonial powers in 1941 and the lightning speed with which she made herself master of the *Nampō* mark the beginnings of the decolonization process in Southeast Asia. Ironically, this process was immensely accelerated by the collapse of Japan as a world power in 1945. Nippon's withdrawal from China (large parts of which she had occupied since the 1930s) and from Southeast Asia occurred before either the Western Allies or the Soviet Union could decisively fill the suddenly vacated Asian space.

In South Asia, Britain voluntarily liquidated her Indian empire, granting independence to India and Pakistan in 1947 (and shortly thereafter to Burma and Ceylon). Russian power in East Asia only sufficed to install a Communist government in the northern part of Korea,

Excerpted from John Bastin and Harry J. Benda, *A History of Modern Southeast Asia: Colonialism, Nationalism, and Decolonization* (New Jersey: Prentice-Hall, Inc., 1968), by permission of John Bastin.

since 1910 a Japanese colony; the Soviets apparently also provided some military aid to the Chinese Communists, for decades embroiled in a civil war with Chiang Kai-shek's Nationalist government. American intervention protected South Korea, but could not prevent the ejection of Chiang from the Chinese mainland to Taiwan (Formosa) in 1949. The consolidation of Communist rule marked the end of a century's foreign dominance over China. A decolonized India and Pakistan, a united China freed from alien control, and a prostrated Japan—these provide the larger Asian setting for Southeast Asian history since 1945.

In turn, that history all of a sudden shed its parochial limitations. Gone was the confining seclusion, the virtual isolation, which the Westerners had imposed on Southeast Asians in colonial times. Gone, too, was Japanese overlordship which, for all the internal upheavals it had caused, had after all kept them more tightly insulated from the rest of the world than ever before. Henceforth, Southeast Asian developments, more volatile than ever before, were destined to be increasingly influenced by political events from the outside. At times, indigenous leaders would seek to involve foreign powers in their domestic affairs, but more frequently still intervention would be injected into the region without local prompting. The global confrontation between two, and latterly three, world powers inevitably came to impinge upon the Southeast Asian scene, the area's internal developments often affecting the course of international affairs.

Even though Southeast Asia's history has become increasingly dominated by the emergence of independent nation states, Western power has not been altogether eliminated from Southeast Asia. As a matter of fact, the first postwar decade witnessed Dutch and French attempts at restoring colonial rule in Indonesia and Indochina, albeit with some belated concessions to nationalist aspirations. The Dutch staged two military campaigns, euphemistically labeled "police actions," against the Indonesian revolutionaries in 1947 and 1948; although they were partly successful militarily, the Dutch finally abandoned these attempts, under considerable international pressure, and transferred sovereignty to Indonesia (with the exception of West New Guinea) in December 1949. French efforts to impose their domination upon the Communist-controlled *Viet Minh* government of Vietnam led to a shattering military defeat at Dien Bien Phu in 1954, followed by France's withdrawal, not only from Vietnam but also from her former protectorates of Laos and Cambodia.

We already noted that the Philippines received their independence from the United States on July 4, 1946, and that the British relinquished Burma in 1948. In Malaya, however, British power was restored without encountering lasting native (as distinct from Chinese-led, Communist) opposition; even there, however, colonial rule ended with the creation of the independent Federation of Malaya in 1957. This left only Singapore and the northern fringes of Borneo—Sarawak, Sabah, and Brunei — under various kinds of colonial and protectorate ties to Britain, and Western New Guinea (Irian Barat, in Indonesian) under Dutch, Eastern New Guinea and Papua under Australian rule. Singapore and the Bornean territories, with the exception of Brunei, merged with Malaya into a wider Malaysian Federation in 1963, Dutch Irian Barat having been incorporated into Indonesia the year before. By the mid-1960s, the Australian-governed territories and the eastern half of the tiny island of Timor—like Goa in India (until the 1960s) and Macao in China, a minuscule but stubborn remnant of Portugal's erstwhile far-flung Asian realm—were all that survived as colonial dependencies in Southeast Asia.

Area-wide national independence did not mean, however, that the Atlantic powers had lost all influence in postwar Southeast Asia. The disappearance of direct French and Dutch military and political control was, indeed, unique, for Britain not only restrained the use of her naval base in Singapore, but independent Malaya, and later Malaysia, remained within the Commonwealth, some countries of which, in turn, provided military personnel for the new state's internal and external defense. The Philippines likewise allowed the continued presence of American ground and naval forces in accordance with a treaty ratified simultaneously with the transfer of sovereignty.

Before long, moreover, the United States—a major Pacific power after World War II, with bases spread over a wide arc from Japan, Okinawa, South Korea, Taiwan, to several Pacific islands—moved into the vacuum created by the French withdrawal from Indochina. Laos and South Vietnam—the country had been temporarily divided by an international agreement in 1954—thus remained within the Western orbit. At the same time, Soviet and Chinese support was injected into North Vietnam, though on a far less massive scale. America's deepening military involvement in mainland Southeast Asia also brought Thailand, the area's only independent state throughout modern history, into a military alliance with the United States with ever larger contingents of American military and other personnel stationed on her soil.

Military involvement to one side, Western economic interests regained a strong position in several parts of Southeast Asia. Thus tin and rubber companies, most of them British, as well as many other enterprises returned in full strength to postwar Malaya, while American business was granted far-reaching privileges in the Philippines. French entrepreneurs continued to play an important role in the Cambodian and, on a diminishing scale, in the South Vietnamese economy after 1954. Thailand in fact granted wider facilities to foreign, notably American, economic interests than they had enjoyed before the war. Economic nationalism, it is true, placed increasing restrictions on the foreigners' economic activities; most governments now levied taxes on aliens and some made the operation of foreign-owned enterprises conditional on their employment of indigenous executive personnel. While such measures undeniably restrict the activities of outside

investors, the Western economic superstructure created during the colonial era continued to function in these new nation states.

In those countries, however, where decolonization assumed a revolutionary momentum—Burma, North Vietnam, and Indonesia—most European economic interests were liquidated in the course of the first postwar decade. North Vietnam, like all Communist polities, nationalized all foreign capitalist concerns outright. In Indonesia the process passed through several stages, affecting Dutch concerns in the first place, followed by British ones in the early 1960s; though these measures practically eliminated Western holdings, some firms, especially American oil and rubber companies, survived the general onslaught. Nationalizations came to a halt—whether temporary or more permanent remains to be seen—when Indonesian politics took a sharp turn in late 1965. By contrast, a succession of Burmese governments took over all foreign-owned enterprises, including British concerns as well as Communist Chinese banks.

The temptation may be strong to discern a causal relationship between military and economic power. Some might argue that the West's continued economic interests demand a similarly continuing military presence. Others might even insist that the retention of economic predominance is one of the real, "neocolonialist" motives for the deployment of Western military might in Southeast Asia. This kind of interpretation, dear to Marxists of all hues, should not be dismissed out of hand: what exactly the interplay between economic interest groups and policy makers in the leading Western countries with a stake in Southeast Asia is, is very hard to know. But it is highly unlikely that such private pressures as are doubtless brought to bear on Western governments are given as great, let alone greater, weight than are economic and above all political and strategic considerations of a higher—i.e., national or even international—order. The very limited size of Western investments in Southeast Asia as a whole makes it unlikely that private and corporate interests are allowed a decisive voice in the formulation of foreign policies affecting this part of the world. But be that as it may, a good case can be made for viewing the fate of Western economic enterprise primarily in the internal context of the decolonization process in the different countries.

4. THE SOUTHEAST ASIA COMMAND

RUSSELL H. FIFIELD

In the course of the Second World War (1939-1945) Southeast Asia became a fixed and practical term even in the United States. Moreover, the region was more and more perceived in collective dimensions having military, political, and other aspects. At the same time this perception should not be exaggerated, for subsequent developments would markedly sharpen it.

The Institute of Pacific Relations founded in Honolulu in 1925 played a significant role in the evolution of the concept of Southeast Asia before the Japanese attack on Pearl Harbour in December 1941, not to mention the establishment of Mountbatten's Southeast Asia Command in August 1943[1]. Prior to the American entrance in the Second World War, the Institute undertook a number of studies on the social, economic, and political problems of Southeast Asia. In 1940 William L. Holland arranged the series of research reports, and in 1941 and 1942 all of them used "Southeast Asia" in their titles.

Possibly the book which did most to popularize the use of Southeast Asia, along with making a major contribution to the concept, was K. M. Panikkar's *The Future of South-East Asia: An Indian View*, published in New York in 1943. This Indian writer on sea power, who later became a diplomat, may have chosen the term Southeast Asia instead of Further India in order to take into account the rising nationalism in the area and thus avoid the embarrassment to his country that the term Further India might bring. As it was, the subsequent leadership role of Prime Minister Nehru and the attitudes of some of his followers were often resented by leaders in Southeast Asia and contributed to the development of the concept there[2].

The creation of the Southeast Asia Command (S.E.A.C.) by President Franklin D. Roosevelt and Prime Minister Winston S. Churchill at the First Quebec Conference in August 1943 was a major step in the military and political identification of the region[3]. It was the British who urged the creation of a "Supreme Allied Command in Southeast Asia". The presumed discussions between Roosevelt and Churchill and certainly between American and British military leaders did not focus on the question of the creation of such a command but on its geographical extent, on command arrangements and relationships, and on associated matters. The British originally wanted French Indo-China in the Command, and Roosevelt

Reprinted in abridged form from *South-East Asian SPECTRUM* 4, no. 1 (October 1975), pp. 42–51, by permission of the author.

at a meeting of the Combined Chiefs of Staff specifically asked if Thailand was included in the China theatre. The appointment of Admiral Lord Louis Mountbatten as Supreme Allied Commander was not debated but the role of General Joseph W. Stilwell, Chief of Staff of Generalissimo Chiang Kai-shek, as Deputy Supreme Allied Commander, was controversial.

In the final report of the Combined Chiefs of Staff to Roosevelt and Churchill on 24 August, approved by the two leaders except for an item on Spain, the "Southeast Asia Command" was established embracing Burma, Thailand, Malaya, Singapore, and Sumatra. French Indo-China remained in the China theatre of Chiang Kai-shek and the rest of Southeast Asia was under the Southwest Pacific Area of General Douglas MacArthur. The Combined Chiefs of Staff would have "general jurisdiction over strategy for the Southeast Asia theatre"[4] but command arrangements and relationships were outlined. It was pointed out in words originally chosen by the British that "the vigorous and effective prosecution of large-scale operations against Japan in Southeast Asia, and the rapid development of the air route through Burma to China, necessitate the reorganization of the High Command in the Indian theatre"[5]. Here is found a reflection of British interests especially in Southeast Asia and of American in China.

Admiral Lord Louis Mountbatten years later commented on the use of the term "South-East Asia" in the "South East Asia Command"[6]. When he was Chief of Combined Operations and a member of the Chiefs of Staffs Committee he and his colleagues were faced with the problem of what to term the area being overrun by the Japanese with the collapse of the ABDACOM (American, British, Dutch, Australian Command). In the discussions the territory came to be geographically referred to as "South-East Asia". Later, Admiral Mountbatten pointed out, the selection of the title South East Asia Command was natural[7].

At the Potsdam Conference of President Harry S. Truman, Marshal Josef Stalin, and Prime Minister Churchill (later replaced by Prime Minister Clement Attlee), 17 July-2 August 1945[8], the changing of the boundaries of the Southeast Command was considered by the British and Americans. The United States Chiefs of Staff on 17 July recommended altering Mountbatten's S.E.A.C. to include Borneo, the Celebes, and Java (with the territory to the East an Australian Command under the British Chiefs of Staff) and to include Indo-China South of the fifteenth parallel. At a meeting of the Combined Chiefs of Staff the next day General George C. Marshall asked the British Chiefs about their reaction to dividing Indo-China. After studying the proposal they indicated on 22 July that the division between S.E.A.C. and the China theatre should be at the sixteenth parallel in view of the "run of communications in Indo-China"[9]. Two days later, at a meeting of the Combined Chiefs, Marshall urged Mountbatten to take over "at the earliest possible moment" his expanded area of command[10].

President Truman and Prime Minister Churchill approved a report of the Combined Chiefs of Staff on 24 July formally defining the new area of the Southeast Asia Command. They noted the division of Indo-China; Washington and London in the arrangement would approach Chiang Kai-shek for his approval; and Mountbatten would take over the expanded territory of his command "as soon as practicable" after 15 August. The Generalissimo subsequently agreed providing the sixteenth parallel was extended across Thailand, a step that was never taken.

It is significant that the new boundaries of S.E.A.C. included all Southeast Asia except the Philippines, northern Indo-China, and the island of Timor. They had military implications for the war and political for the peace. Thus the concept of Southeast Asia was further advanced.

The celebrated Pentagon Papers appearing in 1971 throw more light on the development of the concept during the Second World War and its immediate aftermath in 1945 and 1946[11]. Especially from 1941 many officials in Washington perceived Southeast Asia as being more than a collection of colonial territories, dependencies overrun after Pearl Harbour by the Japanese. This perception was more marked toward the end of US involvement in the war than toward the beginning. At the same time American officials had no standard terminology they could use to express their perception.

American blueprints during the Second World War for Southeast Asia after the defeat of Japan focused on the individual countries but did not exclude broader considerations. President Roosevelt himself was particularly concerned about the future of Indo-China — he opposed its restoration to France and favoured a trusteeship. On occasion he used the term Southeast Asia but his perception of it as a regional entity appears nebulous.

The State Department as well as the War and Navy Departments was involved in 1944 in civil affairs planning in Southeast Asia, planning which concerned political and policy questions[12]. In another direction Secretary of State Cordell Hull forwarded to President Roosevelt on 8 September a far-reaching memorandum on the future of dependencies in the area. It called upon the colonial powers to announce "specific dates when independence or complete (dominion) self-government will be accorded" and to make "a pledge to establish a regional commission"[13]. The reference to "a regional commission" should not pass unnoticed, for it was a farsighted recommendation. According to Hull, Roosevelt "warmly approved" the suggestions. Prime Minister Churchill did not!

Shortly after the President's death in 1945 a lively row erupted within the Department of State over American policy toward Indo-China. A battle of memoranda between 20 April and 9 May between the Division of European Affairs and the Division of Far Eastern Affairs revealed that the latter had a real concept of the emerging dimensions of Southeast Asia while the former thought of the area in terms of European dependencies[14]. In the end the effort to send a memorandum on US policy toward Indo-China to President Truman embracing observations

and recommendations as well as a cable to the American embassy in Paris failed. The drafts of the memoranda battle make fascinating reading today! The Department of State, however, did issue a policy paper on 22 June estimating conditions in Asia and the Pacific (excluding Burma and the Philippines in Southeast Asia) when the war ended and citing policies the United States planned to pursue[15].

On 26 May a shift in the State Department changed the name of the Division of Southwest Pacific Affairs to Division of Southeast Asian Affairs. It reflected a more accurate designation and greater concern over Southeast Asian matters. (The Philippines was a separate division.) As far as jurisdiction in the Department was concerned, there was no change. Until the spring of 1944 the Office of Far Eastern Affairs had no jurisdiction over European dependencies in Southeast Asia since the area was handled by the Office of European Affairs. When the Division of Southwest Pacific Affairs was set up in Far Eastern Affairs in 1944 it had primary jurisdiction for only Thailand and concurrent jurisdiction for the European dependencies in Southeast Asia and the Pacific with European Affairs. This arrangement was highly significant in the formulation of policy in the Department of State. The spelling of "Southeast" in the Division of Southeast Asian Affairs in May 1945, it might be noted, was not an accident. "Southeast Asia" was chosen in place of "South-East Asia" in order not to copy the British[16].

*   *   *

The role of the British in the development of the concept of Southeast Asia should not be minimized. The existence of Admiral Mountbatten's Southeast Asia Command, 1943-1945, with post surrender tasks extending into 1946, caused London to consider more carefully than otherwise the problems of territories in the area outside Burma, Malaya, and British Borneo. Mountbatten found that waging war against the Japanese involved one set of considerations but administering occupied areas brought economic and political problems to the forefront.

On 16 March 1946, Lord Killearn arrived in Singapore as British Special Commissioner in South-East Asia and on May 21 Malcolm Mac-Donald came as Governor-General of Malaya and British Borneo. A British Defence Committee in South-East Asia was established consisting of the Supreme Commander, Governor-General, and Special Commissioner. This early postwar organization reflected a British concern for the region. MacDonald later indicated that the concept of Southeast Asia grew rapidly after the Second World War[17].

Lord Killearn as Special Commissioner played a key role in the economic field[18]. An Economic Organization was created with an Economic Department; Liaison Meetings were held each month at first consisting of representatives from British dependencies and then of additional ones from outside areas. Special regional conferences were convened on topics like nutrition, fisheries, social welfare, and statistics. The organization of rice distribution through a Liaison Conference was one of Lord Killearn's most important tasks. In fact, valuable experience was gained in economic co-operation along regional lines and precedents were set for the future.

On 1 May 1948, MacDonald took over the functions of Governor-General and Special Commissioner with the title of Commissioner-General for the United Kingdom in South-East Asia. From his headquarters in Phoenix Park,

Singapore, he reported to the Foreign Office relative to independent countries and to the Colonial Office on British dependencies. Many of his responsibilities related to advice on the co-ordination of British regional policy in Southeast Asia. He also had co-ordinating and advisory functions for the policy of the United Kingdom from Japan to Afghanistan, including Australia and New Zealand. It seems certain that British military and civilian representatives during and after the Second World War made a major contribution toward the regional concept of Southeast Asia.

Would the concept have emerged without the Second World War and its early aftermath? It has become conventional wisdom for scholars to pinpoint Mountbatten's Southeast Asia Command. Certainly the emerging perception of Southeast Asia as a region in military and political terms in connection with the Second World War should not be underestimated. Indeed, the Japanese conquest of the entire area contributed to the regional concept, for it destroyed the colonial partition of Southeast Asia among the Western powers and necessitated under the circumstances an allied approach toward the expulsion of the Japanese and to a lesser degree toward early postwar problems. Yet it is quite likely that the regional concept of Southeast Asia would have emerged, though much more slowly, without the benefit of the highly stressed Southeast Asia Command.

NOTES

1. Correspondence with William L. Holland.
2. Correspondence with Kenneth P. Landon and interview with Evelyn S. Colbert.
3. For documentation see *Foreign Relations of the United States: The Conferences at Washington and Quebec, 1943* (Washington: Government Printing Office, 1970).
4. Ibid., p. 1130.
5. Ibid., p. 1128.
6. Correspondence with Admiral Lord Louis Mountbatten.
7. It is interesting to note that General R. A. Wheeler who succeeded Stilwell as the senior American in S.E.A.C. knew of no particular reason for calling the Command, the Southeast Asia Command. He believed it was associated with opposition to the Japanese in Southeast Asia. General A. C. Wedemeyer who followed Stilwell in China later called attention to the role of General MacArthur in island-hopping operations from the area of Southeast Asia aimed eventually at the Japanese homeland, operations

that stood in contrast to those of Admiral Chester Nimitz across the Pacific. Correspondence with General R. A. Wheeler and General A. C. Wedemeyer.

8. For documentation see *Foreign Relations of the United States: The Conference of Berlin [The Potsdam Conference], 1945*, 2 vols. (Washington: Government Printing Office, 1960).

9. *Ibid.*, Vol. 11, p. 1319.

10. *Ibid.*, p. 377. The step was taken on 15 August.

11. The Pentagon Papers of 1971 collectively refer to Department of Defense, *United States-Vietnam Relations, 1945-1967*, 12 books (Washington: Government Printing Office, 1971), The Senator Gravel Edition, *The Pentagon Papers: The Defense Department History of United States Decisionmaking on Vietnam*, 4 vols. (Boston: Beacon Press, 1971), and *The Pentagon Papers* (New York: Bantam, 1971) or *The New York Times*, 13-15 June, 1-5 July, 1971. For the Second World War and the immediate aftermath through 1964 the Department of Defense edition is the best.

12. See *Foreign Relations of the United States, 1944*, Vol. V, *The Near East, South Asia, and Africa; The Far East* (Washington: Government Printing Office, 1965), pp. 1186-1198, 1261-1262.

13. Cordell Hull, *The Memoirs of Cordell Hull*, Vol. II (New York: The Macmillan Company, 1948), p. 1600.

14. For documentation see *United States-Vietnam Relations, 1945-1967*, Book 8, pp. 5-25.

15. *Foreign Relations of the United States, 1945*, Vol. VI, *The British Commonwealth; The Far East* (Washington: Government Printing Office, 1969), pp. 556-580.

16. Interview with Lauriston Sharp. Correspondence with John F. Cady. The spelling of Southeast Asia is still a matter of choice. The British generally but not always write South-East Asia or South East Asia and the Americans Southeast Asia. Other variations have been used.

17. Correspondence with Malcolm MacDonald in his later capacity as Commissioner-General. The author has also had correspondence with his successors, Sir Robert Scott and Lord Selkirk.

18. Lord Killearn, died in 1964. The author is indebted to his son, Lord Killearn, for correspondence.

5. POST-WAR REGIONAL CO-OPERATION

PETER LYON

If there were a verb 'to regionalize' then a dispassionate student of regionalism in Southeast Asia might conjugate it thus: past, imperfect; present, indicative; future, indefinite. Regionalism in and/or for Southeast Asia has passed through three stages since 1945 and is still in the third stage.

The first phase, which lasted from the end of the Second World War until the second half of the 1950s, was shaped and characterized mostly by the dominance of the United States and Britain in deciding what of regional associations in and for Southeast Asia there should be. Within Southeast Asia in these years Malaya (and the Borneo territories) and Singapore remained British colonies, thus cordoned off from conducting an independent diplomacy of their own; Vietnam was convulsed by war; Cambodia and Laos were still French colonies until 1954; Burma looked westwards to India or even further to Britain and the United States rather than to Southeast Asia, and relations with the ancient enemy Thailand were quietly cordial though in foreign affairs the Thai leaders were mostly preoccupied with the United States in these years; the Philippines was for all practical purposes a camp-follower of the United States despite rhetorical proclamations in favour of Asian regionalism from 1946 onwards; Indonesia seemed uninterested and uninvolved in Southeast Asia as such — for Sukarno, Bandung and Afro-Asian stages probably seemed more exciting and promising. These were the years which saw the inception of ECAFE and the Colombo Plan -- both worthy in their different ways, but each in their formative years institutionally weak and very reliant on British and American backing. Then, in September 1954, SEATO was formally launched, avowedly a Southeast Asian treaty organization, but with only two full members from Southeast Asia. In these years, then, Southeast Asian initiatives in the matter of creating new regional associations, or in working the few existing ones, were either non-existent, negligible, or merely rhetorical.

The second phase, from the late 1950s until the mid-1960s, as well as witnessing the continuance of ECAFE and the Colombo Plan very much as before,[1] also saw the first significant stirrings of Southeast Asian initiatives in regionalist matters which then led on to some abortive, or to individually undramatic but cumulatively quite important, attempts to create institutionalized co-operation. Two rather different sets of innovation should be

Reprinted in abridged form from Peter Lyon, "ASEAN and the Future of Regionalism", in *New Directions in the International Relations of Southeast Asia: The Great Powers and Southeast Asia*, edited by Lau Teik Soon (Singapore: Singapore University Press, 1973), pp. 156–64, by permission of the author and the publisher.

distinguished. At the level of what might loosely be termed 'high politics' two schemes were launched — ASA and Maphilindo (three, if one adds ASPAC). Both were not to live beyond infancy, though for quite different reasons. A useful account, and — in a sense — an epitaph, on these two experiments was provided in Bernard K. Gordon's book.[2] The second trend, which was to be more durable and probably more significant than the superficially more eye-catching ASA and Maphilindo, was almost completely missed even by Bernard Gordon as well as by myself.[3] This less-than-luminous trend was made by the well-nigh simultaneous launching of a considerable number of functional regional organizations — not only the ADB, which both Bernard Gordon and I noted, or even APO (that little favourite with many Americans), but also AIEDP, AIDC, AIT, AIEPA (see Glossary). Another significant

sign of early gusts that began to make the next prevailing wind was the initiative of Japan in bringing into being not only — or least — the ADB but also MCEDSEA and SEAMEO.

A third phase, of which the present is a part, was formally inaugurated by the inception of ASEAN in August 1967 (though it is arguable, by stressing Japan's role, that the inception of ADB two years earlier was more significant). The most striking and important thing about the launching of ASEAN was Indonesia's active membership in it from the start, symbolizing an end to Indonesia's Confrontation campaign and to her previous indifference to practical regionalism in Southeast Asia. Indeed, Indonesia's participation is a basic precondition of any really important large-scale regionalist enterprise, given that about half the total population of Southeast Asia live in Indonesia.

NOTES

1. For a detailed account of ECAFE until 1955 see David R. Wightman, *Toward Economic Cooperation in Asia: the United Nations Economic Commission for Asia and the Far East* (New Haven: Yale University Press, 1963); and L.P. Singh, *The Politics of Economic Cooperation in Asia: a Study of Asian International Organizations* (Columbia: University of Missouri Press, 1966). Dr Singh's book on the character and functioning of some inter-governmental associations in Asia was mostly about ECAFE and the Colombo Plan. It was indicative of his general view that his last chapter (also labelled 'Part 4 — The Current Situation') was called 'Obstacles to Regional Economic Cooperation and Integration in Asia', and he asserted that Asia was lagging behind all other continents, including Africa, in regional economic co-operation.
2. Bernard Gordon is a well-known enthusiastic academic advocate of regionalism in Southeast Asia. See his book *The Dimensions of Conflict in Southeast Asia*. (New Jersey: Prentice-Hall, 1966), see especially pp. 22-40 and chapters 5 and 6.
3. Peter Lyon, *War and Peace in Southeast Asia* (London: Oxford University Press for the Royal Institute of International Affairs. 1969), see especially pp. 154-8 for ASA, which is mistakenly entitled when cited in full, and pp. 195-8 on Maphilindo.

6.

SEATO, ASA, MAPHILINDO AND ASPAC

NORMAN D. PALMER

Before turning to ASEAN, some reference should be made to four earlier organizations, whose experience — eventually ill-fated — had a pronounced bearing on ASEAN's formation and development. These are the Southeast Asia Treaty Organization (SEATO), the Association of Southeast Asia (ASA), "Maphilindo" (an acronym formed from the first letters of the names of its member countries), and the Asian and Pacific Council (ASPAC). The majority of the members of the first and fourth of these organizations, however, were not Southeast Asian states, and the second and third of these organizations were composed of only three Southeast Asian countries.

SEATO

Formed at the instigation of the United States, with Secretary of State John Foster Dulles in the leading role, SEATO can be more accurately described as a part of the worldwide U.S.-led system of anti-Communist military alliances, or security arrangements, than as a true Southeast Asian regional arrangement. It emerged out of a conference in Manila in 1954, shortly after the Geneva conference on Indochina following

the final victory of the Viet Minh over the French with the fall of Dienbienphu. At this conference the participating nations — Australia, Britain, France, New Zealand, Pakistan, the Philippines, Thailand, and the United States — signed the Southeast Asia Collective Defense Treaty (the Manila Treaty) and proclaimed a Pacific Charter.[1] Although only two nations of Southeast Asia, the Philippines and Thailand, and only one other Asian country, Pakistan, were signatories to the treaty, the "treaty area" was designated as "the general area of Southeast Asia" and a protocol specifically extended the provisions of the treaty to Indochina. The treaty contained provisions for collective action in the event of an armed attack on any of the Southeast Asian countries (much more general and less binding than the comparable provisions in the North Atlantic Treaty of 1949, for countering "subversive activities from without," and even for cooperation in strengthening "free institutions" and the promotion of "economic progress and social well-being."

In a separate protocol the United States made it clear that it interpreted the Manila treaty as a commitment to provide collective defense to Southeast Asia against *Communist* aggression only. In 1962, in another unilateral protocol to the Manila Treaty, the United States

Excerpted from Norman D. Palmer, *The New Regionalism in Asia and the Pacific* (Massachusetts: Lexington Books, 1991), by permission of the author and Lexington Books, an imprint of Macmillan, Inc.

pledged that it would come to the assistance of Thailand in the event of Communist aggression, whether other SEATO members did or did not.

In spite of continuing support from the United States, SEATO became "dead in the water" not long after its formation. It never had much potential as a collective security instrument. Most of its members were reluctant to make the commitment that would be required to achieve this objective. It was widely criticized, not only by the Soviet Union and other Communist states, but also by influential groups within some of its member countries and by most of the non-Communist states of Southeast Asia that were not signatories to the treaty, notably Indonesia.

As the world's political climate changed with the ebbing of the cold war, SEATO gradually lost the support of some of its members. France and Pakistan ceased to take an active role in the alliance, and Britain showed an increasing reluctance to associate itself with any SEATO military preparations and exercises. In a kind of confirmation of Parkinson's Law, SEATO developed an increasingly elaborate organizational structure, mostly based in Bangkok, its headquarters, while it was losing the support of its members and was becoming increasingly irrelevant as a security organization. It never had much relevance in terms of regionalism in Southeast Asia, even though it presumably focused on this region. It is a leading reminder of the problems of developing a really effective collective security arrangement with disparate membership, lacking the essential bases and incentives for cooperation, and of trying to promote any significant regional cooperation from the outside. By the early 1960s it was clearly losing its effectiveness and support. But, as John Stirling noted, "it survived (with occasional military exercises) until 1977, when it was dissolved and its grandiose headquarters in Bangkok taken over by the Thai government."[2] Technically the Manila Treaty, but not SEATO, "is still in force. . . . The alliance remains on paper but in fact is defunct."[3]

ASPAC

Even more ill-fated, and even more irrelevant from the point of view of regionalism in Southeast Asia, was the Asian and Pacific Council (ASPAC), organized in 1966 at the initiative of President Park Chung-hee of South Korea. It did have some significance as perhaps the major example to date of a multi-regional organization designed to bring together most of the leading non-Communist nations of the Western Pacific to deal with external threats (many stemming from the developments in Indochina) and to provide a framework for more widespread cooperation. Its members were Australia, Japan, Malaysia, Nationalist China (Taiwan), New Zealand, the Philippines, South Korea, South Vietnam, and Thailand (with Laos having an observer status).[4] It should be noted that only four of its members were Southeast Asian states and that the largest nation of the region, Indonesia, refused to join. ASPAC was, in fact, never given more than halfhearted support by any participating member except South Korea. Nor were its main objectives and areas of concentration ever clear.

In a joint communiqué issued at the close of the organizational meeting in Seoul, the participating countries announced their "determination to preserve their integrity and sovereignty in the face of external threats"; but at the same time they agreed that the new organization should be "nonmilitary, nonideological, and not anti-Communist." Even the most closely knit regional organization would face difficulties in working toward these conflicting objectives, and ASPAC was anything but closely knit. It is not surprising that it survived for only seven years. What is surprising is that it was formed at all, and that countries of such disparate character would agree to adhere to it. As the Vietnam War gradually began to wind down, with a Communist victory in sight, and, more importantly, as the United States, Japan, and other non-Communist nations began to "normalize" their relations with the People's Republic of China, "the writing on the wall" was clear for all to read. ASPAC was dissolved early in 1973.[5]

ASA AND "MAPHILINDO"

The Association of Southeast Asia (ASA) and "Maphilindo" were different types of organizations, more limited in membership and objectives, each involving only three Southeast Asian states. In 1959 the Prime Minister of Malaya, Tunku Abdul Rahman, formally proposed that an Association of Southeast Asia should be set up. In spite of the fact that most of the Southeast Asian states gave the proposal a cool reception and that China, the Soviet Union, and the Communist states of Indochina denounced it as an offshoot of SEATO, the Philippines and Thailand agreed to join Malaya in forming ASA.

The new organization was launched in 1961. But it had a short life. In 1963, in accordance with a British proposal, two territories on the island of Borneo — Sarawak and Sabah — were brought together with Malaya (which then included Singapore) to form the Federation of Malaysia. The Philippines refused to recognize the enlarged federation, because it had longstanding claims to Sabah. ASA in effect was a victim of this dispute, although a small secretariat continued to carry on a shadowy existence for some time.[6]

The formation of Malaysia was also the *coup de grace* for "Maphilindo," an association of Malaya, the Philippines, and Indonesia, as its name suggests. Its establishment was proclaimed in a declaration of the foreign ministers of the three states in August 1963. It received a mortal blow a month later, when Malaysia came into being. Neither the Philippines nor Indonesia recognized the new federation. Sukarno soon launched a guerrilla war against Malaysia, a bitter and sometimes bloody confrontation — *Konfrontasi* — that lasted until Sukarno's fall in 1967. "Maphilindo" was only one of the many casualties of this conflict, which created the most serious divisions in Southeast Asia until the prolonged war in Vietnam reached new heights shortly afterward.[7]

NOTES

1. For the texts of the Manila Treaty and the Pacific Charter, see *The New York Times*, 9 September 1954.
2. John Sterling, "ASEAN: The Anti-Domino Factor," *Asian Affairs* 7, no. 5 (May/June 1980): 274.
3. Michael Haas, "Alliance," in Ervin Laszlo and Jong Youl Yoo, eds., *World Encyclopedia of Peace* (Oxford: Pergamon Press, 1986), 1:10.
4. See above, chapter 2, 26. See also Norman D. Palmer and Howard C. Perkins, *International Relations: The World Community in Transition*, 3d ed. (Boston: Houghton Mfflin, 1969), 593.
5. Stirling, "ASEAN: The Anti-Domino Factor," 276.
6. Ibid., 275–76.
7. Palmer and Perkins, *International Relations*, 590.

Section *II*

ORIGINS, FORMATION AND ORGANIZATION OF ASEAN

Introduction

Pushpa Thambipillai

The following selections deal with various aspects of the origins, formation and organization of ASEAN, portray the mood and events surrounding the evolution of ASEAN, and highlight various issues and problems the member countries have faced in determining its structure, style, and direction. The selections illustrate how, once initial obstacles had been overcome and ASEAN was created, the next developmental stages posed further questions in the management of regional co-operation.

The articles by Yoshiyuki Hagiwara, Khaw Guat Hoon, C.P.F. Luhulima, Chin Kin Wah, and Muthiah Alagappa illustrate debates that have continued right from the beginning. Nevertheless, these debates and disagreements have been pursued in the "ASEAN way", so as not to disrupt the regional co-operation that has been so carefully nurtured. Thus, the behavioural aspects of regionalism are important factors, as the articles by Pushpa Thambipillai, Estrella D. Solidum, and Purificacion V. Quisumbing demonstrate. The style and substance of intra-regional relations have been built on mutually acceptable modes of behaviour in order to maintain a conciliatory relationship among the participants.

Not only was ASEAN a collective avenue for action initiated by senior government officials and political leaders, it also established the foundation for a network of business sector and community level interactions as the studies by Chng Meng Kng and Johan Saravanamuttu/ Sharom Ahmat explain. However, the vast scope of intra-regional activities at the non-governmental levels is only gradually being realized as national barriers have first to be dealt with. Collectively, as a forward-looking organization of developing countries, ASEAN, since the early 1970s, has also instituted a unique system of bilateral relations with the developed countries, termed the dialogue partners, as discussed by B.A. Hamzah. This process has been gaining momentum in the scope and range of issues covered as well as in membership, with the inclusion of South Korea in 1991.

With the increasing competition in the international economic arena, as well as the need for collaborative action in regional political affairs, ASEAN's internal and external oriented structures, functions and policies have undergone changes and will no doubt see more. Thus, one of the main purposes of this Section is to provide the background to the current level of regionalism, explaining where the concept of ASEAN came from, and where it is heading as it nears the end of its third decade. An understanding of history will direct the proposals for its future development.

As ASEAN seeks to implement some of the recommendations of the Fourth Summit (see Michael Antolik's article), P. Quisumbing's observation remains relevant: that the challenge for ASEAN is the forging of a viable legal framework for smooth intra-regional interaction and effective extra-ASEAN relations. This is, however, not as simple as it appears. The very nature of the six-minus-one principle adhered to by ASEAN recognizes the voluntary participation of each of the member states. As Muthiah Alagappa notes, the gradual and piecemeal development of the consensus method for decision-making clearly reflects a very cautious approach to regional co-operation.

As ASEAN enters the next stage in its evolution, it cannot but adapt to the regional and international influences and strengthen its structures and functions. However, it is unlikely that the founding principles which have steadfastly supported ASEAN since 1967 will be ignored. Organizational innovation is vital, but so is a sense of historical purpose.

7.   THE FORMATION OF ASEAN

YOSHIYUKI HAGIWARA

In 1967, the continually-escalating war in Vietnam, together with China's "Great Proletarian Cultural Revolution," dominated the consciousness of Asia. U.S. military involvement in Vietnam had been accelerated since her air-bombing of North Vietnam in February 1965 and she made use of military bases in Japan, the Philippines, and Thailand. Japan had maintained its mutual security pact with the United States since 1952 and the Philippines and Thailand had been members of SEATO since 1954. Because of these relations, the three governments supported U.S. military involvement throughout the Vietnam war.

In April 1966, the Japanese government initiated the formation of the Ministerial Conference for Economic Development of Southeast Asia,[1] and in June, the Korean government started the Asian and Pacific Council (ASPAC).[2] The former is a regional economic cooperation group under Japanese leadership which will partly substitute its aid for U.S. economic aid to Southeast Asia. ASPAC, in the final communique of the Seoul meeting, was to be for "Greater co-operation and solidarity among the free Asian and Pacific countries in their efforts to safeguard their national independence against communist aggression or infiltration, and to develop their national economies." ASPAC's purpose was to organize the "free" countries in the region to form a "second front" for U.S. military action in Vietnam.

In 1966, in China, the Great Proletarian Cultural Revolution began in August and huge mass movements were continued throughout 1967. This revolution was initiated by Mao T'se-tung to revitalize the revolutionary spirits of the masses particularly in opposition to the Vietnam war.[3]

In such a situation, Malaysia, the Philippines, and Thailand maintained common interests in ASA and ASPAC in 1967. In February 1967, Sukarno invested full power in Suharto and a new military regime based on anti-communism was established in Indonesia. Since independence in 1965, the PAP government of Singapore had been confronted with the "hit-and-run 'Parliament of the Streets' tactics of the pro-communist Barisan Sosialis".[4] These two governments proclaimed a non-aligned foreign policy in principle but because of the anti-communist regime, they could have common interests with ASA governments. What were the common interests at that time? First, the fear of communist influence internally and internationally, secondly the expectation of economic aid from

Reprinted in abridged form from "Formation and Development of the Association of Southeast Asian Nations", *The Developing Economies* XI, no. 4 (December 1973), pp. 443–65, by permission of the author and the Institute of Developing Economies.

the United States, the United Kingdom, and Japan, and thirdly the hope of revitalizing regional cooperation. Thus, in August 1967, five governments agreed to form ASEAN as a regional cooperation group, replacing the moribund ASA and the immobile MAPHILINDO.

The Bangkok Declaration said that the objectives of ASEAN were "to accelerate the economic growth, social progress and cultural development in the region through joint endeavour and partnership in order to strengthen the foundation for a prosperous and equal community of South-East Asian nations; to promote regional peace and stability. . . ."

In spite of this hope, before celebrating its first birthday in August 1968, ASEAN was faced with gloomy prospects. First, a squabble over the possession of Sabah between the Philippines and Malaysia occurred again and secondly, the execution of two Indonesian marines by Singapore government received a strong reaction from Indonesian nationalists. But, these two cases were fortunately held in line and ASEAN survived maintaining its original purpose of cooperation.

In November 1968, Nixon was elected U.S. president and in July 1969 he proposed a withdrawal of the U.S. military presence in Asia after the end of the Vietnam war. He also suggested (in the Guam Doctrine)[5] that the Asian countries take the initiative in creating a defence organization of their own. Besides this U.S. policy, the British Labor government declared in 1968 Britain's east of Suez military withdrawal which would last until 1971. Responding to these policies, in June 1969 the Soviet Union suggested the creation of "a system of collective security in Asia."

In China, the Great Proletarian Cultural Revolution had diminished by 1969 and she began to reconstruct her international relation. And, also, the military clash between China and the Soviet Union took place from June to August of the same year.

With these events in Asia in the background, ASEAN governments agreed to begin a seven-day free visa system for ASEAN members by the end of 1968. In May 1969, they decided to set up several committees in respective capitals: a committee on food production and supply in Jakarta; on civil air transport in Singapore; on communication, air traffic services, and meteorology in Kuala Lumpur; on shipping in Bangkok; and on commerce and industry in Manila. This meant that ASEAN countries followed a rather steady path of cooperation. In March 1970, Sihanouk was expelled from his post as the head of Cambodia, and U.S. forces marched in to Cambodia to help the new regime of Lon Nol.

Responding to the U.S. action, China organized an anti-U.S. front in Indochina, composed of the Pathet Lao, North Vietnam, Vietcong, and Sihanouk supporters. Also, China accused the United States of imperialism and the Japanese of militarism in Asia and was able to improve her relations with the Soviet Union. In this situation, the fourth meeting of foreign ministers of ASEAN was put off until March 1971 in Manila. At this conference, President Marcos proposed the formation of a common market and a payment union for economic cooperation.

Just after the conference, in April 1971, the U.S. pingpong team visited China and in July, Nixon announced that his visit to China would take place before May 1972. In May 1971, at the Sixth Ministerial Conference for Economic Development of Southeast Asia in Kuala Lumpur, Tun Razak presented a strategy to promote peace and prosperity which would neutralize the region, and be guaranteed by the United States, the Soviet Union, and China. At October 1972 U.N. General Assembly Meeting, China's United Nations membership was approved replacing Taiwan as the rightful member. Among ASEAN countries, Malaysia and Singapore supported the Albanian proposal, the Philippines opposed, Indonesia and Thailand abstained from voting.

In November 1971, at the fifth meeting of foreign ministers of ASEAN at Kuala Lumpur, an agreement in principle for Razak's plan was secured and a "declaration of peace and neutrality" of Southeast Asia was drawn up. Malaysia and Singapore formed the ANZUK defence force with United Kingdom, Australia, and New Zealand, which began in effect from November 1, 1971. Thailand and the Philippines kept U.S. military bases in their countries and Indonesia received military aid from the United States.

In February 1972, Nixon visited Peking. Japan normalized diplomatic relations with China in September 1972 and U.S. military involvement in Vietnam ended in February 1973. These historical events seemed to thaw the Asian cold war, which had lasted for more than twenty years since the end of the Second World War. But, basically, the difference between the capitalist and communist regimes exists and a disguised cold war still continues in the region. In April 1973, ASEAN held the sixth meeting of foreign ministers at Bataya, Thailand and it announced five proposals: (1) to deal with the synthetic rubber industry of Japan, (2) to set up a committee for reconstruction of the Indochina region, (3) to set up a central secretariat at Jakarta, (4) to establish the special committee of the central banks, and (5) to have close relations with EC countries. At this conference, the relationship with China and the security problem after the Vietnam war were discussed. But, in the final communique, nothing was mentioned in connection with these serious problems. The different political situations in ASEAN governments made it difficult to form a common stand on these problems. And, in May 1974, the seventh meeting of foreign ministers was held at Jakarta and the possibility of Malaysia's diplomatic relations with China was discussed. But, the communique of this Meeting referred to nothing that would have to do with China and only declared a strengthening of economic cooperation in the region. But, just after this meeting, on May 20, Malaysia normalized the diplomatic relations with China and Tun Razak made his idea of Southeast Asia's neutrality, guaranteed by the United States, USSR, and China a reality. It seems to me that ASEAN has entered a new political and economic era in the region.

NOTES

1. Participants are Indonesia, Japan, Laos, Malaysia, the Philippines, Singapore, Thailand, and South Vietnam.
2. Participants are Australia, Formosa, Japan, Malaysia, New Zealand, the Philippines, South Korea, South Vietnam, and Thailand.
3. Imagawa, E., and Hama, H. *Bunka-daikakumei to Betonamu sensō* [Great Cultural Revolution and the Vietnam War] (Tokyo: Institute of Developing Economies, 1968).
4. Far Eastern Economic Review. *1968 Yearbook, p. 291.*
5. This doctrine was interpreted to mean a decrease in U.S. military forces in Asia to make Asian peoples fight each other [Hayashi, N. "Nihon gunkokushugi fukkatsu no keizai-teki kiso" (The economic basis for the revival of the Japanese militarism), *Gendai to shishō*, October 1970, p. 280]. The South-Vietnamese government announced that around seventy thousand (about 80 per cent Vietcong) soldiers were killed last year, one year after the Paris Armistice of January 1973 [*Mainichi shimbun,* March 16, 1974].

8.

THE EVOLUTION OF ASEAN, 1967–75

KHAW GUAT HOON

The Bangkok Declaration briefly spelled out the aims and purposes of ASEAN, which were primarily social, cultural and economic in nature. However, economic cooperation was clearly given preeminence. Nowhere was it stated that the ASEAN states would cooperate on political matters.

Most of the aims and purposes stated in the Declaration are related to the development needs of the founding-members, each of whom hoped that regional cooperation would contribute to its own economic growth. It should be stressed that while in favour of promoting economic cooperation, the five countries stopped short of making commitments towards economic integration. Indeed, ASEAN did not even have as an objective the creation of a free trade area which is generally considered to be the lowest form of economic integration.

It is also important to note that ASEAN was not meant to be a military alliance. Even cooperation in security matters among the ASEAN countries would be carried out outside the ASEAN framework. Such cooperation exists between Malaysia and Thailand, Malaysia and Indonesia and Malaysia and Singapore along their common borders. Nothing was said about military alliances between individual ASEAN countries and external powers. The only mention of foreign military bases was made in the Preamble of the Bangkok Declaration which noted that "all foreign bases are temporary and remain only with the expressed concurrence of the countries concerned and are not intended to be used directly or indirectly to subvert the national independence and freedom of states in the area".

THE EVOLUTION OF ASEAN: 1967–1975

Shortly after ASEAN's formation, events occurred which showed clearly that cooperation in economic, social and cultural matters was contingent upon political goodwill among its members, and that regional cooperation could be retarded by political tensions. Just a little over a year after its establishment, ASEAN's activities were suspended for nearly eight months as a result of deteriorating relations between Malaysia and the Philippines over the Corregidor Affair and a revival of the Sabah claim.

The Corregidor Affair erupted when a Manila newspaper reported the presence of a secret camp on Corregidor Island where a special

Reprinted in abridged form from Khaw Guat Hoon, "ASEAN in International Politics", in *Politics in the ASEAN States*, edited by Diane K. Mauzy (Kuala Lumpur: Marican & Sons [Malaysia] Sdn Bhd, 1984), pp. 225–63, by permission of the author and the editor.

force of Muslim recruits was being trained. Malaysia alleged that the objective of the Corregidor project was the training of saboteurs who would then be infiltrated into Sabah. Relations between Malaysia and the Philippines reached a new low when the Philippine Congress passed a resolution in September 1968 delineating Philippine territorial boundaries to include Sabah.[1] The Philippines sent a directive to its diplomats attending international conferences to record a reservation concerning Malaysia's competence to represent Sabah. Such a reservation was made at a meeting of the ASEAN Permanent Committee on Commerce and Industry held from September 30 to October 5, 1968. Malaysia's reaction was that it would not attend any further ASEAN meetings until the reservation was retracted. The two countries withdrew their diplomatic representatives from each other's capitals in November 1968.

Diplomats from the other ASEAN countries launched attempts to overcome the impasse. Finally in early 1969, Manila agreed to revoke its reservation. At the Third ASEAN Ministerial meeting which was held in December 1969 a normalization of relations between the two countries was announced.

Tensions also arose between another pair of ASEAN countries — Indonesia and Singapore — in 1968 which were, fortunately, quickly defused. In October of that year, two Indonesian marines, who had been found guilty of acts of sabotage during Confrontation, were executed in Singapore despite appeals from Indonesia and Malaysia. Protests erupted in Indonesia. However, both Indonesian and Singaporean leaders remained calm and relations between the two countries soon improved.[2]

Once political tensions had been defused, the Five could turn their attention once again to cooperative efforts. However, progress in cooperation was slow in the first nine years of ASEAN's existence. Of the hundreds of recommendations proposed in the period from August 1967 to mid–1975, only a small percentage was actually implemented.[3] Little progress was made in expanding intra-ASEAN trade or

promoting industrial cooperation. Indeed, intra-ASEAN trade as a percentage of total ASEAN trade declined from 15.5% to 12.6% during the period 1970–1975. Intra-ASEAN trade was insignificant compared with the total foreign trade of each of the five ASEAN countries.[4] Industrial cooperation did not get underway at all until after the Bali Summit.

While cooperation on regional economic matters did not make much headway, cooperation among the Five in coordinating their bargaining positions with countries outside the region was more successful. The Five agreed to bargain collectively with the industrialized powers in order to obtain economic advantages. For example, in 1972, ASEAN formed a Special Coordinating Committee of ASEAN Nations (SCCAN) to formulate negotiating postures and to undertake negotiations with the European Economic Community. In addition, an ASEAN Brussels Committee, directly responsible to SCCAN, was established for day-to-day contacts. In 1973, the ASEAN countries decided to coordinate their positions at the Multilateral Trade Negotiations under GATT auspices and the ASEAN Geneva Committee was formed in March of that year. The five ASEAN countries moreover collectively approached Japan on the issue of Japanese production of synthetic rubber in 1973–74, and successfully negotiated with Australia on the provision of limited economic assistance to ASEAN as a corporate entity.[5] More dialogues with other countries were conducted in the post-Bali period.

As has been noted, the Bangkok Declaration explicitly excluded political cooperation as an ASEAN aim; it was only at the Bali Summit that political cooperation was formally accepted by the five countries. However, there were already indications of such cooperation in the pre-Bali period, although this was carried on outside the formal auspices of ASEAN at *ad hoc* or special ministerial meetings.[6] One indication was the Kuala Lumpur Declaration of 1971 issued by the five foreign ministers which called for the establishment of a Zone of Peace, Freedom and Neutrality in Southeast

Asia (ZOPFAN). This Declaration, however, was not issued at one of the annual ministerial meetings of foreign ministers provided for in the Bangkok Declaration; it was the result of an *ad hoc* meeting.

ZOPFAN was the modified version of Malaysia's proposal for the neutralization of Southeast Asia. Under the neutralization proposal, Malaysia had called for the neutrality of Southeast Asia to be guaranteed by the U.S.A., U.S.S.R. and China. The proposal was later modified to ZOPFAN under which these three major powers were no longer asked to be guarantors; instead, they were called upon to recognize and respect Southeast Asia as a Zone of Peace, Freedom and Neutrality.[7] The proposal for neutralization and later ZOPFAN was Malaysia's response to the international developments that took place in Southeast Asia in the late 1960s.

Britain's decision to withdraw east of Suez, the American desire to disengage from Vietnam and the Nixon Doctrine indicated that these two western powers were intent on reducing their military roles in Southeast Asia. The Nixon Administration, moreover, was interested in ameliorating American relations with China, a country still considered by Malaysia and, even more by Indonesia, to be a threat to the region. While the western powers aimed at reducing their military roles in Southeast Asia, Chinese and Soviet interest in the region showed no sign of abating. There was a distinct possibility that Southeast Asia could become an arena for a power struggle between these two communist giants. Malaysia under its second prime minister, Tun Abdul Razak (who led the country into the non-aligned movement), proposed neutralization to exclude the region from the disruptive effects of major power intervention and competition.

In November 1971, the ASEAN foreign ministers met in Kuala Lumpur to review recent international developments and to consider the Malaysian proposal. On November 27th, they signed a Declaration that gave cautious endorsement to Malaysia's proposal, announcing that "the neutralization of Southeast Asia is

a desirable objective". It was further stated that:

> Indonesia, Malaysia, the Philippines, Singapore and Thailand are determined to exert initially necessary efforts to secure the recognition of, and respect for, Southeast Asia as a Zone of Peace, Freedom and Neutrality, free from any form or manner of interference by outside Powers.[8]

Although all five ministers endorsed the neutralization concept in the modified form of ZOPFAN, some had considerable reservations. As the Philippine foreign minister, Carlos Romulo, later noted, the foreign ministers had been able to agree "only on the broadest plane of principle".[9]

The convening of special "informal" ministerial meetings in July 1972 and February 1973 to discuss Vietnam was yet another example that the ASEAN countries were conscious of the importance of political cooperation. As in the case of the 1971 Kuala Lumpur meetings, these meetings were not under formal ASEAN auspices. The press statement issued at the conclusion of the July meeting stated, among other things, that the ASEAN countries would explore the possibility of making concrete contributions towards the settlement of the Indochinese conflict. The second "informal" meeting considered the implications of the Paris Peace Treaty of January 1973 on Southeast Asia.[10]

THE BALI SUMMIT

In 1975, the three Indochinese states became communist. The communist victories in Cambodia (renamed Kampuchea), Vietnam and Laos galvanized the ASEAN countries into action. As Lee Kuan Yew commented in his statement at the opening of the Bali Summit Meeting:

> Since April last year, the ASEAN countries have to face up to competition from the Marxist-socialist systems of Vietnam, Laos and Cambodia.[11]

There was a consensus that ASEAN must project an image of itself as a purposeful grouping, an awareness that ASEAN needed concrete achievements if it were to be taken seriously. The Bali Summit of February 1976 reflected the new determination to strengthen ASEAN solidarity and to show the world that ASEAN was serious about fostering regional cooperation.

Three important documents emerged from the Summit — the Treaty of Amity and Co-operation in Southeast Asia, the Declaration of ASEAN Concord and the Agreement for the Establishment of the ASEAN Secretariat. At Bali, the aims and purposes of the Bangkok Declaration were reaffirmed and specific areas for cooperative efforts spelled out in greater detail. Significantly, political cooperation was explicitly recognized as an ASEAN objective. Article 9 of the Treaty of Amity and Cooperation states that

> The High Contracting Parties shall endeavour to foster cooperation in the furtherance of the cause of peace, harmony and stability in the region. To this end, the High Contracting Parties shall maintain regular contacts and consultations with one another on international and regional matters with a view to coordinating their views, actions and policies.[12]

Chapter VI of the Treaty deals specifically with settlement of disputes. The contracting parties agree to refrain from the threat or use of force to settle disputes and instead resort to the mechanisms provided by the Treaty.

The Declaration of ASEAN Concord stipulates a program of action which covers not only the social, cultural and economic fields but also the political. Among other things, it was agreed that "immediate consideration" be given to "initial steps towards recognition of and respect for the Zone of Peace, Freedom and Neutrality wherever possible, that ASEAN machinery be improved to strengthen political cooperation, and that political solidarity be reinforced by "promoting the harmonization of views, coordinating positions and, wherever possible and desirable, taking common actions".[13]

In the economic realm, attention was given to developing preferential trading arrangements and joint industrial projects. The program of action also called for, among other things, common approaches and actions in dealing with other regional groupings and individual economic powers. Other areas of ASEAN cooperation included social and cultural matters.

Finally it was agreed that an ASEAN Secretariat be set up. After nearly nine years of existence, the Association was finally to have a central servicing body.

NOTES

1. Russell H. Fifield, *National And Regional Interests in ASEAN: Competition And Cooperation In International Politics* (Singapore: Institute of Southeast Asian Studies, Occasional Paper No. 57, 1979), p. 12.
2. *Ibid.*, p. 13.
3. For more details, see Saw Swee-Hock and N.L. Sirisena, "Economic Framework of ASEAN Countries" in Saw Swee Hock and Lee Soo Ann, eds., *Economic Problems And Prospects In ASEAN Countries* (Singapore: University of Singapore Press, 1979), p. 18.
4. Wang Ting Min, "Growth Of ASEAN Trade And Tourism" in Saw, ed., *ASEAN Economies In Transition* (Singapore: Singapore University Press, 1980), p. 262.
5. Michael Leifer, "The ASEAN States And The Progress Of Regional Cooperation in South-East Asia" in Bernhard Dahm & Werner Draguhn, eds, *Politics, Society And Economy In The ASEAN States* (Wiesbaden: Otto Harrassowitz, 1975), pp. 8-9.
6. *Ibid.*, p. 7.
7. For a detailed discussion of neutralization, see Dick Wilson, *The Neutralization of Southeast Asia* (New York: Praeger Publishers, 1975).

8. For the full text of the Declaration, see *Facts on ASEAN* (Kuala Lumpur: Ministry of Foreign Affairs, n.d.), pp. 21-23.

9. Roger Irvine in "The Formative Years of ASEAN: 1967–1975" in Alison Broinowski, ed., *Understanding ASEAN* (London: MacMillan Press Ltd., 1982), p. 28.

10. *Ibid.*, pp. 30-31.

11. *Facts On ASEAN*, p. 122. He added that the ASEAN countries "must ensure that differences in political and economic systems between these countries and ASEAN are confined to peaceful competition".

12. For the full text of the Treaty, see *Ibid.*, pp. 24-29.

13. *Ibid.*, p. 40.

9.

THE THIRD ASEAN SUMMIT

C.P.F. LUHULIMA

The first meeting of the ASEAN heads of government which was held in Bali in February 1976 established two important foundations which had since guided intra-ASEAN co-operation: the framework for ASEAN co-operation and the code of conduct for inter-state relations. They were codified in the *Declaration of ASEAN Concord and the Treaty of Amity and Co-operation in Southeast Asia*. The latter one was also intended as a basis for accommodation with the three communist Indochinese states and as a strategic response to the security dynamics of the Indochina-ASEAN region.

The Kuala Lumpur Summit which followed eighteen months later revalidated the mandates and reviewed the progress of the implementation of the Bali programme of action and the Treaty. It provided, however, little additional impetus to ASEAN cooperation. As one study on ASEAN observed, the "final communique of the second summit was lengthy in words but relatively short in substance. No new ground was broken on regional development as a whole or on zonal neutrality. Also, in economic co-operation, the heads of government called attention to accomplishments already reached ... References to cooperation in the social, cultural, and information fields in the com-munique were very nebulous." What the Kuala Lumpur Summit was successful in was the development of its external relations which officially started after the Summit.[1]

After the Kuala Lumpur meeting a great number of political, economic, technological and security developments took place which had their impact on ASEAN. They accentuated ASEAN's concern with peace and stability in the region and severely hampered the progress of the ASEAN economies. It was in the light of these developments that ASEAN felt it necessary to review the major foundations of its co-operation and its machinery to enable it to effectively grapple with the various challenges posed by the Kampuchean problem, the economic downturn and the technological substitution of various traditional commodities. It was with a view to a renewed political commitment of the member countries to ASEAN, the review of ASEAN co-operation and assessments of its success and failures, the submission of novel initiatives and proposals and the redesignation of political, economic, social and cultural co-operation to further deepen ASEAN collaboration towards a more resilient ASEAN that the Third ASEAN Summit was felt to be a *sine qua non*.

The Kampuchean problem that has plagued

Reprinted in abridged form from "The Third ASEAN Summit and Beyond", *The Indonesian Quarterly* XVII, no. 1 (First Quarter 1989), pp. 12–28, by permission of the author and the Centre for Strategic and International Studies.

ASEAN since Christmas 1978 was widely perceived as the major impediment to the realisation of the Zone of Peace, Freedom and Neutrality, including its Southeast Asia Nuclear Weapon Free Zone component, since it had primarily drawn the Soviet Union and the People's Republic of China into the strategic equation in the region, while leaving the United States to tail ASEAN. The interplay of the political and strategic interests of the big powers in the Asia-Pacific region, the People's Republic of China, the Soviet Union, the United States of America and Japan, had a major impact on the strategic environment of Southeast Asia, although that impelling effect is of a balanced character since no power can be singled out as being dominant in the region. The issue of the US bases or military facilities in the Philippines, although primarily a Philippine problem, had widely involved other ASEAN members who had directly or indirectly indicated that they preferred the bases to stay as a visible security guarantee, thus pushing ZOPFAN further into the future, as the ultimate political goal. Mr. Gorbachev's Vladivostok speech of July 1986 and the proclamation of *glasnost* and *perestroika* were additional political variables to be included into ASEAN's review of the framework of political co-operation.

Significant changes in the international economic environment were reflected in equally significant changes in the ASEAN economies both in terms of magnitude and structure. The economies of the ASEAN member countries have expanded tremendously since the Bali Summit. Their GDP structures had been shifting away from agriculture towards manufacturing and to some extent towards services as well, although at different degrees ranging from the Philippines and Singapore at the top of the list to Indonesia at the lower end. Hence ASEAN countries have become augmentably contingent upon external markets for their new export products. However, significant changes in the global economic surroundings had seriously eroded the global trading environ-

ment as well. Developed countries had, in the wake of weakening growth performances, increasingly resorted to protectionist policies, thus creating additional problems for ASEAN and other developing countries.

Equally significant changes in ASEAN's immediate neighbourhood had opened up a whole variety of challenges and opportunities which needed serious consideration. China's four programmes of modernisation; the remarkable economic successes of the newly industrialising economies (NIEs) in East and Southeast Asia; Japan's rise as the most important supplier of capital; the increased involvement of the Soviet Union and other Eastern European countries in the global economy and the perceived emergence of the Asia-Pacific region as the "region of the future," all these developments challenged ASEAN co-operation fundamentally. Thus Singapore's Prime Minister Lee's opening address at the 1987 foreign ministers' meeting emphasised that new paths to growth would be required as a consequence of the fundamental changes in the international system.

Similar changes have also occurred in the global monetary and financial environment with their concomitant effects on the ASEAN countries. Exchange rate fluctuations, unprecedentedly low commodity prices, trade and payment imbalances, increasing protectionism and the prevailing international debt problems had forced a considerable degree of adjustments in the ASEAN economies. And the appreciation of the major currencies had augmented the debt servicing burden of the ASEAN member countries.

Thus ASEAN would have to effectuate the utilisation of regional resources, incrementally increase its self-reliance and hence market-sharing by way of stepping up collaboration in the development of their industries. Effective market opening measures had become more urgent as the deficiency of political commitment to such measures was bound to perpetuate the lack of complementarity among the ASEAN economies.

The significant and major political and

economic developments had led to the necessity of rearranging the magnitude and structure of the social and cultural dimen sions of ASEAN co-operation. The dimensions of regional collaboration should be singularly focussed on the achievement of a greater understanding of ASEAN ideals, of a greater sense of awareness and belonging and of a stronger sense of regional identity for ASEAN to further bolster political and economic co-operation.

The changes had also led up to the necessity of rearranging the ASEAN machinery. The present "two-headed monster" with the foreign and economic ministers each making their own autonomous decisions on how ASEAN is to proceed should be integrated into one comprehensive decision-making mechanism and set of procedures to backup political and economic progress in ASEAN.

THE OUTLOOK

Evaluating the ASEAN Summit and exploring its future development one year after its occurrence is an interesting, yet indispensible exercise. The expectations in the initial stages of the preparations for the Summit ran very high indeed. Towards the end of the exercise the agreements on "novel" initiatives and proposals and some "bold" reformulations of ASEAN programmes of action in the three major areas of co-operation to further deepen ASEAN collaboration could still be categorised as significant. In the field of economic co-operation the Summit succeeded in setting quantitative targets, stipulating regional measures for market liberalisation both as regards the PTA and the Rules of Origin, and standstill and roll back of NTBs, with Indonesia and the Philippines being granted special concessions.

Social, cultural, and science and technology co-operation were reconstituted into functional co-operation with the specific objective of achieving an increased awareness of ASEAN, wider participation of the people in the ASEAN exercise and the development of human resources into national and regional assets. In the field of political co operation, both ZOPFAN and NWFZ were projected further into the future.

These initiatives and proposals were submitted to further foster regional co-operation and solidarity and to strengthen national and regional resilience. Yet these achievement also reflect how fragile the bond among ASEAN nations still is. ASEAN co-operation still has to be nurtured and consolidated carefully. ASEAN still has to determine whether the achievements of the Manila Summit are targeted to maintain the status quo and thus accelerate progress on the national level in terms of GNP per capita, trade performance, far-reaching industrialisation programmes or to move in the direction of a free-trade area by agreeing to the progressive expansion of the items on their inclusion lists of the PTA or of a partial or sectorial integration or towards a common market. Some ASEAN countries are not ready to open up their internal markets to foreign competition on the basis of the infant industries argument, while all ASEAN countries are still concerned about the unequal distribution of gains from trade liberalisation. Thus the status quo will still be maintained for some time to come.

ASEAN also needs to re-formulate the concepts of national interest of each individual member nation in the context of ASEAN regionalism. The principle of concensus in decision-making is essentially a safety device to assure member nations that their national interests will not be compromised. Yet, ASEAN's dependence or rather over-dependence on exports to the developed countries which have increasingly protected their markets despite assertions of allegiance to GATT already have to a certain extent compromised the economic interests of the individual member states of ASEAN. These interests will be further compromised by the global slide towards economic regionalisms of which the most important are the Single European Act and the United States-Canada(-Mexico) free trade area, ASEAN's biggest export markets. Entering these huge markets will almost certainly mean reciprocity, and reciprocity may mean pressure towards one big ASEAN market. ASEAN still consists of six separate markets. Although the Manila Summit declared that "ASEAN shall pursue regional solidarity and co-operation under all circumstances, especially whenever purposes and tensions of any kind, arising from within the region or from without, challenge the capacities, resourcefulness, and goodwill of the ASEAN nations," ASEAN will still have to formulate what it means by "regional solidarity," the "region's potential in trade and development," ASEAN's "efficacy in combatting protectionism and countering its effects." ASEAN will have to ask itself whether these pronouncements have enough weight to face the single European market or the Canada-United States free trade area, particularly if the Canada-United States alliance in trade slides towards the single European market rather than with the Asia Pacific area. ASEAN member countries will have to speed up expanding their individual inclusion lists to move towards a free-trade area, possibly towards sectoral integration of their markets, thus increasing European investments in the region.

Institutionally, this will require strengthening the ASEAN Secretariat. So far ASEAN institutional arrangements have been strongly curtailed by the national interest of each member state. That is the prime reason for the far-reaching decentralisation and geographic distribution of the indefinite number of ASEAN institutions. Such a structure, marked by a web of vertical and virtually independent ministerial prerogatives, has created numerous problems: There is inadequate transsectoral co-ordination at the national level and is compounded by the absence of co-ordination at the ASEAN's committees' level. These shortcomings are accompanied by a cumbersome chain of command at the regional level, a circuitous decision-making process and inadequate follow-up actions. These complexities are the main reason for treating the ASEAN Secretariat more as a symbol than

an effective arm of the organisation. Hence, strengthening the ASEAN Secretariat will primarily mean expansion of the power and authority of the Secretary General, provision of competent manpower on a career basis, adequate funds, but most of all moral support and recognition. This will certainly mean delegation of power on the part of the member states. Although the reluctance is still immense, again external pressure may force ASEAN to compromise as has occurred so often. Moreover, the need for quick decisions will prove that the principle of concensus in all matters and at all levels is a considerable constraint in decision-making.

Politically, the efforts of a settlement of the Kampuchean issue have transcended ASEAN's capability and bargaining power. The negotiations for a settlement on Kampuchea have increasingly passed into the hands of both China and the Soviet Union. This development will certainly complicate ASEAN's political objective of establishing ZOPFAN and NWFZ. Since ZOPFAN represents, primarily perhaps, an assertion of regional resilience, any effort to develop collective ASEAN self-resiliency is a *sine qua non*. ASEAN still has to determine the relationship between national and regional resilience. It still has to harmonise the perception on national resilience to arrive at an ASEAN concept of national resilience in order to be able to formulate the relationship between national and regional resilience and finally the concept of regional resilience and the assertion of collective resilience. Indonesia has taken the initiative by starting an ASEAN seminar on regional resilience in January-February 1989 which will need follow-up actions, since one seminar will not result in a common perception on regional resilience, let alone in the concept of collective regional resilience.

In the field of functional co-operation, the specific objectives of achieving an increased awareness of ASEAN, wider participation of the ASEAN peoples and the development of human resources will require the re-arrangement and the redesigning of the programmes of the

Committee of Social Development (COSD), of Culture and Information (COCI), and on Science and Technology (COST). The current programmes of action were based on the Bali Declaration of autonomously developing socio-cultural activities. The subsumption of social, cultural and science and technology programmes under functional co-operation with the singular objective of complementing and strengthening political and economic aspirations of ASEAN will require far-reaching rearrangements of programmes, something which has hardly begun.

NOTE

1. Russell H. Fifield, *National and Regional Interests in ASEAN: Competition and Co-operation in International Politics* (ISEAS, Occasional Paper No. 59, 1979), pp. 18-19. See also Chin Kin Wah, "The Question of a Third Summit: Pros and Cons, Approaches and Recommendations," paper presented at the *Conference on Regional Development and Security: The Ties That Bind* (12-16 January, 1986, Kuala Lumpur), p. 8.

10.   THE FOURTH ASEAN SUMMIT

MICHAEL ANTOLIK

"Conscientiously, we are turning a new page in the annals of ASEAN history".[1] Thus Thai Prime Minister Anand summarized the sense of achievement at the fourth summit meeting of the Association of Southast Asian Nations (ASEAN) held in January 1992. This gathering in Singapore of the heads of government of Brunei (Sultan Haji Hassanal Bolkiah), Indonesia (President Soeharto), Malaysia (Prime Minister Mahathir bin Mohamad), the Philippines (President Corazon Aquino), Singapore (Prime Minister Goh Chok Tong), and Thailand (Prime Minister Anand Panyarachun) produced agreements that have the potential to reshape the organization, re-energize integration, and enhance the stability of Southeast Asia.

The rapid economic changes, as President Soeharto mentioned in his address to the summit meeting, present new challenges to ASEAN leaders: "Over the past few years, we have vigilantly monitored the currents of economic integration and globalization. This development will have negative effects on the economies of the developing countries if it is followed by the establishment of groups among countries and eventually leads to closed and protectionist economic blocs".[2] The economic changes requiring appropriate responses are, notably, the increased integration of European

states in 1992 and the projected formation of a North American Free Trade Area. Closer to home, new members have been admitted to the region's tentative trade institution, the Asia-Pacific Economic Co-operation (APEC) process — namely, Taiwan, Hong Kong and China — thereby diluting the presence of ASEAN states in that forum.

At the Singapore Summit, the ASEAN states responded with a pledge to establish an ASEAN Free Trade Area (AFTA); but the reasons for this pledge go beyond external economic imperatives. On the political level, two additional developments have induced the ASEAN states to act together. For close to fifteen years, despite ASEAN's role, Cambodia appeared firmly mired in genocide, civil war and occupation. However, this issue has now been removed. Some observers welcome the end of this divisive problem as it will relieve the ASEAN members of the need to reconcile their different perceptions and policies towards China and Vietnam. Others, who saw the Vietnamese occupation as the *raison d'etre* for ASEAN solidarity, fear a declining relevance of the association to each member. Yet, it can be argued, as Philippine Foreign Minister Raul Manglapus did, that Cambodia served as a defence for inaction in economic matters: "We can no longer excuse

Reprinted in abridged form from "ASEAN's Singapore Rendezvous: Just Another Summit?" *Contemporary Southeast Asia* 14, no. 2 (September 1992), pp. 142–53, by permission of the author and the Institute of Southeast Asian Studies.

ourselves by saying 'let's fix Cambodia first'".[3] Moreover, ASEAN cannot claim the Cambodia peace settlement process to be its diplomatic achievement. It flows rather from the end of the cold war and the new co-operation in the United Nations Security Council. While peace in Cambodia will bring benefits, the troubling implication for the ASEAN states is that an important regional issue could only be solved by outside great powers. Perhaps an even more troubling situation which raises questions about the Association's effectiveness and relevance has been the chaos in the Philippines. Here, the ASEAN states' traditional rule of non-interference has led some observers to describe the Association as merely a "comfortable club of convenience".[4]

Nevertheless, the end of the Cambodian stalemate has provided an opportunity, if not a stimulus, for action. Coincidentally, while the Paris Peace Agreement for Cambodia was being signed, much of the ground work for the summit's economic plans was laid at the annual ASEAN Economic Ministers Meeting (AEM) in October 1991, when members decided to take steps towards a free trade area by accepting the Indonesian plan for establishing a Common Effective Preferential Tariff (CEPT).

The CEPT will slash existing tariff rates to 20 per cent within eight years and reduce rates from 20 per cent to 0 per cent in the following seven years. States may, however, delay participation until they are ready.

Reorganization has also touched the centre of the organization's machinery, demonstrating a new commitment to co-operation. An experienced intergovernmental body, the Senior Economic Officials Meeting (SEOM) which had previously worked on preparations for AEMs, will supervise the economic plan. Moreover, this body will now replace ASEAN's five economic committees. The Secretariat has been given new stature; it can initiate, recommend, and supervise policies and action plans. It is now to be headed by the Secretary-General of ASEAN, replacing and upgrading the office of Secretary-General of the ASEAN Secretariat. The position will now be filled by recruitment, instead of the practice of rotation among member states. Finally, summits are to be held on a three-year basis; previously, they were scheduled as the members saw necessary. (Four have been held in twenty-five years since ASEAN was founded in 1967; namely, 1976, 1977, 1987, and 1992.)

NOTES
1. *Straits Times* (Singapore), 28 January 1992; in Foreign Broadcast Information Service, Daily Report/East Asia (hereafter cited as FBIS, DR/EA), 29 January 1992, p. 8.
2. Jakarta Radio Republik Indonesia, 27 January 1992; in FBIS, DR/EA, 28 January 1992, p. 3.
3. Jonathan Thatcher, "ASEAN Seeks New Identity to Stay Together", *Star*, 1 August 1990.
4. Michael Vatikiotis, "Time for Decisions", *Far Eastern Economic Review*, 16 January 1992, p. 23.

11. THE INSTITUTIONAL STRUCTURE

CHIN KIN WAH

THE ASEAN CONSTELLATION, 1967–76

Until major restructuring of ASEAN institutions that took place following the first ASEAN summit in Bali in February 1976, the constellation of ASEAN institutions appeared as depicted in Chart 1. The highest decision-making body as laid down by the Bangkok Declaration was the **Annual Meeting of Foreign Ministers**. This grouping met on a rotational basis in each of the ASEAN capitals and was responsible for policy formulation, coordination of activities, and reviewing of decisions and proposals of the lower-level committees.

The ongoing work of the Association between ministerial meetings was conducted by the **Standing Committee**, comprising the Foreign Minister of the host country as Chairman, and the resident ambassadors of the other ASEAN countries in that host country. The seat of the Standing Committee which rotated annually, conformed with the site of the next Annual Ministerial Meeting. This committee met several times a year and its Annual Report was submitted to the meeting of Foreign Ministers for adoption. Recommendations of committees further down the institutional hierarchy were passed up to the Standing Committee before receiving ministerial consideration.

The Standing Committee was also an overseer of the three special committees that were created to handle the external relations of ASEAN. These were firstly the **Special Coordinating Committee of ASEAN Nations** (SCCAN) created in 1972 to coordinate links with the European Community. This committee, the forerunner to subsequent institutionalized linkages with third countries, was reinforced by the establishment of the **Joint Study Group** in 1975, charged with the task of examining the substance and mechanism of cooperation between the two regional organisations. The other two committees handling external relations and coming under the purview of the Standing Committee were the **ASEAN Brussels Committee** (ABC) and the **ASEAN Geneva Committee**, made up of ASEAN representatives in Brussels and Geneva respectively.

Rotation of the Standing Committee notwithstanding, an element of continuity was preserved by the activities of a more permanent group of officials who were involved in the actual supervision of ASEAN's activities and the preparatory work of the Standing Committee including the screening of recommendations submitted by the various permanent and *ad hoc* committees further down the line.

Reprinted in abridged form from Chin Kin Wah, "The Institutional Structure of ASEAN: Governmental and Private Sectors", in *ASEAN: A Bibliography 1981–85* (Singapore: Institute of Southeast Asian Studies, 1988), pp. xv–xxxv, by permission of the author and the publisher.

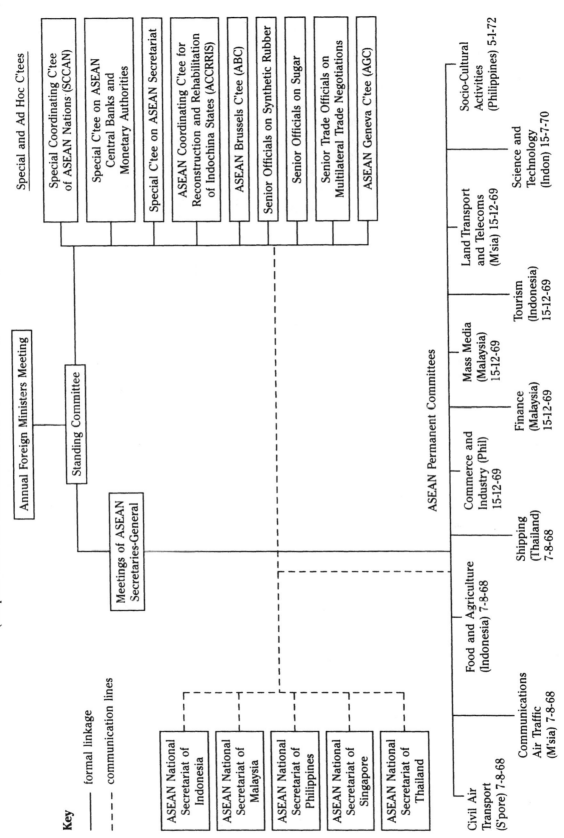

CHART 1

ORGANISATIONAL STRUCTURE OF ASEAN BEFORE BALI SUMMIT (FEBRUARY 1976)

(Adapted from *Ten Years ASEAN*, ASEAN Secretariat, Jakarta, April 1978)

Key

—— formal linkage

- - - - communication lines

Annual Foreign Ministers Meeting

Standing Committee

Meetings of ASEAN Secretaries-General

Special and Ad Hoc C'tees

Special Coordinating C'tee of ASEAN Nations (SCCAN)

Special C'tee on ASEAN Central Banks and Monetary Authorities

Special C'tee on ASEAN Secretariat

ASEAN Coordinating C'tee for Reconstruction and Rehabilitation of Indochina States (ACCRRIS)

ASEAN Brussels C'tee (ABC)

Senior Officials on Synthetic Rubber

Senior Officials on Sugar

Senior Trade Officials on Multilateral Trade Negotiations

ASEAN Geneva C'tee (AGC)

ASEAN Permanent Committees

Socio-Cultural Activities (Philippines) 5-1-72

Science and Technology (Indon) 15-7-70

Land Transport and Telecoms (M'sia) 15-12-69

Tourism (Indonesia) 15-12-69

Mass Media (Malaysia) 15-12-69

Finance (Malaysia) 15-12-69

Commerce and Industry (Phil) 15-12-69

Shipping (Thailand) 7-8-68

Food and Agriculture (Indonesia) 7-8-68

Communications Air Traffic (M'sia) 7-8-68

Civil Air Transport (S'pore) 7-8-68

ASEAN National Secretariat of Indonesia

ASEAN National Secretariat of Malaysia

ASEAN National Secretariat of Philippines

ASEAN National Secretariat of Singapore

ASEAN National Secretariat of Thailand

This group of officials were the Secretaries-General of the five ASEAN National Secretariats established to implement the work of the Association and to service the Annual Ministerial Meeting or other specially covered ministerial meetings and the Standing Committee. Collectively, they were referred to as the **ASEAN Secretaries-General**, each of whom presided over an **ASEAN National Secretariat**. It may be said that this group constituted the pivot of the ASEAN committee system which then existed.

One important group of officials that remained 'invisible' within the formal institutional structure of ASEAN was the **Senior Officials Meeting** (SOM). This committee of senior Foreign Ministry officials (at Permanent Secretary level or its equivalent) was established by the ASEAN Ministerial Meeting in November 1971. They met regularly over the years to discuss the implementation of the Zone of Peace, Freedom, and Neutrality (ZOPFAN) and have now become a regular forum for intra-ASEAN political consultation.

The range of ASEAN programmes which existed in the pre-Bali summit years were reflected by **the eleven permanent committees** of officials and experts which reported to the Standing Committee. The first four of these came into existence in August 1968 and covered Civil Air Transport (first sited in Singapore), Communications Air Traffic (sited initially in Malaysia), Food and Agriculture (Indonesia), and Shipping (Thailand). By December 1969 five more permanent committees were added to the list. These were Commerce and Industry (Philippines), Finance (Malaysia), Mass Media (Malaysia), Tourism (Indonesia), and Transportation and Telecommunications (Malaysia). The last two committees to be established were Science and Technology (Indonesia) in July 1970 and Socio-Cultural Activities (Philippines) in December 1971. The sites of these various committees were rotated once every two or three years. An array of sub-committees and working groups of experts played supportive roles to these committees.

In addition to the permanent committees there were several **special and ad hoc committees**, some of which like the SCCAN and ABC (the former's operational outpost) reflected the growing contacts and negotiations with third countries. The ASEAN Coordinating Committee for the Reconstruction and Rehabilitation of Indochina States (ACCRRIS) formed in February 1973 reflected an intention to assess the economic requirements of the Indochinese states (including the then South Vietnam) and facilitate ASEAN assistance for reconstruction and rehabilitation. Like ACCRRIS, the other committees, for example, the Senior Officials on Synthetic Rubber (created to negotiate with Japan for a reduction in synthetic rubber production), the Senior Officials on Sugar, the Special Committee on ASEAN Central Banks and Monetary Authorities, and the Special Committee on ASEAN Secretariat (created to look into the establishment of a central Secretariat), all had specific functions to discharge, unlike the permanent committees with their generalized functions. The Special and Ad Hoc Committees also differed from the permanent committees in that they did not periodically change their location and chairmanship. Furthermore, they reported directly to the Standing Committee instead of to the Meeting of Secretaries-General.

It is not intended here to discuss the problems of overlapping functions, lack of coordination, unclear lines of authority, and proliferation of these committees.[1] Suffice it to say that these problems together with the acceleration of ASEAN activities from the mid-seventies led to attempts at reorganisation and streamlining of the ASEAN structure. The existing formal structure of ASEAN is derived largely from the major restructuring endorsed at the time of the 1976 Bali summit meeting of ASEAN Heads of Government.

THE EXISTING STRUCTURE OF ASEAN

The Bali summit opened the way to basic

changes in three areas which are reflected in the present institutional structure (see Chart 2). Firstly, since the Bali summit, two other blocs of ministerial meetings have emerged in addition to the Foreign Ministers Meeting. These are the Economic Ministers Meeting of the **ASEAN Economic Ministers** (AEM), and the bloc of **Other ASEAN Ministers** (OAM), a general rubric which covers separate meetings of ASEAN Ministers of Labour, Social Welfare, Education, Information, Health, Energy, Science and Technology, and Environment. Secondly, the permanent and *ad hoc* committees of the pre-Bali period have been regrouped into five economic and three non-economic committees. Thirdly, the ASEAN Secretariat headed by its own Secretary-General and sited in Jakarta came into existence in June 1976.

The **AEM** which is charged with the task of accelerating economic co-operation, is institutionalised by the Heads of Government meeting in Bali in 1976. As such, it is considered a part of the formal institutional structure of ASEAN. The **AEM** is serviced by the Senior Economic Officials Meeting (**SEOM**). Nowadays the **AEM** meets about twice a year to review the progress of the various areas of ASEAN economic cooperation and to consider reports and recommendations of the various ASEAN economic committees.

Although there have been meetings by the other ASEAN ministers, they are not considered a part of the formal organisation of ASEAN. Nevertheless their recommendations are taken up by the ASEAN Foreign Ministers or the ASEAN Economic Ministers but may be referred to the Heads of Government.

The **Annual Meeting of ASEAN Foreign Ministers**, more commonly referred to as the ASEAN Ministerial Meeting (AMM), constitutes a policy-making body responsible for the formulation of policy guidelines and the coordination of all ASEAN activities despite the fact that the Economic Ministers now have the economic committees report directly to them. The status of the ASEAN Ministerial Meeting is enhanced by the fact that it represents the highest repository of the political sovereignties of ASEAN, considering that the **ASEAN Heads of Government** have not been institutionalized as a body with regularized meetings.

There are provisions for the convening of the ASEAN Heads of Government Meetings 'as and when necessary' to give directions to ASEAN. However such meetings have been very infrequent in the life of the Association which had to wait 9 years before the first summit was held in Bali in February 1976. The second summit was convened in Kuala Lumpur in August 1977 but no more summit meeting on the multi-lateral basis was in the making for another 10 years.

It is generally believed that the unresolved Philippine claim to Sabah was one obstacle to the convening of a third summit. No Malaysian Prime Minister had visited the Philippines (which, by alphabetical rotation was entitled to be the next host country) since the claim was revised in the late sixties and despite former President Marcos' declaration of intent at the Kuala Lumpur summit to formally relinquish the claim. Even the gathering of ASEAN Heads of Government in Brunei in February 1984 on the occasion of that country's first National Day celebration, did not result in a formal summit although they met bilaterally and informally.

Since then, the economic downturn faced by practically all the ASEAN states had created new pressure for a summit which it was hoped, would generate momentum and define new directions for economic co-operation. The regime change in the Philippines following the successful civilian-backed military revolt against President Marcos in February 1986 also held out brighter prospects for a resolution of the Sabah problem. Moreover the need to demonstrate collective support for the government of Mrs Corazon Aquino and the desirability of involving newly independent Brunei in the exercise of ASEAN summit diplomacy, also generated political imperatives for the convening of the third summit. Despite persisting concern over the security situation at the summit venue, the ASEAN Heads of Government

CHART 2
ASEAN INSTITUTIONAL STRUCTURE — 1983

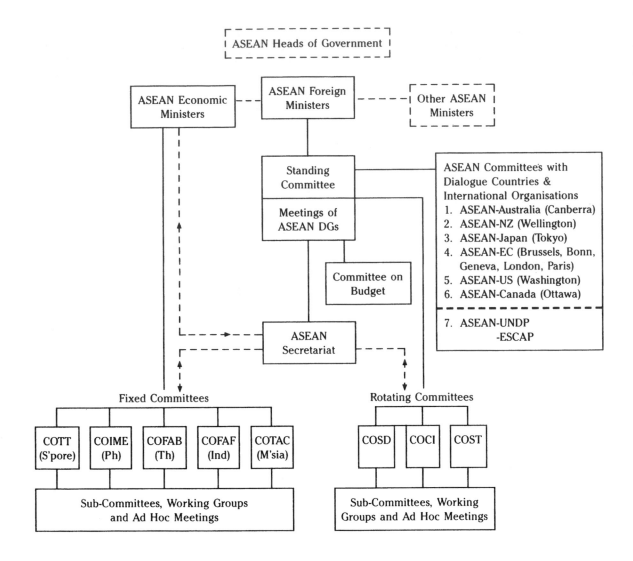

Key

——————— formal linkage

— — — — communication lines

┌ ─ ─ ┐
│   │   uninstitutionalized
└ ─ ─ ┘   arrangements

eventually held their meeting in Manila in December 1987.

Notwithstanding the absence of institutionalized summitries, the ASEAN Heads of Government have met frequently on a bilateral basis outside the formal structure of ASEAN. By one account, ninety-six of these meetings took place between 1967 and 1981 with the largest number occurring between Malaysia and Thailand and the least (only two) between Malaysia and the Philippines.[2]

Given that ASEAN summitry is uninstitutionalized, the ASEAN Foreign Ministers may be considered *primus inter pares* among the ministerial blocs. But since they meet formally as an ASEAN group only once a year unless special or informal meetings are called, the work between ministerial meetings is conducted by the **Standing Committee**, the structure of which (comprising the Foreign Minister of, and ASEAN Ambassadors accredited to, the host country) and the annually rotating location are features carried over from the pre-Bali arrangements. As Chairman of the Standing Committee, the Foreign Minister of the host country is in effect the political spokesman of ASEAN for that year.

Between the Annual Ministerial Meetings, which it services, the Standing Committee handles the routine matters and decides on matters that cannot await the ministerial meeting. It meets about six times a year and submits an Annual Report as well as other reports and recommendations of the various ASEAN Committees for consideration by the Foreign Ministers.

The **permanent functional committees** of ASEAN are grouped into five economic committees and three non-economic committees. A large number of ASEAN programmes and projects are the results of the work of these functional committees, each of which is serviced by an **interim technical secretariat**, the personnel for which are drawn from the bureaucracy of the country that hosts the particular committee. The host country also provides the Chairman of that committee.

The five **economic committees** are the Committee on Trade and Tourism (COTT) based in Singapore; the Committee on Industry, Minerals, and Energy (COIME) in the Philippines; the Committee on Finance and Banking (COFAB) in Thailand; the Committee on Food, Agriculture, and Forestry (COFAF) in Indonesia; and the Committee on Transport and Communications (COTAC) in Malaysia. Among the economic programmes and projects of ASEAN, the ASEAN Industrial Projects (AIP), industrial joint venture schemes (AIJV) and industrial complementation schemes (AIC), come under the general purview of COIME[3] while trade liberalization schemes (AIJV) such as the Preferential Trading Arrangements (PTA) are worked out under COTT. The economic committees report to the AEM.

The **non-economic committees** are the Committee on Science and Technology (COST); the Committee on Social Development (COSD); and the Committee on Culture and Information (COCI). While the economic committees are fixed in location, the non-economic committees rotate among the ASEAN capitals every three years. They report directly to the Standing Committee. In May 1984 the fifth ASEAN Standing Committee meeting held in Jakarta renamed the ASEAN Drug Experts group as the ASEAN Senior Officials on Drug Matters (ASOD). Although ASOD is formally instituted it is not considered an ASEAN Committee. ASOD reports directly to the ASEAN Standing Committee but it has no sub-committee or working group under it. The chairmanship rotates annually according to the host country of the ASOD meeting. The main function of ASOD is to discuss and formulate regional policies, approaches and strategies to combat the drug problem. When ASOD (which meets once a year) is not in session, the coordinating work is carried out by the Narcotics Desk Officer at the ASEAN Secretariat.

Under the functional committees are various sub-committees and working groups which deal with specific projects or areas of co-operation. COIME has by far the largest number of working/experts groups and a regularised Meeting of Insurance Commissioners. COFAF[4] has perhaps the most elaborate organisational structure. Its Sub-committee on Food Handling has four Working Groups and a Food Handling Bureau that deal with the post-harvest (grains), post-slaughter (livestock) and post-landing (fish) stages. The pre-production stages are the responsibilities of 4 other coordinating groups that cover Forestry, Food crops, Livestock and Fisheries.

In addition to the functional committees, there is a **Committee on Budget** which manages and disburses the ASEAN Fund and the budget of the Central ASEAN Secretariat. This committee reports to the Standing Committee.

Separation of the non-economic from the economic committees has meant that the powers of the Standing Committee have been somewhat affected. Decisions of the Economic Ministers and proposals of the economic committees are merely noted by the Standing Committee except where these have implications for political relationships or impinge on relations with third (dialogue) countries in which case they are referred to the Standing Committee which continues to oversee external relations with those countries having official 'dialogue' status.

The third area of major change in ASEAN institutions following the 1976 restructuring concerns the establishment of the central **ASEAN Secretariat** in Jakarta under a Secretary-General who is appointed by the ASEAN Foreign Ministers on a rotational basis for a two-year term. The Secretariat is responsible for the discharge of all the functions and responsibilities entrusted to it by the ASEAN Ministerial Meeting and the Standing Committee. In terms of the overall institutional hierarchy, the ASEAN Secretariat comes directly under the Standing Committee to which it reports. Its terms of reference are set out in the Agreement on the Establishment of the ASEAN Secretariat signed by the ASEAN Foreign Ministers in Bali on 24 February 1976.

Given the diffused nature of ASEAN institutions with most of the ongoing projects initiated and managed by the functional committees and with effective power held by the Standing Committee, the ASEAN Secretariat has very weak functions which have led critics to describe it as a glorified post office. In this respect, it is worthy of note that the **Secretary-General** is not the Secretary-General of ASEAN (that is, he is not the political spokesman of the Association) but only the Secretary-General of the ASEAN Secretariat. In practical terms his powers and functions have fallen short of what is suggested by a straight reading of Article 3 of the Agreement on the Establishment of the ASEAN Secretariat which states that the Secretary-General has the authority to address directly the member governments, ensure that ASEAN committees are informed of current developments in ASEAN activities, and act as a channel for formal communications between the committees. He is also to 'harmonize, facilitate and monitor progress in the implementation of all approved ASEAN activities' and 'initiate plans and programmes. . . .'

The Secretary-General is assisted by three *Bureau Directors* (for Economics; Science and Technology; and Socio-Cultural Affairs) who render supportive roles to the functional committees discussed earlier. Attempts to strengthen the ASEAN Secretariat led to the 1982 AEM's decision (implemented 1½ years later) to establish five Deputy Directors to assist the work of the Economic Bureau Director in servicing and monitoring the work of the economic committees. The areas of purview of these 5 professional officers correspond to the alignment of the 5 existing economic committees. Other home-based staff at the ASEAN Secretariat include a Foreign Trade and Economic Relations Officer, an Administrative Officer, the Public Information Officer, an Assistant to the Secretary-General and since September 1982, a Narcotics Desk Officer who is responsible for collecting data and information on drug activities and helping to implement recommendations of the ASEAN drug experts. Appointments of the home-based staff like that of the Secretary-General (whose tour of duty is now extended to 3 years), are made on a rotational basis. They are changed once every 3 years. In exceptional circumstances the terms of office of the home-based staff may even be renewed.

With the establishment of the ASEAN Secretariat, the Secretaries-General of the various ASEAN National Secretariats have been re-designated **Directors-General** (DGs) to avoid confusion with the ASEAN Secretary-General. However, to all practical purposes the creation of the central secretariat has not altered the lines of authority with respect to the Standing Committee and the national secretariats. The Directors-General still continue their supervisory functions with respect to the ongoing business of ASEAN and facilitate the Standing Committee meetings by their preparatory work. Indeed the DGs and the other members of the Standing Committee meet as a group. The 'invisible' group of Senior Officials Meeting is still being convened periodically.

NOTES

1. For such a discussion, see Hans H. Indorf, *ASEAN: Problems and Prospects*, Occasional Paper No. 38 (Singapore: Institute of Southeast Asian Studies, 1975), pp. 22-38.
2. Estrella D. Solidum, *Bilateral Summitry in ASEAN* (Philippines: Foreign Service Institute, 1982), p. 12.
3. Negotiations for the legal framework of the ASEAN Industrial Projects were actually begun under COFAB, then passed through various expert groups and COIME before receiving approval by the AEM.
4. For a description of the range of activities covered by COFAF see *ASEAN Cooperation in Food, Agriculture and Forestry*, ASEAN Information Series no. 3, ASEAN Secretariat, November 1986.

12.

THE PRIVATE SECTOR

CHNG MENG KNG

A difficult organizational issue in ASEAN relates to the role of the ASEAN private sector. As often stated, ASEAN economies are basically private enterprise economies. Thus, while governments can provide the policy framework and stimulus for complementary regional economic growth, it is only largely through the decisions and actions of businessmen in the private sectors of the ASEAN countries that such growth can be realized. There is thus a need to galvanize the effort and enthusiasm of the ASEAN private sector in ASEAN economic co-operation. It was with such a view that the ASEAN Chambers of Commerce and Industry (ASEAN-CCI) was formed in 1972 with the blessing of the ASEAN Foreign Ministers, and an elaborate machinery has evolved for the purpose not just of inter-country private sector interaction but also for dialogue with official ASEAN bodies. Over the years the ASEAN-CCI has increasingly become a proponent for a more centralized and effective ASEAN machinery, as well as for an enhanced and more direct role for the ASEAN-CCI in official ASEAN decision-making (see, for example, ASEAN-CCI 1981, pp. 34–41).

ASEAN governments have largely accepted the need to incorporate the views of the private sector in their decision-making. In fact the ASEAN-CCI has been actively involved in the formulation of various ASEAN co-operative programmes, especially in the areas of trade and industry such as the ASEAN Industrial Complementation (AIC) and ASEAN Industrial Joint Venture (AIJV) schemes. Beginning with the Twelfth AEM Meeting in January 1982, the President of the ASEAN-CCI formally reports to each AEM Meeting on its views and expectations with respect to the progress of ASEAN economic co-operation. ASEAN Foreign Ministers also formally welcomed the formation of the ASEAN-CCI's Group of Fourteen (G-14) in July 1986 "to study and recommend measures for the advancement of ASEAN economic co-operation and integration" (ASEAN-CCI, 1981). However, despite such developments, ASEAN governments have generally been reluctant to directly involve the ASEAN-CCI in their decision-making at regional level, and official ASEAN organs have generally kept the ASEAN-CCI at arms length. Member countries can of course include private sector personnel in their national delegations (this being their national prerogative) but, at regional level, the ASEAN-CCI is invited to present its views at formal ASEAN meetings only on items of

Reprinted in abridged form from "ASEAN's Institutional Structure and Economic Co-operation", *ASEAN Economic Bulletin* 6, no. 3 (March 1990), pp. 268–82, by permission of the author and the Institute of Southeast Asian Studies.

the agenda on which its views are considered relevant. By and large, the co-operative process among the ASEAN private sectors move on a different track from the official process, with its own speed and direction. How and to what extent should the two dialogue processes be geared to one another in the interest of ASEAN economic co-operation?

Unlike ASEAN governments, the ASEAN-CCI is not finally accountable to the peoples of ASEAN. As an interest group it may present its views but clearly cannot engage directly in the decision-making processes of official ASEAN bodies. As the objectives and ambit of competence of the ASEAN-CCI differ from those of ASEAN governments, its dialogue process naturally has its own dynamics and direction. There should be no question of merging or integrating it into the official dialogue process. The task appears rather one of devising effective channels of communication between the two machineries to facilitate consultation and an appreciation of each others objectives and constraints. However, with six private sectors and six governments, the problems of co-ordinating the relationship at national level with that at regional level is very complex. Different ASEAN countries have different economic philosophies and political cultures, and the dynamics of government-private sector interaction differ from country to country. What is acceptable to one government may not be equally acceptable to another. Consequently, despite the best lobbying efforts at national level, getting governmental consensus at regional level to ASEAN-CCI initiatives is extremely difficult. The effort creates friction within ASEAN and frustration in the ASEAN-CCI. For example, most of the proposals painstakingly worked out in the forums of the ASEAN-CCI for liberalizing intra-ASEAN trade proved unacceptable to COTT despite ostensibly close government-private sector consultations at national levels. In a different instance, but reflecting the same problem, the formal signing of the Basic Agreement on AIJVs was delayed despite the blessing of

the ASEAN-CCI and its final agreement by the AEM because, at the last minute, Malaysian businessmen at national level prevailed upon their government to change certain provisions of the Agreement.

It is inherently difficult to co-ordinate two vertical structures, each with its own internal dynamics, especially when decisions are by consensus and agreements vaguely couched. To achieve greater impact on ASEAN-level policy-making, the ASEAN private sectors should perhaps concentrate more on achieving a higher degree of internal consensus and lobbying more effectively at national level to have their views reflected in national positions than to rely overly on representations from the ASEAN-CCI to official ASEAN organs.

There is perhaps a more fundamental reason for limiting any ASEAN private sector participation in inter-governmental processes at regional ASEAN level. While the ASEAN-CCI is the official representative of the ASEAN private sector, the interest of the organized ASEAN private sector is not necessarily synonymous with the interest of private enterprise which includes maintenance of the market framework and principles of fair and open competition. One of the weaknesses of the ASEAN private sector is, in fact, a chronic tendency towards rent seeking activities. As a long time scholar of Southeast Asian political-economy, Yoshihara Kunio, observed, "South-East Asian capitalism . . . is dominated by rent-seekers. In fact, there are strange breeds of capitalists such as crony capitalists and bureaucratic capitalists. In addition, there are political leaders, their sons and relatives, and royal families involved in business. What they seek is not only protection from foreign competition, but also concessions, licences, monopoly rights, and government subsidies. . . ." (Yoshihara Kunio 1988, p. 3). This was exactly what Goh Chok Tong, then Singapore Minister for Trade and Industry, found from his ASEAN experience. As he noted in a speech to the Fifth Conference of the Federation of ASEAN Economic Associations in October 1980, "Private enterprise generally disdains governmental intervention in business; but when they dream up complementation schemes, they want governments to intervene and protect them from competition. In the end, it was the governments which resisted iron-clad protection for those so fortunate as to be allocated the products under the AICs" (Osborne 1982, pp. 5–6).

ASEAN governments vary in the extent of their intervention in the economy, their commitment to a free market framework and, as noted, in their approach to private enterprise. To prevent the politicization of government-business relationship at regional level, thus complicating the task of economic co-operation, it is also best for ASEAN governments and the ASEAN-CCI to keep one another at arms length and to encourage ASEAN private sector input into the official ASEAN process more at national level.

13.

ASEAN AND THE NGOs

JOHAN SARAVANAMUTTU and SHAROM AHMAT

Our study of the role, philosophy, objectives and activities of the 25 affiliated and 25 non-affiliated ASEAN-based non-governmental organizations has brought out interesting similarities and differences, strengths and weaknesses in the seven categories of NGOs surveyed. The task of this section is to evaluate their overall usefulness and their role in promoting a regional ASEAN orientation on their specialised areas of activities as well as to assess the possible future developments of these organizations and other areas which may be usefully organized in the form of NGOs.

The first category surveyed, the commerce and industry NGOs, are as a group undoubtedly the most organized and coordinated and their contribution to ASEAN cooperation at the private sector level can hardly be disputed. Indeed, from available secondary information as well as from our interviews, it appears that the industry and commodity clubs take off in regional cooperation where inter-governmental efforts fail or dare not to tread. Furthermore, the ASEAN-CCI or its officials have acted as an effective lobby within ASEAN to pressure the ASEAN governments to set up the institutional mechanisms for greater ASEAN economic cooperation among private sector groups. One example we cited was the ASEAN Industrial Joint Venture (AIJV) scheme, which was launched largely on private sector initiative. ASEAN-CCI officials or past officials have also been active in suggesting and influencing the recommendations of the 15 member ASEAN Task Force for future regional cooperation.

To stress the significance of the commerce and industry NGOs is not to imply for a moment that these organizations are trouble-free or are not encountering problems of cooperation. We have touched upon many of these problems in the First Chapter. For example, the failure of the ASEAN Automotive Federation reflects a general problem even among private groups of placing national interests before regional ones or, alternatively, the overwhelming nature of national constraints imposed by governments on such cooperation. Much of the same problems are faced by the second category of NGOs, the Producers' Associations. Furthermore, where the commercial NGOs are concerned, it is clear that projects or programmes which either lack or are unconnected with profit motivation have a poor chance of success. These NGOs are also in general impatient with ASEAN

Excerpted from Johan Saravanamuttu and Sharom Ahmat, *ASEAN Non-Governmental Organizations: A Study of their Role, Objectives and Activities* (Penang: Universiti Sains Malaysia, 1986) by permission of the authors.

governmental tardiness in sanctioning or laying the groundwork for their projects. Such impatience sometimes can cause the premature abandonment of projects.

Be that as it may, the ASEAN-CCI, its industry and commodity clubs and the producers' associations act as important forums and avenues for contacts and exchange among the ASEAN business class and this in itself is already a significant function of these NGOs. Their proliferation suggests that the ASEAN business class is actively seeking new avenues of private sector cooperation even though the level of cooperation may still be rather rudimentary by their own standards. The officials of these clubs, private sector men themselves, are usually their own worst critics. However, it is undeniable that the presence of these NGOs provide a significant complement if not an alternative to inter-governmental cooperation in the economic sphere, which so far has fallen well below expectations in ASEAN.

Given the already wide scope of areas that are covered by the commerce and industry NGOs, ranging from music to banking, the issue is not so much whether new ground could or should be broken by new NGOs but rather that of improving on what is already existing. Apart from the general problems mentioned above, the fact that some of these NGOs have become defunct shows that the lack of a sustained effort in cooperation can be brought about by disinterested, unenthusiastic or even indifferent nationally-based officials. The setting up of secretariats by rotation rather than permanent secretariats is also partially to be blamed for this generalised problem of many ASEAN NGOs.

The NGOs representing the professions are perhaps the most well placed to obviate problems of conflicting national interests and governmental obstacles to regional cooperation since, theoretically at least, their activities and objectives are furthest removed from "non-professional" considerations. We have indeed found them to be an effective and strong grouping of ASEAN NGOs, which have been able to forge a relatively high level of regional

cooperation. They certainly do not deserve the mildly derogatory label of being "social clubs" although like all other ASEAN NGOs they do face the problem of the impermanence of officials and secretariats. Nevertheless, a major disappointment with these professional NGOs is their slowness in drawing up and enforcing professional codes of ethics.

The medical NGOs, which are strictly a subset of the professional NGOs, perform much the same role as the latter. Their numerical strength suggests that medical cooperation is a natural offshoot of overall regional cooperation. As professional bodies, their main activity has been the holding of biennial conferences where scientific medical papers are presented and scientific knowledge exchanged. While there is no doubt about the professional orientation of the medical NGOs, there appears to be a singular lack of regionally-based scientific, medical research or, more pressingly, professional medical training undertaken or even proposed by these NGOs. These NGOs have also been slow in drafting codes of ethics. The overall medical body, MASEAN, is the obvious vehicle for such broad-based activities. It is presently still looking into the area of post-graduate education and the formulation of an ethical code.

ASEAN NGO activity is arguably weakest in the area of education. Apart from the establishment of an ASEAN Academy of Law and Jurisprudence in the University of Philippines and a short spurt of interest in an "ASEAN University" in the late 1970s, no further efforts appear to be forthcoming from the three NGOs — a Teachers' Council, an Economic Association and a non-starter Writers' Association — that occupy the educational realm in ASEAN. The failure of the ASEAN writers to get off the ground is particularly instructive. It epitomises the problem of relying on nationally-based bodies to organize and conduct meetings and activities, the inaugural meeting of which in the AWA case, was never held. Besides room for the establishment of NGOs in any number of educational areas (there being only economics and law so far), an obvious general area for cooperation would be among universities based in ASEAN to establish and map out more scholarly and educational exchange.

Another surprisingly weak area of ASEAN NGO activity is in the socio-cultural realm, which is represented by a mere eight NGOs. There is a strong possibility that the overwhelming presence of ASEAN governmental and inter-governmental activity in this broad area may have stunted the growth of NGOs here. Indeed, many of the socio-cultural NGOs, such as the Confederation of Women's Organizations and the Committee for ASEAN Youth Cooperation are government-linked. Potentially, nonetheless, socio-cultural cooperation through NGO activity is an important area for people-to-people contact in ASEAN and there is a great deal of room for the growth of NGOs which may range from those of the arts to broad socially-oriented movements.

Interestingly, the quasi-governmental bodies in ASEAN are not as assertive nor as effective as one may have expected of these bodies, given governmental support. The most effective group among them, the ports, airports and shippers' associations, involve professionals. Among the rest, we have a likely non-starter in the ASEAN Council of Museums, the broad-based parliamentarians' forum of AIPO, which by its very nature makes no decisions, and the potentially effective petroleum council, ASCOPE.

In conclusion, our survey has found that the ASEAN region is served by a broad and varied array of regionally-based NGOs, augmenting the role of literally thousands of NGOs that now pepper the globe, whether nationally, regionally or internationally-based. The ASEAN NGOs, while generally still an inchoate group, established by and large only in the 1970s, have begun to play a significant role in augmenting and complementing the regional cooperative efforts of the ASEAN governments.

14. INSTITUTIONAL FRAMEWORK
Recommendations for Change

MUTHIAH ALAGAPPA

The gradual and piecemeal development of the Asean institutional framework and the emphasis on the consensus method for decision-making clearly reflects the cautious approach of the member governments to regional co-operation, which has so far been mainly political. In terms of structure and process, the preference has been for a loose framework with negotiations characterising activities at all levels. The loose framework and the consensus method have been posited by some practitioners and observers as positive attributes because of their inherent potential to prevent confrontation and development of intra-associational groups or factions. The loose framework, although making for ambiguity and inefficiency, provides opportunities for 'face saving' which is considered vital for Asean solidarity and cohesion. The numerous bilateral meetings, especially among the Asean heads of state, are viewed as providing the necessary flexibility to allow discussion of sensitive issues outside the formal framework without undermining Asean harmony. The disparate nature of national governments in the region and the strength of nationalist forces in member countries are also deemed to favour a decentralised Asean machinery. The thrust of this approach is that a well-delineated and endowed institutional framework with authoritative procedures is not in harmony with the Asean spirit. Caution should therefore be exercised in advocating changes to strengthen the Asean machinery.

It has, however, also been argued by others that the present Asean machinery and modus operandi suffers a number of shortcomings which must be resolved if Asean co-operation is not to be hampered. The shortcomings identified include the following:

- Lack of an integrated decision-making structure. Apart from providing political direction, the Asean summit characterised by a high degree of protocol and symbolism, has no specific role in the management of Asean co-operation. Consequently the AMM and AEMM have emerged as the two key organs of Asean; but unfortunately the vertical line of responsibility that has evolved has dichotomised the decision-making structure creating problems of co-ordination that seem to erode and debilitate the entire machinery. This situation is further aggravated by the emergence of other parallel

Reprinted in abridged form from Muthiah Alagappa, "Asean Institutional Framework and Modus Operandi: Recommendations for Change", in *ASEAN at the Crossroads: Obstacles, Options and Opportunities in Economic Co-operation*, edited by Noordin Sopiee, Chew Lay See, Lim Siang Jin (Kuala Lumpur: Institute of Strategic and International Studies, 1987), pp. 183–230, by permission of the author and the publisher.

meetings among several other categories of Asean ministers. (For details of these problems of co-ordination see C P F Luhulima's paper on 'Asean institutions and modus operandi: Looking back and looking forward').

- Application of the consensus method to all issues and levels. While the consensus method certainly has its merits and is perhaps the only acceptable method at the highest levels and on major policy issues, it is also a fact the application of this method to all levels and issues has considerably reduced the effectiveness of intra-Asean co-operation even in areas where agreement has been reached at policy level. The need for consensus has also prevented the association from co-operating in areas which may have been beneficial to a substantial number (though not all) of its members.

- The principle of rotation, so heavily emphasised in Asean, has resulted in a machinery that is cumbersome, inefficient and lacking in continuity and expertise. In particular, this has had a debilitating effect on the development and efficiency of the Asean Secretariat. The rotation system relies heavily on the system of national secretariats and creates an Asean network in which the Asean Secretariat is an ineffective outpost as opposed to being the focal point.

- The Asean structure reflects the dominant emphasis on national interests and national representation. There is no provision for representation of the Asean 'community interest'. This lop-sided emphasis on national representation and national gain partly accounts for the very slow development in intra-Asean co-operation. The home-based staff system adopted in staffing the Asean secretariat is a reflection of the emphasis on national representation and one of the reasons underlying the ineffectiveness of the Asean Secretariat.

- The Asean system as a whole suffers from institutional and procedural deficiencies. It also lacks the staff to carry out policy research and advisory functions for the various decision-making bodies; monitoring and implementation functions in relation to accepted policies; and the servicing function for the numerous meetings held annually. For example, the permanent committees which are the main work organs of Asean do not have full-time professional technical staff to identify projects, evaluate proposals, and interact with regional and international bodies. The system whereby the host country provides the interim technical secretariats works against the requirements of continuity and the development of expertise. In many cases, the ITSs have become essentially administrative co-ordinators.

- Excepting the Asean Secretariat and the national secretariats, all other Asean organs (so vital to the advancement of regional co-operation) function only periodically. The AMM and AEMM meet on the average twice a year, the Standing Committee six times a year, and the permanent committees and subcommittees once a year. Although there is in all cases provision for convening special meetings, the format of periodic meetings with minimal or almost no activity in between meetings is hardly a suitable way to advance regional co-operation. The frequent changes in personalities and the system of committees and periodic meetings make for cumbersome and lengthy procedures and thus it often takes a number of years to process major programmes. The system has created much disillusionment especially in the private sector.

- The private sector has been assigned an important role in intra-Asean economic co-operation especially in industry. The private sector may take up to 40 per cent equity in the Asean Industrial Projects (AIPs), it has the initiative to identify and formulate Asean Industrial Complementation (AIC) packages and is assigned the lead role in the Asean Industrial Joint Venture (AIJV) scheme which requires participation of only two member countries. Despite the importance assigned to the private sector, the latter is not allowed to play a formal role in the planning and implementation of Asean projects with which it is involved. While the Asean-CCI can make inputs to the AEMM, attendance is by invitation. The situation is unsatisfactory at the level of the working group where the relationship is informal. Very often the private sector is not consulted on important issues, thus resulting in failure of projects or schemes. For example, the AIC guidelines drawn up without private sector participation have been described as inflexible and impractical by Asean businessmen. The Asean-CCI is also not integrated into official Asean dialogue relations with the dialogue partners, except with the US where the Asean-US Business Council is represented.

- Asean relies almost entirely on a policy regime and does not have a legal regime. Consequently, the rule of the bureaucrat and not the rule of law governs decision-making and also the implementation phase. Asean does not have a charter. It operates on the basis of the 1967 Bangkok Declaration and the 1976 Declaration of Asean Concord. The only treaty is the Treaty of Amity and Co-operation in Southeast Asia. Adoption of a charter is posited as running counter to the consensus principle and likely to introduce tension and rigidity into the Asean system, thereby undermining harmony. The Treaty of Amity and Co-operation has provision for a High Council to enable pacific settlement of intra-associational political disputes but this has remained a dead letter. In the area of trade, Article 14 of the Agreement on Asean Preferential Trading Arrangements (PTAs) provides for a system of consultations to resolve disputes. It includes a bilateral complaints procedure, referral to the Committee on Trade and Tourism (COTT) and finally, a suspension of concessions if the dispute cannot be resolved satisfactorily. Up to now there have been relatively few disputes and these have been resolved through bilateral negotiations. No case has been referred to COTT. Generally Asean countries are sensitive and reluctant to submit issues for adjudication. Therefore, even the very limited efforts to institute mechanisms for conflict resolution have not been implemented.

BASIS FOR CHANGE

Institutional reform is no panacea nor substitute for the lack of political will or deficiencies in policies and programmes for regional co-operation, especially in the economic sector. It must, however, be noted that institutional deficiencies can hamper co-operation and shortcomings, if any, must therefore be rectified. It is also possible to view the structure and process of the Asean machinery as a manifestation of the level of commitment of member countries to regional co-operation. A decision to strengthen the machinery can therefore reflect an increasing level of commitment to regional co-operation. Given the hypersensitivity of Asean states towards any form of supra-nationalism and even strong central institutions, the basis for recommending change shifts from what is logically required and effective to what is feasible and acceptable. Recommendations for change in the structure and process of Asean should therefore take due cognizance of the following:

- The institutional framework must correspond to the objectives and functions of Asean and, more importantly, keep in step with the prevailing commitment and mood of the member states. At the same time the framework must have an in-built capacity and flexibility to allow for the efficient conduct of the association's business and also provide for future development including a higher level of co-operation. It should be noted here that nearly all the present heads of government in Asean have the requisite national standing to authorise and oversee a higher level of intra-Asean co-operation and a correspondingly strong institutional framework. The next generation of leaders may not command such undisputed authority or may take considerable time to acquire such standing. The present period therefore appears opportune to embark on a relatively higher level of co-operation and also to develop a relatively strong institutional framework.

- Recommendations for change should not attempt drastic surgery but build on the existing system wherever possible. In this connection, it should be noted that the key institutions of a framework for regional co-operation are already in place. What is required, therefore, is streamlining of the machinery and process, reconstitution of committees, and refinement of the terms of reference of the various organs to further advance regional co-operation.

- Asean is and will for the foreseeable future continue to be a relatively loose intergovernmental organisation with the primary purpose of strengthening member states as national entities. There is no aspiration towards any form of supranationalism (political or economic integration) although there is now an indication that Asean may be willing to embark on a higher level of economic co-operation. Regional co-operation through Asean is therefore a means and not an end in itself. Co-operation, be it political or economic, will be furthered only when it serves the national interests of all states (or stated alternatively, when it does not damage

the interests of any member). As the dominant concern will continue to be the national interests of member states, the effectiveness of Asean as an institution will therefore be a function of the support of its member states. It is therefore imperative that the institutional framework of Asean provides for the active participation of the national political and administrative elite in the structure and process of the association. The association qua regional organisation is unlikely to develop any significant political authority of its own. Political direction and major policy objectives will continue to be decided by national elites who must be represented in all key decision-making organs and the consensus method must continue to govern all major policy decisions.

- This emphasis on national interest and national representation should, however, be balanced to a significant degree by representation of the collective interests and perspectives of the Asean 'community'. This will facilitate, where possible, an upgrading of the common interest as opposed to merely working on the lowest common denominator at all times. The national elite, however objective they may try to be, will be influenced by national perspectives. Consequently development of an impartial component (the seventh force?) within the structure of Asean to the maximum extent possible has obvious merits. The secretary-general and the Asean Secretariat appear most suited to undertake this promotional function. In addition to their present functions they can act as the exponents of the collective Asean interest in all intra-Asean fora.

- The authority and process for initiation of programmes and projects; research, study and planning; decision-taking; and implementation and monitoring should be clearly defined. The Asean institutional framework must have the necessary capacity and expertise to effectively operationalise these various stages. While decision-making and implementation will continue to be the responsibility of the national elite and the member countries respectively, the Asean Secretariat and the permanent committees should be made responsible and provided with the capacity to initiate and study programmes before the decision-taking stage and subsequently to monitor and report on the implementation phase.

- Method of decision-making is crucial to the effectiveness of any organisation. The consensus or unanimity method ensures the essential interests of all members are taken into consideration. Given the nature of Asean, it is important this method is continued for all major policy (substantive and procedural) issues especially at the political levels of the Asean heads of government and ministerial meetings. Even at the political level and certainly below this level, there is a need to provide for additional methods of decision-making that can be employed for certain categories of issues. However, the system must be characterised by sufficient flexibility and, above all, guided by the Asean spirit of harmony.

- A higher level of intra-Asean co-operation in the economic field (especially a more liberal approach to trade liberalisation, creation of an internal market and movement of services and factors of production across national boundaries) would inevitably increase the number of trade-related disputes among member states (both in the public and private sectors). This is not uncommon to regional organisations but their resolution through bilateral bureaucratic negotiations as is the current Asean practice may not be practical. It is necessary for Asean to develop a more efficient framework for resolution of differences/disputes among member states which may arise from the implementation of accepted policies.

- An important facet of Asean co-operation is its effort to influence the global and regional political and economic environment. This function will become even more significant, especially in the economic field, both in the dialogue relations with major trading partners and in international economic fora and organisations. To facilitate this, the machinery for conduct of Asean's external relations has to be streamlined and strengthened.

- The private sector must be viewed as an important component of Asean economic co-operation: Without private sector participation, economic co-operation especially industrial co-operation will not make headway. Every effort must be made to allow the private sector to participate in the planning and implementation of Asean economic programmes. Similarly the private sector should also invite the public sector to participate in its deliberations and this interaction must take place both at regional and national levels.

15.   DIALOGUE PARTNERS

B.A. HAMZAH

One of the purposes for the Asean link-ups with the industrial world is to create access to their markets and to buy time for regional development. In anchoring to the industrial world the Asean countries also hope to ensure against sudden shifts in global business structure as new business opportunities present themselves. It will be shown in due course that through dialogue partners Asean has built a wealth of experience in multilateral negotiations. Besides confidence Asean has also benefited tremendously from their special relations with the dialogue countries who are Asean major trading partners in the world.

RATIONALE FOR DIALOGUE RELATIONS

Over the years the Asean dialogue partner relations have become a forum for the following:

- technical and development assistance for common Asean projects;
- trade and economic concessions through Asean collective lobbying;
- strengthening of political relations with the dialogue partners; and
- boosting Asean economic standing.

The Asean dialogue partner-relations arrangements with external powers have become a useful mechanism for coordinating Asean common positions on various issues which are primarily economic in nature. This mechanism also reinforces other dealings by Asean with these countries and provides the dialogue countries with a machinery to complement their respective bilateral economic relations. What is yet to be established is the extent to which Asean dialogue partners coordinate their positions towards Asean or the extent to which they plan independently of each other. The evidence for this type of counter-response strategy is meagre at present. Collective efforts on a coordinated and planned basis by Asean trading partners towards Asean are not evident. This is because it is not necessary for the dialogue partners to approach Asean with a common position: the problems facing Asean are not common.

At present, Asean maintains dialogue-relations with the European Community (since 1972), Australia (1974), New Zealand (1975), Japan (1977), Canada (1977), United States (1977) and the United Nations Development Programme (UNDP) (since 1977). The UNDP is a major multilateral agency for funding technical assistance to Asean.

The Asean system of appointing a country or the Asean Secretariat to coordinate policies

Excerpted from B.A. Hamzah, *Asean Relations with Dialogue Partners* (Petaling Jaya: Pelanduk Publications (M) Sdn Bhd, 1989) with permission of the author.

pertaining to dialogue relations on rotation basis has worked very well. Rotating the Chairmanship of the dialogue partners has allayed the fear of complicity and familiarity. The Secretariat takes charge of the UNDP. But this system is deficient in one respect — by appointing one country to look after each dialogue partner, Asean in its present form can only have six dialogue nations. This limitation can be easily resolved by assigning a country to more than one dialogue partner on the same Asean consensus principle of six-minus-X if Asean cannot find a sufficient number of dialogue partners to be equally distributed. A more preferred approach would be to go on issue rather than country basis. A combination of issue-cum-country basis should be ideal for the future.

ASEAN DIALOGUE PARTNER RELATIONS:
ISSUES AND PROBLEMS

Asean talks with its dialogue partners on numerous issues. These are not confined only to economic problems and opportunities. When it was conceived, the idea of Asean-dialogue relations revolved around economic considerations — how to obtain more economic gains through direct investment, trade and technical assistance for the Asean countries. Non-economic issues are now often included in the dialogue discussions. For Asean, such a forum is extremely useful for airing its views on issues of vexing international relations — especially when such issues have a direct bearing on Asean's overall destiny. Asean has been known to explore all possibilities and has left no stone unturned whenever such an opportunity arises for it to focus on particularly controversial political issues like Kampuchea, superpower relations and North/South dialogues. Nonetheless, for very obvious reasons, economic matters continue to dominate Asean-Third Countries dialogue partners talks.

A look at the Asean-dialogue partner relations reveals Asean's growing maturity and confidence in its dealings with its dialogue partners. These newfound characteristics have enabled Asean to treat itself as its dialogue partners' equal or near equal.[1] In practice this involves a combination of the following:

a) Asean is now more prepared to shift intergovernmental dialogue towards issues of mutual market access, and the facilitation of private sectors;

b) the relationship has moved beyond the unilateral dimension. It has developed into a strong partnership for mutual benefit; and

c) Such a relationship has also helped to defuse other sensitivities with the dialogue partners in other international fora. Asean always votes as a bloc especially on issues of immutable principles in international relations. Asean bloc voting and lobbying are significant in offering reasonable trade-offs.

The dialogue partners are happy with dialogue relations for a number[2] of reasons. Some of these are:

a) to emphasise the importance these countries attach to their relations with Asean by a frank and open exchange of views on economic matters of common concern;

b) to move further along the road toward a much more mature and reciprocal relationship with the Asean countries — emphasising in particular that market access and a favourable investment climate are two-way streets;

c) to emphasise the limitation the public sector faces in transacting business. In the free enterprise system business remains the major concern of the private sector. Therefore, the dialogue partners are mainly concerned with promoting the idea that the private sector performs a primary function in economic relations. Hence their continued insistence for some kind of private representation in Asean-Third countries dialogue process;

d) for the dialogue partners, such meetings are useful for them to inform Asean and at the same time create better understanding of their own external policies on issues such as GATT, GSP, import limitations of certain products, investment policies and issues relating to domestic constituencies;

e) All dialogue countries see Asean as a strong bloc that they can rely on to support certain objectives. For example, the United States is keen to encourage Asean accession to the full range on MTN codes and get Asean to co-operate in the new GATT round;

f) to review regularly the status of ongoing projects; and

g) dialogue partners are interested in having access to an enlarged Asean market. The dialogue partners are hoping that Asean will integrate its disparate markets into a common system. The advantages of a single Asean market from the investors' point of view are too obvious.

ACHIEVEMENTS

Considering the number of approved technical projects, the achievements of Asean dialogue relations are numerous but insignificant in substance. This is because Asean countries put too much effort on technical assistance and do not venture positively into much more significant business areas. As a mechanism for defusing trade differences the system of dialogue relations can be said to have made an impact but at times it fails to work. The Australian aviation policy is a good case in point.

NOTES

1. Asean is now more vocal. It complains a great deal about policies which it considers offensive and inimical to its advancement. For example, Asean recently took a firm stand on the question of EEC countries levying a tax on palm oil. The Minister of Primary Commodities of Malaysia, Dr Lim Keng Yaik, has even suggested "retaliatory measures" against EEC in the form of trade boycotts should EEC go ahead with its policy.

2. See Progress Report submitted by *Asean-Australia Economic Co-operation Program Committee*, Aug. 1986 (limited circulation). Also, *Asean-CCI Handbook, 1986/1987.*

NEGOTIATING STYLES

PUSHPA THAMBIPILLAI

DECISION-MAKING: THE CONSENSUS MODEL

When one studies decision-making in ASEAN, one invariably comes across numerous committees and meetings, with, one can correctly assume, an ascending scale of importance of the issues corresponding to the ranks of the participants; for example, senior officials may discuss issues of lesser significance or be only involved in preparatory meetings, while Ministers may take up more important issues. Given the lack of structural and legalistic norms to regulate procedures, coupled with the presence of numerous levels of meetings among government officials, a peculiar system of decision making has evolved within ASEAN:

(i) decision-making through small groups and committees, and
(ii) procedurally following what is called the consensus model.

Culturally, this particular model can be identified as being part of the regional social system. That part of Southeast Asia that constitutes ASEAN has one ethnic and culturally dominant group — peoples of the Malay stock. Hence a basic culture shared by the majority of the inhabitants of the region prevails, together with other features superimposed from outside the region.

The consensus approach and the two basic terms of *musyawarah* (the process of decision-making through discussion and consultation), and *mufakat* (the unanimous decision that is arrived at) are associated with traditional, especially village politics in certain parts of Indonesia and to a lesser degree in Malaysia and the Philippines.[1]

From the societal and village level analysis we could apply this particular style of decision-making to the national or international level. In the international context the consensus approach implies that negotiations and decision-making are also conducted in a manner to "save face" and maintain a conciliatory relationship among the participants.

The nature of consensus building, the role of individuals and the changing environmental influences on decision-making will be discussed later in relation to the ASEAN case.[2]

When one discusses the issue of decision-making and negotiations with ASEAN officials, one gets the impression (when one succeeds in talking to them and getting some response), that generally there is no problem as decisions are arrived at through consensus. "Consensus"

Excerpted from Pushpa Thambipillai, *ASEAN Negotiations: Two Insights*, by Pushpa Thambipillai and J. Saravanamuttu (Singapore: Institute of Southeast Asian Studies, 1985), by permission of the author and the publisher.

seems to be the catch-word, a mask to hide actual problems and disagreements since there is no open vote counting. The unmasking is a long and patient process, frustrating but sometimes revealing certain inner aspects of negotiations.

Reluctance, on the part of officials, to discuss details could be a sign of inherent problems. What appears on the surface, or what is described by officials may not reflect actual discussions. It is only the sudden outbursts or glimpses by third parties that reveal some of the processes involved. Nevertheless, the cultural model of not revealing disagreements as well as the frank opinions of a number of respondents, have given some insight into the various aspects of negotiations.

It must be made clear at the outset that there is no single ASEAN policy that emerges from any particular meeting. What we perceive as an ASEAN policy is actually some form of a synthesis or amalgam of the policies of the different members so that a common stand is projected. Thus the components of the resulting ASEAN policy maintain their identity while encompassing the general thrust, allowing each member to diverge within a certain acceptable boundary. A policy, be it economic or political, once it is decided that it should be pursued collectively, undergoes different stages of formulation and acceptance at the national as well as regional levels. Surprisingly, it is not the political but the economic or technical issues that seem to face more obstacles. For example, a political issue whether or not to support the formation of the Coalition Government of Democratic Kampuchea was of concern, it appeared, only to a core of political leaders in each country, limited perhaps to the executive and foreign offices. However, economic issues, such as the expansion of regional trade may have its supporters and opponents in various related sectors of each country, for example, trade, industry, or labour offices. The larger the country, the more distributed the functions and activities, and the more difficult it seems to arrive at a national policy that would be supported by the different sectors. Thus, there could be inter-departmental competition in a bid to represent national interests. For instance, one Indonesian official cited an example of sectoral interests in the debate on freer trade for a commodity versus protection for an industry in that specific commodity, to explain why some would support free trade while others would not. Smaller states like Singapore seem to have less problems in arriving at national positions since a more cohesive and relatively smaller group of people is apparently in charge of the major sectors, and priorities are clearly defined by this score.[3]

National consensus-building is thus the first stage before a country stand can be adopted and introduced to the regional meeting. The input in consensus-building varies from country to country and from issue to issue. What appears at a particular regional meeting is a set of different country positions. (No country position papers on any topic were ever disclosed to a researcher.) If we were to use the algebraic example, then each country position is somewhat like $x + 1$, or $x - 1$, or $x + 2$ (rather than x, y, z), based on a common outlook but with variations on the shared viewpoint.

The fact that the member countries arrive at a meeting with some common denominator is in itself an achievement and is partly explained by the consensus model discussed above where "sending out feelers" to the member countries is important. The consensus model holds that through some degree of manipulation and informal bargaining an acceptable formula is arrived at by adjusting each member's respective policy stand so that at a later more formal meeting a synthesis of the varying opinions can be easily adopted. The ASEAN negotiations have some similarities with this process.

According to ASEAN officials a great deal of note-comparing and adjustments occur during and after the national decision-making stage before an issue is brought to the regional meeting. Through informal channels ("feelers") the likely position of a particular ASEAN country on an issue will be known in advance. If the reaction seems unfavourable and with little chance of modification, then, that particular issue or a particular position will not be pursued or would be presented in a slightly modified version. Sometimes it will be pursued more obliquely if it is important to a particular country. This is to pre-empt the emergence of confrontational issues at regional meetings, where failure to reach a common agreement could be interpreted negatively and cast doubt on the workings of the organization. In short, only issues with some degree of acceptability will be presented at the regional level.

For issues relating to economic and technical matters, specific committees in each country are entrusted with the early stages of negotiation. For example, Preferential Trading Arrangements related matters are taken up by officials assigned to COTT. Depending on the significance of the issue and the prerogatives given to the negotiators, certain decisions are made. If the issues deal with important or sensitive matters, then they are left to the ministers concerned since the officials at the committee levels "do not have the mandate from the government to make major decisions affecting national interests", as one official commented. Besides, if the negotiators from a particular member country (or from all member countries) were junior in rank they would not be able to make alternative decisions if the ones they came prepared with were unacceptable. Another instance when it is referred to the ministerial level is when no decision can be arrived at during the committee stage, thus passing on the tasks to higher authority, hoping that the "delay tactics" would lead to certain settlements at the higher level. It appears, that, rather than enter a definite "No" at the end of the meeting, a postponement seems to save the day; under the consensus set-up it is important to "save face", and not to be in a confrontational or directly contradictory situation.

How much flexibility does a negotiator enjoy? It depends on his position in the official hierarchy. It is the senior bureaucrats in the various ministries, including the directors-general, who are in fact the main policy makers for the ministers and hence, are aware of the background of various policies. They have the capacity to decide as to how much they can alter or modify their stand during the regional meetings. But if they, too, cannot decide or do not wish to commit themselves, "there is always the excuse that they have no mandate to make decisions and thus have to consult their ministers".

One conclusion we can draw from this particular procedure is that the very fact that negotiations occur at different levels is an asset towards consensus formation. From the committees to the senior officials and finally to the ministerial meetings — at each level consensus is sought. By the time the final meeting on an issue occurs, basic differences would have been ironed out and the public would only hear of the common areas of co-operation agreed upon or the policy statements on a particular issue. However, it does not seem to terminate here; the process seems to go beyond eloquently worded communiqués. In fact an official suggested that one has to look at the process covering the "before-during-after" of a particular decision to understand ASEAN negotiation styles, their influence and their outcome.[4]

POLITICAL CULTURE/SYSTEM

Although individual cultural traits are downgraded (though not entirely eliminated) there seems to be a general consensus on certain traits of country behaviour directly reflecting on the representatives but not explicitly stated. In rank order, Singapore followed by Malaysia seems to take one extreme (on points like preparation, clarity, etc.) while Indonesia and the Philippines take the other.[5] Singapore with its group of relatively young but trained personnel seems to be the most articulate with well substantiated arguments and facts to support claims (especially in economic/technical issues).

Hence the negotiators are direct and forthright. It was difficult to decide if this is a cultural trait or characteristic of a country that is modern and industrializing. Singaporean negotiators, although from different ethnic groups do not seem to portray distinct cultural traits for each of the ethnic group. It is a collective "Singapore trait" that is exhibited during negotiations. It could be the level of "professionalism" that is referred to. On the other hand the participants from the Philippines (according to respondents) generally seem less specific, not too clear as to their wants and tend to dwell on much "rhetoric". Perhaps this is the only case of any "clear" indication of some trait.

Malaysia, despite the fact that it has a reputation for able negotiators seems to be affected by its political culture and domestic system. This portrays the Malaysian negotiators as less "open", and more rigid. They seem to be restricted by a number of domestic priorities governed by law or policies on ethnic issues. They have a tendency to "frequently consult home". Nevertheless, Malaysians and Singaporeans are described as "tough" negotiators, implying that they will stand by their decisions, giving long explanations to back their views.

Despite the differences, there is a growing realization that a web of interlinked relationships bring these countries together, either shared historical experiences (Malaysia and Singapore), dominant religious and ethnic similarities (Indonesia and Malaysia) or ideological orientations (all of them), and no one factor dominates. Thus there is no specific indication that there is a permanent or quasi-permanent coalition formation among the five during regional negotiations. Support or disagreements within the group vary according to the issues and the interests at stake.

NOTES

1. Similar forms of behaviour are also reported to be prevalent in Thai social practices.
2. Other studies that have discussed ASEAN decision-making and negotiating styles, elaborating on the consensus model are: Thakur Panit, "Regional Integration Attempts in Southeast Asia: A Study of ASEAN's Problems and Progress", Ph.D. dissertation, Pennsylvania State University, 1980; Peter J. Boyce, "The Machinery of Southeast Asian Regional Diplomacy", in *New Directions in the International Relations of Southeast Asia. The Great Powers and Southeast Asia*, edited by Lau Teik Soon (Singapore University Press, 1973), pp. 173–185. Also, Hans H. Indorf, *ASEAN: Problems and Prospects* (ISEAS: Occasional Paper No. 38, 1975), and Russell H. Fifield, *National and Regional Interests in ASEAN: Competition and Co-operation in International Politics* (ISEAS: Occasional Paper No. 57, 1979).
3. Sufficient research has yet to be done on this stage of national decision-making, the processes, the participants and the outcomes.
4. This is in fact a very interesting topic to study, but from personal experience, I would add that it would also be a frustrating one, given the lack of access to information.
5. It could be a methodological fallacy given the fact that most of my respondents to this question were Thais; perhaps there is a tendency to place oneself somewhere in the middle — a cultural trait?

17. BILATERAL SUMMITRY

ESTRELLA D. SOLIDUM

NATURE OF THE BILATERAL MEETINGS

What we brought out for discussion in this paper are the bilateral meetings of heads of states or bilateral summitry in ASEAN which consist of the numerous visits made between presidents or prime ministers of ASEAN states. These leaders visited with one another on certain matters. Some of those visits were made formally but many of them were done in rather informal setups, without the protocol, elegance and fanfare that characterize state visits. In some instances, the political leaders, dressed in work clothes, held their meetings at some small distant island or town. A number of the visits were considered routine but necessary, especially those made by incoming Thai Prime Ministers who had to explain to other leaders the policies which they were adopting and to assure them of their country's continuing commitment to ASEAN. All the leaders who were involved in the bilateral meetings expressed faith in the belief that strong bilateral relations constitute one of the bedrocks for regional solidarity. These meetings found a culturally-based support in the value of kinship which always evokes strong loyalty among them. And as among kins, the political leaders took counsel with one another, advised and restrained one another, and encouraged each one to proceed to other aspects of cooperation especially to areas which the functional committees could not have competence on.

USEFULNESS

Bilateral meetings of heads of states are perceived to be useful to ASEAN and to its regional objectives of peace, progress, and security. The usefulness to the organization may be understood in terms of enhancing ASEAN's effectiveness defined as the ability to maintain its level of work and its capability to expand its scope of concern without sacrificing the fundamental principles which underlie the life of the organization.

Bilateral summitry enhances the effectiveness of ASEAN if the outcome 1) gives direction to ASEAN's policies such as by contributing to the preservation of its fundamental principles and enabling it to accept new responsibilities for mutual benefit; 2) smoothens its processes such as by facilitating transactions and cutting down time for decision-making and action; 3) provides a congenial environment for the members by increasing their vitality to work, their mutual responsiveness, and their will to play down conflicts; 4) increases the members'

Excerpted from Estrella D. Solidum, *Bilateral Summitry in ASEAN* (Manila: Foreign Service Institute, 1982), by permission of the author.

desire to search for new areas of cooperation and for new collective efforts, and 5) improves the quality and quantity of ASEAN's resources, to include the credible identitive assets such as symbols and values which create ASEAN's appeal.

The usefulness of bilateral summitry to ASEAN's regional objectives of peace, progress, and security may be understood in terms of capability of the outcome to help bring about conditions that promote 1) general well-being, congeniality, spread of benefits which are products of collaborative efforts, mutual understanding, mutual respect among states, and acceptance of peace and friendly relations (peace); 2) advancement in various aspects of life (progress) and 3) reduction of conflict situations in the region through conflict resolutions and prevention of spill over of conflicts to other areas, as well as bring about the satisfaction of people's values (security).

DATA BASE

To understand the beneficial role of bilateral summitry one has to know the nature of concerns that have been taken up and their impact on ASEAN. This study looked at the subjects discussed in the ninety-six meetings between heads of states from 1968 to 1981. Data for this came from documents such as speeches and joint communiques issued on the occasion of the meetings, and from periodicals which carried statements made by the political leaders before and after their meetings to journalists. Other media treatment such as editorials and columns provided some insights into the business that were taken up. Data show that in general, the concerns were characterized by one or more of the following: 1) high sensitivity, tending to escalate any conflict which were contained in the situation;, 2) specificity of impact, meaning to say that the effects involved only two or three states at a time; 3) delicateness because it involved change of policies of states or need for secrecy; 4) counterproductiveness if taken up on an ASEAN-wide scale; and

5) broadness of dimension because the issue cut into national or regional interests or into economic and political interests of the members.

Were these bilateral meetings related to ASEAN at all? Data show that they were able to take place because ASEAN was in existence or that they were held to assist ASEAN to achieve its goals. Some meetings took care of issues whose resolutions were needed in order that ASEAN's mechanism could be strengthened. On other matters, the leaders were able to discuss or negotiate on their problems because ASEAN had provided the context for their behavior, especially on situations which necessitated some harmonization of national interests with regional objectives. Statements to this effect were made by the leaders themselves at their bilateral meetings and constitute the proofs that the bilateral meetings of heads of states were indeed related to ASEAN's existence and were not events that took place apart from it.

Since 1967 up to 1981 there have been about ninety-six of these meetings. The most number of meetings, around nineteen of them, were made between Malaysia and Thailand, and followed by Singapore and Thailand which had fourteen. Singapore had about twelve meetings with Malaysia, and thirteen with Indonesia. Thailand and Indonesia had nine meetings between them. The Philippines had the lowest number of bilateral meetings of heads of states, namely, seven with Indonesia, six with Thailand, five with Singapore, and two with Malaysia. Below is a tabulation of the meetings that have been looked into.

Malaysia — Thailand	19
Singapore — Thailand	14
Malaysia — Indonesia	13
Singapore — Malaysia	12
Indonesia — Thailand	9
Indonesia — Singapore	9
Philippines — Indonesia	7
Philippines — Thailand	6
Philippines — Singapore	5
Philippines — Malaysia	2
Total	96

The highest number of bilateral meetings of heads of states occurred in 1976 when there were sixteen of such visits. The leaders held eight meetings solely on consultations about the coming Bali Summit Meeting in February 1976. The other topics taken up in 1976 were the political conditions as aftermaths of the Indo-China war, possible relations with China, and growing communist insurgencies in each ASEAN state. 1978 saw twelve meetings on the developments involving Vietnam and Cambodia, Vietnam and China, and pressures on Thailand. In 1975, there were eleven meetings which touched on the general situation in Southeast Asia, relations between Vietnam and Cambodia, and proposals for the first five heads of state meetings of ASEAN. By 1979, nine meetings were held, touching on oil supply from partners, Indo-Chinese refugees problems and the Indo-China situation. In 1980, eight meetings were held, still on the Cambodian problem, assurances of oil supply for needing partners, and problems along their boundaries. In all these meetings other intra-ASEAN matters were also discussed.

To summarize, bilateral meetings occurred in the years as follows:

1968 — 5		1.	1976 — 16
1969 — 0		2.	1978 — 12
1970 — 5		3.	1975 — 11
1971 — 2		4.	1979 — 9
1972 — 4		5.	1980 — 8
1973 — 5			
1974 — 6			
1975 — 11			
1976 — 16			
1977 — 7			
1978 — 12			
1979 — 9			
1980 — 8			
1981 — 6			
96			

In this study, the subjects that were taken up in the various bilateral meetings of heads of states have been classified into six major groups. In the order of the frequency with which they were discussed, these groups are as follows:

1. ASEAN cooperation, including specific and general proposals for economic cooperation, the need for mutual understanding to enhance cooperation, and the necessity to achieve unity in many matters.
2. Intra-ASEAN problems which were too sensitive for formal ASEAN-wide discussions; such as secessionism problems, borders, territorial claims, problems on territorial waters, friendship and other treaties.
3. Foreign policy, the adoption of a policy of non-alignment, promotion of the idea of neutralization, explanation of new policy shifts, state and ASEAN policy towards Vietnam, Laos, Cambodia, and China.
4. Security problems which included the status of American bases in the Philippines, SEATO, military cooperation in ASEAN, bilateral military cooperation outside of ASEAN, and communist and ethnic insurgencies.
5. International developments as they affected ASEAN and the rest of the region, such as the establishment of socialist governments in Vietnam, Laos, and Cambodia, China's renewed interest to improve relations with Southeast Asian states, and problems arising from the confluence of the hegemonic interests of the big powers in the region.
6. ASEAN organization itself, five-state summit meetings, and the restructuring of ASEAN.

18.

ROLE OF LAW IN ASEAN DEVELOPMENT

PURIFICACION V. QUISUMBING

The Bangkok Declaration of 1967 which formally announced the existence of the Association of Southeast Asian Nations (ASEAN) states that one of the basic purposes of the Association is "to promote regional peace and stability through abiding respect for justice and the rule of law in the relationship among countries of the region."[1] More than mere legal rhetoric, this declaration of intention by the founders may well be the biggest challenge for ASEAN leaders because it posits the forging of a viable legal framework for smooth intra-regional interaction and effective extra-ASEAN relations, clearly a requisite to fulfill if a sense of community within the treaty region is to develop.

This paper intends to identify some of the problems attendant to developing regional law and the prospects for achieving the above stated objective of the Association. The emerging legal framework for regional dispute settlement provided in the Treaty of Amity and Cooperation for Southeast Asia is then analyzed in the context of other regional agreements, an exercise which could be of some usefulness in understanding the ASEAN "legal style" and approach to conflict amelioration.

The key role of law in ASEAN goes beyond the fact that the association itself is a creation of the "law" or agreement among member states for it is both the basis of cooperation as well as the object of such collaboration. The significance that ASEAN leaders put in legal development is reflected in several basic documents. The Declaration of ASEAN Concord adopted as a framework for cooperation the "study on how to develop judicial cooperation including the possibility of an ASEAN extradition treaty." It also calls for a "study of the desirability of a new constitutional framework for ASEAN."[2]

For most programs of action to be implemented would necessarily involve legal issues that have not only regional import but, more importantly, national impact. Take for instance the declaration of ZOPFAN (Zone of Peace, Freedom and Neutrality.)[3] Theoretically desirable, the policy if implemented in the Philippines would require not merely policy revisions but a whole series of acts to revamp several treaties and legislation affecting national security and security arrangements.[4] Even the general statement calling for the "strengthening of political solidarity by promoting the harmonization of views, coordinating positions and, where possible and desirable, taking common actions"[5]

Reprinted in abridged form from Purificacion V. Quisumbing, "Problems and Prospects of ASEAN Law: Towards a Legal Framework for Regional Dispute Settlement", in *ASEAN Identity, Development and Culture*, edited by R.P. Anand and Purificacion V. Quisumbing (Honolulu: East-West Center, 1981), pp. 300–18, by permission of the author and the publisher.

can have profound legal ramifications. One might even say that all aspects of the program of action provided in the ASEAN Concord, all areas of regional cooperation — economic, political, social, cultural and information, security and improvement of ASEAN machinery — necessarily involve changes or adjustments in member states' national laws, and in some cases call for the enactment of new legislation in order to carry out regional arrangements.

Development of ASEAN law is bound to be a complex and difficult task, given the circumstances in and forces acting upon the region. There are but few predisposing factors to building a community law. Among these is ironically the "common colonial heritage" of Western legal concepts and institutions.

Commonalities in pre-colonial societal organizational patterns and system of values which formed the bases of relational structures have survived imposed colonial legal systems, particularly among some ethnic groups and people in the countryside, so that customary laws often co-exist with other legal orders within the Southeast Asian countries. It is these elements in the legal cultures[6] that serve as the connecting links toward an ASEAN legal system. One example of such shared value in the region's legal cultures is preference for certain dispute settlement or conflict management modes which are non-adversary, non-formal in the Western traditional sense, a subject which will be discussed further in relation to the regional law on dispute settlement.

Countervailing forces that militate against communal law for ASEAN are more readily perceivable, partly because it has long been fashionable and politically expedient for dominant powers to stress diversity and downplay any unifying characteristics of the region. Many scholars, taking their cue from the prevailing sentiment and literature on Southeast Asia, had for long looked for and wrote about fragmentation of the region's peoples and cultures. It is somewhat like how one looks at a collage or mosaic composition. One could see the elements and never see nor sense the message that is the composition.

This is not to say that differences do not matter. For in the area of legal development for the treaty region, diversities of legal cultures and systems among member nations are proving to be hurdles to be overcome with great care and skill if law is to serve communal concerns and interests.

Even just a brief survey would readily illustrate the intricate mosaic of legal systems in the region. Indonesian jurisprudence is founded on Islamic, Hindu and Adat law, with selective retention of Dutch law. Malaysia and Singapore share traditions of British law superimposed upon Islamic legal foundations and now modified by modern, indigenous legal innovations. The Philippines has a legal system which is a peculiar blend of Roman and Canon law, Civil law of the Iberian strain, Anglo-American law, Islamic and Adat law (only recently elevated to positive law with the enactment of the Muslim Personal Law Code for Muslim Filipinos). Thailand has its indigenized electric legal system which has integrated concepts from Khmer, Indian, French and British legal systems.

The problem of an entity's "legal personality" is always a fundamental one in law because it determines status and capacitation. Quite unlike other regional organizations, ASEAN has *deliberately* chosen not to adopt a formal "charter". A standard charter generally would have contained provisions on machinery and institutions with defined duties, powers and functions; provide for the legal capacity of the organization; mandate the creation of a secretariat empowered to act in behalf of the Association in its concourse with other international entities; prescribe an amendatory procedure and perhaps even specify the lifetime of the organization. That all these are not part of ASEAN initial development was surely not a result of incompetence. One might even say that it was a stroke of genius because it is now beyond doubt that it was the lack of rigid structures in the organizational setup that allowed for the necessary flexibility and resilience which ASEAN needed in responding to the many buffeting forces interacting in the region. Subsequent to the Bangkok Declaration there was in fact a move to adopt a formal charter for ASEAN. But after careful deliberation and consultation, the idea was set aside and the Council of Minister reaffirmed that the original Declaration and other subsequent basic documents were adequate to constitute the foundation of the Association.[7]

Clearly, ASEAN law has two components, regional and national. Changes in each will more and more affect the other. Legal problems and issues related to and arising from intra-regional transactions as well as those involving extra-ASEAN elements promise to become more complex as interactions become intensive. At this stage it is not appropriate to speak of an ASEAN community law originating from a supranational level and having direct import and binding effect on individuals and legal persons in member states. And unless it is to better explain ASEAN's uniqueness as a regional arrangement, comparison with the European Communities and the law emanating from the various community institutions would not only be odious but misleading. However, if ASEAN law as used here refers to the agreements, treaties and declarations which guide and shape the patterns of interaction within and of the Association, it is the position of this paper that such a law is emerging and one important component is the Treaty of Amity and Cooperation if only because it contains the seed that might well spring forth as the legal framework for regional dispute settlement in Southeast Asia.

That no community can long continue to exist without a conflict amelioration mechanism is axiomatic. Speaking recently on his idea of an incipient Pacific Community, former East-West Center President Kleinjans identified what he considers the ten basic characteristics of any kind of community:

> First, a community is made of people, who secondly, inhabit a territory. Third, these people share a fund of knowledge. Fourth, they have a vehicle of communication — a language. Fifth, they have a common heritage — a history. Sixth, they respond to a set of symbols. Seventh, they share a core of

common values. Eighth, they are linked in a network of institutions. Ninth, they have *ways of settling conflicts among, themselves*, and tenth, their society has form or order.[8]

An ASEAN community undoubtedly is being forged into existence. One only has to examine the basic documents which predicate the Association on the region's common culture, history, aspirations, and common will. Taking the position that a viable mechanism for settling disputes and ameliorating conflicts within the community is a *sine qua non* to the community's survival, this paper proceeds to examine what ASEAN has done toward developing regional law to bring this about.

Promulgated in February 1976, the Treaty of Amity and Cooperation contains the basic law on the pacific settlement of disputes for the treaty region.[9]

Chapter IV of the ASEAN Treaty of Amity, titled "Pacific Dispute Settlement," has five articles providing for the establishment of "regional processes" for settling disputes and managing conflicts and broadly outlines the framework of that process, i.e. parties and their obligations, disputes within the jurisdiction of the mechanism, and the mechanism of dispute settlement itself. It also sets the rule of construction and controlling language. For purposes of the workshop's objective — to discuss cultural development in the treaty region — these provisions are analyzed here not for their legal import as for the light they might throw on understanding ASEAN's legal style. Attempt is made to reflect on the Association's preferences for certain approaches to dispute settlement and the cultural moorings of such choices.

The mere act of successfully concluding the Treaty held great significance for ASEAN for it marked a maturation stage for the Association where the members had sufficiently become confident of the stability and strength of their relations *inter se*. By providing a framework for settling disputes, moreover, the members in effect had acknowledged the existence of disruptive forces within the region which, if not confronted, would erode whatever gains had been attained. They had gone past the stage of building and nursing the fragile foundations of the early stages and in the now familiar "step-by-step ASEAN approach" to region-building they set out to shape the framework for peaceful solutions to outstanding conflicts. Thus, as an event the Treaty might well represent one of the major achievements of ASEAN.

NOTES

1. ASEAN DECLARATION, Bangkok, 8 August 1967.
2. Declaration of ASEAN Concord, Kuala Lumpur, February 24, 1976.
3. Declaration of the Zone of Peace, Freedom and Neutrality, Kuala Lumpur, 1971; ASEAN Concord, 1976.
4. The Philippines has a series of security treaties with the United States of America. For the moment, political and security realities in the region have converged to favor the continuance of American bases in the country.
5. ASEAN Concord.
6. Legal cultures, as distinguished from legal systems which refers to the formal system of laws is used here to mean both the formal and non-formal aspects of the legal order.
7. This decision is reflected in the Joint Communiques issued by the Foreign Ministers Council.
8. Extracted from President Everett Kleinjans' talk to the Asian/Pacific Roundtable in Washington, D.C. and his letter to Richard Mallery. (Emphasis supplied.)
9. Treaty of Amity and Cooperation, Denpasar, Bali, Indonesia, 24 February 1976. The Joint Communique of the Ninth ASEAN Ministerial Meeting, Manila, June 24-26, paragraph 8, expressed gratification at the ratification of the Treaty by all signatories.

THE POLITICS OF ASEAN

Introduction

Chandran Jeshurun

Given the background of Southeast Asian history particularly in terms of its decolonization process and the emergence of modern states, it is not surprising that their domestic politics and their bilateral relations within the region have been the focus of much scholarly attention among regional specialists. Apart from the obvious division of Southeast Asia into socialist and non-socialist states that was in a way reflected by the formation of ASEAN itself, it cannot be denied that even among the member states of the organization there has existed a wide range of contentious issues based on both historical grounds as well as their post-independent experiences. In these circumstances, it is understandable that scholars have attempted to unravel some of the less known sources of political problems within ASEAN and also examine the structural factors within the organization that have contributed to ameliorating intra-ASEAN differences.

In view of the fact that internal self-examination is often a rather delicate matter, most of the in-depth studies of this aspect of ASEAN tended to be undertaken only after an initial period of consolidation and substantial progress when it seemed to be appropriate to adopt a more critical review of the organization's future development. The late Hans H. Indorf, who had been following ASEAN's birth and early evolution with a special interest in its organizational structure and its potential internal difficulties precisely because of his keen awareness of the strong pulls of sovereignty and historical self-images, published a study for the Institute of Southeast Asian Studies in 1984 which provides a useful starting point. This is followed by two more selections, one of which by Chan Heng Chee covers a broad sweep of the recent experience of intra-ASEAN co-operation in the main critical areas of politics, security and economics, while the other by Zakaria Haji Ahmad reaffirms many of Hans Indorf's early predictions about the primacy of national interests. By focusing on the decision-making process, Zakaria's contributions also stands alone among the literature on the internal goings-on of the ASEAN member states in having utilized empirical data based on interviews with senior officials of the time in a systematic manner.

As the idea of the state and the question of the legitimacy of governments are prominent in the discussion of regional stability in Southeast Asia, it is inevitable that the political taxonomy of the ASEAN states has also been the subject of scrutiny by scholars. Ranging from those with deep historical roots such as the Kingdom of Thailand on the one hand to those that were created through political disunity, such as Singapore, ASEAN does constitute a somewhat unique mix of different forms of the concept of nationhood. However, all the existing regimes that govern these states have had to confront the challenge of legitimacy within the context of their own internal politics at one time or another. This complex intellectual problem is dealt with in the thoroughly researched and eloquently argued essay of Sukhumbhand Paribatra and Chai-Anan Samudavanija. In a related context, the military as a national institution also deserves to be taken into account within ASEAN particularly in its perception of and contribution to national security. Finally, those who have studied the ASEAN formula for regional co-operation have either been impressed with its comparative success or tend to bemoan its many shortcomings. Nevertheless, the organization does possess certain intrinsic typically Southeast Asian qualities that sometimes defy clear description but somehow have had a signal effect on preserving its cohesion and common long-term purpose. This futuristic view of the prospects for ASEAN's further growth and strengthening is provided by Michael Antolik.

19.

POLITICAL RELATIONS WITHIN ASEAN

HANS H. INDORF

Ample evidence in these pages suggests that ASEAN member countries will act as sovereign states, largely unencumbered by the aggregate obligations of a regional organization. Perceived national interests dominate political planning and executive action. This is as it should be in a world governed by diverse egocentric policies and an escalating interdependence increasingly spilling beyond the geographic confines of a region. Consequently, it is natural to assume that intra-ASEAN relations would be characterized by the aberrations and intemperances of conflicting national objectives. Yet, the question remains as to how such confrontational international behaviour can conform to the professions of regional unity so often enunciated by government leaders. An immediate reaction would be that the unmitigated exercise of national sovereignty and regional unity are generally incompatible. Some sacrifice for common ideals is necessary to justify a credible standing in a collective enterprise. Under what circumstances can it be expected?

Any answer would have to take account of two diverging views of regionalism: one is centrist and the other intergovernmental. The former would expect the emergence of joint institutions with controlling propensities, focusing upon a problem-solving orientation that may necessitate submergence of state priorities. The latter implies inter-governmentalism that seeks to harmonize interests, in the process of which the limits of potential co-operation will inevitably be discovered. This view incorporates bilateral disagreements as an enervating function of international intercourse, and assigns to regional institutions only a secondary, co-ordinating role. The continued and parallel existence of both views among ASEAN member states has created a teleological ambiguity that invites further friction.

In the concluding sections to follow, an attempt is made to synthesize the bilateral problems within ASEAN with the ameliorating features provided by accident or by design. When grafted onto the extra-regional dimension of anticipated cohesion and economic attraction, a less controversial form of regionalism may crystallize for ASEAN. Instead of castigating the organization for ineptness, it may have to be accepted that member governments prefer a perpetuation of political pluralism to a more cohesive supranationalism. As a result, intra-ASEAN problems will persist but, hopefully, their effect can be mollified by a deeper appreciation of inevitable limitations to regionalism.

Excerpted from Hans H. Indorf, *Impediments to Regionalism in Southeast Asia: Bilateral Constraints among ASEAN Member States* (Singapore: Institute of Southeast Asian Studies, 1984), by permission of the publisher.

PATTERNS OF BILATERAL CONFLICT

There is no doubt that the existence of ASEAN, and its practice of consultation, have conditioned regional leaders to be more sensitive to the interests and commitments of their neighbours. Despite the self-imposed restraint, however, frictional situations abound, involving all member states with increasing frequency for widely divergent reasons, and for very basic causes[1] An analysis of the variables of disputes among the ASEAN countries, be they motivations, actual substance, timing or parties involved, can lead to some interesting conclusions.

Fundamental to the disparate bilateral problems prevailing in ASEAN is the recognition that member states project and preserve their national interests regardless of common bonds stipulated under the multilateral umbrella of a regional organization. Although not consciously admitted, the emphasis is upon intergovernmentalism in which national interests converge only coincidentally, and felicitously, with regional objectives. Obviously, such convergence attains different shades of accomplishment, but the important difference is one of intent. If it points to a strengthening of centrist institutions, it would have to retain the representational character of participating governments to ensure intergovernmentalism. More likely, the intent will be aimed at problem-solving for national benefit, with regional gains remaining incidental.

ASEAN's interest is a compound of national interests. For political reasons, they are more concerned with short-term results, the aggressive pursuit of which, by some elected leaders, can undermine mutual confidence.[2] In this climate, national disagreements are more likely to occur, and to linger on, in the absence of harmonized systems for their management. State interests remain paramount even within a system of regional co-operation.

This becomes evident when examining the substance of intra-ASEAN friction. Most clearly delineated are state claims involving the territorial imperative, which is advanced for reasons of history or actual possession. Underlying these assumptions are the more volatile arguments of security and resources which are strictly nationally managed prerogatives. Superficially, it appears that conflicts over borders could easily be settled since they involve something measurable for which compromise is mathematically achievable. Yet, boundary demarcations are lacking despite the availability of joint border committees and the governmental realization that this divisive issue continues to be an obstacle to good neighbourly relations. So far, competing claims remain sub rosa.

Economic differences cut even deeper into regional cohesion. At stake are material gains — or losses — impacting directly on citizens and the business community. Consequently, the ASEAN governments have been uncustomarily intransigent in pressing for acceptance of their national positions, at the expense of conciliatory solutions. In this instance of conflictual substance, more than in any other, dispute situations were marked by incomprehension of another nation's justification for its policies. Worse was the fact that, in economic matters, there was a general unwillingness to concede to the greater good of all.

It has been argued by officials and the local media that the recessionist trends in the industrialized world have severely affected national economies in Southeast Asia, which are still too dependent upon soft commodity exports.[3] With drastic reductions in export earnings, budgetary appropriations have fallen alarmingly, and external government debts have assumed dangerous proportions. Under these circumstances, any co-operative action within ASEAN, it is believed, could only have near-term cosmetic effects, leaving structurally corrective measures to national initiatives. Yet, there is no convincing evidence that ASEAN has been given a serious opportunity to deal with industrial competition, joint markets, the regional movement of labour or a co-ordination of development plans. On the contrary, economic nationalism appears to be more determined than ever, with an increasing number of intra-ASEAN economic conflicts in its wake.

While territorial and economic issues have been major reasons for Southeast Asia's simmering disagreements, the communal and religious dimensions have added a publicly subdued emotional undercurrent that, because of its intangibility, will make solutions for intractible problems even less certain. To mind comes the close association between Malaysia and Indonesia, and its effect on minorities in Thailand and the Philippines. Pragmatic leaders have kept doctrinal excesses within manageable limits, but should Islamic militancy gain influence over some governmental decisions, the effect on regional co-operation could be debilitating. Likewise, Singapore's commercial practices are not always credited to an imaginative leadership but to the idiosyncrasies of a Chinese society. This fallacy will be compounded by other erroneous communal assumptions as the city-state's economic fortunes become even more disproportionate to the rest of ASEAN.

One astounding fact concerning intra-ASEAN disagreements is that the density of their occurrence did not noticeably fluctuate in accordance with major developmental trends of the organization. For example, it could have been expected that the 1967 inauguration of ASEAN would introduce an all-pervasive goodwill, yet the basic communal issues festered on, particularly over Sabah and Singapore. After the Bali summit of 1976, the euphoria over new co-operative ventures soon dissipated when more direct economic interaction produced greater opportunities for friction. Even the external pressures generated by Vietnam and the Soviet Union in the 1980s did not bring about the proverbial unity within the region. A public consensus was reached to support Thailand and to utilize the United Nations processes, but divergent national views persisted regarding details in the approaches to the Khmer coalition, Vietnam, and China.[4]

In other words, the timing of bilateral disputes was not appreciably affected by the rate of ASEAN progress. Southeast Asian nations consider their sovereign interests as the cardinal motivator which determines the form and substance of their international relations. Membership in a regional organization remains just one tool in the arsenal of measures and methods available for interstate behaviour. ASEAN as a collective entity cannot as yet significantly influence the tactics and policies of its members.

Of the four variables which characterize disagreement, that is, motivation, substance, timing, and implicated agent, it is the last which seems to exceed the other three in importance. Although all the countries in the area are party to one conflict or another, it is Malaysia and Singapore which are numerically most frequently involved. There are manifold reasons for this situation, but it does not suggest by any means that the two countries aim to be the major source of trouble within ASEAN. Circumstantial evidence can provide a partial explanation.

As previously indicated, Malaysia has land or maritime borders with all the other ASEAN states. As a major supplier of key raw materials, it can play a decisive, and disagreeable, role on the world market. In a communally divided society, the government has been forced to emphasize rapid progress in development as well as Malay nationalism — both factors that lend themselves to passive confrontation. National leaders have shown a preference for resoluteness in policies, which set them apart from the more accommodating traits of their neighbours.

Some of these features are replicated in Singapore, especially resolute leadership and the unswerving pursuit of economic advancement. Yet, there are other factors which make Singapore frequently, but unwillingly, a party to regionally contentious issues. As the youngest and smallest state within the region, it has to act without the moderating influence of history and tradition. For a city-republic, the question of survival is more eminent than for larger countries nearby, and being a rather homogeneous Chinese society with only a very small proportion of other Asian racial communities has not made social intercourse any easier. The chief obstacle to good relations, however, appears to have been Singapore's effective economic practices and, for lack of raw materials, its position as the commission merchant for the area. As in the case of Malaysia, the conditions which made both countries reluctant parties to intra-ASEAN disputes are largely immutable.

The pattern of bilateral conflict that emerges in Southeast Asia is determined by considerations of indivisive sovereignty, primarily focusing on territorial rights and economic interests without any particular time constraints. The Association's contribution was a diminution in dimension rather than an outright elimination of conflict. Since most disagreements seemed to coalesce around Malaysia and Singapore, it leaves room for optimism that remedial steps can be found to reduce the incidents of bilateral friction.

THE AMELIORATION OF CONTENTIOUS ISSUES

Regional relations in Southeast Asia are regulated by intergovernmentalism rather than by a search for a common destiny. Consequently, the clash of sovereign interests will remain an inevitable by-product of political life. The fact that countries have chosen to collaborate within the mutually accepted framework of ASEAN has increased the likelihood that conflicts of peripheral national value would not explode into open confrontation, and that those of a more serious nature would not tear the organization asunder. Personal consultations and periodic meetings have had a mitigating effect on potential bilateral hostilities.

Yet, recognizing that problems exist, and hoping for the emollient influence of ASEAN may not suffice for building a resilient regionalism. Positive measures need to be considered and accepted which can transform the institutional palliative of impact reduction to one of constructive co-operation. In the light of

the conflictual patterns that can be discerned, some remedies seem to suggest themselves. These can be briefly sketched and conveniently grouped under leadership, national policies, and collective actions.

It is almost mandatory to understand that interstate difficulties in Southeast Asia are the products of governments which condone and control them. In a quasi-authoritarian setting, it is the leaders of these governments who can effectively induce the process for accommodation. Subordinates implement and interpret existing regulations, but they cannot voluntarily compromise. The weight of bilateral relations is on the shoulders of the heads of government. A redress of grievances has to commence at this level.

Periodic visits should accomplish the task if they could be changed from itinerant social occasions to regular business meetings. If regional matters deserve priority, a definite schedule of annual contacts, occasionally with selected Cabinet members, would be justifiable in the context of domestic policy considerations. No doubt, the exercise would be more time consuming than summitry but would at least allow for greater privacy; misunderstandings can arise among those not present (as the 1980 Kuantan meeting demonstrated) but rotating visits could reduce this possibility. As it is, joint statements invariably stress "the need for frequent exchanges of views among the ASEAN heads of government."[5] It is time that leaders follow their own declarations.

However, heads of government can only set the tone, indicate similarities in perception, and stress the areas for likely agreement. The Malaysia-Singapore precedent of establishing a high-level intergovernmental committee, charged with preparing acceptable propositions within a definite time-frame, and reporting these directly to their prime ministers, is an excellent device worthy of duplication between other regional capitals. Attention to bilateral disagreements must be upgraded; lingering suspicions, mistrust, and prejudices will impede national development.

While leaders and ministerial technocrats should show a greater resolve for settling problems instead of perpetuating the present custom of postponing mutual consultations, the citizens themselves will ultimately have to be mobilized for comprehending, if not supporting, the resolution of contentious issues. Whether the disputes concern border irredentism, fishing in extraterritorial waters, or illegal immigration, the masses are woefully uninformed, often as the result of a conscious policy of depoliticization.[6] This blissful unawareness of neighbourly frictions, and ASEAN objectives for regional co-operation, can be overcome. Means of communication are available to undertake a broad effort in public relations to explain regional affairs and their close linkage to domestic policies. An unemployed Malaysian worker is entitled to be made aware of the implications of the Indonesian guestworker programme beyond a mere economic rationale. Consensus building begins at home.

A final aspect involving heads of government in the elimination of bilateral problems is the much maligned summit of ASEAN leaders which itself has become a source of conflict because of its *ad hoc* arrangements. Perhaps there should be an agreement which institutionalizes summit meetings as a necessary prerequisite for productive regional co-operation. Most likely, summit conferences could benefit from being deformalized and held whenever justified by circumstances which, in turn, require a clearer definition. Ambiguities are liable to cause irritation, and the preparatory process for the next ASEAN summit has been no exception. It may also serve a useful purpose to make the convening of a meeting the exclusive responsibility of the next host government (as determined by alphabetical rotation) which has to submit detailed proposals for the agenda. This procedure would have a decided advantage over the current amorphous multilateral understandings. It would locate the obligation for initiating exploratory bilateral consultations with only one government, forcing it to formulate substantive reasons which are subject to unanimous consent. It would also relinquish

the practice of a less than dignified public campaign for holding a summit.

Aside from leadership input which can assist in the amelioration of conflict situations, tangible national measures could be contemplated as long as it is recognized that some of the intergovernmental disagreements are caused by differing concepts of national sovereignty which are not easily allayed by legal mechanics. For instance, border demarcations, which began years ago, have made only slow progress. The only land boundaries in ASEAN are those between Malaysia and Thailand in the north and Malaysia and Indonesia in Kalimantan. A more concentrated effort could bring expeditious benefits. Extra troublesome are maritime borders but since all the ASEAN countries have signed the new international Law of the Sea Treaty in December 1982, a regional adherence to its provisions prior to ratification could eliminate some uncertainties. Furthermore, Malaysia is in the process of printing yet another national map which may specify its own claims but again invite counterclaims. Procrastination and the absence of consultations for their resolution can draw unnecessarily from a dwindling residue of goodwill. A mutually agreed-upon timetable for settling territorial disputes could minimize conflict.

There is still an observable reluctance to enter into bilateral agreements with neighbouring states, whether on joint exploration, marketing, purchasing, research, or other activities. Preference is given to negotiations on an all-ASEAN basis instead of using the often more profitable interstate mechanisms. In the realm of security, bilateral commitments have reached a high degree of comprehensiveness. Why could not the same amount of energy and determination be devoted to foreign investment strategies, currency convertibility, or manpower planning? Many of these potential joint endeavours are being examined by the ASEAN Permanent Committees; some have been for years, others will be in the future. A good case could be made for starting co-operative experiments at the bilateral level, whether they be complementary schemes or joint industrial enterprises, before elevating them to the multilateral sphere. It would reserve more initiative for intergovernmental action, reduce the workload of ASEAN committees, provide data-yielding experience for eventual ASEAN projects, and still make a sound contribution to promoting regionalism.

It has been said that fences make good neighbours; Malaysia has been constructing such a barrier at the Thai border. Since the fence was not erected exactly on the boundary line but inside Malaysian territory, the resulting no-man's land was illegally settled by thousands of Thai Muslims. Now Bangkok has decided to build its own fence and, thus, presumably force the settlers to make a choice.[7] Will it really terminate the problem? Fences were also meant to curb border smuggling. The Malaysian gates are reportedly opened for the "Golden Hour" when smugglers can purchase their way through the guards, only to form convoys of contraband on the Thai side, where an additional fee will let them enter the country. It is obviously a revenue enhancing measure but for whose benefit? Smuggling remains a serious problem but effective joint actions could drastically curtail this painful regional activity.

When existing bilateral problems are measured against the reality of ASEAN solidarity, two facts stand out: a frailty in the collective will, and unutilized opportunities for co-ordinate problem-solving. Reference to the former must include the observation that ASEAN has demonstrated an obsession with institution-building at the expense of focusing upon common policies. Despite the Bangkok Declaration and subsequent joint agreements, an explicit understanding regarding the final objective of regional co-operation is missing. Thai requests for a common market, Philippine suggestions for a customs union, and a general clamour for an equitable division of industrial development, point towards a trend for increasing regional interaction. Other members stress national resilience, independent ventures and even commercially protective measures which view ASEAN as a subordinate edifice for furthering state policies. Both propositions

have merit but as long as discussions are marked by a lack of perspicuity as to the ultimate goal, the acceptance of joint projects will be less than unanimous.

Specifically, ASEAN could assist national governments by much more vigorously involving the non-governmental sector in its planning. Intelligence and funding are not the sole preserve of public agencies. Long-term economic development can be accelerated by exchanging regionally available resources, from management experience to project expertise. A regional manpower study could examine the inter-country flow of labour, recruitment standards, uniform work permits, benefits and compensation. It might even be preferable not to declare a joint venture as an ASEAN project if it fails to receive an absolute consensus, thereby avoiding aggravation and giving bi- and tri-lateralism a chance. A respect for diversity within a common framework could alleviate many of the present difficulties. Should leadership initiatives, national policies, and collective action fall short of expectations by not providing relief for bilateral friction, there is always the Treaty of Amity with its dispute-settlement provisions.[8] It would be a last resort, even if undesirable, because of its final formality.

THE INTERNATIONAL PERCEPTION OF INTRA-ASEAN COHESION

So far, the prevalence of bilateral conflicts among the ASEAN member states has been viewed as the outcome of inflexible national policies, justified by sovereignty endured in preference to violent alternatives, and quietly condemned for its dysfunctional effect upon ASEAN itself. Yet, there is an external dimension to internal disagreements, one affecting security and the other, the image of the organization.

First is the proposition that a regional association which projects a cohesive front, which is united in its policies and predictable in its actions, is less likely to invite adventurism against any one of its member states. ASEAN reality, however, does not yet reflect such a perfect combination of elements. Instead, an interested outside observer perceives in ASEAN a dynamic pluralism in which conflicting national policies continue to supercede aspects of burden-sharing and the voluntary imposition of limits on self-interest, which are accepted as a *sine qua non* of regionalism. The Association as a group has not been able to exert the molecular attraction which could induce member states to act predictably in unison. Common approaches, whether to a trading partner or a presumed antagonist, were only possible when the unifying denominator promised the highest possible return. Unity frequently broke down when the first offer was rejected and negotiations had to take its place, an ordinary occurrence in an organization of co-equals.

Another ASEAN feature which cannot escape the notice of foreign observers is the belief in the spillover concept. It stipulates a gradualist approach, often asserted by regional leaders when member governments are admonished to focus upon the construction of national resilience which, in turn, would produce an area-wide resilience.[9] If the practical application of the concept is taken at face value, it would also cover negative aspects other than national resilience. Could a spillover effect not also be anticipated of the many bilateral disagreements which have become a fact of Southeast Asia's political life? The conclusion for external actors, be they Vietnam or Japan, is that intra-ASEAN differences can make collective action vulnerable to individually isolating approaches. Openly exploiting this ASEAN weakness may not always be advisable but it appears to have been done.

Most prominent were the attempts made by Vietnam's Foreign Minister Nguyen Co Thach during his periodic rounds of ASEAN capitals, when he tried to enlarge upon incipient differences concerning Kampuchea. Hanoi's willingness to play host to various covert visits by Indonesian delegations and to make concessionary gestures regarding its claims to the Indonesian-occupied Natuna Islands, led some observers to suspect another form of an ingratiating approach. But pursuing divisive tactics was not limited to Vietnam. Negotiating a textile quota with the European Economic Community (EEC) during 1982 became an exceedingly protracted task since ASEAN member states could not agree among themselves on a general set of conditions.[10] Finally, Thailand reached a separate agreement in an apparent exchange for an advantageous arrangement for the export of manioc. There are also the earlier Japanese overtures to the Philippines, among other illustrations, when it sought to divorce Manila from ASEAN's united-front demands on production limits for synthetic rubber.

Although many of these divisional attempts failed to attain the desired results, disputes within ASEAN can nevertheless create added opportunities for the rest of the world to disrupt the progress towards regionalism. This could have been the reason for Mr Lee Kuan Yew's prophetic warning:[11]

> In the intermediate term, by the late 1980s or early 1990s, however, it is possible that there could be outside forces eager and capable of exploiting any differences that may arise between us. Such outside forces can create difficulties for all of us. Hence, it behoves us to use these intervening years to strengthen our cooperation and solidarity.

Dissension and some mistrust within ASEAN have characterized negotiations with the Association's seven Dialogue partners, from New Delhi to Ottawa. ASEAN's economy is an integral part of the world system. Whenever conflicts of interest among member states prevented a successful joint approach, single countries have pursued their own external trade links — even at the expense of their neighbours — covering such diverse commodities as rice, rubber, and diesel engines.

Residual wariness of each other may also have discouraged the ASEAN member countries from agreeing upon a single channel for trade negotiations. It must be remembered that the original practice of using member governments as contact points for foreign governments has now been largely replaced by ASEAN ambassadorial committees in the capitals of the industrialized countries. This insistence upon equal representation in almost all significant ASEAN initiatives is probably a contributing factor for the organization's disinclination to establish itself as a legally constituted body. One of the consequences is that extra-regional governments are forced to deal with five member states instead of with a single entity, thereby directing relations into a bilateral pattern which could encourage inequitable trading terms.

ASEAN's inability to eliminate some of its intramural problems has no doubt affected the perceptions of its Dialogue partners. American officials spoke charitably of ASEAN, as "sui generis" with "competing economies", and "protectionist pressures". The absence of a joint investment code in ASEAN has made its members fair game for economic rivalry among one another when offering suitable incentives to foreign businessmen.[12] Such competition can exacerbate ASEAN relations, and benefit to some extent the overseas capital market.

NOTES

1. An interesting study by Richard N. Lebow, *Between Peace and War* (Baltimore: Johns Hopkins University Press, 1981) comes to the conclusion that conflict arises out of need and not opportunity. Lebow argues that weak nations are more likely to act aggressively, frequently by underestimating an adversary's resolve.

2. On this basic concept, there are many parallels to trends in the EEC, as explained by Paul Taylor in, "Intergovernmentalism in the European Communities in the 1970s: Patterns and Prospectives". *International Organization* 36, no. 4 (Autumn 1982): 741-66.

3. For an elaboration of these views, see "Community Begins at Home", *Far Eastern Economic Review (FEER)*, 10 December 1982, pp. 67-69; and "Viability of ASEAN in Question", *ASEAN Forecast* (February 1982), p. 24

4. A recent illustration was the idea advanced by Foreign Minister ACM Siddhi Savetsila which asked Vietnam to withdraw its troops 30 km from the Thai border as a gesture of good faith, followed by Siddhi's visit to Hanoi. The Sixteenth Ministerial Meeting in Bangkok in 1983 failed to adopt the concept and, in its Communiqué (para 15), merely "endorsed" the national initiative. Dr Mochtar pointedly referred to the idea in his opening address as "YOUR proposal . . . demonstrates the desire of YOUR government . . ." (emphasis added): see *Bangkok Post*, 25 and 26 June 1983.

5. A "typical" communiqué was issued at the end of Mr Lee's visit to the Philippines in February 1980, in which they "agreed to consult" the other leaders, emphasized "frequent exchanges of view" and "the holding of a summit meeting . . . in 18 to 24 months". See *FBIS* [Foreign Broadcast Information Service] IV (3 March 1980), p. 02.

6. R.S. Milne. 'Technocrats and Politics in the ASEAN Countries", *Pacific Affairs* 55, no. 3 (Fall 1982: 403-29. A relevant analysis is provided by Joan S. Black in "Opinion Leaders: Is Anyone Following?" *Public Opinion Quarterly* 46 (Fall 1982): 169-76, and *Business Day* (Manila), 10 August 1982, p. 11, reaches the conclusion that ". . . the man in the street could not care less . . . even if he knew . . . what ASEAN was all about."

7. *Bangkok Post*, 16 September 1982, p. 1, vividly described the dilemma.

8. ASEAN Documentation Series 1981, *Treaty of Amity and Co-operation in Southeast Asia* (Bali, 24 February 1976), especially Chapter IV.

9. The limitations of this argument are explored in Hans H. Indorf, "Some Speculation on a Second Blueprint for ASEAN", *Contemporary Southeast Asia* 3, no. 2 (September 1981): 144.

10. See Hans H. Indorf, "Political Dimensions of Intra-Regional Co-operation: the Case of ASEAN and the EEC", *Asia-Pacific Community*, no. 19 (Tokyo: Winter 1983) 89-107.

11. Departing remarks on the occasion of Dr Mahathir's visit to Singapore, in *Straits Times*, 19 December 1981, p. 14.
12. Quotes from *Testimony Before U.S. Senate Foreign Relations East Asian Subcommittee* (Washington, D.C., 8-10 June 1982). See also Derek Davis, "From the Littoral of Pragmatism", *FEER*, 10 December 1982, pp. 73-74; Hans H. Indorf, "U.S.-ASEAN Relations", in *Thai-American Relations in Contemporary Affairs*, edited by Hans H. Indorf (Singapore: Executive Publications Ltd, 1982), pp. 159-75.

20.

THE STRUCTURE OF DECISION-MAKING*

ZAKARIA HAJI AHMAD

The national bureaucrats who work on ASEAN affairs might appropriately be called the "decision-makers" of the regional organization, for it is they who carry out the day-to-day chores — formulation of policy and viewpoints, attendance and deliberation at meetings, negotiations and discussions, and implementation of decisions.

Primarily, these decision-makers are the staff of the ASEAN National Secretariat (ANS) in each of the member states' Ministry of Foreign Affairs (MFA). According to Nishikawa, after 1976 the ANS had been changed to the "Office of the Director-General, ASEAN (name of member country)",[1] although he observed that "these offices continue their previous functions and work effectively to complement the work of the ASEAN Secretariat in Jakarta".[2] However, reference to the ANS was constantly made by respondents interviewed in the course of this study. Even in the Philippines, where the Ministry of Foreign Affairs was reorganized in late 1982, with the "ASEAN National Coordinating Commission" being renamed "Office of ASEAN Affairs", this will "not affect the ASEAN desk".[3] ASEAN work is usually conducted through negotiations at ministerial level, and within the Standing Committee (which is formed in the country where the Foreign Ministers' Meeting

is held) and the "permanent" committees (of which there are nine).[4] However, it is the ANS that "coordinates" each country's position at ASEAN deliberations.

Outside each MFA, decision-makers dealing with ASEAN come basically from "technical" agencies such as the departments or ministries handling economic development and planning, trade and industry, transport, communications, health, forestry, science and technology, energy, agriculture, and primary industries. Usually, these "secondary level" officials deal with matters handled by the specific ASEAN committees. (In some cases, however, some ANS officials also deal with specific technical matters.)

In all the three countries studied, ASEAN matters are also attended to by some of the most senior MFA officials, although most of the work is done by the national secretariat. The MFA's advice is sought on all matters relevant to ASEAN, indicating the primary influence and position of the MFA's bureaucrats.

However, although it is possible to picture concentric circles of ASEAN decision-makers, with MFA top officials at the core surrounded by ANS officials as a primary circle and technical officials as the outer ring, the locus of authority remains blurred. During ASEAN meetings, this blurring may occur because of the nature of

Reprinted in abridged form from "The World of ASEAN Decision-Makers: A Study of Bureaucratic Elite Perceptions in Malaysia, the Philippines and Singapore", *Contemporary Southeast Asia* 8, no. 3 (December 1986), pp. 192–212, by permission of the author and the Institute of Southeast Asian Studies.

a member-state's governmental system — for example, competition or rivalry between ministers can hinder the decision ANS officials can make or convey without clearance from the highest authority of that country. The administrative style of a particular country has some relevance as well, as will be seen below.

The conceptual distinction between primary and secondary agencies appears most valid in the Malaysian and Singaporean cases. In the Philippine case, however, it has been observed that there has been a steady erosion of the MFA's role and influence in foreign policy, including ASEAN matters, as a result of a heightened sense of the importance of economic parameters in external relations and the advent of "development diplomacy".[5] The role of the Philippine MFA may, therefore, be subject to contending rivalry from other agencies, especially the National Economic Development Agency (NEDA), a situation that seems amplified by the view of one Filipino respondent that "economic planning officials had much influence on questions relating to regional cooperation in as much as it related to economic matters". In this case, then, the MFA's role as a primary locus of decision-making may be shared by other agencies and subject to the nature of inter-agency relations.[6] However, according to the Filipino respondents, the MFA's role was still important in an overall sense although it was also clear that policies of an economic nature were more within the sphere of NEDA. Indeed, one respondent described the MFA's role as important in the "political aspects" of ASEAN, and that there was "no inter-agency struggle because of the close relationship between NEDA and the MFA".

Although the MFAs in all three countries usually have the "final say", in a number of instances the agency that is designated as the co-ordinating body for a particular agenda attempts to "take the lead". One MFA respondent who dealt with "technical" matters asserted that although 80 per cent of ASEAN business concerned economic issues and the other 20 per cent political, the latter was "glamourized" by the press. This is significant not only in terms of the perception, but also because it again raises the question of the exact locus of authority and decision-making within the agencies dealing with ASEAN affairs.

It is apparent that the machinery for ASEAN decision-making has become increasingly complex: so much so that there is an ongoing attempt at reorganizing ASEAN procedures. In several instances, certain problems have become so big that an individual ASEAN country is simply assigned to deal with it. In other areas, one country has been allowed to chair a committee, rather than rotate the chairmanship. Decision-making resides in committees in which all ASEAN members are represented, but the work of these committees is slow and tedious, so verbal consensus is often achieved prior to the actual working out of details. Although there are already five committees established under the aegis of the economic ministers, it is felt that a sixth — on energy — should be set up. Decisions made by the committee are then affirmed by the respective ministers and standing committees. That agreement can be reached almost informally indicates an air of ease in ASEAN decision-making.

If certain national circumstances render it difficult to pinpoint the exact locus of authority, it was also revealed by a senior ASEAN Secretariat official that, for the grouping itself, the relative importance of the foreign and economics ministers remains to be established. It is thus unclear whether the deliberations of the meetings of the five (later six) foreign ministers or of their economic counterparts holds greater weight.[7]

The "ASEAN officials" of the respective MFAs represent their countries' interests at ASEAN deliberations but the platform, as it were, on which they interact is governed by what may be called "codes of behaviour". Essentially, these "codes" have been set by the Bangkok Declaration of 1967, the ASEAN Concord and the Treaty of Amity and Co-operation as well as supplementary agreements. Interestingly, however, such a revelation came only from one source — a Malaysian respondent. This might mean that such codes of behaviour are assumed to be obvious, or it could reflect the fact that Malaysian decision-makers operate in what they understand as a "formal" context, whereas other respondents presumably did not feel so inclined. In a related sense, Singaporean respondents had also a notion of the "formal" nature of organizations, and in identifying problems faced by ASEAN one noted that there were "serious problems in administrative matters such as budgeting". He opined that Malaysian and Singaporean administrative styles "exercised more control" over such matters whereas the Filipino and Indonesian approaches were "rather loose". Malaysian and Singaporean respondents apparently thought that such problems had to be dealt with before any expansion of ASEAN could be undertaken.

The views and opinions of these decision-makers underscore the structure of decision-making on ASEAN affairs in their respective countries. As one Malaysian respondent put it, decision-making in Malaysia is "tilted in favour of bureaucrats", a style that corresponds with the heavy influence of the bureaucracy in what Esman called "an administrative state".[8] This was not, however, the impression gained from Singaporean respondents, indicating more direct control by political ministers over bureaucratic decision-making. In the Philippines, control over bureaucrats would seem to be subject to at least seven major groups,[9] although respondents who were "secondary" officials indicated a more direct concern by ministers (who are largely economists) over issues of economic co-operation. Indeed, Manila has established a ministerial and technical committee on ASEAN economic co-operation, chaired by the Prime Minister. Nonetheless, it is apparent even in the Philippines that the views and advice of its bureaucrats are heavily relied upon.

Members of each country's ANS attend ASEAN meetings, having prepared briefs according to their respective national viewpoints. Given that each national position on any particular issue would have to be vetted by the higher echelons of each country's MFA, it was not clear from the views obtained whether the ANS staff's views were always readily accepted or were sometimes altered. But the impression gained was that the ANS views often had some weight. In this regard, the "style of administration" in each particular country is probably important. The Malaysian and Filipino respondents were more "open" in their discussion of viewpoints, whereas the Singaporeans were rather reluctant. This could mean that the "vetting" procedure is more rigorous in the Singaporean situation but much less so in the Malaysian and Philippine contexts.

The degree of control in each situation also depended on the seniority of the ANS official concerned. The more senior the official, the less rigorous the vetting. For example, in the early years of ASEAN, Singapore's ANS was a "one-man show" and the span of decision-making was small; indeed at one time the ANS Director-General was *the* most senior MFA official. Given also the priority now accorded to ASEAN, it seems likely that officers assigned to an ANS will have a fair degree of seniority: this was certainly the case for all the respondents interviewed. Because of the small span of authority, ASEAN officials are in very close communication with their bureaucratic superiors and political masters. The degree of control was, therefore, a question of not only the extent of seniority but also of the very compact nature of organization of ASEAN activities in each country. The ASEAN bureaucratic decision-maker as such occupied a critical place in each member state's decisions on ASEAN-related issues.

It may be presumed that each ASEAN decision-maker acts and makes decisions according to what he perceives to be the best interests of his country. It appears, from one source, that such a predisposition also exists amongst the ASEAN officials nominated to conduct ASEAN's affairs *on behalf* of ASEAN. According to the regulations, such an official "cannot participate in politics" but can "facilitate matters" in his or her own country. The impression gained from the self-assuredness of the respondents is that although they represent their respective countries, their style is individual, not national. Thus, while each decision-maker is an individual who sees his country's interests as tied in to ASEAN, no decision-maker acts purely in the interests of ASEAN.

The representation of one's national interest(s) is an important component of each individual's self-awareness of his or her own role in the regional organization. Generally, respondents affirmed this role of maximizing their own national interests in ASEAN's deliberations, but rationalized this as a necessary step — not doing so would be "harmful" to one's own country, and in any event such maximization of national interest was not seen as damaging to the regional organization.

In more "technical" areas, it was admitted that competition among ASEAN member states was necessary, but that at the same time joint efforts were being made to minimize the effects of this on regional co-operation. Decision-making is being structured in terms of collaboration, not co-operation. An example of this relates to an ongoing attempt to establish a joint ASEAN shipping service through equity participation, a proposal being mooted by the Federation of ASEAN Shippers' Councils to the Federation of ASEAN Shipowners' Associations.[10] Interestingly, this proposal is being proposed as an alternative to the Far East Freight Conference (FEFC), whose rates are considered too competitive for the individual, nascent shipping lines of ASEAN.

If national interest is regarded as an important component of the decision-maker's stances, are there frictions in the process of ASEAN decision-making? This is an issue that cannot be resolved or answered on the basis of the available interview evidence. Different national

interests led to different nuances but there emerged a perception that "openness" is important. One source stated that no suspicions existed in the decision-making corridors of ASEAN but that one "could tell what another was driving at". It is also pertinent that there is a view that the leaders of ASEAN prefer not to allow bilateral issues within the organization to emerge as stumbling blocks in discussions. Perhaps, indeed, there is a notion that certain problems are best swept under the carpet, a style that might conceivably be regarded as non-Western or even indigenously Southeast Asian.

Nonetheless, the question of national interest is probably a central factor in the process of ASEAN decision-making. Sometimes the notion is that, as bureaucrats, these decision-makers perform only their assigned tasks and nothing more. Style of course is important. One view classified the Filipinos as "liberals" who acted more like the "private sector" of their own country. They thus pushed for free trade just as the private sector would. But other nationals saw the issue differently, and analysed it cautiously. This had to do with "national style" as well — the inaccuracy of statistics (except for Malaysia and Singapore) was viewed as a national element that sometimes made discussion a lot more difficult. If an issue became too difficult to negotiate at meetings, it was pushed on to be deliberated by the respective ministers; such deliberations did not involve bureaucrats, who were only informed of the outcomes later. This also implied that ASEAN decision-makers are generally more "rigid", perhaps even pushing their national interests further than necessary. Such rigidity can be explained by a view that, notwithstanding a prevailing spirit of "give and take", ASEAN should not violate the national interests held sacrosanct by its members.

NOTES

* This paper was originally prepared for the ASEAN Economic Research Unit Project, "An Inquiry into the Political Factors in Regional Integration: A Study of ASEAN". As the research was conducted prior

to the inclusion of Brunei in ASEAN in 1984, interview citations refer to the original five member states of ASEAN.

1. Jun Nishikawa, *ASEAN and the United Nations System* (New York: UNITAR, 1983), p. 14.
2. Ibid.
3. *New Straits Times*, 23 December 1982.
4. Nishikawa, op. cit., pp. 12–14.
5. Richard Kessler, "'Development Diplomacy': The Role of the MFA in the Philippines", *Philippine Journal of Public Administration* 24, no. 1 (January 1980): 26–46.
6. On inter-agency relations, see ibid.
7. The analysis by Nishikawa, op. cit., pp. 12–13, does not clarify this issue. His chart of the organizational structure of ASEAN on p. 13 equates the standing of the two groups of ministers, and his statements that "the highest policy-making body of ASEAN is the Meeting of Foreign Ministers" and that "the meeting of ASEAN Economic Ministers is a supreme decision-making body in the field of economic cooperation", on p. 12, are contradictory.
8. M.J. Esman, *Administration and Development in Malaysia* (Ithaca: Cornell University Press, 1972).
9. Kessler, op. cit., p. 32.
10. Both these organizations are private or non-governmental ASEAN bodies. However, their activities are closely monitored by the respective ASEAN governments.

21.

INTRA-ASEAN POLITICAL, SECURITY AND ECONOMIC CO-OPERATION

CHAN HENG CHEE

BILATERAL POLITICAL COOPERATION

The emergence of ASEAN as a political community in the course of the dramatic maneuvers over Cambodia has tended to overshadow the more substantial progress achieved in bilateral political cooperation among the five partners. Since 1967, assiduous efforts have been directed toward structuring procedures and formalizing processes to resolve contentious issues among themselves. To a large extent, traditional animosities have receded and bilateral difficulties have been contained and resolved by invoking the ASEAN "spirit." It would not be an exaggeration to say that in the present ASEAN political ambience, it is difficult to conceive of any two or more members resorting to the use of physical force as a means to solve a problem.

The most remarkable improvement in relations occurred between Singapore and Malaysia. Since the dark, grim days of separation, the historically difficult relationship has taken a more cordial turn, based increasingly on pragmatic, functional ties. In 1980, the two governments agreed in principle to set up an intergovernmental committee (IGC), directly responsible to both prime ministers, to increase the level and quality of cooperation between the two countries. The aim was also to prevent minor problems from being exaggerated beyond control by adverse publicity and to prevent such issues from reaching the stage of intractability. It is under the Mahathir government, however, that Singapore-Malaysia cooperation moved to a new plane. Recognizing that "an unhappy Singapore can be destabilizing to Malaysia" and that "likewise, discontent in Malaysia can affect Singapore,"[2] Mahathir, in his first visit as prime minister, swiftly settled many outstanding bilateral issues with his Singapore counterpart. As a barometer of the newfound trust, Malaysia for the first time allowed Singapore access to training in the Kota Tinggi Jungle Warfare School.

Friction between Malaysia and Thailand has perennially erupted over security cooperation on the Thai-Malaysian border because of the lack of common agreement on who constitutes the common enemy. Thai suspicions that their Malaysian ally is not interested in the suppression of the Muslim separatists operating in the south — indeed, that Malaysia may even be secretly succoring their cause — is matched by Malaysian concern that Thai effort in the containment of communist insurgents is ineffective.[3] Occasionally, an open outburst of frustration such as that expressed by leading Thai security personnel — Supreme Commander

Reprinted in abridged form from Chan Heng Chee "ASEAN: Sub-Regional Resilience" in *Security Interdependence in the Asia Pacific Region*, edited by James W. Morley (Lexington, Mass.: D.C. Heath, 1986), pp. 111–43, by permission of the author and Lexington Books, an imprint of Macmillan, Inc.

of the Armed Forces, General Saiyud Kerdphol, Minister of Interior Sitthi Jirarote, and Lt. General Harn Leenanond, Commander of the Fourth Army Region (in the south) — that the Thai–Malaysian General Border Committee meeting in August 1982 was "unsatisfactory" creates the impression of crisis in bilateral relations; but political leaders have been swift to reaffirm close bilateral ties by immediate consultation to iron out differences. In seeking to control subversion in the south, Malaysia and Thailand are fully aware of the interdependence of security efforts. Both countries have agreed to look into the development of the Golok Basin along the common border to underpin security.

Although a new start in Malaysian-Philippines cooperation was promised when President Marcos dramatically renounced the Philippine claim to Sabah at the 1977 ASEAN heads of government meeting in Kuala Lumpur, nothing developed from that statement. The Philippines legislature is yet to legalize its president's offer. In 1981, accusations surfaced that Muslim separatists were allowed to operate from Sabah and that the eastern state of Malaysia was a source of arms flow to the rebels, leading some Philippine assemblymen to argue for a reactivation of the Sabah claim. In reaction, some Sabah pressure was put on the federal government to break diplomatic ties. That the issue did not blow up was due in no small part to the efforts of the Malaysian prime minister, Dr. Mahathir, to actively defuse the issue. There is every indication that the Philippine willingness to formalize the renunciation is tied to a Malaysian agreement on a border patrol pact, which would stem the arms flow from Sabah to the Muslim separatists in the Mindanao-Sulu region.[4] Although the Sabah claim survives as an irritant in Malaysian-Philippine relations, it does not seem to stand in the way of overall ASEAN cooperation.

On the thorny questions of border demarcation and territorial claims — traditionally, issues that hold the greatest potential for conflict between neighbors and that are the most susceptible to military solutions — the ASEAN states appear to have worked out an amicable settlement among themselves. Through the Joint Thailand-Malaysia Land Boundary Committee, Thailand and Malaysia have been establishing the borderline between the two territories. Since the beginning of the joint effort in 1975, 58 percent of the total common border has been demarcated.[5] In the case of Indonesia and Malaysia, the two nations signed an agreement in February 1982 whereby Malaysia became the first country to accept Indonesia's jurisdictional claims under its archipelagic principle. Indonesia, by the same token, agreed to recognize Malaysia's right to use waters in the Indonesian territorial sea lying between Western and Eastern Malaysia.[6]

During Mahathir's visit to Singapore, the two prime ministers agreed that once the boundary line was fixed in the Straits of Johore upon completion of a hydrographic survey presently being undertaken, the line would be adhered to and would not change with the shifting channel. However, Malaysia still has to work out an agreement with the island republic on Pulau Batu Putih in the Singapore Straits. With regard to the Philippine-Indonesian claims, the main point of contention is the island of Palmas, or Pulau Miangas (the Indonesian name), which is situated where the archipelagic baselines of Indonesia and the Philippines overlap. However, there is no move on either country's part to force a resolution of the problem at the moment. The Philippines has a dispute with Malaysia over official continental shelf maps that involve the Kalayaan group in the South China Sea, but both sides will rely on negotiation to solve the problem. By contrast, the ASEAN states' territorial disputes with China and Vietnam over the Spratly Islands have been less peacefully settled. The Philippines has occupied seven islands to forestall counterclaimants,[7] and Malaysia dispatched troops to the Layang Layang atoll under cover of a naval exercise in late November 1983.

SECURITY COOPERATION

Although it was founded as an economic, social,

and cultural grouping, ASEAN has been fundamentally exercised by security concerns encompassing threats to the subregional environment as well as threats to the domestic order of member states. Paradoxically, there is hardly any mention of security cooperation in the ASEAN official documents, except in the Declaration of ASEAN Concord, which deals with the subject in one line, prescribing "continuation of co-operation on a non-ASEAN basis between the member states in security matters in accordance with their mutual needs and interests." That security questions were considered best left outside the ASEAN format indicates ASEAN's allergy to the formation of a military alliance.

Over the past 16 years, however, member-states have stepped up bilateral security co-operation on a wider scale to meet internal subversion and to strengthen the external defense capabilities of the state. Since the Vietnamese invasion of Kampuchea, bilateral air, land, and naval military exercises have become commonplace: Thailand conducts joint air exercises with Indonesia, Singapore, the Philippines, and Malaysia, and also permits Singapore military personnel to train on Thai soil.[8] Malaysia and Singapore hold naval exercises in the strategic Straits of Malacca and belong to the Five Power Defense Arrangement.[9] Indonesia and Malaysia cooperate along the Kalimantan border between East Malaysia and Indonesia against Communist insurgents under the auspices of the 1972 General Border Committee, and air exercises are conducted by Singapore and Indonesia. There is greater exchange and coordination of security intelligence, simultaneous strengthening of the armed forces, and moves toward the standardization of arms and the working out of "uniform operating procedures" against the common enemy, all of which point to a possible eventual scenario of resource pooling.

Nonetheless, ASEAN's security cooperation conscientiously stops short of forming a military pact. In September 1982, the Singapore prime minister's suggestion at the end of a state visit to Jakarta — that the time had come for greater military cooperation in ASEAN, leading up to "multi-lateral exercises encompassing all members" — was publicly and vigorously rejected by the older ASEAN partners.[10] This decisively stopped speculation that a military pact was imminent. ASEAN's adamant refusal to contemplate a pact arises from the belief that far from enhancing regional security, such an alliance would have a provocative value, hastening counteralliances. In the discussions on the evolution of ASEAN into a security organization, it is often forgotten that the existing framework of ASEAN does not allow for activities in this direction. Should ASEAN reach a stage when a military alliance is considered in order, the alliance would have to be formulated outside the present ASEAN organization, not unlike NATO's relationship to the EEC.

ASEAN ECONOMIC COOPERATION

In contrast to the close cooperation in the political and security areas, actual progress in economic regionalism is slow, if not disappointing. At Bali, new vistas in trade and industrial development were opened, the former through selective trade liberalization in the Preferential Trade Arrangements (PTA), the latter through ASEAN Industrial Complementation (AIC) projects and ASEAN Industrial Projects (AIP). In addition cooperative programs have been launched in tourism, food and agriculture, mining and energy, transport and communications, and banking and finance. The translation of the aspirations into economic practicalities, however, have been more problematic.

At the fifteenth ASEAN economic ministers' meetings in October 1983, the Thai prime minister, General Prem Tinsulanond, gave a figure of 18,933 items as tariff preferentials.[11] Since 1977, the tariff cuts on trading products have been wider and deeper, beginning with 10 percent for most products, and now are generally 20 to 25 percent across the board. This means the PTA are now more than just cosmetic, suggesting that the failure of intra-ASEAN trade to take off is more fundamental. According to the Singapore prime minister, "PTA imports accounted for 1.5% of total ASEAN imports in 1978 and increased to 2% in 1979."[12]

ASEAN Industrial Projects have not met with greater success. The idea, adopted from a UN study on ASEAN cooperation, envisaged an ambitious plan for something close to regional import substitution. Each ASEAN state would set up a large industrial plant to meet the region's need in a designated product. The projects proposed are the ASEAN Urea Project in Indonesia and Malaysia, the ASEAN Rock Salt-Soda Ash Project in Thailand, the Copper Fabrication Project for the Philippines, and the Diesel Engine Project for Singapore. So far, only the Indonesian project is close to completion, and Malaysia's project is about to enter the construction stage. The Philippines has been switching projects and is therefore only at the early stages, and Singapore dropped the project assigned to it. The slow progress in the AIPs has been said to be due to poor project identification, financing problems, and implementation problems.

Equally weak is the industrial complementation scheme, which is based on the idea of each member-country producing specific components to produce a single ASEAN product. The major thrust in the automotive industry to produce the ASEAN car, adopted after a lengthy process of refinement and discussion, has been jeopardized if not abandoned in the wake of Malaysia's plan to build its own car. Even without Malaysia's problem, industrial complementation has been held back by Singapore's reluctance to participate. As an island economy whose prosperity is based on free trade and manufacturing, Singapore disagrees with the extension of monopoly rights and protection extended to products manufactured under the complementation scheme. To circumvent the unanimity principle and to absolve itself from the charge of sabotaging AIC projects, Singapore's prime minister, Lee Kuan Yew, proposed in 1980 that ASEAN consensus should be redefined to include a "5–1" formula; that

is, consensus is considered achieved even when one member-state declines participation.

The foregoing facts simply highlight the obstacles in the way of economic regionalism and are a reflection of the diverse interests that result from economies at different stages of development and efficiency and with competitive rather than complementary patterns of trade. If ASEAN founders had envisaged the association as a vehicle to buttress the economic base of the subregion through economic cooperation, ASEAN must be judged as less than effective. Economic cooperation schemes mounted under the auspices of the treaty have been deferred in one way or another. What seems to be demonstrated is that although different strategic perspectives may not prevent political cooperation nor undermine its vitality, different economic perspectives have been more difficult to overcome. That Indonesia is the largest and yet economically among the weakest in the community is a significant constraining factor in subregional economic endeavor, setting the pace of economic cooperation in ASEAN.

But without doubt, ASEAN is a case of successful economic development. ASEAN countries have enjoyed high GDP growth rates, averaging 7.3 percent in the period 1970–80. Singapore's average GDP growth rate was the highest, at 8.5 percent, with Malaysia managing 7.8 percent, Indonesia 7.6 percent, and Thailand 7.2 percent. Even the Philippines, by far the weakest economy of the five, recorded a 6.3 percent growth rate. And even though the direct contribution of ASEAN economic policies to these rates may be small, it cannot be denied that, as Singapore's foreign minister, S. Dhanabalan, put it: "ASEAN has created a regional climate that has enabled each of us to get the maximum out of our national economic policies. Thus, our economies have grown at a rapid rate."[13] Again, if we go beyond official programs to evaluate the economic significance of ASEAN, there is clear evidence of a trend for local businesses to invest profits in their home countries and within the subregion. Joint ventures between private groups from ASEAN states and ASEAN multinationals have been established, which indicates that the private sector is developing a growing confidence and stake in the subregional system. This would not have occurred if there were a sense of interstate conflict and tension within the subregion — a situation ASEAN has gone out of its way to avoid.

The climate of security engendered by co-operative solidarity has also intensified American and Japanese economic interests in the sub-region. ASEAN is the fifth largest trading partner of the United States, and direct private American investment increased from U.S.$730 million in the mid-1960s to U.S.$4 billion at the end of the 1970s.[14] In the case of Japan, imports from ASEAN increased from 10 percent of total Japanese imports in 1965–70 to 15 percent in 1980; on the ASEAN side, a quarter of the subregion's trade is with Japan.[15] In addition, Japan is the leading investor in the subregion, with Japanese direct foreign investment amounting to $7.021 billion in 1980.[16]

NOTES

1. *Straits Times*, 14 May 1980.
2. *Straits Times*, 18 November 1981.
3. *Bangkok Post*, 3 September 1983 and 12 September 1982.
4. V. Selvaratnam, "Malaysia in 1981: A Year of Political Transition," in *Southeast Asian Affairs, 1982* (Singapore: ISEAS, 1982), p. 271.
5. *Bangkok Post*, 9 September 1982.
6. *Indonesian Observer*, 26 February 1982.
7. *Far Eastern Economic Review*, 13 August 1981.
8. *Bangkok Post*, 1 January 1981.
9. *Asiaweek*, 22 October 1982.
10. Ibid.
11. *Straits Times*, 18 October 1983.
12. Speech by Prime Minister Lee Kuan Yew at the opening of the fifteenth ASEAN ministerial meeting, 14 June 1982, Singapore.
13. Opening statement by S. Dhanabalan, minister of foreign affairs of Singapore, at the fifteenth ASEAN ministerial meeting, 14 June 1982, Singapore.
14. *Straits Times*, 6 March 1982.
15. Kiyoshi Abe, "Economic Co-operation among the ASEAN Countries and Japan," in *Security in the ASEAN Region: Proceedings and Papers of an International Symposium* (Tokyo: Takushoku University, 1983), p. 85.
16. Sueo Sekiguchi, "Japanese Direct Foreign Investment and ASEAN Economies: A Japanese Perspective," in Sueo Sekiguchi, ed., *ASEAN–Japan Relations: Investment* (Singapore: ISEAS, 1983), p. 233.

22. THE PROBLEM OF LEGITIMACY

SUKHUMBHAND PARIBATRA
and CHAI-ANAN SAMUDAVANIJA

The first, and perhaps the most crucial, internal dimension of Southeast Asian countries taken as a whole, is the lack of what has been aptly termed 'unconditional legitimacy'.[1] Although, as pointed out above, the post-independence map of Southeast Asia has not been much revised and outside of Indochina no major revolutionary transformation has successfully taken place, there exist challenges, both armed and unarmed, to the prevailing state boundaries as just and definitive lines of political, social and economic division; to the ruling regimes as appropriate orders of distributive justice; and to governments as fair and effective instruments of security and progress. Table 3.1 lists the major armed rebellions which have taken place or are still taking place in post-independence Southeast Asia.

One set of explanations for this lack of unconditional legitimacy may be termed 'structural'. As has been pointed out,[2] one meaning or component encompassed by the Weberian concept of legitimacy is a *common belief* in a given political and social order. For a number of reasons this common belief has been absent or weak from the time of independence.

The first reason is the artificial creation of modern 'nation-states' in Southeast Asia. Today's state boundaries, together with their underlying philosophy, concepts, norms and aspirations concerning nationhood, have been superimposed for administrative convenience by the colonial powers on a region of immense heterogeneity, where at least 32 ethnolinguistic groups and all the world's major belief systems are to be found, and these boundaries in most cases do not correspond to the actual ethnolinguistic and religious dividing lines (see Tables 3.2 and 3.3). Thus, there exist within each Southeast Asian state enclaves of minorities who are not always willing to accept or identify with such an 'alien' construct as a matter of conviction or habit, especially since acceptance or identification often entails subjugation by another ethnolinguistic or religious group. Although the existence of a minority ipso facto does not mean that there will necessarily be an armed rebellion or that if there is an armed rebellion it will inevitably succeed, there have been sufficient cases of ethnic or religious dissidence to suggest that there is an absence of basic consensus

Reprinted in abridged form from Sukhumbhand Paribatra and Chai-Anan Samudavanija, "Internal Dimensions of Regional Security in Southeast Asia", in *Regional Security in the Third World: Case Studies from Southeast Asia and the Middle East*, edited by Mohammed Ayoob (London: Croom Helm Ltd., 1986), by permission of the authors and the editor.

TABLE 3.1: Major Armed Rebellions in Post-Independence Southeast Asia

Country	Armed Rebellion (dates of rebellion)	Objective of Challenging	
		State[1]	Regime[2]
Burma	1. Burma Communist Party (1948–)		x
	2. Ethnically-related armed rebellions (1948–)[3]	x	
Cambodia	1. Khmer Rouge (1970–5)		x
	2. Khmer Rouge/Khmer People's National Liberation Front/ Moulinaka (1979–)		x
Indonesia	1. Madiun Communist rebellion (1948)		x
	2. Darul Islam (1948–62)		x
	3. PRRI Permesta (1958–61)	x	
	4. Organisasi Papua Merdeka (1963–)	x	
	5. PKI (1965)		x
	6. Aceh Merdeka (1976–9)	x	
	7. Fretilin (1976–)	x	
Laos	1. Pathet Lao (1951–75)		x
	2. Le Ligue de Résistance Meo (1946–75)	x(?)	x
Malaysia	1. Communist Party of Malaya (1948–)		x
	2. North Kalimantan Communist Party (1950s–)		x
Philippines	1. Huks (1946–54)		x
	2. New People's Army (1969–)		x
	3. Moro National Liberation Front (1972–)	x	
Singapore	none		
Thailand	1. Barisan Revolusi Nasional (1960–)	x	
	2. Communist Party of Thailand (1965–)		x
	3. CPT-related minority group (1965–)	x	
	4. Pattani United Liberation Organization (1967–)	x	
	5. Barisan Nasional Pembebasan Pattani (1971–)	x	
Vietnam (South)	1. National Liberation Front (1958–75)	x	x
	2. Le Front Unifié de Liberation des Races Opprimées or FULRO (1964–75)	x	
	3. Le Mouvement pour l'Autonomie des Hauts-Plateaux (1961–75)	x(?)	x

NOTES:
1. Armed rebellions with overt intentions of 'revising' the existing relationships with central governments or the prevailing state boundaries by setting up more autonomous regional administration, seceding to form an independent state, or seceding to join another state, are considered to be challenging the state as an institution.
2. Armed rebellions with overt intentions of changing in a more or less comprehensive way the political, economic and/or social order prevailing in a given state are considered to be challenging the existing regime as an institution.
3. According to one authority, since 1948, there have been at least 24 ethnically-related rebel groups. See David I. Steinberg, 'Constitutional and Political Bases of Minority Insurrections: Burma', presented at the Workshop on 'Armed Separatist Movements in Southeast Asia' organized by the Institute of Southeast Asian Studies, on 7–9 December 1983 in Singapore.

TABLE 3.2: Ethnolinguistic Composition of Southeast Asian States, 1976

State	Ethnolinguistic Groups	Percentage of Population
Burma	Burman	75
	Karen	10
	Shan	6
	Indian-Pakistani	3
	Chinese	1
	Kachin	1
	Chin	1
Cambodia	Khmer	90
	Chinese	6
	Cham	1
	Mon-Khmer tribes	1
Indonesia	Javanese	45
	Sundanese	14
	Madurese	8
	Chinese	2
Laos	Lao	67
	Mon-Khmer tribes	19
	Tai (other than Lao)	5
	Meo	4
	Chinese	3
North Vietnam	Vietnamese	85
	Tho	3
	Muoung	2
	Tai	2
	Nung	2
	Chinese	1
	Meo	1
	Yao	1
South Vietnam	Vietnamese	87
	Chinese	5
	Khmer	3
	Mountain chain tribes	3
	Mon-Khmer tribes	1
Malaysia	Malay	44
	Chinese	35
	Indian	11
Philippines	Cebuano	24
	Tagalog	21
	Ilocano	12
	Hiligaynon	10
	Bicol	8
	Sumar-Leyte	6
	Pampangan	3
	Pangasinan	3

Table 3.2 (continued)

State	Ethnolinguistic Groups	Percentage of Population
Singapore	Chinese	75
	Malay	14
	Indian-Pakistani	8
Thailand	Thai	60
	Lao	25
	Chinese	10
	Malay	3
	Meo, Khmer and others	2

TABLE 3.3: Distribution of Ethnic Groups in Southeast Asia

Name of Ethnic Groups	Country of Residence	Approx. Number
Meo		
Other names: Miao, Hmung,	China	2,500,000
Hmong, Hmu Meo, Mlao,	North Vietnam	219,514
Mnong, Miao-Tseu, H'moong,	Laos	300,000
Meau, Mong, Lao Som	Thailand	58,000
Yao		
Other names: Kim-Mien, Kim	China	660,000 to 745,985
Mun, Yu-Mien, Mien, Mun,	North Vietnam	186,071
Man, Zao	Laos	5,000
	Thailand	19,000
Kachin		
Other names: Chingpaw,	China	100,000
Jingpaw, Singhpo, Kakhieng,	Burma	350,000
Theinbaw		
Lahu		
Other names: Mussur, Musso,	China	139,000
Laku	Burma	66,000
	Thailand	18,000
	Laos	2,000
Karen		
Other names: Karean,	Burma	2 to 3 millions
Kariang, Kayin, Yang	Thailand	200,000
Under following groups		
(a) Kayah		
Other name: Karenni	Burma	75,000
(b) Pao		
Other name: Thaungthu	Burma	200,000

Table 3.3 (*continued*)

Name of Ethnic Groups	Country of Residence	Approx. Number
Chin Other names: Lushai, Kuki Koochie, Mizo	India Burma	821,000 200,000
Naga	India Burma	550,000 75,000
Mon Other names: Mun, Peguan, Taleng, Talaing	Burma Thailand	350,000 60,000
Thai Names of different groups: Thai Yia or Shan Thai (black, white, red)	China Burma Thailand South Vietnam Laos	About 9,500,000 Thais distributed among all 1,000,000 50,000 385,191 235,000
Tay	North Vietnam	503,995
Nung	North Vietnam	313,998
Ahom	India	345,000
(a) Rhade	South Vietnam	100,000
(c) Jarai	South Vietnam	150,000
Groups of primitive autochthonous hill tribes speaking one language of origin, i.e. Mon-Khmer		
(1) Kha or Lao-Teng	Laos Thailand	750,000 16,000
(2) Phnong or Khmer Loeu	Cambodia	54,000
(3) Moi	South Vietnam	500,000
(4) Wa or Kawa	China Burma	286,000 334,000
(5) Paulang Aborigines	Burma Malaysia	60,000 50,000

SOURCE: Martial Dasse, *Montagnards Revoltes et Guerre Révolutionaries en Asie du Sud-Est Continentale* (D.K. Book House, Bangkok, 1976), pp. 236-8, translation from French by authors.

concerning what constitutes nationhood and that such an absence, when joined with certain political and socio-economic factors, can lead to a violent rejection of the existing nation-state as an institution.[3]

The second reason is the artificial insemination of western ideas. Partly due to colonialism and partly due to the growth of communications in the post-war world, influences of such beliefs as liberalism and socialism have penetrated the region. This induces a breakdown in basic consensus concerning the values of distributive justice, for not only do such western ideas conflict with each other fundamentally but they also challenge, and often provoke reactions from, the traditional belief systems, particularly religious. At the same time, by clearly holding forth attractive images of ideal political and social orders they are apt to create radical discontentment with the existing, transitional ones. Armed Communist rebellions, which have occurred in every Southeast Asian state with the exception of Singapore, and armed 'religious' rebellions, such as Dar'ul Islam and the Moro National Liberation Front, are the most dramatic, but by no means sole, manifestations of the absence of basic value consensus in the domestic politics of the region.

Apart from these structural factors, the lack of unconditional legitimacy can also be explained in terms of 'process'. Three other meanings encompassed by the Weberian concept of legitimacy are: a *claim* by an individual or a group of individuals to the right to rule over a given political and social order; a *justification* for the existing form and pattern of political rule or domination which entails unequal shares of scarce values, rights, privileges and opportunities for self-advancement in society; and *promises*, overt or implied, that that form and pattern of political rule or domination will contribute justly and effectively to the material and spiritual well-being of the ruled.[4]

Partly because of the structural problems discussed above, partly because of their own failings and impatience, and partly because of additional problems generated in the process of change, regimes and governments in Southeast Asia have seldom been able fully to justify their claim to the right to rule and make good their promises to confer benefits to the ruled.

In the immediate aftermath of independence, 'national self-determination', 'civil liberties' and 'individual rights' were justifications and promises made by the regimes and governments to make good their right to rule. However, these 'political goods' have not been fully delivered. Structural problems brought forth pains of birth and adolescence, as it were, and because they could not be easily coped with, concerns for 'unity', 'stability', 'order' and 'security', which were all too often identified with regime preservation, became of paramount importance. Accordingly, national self-determination came to mean little more than an imposition of the most powerful ethnic group's will upon the rest for the sake of 'national unity'; democracy and political participation became at best 'guided' in accordance with the values of distributive justice of the rulers for the sake of stability and order; and civil liberties and individual rights became circumscribed by more or less coercive and repressive measures for the sake of 'national security'. In this way, what might be termed an impulse towards authoritarianism has acted as an antithesis to the process of legitimation as originally conceived by Southeast Asia's regimes and governments.

In more recent years, the focus of the legitimation process especially in non-Communist Southeast Asian countries has shifted, though not entirely, to the economic sphere. Justifications and claims to the right to rule are now predominantly based on promises of economic performance which would bring 'development', 'progress', 'justice', 'resilience' and 'security' to the ruled. To a certain extent a good deal of success has been achieved, particularly in terms of economic growth (see Table 3.4). However, a number of problems have arisen in the process of economic change which serve to undermine the quest for legitimacy through promises to deliver 'economic goods'.

One such problem is the issue of distribution

TABLE 3.4: Average Growth of Gross Domestic Product

Country	Average Growth Rates (per cent)*	
	1960–70	1970–81
Burma	2.6	4.8
Indonesia	3.9	7.8
Malaysia	6.5	7.8
Philippines	5.1	6.2
Singapore	8.8	8.5
Thailand	8.4	7.2

* Average growth rates are weighted by country GDP in 1970 dollars.

SOURCE: The International Bank for Reconstruction and Development, *World Development Report 1983* (Oxford University Press for IBRD, New York, 1983), pp. 150–1.

or equity. Development strategies generally chosen and implemented by non-Communist Southeast Asian governments are aimed at bringing about rapid economic growth with focus on urban-based industrial promotion and utilization of advanced technology in an environment of free enterprise. The underlying assumption is that sooner or later there will be 'trickle-down' effects and any maladjustments in terms of distribution will automatically be corrected. In that eventuality equity in terms of equal shares will not be achieved, but everyone's demands and requirements will be 'satisfied' and there will be further incentive to work for another round of growth and trickle-down effects.

However, this 'percolation theory', as it

were, has not fully worked in practice. The 'self-adjusting' mechanisms have not operated quickly or effectively enough, and consequently large and growing disparities in income and wealth exist between those who have and those who have not, in particular between the urban-industrial sector and the rural-agricultural sector (see Tables 3.5 and 3.6). Despite many a declaration of good faith by the governments that they would attempt to minimize the trade-off between growth and equity, for example by redistributional measures such as land reform, promotion of agricultural productivity and rural development, and progressive taxation, little has been achieved because the regimes concerned have not been willing to take the political risks inherent in such measures, and indeed themselves have vested interests in the continuation and preservation of the status quo. Since the justification for their rule has been based on promises to bring progress to all, failure to bring about a more just distribution of benefits cannot but serve to undermine the process of legitimation. The crucial importance of failure is underlined by the fact that with a few exceptions, minority groups which, as discussed above, already have grievances against central governments, are seldom beneficiaries of overall economic growth.[5]

The second problem concerns dynamic socio-economic forces unleashed in the process of economic growth and change especially in non-Communist countries. During this process

TABLE 3.5: Income Distribution

Country/Year	60% Lowest Income Households' Share of Total Household Income (per cent)	10% Highest Income Households' Share of Total Household Income (per cent)
Burma	n.a.	n.a.
Indonesia 1976	27	34
Malaysia 1973	23.6	39.8
Philippines 1970–1	27.0	38.5
Singapore	n.a.	n.a.
Thailand 1975–6	29.1	34.1

TABLE 3.6: Sector Distribution of Production and Population in 1960 and 1981

Country	Agricultural Production as % of Total GDP		Rural Population as % of Total Population		Industrial Production as % of Total GDP		Urban Population as % of Total Population	
	1960	1981	1960	1981	1960	1981	1960	1981
Burma	33	47	81	72	20	23	19	28
Indonesia	50	24	85	79	25	53	15	21
Malaysia	36	23	75	70	27	54	25	30
Philippines	26	23	70	63	48	62	30	37
Singapore	4	1	—	—	30	71	100	100
Thailand	40	24	87	85	32	48	13	15

SOURCE: *World Development Report 1983*, pp. 152–3, 190–1.

TABLE 3.7: Demographic Indicators

Country	Population in Mid-1981 (million)	Projected Population (million)		Average Annual Growth Rate of Labour Force (per cent)			Average Growth Rate of Urban Population (per cent)	
		1990	2000	1960–70	1970–81	1980–2000	1960–70	1970–81
Burma	34.1	42	52	1.1	1.4	2.2	3.9	3.9
Indonesia	149.5	179	216	1.7	2.5	2.0	3.6	4.0
Laos	3.5	4	6	1.0	0.7	2.7	3.7	5.2
Malaysia	14.2	17	21	2.8	2.9	3.1	3.5	3.3
Philippines	49.6	62	76	2.1	2.5	2.9	3.8	3.7
Singapore	2.4	3	3	2.8	2.7	1.3	2.4	1.5
Thailand	48.0	58	69	2.1	2.8	2.3	3.5	3.4

SOURCE: *World Development Report 1983*, pp. 148–9, 184–5, 188–9, 190–1.

the economies become complex with growing division of labour between various sectors, criss-crossing patterns of production and exchange, and formation of interest groups; significant movements of population from rural to urban areas taking place (see Tables 3.6 and 3.7); and, partly as a result of higher standards of living and partly as a result of this country-to-town migration, a rapid expansion of literacy and higher education ensues (Tables 3.7 and 3.8).

These trends have three major consequences. One is that a pluralism of conflicting and irreconcilable demands, requirements and interests, often with elite groups, is created. The second

TABLE 3.8: Education

Country	% of Population Enrolled for Higher Education		Adult Literacy Rate	
	1960	1979	1960	1980
Burma	1	4	60	66
Indonesia	1	n.a.	39	62
Laos	n.a.	n.a.	28	44
Malaysia	1	3	53	60
Philippines	13	25	72	75
Singapore	6	8	n.a.	83
Thailand	2	13	68	86
Vietnam	n.a.	3	n.a.	87

SOURCE: *World Development Report 1983*, pp. 196–7

is that social mobilization takes place at a fast pace, creating rising expectations, which are political as well as economic, and also rising frustrations where those expectations are not fulfilled. The third is that an ever increasing number of people are uprooted from their traditional, land-based values and, while still imperfectly acculturated to the 'new world', remain an unpredictable factor, a potential source of dissent and discontent.

In this context the parameters of the legitimation process become transformed. Regimes and governments may be able to continue to deliver more economic goods, but for some 'more' may not be 'enough', either because a greater share is going to another interest group or because much more is expected not only in terms of economic well-being but also in terms of political participation or freedom, while for others more may be 'too much', given many Southeast Asians' innate conservatism, as evident from the growth of Islamic fundamentalism in the region. The transformation of the parameters of the legitimation process puts regimes and governments squarely in a dilemma. On the one hand, continued economic growth and development are still seen to be necessary for their legitimation, but, on the other hand, socio-economic changes generated by economic growth and development greatly complicate and indeed undercut the quest for legitimacy. This dilemma in all probability can only be resolved by implementation of thoroughgoing institutional and political reforms which, given Southeast Asian leaders' impulse towards authoritarianism, may not be easily or painlessly forthcoming.

The third problem, which has emerged in the process of economic change to undermine the quest for legitimacy through promises to deliver 'economic goods', is the growth of interdependence. Economic strategies based on high growth and free enterprise serve to open up the economies of non-Communist countries and increasingly link them to the world trade, investment, credit and energy systems (see Tables 3.9, 3.10, 3.11, and 3.12),

TABLE 3.9: Growth of Exports and Imports of Non-Communist Southeast Asian Countries

Countries	Exports (million US$)	Imports (million US$)
Indonesia		
1965–7	731	620
1971–3	2,063	1,654
1977–9	12,692	6,700
Malaysia		
1965–7	1,232	1,131
1971–3	2,146	1,854
1977–9	8,179	6,009
Philippines		
1965–7	843	923
1971–3	1,348	1,446
1977–9	3,699	5,297
Singapore		
1965–7	1,007	1,253
1971–3	2,515	3,760
1977–9	10,610	13,802
Thailand		
1965–7	645	1,015
1971–3	1,159	1,615
1977–9	4,276	5,728

SOURCE: Rechain Chintayarangsan, 'ASEAN's Primary Commodity Exports', in United Nations Economic and Social Commission for Asia and the Pacific *ASEAN and Pacific Economic Co-operation* (UNESCAP, Bangkok, 1983), p. 22.

as well as, inevitably transnational influences of tastes, ideas and belief-systems. The trend has two major consequences. One is that regional economies become increasingly sensitive or vulnerable to fluctuations in the world market, monetary system and energy supply, as well as a long-term decline in the terms of trade (see Table 3.13). The other is that domestic socio-economic systems become mirror images, albeit somewhat distorted and on a reduced scale, of the global systems with their pluralism of demands, requirements, interests and issue-specific or functional group formations; or to put it another way, the openness of the regional economies accelerates the trend towards domestic pluralism.

TABLE 3.10: Private Direct Investment Inflows for Non-Communist Southeast Asian Countries 1967–1980 (million US$)

Year	Indonesia	Malaysia	Philippines	Singapore	Thailand
1967	−10	43	−9	34	43
1968	−2	30	−3	26	60
1969	32	80	6	38	51
1970	83	94	−29	93	42
1971	139	100	−6	116	39
1972	207	114	−21	191	68
1973	15	172	54	389	77
1974	−49	571	4	596	189
1975	476	350	97	611	86
1976	344	381	126	331	105
1977	235	406	209	335	106
1978	279	467	163	739	53
1979	219	647	73	911	50
1980	184	928	40	1,454	186
Cumulative Total 1967–80	2,152	4,383	704	5,864	1,155

SOURCE: Development Planning Division, UNESCAP, 'ASEAN Investments from Pacific Sources' in *ASEAN and Pacific Economic Co-operation*, p. 188.

TABLE 3.11: Foreign Capital Borrowing of Non-Communist Southeast Asian Countries (outstanding, end of year)

Country	Foreign Capital Borrowing
Indonesia (1979)	17,002.0
Malaysia (1980)	4,696.3
Philippines (1980)	9,637.2
Singapore (1977)	1,188.5
Thailand (1980)	5,921.9

SOURCE: Yen Kyun Wang, 'Monetary Interdependence among ASEAN and Pacific Countries' in *ASEAN and Pacific Economic Co-operation*, p. 258.

TABLE 3.12: Energy Consumption and Import of Non-Communist Southeast Asian Countries

Country	Average Growth Rate of Consumption (%)		Per Capita Consumption (KG coal equivalent)		Energy Import as % of Merchandise Exports	
	1960–74	1974–80	1960	1980	1960	1980
Burma	4.3	5.8	60	87	4	n.a.
Indonesia	4.3	9.0	129	266	3	8
Malaysia	4.1	7.7	616	818	2	13
Philippines	9.7	4.4	159	380	9	41
Singapore	10.1	6.6	2,111	8,544	17	36
Thailand	16.3	6.5	63	370	12	44

SOURCE: *World Development Report 1983*, pp. 162–3.

TABLE 3.13: Terms of Trade of Non-Communist Southeast
Asian Countries

	Terms of Trade (1975=100)	
Country	1978	1981
Indonesia	95	154
Malaysia	109	101
Philippines	98	68
Singapore	102	n.a.
Thailand	87	62

SOURCE: *World Development Report 1983*, pp. 164–5.

In this context, the parameters of the legitimation process are further transformed. Delivery of promises is not only made dependent on uncontrollable, unpredictable, exogenous factors but also rendered more complicated and difficult to attain by transnationally induced pluralism. Once more regimes and governments are put squarely in a dilemma. On the one hand, openness is necessary for the process of legitimation, but, on the other hand, if uncontrolled it may undercut the very quest for legitimacy.

Thus, the shift in focus to the economic sphere in the process of legitimation has not been without difficulties despite the relatively high economic growth within the region, and there is no reason to surmise that these difficulties will diminish in the years ahead. On the contrary, with the average growth rates of the labour forces predicted to be mostly above 2 per cent for the rest of this century (see Table 3.7) and the approaching exhaustion of agricultural land frontiers, especially in Indonesia and Thailand, and indeed of a number of raw materials, the demands and

constraints on the economies and economic planners are likely to multiply and not subside. In this connection, it should be pointed out that although the discussion concerning claims and justifications being based on promises to deliver economic goods is mainly concerned with the non-Communist countries of Southeast Asia, most notably the five original members of ASEAN (Indonesia, Malaysia, Philippines, Singapore and Thailand), it may in a not so distant future also to a degree apply to the Communist countries: as illustrated by the existence of a large black market economy in Vietnam, to a certain extent the demand for the delivery of economic goods especially consumer items is already there and may increase once the economy is demobilized from its war-footing.

The foregoing suggests that for reasons of structure and process there is in Southeast Asia a relative lack of unconditional legitimacy which is usually enjoyed by western states. It does not follow that regional states are weak in terms of disposable power and likely to disintegrate or that their regimes are always unstable and shortlived. But it does follow that Southeast Asian states are more or less fragile in nature, and this fragility is reflected in the absence of effective political institutionalization, last-resort dependence on instruments of coecion however subtly disguised and manipulated,[6] and propensity towards delegitimation, or 'the process of making explicit, self-conscious rejections and attacks on the ultimate grounds on which a system of legitimacy is predicated',[7] with the potentiality for domestic violence that such a process entails.

NOTES

1. Mohammed Ayoob (ed.), *Regional Security in the Third World*, Chapter 1.
2. Joseph Bensman, 'Max Weber's Concept of Legitimacy: An Evaluation' in Arthur J. Vidich and Ronald M. Glassman (eds), *Conflict and Control: Challenge to Legitimacy of Modern Governments* (Sage Publications, Beverly Hills, Ca., 1979), pp. 17–48.
3. For further elaboration, see Sukhumbhand Paribatra and Chai-Anan Samudavanija, 'Factors behind Armed Separatism: A Framework for Analysis' in Lim Joo Jock with S. Vani (eds), *Armed Separatism in Southeast Asia* (Institute of Southeast Asian Studies, Singapore, 1984).

4. See Bensman.
5. See Paribatra and Samudavanija.
6. This is one of the points which emerged from the project on 'Development, Stability and Security in the Pacific-Asian Region', organized by the Institute of East Asian Studies, University of California at Berkeley, and the Centre for Strategic and International Studies, Jakarta, for which a final conference was held from 17–21 March 1984.

   Political institutionalization has been well defined by one eminent authority as 'a process whereby a political structure is made operational in accordance with stipulated rules and procedures, enabling regularized, hence predictable performance with respect to such key functions as the selection of leadership, the making and implementation of policies and execution of justice. Ideally, political institutionalization enables a movement away from the erratic practices and arbitrary decisions stemming from a high dependence upon personalized rule. In its success, it also precludes abrupt, drastic changes in basic structure, including revolution, since change is made possible in a legal, evolutionary manner via established procedures.' See Robert A. Scalapino, 'Political Institutionalization in Asian Socialist Societies', a paper prepared for the project cited above, p. 1.
7. Bensman, p. 40.

23.

THE MILITARY AND NATIONAL SECURITY

CHANDRAN JESHURUN

The background of national security concerns in ASEAN and the nature of threat perceptions among the different members in a region as unpredictable as Southeast Asia makes it apparent that the development of civil-military relations has followed its own rather original course. One view has contended that the proper nomenclature for studies of this nature, which probe into the intricate pattern of relationships between the civilian and military sectors of developing societies, should be "military-civilian," on the grounds that the more accepted form "may not be theoretically useful as militaries that do not intervene in the political process may very well have a political role as well."[1] There is in ASEAN today clearly only one leadership that can be described as a military one, although the position of President Suharto is technically an elected one, the Sultan of Brunei is a civilian Prime Minister while also holding the titular post of Supreme Commander of the Royal Brunei Armed Forces, and Prime Minister Chatichai Choonavan of Thailand is an elected representative of the people and a former retired Major General from the Royal Thai Army.[2] Whichever approach is taken, however, the purpose of this paper has been to set the proper historical and strategic context within

which to gauge the evolution of civil-military relations in ASEAN, particularly as they have impinged upon the question of national security.

Both the direction of recent events in countries such as Thailand and the established pattern of civilian supremacy in government and politics that is to be found in Brunei, Malaysia, Singapore, and the Philippines would be strong grounds for contending that the future of the military in ASEAN is most likely to remain subservient to civil authority in the foreseeable future.[3] For this reason, it would be worthwhile to explore the major issues of national security that the countries above have had to face, with a view to better understanding the general lines of conduct that have come to be agreed upon between the civilian and military sectors in dealing with a variety of threats to the national well-being of their countries.[4] To begin with, it may be safely surmised that the recent history of civil-military relations in ASEAN has been largely conditioned by the twin factors of rapid changes in the external strategic environment and the equally pressing demands of domestic situations. In both these vital areas, events and trends over the past 40 years have impinged directly on the national security concerns of the ASEAN members. As a consequence of these external and internal

Reprinted in abridged form from "Civil-Military Relations and National Security in ASEAN", *Pacific Focus* IV, no. 2, (Fall 1989), pp. 75–98, by permission of the author and the Center for International Studies, Inha University.

influences on the development of civil-military relations, it would be appropriate to examine the changes that have occurred at three different levels: the predominantly civilian-dominated pattern; the situation in which the military has had the upper hand; and the instances of a combined civil-military approach to national security problems.

The two countries in ASEAN which have an impressive record of predominantly civilian management of security issues are undoubtedly Malaysia and Singapore. Brunei could possibly be included in this category, but its experience in individually coping with its national security needs is somewhat limited for the purpose of this analysis.[5] It is much more difficult to exclude the Philippines, as it has nominally practised what is purportedly a political system in which civilians have been in command of decision-making in and management of national security problems. However, an exception could be made in its case in view of the unusual fact, in comparison with Malaysia and Singapore, of its police force, the Philippine Constabulary, being an integral part of the AFP.[6] As will be discussed later, one of the unique features of the set-up in Malaysia and Singapore is that, in accordance with traditional British security directives, the police have always remained a civilian force, although uniformed and generally armed since the 1970s. Indeed, it could be said that the Royal Malaysia Police (RMP) and the Singapore Police Force (SPF) are two of the oldest civilian peace-keeping organizations in the region, and the former also possesses a credible paramilitary strike capability.[7] It cannot be denied that the preservation of this division of labour between the law-and-order role of the police and the professional military has been largely instrumental in enabling the governments of Malaysia and Singapore to maintain the tradition of civilian supremacy in politics.

At the operational level, too, it must be remembered that neither in Malaysia nor in Singapore has the security situation ever entailed the need to send military forces across borders to counter an enemy offensive, notwithstanding the brief episode of Indonesian Confrontation in the mid-1960s. The only overseas military duties that the MAF have had to undertake were the several occasions since 1960 when Malaysian troops have served under the United Nations flag in the Congo, Iraq, and Namibia.[8] On the whole the preoccupation of Malaysian security planners has been to deploy their forces in a counter-insurgency role, which has essentially meant jungle operations using counter-insurgency warfare (CIW) tactics and a limited amount of coastal naval patrolling as well as air force supply dropping sorties.[9] In these circumstances, the bulk of the security operations belonged to those elements of the government apparatus which dealt with intelligence gathering and selected elimination of CPM agents and its guerilla assault units. Thus, the pre-eminence of the RMP and especially its Special Branch and Jungle Squads, the precursors of the later Police Field Force (PFF), was virtually unchallenged throughout the period of the Malayan Emergency, from 1948 to 1960, and in the years of revived communist activity in the 1970s.[10] This very distinct operational feature of the national security situation in Malaysia has left an indelible mark on the structure of the command and policy apparatus of the Malaysian security system.[11]

The MAF have always been represented in the National Security Council, and military units have been routinely deployed in CIW duties, including all three Services, but they have never had to assume sole responsibility for national security. Even in the desperate days of the post-May 1969 period, when race riots had caught the RMP by surprise, the military was called in to lend support in aid of the civilian authority as provided for in the Constitution. Under the supra-constitutional regime of the National Operations Council (NOC), which ruled the country during the parliamentary interregnum from May 1969 to January 1970, the MAF's chief of staff and other individual senior personnel played an integral part in government by decree, but were always subject to the civil authority.[12] This, then, is the special case of Malaysia, which is similar in almost all respects to the system that has been nurtured in Singapore, where the concept of "Total Defence" is a further safeguard against any form of unilateral initiative on the part of the SAF in the management of national security.[13]

It must be admitted that the political leadership in both countries has been solidly committed to the principle of civilian supremacy, as the Prime Ministers of Malaysia and Mr. Lee Kuan Yew in Singapore have kept a close hold over their national military forces through the Ministry of Defence. This strategic portfolio has always been in the hands of the Prime Minister himself or else entrusted only to his closest political aide, who at times has been related to him by family ties.[14] Alternatively, a system of succession to armed forces leadership was also skillfully instituted and ensured the position of Armed Forces Chief being held invariably by someone who had close kinship ties with the political elite. The intrinsic importance of strategic military commands in Peninsular Malaysia, for example, is amply illustrated by the carefully scrutinised selection process before the appropriate officer is appointed, for once an officer attains such acceptance, he is normally considered to be in line for higher appointments in the military.[15] Finally, the administrative separation of the MAF, who are under the Ministry of Defence, and the RMP, who come under the Ministry of Home Affairs, with two different ministers further confirms the authority of the civilian sector. However, as a balance to the civilian authority, the system of constitutional monarchy in Malaysia provides for officers' commissions in the MAF being awarded by the Yang Dipertuan Agong (the Paramount Ruler), who is also the Supreme Commander of the MAF in his capacity as titular head of state.

Turning to the norm that is observed in Indonesia and Thailand, however, one finds that military authority is the real source of all power in the state, even though there are all sorts of constitutional provisions for a dispersion of powers. The basic reasons for this dominant role of the military in all matters that are related to national security naturally differ somewhat between the two countries. The longer-established pattern in Thailand has its origins directly in the post-1932 period and in the Royal Thai Armed Forces' (RTAF) constitutional and ceremonial links with the monarchy. It is also effectively bolstered by the Thai military's undisguised involvement in conducting commercial enterprises and in major business interests. For that reason alone, if not for any other, the RTAF has been able to function as an independent force outside the pale of other ordinary government administrative machinery.[16] This unique status was further enhanced by the greatly heightened security threats that Thailand encountered from the late 1960s onwards, thus providing a more plausible rationale for the military to assert itself completely in the sphere of national security planning and implementation. Two agencies that are central to this purpose, the National Security Council (NSC) and the Internal Security Operations Command (ISOC), formerly known as the Communist Suppression Operations Command, have played a critical role in maintaining military supremacy in Thai national security. The workings of ISOC at the height of the CPT's insurgency enabled the RTAF to involve itself from the highest policy and command circles in Bangkok to the entire country at the provincial and district levels, where it oversaw not only the purely CIW function, but also a range of civic-action programmes to win over the hearts and minds of the local inhabitants.[17] In later years, as the CPT's strength and its potential threat to national security waned distinctly, there were indications that the initiative had moved over to the NSC, in which, once again, it was the military element that played the dominant role.[18]

Under the newly-installed civilian government of a year ago, it would be interesting to know just how much of the military's hitherto unquestioned authority in national security planning and execution has been taken over by civilian functionaries or institutions. There is sufficient evidence to indicate that the RTAF's influence over foreign policy formulation has been on the decline for more than a decade, and this is not entirely surprising given the more public discussion of international and regional questions among Thailand's literate classes. However, in the area of the suppression of communist and separatist activities, the RTAF continues to be at the forefront, as reflected in its recently launched campaign to win over the Muslim populace in the South, called "Harapan Baru" (New Hope). As long as the conditions in Indochina remain basically unstable and the long-term motives of the Vietnamese unpredictable, it can be safely assumed that the military in Thailand will maintain a dominant position in the direction of national security policy.

In Indonesia, the original and shrewd philosophical justification of ABRI's extra-military role that is embodied in the concept of "dwifungsi," which literally justifies its participation in the social, economic, and political life of the country, remains the main basis for military domination of the management of national security. Admittedly, the post-Gestapu situation in 1965-66 was fraught with danger for the still-fragile nature of Indonesian nationhood, and it was the unhesitating action of the ABRI leadership that brought back conditions of relative normalcy to the country by the early 1970s. Since then, under the New Order, the ostensible purpose of the military has been to legitimize its role, and more particularly that of the Suharto leadership, both in the face of a possible resurgence of disaffection among pro-Sukarno and pro-PKI elements in the society, as well as the more overt opposition of disenchanted senior members of ABRI itself.[19] National security itself has become much more broadly defined under the New Order in Indonesia, owing partly to the dramatic changes in the regional strategic environment since the 1970s and to some extent to the two major military and CIW campaigns that were waged first in the former Portuguese colony of Timor and subsequently in Irian Jaya.

In these circumstances the composition and qualitative nature of ABRI itself have undergone some basic transformation over the past two decades, with a selective trimming-down of its rather unwieldy size since the Sukarno years being one of the earliest measures adopted by the military leadership. The organization of its formations and deployment throughout the country have also clearly reflected a more precise strategic perception of ABRI's national security role, not to speak of the development of special rapid deployment strike units for the purpose of putting out brush-fire outbreaks in different parts of the country.[20] There has also been a new emphasis on achieving a credible naval capability in view of the archipelagic concept of Indonesian defence coupled with the growing seriousness of international disputes involving sea lanes, strategic straits, and EEZ claims. Another significant change that has occurred is in the character of the senior officer corps itself, as the '45 generation, which fought for independence, has made way in stages to a new crop of post-1945 generals. While it is difficult to calculate precisely how all these new configurations have affected the management of national security in Indonesia, it is, nevertheless, clear that the supremacy of the military over the civilian elements in government has not diminished in any way.

Viewed from the deliberate steps that have been taken by the Suharto government to civilianize the day-to-day government and politics of the country, especially with scheduled elections being held regularly for membership of the DPR (Lower House) and MPR (Upper House), this is indeed a somewhat contradictory outcome. To some extent at least, therefore, it must be admitted that the main reason for the lack of a civilian role in questions of national security is the adamant view of the military leadership that these are within their professional purview and far too critical to be handled in a strictly administrative fashion. As if to strengthen this standpoint, it will be found that all the state apparatus for national security, beginning with the Ministry of Defence (HANKAM) and including such bodies as the recently dissolved KOPKAMTIB (Command for the Restoration of Peace and Stability), has been closely controlled and manned by ABRI itself with hardly any civilian component. Similarly, the principle of "dwi-fungsi" has ensured that all vital installations and particularly strategic administrative positions, such as the governorship of Jakarta, are under the charge of military officers. There is, thus, a very blatant policy of military domination with civilian participation kept to a minimum in all matters concerning national security. The only exception to this trend has been the management of Indonesian foreign policy by the DEPLU (Department of Foreign Affairs), and even here there were occasional instances of military interference, especially when it involved delicate issues such as relations with Vietnam and the PRC.

The third pattern that has gradually become discernible in civil-military relations in ASEAN is a more problematical one as there is insufficient evidence to support the thesis, but a close examination of security developments in individual countries, as well as the responses of the organization itself to regional security crises, does reveal a new trend. This is the concept of combined civil-military approaches to problems of regional security which has been subsequently translated to function in national situations, and it is in part, at least, based on the old Indonesian rhetoric of "national resilience" and "regional resilience". There are several important factors that have indirectly contributed to the growth of greater security cooperation between the civilian elements in governments among the ASEAN countries and their military counterparts. Of these, as alluded to earlier in the case of Thailand, the fast-changing nature of regional politics and the unpredictability of the usual strategic analyses have alerted both the military and civilian leadership to be more cautious and perspicacious in security planning. Another reason for such cooperation is the unavailability of ready advice from friendly big powers as had been the case in the past, making it extremely important for

the individual member states of ASEAN to form their conclusions regarding the security scenario devoid of the number of optional inputs that had previously been available. Moreover, the military establishments too have come to appreciate that the security threats in the region are much more complex, particularly with the experience of the proxy-wars between the communist powers themselves, and this has made them more amenable to advice from and consultation with civilian planners and policy-makers. Undoubtedly, there is a large element of truth in the belief that foreign policy has become increasingly enmeshed with security matters in Southeast Asia, and ASEAN has willy-nilly been embroiled in the most critical issues, such as the Cambodian question.

At the domestic level, too, there is a strong perception that matters of national security cannot be managed effectively if they are viewed exclusively from a military perspective, and the growing demand in the region, after such events as the fall of President Marcos in the Philippines in February 1986, for greater participatory politics has served to forewarn governments of the need to have a broader appreciation of security questions. In fact, even among the traditionally civilian-led governments in ASEAN, such as Malaysia and Singapore, there have been early moves in the direction of establishing mechanisms for closer collaboration between their police forces and the military since the mid-1970s. In one particular case in Malaysia, when a small-scale but potentially dangerous communist insurgency had broken out in the east Malaysian state of Sarawak, the government created a precedent by forming a combined operations command under the civil service, the police, and the army which was known as RASCOM (Rejang Area Security Command). Since then, such forms of combined responses to national security needs have become common, and the military itself is now represented in all government security coordinating bodies from the national to the district levels. This trend among the civilian regimes will probably be emulated by the military-dominated governments as its relevance and practicality become evident, given the likelihood of new forms of threats to the region emerging in the future. The constant interaction that occurs within ASEAN at a variety of levels, but most significantly over questions of regional security, will inevitably create an atmosphere that is conducive to regular civil-military cooperation in managing their individual national security demands.

NOTES

1. Zakaria Haji Ahmad, "Configurative and Comparative Aspects of Military-Civilian Relations" in Ahmad and Crouch (eds.), *Military-Civilian Relations*, p. 2.

2. While President Soeharto was a full-serving general at the time he became Acting President in 1966, he had, of course, formally retired from that rank when he became the substantive President later. The Sultan of Brunei is Sandhurst-trained, and as the hereditary ruler, he is by office also the Supreme Commander, but under the constitutional arrangements that Brunei introduced as an independent state, he also serves as the Prime Minister and Minister of Defence. The case of General Chatichai is, on the other hand, much more straightforward, as he had long retired from the RTAF when he went into active politics. Nevertheless, the tradition of the military having a role in government both in the case of Thailand and Indonesia does encourage outside observers to sometimes assume that the Indonesian leadership in particular is a military one.

3. This was not the general conclusion that was arrived at by the authors of the compilation of civil-military studies published as Ahmad and Crouch, *Military-Civilian Relations*.

4. It will, of course, not be possible in a paper such as this to be either thorough or comprehensive, and the cases that will be highlighted are those that are more popularly known and also which have had an international impact.

5. See, for example, Zakaria Haji Ahmad, "The Military and Development in Malaysia and Brunei, with a short survey on Singapore," in Djiwandono and Yong (eds.), *Soldiers and Stability*, pp. 231-54.

6. Richard J. Kessler, "Development and the Military: Role of the Philippine Military in Development" in Djiwandono and Yong, (eds.), *op. cit.*, pp. 213-27.

7. Zakaria Haji Ahmad, "The Bayonet and the Truncheon: Army/Police Relations in Malaysia" and Stanley S. Bedlington, "Ethnicity in the Armed Forces in Singapore" in DeWitt C. Wllinwood and Cynthia H. Enloe (eds), *Ethnicity and the Military in Asia* (New Brunswick, N.J.: Transaction Books, 1981), pp. 193-241 and 242-66. See also Robert L. Rau, "The Role of the Armed Forces and Police in Malaysia" in Edward A. Olsen and Stephen Jurika, Jr. (eds), *The Armed Forces in Contemporary Asian Societies* (Boulder, Colo.: Westview Press, 1986), pp. 153-69 and Mohd. Reduan Hj. Aslie and Mohd. Radzuan Hj. Ibrahim, *Polis Diraja Malaysia: Sejarah, Peranan dan Cabaran* [Royal Malaysia Police History. Role and Challenge] (Kuala Lumpur: Kumpulan Karangkraf, 1984).

8. The Malaysian Special Force, as it was called, which was up to brigade strength, was deployed in the former Belgian Congo from 1960 to 1963 at the invitation of the United Nations. A small U.N observer group was sent to Iraq under U.N. auspices in 1988, and an army battalion is now serving in Namibia.

9. Anon, "1933-1983: 50 Years of the Malaysian Army," *Sorotan Darat* (The House Journal of the Malaysian Army), No 1, (March 1983), pp. 28-37.

10. Richard Clutterbuck, *Conflict and Violence in Singapore and Malaysia, 1945-1983* (Singapore: Times International, 1984). See also, Richard Stubbs, *Hearts and Minds in Guerilla Warfare: The Malayan Emergency, 1948-1960* (Kuala Lumpur: Oxford University Press, 1989).

11. "National Security" in *Malaysia, A Country Study*, edited by Frederica M. Bunge (Washington, D.C.: U.S Government, 1985), pp. 235-315.

12. Karl von Vorys, *Democracy without Consensus: Communalism and Political Stability in Malaysia* (Princeton: Princeton University Press, 1975).

13. Chan, "Singapore" in Ahmad and Crouch (eds.), *Military-Civilian Relations*, pp. 136-56.

14. Chandran Jeshurun, "Development and Civil-Military Relations in Malaysia: The Evolution of the Officer Corps" in Djiwandono and Yong, (eds.), *Soldiers and Stability*, pp. 266-9.
15. Ibid., pp. 262-5.
16. Suchit Bunbongkarn, *The Military in Thai Politics, 1981-1986* (Singapore: Institute of Southeast Asian Studies, 1987).
17. Kusuma Snitvongse, "Thai government responses to armed communist and separatist movements" in Jeshurun (ed.), *Governments and Rebellions*, pp. 247-72.
18. Chai-Anan Samudavanija and Sukhumbhand Paribatra, "In Search of Balance: Prospects for Stability in Thailand during the Post-CPT Era" in Kusuma Snitvongse and Sukhumbhand Paribatra (eds.), *Durable Stability in Southeast Asia* (Singapore: Institute of Southeast Asian Studies, 1987), pp. 187-233.
19. Dorodjatun Kuntjoro-Jakti and T.A.M. Simatupang, "The Indonesian Experience in Facing Non-Armed and Armed Movements: Lessons from the Past and Glimpses of the Future" in Snitvongse and Paribatra (eds.), *Durable Stability*, pp. 96-116.
20. Harold Crouch, "Indonesia" in Ahmad and Crouch (eds.), *Military-Civilian Relations*, pp. 50-77.

24.

THE PROSPECTS FOR
ORDERLY CHANGE IN ASEAN

MICHAEL ANTOLIK

ASEAN has an enviable vitality because its members draw benefits from all its dimensions. As a consultative process, operating on bilateral and multilateral levels, it facilitates accommodation; it symbolizes the resultant, commonly achieved stability and prosperity; and it is the regional organization that institutionalizes the political process. Each is a facet of ASEAN, inseparable and intertwined. The successful association confirms their consciousness that the states are part of a culturally interdependent entity, identified as the ASEAN subregion. Success further realizes their aspirations for peace and stability and so provides the incentive to participate in the ASEAN organization, whose consultative machinery facilitates the political process.

Symbolism is central because these states, reflecting a cultural predisposition, prefer indirect approaches to conflictual situations. From the start in 1967 ASEAN served as an indirect nonaggression pact to conclude *konfrontasi* and, as states still face intramural security problems, suspicions, and rivalries, the organization still fulfills that function of indirect reassurance. The Association's charter holds the promises important to managing competition. Members pledged in the Bangkok Declaration "that they are determined to ensure their stability and security from external interference in any form or manifestation in order to preserve their national identities [and] to promote regional peace and stability through abiding respect for justice and the rule of law."

The states fulfill the promises to refrain from interference and to respect each other because the regional organization unites them in a higher common interest, a peaceful and stable environment. The organization is first an escape from distasteful realities, whether they be intramural differences or problems with outsiders. The Association speaks in positive language; it points to opportunities and benefits that economics and cultural cooperation can bring. To achieve these spoken and unspoken objectives, ASEAN states willingly participate in an "ongoing conclave," the political process.

Their commitment, however, rests not on hopes for the future, but on past experience, which created the common awareness that competition is futile, foolish, and costly. Specifically, states fear competition first among themselves — this is the lesson of *konfrontasi* — and then with outsiders who might exploit their vulnerabilities, namely, social cleavages, economic discontent, and insurgencies. Successful association, then, is predicated on the basic principles of restraint, respect, and responsibility.

Excerpted from Michael Antolik, *ASEAN and the Diplomacy of Accommodation* (Armonk, N.Y.: M.E. Sharpe Inc., 1990), pp. 155–67, by permission of the author and the publisher.

In 1967 this meant states do not interfere in other states, either by war, aid to insurgents, challenges to legitimacy, and comments about personalities. Down to the present, reciprocal restraint serves each government's domestic interests: each can focus on internal problems, such as insurgency, corruption, development, and internal political challenges. Some minimal rules follow: States will deny sanctuary to insurgents from a neighbor state and refrain from challenges to others' territorial integrity. Also, there will be no public challenges, comments, or criticisms of other regimes' legitimacy, domestic systems, conduct, policies, or style.

Besides restraint shown in tolerance, an accommodative relationship requires respect. States first show this through diplomatic acceptance, that is, they attend public consultations with their partners. ASEAN meetings and bilateral summits demonstrate both awareness of interdependence with neighbors and willingness to forgo individualism by seeking others' advice and concerns. Respect is evident in the customary approaches to decision making, consensus and ambiguity, both of which assuage the irritations of interdependence. The group makes no decision unless all agree to it, thus respecting each participant's sovereignty. A final principle of ASEAN accommodation, and one that demands the highest sensitivity to interdependence and a spirit of sacrifice, is responsibility — states must consciously consider the effects their domestic policies might have on a neighbor. Governments have come a long way in this matter of sensitivity; Singapore's 1968 execution of marines, despite President Suharto's plea, contrasts with the 1989 commutation of a caning judgment against a Thai illegal worker after the case raised popular outrage in Thailand. States may even help another government with a domestic difficulty by sharing intelligence information, advocating their partner's case with outside powers, or interceding with minority groups in that country.

Several tactics flow from the practice of these principles. Ambiguity is the handmaid of consensus; in language it allows participants to reach common stands and, subsequently, to hold their own interpretation of so-called common stands. Similarly, codewords allow participants to speak of harsh realities, threats, or understandings, and to make rallying calls in acceptable common language. So too, "ambiguous association," used in displays of solidarity, shows strength and cohesion at the moment but leaves no definite restriction on the future. Other tactics are postponement, quiet diplomacy, and compartmentalization. Postponement allows the participants to avoid a divisive issue; quiet diplomacy permits governments to negotiate without external interference or domestic pressure. Compartmentalization safeguards the larger political process from bilateral disputes. And in the broadest sense of compartmentalization, the regional organization and its economic agenda serve as a veil for politics, providing participants with a neutral reason for associating.

Developed in the context of intramural relations, these principles and tactics also enable ASEAN states to determine common policies toward external actors. They are critical to the political process because the states are reluctant to pursue common foreign policy. As small, developing states, they tend to be reactive and preoccupied with domestic issues. They know that they have divergent threat perceptions and policy preferences. Nevertheless, when external crises threaten the process with disintegration and defection, they coordinate foreign policies. Such rallies go to the origins of ASEAN. When the end of colonialism presented these new nations with the challenge of dealing directly with each other, they established the ASEAN process in 1967 for these purposes. In the final phase of the Vietnam War, when they feared a power vacuum and the danger of great-power competition, ASEAN members came up with the first common initiative, Zopfan. Subsequently, with the fall of Saigon and the end of the U.S.-supplied front line in Indochina, they reaffirmed intramural relationships and symbolically shored up their own front line, Thailand, with a summit in 1976. Since the Vietnamese occupation of Cambodia in 1979, they have demonstrated solidarity through meetings and collective political stands in support of Thailand.

Giving primacy to intramural dynamics and the art of accommodation answers some questions about ASEAN politics. Common foreign-policy stands had a slow and guarded development because division of opinion and perception within the grouping made finding compromises difficult. These same factors explain why ASEAN states have not moved toward a collective defense arrangement, states differ about sources of danger, do not have sufficient military counterforce, and, in some cases, hope that the rationality of accommodation can persuade Vietnam to renounce confrontation. ASEAN's Treaty of Amity and Friendship is still open to all in Southeast Asia, including war-weary, indebted Vietnam — a prime candidate to realize that competition is futile, foolish, and costly.

ASEAN'S success in multilateralism means that differences that are to be expected in a gathering of several governments have been accommodated. The important common and mutual interest, the control of insurgency, does link many members. The ASEAN process rests on the confidence engendered by the bilateral endeavors between several pairs of members to suppress insurgencies that cut across borders. The four states along the Malacca Straits developed strong bilateral ties as they cooperated in border patrol agreements and regular summits. Moving east, Indonesia and Malaysia cooperated in stabilizing Borneo. The insurgency problem again played a central but not so positive role, in linking the Philippines to the ASEAN process through its shared problem with Malaysia. Manila and Kuala Lumpur have abided by the general principles of restraint, respect, and responsibility; but the two have not moved onto a higher, more cooperative plateau like other pairs. Multilateralism has been more significant in this bilateral relationship; ASEAN partners help the two to manage their bilateral differences.

Regionalism, as a conceptualization of cultural bonds and security interdependence, also helps mitigate suspicions through its positive symbolism — the "spirit of ASEAN."

This dynamic extends to all, as multilateral association takes on a life of its own. The Association dynamic, summarized as "a friend of my friend becomes my friend," provides a rationale to cooperate for those states not directly intertwined by an insurgency interdependence. Manila, Singapore, and Bangkok are brought into much more regular and close contact with each other through ASEAN than would be the case without the organization. ASEAN also creates a neutral context and forum in which smaller states, like Singapore, Brunei, and, in some respects, the Philippines, jointly deal with Indonesia. Together they feel less outclassed by the larger state without forming a potentially polarizing coalition in the region. Multilateralism is further bolstered by the appeals of regional cooperation; Europe serves as a model and the United States encourages the trend. Moreover, regionalism assuages irritations and suspicions by clothing sacrifices and policies in language of partnership, kinship, and friendship. The costs of restraint, respect, and responsibility are balanced by benefits derived from national acceptance, regional stability, and international recognition.

This intramural stability, the first achievement of ASEAN politics, is the foundation of the ASEAN process. It puts aside all charges that the early years of ASEAN were moribund; states were successful in recovering from *konfrontasi*. Second, these states concentrated on improving relationships, using gestures and approaches from their cultural milieu. As a non-Western approach, it was ad hoc; there is no precise treaty commitment concerning political or security matters, and politics are veiled by an economic-cultural organization. A consequence is that participants are open to gradual, incremental change. A negative effect, however, is that participants and observers develop different expectations of the process, most notably in the area of economics. Third, strong and cooperative bilateral ties between most contiguous neighbors — those bound in "need-suspicion" relationships — form a skeletal foundation for the larger political process. Where insurgency interests converge, relationships are strong. But, because interdependencies vary in nature and intensity, each participant, depending on the number and importance of neighbors, has a different stake in the process. Likewise, some states are more important to the process than others. The Philippine-Malaysian cleavage has been tolerated because the stakes are not as high on the east flank, unlike the highly interdependent areas in the west — the core of ASEAN — where accommodation is essential. In brief, the ASEAN process has worked because it has satisfied participants' self-interest. However, "self-interest is a powerful motivating force, but it comes in many shapes: short-term and long-term; narrow and broad; intelligent and stupid; and altruism may emerge when all else fails."[1] Fortunately, ASEAN leaders have perceived their self-interest in regional terms through the "ASEAN" symbol, which broadens and raises individual self-interest to higher common levels. "ASEAN" serves as a diplomatic leitmotif helping to create long-term, broad, intelligent, and even altruistic policies among the participants. "ASEAN" recalls years of benefits and good faith; it reminds governments that they are interdependent — thus, the "spirit of ASEAN" influences national behavior. It is assisted by the framework of the ASEAN organization, which provides the context for long-term reciprocity and a means of easier communication. Together, spirit and organization speak the higher common interest; participants need and enjoy, to the envy of many, good relations with neighbors.

In sum, this symbol of unity and community insures that the political process built upon accommodation continues. ASEAN is truly a myth in the classical sense; under its facade of smiles and stories of friendship lie the basic truths. It is the acceptable public expression for cooperation between governments that have yet to overcome feelings of suspicion and rivalry in their search to control insurgency and subversion; it is the public record of good faith demonstrated over the past two decades and pledged for the future; it is a reputation of international influence and respect in diplomatic and economic bargaining forums; it is collateral backing promises of good behavior. All these images and benefits serve as higher interests to assuage potentially explosive historical, racial, religious, and economic suspicions that still divide ASEAN members. These interests are aggregated in an indirect, positive, and successful symbol, "ASEAN."

NOTE

1. Leonard Silk, "Getting Back to the Real World", *New York Times*, November 16, 1983.

Section *IV*

SOCIAL AND CULTURAL ISSUES IN ASEAN

Introduction

Ananda Rajah

A problematic issue in ASEAN has been the definition of what constitutes the "social" and "cultural" as contained in the ASEAN Declaration of 8 August 1967. The Declaration states that the objectives of ASEAN are "to accelerate the economic growth, social progress and cultural development in the region". It seems reasonable to assume that the signatories to the declaration were not unaware of the ambiguities entailed in the use of the terms "social progress" and "cultural development". Given the prevailing political conditions of the times in Southeast Asia, it is conceivable that the general references to social progress and cultural development were preferable to objectives such as "economic integration" or "political development and integration", objectives which would have been impossible to realize. The significance of these references, which many analysts have missed, lies precisely in the fact that they represent the avoidance of enunciating political objectives of any kind which could possibly become the focus of dissent or disagreement.

The enunciation of social and cultural objectives, however, raised a host of complex issues which consequently had to be addressed within the framework of ASEAN. In terms of what has in fact been done, it is apparent that, as with the Declaration and the various ASEAN summits since then, a sense of pragmatism has prevailed. ASEAN has attempted co-operation on social and cultural matters, which have been *operationally* and *functionally* defined (as against social science definitions of what constitutes the "social" and the "cultural"), so as to be manageable and achievable in the wider context of an association of sovereign nation-states. This has meant specific undertakings which the member states might reasonably agree to co-operate on and this includes the activities undertaken by (1) the Committee on Social Development (COSD); and (2) the Committee on Culture and Information (COCI).

It is evident that the very nature and complexity of social and cultural issues in the region have precluded greater co-operation among the ASEAN states beyond that which is feasible and practicable whilst also needing to recognize the sovereign rights, legitimate interests, and sensitive domestic issues of the member states. For this reason, however, the fact that co-operation has been possible at all and in some instances successful is in itself worthy of note.

The excerpts in this Section illustrate the range and import of these social and cultural issues against which formal ASEAN co-operation might be considered and evaluated.

The selections represent scholarly perspectives on the social and cultural underpinnings, issues and implications of what is entailed by a regional grouping of sovereign nation-states marked by ethnic and religious heterogeneity, different historical trajectories, different stages of economic development, and different political institutions. At the same time, the selections are intended to illustrate some of the more important issues which have emerged in the course of the development and maturing of the ASEAN states, both separately and as states bound together by perceptions of, increasingly, common economic and political interests which have had consequences for how social and cultural issues have come to be defined.

Sharon Siddique's paper sets out succinctly the principal concerns which lie at the heart of social and cultural issues in the ASEAN states: definitions of the identity of sovereign nation-states, modernization, cultural change, and "Westernization" which was, and continues to be, viewed with concern in the ASEAN states. Patya Saihoo's paper may be seen as an elaboration of some of the issues contained in Siddique's paper. The paper is noteworthy for the distinction it makes between élite and popular consciousness of ASEAN "cultural unity" and the insight that any consciousness of "cultural unity" on the part of the élite in ASEAN may well be a product of the acquisition of modern, "Western" knowledge and an "international culture". Lau Teik Soon's paper, on the other hand, while recognizing that the region is an enormous cultural mosaic, sets out what has been achieved within the institutional framework of ASEAN bodies despite this cultural diversity.

The paper by Aline K. Wong and Paul P.L. Cheung reviews demographic trends in the ASEAN states (with the exception of Brunei). Trinidad S. Osteria's paper complements that of Wong and Cheung in tracing trends in, and the future of, urbanization in four ASEAN states (Indonesia, Malaysia, the Philippines and Thailand).

"Social justice" is a term explicitly used in the Bangkok Declaration and in the ASEAN Declaration of 8 August 1967. John E. Walsh's paper is a careful exploration of this complex notion which continues to pose formidable problems of definition and measurement, let alone effective and realistic implementation.

The paper by Ungku A. Aziz deals with a subject which has for long been considered an important, if not indispensable, and highly promising focus of ASEAN social and cultural co-operation. Notwithstanding this, initiatives and efforts at co-operation on education in ASEAN have tended to be limited in scope.

Wang Gungwu's essay deals with two issues of perennial significance and concern in the region — ethnicity and religion — because of their potential for conflict. The essay is instructive for its discerning identification of phases in the recent history of the ASEAN region, how ethnic and religious issues may be situated in relation to these phases, and how the fact of being a regional association of states has provided member states — each of which has had to grapple with ethnic and religious problems — not only with a comparative perspective on ethnic and religious rights but a sensitivity to wider common issues thus enhancing regional co-operation.

Jakob Oetama's paper deals with an issue of considerable importance in the region because of the social, cultural, and political implications of the role of the press and because of competing definitions about what such a role should be. The role of the press has been a contentious one in many ASEAN countries and, as Oetama's reflections indicate, the issues are hardly simple.

Although the selections in this Section do not cover the entire range of social and cultural issues in ASEAN, they none the less describe their major features and contours. If generalizations may be made on the basis of these papers, there would undoubtedly be broad agreement that social and cultural issues are intimately linked to economic and political issues. At the same time, it is also evident that in these states, individually and collectively, there has been an ongoing dialectical process, in which nation-state formation and new constructions of the meaning and significance of what constitute social and cultural issues are held together in a mutually-defining relationship. It is a process intrinsic to the building of nation-states and the constituting of a regional association of nation-states — intrinsic, that is, to attempts at realizing what are indisputably newly "imagined communities" in Southeast Asia.

25.

CULTURAL DEVELOPMENT
An ASEAN Overview

SHARON SIDDIQUE

It is ironic that since the attainment of political independence Southeast Asian nations are being more profoundly challenged by the West than ever before. Technological advancements in agricultural production, industrialization, urbanization and the introduction of modern business and banking facilities have initiated profound changes in Southeast Asian societies. There is an increasing sense of urgency reflected in discussions on the need for cultural development. This urgency is, in a sense, a response to the cultural changes which have been the inevitable consequence of the modernization process. There is a feeling that the challenge of increasing Westernization can only be met through a dynamic programme of cultural development which would be directed to adapting traditional cultural values and norms to the new social and cultural milieu in which people find themselves. This sense of urgency is also reflected in the fear of a cultural vacuum in which traditional cultural norms are no longer found relevant to new socio-economic conditions. In fact, the preference for the term cultural development to refer to the process of cultural change reflects a fundamental alteration in the manner in which

Southeast Asian leaders — as well as Western commentators — perceive this process. No longer is cultural change conceived of as a natural, gradual process of diffusion and assimilation. It is now perceived as something which requires active, dynamic cultural engineering.

The former Indonesian Minister of Religion, Mr. Mukti Ali, captured the essence of this attitude in a speech which he delivered at the Goethe-Institute in September 1971 in Jakarta: "We, the Indonesians, are in the process of development . . . We may fail before the challenge of modern technology, with its perplexing threat to the human spirit; or we may succeed. But if we do succeed, it will be in continuity from our own past in our own self-interpretation . . ."

This challenge of modernization is a general preoccupation in all ASEAN countries. This seems to be translated, at the national level, into a preoccupation with two important aspects of nation-building — first the emphasis placed on the need for a national identity, and second, on a concern for achieving national integration. Representatives from ASEAN countries who attended a one week seminar in February 1976 at the Cultural Documentation Centre for UNESCO,

Reprinted in abridged form from Sharon Siddique, "Culture Development in ASEAN: The Need for an Historical Perspective", in *ASEAN Identity, Development and Culture*, edited by R.P. Anand and Purificacion V. Quisumbing (Diliman, Q.C.: University of the Philippines Law Center and East-West Center Culture Learning Institute, 1981), pp. 68–85, by permission of the author and East-West Center.

stressed the importance of cultural development efforts in promoting national identity and national integration.[1]

This search for a national identity is in part reflected by the necessity to establish an identity separate from the colonial heritage. This is reflected in a resurgence of interest in indigenous cultural heritage. From this perspective, we can talk about the choice of a national language, a national culture, a national dress, and a national credo. Both Malaysia and Indonesia have opted for a national language (Bahasa Malaysia and Bahasa Indonesia respectively) which is based on the Malay language. Many regional languages and dialects, including the national language of the Philippines, belong to the Malayo-Polynesian language group.[2] In an effort to create the basis for a national identity which transcends the cultural and ethnic differences of their populations, Malaysia and Indonesia have also adopted a national credo, which reflects the basic principles of their national ideologies (*Rukun Negara and Panca Sila*, respectively).

One of the most important regional implications of this search for national identity through a resurgence of interest in indigenous "roots" is the regional revival of the cultural heritage of the Muslim world of Southeast Asia. Although Muslim political power was eroded by the colonial powers, and also by the emergence of the nation-states, the Islamization process left a legacy which can be seen in contemporary socio-linguistic, legal and educational institutions which continue to integrate and unite the Muslim population of ASEAN. One of the most important of these legacies is the collections of historical chronicles (called *babad, hikayat* or *sejarah*) which narrate the coming of Islam, the founding of the various

Islamic principalities, and their interrelationships. Islamic educational institutions — called *pondok, pesantren, pondok-pesantren* and *madrasah* — are also important in forming a sense of Muslim identity transcending national boundaries. According to Professor Syed Naguib Al-Attas, the choice of Malay as the main language of religious propagation in the region had a profound effect on the language as it was refined to provide a linguistic vehicle for religious expression.[3] The Malay-Muslim world of Southeast Asia, which cuts across national boundaries, and stretches, as we pointed out, from southern Thailand to the southern Philippines, will be a significant factor in cultural development and communication in the region.[4]

There is one other important insight to be gained from approaching cultural development in ASEAN from a historical perspective. This has to do with the second preoccupation of nation-building mentioned above — national integration. We have shown that the present indigenous cultural resurgence is a process which is quite in keeping with the need to create a national identity. It is, however, an unavoidable fact that the composition of the population of many ASEAN countries was fundamentally altered by colonial rule. Here the historical perspective gained through a discussion of the term plural society is particularly relevant. Just as we must recognize the fact that ASEAN states have a rich cultural heritage which predates colonial experience, we must also be cognizant of the fact that an important legacy of the colonial era is a fundamentally altered ethnic-composition of Southeast Asia. Plural societies created as a result of colonial expediency have had to be integrated into the fabric of independent nation-states.

NOTES

1. *Cultural Planning in Asia*, (Tehran: Asian Cultural Documentation Centre for Unesco, 1977), 2 vols.
2. Dr. Septy Ruzui, *A Survey of Relations Between Indonesian, Malay and Some Philippine Languages* (Kuala Lumpur: Dewan Bahasa dan Pustaka, 1968).

3. Dr. Syed Naguib al-Attas, *Preliminary Statement on A General Theory of the Islamization of the Malay-Indonesian Archipelago* (Kuala Lumpur; Dewan Bahasa dan Pustaka, 1969).
4. Sharon Siddique, "Contemporary Islamic Developments in ASEAN" in *Southeast Asian Affairs 1980* (Singapore: Heinemann Asia Pte. Ltd., 1980).

26.
PROBLEMS IN CULTURAL DEVELOPMENT

PATYA SAIHOO

In the ASEAN region there is no nation which consists of only one ethnic group, and in each nation can be found problems of ethnic identity which makes national unity less than perfect and national cultural identity an assorted picture with possible complaints at all times from some or all component ethnic groups about the inequitable share of their ethnic identity in the final. picture of the national culture. Such complaints may or may not always appear in the national press, but cases are familiar to close observers and students of the problem of nation-building, which requires the development of a national consciousness, identity and sense of community of which no nation can so far claim complete achievement.[1]

A regional grouping, such as being developed in Southeast Asia or Europe of Africa, stands in the same relation to its component nations as does a nation to its ethnic groups, with perhaps one difference in that no one nation may take the dominant position at the expense of other member nations in the association as an ethnic group may do in a nation. Hence, there should be less of a likelihood that some nation (or nations) may resent the sacrifice of its (or their) national (or cultural) identity in the process of achieving a common regional group identity. Whereas a nation may have need of a common national language or give a dominant place to one religion at the expense of some member ethnic groups, a regional association does not have such a need. Although it could be argued that possession of such common features should more greatly facilitate the creation of a common consciousness, identity and sense of community, such as found to unify an ethnic group, the opposite can also be true that a people sharing all common cultural features may be so politically divided and split into two nations, such as Korea or Germany, or nations purportedly sharing the same cultural tradition, such as Western Europe, could, as during World War II, be at war with one another.[2]

So it must seem that creating a national consciousness among the nation's ethnic groups is a different undertaking from creating a regional consciousness among the region's member nations, since a nation's demand on its members may affect more areas of life's activities than does the demand of a regional association on its members. But because of this more far-reaching demand of a nation on its members, there is a greater consciousness of the national entity than there is a consciousness

Reprinted in abridged form from Patya Saihoo, "ASEAN Identity, Development and Culture, edited by R.P. Anand and Purificacion V. Quisumbing (Diliman, Q.C.: University of the Philippines Law Center and East-West Center Culture Learning Institute, 1981), pp. 109–29, by permission of the author and East-West Center.

of a regional entity among the public of its member nations.

CULTURAL, ECONOMIC AND POLITICAL INTERESTS

A regional association is usually formed to serve common political and economic interests which need not interfere with the general cultural life of its member nations at all, and a successful regional association of nations does not require a common cultural unity in the popular sense among its members, so long as it fulfills the expectation of such political and economic interests that brought them together in the first place. Any extension of such alliance into cultural activities at all only has a secondary function for closer relations once the primary objectives appear to be viable. By themselves cultural activities, such as normally interpreted and included in the treaty provisions, are not the focus of the treaty interests, and it would be a rare treaty indeed to have no other objectives but cultural interest.

Thus the consciousness of a regional identity involved in a regional treaty is usually one of political and/or economic interests, without which no amount of the consciousness of "common ties of race and culture" can be sufficient to sustain the existence of such an association.

In the text of the ASEAN Declaration there is no mention of political *raison d'etre* of the treaty, and only "economic growth, social progress and cultural development in the region through joint endeavours" are given as the first aim and purpose of the association, but such conventional statement should not conceal the true interests that underlie the treaty formation which are mainly political.

This insistence is not intended to detract our attention from the main subject-matter of our discussion, which is "cultural development", but only to remind that the same desire and definition may not be equally insisted upon by the respective governments or the general publics of the treaty members.

As all national leaders are aware, the cultural unity of the nation that they see is often different from what the common citizens see. If "cultural development" to such national leaders should mean "the development of a national culture," which transcends the persistence of local and ethnic cultures, then reference to a common racial and cultural heritage may not serve the desired objective and more appropriate strategy may be found in speaking less of mutual cultural understanding and appreciation and more of equitable political and economic benefits for all citizens regardless of racial and cultural origins and identities.

It is in such terms as common political and economic interests that the masses with different ethnic and cultural backgrounds are aware of the meaning and identity of the nation to which they must all belong as citizens. Although mutual understanding and appreciation of each other's culture are desirable and self-enriching, and could help to smooth inter-personal and inter-group activities and relations even in political and economic matters, this is not an absolute condition. Instances have been known that effective symbiotic relationship in economic matters can develop and endure between a Chinese village-storekeeper and his Thai or Malay clients in villages of Thailand and West Malaysia, without each understanding thoroughly of the other's culture as long as both can find mutually satisfactory benefits in their commerce.[3] Successful political relations can be established between two nations of entirely different cultures, with the leaders of either nation-knowing, understanding and appreciating only superficially of the other's culture, provided that in political matters each nation is getting what it wants from the other.

Or perhaps that is not entirely true? Some knowledge of the other's culture is necessary for at least one party who receives rather than gives. Perhaps that is why the Chinese expatriate always masters the vernacular and knows some local customs of his indigenous customers pertinent to his business, and not vice versa. The same reason explains why leaders of the developing East are more familiar with the language and the way of life of their counterparts of the developed West, and not the other way round. This is only to accept that cultural knowledge helps in personal and group relations, but only as long as the priority economic or political objectives are achieved.

The main point of this part is that the consciousness that binds two persons or groups of different cultures, be it in the same nation or in a regional association of several nations, is that they share some common economic and political interest that promises mutual benefit. If faced with a threat from a third party outside of their partnership to upset their interest and deprive them of the expected benefit, the consciousness of that bond is strengthened if both partners believe that they could overcome the threat only by being united in their association. Without such mutual benefit, an external threat, and a conviction that only a cohesive unity of their association can ride the storm, no sense of belonging to the same community, no shared identity, and no consciousness of one and the same entity with a common destiny can ever develop among the members of the association.[4] Therefore, if "cultural development" is the development of regional ways of thinking and valuing which would lead to the deepening and strengthening of an ASEAN regional consciousness, identity and sense of community, then we should feel less concerned about the development in the various forms of the arts and pay more attention to the development of knowledge and information on the areas of common interests and mutual benefits of political and economic nature rather than those of artistic and cultural (in popular usage) character. Perhaps this is exactly the priority set by the ASEAN Secretariat and the budget allocated so far for the various programs of activities.[5]

ELITE CONSCIOUSNESS VS
POPULAR CONSCIOUSNESS

The elite of any nation are supposed to have a wider and farther view of things than the popular masses who are absorbed in parochial interests within the narrow confines of their families, kin groups, village community, occupation, religious sect, tribal territory, or ethnic fraternity. It is less realistic, therefore, to expect among the masses in each ASEAN nation an awareness of the ASEAN entity and a sense of ASEAN community with their limited school knowledge of human and cultural geography. We must instead look to the elites for a more helpful indication.

Among the topmost political elite — prime ministers and foreign ministers especially — there is no doubt, although the awareness of ASEAN viability may have had its lull moment before the fall of Indochina compared with after. It is hoped that among political parties both in and out of power this awareness is equally shared. The series of events in Indochina up to now seems to have promoted it, and one must admit that this is largely a political interest that all existing regimes of the ASEAN nations share. This consciousness of a common political destiny would last long as there is no radical change in any of the ASEAN regimes. Should that once occur — for the sake of argument — this sense of a common political community would immediately show up its fragility.

The economic elite of ASEAN may be less united. With each ASEAN nation developing its economy with unequal resources and different production and consumption needs, a few areas of common interests may be identified, but to enlarge these areas sufficiently to create a clearer sense of a unified economic community is not yet in evidence among the more knowledgeable economic-minded section of the public, let alone the masses. In any case, economic interest and economic interest groups being what they are, a united front of ASEAN business and industries, which forget to share their profits equitably with the public, may only result in an internal political and social division within each and all ASEAN countries that does not really serve the cause of ASEAN unity that we desire.

Social, cultural, educational, and mass media and communication elites of ASEAN countries may be aware of a common and comparable background of their Southeast Asian heritage and cultural influences of India and China, and in their respective spheres of activities there could be a close feeling of camaraderie and professional brotherhood. But to what extent beyond the impersonal sharing of a common Southeast Asian traditional life-style, basic philosophy, artistic tradition, etc., exist personal contacts and relations that are more important for a meaningful sense of community? Diplomatic families usually mix freely with the local social and cultural elites, some members of whom in turn are in more advantageous position than their fellow-countrymen of the masses to travel and meet their peers in fellow ASEAN countries, thus making personal association a reality. But again the question remains whether these limited contacts in time and space of the elite minority can bring about the desired consciousness of ASEAN identity and sense of a real community without a larger popular participation. Or perhaps the larger public could be safely ignored, since international relations are as a rule results of elite decisions. If this is so, one could further ask if the decisions of social and cultural, etc., elites are as ever important as those of the political and economic elites.[6]

One could perhaps fairly say that although the masses have their own sentiments and parochial prejudices, these only become overt actions following the leadership of their elites. As long as the elites are united in their convictions about the common destiny of an extra-ethnic, extra-national community, and as long as the elites are not alienated from their own masses, only their common consciousness is what counts, and this should be promoted if it is deemed to be desirable and is found to be wanting.

PROBLEMS OF CULTURAL UNITY AND
DISUNITY OF ASEAN

Though ASEAN may have a past cultural unity, over the ages absorption of foreign cultural elements has introduced considerable differences that may now outweigh similarities. The great challenge for ASEAN studies is how to reconcile these differences in order to reach the desired ASEAN goals.

Perhaps one really common cultural feature of all ASEAN peoples, earlier settlers or later arrivals, is the primordial animism that persists despite the more recent formal acceptance of the major world religions. The masses of ASEAN peoples, be they Thai Buddhists, Filipino Christians, or Indonesian Muslims, do not deny some animistic beliefs. This may provide a basis of cultural unity which the religious elites of all these societies are not very proud of, and here we enter an area of cultural differences. Though fundamentally all major world religions share many similar values, religious differences even between different sects of the same faith have been used to divide rather than unite. The subject of religion in national development has been increasingly discussed in various quarters. Now may be the time to widen the scope of discussion to examine the role of religion(s) in regional development such as that of ASEAN.

ASEAN countries do not have linguistic unity, even though Malay has now been adopted as the national language of Indonesia and Malaysia, and an ASEAN *lingua franca* may have to be a non-ASEAN language, such as English. Similarly, not all ASEAN countries admit equal cultural debts to the two great civilizations of India and China, the Philippines being a clear exception, but with regard to the influence of these two great cultures a more important issue for consideration is the human elements that have penetrated the ASEAN region in more recent times rather than the study of the more impersonal elements that have been assimilated into local cultures long ago.

With the impact of modernization one might say that the modern elites of ASEAN now have a greater cultural unity than their masses from the acquisition of modern, "western", knowledge and an "international" culture. This common character may help to minimize the traditional cultural differences of their diverse ethnic origins. In contrast, one might say that the traditionalist elites of ASEAN would emphasize the differences that give them their cultural identity.

The question of ASEAN cultural unity or disunity can have no quick and easy answer, and one must hope that the promotion of Southeast Asian studies will eventually clarify the issue for us. For the sake of the desired ASEAN goals the scholars must show us unifying elements for the future in the diversity of the past and the present.

NOTES

1. A book such as P. Kunstadter (ed.), *Southeast Asian Tribes, Minorities, and Nations*, (1967), describes enough to tell a story even without a full coverage of all groups or all countries (Indonesia and the Philippines being omitted).

2. Malaysia and Indonesia had their differences during the "konfrontasi" of the early 1960's. Arab nations today do not agree on all things.

3. This is common knowledge among local residents that does not appear in published reports, but a study such as Louis Golomb, *Brokers of Morality: Thai Ethnic Adaptation in a Rural Malaysian Setting* (1978), gives a thorough account of symbiotic relations of Thais, Malays, Chinese, and Indians in the same community setting.

4. The now defunct Southeast Asia Treaty Organization (SEATO) is a case in point. The Asia and Pacific Council (ASPAC) is another. In Europe, the North Atlantic Treaty Organization (NATO) or the European Economic Community (EEC) still exist for the same reason.

5. For instance, a permanent committee on Socio-Cultural Activities of ASEAN was only set up in 1972, five years after the formation of ASEAN and after other economically-oriented committees. A Cultural Fund of about U.S.$5 million promised by Japan in 1972 to promote cultural relationships among ASEAN states only had its first work projects in 1979. See Patya Saihoo, "Problems in ASEAN-Japan Cultural Exchange," in *Asia Pacific Community*, No. 5, 1979.

6. In a different time and place, T.S. Eliot, a member of the English (and European) literary elite, expressed his views on the role of social and cultural elites *vis a vis* the political elite that might not be congruent in cultural matters in his *Notes towards the Definition of Culture* (first published in 1948), and especially in *The Unity of European Culture*, as an appendix, about the fate of European writers before World War II. In the ASEAN context, Estrella D. Solidum, *Towards a Southeast Asian Community*, (1974), has much to report on the political elite attitudes and interests in regional cooperation in Southeast Asia during 1959-1969. (Chapter 3, pp. 23-168). It would have been interesting to learn the attitudes of other types of elites on the same subject also had they been studied. It may be now time for another more comprehensive study.

27.

CULTURAL CO-OPERATION BETWEEN THE ASEAN STATES

LAU TEIK SOON

A SEAN is a huge cultural mosaic reflecting the vast richness and philosophical basis of its various societies. And over the years since independence, each of the governments has attempted to mould a national identity out of the cultural diversities which exist as a permanent feature of their societies. There are, of course, tremendous problems in the way of the nation-building programmes of each government in ASEAN, but with leadership, dedication and determination, these problems will be surmounted.

In the process of national building, however, each of the ASEAN countries faces the common problem of modernization or urbanization and with it the westernization of their societies. It must be noted that with the exception of Singapore, the ASEAN states are mainly rural in nature, with varying degrees of urbanization. In Thailand, 77% of the population are working in the agricultural fields, in both Indonesia and the Philippines, 70% of the population are engaged in agricultural activities, and in Malaysia, 57% of the population work in the rural areas. Even in Singapore, 8% of its population are engaged in agriculture. Urbanization, of course, has been concentrated in the major towns and cities of the ASEAN

countries, and it is here that western cultures have made their presence felt. But accompanying this development is the gradual breakdown of the traditional societies — traditional authorities, cultures, customs, values and way of life. The dilemma then which exists for each of the ASEAN countries is to strike the appropriate relationship between urbanization-cum-westernization and the maintenance of the traditional cultures.

As urbanization is proceeding, there is in ASEAN today a great concern for the preservation and development of the various cultures. After political independence, the governments in ASEAN have been concentrating on the development of their economies, but some attention has been given to the area of social and cultural development in each country. Among themselves in the ASEAN organization, cultural co-operation is vital for the following reasons: firstly, the need to understand each other's cultures, value systems, nuances and sensitivities; secondly, the need to promote the cultural heritage of ASEAN to their nationals and to others outside of the region; and thirdly, the need to protect the rich cultural heritage from the vagaries of nature and modernization.

It is against the above background that we

Reprinted with slight abridgement from Lau Teik Soon, *Cultures in Encounter: Germany and the Southeast Asian Nations. A Documentation of the ASEAN Cultural Week, Tübingen, Summer 1977*. Studies in International Cultural Relations, no. 6, edited by Institute for Cultural Relations Stuttgart. (Horst Erdmann Verlag, 1978), pp. 50–55, by permission of the author and the Institut für Auslandsbeziehungen, Stuttgart.

can understand the aspiration of the ASEAN peoples to promote cultural co-operation among themselves. In August 1967, at Bangkok, the ASEAN governments declared that they would co-operate to accelerate the economic growth, social progress and cultural development in the region. This aspiration in the cultural field was further spelt out at the Bali Summit in February 1976. The Declaration of ASEAN Concord stipulated, inter alia:

> Introduction of the study of ASEAN, its states and their national languages as partner of the curricula of schools and other institutions of learning in the member states.

> Support of ASEAN scholars, writers, artists and mass media representatives to enable them to play an active role in fostering a sense of regional identity and fellowship.

> Promotion of Southeast Asian studies through closer collaboration among national institutes.

Towards the achievement of these objectives, the ASEAN organisation has established two permanent committees, namely, the Permanent Committee on Socio-Cultural Activities established in 1971 and the Permanent Committee on Mass Media set up in 1973. At the Bali Summit, an Agreement on the Establishment of the ASEAN Secretariat was signed and included in the administrative structure of the ASEAN Secretariat is the Social and Cultural Bureau. At present, a Singaporean has the honour of being the Bureau Director and within the purview of the Director are the activities of the permanent committees, ad hoc committees and expert groups dealing with socio-cultural matters.

ASEAN co-operation in the cultural field has been quite impressive if one takes into consideration the fact that ASEAN is only ten years old and that before 1967, the ASEAN countries had little, if any, co-operation in cultural matters among themselves. A review of the cultural co-operation of the ASEAN countries will indicate that the projects implemented have been in the following areas:

> Those concerned with the preservation and propagation of the ASEAN cultural heritage through the establishment of ASEAN cultural institutions in member countries;
> exchange of cultural items and artistes; and hosting of film festivals in member countries and the joint participation in film productions.

Let me deal briefly with each of these aspects of the cultural co-operation in the ASEAN countries.

In the field of the preservation and propagation of the ASEAN cultural heritage, the initial years saw ASEAN attempting to promote the understanding of each other's varied cultures. Thus, in 1971, the ASEAN Journal, a quarterly magazine, was first published. It has proved to be one of the most useful media in publicising the cultural heritage of member countries. Then in 1972, a National Depository for ASEAN Publications was established in each of the member countries. More specifically, efforts were made to understand, learn and study the past, the traditions, the dance and music of the ASEAN countries. In May 1973, the First Summer Field School of Archaeology was conducted for about a month in Balayan, Batagas in the Philippines. In June 1975, a training course in traditional dancing and music was held in Indonesia. A year later, ASEAN experts on design and crafts met in Jakarta. In 1975, two meetings among the museum experts were held in Jakarta and Manila and these efforts culminated in the formation of the ASEAN Association of Museums in December 1976. Finally, to encourage literary pursuits as a means to further promote mutual appreciation and understanding of ASEAN cultures, an ASEAN Literary Awards Programme has been established. Three awards of US$1,500 each are to be granted every three years for outstanding works of literary merit in the field of fiction, non-fiction and poetry-drama This project is being implemented this year.

In the area of cultural exchanges among the ASEAN countries, there have been a few successful projects. Since 1971, exchanges of radio programmes on socio-cultural, economic and general interests have been implemented among member countries. The First Exchange of Radio-Television Artistes Programme was held in September-October of 1975. Under the programme, five top radio and television artistes from each member country formed a travelling troupe and gave public performances in the ASEAN capitals. Their performances were televised live, thus enabling a wider public participation in the programme aimed at understanding ASEAN cultures in songs, music and dance. A second exchange programme took place in October-November last year. Then, there was the First ASEAN Art and Photographic Exhibition held in member countries from January to August 1974. This was another travelling exhibition aimed at introducing ASEAN works of art to a wide section of the public in the ASEAN countries. A second exhibition is being planned for 1978.

Realising that film is one of the most effective media in bringing about cross-cultural enrichment, member countries have hosted in rotation the ASEAN Film Festival since 1971. At these festivals, both documentary and theatrical films of a non-political and non-religious nature are screened. At the last Film Festival, held in Manila, documentary films submitted were screened over television to reach a wider audience. As a result, the screening of documentaries on television after each Festival will be standard practice in the future. Finally, the venture into film production was undertaken very recently. A documentary entitled "Ten Years of ASEAN" was produced by member countries, with each responsible for the production and cost of its respective segment of the film and the Philippines undertaking all post-production work. The film was telecast in member countries on 8 August 1977 to commemorate the tenth anniversary of the Association. Following the success of this joint venture, funds have been approved for the production of three more documentaries dealing with (a) the formation of ASEAN, (b) the socio-cultural structures of ASEAN, and (c) the economic-industrial structure of ASEAN.

The above summary of the cultural co-operation in the ASEAN countries shows that in the field of cultural co-operation progress has been satisfactory. There is abundance of enthusiasm and commitment on the part of the member countries to achieve their objective of cultural co-operation. However, there is still much that can be done. One area which has occupied the minds of the ASEAN officials is whether or not a distinct ASEAN cultural identity can be evolved, by way of having a common language to communicate with one another, a greater blending of the art forms, for example, in music, dance, literature, drama, painting and sculptures, and by way of giving greater emphasis to the adoption of traditional cultural values. Thus, for example, there are common elements in the melodies, the musical instruments used and the mode of orchestration adopted in the traditional music of the region. In dance, the art form is basically traditional or folk, reflecting either the rural nature of ASEAN society or the cultural characteristics inherited from the mainstream of Malay, Chinese, Indian and Western civilizations. In working towards a distinct ASEAN cultural identity, there have to be certain sacrifices and integration of the various traditional cultures. These are practical problems which have to be faced but they are challenges which can be overcome.

The member countries of ASEAN are diverse in character, in terms of the size and the heterogeneity of their populations, the many religions practised, the number of languages used and the historical circumstances which were experienced by each of them. As each member country is engaged in strengthening its social fabric, moulding and consolidating its own national identity, they are nevertheless committed to cultural co-operation in ASEAN. They have pledged themselves to develop vigorously an awareness of a regional identity and to exert all efforts to create a strong ASEAN community. In reviewing the years of cultural co-operation, the peoples of ASEAN are justified in having the confidence that, armed with the traditional ASEAN spirit of solidarity and friendship, and following the guidelines laid down in the Declaration of ASEAN Concord and the Treaty of Amity and Co-operation in Southeast Asia, they can look forward to the successful creation of the ASEAN community.

28

DEMOGRAPHIC AND SOCIAL DEVELOPMENT
Taking Stock for the Morrow

ALINE K. WONG and PAUL P.L. CHEUNG

DEMOGRAPHIC DEVELOPMENT

Demographic development in the ASEAN region[1] in the past two decades is notable for two features: accelerated progress in mortality reduction, which commenced after World War II, and remarkable success in lowering fertility and curbing population growth. As a result, the region as a whole is making rapid strides towards the completion of the so-called "demographic transition," the movement from high fertility and mortality to low fertility and mortality conditions. It is notable that Singapore, the demographic forerunner, completed the transition in barely 20 years and lowered its fertility by 1975 to the replacement level—2.1 children per woman, the number necessary if she and her husband are to be just replaced in the next generation, allowing for mortality.

The reduction in mortality has been rapid in all ASEAN countries, which is not surprising given the spread of modern public health and medical technologies throughout the world since World War II. Table 2.1 documents the upward trends in life expectancy at birth and the decline in infant mortality from 1960 to 1985. Note that although the absolute gains are similar, between-country differentials remain large, reflecting divergent stages of socioeconomic development within the region. Indonesia had a fairly low life expectancy of 42.5 years in the 1960s. Steady gains were made in the early 1970s when life expectancy was raised by five years to 47.5, and, by the early 1980s, another five years were added. In the 1960s, Malaysia, the Philippines, and Thailand already had life expectancies of around 55. By the early 1980s, the life expectancies in these countries had risen to 66.9, 64.5, and 62.7 years respectively. Among the three, Malaysia has shown the largest gain and enjoys the second highest life expectancy ·in the region. Singapore's mortality level is fast approaching the level of the developed countries, with a life expectancy of 72.2 years and an infant mortality rate of only 11 infant deaths per 1,000 live births.

The rapid decline from high to moderate or low mortality is associated with three factors: the effective implementation of public health and disease control measures, better access to and utilization of medical services, and the general improvement in the standard of living as reflected in the increase in average daily protein and caloric intake.[2] Future mortality

Reprinted with slight abridgement from Aline K. Wong and Paul P.L. Cheung, *The ASEAN Success Story: Social, Economic and Political Dimensions*, edited by Linda G. Martin (Hawaiii: East-West Center, 1987), pp. 17–36, by permission of the authors and the publisher.

TABLE 2.1: Selected Mortality Indicators, 1960–85

	Life expectancy at birth (years)			Infant mortality rate (deaths per 1000 live births)		
	1960–65	*1970–75*	*1980–85*	*1960–65*	*1970–75*	*1980–85*
Indonesia						
Both sexes	42.5	47.5	52.5	145	112	87
Males	41.7	46.4	51.2			
Females	43.4	48.7	53.9			
Malaysia						
Both sexes	55.7	63.0	66.9	63	40	29
Males	54.2	61.4	65.0			
Females	57.4	64.7	68.8			
Philippines						
Both sexes	54.5	60.4	64.5	97	68	50
Males	52.9	58.8	62.8			
Females	56.2	62.1	66.3			
Singapore						
Both sexes	65.8	69.5	72.2	30	19	11
Males	64.1	67.4	69.1			
Females	67.6	71.8	75.5			
Thailand						
Both sexes	53.9	59.6	62.7	95	65	51
Males	51.9	57.7	60.8			
Females	56.1	61.6	64.8			

SOURCE: United Nations, *World Population Prospects: Estimates and Projections as Assessed in 1982* (New York: United Nations, 1985).

reduction on a national basis, of course, will depend on the continuation of these efforts. Furthermore, research has shown the persistence of significant mortality differentials by localities and socioeconomic characteristics (Herrin et al. 1981). The extension of cheap, easily available health services to the rural areas and to the lower class is as much a prerequisite for future mortality reduction as the adoption of advanced medical technology. However, as experiences in other countries have shown, the size and the tempo of future reductions are likely to be smaller and slower unless there is significant improvement in the standard of living among the majority of the population (Palloni 1981).

The region's pattern of fertility decline, especially its magnitude and tempo, has received considerable research attention. For example, Singapore's total fertility rate (TFR) stood at 6.5 children per woman of reproductive age in 1957. As Table 2.2 shows, it declined to 4.9 in the early 1960s, and by the early 1980s it was 1.7—below-replacement fertility, as defined above. Singapore's fertility is now among the lowest in the world. Thailand and Malaysia have shown equally remarkable drops in their total fertility rates, from a high of around 6.5 children per woman in the early 1960s to less than 4.0 in the 1980s. The decline has been less swift in the cases of Indonesia and the Philippines. Nonetheless, significant

TABLE 2.2: Selected Fertility and Population Growth Indicators, 1960–95

	1960–65		1970–75		1980–85		1990–95	
	TFR[a]	Annual growth rate (percent)	TFR	Annual growth rate (percent)	TFR	Annual growth rate (percent)	TFR	Annual growth rate (percent)
Indonesia	5.4	2.1	5.5	2.4	3.9	1.8	2.9	1.5
Malaysia	6.7	3.0	4.9	2.5	3.7	2.3	2.9	1.9
Philippines	6.6	3.0	5.0	2.5	4.2	2.5	3.3	2.1
Singapore	4.9	2.8	2.6	1.7	1.7	1.3	1.7	1.0
Thailand	6.4	3.0	5.0	2.6	3.6	2.1	2.6	1.7

[a] TFR stands for the total fertility rate, which is measured in terms of children per woman.

SOURCE: United Nations, *World Population Prospects: Estimates and Projections as Assessed in 1982* (New York: United Nations, 1985).

fertility reductions were made in these two countries. By 1995, if current trends continue, the ASEAN countries (with the exception of the Philippines) are expected to have TFRs of below 3.0.

Three additional features characterize the fertility decline in the ASEAN region. First, the impressive decline is due largely to a drop in marital fertility, with the increase in age at marriage playing a secondary role (Herrin et al. 1981). This change in marital fertility signifies the increasingly widespread adoption of modern contraceptives for the explicit purpose of birth control. Second, the decline in marital fertility is thought to have begun among older women in the prevention of unwanted births and to have been followed by the lowering of the number of wanted births through a downward shift in fertility preference. Third, the diffusion of modern contraceptive technology has been rapid and pervasive across geographical and socioeconomic boundaries. The rapid decline in marital fertility among rural populations and the less educated has been noted especially in the cases of Thailand and Indonesia (Knodel et al. 1984; Hull et al. 1977).

The decline is the outcome of interplay between social and economic changes on the one hand and governments' intense efforts on the other (Bulatao 1984). Demographers in

the region have generally acknowledged the effectiveness of governmental involvement in organizing and promoting fertility control measures. The concern over rapid population growth led Singapore in 1965, Malaysia in 1966, Indonesia in 1968, and Thailand and the Philippines in 1970 to adopt official anti-natalist policies. Subsequently, all ASEAN countries instituted country-wide family planning programs, with well-developed organizational infrastructure. The programs in Indonesia, Thailand, and Malaysia have been particularly commendable in their effective delivery of services to rural residents through health stations or outreach networks. In Indonesia, the involvement of community leaders in the program has resulted in strong community-wide participation. In Singapore, the program is reinforced by a wide-ranging set of social policies with anti-natalist intentions.

The systematic introduction of modern contraceptives, though legitimized by the government, could not have wholly accounted for the fertility decline. Latent demand for birth control is clearly met by the program, and the prevention of one or two unwanted births per woman could amount to a noticeable aggregate fertility reduction. However, unless fertility preferences are substantially lowered, rational birth control could do little to effect a significant fertility decline. In the ASEAN region, research has shown that fertility decline is probably precipitated by a downward shift in fertility preference (Knodel et al. 1984).

Changes in fertility preferences are indicative of the changing balance in the familial calculus of the value and cost of children. Reduction of the economic contribution of children to the family, partly because of a gradual shift to a wage economy and the constraints on land utilization imposed by the size of landholdings, places a limit on the economic value of children. At the same time, parents, with higher education than past generations and having still higher aspirations for their children, are increasingly aware of the rising cost of educating their children up to expectation. The net result of these changes is that large family size is increasingly viewed as an avoidable economic burden. This realization, coupled with the growing emphasis on the psychological value of children, may have tipped the balance in trading quantity for quality of children.[3]

Changes in fertility preference over time have not been documented in a comparative framework,[4] but the decline for each country is nonetheless noticeable. Among Chinese in Singapore, the desired number of children dropped from an average of 3.6 in 1973 to 2.6 in 1982. The evidence from Thailand also indicates a significant drop in the past two decades, but the number has leveled off at about two to three. The leveling off of fertility preference will no doubt pose a constraint to some countries' efforts to control the size of their populations.

The issue is, therefore, whether the governments concerned will be able to devise additional measures or policies to encourage further declines in fertility preference. The case of Malaysia constitutes an interesting and exceptional reversal of the ASEAN countries' population control policies. The recent pro-natalist shift in Malaysia's population policy, if implemented rigorously, may reverse that country's fertility trend. For successful implementation, it would require some strong inducements at the family level in order to counter the past trend of fertility decline. Pending further developments, it is unclear how such a pro-natalist shift would alter the relationship between Malaysia's population, resources, and economic development.

As for Thailand, Indonesia, and the Philippines, further fertility declines would require not just continuing government efforts to promote family planning programs, but also accelerated growth in standards of living and social infrastructural development, which facilitate the decline in fertility preference. In any case, the data suggest that it would be unlikely for these countries to reach replacement levels of fertility in the immediate future.

The case of Singapore illustrates the population concerns the other countries may face in the long run. With its below-replacement fertility, Singapore has been sensitized to the quality of its future cohorts. Its recent attempts to adjust the "lopsided" procreation pattern as related to educational levels, i.e., the tendency of more-educated women to have fewer babies, and attempts to search for talent through overseas recruitment exercises, provide some indication of the future direction of Singapore's population policy. At the same time, the sustained declines in fertility and mortality have led to concern about an aging population, with far-reaching implications for the welfare burden of the aged, the shortage of labor, adjustments in infrastructural provisions, as well as the socio-cultural ethos of the society (Martin 1985).

LITERACY AND EDUCATION

Another major aspect of ASEAN's social development is its educational transformation. In the postwar era, both the process of education and the distribution of schooling opportunities have undergone significant changes. The trend toward broad-based and longer formal education is clearly evident in all ASEAN countries. Table 2.3 shows that younger age groups in

TABLE 2.3: Proportion Attained Primary and Secondary Schooling, by Age and Sex

	Ages 15–19		Ages 20–24		Ages 25–34	
	Primary	*Secondary*	*Primary*	*Secondary*	*Primary*	*Secondary*
Indonesia (1980)						
Total	.60	N.A.	.57	.24	.54	.22
Male	.63	N.A.	.62	.30	.60	.26
Female	.57	N.A.	.52	.19	.51	.17
Malaysia*a* (1980)						
Total	.93	N.A.	.90	.30	.85	.19
Male	.95	N.A.	.93	.33	.91	.23
Female	.92	N.A.	.87	.27	.79	.15
Philippines (1985)						
Total	.96	N.A.	.96	.48	.94	.37
Male	.96	N.A.	.96	.48	.94	.40
Female	.96	N.A.	.96	.48	.93	.35
Singapore (1980)						
Total	.92	N.A.	.89	.32	.85	.29
Male	.93	N.A.	.91	.30	.89	.31
Female	.92	N.A.	.88	.33	.81	.27
Thailand (1980)						
Total	.97	N.A.	.96	.23	.94	.15
Male	.97	N.A.	.97	.27	.96	.19
Female	.96	N.A.	.95	.20	.93	.12

N.A.: Not applicable.

a Malaysia figures from Khoo Teik Huat, *General Report of the Population Census* (Kuala Lumpur: Department of Statistics, 1983).

SOURCE: United Nations, *Demographic Yearbook, 1982* (New York: United Nations, 1983).

each country are more likely to have received primary and secondary education. With the exception of Indonesia, the ASEAN countries moved rapidly in the 1960s to universal primary education. Thus, young people just entering the labor force in the late 1970s and early 1980s were equipped with at least a primary education. For countries that already had a high level of primary education, significant progress in the attainment of secondary education can be observed in the same period. Even in the case of Indonesia, the proportion of primary-school-age children who were actually in school in 1980 stood close to 100 per cent,[5] suggesting that the steady gain in primary education had quickened in the decade.

A notable region-wide phenomenon in the educational transformation is the diminishing sex differential in educational attainment. Table 2.3 shows that for most countries the gap between the sexes has narrowed. In the case of the Philippines, studies have shown that a crossover may have occurred in favor of females (Smith and Cheung 1981), and the data in Table 2.4 substantiate it. Similarly, signs of a crossover are already apparent for Singapore, but enrollment figures shown in Table 2.4 suggest that crossover is not likely

TABLE 2.4: Enrollment Ratios at Primary and Secondary Level by Sex, 1970–80

	Primary			Secondary		
	Total	*Male*	*Female*	*Total*	*Male*	*Female*
Indonesia						
1970	77	83	71	15	20	10
1975	83	90	76	19	24	15
1980	112	119	104	28	33	22
Malaysia						
1970	87	91	84	34	40	28
1975	91	93	89	43	48	39
1980	92	93	91	51	52	49
Philippines						
1970	108	N.A.	N.A.	46	N.A.	N.A.
1975	108	N.A.	N.A.	54	N.A.	N.A.
1980	110	111	108	63	58	68
Singapore						
1970	106	110	102	46	47	45
1975	111	114	107	53	52	53
1980	107	108	105	59	58	61
Thailand						
1970	83	86	79	17	20	15
1975	84	87	81	26	28	23
1980	96	98	94	29	30	28

NOTE: The enrollment ratio is the number of students enrolled divided by the appropriate school-age population. It is possible for the ratio to exceed 100 because of age-grade retardation; i.e., the number of students at a given level could exceed the population of the expected schooling age for that level.

N.A.: Figures not available.

SOURCES: 1970 and 1975 data—United Nations, *Demographic Yearbook*, 1982 (New York: United Nations, 1983). 1980 data—United Nations Educational, Scientific and Cultural Organization, *UNESCO Statistical Yearbook, 1984* (Paris: UNESCO, 1984).

to occur in the other ASEAN countries in the immediate future in spite of some recent rapid gains made toward a balanced sex ratio at the tertiary levels in Malaysia and Thailand. In general, sex inequality in educational attainment is not yet totally removed, especially at the family level where educational investment decisions have to be made for the children. In Indonesia, Malaysia, and the Philippines, research has revealed a tendency for poorer families to favor boys in the allocation of scarce family resources for education (Mani 1983; Smith and Cheung 1981; Wang 1980).

Underlying this transformation is a subtle shift in the premise of social stratification by education in the region. Clearly, the distribution of primary education has become more equitable across socioeconomic strata. A child from a poor family now stands as much chance of beginning and completing primary education as his well-off counterparts. This equality in access provides a definite avenue of upward mobility for the more able from the lower socioeconomic groups. However, the relevance of inherited social advantages has persisted. Research has shown that family background characteristics remain important determinants in the attainment of post-primary education, especially at the tertiary level (Smith and Cheung 1986). School performance and educational aspiration are also positively associated with family background, giving the well-off an added advantage. In the case of the Philippines, where progression to tertiary level is common, socioeconomic status determines to a large extent the quality of college education received, which in turn is reflected in the ability to be admitted to quality schools. It is therefore not surprising to find that, within a given level of educational attainment, the perceived quality of the school becomes an important determinant of the ease in job search and labor market entry.

A critical problem that has surfaced in the midst of the educational transformation is the dearth of opportunities for the effective utilization of the educated. For example, in Indonesia and the Philippines economic development has not proceeded at a pace that allows adequate absorption of the college-educated. The limited absorptive capacity of the labor market in general will undoubtedly have a dampening effect on the future growth of average educational attainment. On the other hand, as in the case of Singapore, rapid economic growth has resulted in a shortage of highly qualified personnel, thus necessitating programs of expansion of educational opportunities and emphasis on science and technology, as well as intensive efforts in foreign recruitment.

THE RISE OF THE MIDDLE CLASS AND INCOME INEQUALITY

Rapid economic growth is inevitably associated with a diversification and further differentiation of the occupational structure. New occupational roles arise because of emerging societal needs, while traditional roles may become obsolete. Associated with these changes is the broadening of the social mobility process, and perhaps the movement towards equality in the distribution of monetary rewards among the population.

Observers have noted that the pace of diversification and differentiation of the occupational structure in the ASEAN region has quickened only in the past two decades. Prior to that the process had been slow, with the proportion of nonagricultural workers remaining at about the 20 percent level in the agriculture-based countries (Evers 1973). The substantial shift of workers from agricultural to nonagricultural occupations is a product of both industrialization and urbanization. Among the non-agricultural occupations there has been an increase, in proportion as well as in absolute numbers, of administrative, managerial, and professional workers. All the ASEAN countries witnessed a doubling in the number of this group of workers in the decade 1970–80. If these workers can be considered constituents of the middle class then the social stratification in ASEAN countries has indeed witnessed a thickening of the middle layers.

The broadening of the middle class over time has profound social implications. First, the attainment of administrative, managerial, and professional occupations is usually indicative of an open system of social mobility based on educational level and individual merits. The new professionals are therefore markedly different from their older counterparts, who tend to be indigenous aristocrats transferred to modern occupational roles (Evers 1973). The opening-up of the social mobility process to the lower classes is an important structural transformation. While rapid social mobility represents the fulfillment of popular aspirations and raises the sense of well-being in society, it is important to note that social unrest could easily result from the frustration of these aspirations brought about by a slowdown in the rate of economic growth. Second, members of the middle class, partly because of their education and partly because of their access to scarce resources, are prone to external influences on their values and life styles. In a sense, they become social trend-setters and cultural innovators. Their impact on traditional orientations to life should not be underestimated.

The emergence of the middle class does not mean that an equitable distribution of societal rewards and benefits is in effect. Observers have often noted the coexistence of an emerging middle class and a greater inequality in income distribution in some of the ASEAN countries. With the exception of Singapore, the equity performance in ASEAN countries has not kept pace with economic development (Wong and Wong 1984). In the Philippines, income inequality, as measured by the Gini ratio, has shown only a small decline from the early 1960s to the mid-1970s; the Gini ratio dropped from around .50 in the 1960s to .45 in 1975. This slight decline occurred while the Philippine economy was undergoing rapid expansion and growth. In Indonesia and Thailand, the trends show an increase in inequality, with the ratios deteriorating from .35 in 1965 to .41 in 1976 for Indonesia, and from .56 in 1963 to .60 in 1972 for Thailand, although recent evidence in Thailand seems to show that the situation has improved since 1972. In Malaysia, the Gini ratio increased between 1957 and 1970, after which it started on a downward trend (from .50 in 1970 to .44 in 1973) in part because of

the redistribution-oriented New Economic Policy. In Singapore the trend has shown rapid progress toward greater equality; the ratio decreased from .50 in 1966 to .38 in 1977. This is attributable to an industrial economy with nearly full employment over a long period of time.

It should be emphasized that summary measures such as the Gini ratio should be interpreted with great care, because any change in the pattern and trends of income inequality of a country has to be analyzed in the context of its particular structural and institutional characteristics, which in turn provide the source of such inequality. Suffice it to say that for four of the five ASEAN countries considered here the disturbing feature is that income inequality has been reduced slowly or has even increased during the period in which all of these countries have experienced impressive economic growth. The serious implications for their social and political stability, should economic growth slow down for sustained periods in the future, are obvious. It is, however, heartening to note that since the 1970s there has been a growing awareness among the ASEAN governments of the equity issue, and that they have explicitly incorporated the reduction of inequality and poverty as important objectives in their various development plans.

NOTES

1. This paper does not cover Brunei, which joined ASEAN in 1984 as the sixth member, because of the focus on *past* development trends in ASEAN.

2. The increase in average daily caloric intake is largest in Indonesia and the Philippines, where daily intake increased from below 2,000 to around 2,400 between 1965 and 1981. For the same period, the increases for Singapore, Malaysia, and Thailand were also substantial. See Asian Development Bank (1984).

3. For a detailed discussion on the value and cost of children and their effect on fertility decisions, see publications in the seven-volume series *The Value of Children: A Cross-National Study*, published by the East–West Population Institute on various dates between 1975 and 1979.

4. Some estimates are presented in a World Fertility Survey report on family size preferences. See Lightbourne and MacDonald (1982).

5. This is a net enrollment ratio, adjusted for age-grade retardation.

29. RECENT TRENDS IN URBANIZATION

TRINIDAD S. OSTERIA

The six constituent countries of ASEAN (Brunei, Indonesia, Malaysia, the Philippines, Singapore, and Thailand), now a major regional group in Asia, each having different cultural and historical backgrounds, emerged in the post-war period with several common problems associated with urbanization and rural-urban migration. Except for Singapore, these countries are predominantly rural with extremely uneven population distributions. Since the 1960s, the countries of the region have been characterized by rapid population increases as a result of continued declines in mortality rates while fertility levels remained high. The governments of these countries have adopted family planning measures to reduce the high rate of natural increase. With the astounding growth of the population in the post-war era, there was an increasing influx of population into urban areas. As population increase accelerated, the attendant implications of migration to cities and towns attracted the attention of scholars and policy-makers.

Urbanization in the ASEAN region has been characterized by the functional dominance of one great city. However, unlike the Western experience where urbanization was accompanied by industrialization, urbanization in ASEAN countries has not necessarily been attended by a similar process. The ASEAN region's urban areas are better regarded as "subsistence-oriented" with sectoral lags where different economic sectors develop at varying rates. The pattern of uneven development is characterized by a dominant tertiary sector with a large number of marginal occupations exemplified by the presence of hawkers, pedicab drivers, porters, etc.[1] Furthermore, with the exception of Thailand, there has not been a history of significantly rapid urban growth in the other countries of ASEAN. The growth of cities and towns in these countries only accelerated under colonial rule with the pace of urbanization varying from one country to another according to the policies of the European powers.

This paper examines recent trends in urbanization in four selected ASEAN countries — Indonesia, Malaysia, the Philippines and Thailand.

Since the 1950s, there has been considerable interest in the process of urbanization in the ASEAN region. Basic to the focus is the assertion that natural increase has contributed a higher proportion of the total increase of city populations because improved techniques of medical prevention of death have lowered the

Reprinted in abridged form from Trinidad S. Osteria, "Recent Trends in Urbanization in the ASEAN Region", *Southeast Asian Affairs 1987* (Singapore: Institute of Southeast Asian Studies, 1988), pp. 63–82, by permission of the author and the publisher.

mortality rates, particularly the infant mortality rate. The combination of pre-industrial fertility and post-industrial mortality has resulted in high rates of natural increase in contemporary ASEAN cities. However, rural to urban migration also proceeded apace, resulting in a swelling tide of population movements to cities.

SCALE AND PACE OF URBANIZATION IN
SELECTED COUNTRIES OF THE ASEAN REGION

While there has been increasing evidence in recent years of a relatively rapid decline in the rate of population growth in the ASEAN region, variations have been noted from 1.6 per cent

in Indonesia to 2.4 per cent in the Philippines. Except for Indonesia, the present growth rates are considerably higher than the contemporary developing region of the world. Although the population growth rate in Indonesia is the lowest, among ASEAN countries, its population base which is largest results in the largest net addition to population among the four countries. It is estimated, for example, that there will be a net increase in Indonesia's population of 50.7 million between 1980 and 2000 (Table 1).

In all these countries, a marked increase in population was noted particularly between 1950 and 1960 although there are incipient declines in growth rates from 1970 onward.

TABLE 1: Changes in Total Population and the Annual Growth Rate in Four Selected ASEAN Countries, 1950–2000*

Country	Year					
	1950	1960	1970	1980	1990	2000
Indonesia						
Total population (millions)	80.02	109.71	122.21	148.03	173.53	198.69
Growth rate (%)		2.00	2.24	1.92	1.59	1.36	
Malaysia						
Total population (millions)	6.25	8.17	10.86	14.07	17.69	21.27
Growth Rate (%)		2.68	2.85	2.59	2.29	1.84	
Philippines						
Total population (millions)	20.86	28.10	37.54	49.21	62.83	77.04
Growth rate (%)		2.98	2.90	2.71	2.44	2.04	
Thailand						
Total population (millions)	20.97	27.23	36.50	47.06	57.89	68.61
Growth rate (%)		2.61	2.93	2.55	2.07	1.70	

* It should be noted that although these four ASEAN countries conduct their population censuses on a periodic basis, the timing differs from country to country. For this reason, the results of population projections prepared by the United Nations in 1980 were used for comparative purposes. This also applies to Table 2. For instance, the intercensal annual population growth rate from the last two population censuses for each country is as follows: 2.42 per cent for Indonesia (1971–80); 2.32 per cent for Malaysia (1970–80); 2.71 per cent for the Philippines (1975–80); and 2.56 per cent for Thailand (1970–80).

SOURCES: United Nations, *World Population Prospects as Assessed in 1980* (New York, 1981), in N. Ogawa, "Urbanization and Internal Migration in Selected ASEAN Countries. Trends and Prospects", in *Urbanization and Migration in ASEAN Development*, edited by P. Hauser, D. Suits, and N. Ogawa (Hawaii: University of Hawaii Press, 1985).

Urban populations in all four countries grew considerably faster than total population although the differences narrowed from the 1950s to the 1960s and widened thereafter (Table 2). Except for the Philippines, annual growth rates of urban populations in the 1970s for the ASEAN countries were considerably higher than that of the selected developing countries in the United Nations studies. The annual urban growth rates of the four ASEAN countries, which ranged between 4 and 5 per cent, exceeded by a considerable margin an estimated annual growth rate of 3.99 per cent for the developing region estimated by the United Nations for the period 1970–80. These

results indicate an accelerating pace of urbanization in the ASEAN region.[2]

Malaysia. Although the overall level of urbanization in Peninsular Malaysia increased from 20.4 per cent in 1950 to 29.4 per cent in 1980, there were nevertheless considerable variations in the rate and tempo of urbanization among the ten states. Between 1947 and 1957, all ten states with urban areas experienced an increase in the level of urbanization — the largest increase being registered in Pahang followed by Selangor. During the period 1957–80, the tempo of urbanization in all states had slowed down compared with the preceding

TABLE 2: Changes in Urban Population, Annual Growth Rate, and Level of Urbanization in Four Selected ASEAN Countries, 1950-80*

Country	Time Period						
	1950		1960		1970		1980
Indonesia							
Urban population (millions)	9.93		14.25		20.86		29.91
Growth rate (%)		3.68		3.88		3.67	
Urbanization level (%)	12.41		14.59		17.07		20.21
Malaysia							
Urban population (millions)	1.27		2.06		2.93		4.13
Growth rate (%)		4.94		3.59		3.49	
Urbanization level (%)	20.36		25.22		26.97		29.36
Philippines							
Urban population (millions)	5.66		8.51		12.37		17.86
Growth rate (%)		4.17		3.80		3.72	
Urbanization level (%)	27.13		30.30		32.94		36.21
Thailand							
Urban population (millions)	2.20		3.41		4.82		6.76
Growth rate (%)		4.49		3.54		3.44	
Urbanization level (%)	10.43		12.51		13.22		14.37

* These estimates and projections are heavily influenced by definitions of localities and their classification as urban. Although there are pronounced differences among countries in these definitions and classifications, these United Nations results are based on the same definitions and classifications throughout the entire period 1950–2000. For this reason, the numerical values in some cases shown in Table 2 are considerably different from those obtained in population censuses.

SOURCES: United Nations, *Estimates and Projections of Urban, Rural and City Populations, 1950–2025: The 1980 Assessment* (New York, 1982), in Ogawa, op. cit.

intercensal period. However, the Federal Territory, Selangor, and Pahang remained as the three main receiving states and Malacca, Perak, Kelantan, and Kedah, as the four primary out-migration states.[3]

The inflow of migrants into Selangor and Pahang can be traced to two major factors, namely, the rapid economic development of Selangor and the extensive land development programmes undertaken in Pahang.[4] The pull force of Selangor on migrants from neighbouring states like Perak and Negri Sembilan was further enhanced because Kuala Lumpur, the nation's administrative and cultural capital, is situated in Selangor itself aside from the fact that Selangor, being heavily industrialized, provided greater attraction to migrants searching for better employment opportunities.[5]

One of the factors underlying such changes in migratory patterns is Malaysia's urban-biased industrialization efforts that were launched in the early 1970s. Another is the New Economic Policy (since 1970) which resulted in a large number of rural Malays moving to urban areas to take advantage of expanded employment opportunities particularly allocated for them. In fact, the proportion of rural-urban migration among Malays has been rapidly rising in the recent past: 16.4 per cent for 1970–80, and 17.1 per cent for 1975–80. A comparison of urban population growth by ethnic groups indicates conclusively that the Malay urban population increased the fastest among all ethnic groups, constituting about 37 per cent of the urban population in 1980, compared with only 27 per cent in 1970.

The Philippines. Urbanization in the Philippines was not always a continuously even process. At the turn of the century, there were periods of relatively moderate (1903–39), rapid (1939–80) tempos of urbanization as indicated by the growth of both urban and rural populations. While an overall slackening in the tempo of urbanization is noticeable despite the recent pattern of rural-urban transfers of population, urban concentrations none the less

have increased considerably. This is demonstrated by the primacy index measuring urban growth in Metro Manila and the three next largest cities, namely, Cebu, Iloilo, and Bacolod. While the reclassification of urban areas accounted for a significant portion of urban growth (as exhibited in census data) in earlier periods, natural increase later became the most important factor in accounting for urban growth after these re-classifications. As might be expected, migration was also a significant contributory factor to the growth of Metro Manila and other big cities.[6] It is projected that the level of urbanization will be approximately 49 per cent by 2000, a large proportion of which will be the result of rural-urban migration. Furthermore, it is also estimated that 62 per cent of the total urban population or about 16 million people will be concentrated in Metro Manila. This migration type will continue to feature a rise in illegal squatter settlements in the heart of the city as it has in the past.

The Philippines urban population was estimated at 12.4 million in 1980, registering an almost 4 million increase to 8.5 million in 1960. Thus, while the Philippine population was growing annually at a rate of 2.7 per cent, that of the urban sector was almost twice as fast at 3.7 per cent. The increase in urban populations was due not only to high migration rates but also to natural increase in cities because the fertility rates in Philippine cities, though lower than those in the rural areas, nevertheless have remained high. In 1960, 30 per cent of the nation's population were living in urban areas. The percentage increased to 32.9 by 1970 and 36.1 by 1980 indicating that more than 1 in 3 Filipinos now live in urban areas.

Compared with Indonesia and Malaysia, the Philippines has a considerably higher level of urbanization and greater rural-urban mobility. According to the 1970 census, the proportion urban was 31.8 per cent, and the rate of lifetime migration was 24.3 per cent. In the 1950s, the major migration streams were represented by the northward and southward movements from the Visayan regions to Luzon, and to the sparsely settled territories of Mindanao respectively. Throughout the 1960s, however, this pattern of migration gradually changed, and in the early 1970s, there was a substantial decline in the southward movement, whilst the Visayan migration to Luzon became increasingly pronounced. This pattern reflected the effect of industrialization in Metro Manila and its adjacent areas.[7]

Indonesia. The post-independence period witnessed the retention of the features of a dependent economy which marked the years of colonial rule, namely, an emphasis on the export of raw materials and the import of processed goods along with an associated, extremely limited development of secondary industries — a situation that favoured Jakarta's movement towards primate status. In this period there has also been a greater centralization of activities in the national capital. Widespread improvements in transport and communications made possible a much greater degree of centralization of administrative and commercial activity in the national capital. In the first half of the 1970s the city had grown at a rate of 3.25 per cent per annum — more than 80 per cent greater than the overall rate of growth of the national population over the 1971–76 period. Jakarta is now the largest ASEAN city.

A number of trends are noticeable in the urbanization of the country. Since independence, regions have become progressively more urbanized, although the rate at which this has occurred varies both between regions and within regions. Kalimantan has been consistently the most urbanized region from the colonial era until the present. However, the tempo of urbanization in Kalimantan was below the national average until the 1971–76 period. Inner Indonesia has generally been more urbanized than the nation as a whole, although the margin of difference has been progressively reduced as indicated by successive censuses until 1976 when the urban-rural ratio was slightly below the national average. Several centres in Sulawesi

experienced very rapid growth in the 1950s partly due to the influx of refugees fleeing from rebel groups dominating extensive sections of rural Sulawesi.[8] The 1980 Census showed that Jakarta's population has continued to grow at almost twice the national average. The major reason for this is the increased volume of non-permanent migration to the capital from well outside its commuting range. In addition, Jakarta has overspilled its boundaries into the adjoining *kabupaten* (districts) of Bekasi, Tanggerang, and Barong. The overspill and its consequences have required the formation of a new administrative unit with limited municipal powers. The growth of Surabaya and Bandung was reduced somewhat during the 1970s but again inadequacies in definition of urban areas constitute something of a problem.[9] In Indonesia, the rate of natural increase in urban areas is high.

Thailand. Even when an underestimation of the urban population in Thailand is taken into account, the overall level of urbanization in the country remains quite low at less than 25 per cent. Nevertheless, the rate of urban population growth is high. Using designated municipal areas as the equivalent of urban places, the average annual rate of urban population growth between 1960 and 1970 was 3.4 per cent, whereas the rural population grew by 2.6 per cent each year. Between 1970 and 1980, the urban population increased at an average annual rate of 5.3 per cent compared with 2.1 per cent for the rural population. It should be noted that, for both periods, although the urban growth rates exceeded those of rural places, the differentials between the two rates increased. The tempo of urbanization increased from 0.6 for the former period to 3.2 for the latter period.[10]

When the regional variations in the growth of urban population and rate of urbanization are examined for the period between 1970 and 1980, the data show that the average annual growth rate of the urban population exceeded that of the rural population in all regions. Focusing only on the growth of the urban population,

the data indicate clearly that the urban population in the central region as a whole grew much
faster than those of the other three regions.
For the period under study, the average annual
growth rate of the urban population in the
central region was 4.2 per cent, whereas the
other regions grew at rates ranging between
4.3 per cent in the south to 3.3 per cent in the
northeast. When Bangkok is excluded from
the central region, however, the average annual
growth rate of the latter of 2.8 per cent falls
below this range, again showing the capital's
role in suppressing urban growth in its vicinity.

These regional changes are but slight compared with the acceleration in the growth of
the Bangkok metropolitan area. Even given the
redesignation of boundaries, an average annual
urban growth rate for the central region as
a whole of 5.7 per cent is very rapid indeed.
These data confirm the earlier conclusion that
Bangkok dominated the country's urban system
and is responsible for the substantial differences
in urbanization and urban growth between
the central region and the other three regions.
When the metropolis is excluded, there are
only slight regional variations in urban growth
in Thailand.[11]

The growth rate of urban areas has increased,
over the last twenty years, from an average of
3.3 per cent per annum during the 1960–70
intercensal period to 5.2 per cent per annum
during the 1970–80 period. The data also
suggest that the larger towns are growing
faster than the smaller towns. However, this
conclusion needs to be qualified with the pro-
viso that small towns were reclassified and
placed in the larger town category during the
periods under consideration, and that fewer
new towns were created at the lower end of the
hierarchy. Although Bangkok unquestionably
dominates the urban structure in Thailand,
and its growth rate at over 4 per cent per
annum adds in absolute terms each year the
equivalent of about twice the population of
the second largest city in the country, there
is certainly significant urban growth in the
other regions. The provincial centres, once

given realistic urban boundaries, appear to
have been growing very quickly indeed during the 1970s. It is likely that an articulated
urban system is evolving, clearly dominated
by the primate city but serving regional and
local markets with essential services through
a network of urban centres. Accordingly, some
degree of decentralization of administration
and marketing mechanisms may quite possibly
emerge in the future.

Future pace of urbanization. Table 3 presents
the 1980 United Nations projections of urban
population, its annual growth rate, and the level
of urbanization for each of the four ASEAN
countries over the period 1980–2025. The
urban populations of these four countries are
expected to increase steadily. Thailand, which
had the smallest urban population of the four
in 1980, is projected to undergo the largest
relative gain. Having the largest urban population among these countries in 1980, Indonesia
is expected to see an increase of this population
by 4.3 times. Although these four countries
will expand their urban populations continuously, the tempo of growth is expected to differ
considerably. The projected peak of urban
population growth in Indonesia is 3.90 per
cent per annum over the period 1990–95. For
Malaysia, it is 3.88 per cent from 1985 to 1995;
for the Philippines, 3.88 per cent from 1980
to 1985; and for Thailand 4.59 per cent from
1995 to 2000.

The urbanization level is projected to continue to rise in all four countries over the
entire period. The Philippines is now the most
urbanized, and by the year 2025 two out of
three persons are expected to reside in urban
areas. Malaysia, the second most urbanized,
is projected to double its level of urbanization
over the next forty-five years. Indonesia, third
ranked in urbanization, is estimated to have
slightly more than half its population resident
in urban areas by 2025. Thailand, the least
urbanized in this group, is expected to almost
triple its urbanization level over the projected
time period.

TABLE 3: Estimates of Urban Population, Annual Growth Rate, and Level of Urbanization in Four Selected ASEAN Countries, 1980–2025

Country	Time Period									
	1980	1985	1990	1995	2000	2005	2010	2015	2020	2025
Indonesia										
Urban population (millions)	29.91	36.04	43.68	53.09	64.09	76.01	84.45	101.48	114.75	128.26
Growth rate (%)	3.73	3.84	3.90	3.77	3.41	3.03	2.75	2.46	2.23	
Urbanization (%)	20.21	22.44	25.17	28.44	32.25	36.20	40.20	44.20	48.14	51.96
Malaysia										
Urban population (millions)	4.31	4.98	6.05	7.34	8.85	10.46	12.15	13.90	15.63	17.34
Growth rate (%)	3.75	3.88	3.88	3.72	3.36	2.99	2.69	2.35	2.08	
Urbanization (%)	29.36	31.46	34.19	37.58	41.59	45.57	49.47	53.24	56.84	60.25
Philippines										
Urban population (millions)	17.82	21.63	26.16	31.57	37.78	44.24	51.03	57.84	64.65	71.20
Growth rate (%)	3.88	3.80	3.76	3.59	3.16	2.85	2.51	2.23	1.93	
Urbanization (%)	36.21	38.66	41.64	45.12	49.04	52.82	56.44	59.88	63.10	66.11
Thailand										
Urban population (millions)	6.76	8.20	10.10	12.64	15.91	19.62	23.76	28.26	33.10	38.14
Growth rate (%)	3.86	4.17	4.48	4.59	4.19	3.84	3.47	3.16	2.83	
Urbanization (%)	14.37	15.63	17.45	19.93	23.18	26.70	30.44	34.33	38.31	42.32

SOURCES: United Nations, *Estimates and Projections of Urban, Rural and City Populations, 1950–2025: The 1980 Assessment* (New York, 1982), in Ogawa, op. cit.

A cause of concern is the role and scope of regional development plans in each ASEAN country. For instance, Indonesia's regional development plans have already induced noticeable changes in the pattern of migratory flows in recent years. In the Philippines, a set of regional development plans, which were implemented in the 1970s to rectify the migratory stream predominantly into Metropolitan Manila, are expected to gradually attenuate such movements. Malaysia, having a diversified range of regional development plans, has been redistributing the population in both rural and urban areas.[12]

As distinct from the pattern of urban growth in industrialized countries, urban areas in ASEAN contain relatively small modern sectors and rapidly growing urban informal sectors with a rapidly growing population of urban squatters.

NOTES

1. Y.M. Yeung and C.P. Lo, *Changing Southeast Asian Cities: Readings in Urbanization* (Kuala Lumpur: Oxford University Press, 1976), pp. *xvii–xviii.*
2. N. Ogawa, "Urbanization and Internal Migration in Selected ASEAN Countries. Trends and Prospects", in *Urbanization and Migration in ASEAN Development*, edited by P. Hauser, D. Suits, and N. Ogawa (Hawaii: University of Hawaii Press, 1985), pp. 83–104.
3. Ogawa, op. cit.
4. Nor Laily Aziz, "Malaysia: Population and Development", mimeographed (Malaysia: National Family Planning Board 1981).
5. Lai Yew Wah and Tan Siew Ee, "Internal Migration and Economic Development in Malaysia", in *Urbanization and Migration in ASEAN Development*, op. cit., pp. 264–87.
6. E. Pernia, *Urbanization, Population Growth and Economic Development in the Philippines* (Westport, Connecticut and London: Greenwood Press Inc., 1977), p. 209.
7. Ogawa, op. cit.
8. Pauline Millione, "Contemporary Urbanization in Indonesia", in *Changing Southeast Asian Cities*, op. cit., pp. 91–99.
9. United Nations, *Migration, Urbanization, and Development in Indonesia* (1981), pp. 63–66.
10. United Nations, *Migration, Urbanization, and Development in Thailand.*
11. Ibid.
12. Ogawa, op. cit.

30.

CULTURAL COMPONENTS OF THE SEARCH FOR SOCIAL JUSTICE IN ASEAN
A Westerner's View

JOHN E. WALSH

SOCIAL JUSTICE

There are, at least three things that can be said about social justice in general and I would like to enlarge briefly on each of them.

The first is that every society or culture has some concept of social justice. This means only that every society has some way of distributing the benefits and burdens of group life according to criteria which it regards as fair and equitable.

The second is that the essence of social justice, like all other forms of justice, is the exclusion of arbitrariness. As Rawles has already indicated for us, the difference in concept between social justice and social injustice hinges on whether a society's social institutions distribute social benefits and burdens arbitrarily or according to some accepted principle of fairness and equity. According to this analysis, it is simply inconceivable that an arbitrary distribution of benefits and burdens could be considered fair and just.

The third is that the concepts of social justice and of development, contrary to much popular opinion, are not synonymous. As concepts, both social justice and development apply not only to material economic goods and benefits but also to intangible good and benefits — such as prestige, self-respect, and feelings of sharing and good will. However, development is an aggregative concept and social justice is a distributive concept. Development seeks to increase the net or aggregate amount of all goods or benefits of society. Social justice is concerned with making sure that the goods and benefits of society, whatever its stage of development might be, are fairly or equitably distributed. Thus social justice and development differ particularly in their goals or objectives. There is no magnitude of increase of the goods of benefits of a society which in itself guarantees that these goods and benefits will be equitably not arbitrarily — distributed.

IN ASEAN ...

One of the many impressive and distinctive things about ASEAN, from a Westerner's point of view, is that it may be the only regional organization or association that has made a formal commitment to the achieving of social justice at the regional level. Both the ASEAN

Reprinted with slight abridgement from John E. Walsh, *ASEAN Identity, Development and Culture*, edited by R.P. Anand and Purificacion V. Quisumbing (Diliman, Q.C.: University of the Philippines Law Center and East-West Center Culture Learning Institute, 1981), pp. 173–98, by permission of the East-West Center.

Declaration of August 8, 1967 and the Bangkok Declaration of July 31, 1961 refer in their *preambles* to the "cherished ideals of peace, freedom, *social justice* and economic well being". (Italics mine). But it is Article 7 of the Treaty of Amity and Cooperation in Southeast Asia of February 24, 1976 which makes the commitment to the achieving of social justice formal, official and binding among the five states party to the treaty. Article 7 reads in full:

> "The High Contracting Parties, in order to achieve social justice and to raise the standards of living of the peoples of the region, shall intensify economic cooperation. For this purpose, they shall adopt appropriate regional strategies for economic development and mutual assistance."

There may be some question as to how binding in a legal sense this commitment is and as to what remedies would be possible if one or the other parties should default; but it is an unmistakable commitment. The reason for intensifying economic cooperation is to achieve social justice and to raise the standards of living of the peoples of the region. It suggests that achieving social justice and raising the standards of living of the peoples of the region would be either more difficult or impossible if appropriate regional strategies for economic development and mutual assistance are not adopted. As is the case with all treaties, the commitments made in Article 7 of the Treaty of Amity and Cooperation in Southeast Asia are intended to be binding on the states themselves as continuing political and legal entities and not just on the particular governments that entered into the agreements.

A careful reading on Article 7 also leads to a further conclusion. The Article states that economic cooperation in the ASEAN region is to be intensified in order to achieve social justice *and* to raise the standards of living of the peoples of the region. A Treaty is not a philosophical document. It is possible to read into it more than the authors themselves intended. Nevertheless, Article 7 appears to be

saying that the achieving of social justice and the raising of the standards of living of the peoples of the region are two separate and distinct, though no doubt closely related, objectives. ASEAN has committed itself both to social justice and to development on a region-wide basis.

The question might well be asked, "Is it possible at all to speak of ASEAN-wide cultural principles at this time since the ASEAN Agreements are, relatively, of such recent origin?" In my opinion it is not only possible but necessary. Speculatively, it would be hard to imagine how the ASEAN Agreements themselves could have come into force if they had not been based on wide and deep consensuses throughout the region, that is, shared perceptions, values, feelings, aspirations. More importantly, however, The Treaty of Amity and Cooperation itself indicates explicitly that the framers and signatories of the Treaty were well aware of these consensuses. The very first sentence of the *Preamble* to the Treaty declares that the High Contracting Parties are "Conscious of the existing ties of history, geography and culture, which have bound their peoples together".

This is not to say the formal agreements are unnecessary. If, as the author believes they do, they reflect previously existing but perhaps not fully articulated consensuses, they also further strengthen, vivify and expand those consensuses by making them a matter of public record and legal status.

CULTURAL ELEMENTS IN THE ASEAN REGION

The very signing of a treaty, by which the leaders of five independent sovereign nations commit themselves and their countries to a mutual and reciprocal search for social justice, can in itself be seen as an action with dramatic energizing significance.

The attempt here, however, is to seek out the underlying cultural principles that made such a dramatic action possible in the first place. Since people have no way of thinking and acting other than in accordance with their own cultural principles, the same principles that made it possible to reach agreement on a region-wide commitment to the achieving of social justice will determine to a very large extent what the nature of the search for social justice is, what forms it takes, and what distributive practices come to prevail. It should be repeated here that our concern is not with either the substance or process of social justice themselves but with the cultural principles that appear to influence and shape them both. One cannot hope to understand the ASEAN search for social justice unless one first understands the principles that guide that search.

The peoples of ASEAN might themselves word these cultural principles differently and they might well question the grounds on which this or that principle is perceived by this Westerner to be central to the search for social justice in ASEAN. Nonetheless, to him at least, it would appear that the following six components of ways of seeing and doing things are consciously or unconsciously part of the framework of discussions of social justice in ASEAN and part of the framework of discussions of social justice in ASEAN and part of the motivating force for arriving at decisions about policies and programs. These principles are not mutually exclusive and indeed each supports and reinforces the others. The six are: 1. Openness to pluralistic thinking. 2. Desire for autonomy and indigenization. 3. Readiness for development. 4. A tradition of sapiential concern. 5. Collectivistic rather than individualistic orientation. 6. Spirit of cooperation.

OPENNESS TO PLURALISTIC THINKING

Pluralism in this context is taken to mean a recognition and acceptance of the fact that there is a great variety of possible explanations or interpretations of events and a great variety of ways of doing almost everything. The term pluralism is perhaps best understood in contrast to its opposite, namely, exclusivism,

ideology or dogmatism all of which imply that there is only one correct and valid way of seeing and doing things. In these latter systems all answers are to be found not so much by consultation, by experience and examining the facts, by learning from others, and by seeking to accommodate different points of view, but by reference back to some supreme authoritative source.

The point here is that one finds throughout ASEAN an unusually high degree of openness to pluralistic ways of thinking and ways of doing things. The ASEAN documents themselves are steeped in expressions indicating this openness to pluralism — for example, the spirit of equality trust, mutual respect, partnership, cooperation and the rule of law. All of these imply a willingness to compromise or to look to alternative solutions to specific problems. ASEAN as an organization may be seen as one of the fruits of this openness.

DESIRE FOR AUTONOMY AND INDIGENIZATION

The second cultural principle or consensus in ASEAN is the clear desire among the ASEAN political leaders, intellectual leaders, public opinion leaders, and large numbers of people in an walks of life, to manage the affairs of ASEAN by themselves. All of the countries of ASEAN, except Thailand, have been subject to colonial domination and this principle may be seen as a strong negative reaction to the injustices and indignities of colonialism. Having now gained their independence, the ASEAN countries are determined to preserve their autonomy, to withstand any kind of physical, cultural or economic imperialism, and to prove that they are perfectly capable of handling their own concerns in their own way. Coming together in ASEAN is perceived as a way of insuring the largest possible measure of national autonomy within a regional structure and of gaining at the same time the benefits that come from intra-regional cooperation. Autonomy is not seen as the same thing as isolation or protectionism. ASEAN as a whole and the nations within it fully intend, as the etymology of the word autonomy suggests, to play a part in the "making of the laws" not only by which they govern themselves but also those by which they participate in the broader world community.

The desire for indigenization is as strong as the desire for autonomy and the two are, in fact, closely related. Indigenization implies a return to the beginnings or to what was first there as a way of discovering the deeper sources of pride, self respect and identity. Just as autonomy does not necessarily imply isolation, indigenization does not necessarily imply a return to the past. Rather it implies a throwing off of the overlay of alien or foreign elements that prevented the indigenous culture from developing and flourishing in accordance with its own inner dynamics and tendencies.

More specifically in the ASEAN context, indigenization suggests two things: One, the search for and rediscovery of both local and common regional cultural values, and, two, awareness of the fact that ASEAN itself is an indigenous creation.

READINESS FOR DEVELOPMENT TAKE-OFF

If there is any one single characteristic, element of consciousness, cultural principle, or inspiring force more pronounced than the others in the ASEAN region it is a generalized feeling that the region is ready for what is called development take-of. It might well be said that the very existence of ASEAN as an organization is both an indication of and a response to this feeling of readiness.

There is at least three ways of characterizing the cultural principle, here called readiness for development take-off, in ASEAN. The first is the growing attitude that development, even in purely economic terms, is *possible*. No one can say what percentage of the people has this attitude or outlook or how deeply they have it, but it is possible to speculate about the immense amount of psychic and physical energy released by the beginnings of progress and the thought that further progress can be achieved.

The second characteristic of readiness for development take-off in ASEAN is really a part of the overall determination to indigenize. Development in the economic sphere, as in other spheres, is to be what the ASEAN countries want it to be and not what others say it should be. "Trade not Aid" has become an ASEAN catchword. So has the word "Complementarity". Dialogues between the ASEAN community and the European Common Market, Japan, and the United States have been established, with the word *dialogue*, itself, carrying the meaning that economic and trade relationships will be conducted on as a two-way rather than a one-way basis.

The third characteristic of readiness for development take-off is the recognition of development as a holistic or inclusive process.

RESPECT FOR THE SOURCES OF WISDOM

To say that "respect for the sources of wisdom" is an evident cultural principle in ASEAN is not to say that respect for those persons and institutions considered to be the sources of deeper values and meanings is limited to ASEAN. It is only to say that it exists in ASEAN in a remarkably high degree.

If "respect for the sources of wisdom" is indicated by the amount of respect shown for those whose profession it is to show the ways of wisdom, of enlightenment, redemption and salvation, then respect for the sources of wisdom in ASEAN countries is very much in evidence.

If "respect for the sources of wisdom" is also indicated by the amount of respect shown for those members of society who are in the best position to have acquired wisdom, then "respect for the sources of wisdom" is also evidenced by this criterion. Great respect is shown in the ASEAN countries to the aging and the elderly. The underlying assumption appears to be that wisdom is most often acquired through experience and that experience can only be acquired with age. Wisdom is taken to be that intellectual habit or ability which enables people to see things in the light of their ultimate meanings and deeper realities and of knowing how to live as well as how to make a living. The aging are respected because they have survived the many interior and exterior terrors with which the world will have inevitably confronted them and because the younger members of society can benefit from their example and their insights.

COLLECTIVE RATHER THAN
INDIVIDUALISTIC ORIENTATION

The cultural principle that the ASEAN region as a whole is more collectivistically than individualistically oriented has been commented on so often as to need little elaboration here. For example, Soedjatmoko of Indonesia, in speaking of individual rights and collective obligations in Asia, takes the collectivistic orientation of Asian societies for granted and says of them that they are ". . . societies which do not see the degree of individualization achieved in the West either desirable or possible.[1]

Perhaps the most evident explanation for the cultural principle here termed "Collective Group of Societal Orientation" is the relatively high value placed in the ASEAN countries on the extended family. The family is as it were, a primordial social and economic unit based on blood and love relationships as well as common needs. It is therefore almost always the first identified "we" or "us" as contrasted with "them" or "those".

One further word of explanation is necessary. The very stating of this cultural principle as a collectivistic rather than an individualistic orientation is likely to be misleading. It implies a distinction between the individual and society that the people of ASEAN themselves do not recognize. In other words the very distinction between the individual and society can be regarded as a product of Western logic or more broadly of Western culture itself. The question often asked in the West — does the individual exist for society or society for the individual? — could not even rightfully be asked in ASEAN, much less answered.

SPIRIT OF COOPERATION

The final cultural principle to be singled out here can be seen to be closely related to the others and even derived in some way from them. It is the spirit of cooperation. Article I of the Treaty of Amity and Cooperation in Southeast Asia says that "the purpose of this Treaty is to promote perpetual peace, everlasting amity and cooperation among their peoples which would contribute to their strength, solidarity and closer relationship." The Article, in so stating, was recording the fact that a certain degree of the spirit of cooperation was already manifest — witness the treaty itself — and that one purpose of the Association was to further cooperation and specify some of the forms it might take.

The point here is that ASEAN as a regional organization is building on a feeling, outlook, attitude, or "spirit" which is already deeply ingrained in the consciousness of the people of the region. So deep are cooperative tendencies and sentiments that it might almost be said that in ASEAN getting things done is not as important as the way in which they are done. As an organization ASEAN has already shown a marked preference for getting things done by persuasion and through consensus rather than by one side's outvoting the other and thus possibly losing the cooperation necessary to successful completion of the venture.

CONCLUSION

A conclusion that might be drawn from all this is that ASEAN is now undertaking to formulate its own concepts both of what social justice means and of how to go about achieving it.

This is very much in keeping with its cultural principle of autonomy and indigenization. It is also, as has been indicated, something from which other nations and regions may have much to learn.

Given sufficient time and favoring circumstances, a theory of social justice may emerge in ASEAN which is:

Pluralistic in at least two senses: a) It sees both social justice and development as including many more elements than the strictly economic or material ones; and b) It corporates the ideas, needs and values of all persons in the society since, as Abueva puts it, the human being is regarded as an end and not only the means, the subject and not merely the object, an active participant and not merely a spectator.

Indigenous to ASEAN in that it is based on deeply felt, authentic ASEAN values, which above all see the individual not as an atom adrift and alone in the world but as finding his fulfillment in society.

Developmental in that it takes advantage of the rich natural resources of the region as a way of meeting the material needs of all the people. Sufficiency for all, rather than affluence, seems to be the goal.

Wisdom-centered in that it values over quality, over quantity, work over money, human needs and concerns over a de-humanizing technocracy, community service over the storing up of wealth, and the freedom and dignity of the individual over government control and direction.

Collectivistic in that the achieving of social justice comes to be seen as an effort which all economic class, caste, ethnic, or linguistic, religious, or age group share both the benefits and the burdens.

Cooperative in that, as a social function, the achieving of social justice requires the good will, discipline, and sacrifice not of just a few but of all members of society.

What form a distinctively indigenous theory of society or of social justice will take in the ASEAN region depends finally on the thinking and the values, that is, the cultural principles of the peoples themselves. To a westerner it appears that the combination of the six fundamental cultural principles were perceive as prevailing in ASEAN exists in the same way in no other place in the world. As the peoples in the ASEAN region continue their search for social justice in ways that arise organically and integrally from their own cultural principles, they may very well contribute to the better understanding of this never — ending search in other parts of the world as well.

NOTE

1. Soedjatmoko, "Peace, Security and Human Dignity", Background Paper prepared for the Asian Conference on Religion and Peace. Singapore, November 25, 1976. p. 17.

31. CO-OPERATION ON EDUCATION IN ASEAN

UNGKU A. AZIZ

Creating Asean-Mindfulness Through Co-operation on Education

There can be no co-operation without a strong sense of commitment. Commitment begins in the mind. There is a need to strengthen the notion of Asean among all its members. In practice this means that there is a need to sharpen the image of the concept of Asean in the minds of those who play leadership roles in each of the Asean countries. This category of leadership ranges from heads of states, politicians, statesmen, commanders of the armed forces, administrators, entrepreneurs, mass media and creative individuals as well as academicians. Every elite personality in the Asean countries should have not only a clearer concept of Asean and what it does, especially in his own field of interest, but he should also be perceptively motivated towards strengthening regional institutions.

Motivation comes from the mind. More activities will result if those responsible for making public policy and those who think they can influence public opinion are more clearly Asean-minded. A major obstacle to the enhancement of Asean activities in education or in any field is the indifference that exists at many levels.

This paper may be considered a preliminary exercise towards the establishment of an idea in the minds of those concerned with developing regional co-operation on education. While the abstract notion of Asean and its solidarity is a prerequisite for thinking about regional co-operation, the idea can become more influential in the minds of the Asean elite if there are concrete proposals for some form of active collaboration.

There is a need to create a strong sense of Asean-mindfulness especially in the field of regional co-operation on education. The lack of this sense is an obstacle towards effective regional co-operation. The stronger the sense of Asean-mindfulness is, the better will be the regional co-operation on education. It follows, too, that once regional collaboration on education becomes a clear aspect of Asean co-operative activities the more likely it is that there will be a readiness to think seriously about regional co-operation in education.

In exploring the notion of enhancing Asean-mindfulness, it must be realised there is an interacting and cumulative relationship between Asean education and Asean-mindfulness. As teachers at all levels in the respective Asean national educational systems learn more

Reprinted with slight abridgement from Ungku A. Aziz, *ASEAN at the Crossroads*, edited by Noordin Sopiee, Chew Lay See, and Lim Siang Jin (Kuala Lumpur: Institute of Strategic and International Studies, 1987), pp. 395–414, by permission of the author and the publisher.

about Asean and the significance of regional co-operation, then so will administrators, diplomats and statesmen begin to appreciate the advantages of regional co-operation through the rapid and effective realisation of teaching programmes, provision of teaching materials, etc. Although this process may take several years, the first step is to realise that co-operation begins in the minds of the leaders. The motivation for effective co-operation will become stronger as specific projects are designed and successfully carried out.

It would not be out of place to touch briefly on another aspect of Asean-mindfulness. It is this author's belief that it will be stronger when there is a more perceptible feeling of self-reliance. Conversely people may be less serious, if they are over-dependent on others. For example, if people are entirely dependent on donors and a project is wholly financed from a grant from one government or an international foundation, then the national administrators of the project may become excessively concerned with the maintenance of a favourable image with the donors and less concerned with the real impact of the project. When such attitudes have a regional orientation, then all plans and activities are carried out at the level of the lowest common denominator.

TRACES OF CO-OPERATION
IN EDUCATION IN THE PRESENT

Co-operation on education in the Asean region is a well-ploughed area. There is considerable evidence that co-operation has been successful at the governmental as well as non-governmental levels over the last 20 years. While this paper cannot hope to offer an evaluation of the results of such co-operation it can provide a checklist of such efforts together with some description of the reported scope of their respective activities. The full description of each organisation's activities during the past decade together with some analysis of the

financing and, more importantly, the achievements would require on-the-spot investigations in each of the Asean capitals. The empirical evaluation of the reported achievements may require even more resources of manpower, time and finance.

We can begin with an attempt to answer the question: 'Who has been co-operating on education in the region?' The answer can be found in the work of five groups of organisations:

- UN agencies especially Unesco and ACEID;
- Inter-governmental agencies — SEAMEO, RIHED, etc;
- Non-governmental agencies such as ASAIHL, SEACEN etc;
- Educational institutes with a regional scope such as the Asian Institute of Technology (AIT) in Bangkok, Asian Institute of Management (AIM) in Manila and Colombo Plan Staff College for Technician Education (CPSC) in Singapore; and
- Asean's anagramatic committees that range from COST (Committee on Science and Technology) to NGOs like ASCOJA (Asean Council of Japan Alumni) which is composed of senior officials and entrepreneurs from the member countries.

Even the above list may not be comprehensive. No directory of educational institutions in Asean or Southeast Asia appears to have been published recently.

United Nations Agencies

Virtually every UN agency has had some interest in co-operation on education in the region at some time or other. The World Bank has promoted studies and provided financial resources for specific country studies, some of which may be relevant to neighbouring countries in the region. However, this paper will be confined to the work of Unesco in Asean. A fairly comprehensive description is available in a recent book entitled, *Education in Asia and the Pacific — Retrospect: Prospect* by Raja Roy Singh published by Unesco Bangkok in 1986.

The region covered by the Unesco Conference of Ministers of Education and those responsible for Economic Planning in Asia and the Pacific or MINEDAP, is considerably larger than Asean. MINEDAS was established in 1962. Without becoming facetiously involved in acronyms, MINEDAS metamorphosised into MINEDASO, and is currently MINEDAP (Ministers of Education and those responsible for Economic Planning in Asia and the Pacific).

We should be aware of the existence of APEID which is said to be a mode of inter-country co-operation for practical help in education endeavours [Raja Roy Singh, p 13]. APEID has associate centres which are institutes of member states or international bodies of member states . It also has national development groups and promotes regional consultational meetings. In the Unesco regional office, ACEID serves as a catalytic agent for collection, innovation, identifying gaps and growth points in national efforts besides developing educational materials and promoting the educational exchange of media resources.

Inter-Governmental Agencies

SEAMEO. The Southeast Asia Ministers of Education Organisation was established on Nov 30, 1965. The experience of SEAMEO should be of considerable interest to this conference because its membership almost fits the Asean circle. (Additional members are Democratic Kampuchea and the Lao Peoples Democratic Republic). Significantly, its regionally-oriented institutes are good examples of co-operation in education. It also allows for associate membership (Australia, France and New Zealand) and affiliate membership. Besides this, it seeks donations on a global scale.

SEAMEO has seven centres and projects: BIOTROP (Regional Centre for Tropical Biology) in Bogor; INNOTEC (Regional Centre for Educational Innovation and Technology) in Manila;

RECSAM (Regional Centre for Education in Science and Mathematics) in Penang; RELC (Regional Language Centre) in Singapore; SEARCA (Centre for Graduate Studies and Research in Agriculture) in Manila; SPAFA (Project in archaeology and fine arts) in Bangkok; and TROPMED (Tropical Medicine and Public Health Project) in Kuala Lumpur.

A number of regional centres have collaborative institutes in the member countries. They provide research and teaching facilities for personnel from other member countries.

It is useful to study the funding adopted by SEAMEO. During the decade 1971-82, the member countries met 86 per cent of operating funds (in 1981/82 the total was US$54.5 million) and 58 per cent of capital funds totalling US$426.5 million. During the same period international aid provided 49.9 per cent of special funds amounting to US$18.1 million. The donors included CIDA of Canada, DANIDA of Denmark, DAAD of the Federal Republic of Germany, the Netherlands and the US. It is also significant that Asean is listed as providing US$357,000 in this category.

The SEAMEO centre maintains a library and a data base that has materials relevant to education and research in the region. The SEAMEO Educational Development Fund was established as a repository for donations for the support of special fund requirements. It comprises an endowment fund and a fund for immediate use. Both tied or untied contributions are accepted.

RIHED. The Regional Institute of Higher Education and Development, established in 1970, is supported by three governments (Indonesia, Malaysia and Thailand). Singapore has withdrawn its membership. The main source of funds comes from contributions by member governments. If one single institution were to be selected for a detailed case study of its effective impact on higher education in the region as well as its life cycle, RIHED would be the neatest example to be selected. Incidentally, its report on the proceedings of a regional conference entitled 'Regional Co-operation in Advanced Studies in Southeast Asia' (Singapore: Dec 20-22, 1976) is germane to discussions about co-operation on education in Asean.

Non-Governmental Organisations

Co-operation on education by non-governmental organisations deserves some attention.

ASAIHL. The Association of Institutions of Higher Learning in Southeast Asia was founded by the heads of eight state universities in Southeast Asia in Bangkok in 1956. Its purpose is to assist member institutions to strengthen themselves through mutual self-help. It has achieved international distinction in teaching, research and public service. In the region it is the oldest NGO solely concerned with co-operation on education. Membership is limited to recognised universities in the region, that is, the Asean countries with the addition of Hong Kong. Affiliated member universities come from Japan, the US and Australia. Occasionally, ASAIHL receives grants from national or international foundations for the funding of international conferences. ASAIHL's list of publications is an indication of the topics of current concern to the region's top university administrators. The ASAIHL secretariat is located in Bangkok.

Education and Training Institutes

There are a number of specialised institutes which have a regional orientation. Although they may have been set up by Asean member governments as national projects, they accept students or research workers from throughout the region and are able to carry out academic work as well as professional training of a high quality.

- The Asian Institute of Management (AIM) in Manila offers a post-graduate degree in business administration and short-term courses.

- The Asian Institute of Technology (AIT) in Bangkok provides post-graduate training and other courses in engineering technology and computer science.
- The SEACEN Research and Training Centre in Kuala Lumpur provides training in central banking. It has a wide membership which ranges from Nepal to the Philippines. It is administered by a board consisting of the governors of the participating central banks.
- The Colombo Plan Staff College (CPSC) for Technical Education in Singapore was established in April 1974 as a joint co-operative enterprise of 27 member countries including all Asean countries, except Brunei. The college does not only instruct participants in the knowledge and techniques of the relevant field in a formal way but also develops their analytical and problem solving capabilities to help them initiate and carry out improvements in their respective fields of operations. The college has a library, carries out research and provides consultancy services. There is an agreed funding formulae for different type of costs.

Co-operation on Education in Asean

We shall begin by reviewing basic data relating to education in the region as presented in Table 1.

The Asean Declaration of Aug 8, 1967 states, among others, these aims and purposes of Asean:

1. To accelerate the economic growth, social progress and cultural development in the region through joint endeavours in the spirit of equality and partnership in order to strengthen the foundation for a prosperous and peaceful community of Southeast Asian nations;
3. To promote active collaboration and mutual assistance on matters of common

TABLE 1: Asean Population and Education Data

| Country | Population 1986 | Students | | | Education as % of Total Public Expenditure |
		Primary	Secondary	Tertiary	
Brunei	0.2	34,373[a]	18,565[a]	1,192[a]	14.1[c]
Indonesia	168.4	29.27m[b]	8.04m[b]	1.02m[b]	9.4[d]
Malaysia	15.8	2.19m	1.29m	43,258	13.0
Philippines	58.1	8.99m	3.51m	1.59m	12.8
Singapore	2.6	278,060	190,328	39,693	12.5
Thailand	52.8	7.82m	2.24m	379,648	26.2
Total	297.7	48.58m	15.29m	3.07m	—

NOTES: [a] 1984
      [b] 1984/85
      [c] 1982
      [d] 1983

SOURCE: Asia 1987 Yearbook, pp 6-8

interest in the economic, social, cultural, technical, scientific and administrative fields;
4. To provide assistance to each other in the form of training and research facilities in the educational, professional, technical and administrative spheres;
6. To promote Southeast Asian studies.

In the Declaration of Asean Concord (1979) it is stated:

Member states shall vigorously develop an awareness of regional identity and exert all efforts to create a strong Asean community, respected by all and respecting all nations on the basis of mutually advantageous relationships, and in accordance with the principles of self-determination, sovereign equality and non-interference in the internal affairs of nations.

The following programme of action on culture and information was adopted as a framework for Asean co-operation:

1. Introduction of the study of Asean, its member states and their national languages as part of the curricula of schools and other institutions of learning in the member states.
2. Support of Asean scholars, writers, artists and mass media representatives to enable them to play an active role in fostering a sense of regional identity and fellowship.
3. Promotion of Southeast Asian studies through closer collaboration among national institutes.

We should also note Article 8 of the Treaty of Amity and Co-operation in Southeast Asia (Bali, Feb 24, 1976):

The High Contracting Parties shall strive to achieve the closest co-operation on the widest scale and shall seek to provide assistance to one another in the form of training and research facilities in the social, cultural, technical, scientific and administrative fields.

The 12th meeting of Asean foreign ministers in Bali (June 28-30, 1979) had the following to say about co-operation with third countries/international organisations:

The Foreign Ministers commended the Asean experts in education and in population and family planning for the comprehensive Asean education programme and the Asean population and family programme respectively, which are under the Asean-Australia dialogue. The meeting looked forward to the immediate implementation of the projects and activities.

These are clear statements of the intention to co-operate in the field of education. Further study, perhaps at the Asean Secretariat, is needed to compile a list of programmes and projects that have been initiated or successfully completed in the field of education. Similarly, further work is required to identify activities and discussions under Asean sponsorship that have taken place with the aim of co-operating on education.

There has been considerable activity in the formation of NGOs and private organisations in many sectors of commercial, legal or social affairs in Asean. A list of 27 Asean non-governmental private organisations is given below:

1. Asean Tours and Travel Association
2. Asean Motion Picture Producers' Association
3. Asean Inter-Parliamentary Organisation
4. Asean Council of Museums
5. Asean Women Circle of Jakarta
6. Asean Port Authorities Association
7. Asean Council of Petroleum Co-operation
8. Asean College of Surgeons
9. Asean Cardiologists Federation
10. Asean Consumers Protection Agency
11. Asean Steel Community
12. Asean Federation of Jurists
13. Asean Bankers Association
14. Asean Trade Union Council
15. Asean Federation of Women
16. Asean Automotive Federation
17. Asean Paediatric Federation
18. Asean Federation of Accountants
19. Asean Council of Japan Alumni
20. Confederation of Asean Chambers of Commerce and Industry
21. Confederation of Asean Journalists
22. Committee for Asean Youth Co-operation
23. Federation of Asean Shippers' Councils
24. Federation of Asean Shipowners' Associations
25. Federation of Asean Newspaper Publishers
26. Federation of Asean Economics Associations
27. Federation of the Asean Public Information Organisation.

An observer of Asean has commented that almost every time you turn around, so to speak, they form another committee or special group in Asean to deal with some specific subject or problems. And each time one of these new groups is formed, there seems to be a sort of collective sigh and moan of 'oh no, not another one'.

It may be a little harsh and even impolite to suggest that it is an Asian habit, derived perhaps not from the colonial heritage but from the international agencies, to form a committee, task force, study group or work party whenever some thinking or action seems to be needed. It would be natural for Asean members to transfer such habits that appear entrenched in their respective cultures to the communality of action. Hence we have not only a plethora of committees and organisations but these are also bestowed with mellifluous acronyms so much so that one study soon to be needed will be a directory of acronyms in education in Asean.

One useful first step would be to review the work of the committees and organisations that have been established and to terminate those whose results do not seem justified. In a sense, the act of forming such committees and organisations may itself hinder positive results The initiators often stop at that point either because their creative energies are drained in the process or, considering their duty done, they feel they can leave the rest of the task to the experts. The formation of committees should not be a substitute for co-operative action in realising a programme.

AGENDA FOR ACTION

Co-operation on Education to Enhance the Learning Process

In its simplest form, the learning process involves

the transmission of knowledge and intellectual interaction between the teacher and the student. Enhancement is likely to occur if teachers can interact with other teachers in different environments. The learning horizons of students are extended by contact between teachers and students from other environments.

In spite of, or in some instances because of, various 'educating' tendencies, genuine indigenous development of learning emerged in the region during the previous half century. This could only happen when education policy was formulated by the national leaders of the countries in the region and not by the colonial administrators.

Here we are concerned with enhancing the learning process by co-operative activities in education specifically by increasing the qualitative and quantitative flow of learners in the region.

The first step would be to define the areas in which co-operation to enhance academic mobility would be useful and commonly desired. Various forms of academic mobility will be discussed.

The second step would be to create an Asean Education Co-operation Fund (AECF). This fund could be accumulated by agreed annual contributions from the members and its board could be empowered to receive donations from foreign foundations and private enterprises interested in Asean. It would be responsible for meeting all the costs of fellowship schemes described below. The AECF should not only pay for tuition fees, transport and stipends for fellows, it should consider making grants up to an agreed maximum for the pursuit of research projects relevant to Asean development. The fund could be administered by an independent board consisting of six members, one from each Asean nation, appointed for a six-year term. The chairman could be appointed on rotation from among the members. Appointments should be staggered in the first instance so that every two years some members are replaced. No member should serve for two consecutive

terms. The board would be assisted by the Asean Secretariat.

Six forms of academic mobility are suggested: Travelling lectureships, fellowships, student scholarships, student visitorships, conferences and exhibitions.

PEERING INTO THE FUTURE

Short of a nuclear holocaust, it is unlikely that there will be serious future shocks for Asean during the rest of this century. Nevertheless, Asean needs to recover the tempo of development it had before the current global recession by restructuring its respective national economies to meet the trends in the advanced economies. There is no lack of international co-operative activity on education. Some of the co-operative arrangements are as light as spiders' webs while others are powerful networks in every sense of the term. There may be areas where co-operation seems to be lacking simply because no clear targets have been set. There may be other areas where co-operation has been lagging because motivation has been dissipated or energies have been diverted into other lines. Then again there may be a third type of lacunae where certain subjects are not taken up because they are feared by some and the Asean community prefers to decide matters according to *musyawarah* or consensus.

Initially, it may be useful to commission a thorough review of the actual attempts at regional co-operation on education that have taken place since the establishment of Asean. Some of the projects should be studied in depth so that the obstacles and the problems that have arisen could be used as guidelines for programmes to be considered in the future. Although this paper recommends the generation of further studies, it would be difficult for future technocrats to prepare effective programmes and to implement them without empirical data and objective evaluation.

In the meantime, the linkages between

between institutions of higher learning in the region should be further strengthened. New strands should be added to the cables that bind the network together. Every member could designate one participant and all the institutions of higher learning in each country could form their own national network around these participants. Then the process of dissemination or discussion and participation would be smooth and known to all. Each member may consider forming an institute of Asean studies or designate an existing university department or faculty as such an institute. These institutes could be linked to each other through a bureau in the Asean Secretariat. The movement of scholars and students through the region should be encouraged in every possible way. This is a good way to create Asean-mindfulness.

Finally, when co-operation on education is considered to have reached a stage of sufficient maturity, then discussion could be initiated for the enhancement of co-operation in education.

32. ETHNICITY AND RELIGION IN SOCIAL DEVELOPMENT

WANG GUNGWU

Islam is ASEAN's largest religion, though it is not predominant in all six countries. Next are Christianity, Buddhism, and the Chinese religions based on varying mixes of Buddhism, philosophy, and folklore, most notable in Malaysia and Singapore. The noteworthy point is that ASEAN subscribes to religious tolerance, and religion has never been allowed to affect the good relations between its members, in which secular considerations are paramount.

Problems of ethnicity in the ASEAN countries (except for Singapore, where migrant peoples form the majority) derive mainly from two sources: firstly, from migrant minorities (mainly urban-based Chinese and Indian), whose problems have nothing directly to do with religion; and secondly, from territorially based minorities, whose religious differences with the majority peoples have led some of them to challenge the authority and legitimacy of the nation-state, as in the case of the Moslem populations of southern Thailand and the southern Philippines.

With this background in mind, and before considering the political implications of religion and ethnicity in ASEAN, some historical observations are in order.

HISTORICAL PHASES

Recent history in the ASEAN region breaks down broadly into three phases: an external first phase, an internal second phase, and an external third phase, summarized as follows:

1ST PHASE: 1950–65, characterized by reaction against external influence, whether in the form of colonial ideas and institutions or neocolonial interference, and by fear of external subversion, especially communism.

2ND PHASE: 1965 to the late 1970s, which saw a shift of emphasis to issues of internal control, of order, of balancing democracy, and of economic development. During this period, ASEAN countries confidently opened themselves to the world economy.

3RD PHASE: The late 1970s to the mid-1980s, in which there has been renewed concern not only about external factors, especially vulnerability to foreign economic power, but also about threats to indigenous cultural values.

Examining the role of religion through the three phases, it can be observed that:

1. Buddhism in Thailand does not seem to

Reprinted with slight abridgement from Wang Gungwu, *The ASEAN Success Story: Social, Economic and Political Dimensions*, edited by Linda G. Martin (Hawaii: East-West Center, 1987), pp. 40–43, by permission of the author and the publisher.

have been affected by the shifts of emphasis through the phases.

2. Minority Chinese and Indian religions were affected in the second phase by the weakening of direct ties with China and India.

3. Christianity was favored through the first phase but weakened as controls and restrictions were imposed upon its external links.

4. Islam was purposefully controlled if not suppressed by colonial powers until well into the first phase, but was widely revived in the second phase, and the revival was largely generated from within each country. There is some current interest in whether the resurgence of Islam in ASEAN since the late 1970s was externally stimulated by West Asian influences. I believe it was generated initially by political factors within each country; for example, by feelings of neglect and discrimination in Thailand and the Philippines and by the perceived threat from migrant communities in Malaysia. But today it is also a cultural and spiritual response to rapid economic change perceived as threatening traditional values. I also believe that the ASEAN grouping has been a moderating check on the excesses of radical and revolutionary Islam.

ETHNIC IMPLICATIONS

Issues of ethnicity can also be analyzed using the same three phases. If local and territorial ethnic minorities still constitute problems today, they can be managed internally. Migrant minorities, however, and notably the Chinese, certainly went through the first phase as threats to the new nation-states (when there was fear of communist subversion) to the second phase in which they became internally manageable problems for each country. This transition was the case even in Malaysia, whose Chinese minority was the largest in the region. The question is: has the third phase (of renewed concern about their external links) been reached now that China has adopted an open-door policy? Are there fresh external pressures on

the ASEAN minorities of Chinese descent? And the minority question apart, is China an economic threat? Is there cause for alarm?

I would suggest that if there is an economic slowdown—or simply the fear of economic stagnation—then China offers growth opportunities that may provide mutual benefits for both the ASEAN states and China. Moreover, while individual ASEAN countries may be justified in feeling concern, ASEAN as a group need have no fears, partly because ASEAN's economic development is more advanced than China's and partly because ASEAN's ethnic Chinese businessmen seem to prefer to advance their fortunes in their ASEAN homes and with ASEAN's established partners.

All the same, it is worth noting the interesting juxtaposition between ASEAN's containment of Islam in its radical form and as a political force, and ASEAN's resistance to the pull of China (for ethnic Chinese) by acting in concert and gaining diplomatic leverage with China.

POLITICAL IMPLICATIONS

My second main comment is with regard to the political implications of religion and ethnicity. The relationship between religious faith and the power of the modern state seems to vary among countries in ASEAN. For example, in countries that have one clearly dominant faith (as in Thailand, the Philippines, and Indonesia) there has been a trend toward a secular state that acknowledges the diversity of religious groups whether large or small. Such states play down the political role of religion and encourage religions to provide educational services and to support the spiritual life of citizens. The dominant religion is strong, but it is neither dependent on nor does it seek to control the state.

The political implications of ethnicity are bound up in three kinds of rights that apply to the ASEAN states. First, there are traditional rights, which were often taken away by the colonial powers. For different ethnic minorities, they included tributary rights, feudal rights, and special trading-port rights for alien or migrant communities, sometimes accompanied by some kind of extraterritoriality allowing these communities to be governed by their own laws and customs. Such traditional rights evolved over centuries and lasted until the onset of World War II.

The second kind of rights are the new citizenship rights of republican or nationalist states. These are largely legal and political rights and, in theory, are equal and nondiscriminatory. But they are often difficult to implement fairly for minorities, especially in the early stages of nation-building. In the period of modernization, most ASEAN states experienced these difficulties.

The third kind of rights are minority rights, derived more recently from the abstract philosophical idea of "human rights" as a universal phenomenon. Exponents of such rights have sometimes claimed the necessity of international intervention on their behalf, and the resulting debate has had an effect on the question of ethnicity in multicultural societies in many parts of the world.

ASEAN has thus far been successful in projecting an image of growth, security, and confidence. Its existence provides a comparative perspective on ethnic and other rights. Its experience with its members' social, cultural, and political issues has heightened its sensitivity as a group to wider common issues.

33.　THE PRESENT AND FUTURE ROLE OF THE PRESS

JAKOB OETAMA

What are the problems confronting the ASEAN Press? What are the positions, functions and problems of the Press?

Institutions including the press in ASEAN Countries are still in the making. They have to shape themselves. The press system is not exempted from the process.

The population of the 5 ASEAN countries numbers about 250 millions. The circulation of newspapers and magazines is less than 10 millions. It is far below the minimum standard of Unesco, which counts 1 newspaper for every 10 people.

The infrastructure in terms of management, newsprint, printing machines and manpower is still inadequate. The hardware as well as the software is to be developed.

No less interesting is the problem of press freedom. This is of course a perennial issue. For the developing countries, however, it demonstrates specific characteristics.

They all adhere to the notion of a free and responsible press. The degree and the substance might be of different levels. The press system is a part of the political system; when the political system is communist, then the press system will be also a communist one. When it is a democratic or an authoritarian system, the press follows the same patterns.

To which category does the political system in ASEAN countries belong? It is indeed a very complicated and touchy problem. Consistent with the conception of a developing nation, it is fair to assume that the political system in ASEAN countries is subject to development.

The political system is confronted with a number of not always compatible tasks. It should be strong and effective. But it must also be clean and able to provide an opportunity for the participation of the people in the process of government.

Sometimes they face the fact that political institutions among the people are inadequate. It is quite often the case, that with all its weaknesses, the press is called to fulfil a bigger role.

The press is a part of the political system. It is, however, not a passive and subordinated one. It should have its autonomy. It should contribute actively to the development of a democratic political system. The press must enjoy freedom with responsibility. It is sometimes a very delicate position, more complicated than that of the press in the established countries.

A new approach has been introduced on

Reprinted in abridged form from Jakob Oetama, *Cultures in Encounter: Germany and the Southeast Asian Nations. A Documentation of the ASEAN Cultural Week, Tübingen, Summer 1977*, Studies in International Cultural Relations, no. 6, edited by Institute for Cultural Relations Stuttgart (Horst Erdmann Verlag, 1978), pp. 124–30, by permission of the author and the Institut für Auslandsbeziehungen, Stuttgart.

the concept of the freedom of the Press. Some people called it a freedom of the press which is closely related to the press functions. The freedom of the press was perceived as an essential constituent of the so called "Development Journalism".

The new approach has gained more importance from journalists in many developing countries. The same approach has also acquired some sort of recognition by journalists in the Southeast Asian Region.

Coincidentally, a new school of thought has also been developed within the mass communication science. The new school of thought has some resemblance to that of Development Journalism. Experts call it "functional communication", which has a number of basic elements, such as, that communication should be conducted in two ways — from the communicators to the receivers and simultaneously from the receivers to the communicators.

The other element worth mentioning here is that functional communication lays emphasis on the communication process into the society. In other words, the communication process is being used to energize dynamic and creative potentials prevalent in the society. And we all know that the development process requires social dynamic potentials, without which a development would not gain momentum.

Now, we have to probe into the problems facing the Press in this sector. One of the most salient points in this respect is the lack of perspective capability and the right technique on the part of the Press itself to practise development journalism. The Press ability to put development journalism into practice has still to be upgraded.

Practical problems arise as to how the freedom of the press should be executed creatively in the reporting of development events, in seeking and introducing creativeness to society, in developing public opinion conducive to the efforts of improving people's livelihood. So, it is now clear that our problems centre mainly on how to make use of the existing freedom of the press.

The criticism, control and correction towards the government and society should be conducted. However, all these have to be implemented within the framework of providing service to the people, and of implementing development.

I would like to cite one practical topic that should be repeated over and over again, that is the fact that "power tends to corrupt". It has been historically proven that power or authority are prone to being malpractised and misused for self-interest. It is, therefore, quite clear that control and corrective measures are needed. Qualitatively good control and correction would be more effective.

PRESS FUNCTIONS

Let us go further into the details of the functions of the Press. This will become much more evident if we take into account some of the social problems.

ASEAN consists of pluralistic societies. The heterogeneity of the pluralistic societies constitutes a source of national creativeness. But heterogeneity could also harbour social sensitivity. The publicity of a sensitive issue would not necessarily cause conflicts of greater magnitude. Self-restraint is unquestionably needed. On the other hand, the Press should adopt as its main task promoting the process of nation building.

The infrastructure of democracy will grow stronger and firmer if the national building runs smoothly.

The readership in ASEAN countries is also pluralistic. In this context, the Press should function as a forum for exchanges of views, introduction of social leaders. In this way, we could expect to promote mutual understanding among the various social groups and to minimise prejudice which usually goes with the process.

Social infrastructures are decisive in the promotion of democracy. This was proven in the history of west European nations. This was also true in the history of various developing countries.

Included in the list of significant social infrastructures is the people's political awareness. Political awareness implies the consciousness and understanding of one's rights and duties as a citizen. A politically aware person knows and understands the political system and process of his own country. The Press has to contribute to the political socialization.

Ever since Dr. Wilbur Schramm was first assigned by UNESCO to conduct a comprehensive study on communication for development, much has been discovered on the relations between the process of communication and development.

Research has been done. Dr. Daniel Lerner of the Massachusetts Institute of Technology, Boston, conducted similar research and study in the Middle East. I am interested in Lerner's theory on the process of psychological transformation required for development. Lerner used the term "empathy" — the mental ability to project oneself into the role of other people who have progressed further. A farmer projects himself into the picture of another farmer who is much more progressive through the deployment of all improved agricultural methods. The projection helps the farmers to go forward in the role of progressive and effective farmers.

Mass communication through the Press should help the Press to open new horizons and dimensions for the people. The Press is to encourage the process of empathy.

The major underlining aspect of development is to transform the imagination of the people towards the creation of a new role.

Development is generated by the government in developing nations. To reach the stage of self-sustaining growth, the initiatives from above must be responded to by the people. Participation from below is a must. Politically speaking, it means development within the democratic pattern. The Press has to encourage the participation of the people.

Development can be hampered by the government as well as by the social forces in the society. The press should be the watchdog to both sides.

To summarize: a press system functions within the social fabric of a country. The political system in developing nations is subject to development. The goal of the development is prosperity, security, democracy, distributive justice.

The press has to develop into an adequate institution. At the same time, it should play its appropriate role. The essence of its role is to promote the implementation of the common goals of development. It is a necessity that the Press should be autonomous and free to be able to fulfil its appropriate role.

The nation of a free and responsible press, however, is to be perceived within the frame of development.

ECONOMIC CO-OPERATION
STOCKTAKING, ISSUES, AND TRENDS

Introduction

Joseph L.H. Tan

At the Singapore Summit (January 1992), it was clear that there is a strong desire to propel ASEAN forward on the economic front. The future source of ASEAN solidarity and strength is likely to be derived from this "economic bonding" process. Dramatic events particularly in Europe, the Americas and Indochina are also presenting new challenges and opportunities for economic co-operation in ASEAN. From the First ASEAN Summit (Bali, 1976) and the Second ASEAN Summit (Kuala Lumpur, 1977) to the Third ASEAN Summit (Manila, 1987), ASEAN economic co-operation had been evolving at a slow pace. Yet the pace of accumulation of the literature on ASEAN economic co-operation since the establishment of ASEAN in 1967 has been most impressive. The selections in this Section provide a broad view of the "forest", while the next two Sections take the "ASEAN-watchers" closer to the "trees", that is, the various aspects of intra-ASEAN economic co-operation and ASEAN's external economic relations.

This Section consists of eight selections, three of which are "outsiders'" perspectives by non-ASEAN economists, while the remaining five provide a diversity of perspectives of ASEAN economists. The first of these "outsiders", Rolf J. Langhammer, conducts a valuable stocktaking exercise, which applies the theory of international organizations to assess the performance of ASEAN as a regional body of integration and co-operation. Under the criteria of public versus private goods and national versus supranational goods, he draws out various recommendations for changes to ASEAN's policy instruments.

ASEAN economic co-operation becomes the more compelling in light of a rapidly changing international economic environment, including opposing trends of increased globalization and interdependence and heightened protectionism and bilateralism. Given these circumstances, Seiji Naya and Michael G. Plummer proffer a number of major options and imperatives for ASEAN in the 1990s. They conclude by underlining the urgency for ASEAN to improve its intra-regional co-operation programmes, and the need to consolidate itself into a more cohesive "bargaining bloc" in international negotiations.

The third "outsider's" perspective comes from Hal Hill, whose extract was written just before the Third ASEAN Summit in Manila in December 1987. Hill discusses three propositions. First, he argues that progress in ASEAN economic co-operation has not been particularly important in contributing to the group's remarkable economic performance, either individually or collectively. Second, he develops the theme that much scope for increased economic co-operation still exists. Third, although there are measures available which would promote closer ASEAN economic co-operation, Hill cautions against forcing the pace of economic integration (a point which Langhammer and other contributors underscored repeatedly). In addition, he offers two recommendations which have continuing relevance: ASEAN could promote services-led co-operation, with a spin-off for merchandise trade (including shipping and civil aviation services); and ASEAN could pool its resources along with external assistance to create a structural adjustment facility to stimulate the ASEAN economies, individually and as a whole. ASEAN is presently undergoing major internal changes, with its member states implementing policies of economic liberalization, export promotion and greater participation in the international market-place.

The next five selections represent reflections from "ASEAN-insiders", beginning with Florian A. Alburo who poses a number of crucial questions that have enduring relevance beyond the context of the Third ASEAN Summit. Will integration in ASEAN be realized? Can the benefits of integration, as noted in trade theory, be achieved? Will the initiatives around a Preferential Trading Arrangement (PTA) be superior to say, a customs union? These questions guide his reviews of previous attempts at ASEAN economic co-operation, as well as prospects for enhancing it.

Mohamed Ariff's contribution also uses the Third ASEAN Summit as a benchmark, but he provides a somewhat different set of observations. Ariff argues that the long-term vision of ASEAN economic co-operation is unclear, and that regional economic integration might do more harm than good if it renders the group too inward-looking. He argues that (a) the long-term vision of ASEAN economic co-operation is unclear. "The textbook customs union model, the common market framework, and the economic union concept are not necessarily good

for ASEAN. ASEAN is too heterogeneous a group to feel comfortable in any of these standard outfits"; (b) regional economic integration can do more harm than good as it might render the group more inward-looking; (c) the second-best theory clearly indicates that regional economic co-operation is not without a cost and should be regarded as only a means and not an end in itself; (d) ASEAN should continue to liberalize its trade and investment policies and allow market forces to drive the operations of its individual economies.

The next contribution by Narongchai Akrasanee and Somsak Tambunlertchai addresses Mohamed Ariff's concern that market forces operating through the private sector should play a larger role in the economic systems of ASEAN countries. They examine the rationale for closer government-private sector co-operation, and suggest ways to improve the interaction and co-operation between ASEAN governments and the private sector.

Taking a fresh perspective on intra-ASEAN economic co-operation, Mari Pangestu, Hadi Soesastro and Mubariq Ahmad examine various approaches for enhancing such co-operation, including the feasibility of the ASEAN Free Trade Area (AFTA), and the Johor-Singapore-Riau Growth Triangle. They also touch on the need for an ASEAN Economic Treaty.

Finally, John Wong's assessment of the effectiveness of ASEAN as a regional economic grouping provides some cautious lessons for other emerging regional groupings. He discusses two "gaps", one of expectation, and the other in implementation. Even if such gaps can be overcome, Wong cautions that regional economic co-operation in ASEAN or any other regional grouping in the Third World "is destined to be a long and laborious process".

34.   ASEAN ECONOMIC CO-OPERATION
A Political Economy Point of View

ROLF J. LANGHAMMER

A SEAN is standing at a watershed between widening its membership (towards Indo-China) and deepening co-operation and/or integration internally (for example in a defensive reaction to emerging trading blocs in other parts of the world). At the same time, it has to redefine its role as a sub-regional institution in a wider Asia-Pacific grouping.

To decide whether to go various ways simultaneously or not requires a stock-taking of achievements and failures. The theory of international organizations (IOs) offers some clues to assess the output of IOs and their underlying political rationale.

THE RATIONALE FOR FOUNDING AND
OPERATING INTERNATIONAL ORGANIZATIONS:
NATIONS AS INDEPENDENT ACTORS

To start with, the dominant approach in the political economy of IOs is that nations are independent (and selfish) actors and that it is the national benefit and not the grouping's benefit which determines the decision to join a grouping (Olson and Zeckhauser 1966; Sandler 1980; Fratianni and Pattison 1982; Frey 1984, Vaubel 1986).[1]

Second, an IO provides valuable services which are not supplied by the individual nation. Otherwise such services would preferably be offered by the nation state which then would not have to bear costs of compromising. National security is one of such services, access to information on policy positions and reaction patterns of partner countries is another one (Fratianni and Pattison 1982; 1990), collective bargaining power against non-member countries a third one. The more such services are genuinely public and supranational,[2] the more it is likely that the IO enjoys a monopoly. To prevent monopolistic inefficiencies, one needs (1) more competition between different IOs, (2) easier options for exit (that is rules enabling member countries to fully or partially withdraw from the IO), less indivisibilities of output of the IO[3] and more voting rights for member countries which pay more.

Third, large member countries tend to be exploited by small countries which behave like free riders. Again, this may spur inefficiencies. A country, for instance, which pays very little into the common budget but enjoys the same voting right as the large contributor (the UN case) would always be well-advised to opt for the expansion of the budget even if it benefits little from new activities.

Fourth, the smaller the grouping in terms of

Reprinted in abridged form from "ASEAN Economic Co-operation: A Stock-Taking from a Political Economy Point of View", *ASEAN Economic Bulletin* 8, no. 2 (November 1991), pp. 137–50, by permission of the author and the Institute of Southeast Asian Studies.

membership, the more likely it is that the share of the benefits accruing to an individual country to those accruing to the whole IO is large. It decreases with increasing membership because of costs of compromises and decision-making.

Fifth, the "output" of an IO cannot be measured objectively. Let us assume that ASEAN country A, for instance, gives priority to internal trade liberalization (TL) over collective bargaining with third countries (CB) and to CB over regional industrialization (RI), while ASEAN country B gives priority to CB over RI, and to RI over TL, and finally ASEAN country C prefers RI to TL and TL to CB. Then Arrow's impossibility theorem (Arrow 1951, Chapter 111) holds so that it is not possible to define an aggregate output function of ASEAN. Only if preferences of member countries were identical or if a hegemonic power would enforce its preferences, such a function could be derived and the output could be measured.

LESSONS FROM THEORY FOR ASEAN

The fifth theoretical aspect mentioned above is very relevant as it denies direct access to stock-taking of an IO like ASEAN. Given the large differences in resource endowment, size, per capita income level and political heritage, ASEAN countries never had identical preferences. Nor had there been a hegemonic power within ASEAN which enforced its preferences. Fixed contractual arrangements did not exist as the 1967 Bangkok Declaration cannot be understood as such a contract. Instead, ASEAN from its very beginning was based on the principle of voluntary consent without majority rule and without binding contractual commitments.

Given this situation, one could be tempted to measure the performance of ASEAN by using proxies, for instance, its attractiveness for neighbouring countries or simply its survival, or, alternatively, its international reputation. Yet, the latter approach would be confronted with the legitimate question "how can one measure

reputation", and the former would be economically meaningless if ASEAN had not to struggle with other IOs for survival. Indeed, for a long time ASEAN had no other IO as a regional competitor. Yet, in the absence of competition, using growth or survival of ASEAN would mean to use input rather than output as a performance indicator which is a bureaucratic proxy and typical for non-traded government services.

However, over the last decade ASEAN has operated those five services (or measures) mentioned above. At least three of them are instruments of co-operation (the dialogue partner system, the AIPs and the AICs) and only the PTA is a clear trading bloc instrument, that is an instrument of integration. The AIJV is a borderline case as by its nature it aims at co-operation (yet, between private companies not between public authorities). But its incentive primarily relies upon the effectiveness of the only integration instrument, the PTA preference margins.

All measures can be confronted with two questions derived from the theory of IOs. These questions are relevant yardsticks to a stock-taking of ASEAN.

First, and most importantly, did the measures really produce a supranational good or service or only a disguised national one? Would it have been more effective to let the individual ASEAN state do the job for itself? This question leads us to the so-called subsidiarity principle which is most useful for decentralized market economies (as ASEAN countries are). The principle requires that policy-making and regulations should be at the regional level only insofar as it is inappropriate or impossible to implement policies at the national level. Related guidelines of this principle are "home country rule", "country-of-origin principle" and "mutual recognition of national policies"; all principles applied in the EC 1992 programme (see Pelkmans and Sutherland, 1990: 99).

Hence, predominantly it is the nation state which is responsible for policy-making. The less the effectiveness of national policy-making is hampered by policies of a member state, the less there is need to co-ordinate national policies or even to shift responsibility from the national to the regional level (thereby negotiating a common policy).

Secondly, are services provided by ASEAN private or public ones? Would private actors be more efficient producers? Are they hindered, or discriminated against, by public authorities who have an interest to define their tasks as widely as possible in order to justify their drain upon the financial? *A priori*, such questions are more difficult to answer than the first one as the borderline between private and public services cannot be precisely defined (for instance, customs clearance can be managed by a private company as in Indonesia as well by public authorities as in other ASEAN countries).

Without forestalling the analysis, it appears that this question has more relevance for services like information which the various ASEAN committees provide than for the five instruments. To put the question differently, is information — as a result of the committee activities — worth the costs or would private suppliers be able to offer the same amount and quality of information at lower cost?

As a result of stock-taking under these questions, we expect to come to a ranking of ASEAN instruments from genuine public and supranational ones to measures which would have been better left to the private sector. Under the assumption that all ASEAN countries would not have received such over-proportionate records in economic growth without allocative efficiency, it may be hypothesized that ASEAN incurred failures in those instruments which misleadingly were to be shifted to the Community level, though they actually were jobs of national policies. Yet, negative effects on resource allocation could be contained because policy mistakes were pragmatically recognized and Community policies were no longer pursued. Better results are expected for those instruments which truly went beyond national capacities and thus showed a positive value added when ASEAN as a whole took care of them.

ASEAN Policy Instruments in Retrospect: Synopsis and Lessons

A synopsis of ASEAN policy instruments under the criteria of private versus public good and national versus supranational good leads to a clear result. The ASEAN Dialogue Partner System is the only co-operation instrument which provides both a public and supranational good. Thus, it is the only one which conforms with the principle of subsidiarity. All other instruments would have been better implemented by the private sector or by the national public authorities.

Lessons from this synopsis and recommendations for changes could be as follows:

1. The focus should be on co-operation not on integration.
2. Within co-operation, ASEAN should concentrate on truly collective goods which cannot be produced by individual ASEAN states.
3. Top priority is to be given to macroeconomic stability and open market principle in all ASEAN member countries as a co-operation target.
4. One should differentiate between co-operation towards non-member countries and co-operation for ASEAN-internal purposes.
5. Given internal policy constraints, co-operation towards non-member countries (Dialogue Partner System, Asia-Pacific policy consultation and co-ordination) seems easier than internal co-operation which includes all member countries.
6. Sub-regional co-operation is particularly promising (the "growth triangle" or the Singapore-Malaysia and Singapore-Indonesia agreements on water supply are good examples).
7. If integration is politically acceptable, priority should be given to measures towards more factor mobility (lowering costs of capital transactions).
8. ASEAN should establish itself in international fora (for instance, common ASEAN

armed forces under UN supervision; common ASEAN task force for disaster relief) and it should provide more identification symbols for ASEAN citizens.

This list rests on three essential assumptions. First, ASEAN will remain an open and non-discriminatory co-operation agreement. It will not become an integration bloc treating members and non-members unequally by definition. Sub-regional initiatives will gain in importance.

Second, it will continue to rely primarily on the existing institutional framework. Thus, no messy bureaucratic regional body will be established.

Third, it will open its dialogue system more to East Asian economies than in the past. Some ASEAN countries may join newly founded East Asian groupings and this will raise questions of overlapping memberships, trade-offs and need for broader formula compromises.

NEW AREAS OF CO-OPERATION

There are some ideas and priorities which arise from an outsider's view. Broad areas for co-operation will be the following ones:

- to co-ordinate macroeconomic policies and to dismantle restrictions against factor mobility on the one hand, and
- to economize on regionally mobile resources and share the financial burden in large infrastructure projects of common interest on the other hand.

Fields for mutual consultation are medium-term policies which are expected to have a direct or indirect impact upon partner country economies and could cause countervailing reactions, for instance, development planning, fiscal policies, credit market policies, exchange rate regimes and labour legislation. The idea behind consultation is to stabilize expectations through pre-announcement, to rule

out deliberate "beggar-my-neighbour" policies, and not necessarily to come to concerted actions or even policy harmonization. Competition between economic policies of ASEAN countries should not be suppressed by stabilized expectations but established on a more rational basis.

Project-oriented co-operation that is truly supranational and public goods is the second area of action. Environment, energy and education, for instance, are scarce resources which are supranationally mobile. Isolated national policies may produce external costs for other ASEAN member countries as well as for a region as a whole (through excessive pollution, overfishing, outflow of skilled personnel, and energy waste).

To come to grips with such issues which require norms, standards and rules leaves two possibilities open, that is either national treatment (the rules of the importing country apply equally to residents and non-residents) or mutual recognition of national rules subject to common minimum standards. In the latter case, all ASEAN member countries (or those which are affected) negotiate minimum standards to be met in all national regulations. Beyond such standards, each country is free to apply its own tougher standard on its home market. Exports of goods and services based on national regulations which meet the minimum standards are accepted by the partner countries. The EC example provides vast evidence for the importance and the scope of this "mutual recognition" principle. It covers standards of environmental protection, health, safety, security, education (recognition of diplomas), residence and asylum, to list the most important issues only.

The principle which is consistent with market forces is to fix the threshold level of minimum standards as low as possible and to allow for as much competition between national rules as possible.

Finally, common infrastructure projects (energy grids, highways, water conservation, maritime mining) could call for managerial and financial burden-sharing among ASEAN member countries. Likewise, externally-induced changes in the economic environment (protectionism could require common retaliatory actions. The scope of the latter field stretches from agriculture to air transport. The final results of the Uruguay Round will make this field more transparent.

OUTLOOK

A stock-taker is tempted to assess the face value of assets and liabilities prudently, that is to overrate past conflicts and future risks and to underrate past achievements and future prospects. Thus, the balance sheet may contain a number of undisclosed reserves.

When reassessing ASEAN as a trading bloc or as a loose, non-binding co-operation scheme, there is no convincing economic argument saying that ASEAN should move on with institutionalized trade integration the core of which would be the PTA. Clearly, the past has shown that ASEAN countries' trade policies are national jobs and that national authorities proved their capability to do such jobs very efficiently. Except for Singapore and Brunei, ASEAN countries are not free traders but over the years they continuously freed imports and thus lowered implicit taxes on exports.

Given the fact that the dynamics of trade are outside ASEAN rather than within the grouping, there is no reason why the dominance of the national authorities in trade policies should not be continued. The external threat of a possible failure of the Uruguay Round would not bring better economic arguments as ASEAN is too small to retaliate with an FTA even if it could be rapidly implemented.

If trade integration and its deepening is ruled out, integration of factor markets remains as an alternative. Yet, full labour mobility is not acceptable within ASEAN and thus only minimum standards for certain segments of the labour market may be negotiable. With labour-abundant candidates for membership in Indo-China in the offing, ASEAN countries will have to clear their views in this aspect since labour migration is bound to become a worldwide and not only regional issue.

Liberalizing capital transactions has been underlined above as an important incentive for savings mobilization and efficient credit allocation in ASEAN countries in the nineties. While the main part of this policy challenge rests with the national authorities, some common guidelines for timing and sequencing may be discussed on the level of ASEAN ministers.

Beyond that, there doesn't seem to be much scope for institutionalized integration through a legally fixed framework or through deadlines. Legalism in the EC sense has never been a strong point of ASEAN in the past, and is unlikely to be accepted as a guiding principle of integration in future. Traditionally, markets in East and Southeast Asia have become less segmented through market forces (technological improvements, lowered costs of uncertainty and information, declining costs of transportation, lower trade barriers on MFN basis) and not through concerted political actions.

The ongoing discussion on ASEAN as a sub-regional entity in a wider Asia-Pacific context and the question of new — very much poorer — members (or associates) will make institutionalized integration even more unlikely than in the past. Instead, project-specific co-operation which does not necessarily comprise all ASEAN member countries but only those which are definitely interested in concrete across-the-border projects, is expected to become the future backbone of ASEAN.

Such projects should concentrate on human and physical infrastructure, not on industrial planning. The failure of the AIPs and AICs bears witness to the responsibility of national authorities for industrial policy guidance and of the private sector for implementation. There is no ASEAN role to play in industrialization targeting.

Outward co-operation will remain essential not only *vis-à-vis* the OECD countries in the ADPS but increasingly *vis-à-vis* other East Asian countries (or groupings) too. To maintain the ASEAN profile as an open, growth-oriented and macroeconomically stable association is an essential prerequisite for meeting competition with the new emerging groupings. There is no way to substitute regional "actionism" for economic performance of the individual member countries. This is the message conveyed by Latin American groupings. Hence, a stock-taking of ASEAN will always be a stock-taking of individual ASEAN countries and their national achievements.

NOTES

1. Recent modifications of this theory are based on the principal-agent approach. This approach decomposes the relationship between the principal, that is the citizen, and the agent, that is the international organization into four pairs of relations (and vested interests): citizen-governments (within a country); government-national representative to an international organization; national representative-management of an international organization; and finally, management-employees within an international organization. An inquiry into these relations seems particularly useful for contractually-based institutions with a large permanent staff such as the United Nations, the EC, the World Bank and the IMF but not for consensus-driven loose arrangements with little administrative overheads such as ASEAN. See Frey and Gygi (1990) for such modifications.
2. The well-known conditions of public goods (that is non-rivalry and non-excludability) hold and deter private producers from supplying the service. Furthermore, an individual state is unable to provide such services.
3. This would mean that a member state can choose between those services which it likes and those which it does not need.

35. ASEAN ECONOMIC CO-OPERATION
The New International Economic Environment

SEIJI NAYA and MICHAEL G. PLUMMER

While the Association of South East Asian Nations (ASEAN) was founded in response to the threat of communist expansion in Indochina, accords on greater economic co-operation have often been spurred by political considerations. Advocates of greater economic co-operation stress the dynamic gains that could be achieved through greater economic co-operation, and they have criticized the relatively slow pace of intra-regional co-operation without fully understanding the political motivations and constraints. Pessimists argue that greater economic integration is either politically unrealistic or undesirable because of the discriminatory nature implied by an "ASEAN trade bloc". In any event, as the regional political situation stabilizes, the policy agenda will increasingly focus on economic issues. In many ways, ASEAN is at a watershed.

Indeed, a common strategy on domestic economic policy may be a prerequisite to enhancing regional co-operation that will facilitate intra-ASEAN trade and investment liberalization in the future.

The greater internationalization of the ASEAN economies has rendered them more sensitive to changes in international economic policies and trends. Concerns about rising protectionism in developed countries, the increase in bilateral trading blocs, and the outcome of the current Uruguay Round of GATT, have important implications for the economic growth prospects of ASEAN.

The potential for deleterious effects on ASEAN (as well as the rest of the world) of increasing bilateralism in the developed world cannot be ignored. Hopefully, the EC-ASEAN Co-operation Agreement and the ASEAN-EC Economic Dialogues will serve as effective forums for the EC and ASEAN to discuss any observed problems and address any fears of a Fortress Europe.

EC 1992 and the U.S.-Canada Free Trade Area, along with a plethora of proposals for bilateral arrangements in the Pacific which may or may not include ASEAN, have made ASEAN somewhat nervous with respect to its international trade prospects. Recently, ASEAN has been participating in the newly-formed Asia-Pacific Economic Co-operation (APEC) Ministerial group, the offspring of an Australian initiative resulting in a first conference in November 1989. The next meeting was held in July 1990 in Singapore, a testament to the importance of ASEAN in any Asia-Pacific regional forum. Although some in ASEAN were initially concerned that it might be dominated by developed countries and that it could dilute

Reprinted in abridged form from "ASEAN Economic Co-operation in the New International Economic Environment", *ASEAN Economic Bulletin* 7, no. 3 (March 1991), pp. 261–76, by permission of the authors and the Institute of Southeast Asian Studies.

ASEAN economic co-operation, APEC presents an important opportunity for ASEAN to discuss its needs and worries with its most important trading partners, and opens up new potential avenues of co-operation. Moreover, the Pacific Economic Co-operation Conference (PECC), established in 1980, continues to be an important forum for academics, private-sector representatives, and government officials in a private capacity from ASEAN countries to consult, exchange ideas, and undertake joint research with their Asia-Pacific counterparts. Given its "tripartite" structure and unofficial status, PECC complements APEC and serves as an important source of timely and comprehensive information.

ASEAN OPTIONS AND IMPERATIVES

The avenues open to ASEAN in the 1990s to stimulate economic growth through international trade and investment are at least four-fold. First, the most effective, and in the long run the most promising, path to economic development in ASEAN is for all countries to continue to pursue trade and investment liberalization policies at the national level. This route leads to a more competitive and efficient economy, a more equal sharing of the national wealth, and a greater inflow of needed foreign capital and its associated technology transfer. In short, unilateral liberalization of both external and internal sectors will provide for a healthier economy in the long run.

Among the developing countries, the most salient success stories of trade and investment liberalization have been experienced in Asia, and ASEAN is no exception to this. Along with Hong Kong, Singapore has the reputation of being one of the most open economies in the world, and few would disagree that this was the prime impetus to its phenomenal economic success. Thailand's programme of trade and investment liberalization has played a part

in its recent double-digit economic growth performance and has now, along with Malaysia and the NIEs, been labelled a "dynamic Asian economy" (DAE) by the Organization for Economic Co-operation and Development. Through the same means, Malaysia has been able to recover from its commodity-price-induced recession of the mid-1980s by, for example, liberalizing foreign trade and investment and creating a "one-stop investment centre" for foreign investors. Now Indonesia has embarked on an aggressive programme of tariff and non-tariff barrier reductions, financial liberalization and deepening, foreign investment promotion, and freeing of domestic investment. It is currently recording great successes out of its dramatic structural change in the late 1980s. Perhaps the Philippines is the only exception to this trend. Beginning in the early 1980s, the Philippines launched a programme of trade and investment liberalization that was put on hold in the mid-1980s because of the political situation. While there are signs that the Philippines intends to continue its outward-looking trade orientation, many of the same obstacles that have undermined past efforts at liberalization remain. Strong support still remains for an inward-looking, "Filipino-first" policy that has resulted in the Philippines moving from first to perhaps last place in ASEAN.

Moreover, as part of national economic liberalization, the governments of ASEAN should continue to forge a co-operative relationship with the private sector. While there are dangers associated with government-private sector collusion that cannot be ignored, mechanisms are needed in order to understand and evaluate the needs of the private sector as the prime catalyst in economic development, and to maximize its social contributions. This sort of co-operation is already being promoted through the establishment of government-private sector councils throughout ASEAN and through the national Chambers of Commerce and industry clubs in ASEAN.

Second, ASEAN member-states, individually and as a group, should continue to pursue their interests at the current Uruguay Round of GATT. ASEAN and other developing countries have been participating much more intensively at this round than at any other. This is a testament to the new consensus that developing countries will only reach impasses with demands for a "new international economic order"; rather, they should pursue multilateral agreements in partnership with the developed countries in lieu of conflict. We have now entered the "trade-not-aid" era. By aggressively working in the various GATT committees, which cover a wide variety of extremely relevant topics for ASEAN — such as tropical products, intellectual property protection, trade in services, trade-related investment measures, nontariff barriers, and orderly marketing arrangements — the ASEAN countries can ensure more liberalized access to their most important markets. In many ways, the Uruguay Round presents a critical phase in the postwar international trade experience; never has the need to counteract the rise of protectionism and managed trade been greater. Hence, ASEAN needs to safeguard its interests, and as it is even unilaterally liberalizing its markets, it has much to offer at the bargaining table.

Moreover, as already mentioned, by working together as a "bargaining bloc", ASEAN can ensure that its bargaining power will be maximized. Independently, ASEAN countries are small; together, they are a force to be reckoned with. Indeed, ASEAN has not been able to advance effectively its common interests at the Uruguay Round, except in agriculture as part of the Cairns Group.

Third, while ASEAN should continue to press for "first-best" solutions by promoting international trade and investment liberalization ASEAN can supplement this process by expanding more vigorously its intraregional trade and investment links to pool markets and resources and stimulate economic growth. Of course, ASEAN's principal trading partners are and will continue to be outside the region and, hence, it should not seek to isolate itself

through the creation of an inward-looking trading bloc. Such a move would be against its interests due to possible trade diversion and other associated efficiency costs.

One way of increasing trade and investment links is through economic co-operation programmes. As mentioned above, these programmes have thus far not been effective in sewing the economies together. Moreover, discriminatory trading arrangements do have some efficiency costs, making them second-best solutions to multilateral liberalization. Nevertheless, empirical studies (Devan 1987; Imada 1990), as well as theoretical predictions,[1] show that trade liberalization can increase economic efficiency in the region. The EC serves as a shining example of how, under certain conditions, a preferential trading bloc can lead to net economic gains and progress. Of course, intraregional integration will impact negatively on certain sectors in all countries; structural adjustment toward efficiency is never costless. However, winnings should outweigh losses by the definition of greater efficiency, and such transformations are in the long-term interest of the economy.[2] It is likely that the time is not ripe for a free trade area in ASEAN, but current trends in economic liberalization make the potential for such an agreement more logical.

Moreover, as ASEAN becomes more economically integrated through co-operation programmes, it can act more in unison in international negotiations and, hence, can increase its bargaining power. Again, the EC experience is exemplary; in international negotiations, the whole is greater than the sum of the parts.

On the industrial programmes front, much progress can be made toward knitting the ASEAN economies together to increase competitiveness. The AIP programme does not have much of a future for at least two reasons. First, government-to-government projects of this type are generally difficult to negotiate between all ASEAN countries as they tend to maximize bureaucratic interference. Second, to the extent that they compete (or potentially compete) with private sector production, AIPs can be detrimental to private sector development; these projects are inherently inconsistent with the current privatization trend in ASEAN. Nevertheless, the AIC programme and the AIJV programme do have potential as private-sector initiated and implemented projects that take advantage of a regionalized division of labour. As mentioned, the AIC now has two active projects in automobile assembly, and Mercedes Benz and Volvo as well as others, are currently considering applying for AICs. Being itself private sector-oriented and geared to attract foreign investment, the AIC programme can be used as an efficient means of rationalizing production in the region and taking advantage of specific endowments of all countries involved.

However, the AIJV programme has, perhaps, the greatest potential even though its success has been limited. It can be much more flexible in scale, involve fewer countries, and currently has a very attractive foreign ownership scheme. Twenty-one projects have been approved to date, and the Committee of Industry, Minerals, and Energy (the ASEAN permanent committee under whose jurisdiction AIJVs come) has been approving additional AIJVs. Nevertheless, the programme needs to be improved in order to approach its potential.[3]

In addition, greater efforts should be made to integrate the ASEAN trade and industrial programmes. As the PTA and the AIJV both have the goals of pooling regional markets and resources, benefits can be derived by combining the programmes. After all, if the PTA's margin of preference were increased to 90 per cent in any good, a main attraction of the AIJV programme for that category would become redundant.

In short, increasing ASEAN regional economic co-operation can be an effective way of increasing the competitiveness of the ASEAN economies in the international marketplace, as well as providing additional markets for itself. And even though intra-ASEAN trade and investment is relatively small, as these countries develop, the potential for greater intra-industry trade will be added to that of inter-industry exchange.

Fourth, ASEAN can continue to explore economic co-operation agreements with its trading partners, based on the concept of open regionalism, i.e. agreements which do not cement ASEAN into various trade blocs. For example, the U.S. Government and ASEAN are currently exploring this sort of agreement. It was argued that the negotiation of a framework agreement would facilitate flows of direct foreign investment and technology, reduce uncertainty, increase market information, mitigate bureaucratic restrictions, reduce equity restrictions, encourage innovation and technology transfer through the protection of intellectual property rights, and increase export consciousness (Naya et al. 1989). While the negotiation of a U.S.-ASEAN agreement will most likely be relatively modest at first, it is noteworthy that such discussions are taking place and is an indication of the need for a more formal consultative forum. Moreover, such an agreement could be used as a model for agreements with ASEAN's other dialogue partners, and, perhaps, even for an Asia-Pacific agreement.

While economic interdependence has increased greatly in the Asia-Pacific over the past few decades, no forum for consultation has emerged in the Asia-Pacific to deal with the resulting frictions that naturally arise from such a process. Economic interchange has been booming in recent times; means need to be found to mitigate tension arising from increasing interdependence, foster greater co-operation, and stimulate new opportunities. As was mentioned earlier, PECC has been an effective conduit for discussions on regional economic issues between academics, private sector representatives, and government officials in a private capacity. ASEAN, all of whose members are represented in PECC, has been a significant and active participant in PECC-associated activities. But while PECC does present member-governments with important and timely information, it has only indirect government input.

The realization of the need for a formal consultative body at an even higher level has led to the creation of APEC. It is too soon to say which direction APEC will take; the participating countries have necessarily been taking a very cautious approach, as many obstacles need to be skilfully overcome. Essential questions ranging from membership to the type of economic arrangements will have to be dealt with in time.

In any event, there is no question that ASEAN will play a pivotal role in the process, as it has in PECC, and APEC presents an enormous opportunity for ASEAN in terms of both diplomacy and economics. As discussed at length above, the increasing tensions between the powers in the Asia-Pacific, trends toward bilateralism, and protectionism threaten to impede the outward-looking economic development strategies and goals that ASEAN has espoused. A forum to diffuse these tensions would serve to enhance international trade and investment, reduce any threats of a trade war, and make the future more certain.

However, it is not in ASEAN's interest to actively seek the creation of an Asia-Pacific preferential trading bloc to rival the one brewing in Europe. Until last year, the world was essentially split between the East and the West; the dramatic revolutions in the East have laid the ground-work for a new economic order void of divisions marked after World War II. Recently, Eastern Europe has launched efforts to reinvigorate their economies based on a market system and international trade and investment. It would be in no country's interest, ASEAN members included, for the world to be split again into Europe on the one hand and the Asia-Pacific on the other, with the others

left behind. Gains from trade will be maximized through an efficient international division of labour, not a regional one. Markets for exports and sources of investment and imports do exist beyond the confines of the Pacific.

CONCLUSION: ASEAN IN THE NEW INTERNATIONAL ECONOMIC ENVIRONMENT

The ASEAN countries have experienced great changes since the early 1980s. Their outward-looking economic development strategies which are based on economic efficiency and private sector development have been generating significant rewards in terms of economic growth and welfare. The stage has been set for even greater milestones in the 1990s. Indeed, ASEAN is already being labelled the next tier of NIEs.

However, economic prosperity is never guaranteed; ASEAN will have to step up its efforts to safeguard the international institutions and principles that have guided the postwar trend toward freer markets. Increasing economic interdependence, particularly in the Asia-Pacific, has led to greater economic conflicts, which need to be diffused in order to preserve a healthy atmosphere for international trade and investment. Moreover, given its size and stature in the region, ASEAN will need to play a key role in promoting regional endeavours to enhance economic co-operation and consultation.

ASEAN can also improve its intraregional co-operation programmes in order to take better advantage of its own markets and resources. Although progress is being made despite many inherent difficulties, economic co-operation remains at an elementary level. In addition, a more cohesive ASEAN entity would strengthen its position in international and dialogue-partner negotiations and discussions.

NOTES

1. If countries with similar economic structures (homogeneous economies) integrate in, say, a free trade area, the potential for trade creation is greater, and for trade diversion less, than if the economies

had heterogeneous economic structures. This is why empirical studies on the creation of the EC and the First Enlargement (to include the United Kingdom, Denmark and Ireland), each of which involved integration of homogeneous economies, yielded net trade creation (greater efficiency), but studies on the Second Enlargement, which integrated heterogeneous economies (Spain, Greece, and Portugal with the advanced EC 10), generally yield net trade diversion (less efficiency).

2. It is necessary to note that these gains will not necessarily be reaped in the short run, and hence for a given discount rate, it is possible to construe a scenario where integration would yield net losses to some country(ies). However, this point can be made for any trade liberalization programme, and empirical evidence has shown that such programmes do benefit participating countries.

3. For a series of recommendations to improve the AIJV programme, see Driscoll et al. (1990).

36

CHALLENGES IN
ASEAN ECONOMIC CO-OPERATION
An Outsider's Perspective

HAL HILL

Asean economic co-operation encompasses a range of complex, and even delicate issues which are perhaps best left to Asean nationals rather than to outside observers. And I am also mindful of the fact that economists not infrequently dispense hard-headed, politically uncompromising advice to other countries, but recoil from doing so in their own countries where they see much more clearly the political and social obstacles to 'first-best' economic policy advice.

In this paper I propose to advance three propositions:

- Asean has been a remarkable success. Its economic performance has by and large (and until recently) been very good, and Asean has been a particularly cohesive grouping on political and strategic issues and on its economic relations with its major dialogue partners. However, progress in Asean economic co-operation has not been an important contributory factor to the group's success, both within and beyond the region.
- There is enormous scope for increased economic co-operation, and this goal will be achieved most effectively by maintaining the current thrust towards unilateral liberalisation. Such a thrust will not only promote economic recovery in the region, but will also spill over into stronger regional ties.
- There are a good many measures which could be introduced, specifically to encourage closer Asean economic co-operation. However, measures which force the pace of economic integration could prove costly and difficult to implement, and should be approached most cautiously.

ASEAN ECONOMIC CO-OPERATION: RATIONALE AND RECORD

There are at least four reasons why neighbouring countries might wish to forge some kind of regional association. Each reason has been invoked to some extent in the Asean case.

The first is the argument that it makes sense to get on well with one's neighbours. After decades of turmoil this was first and foremost the motive underlying the formation of the European Economic Community (EEC). It was also an important consideration in the 1967 Bangkok Declaration (the second aim being

Reprinted in abridged form from "Challenges in Asean Economic Co-operation: An Outsider's Perspective", in *ASEAN at the Crossroads*, edited by Noordin Sopiee, Chew Lay See, and Lim Siang Jin (Kuala Lumpur: Institute of Strategic and International Studies, 1987), pp. 81–89, by permission of the author and the publisher.

'to promote regional peace and stability'), as it has been in other organisations, most recently including the South Asian association.

The second is the argument that trade creation developing out of closer economic ties will confer substantial economic advantages (through scale economies, etc), and that these benefits will outweigh the costs of trade diversion, which arise because importers may not be able to buy from the cheapest source and exporters to sell at the highest price.

The third reason is based on the belief that regional liberalisation is politically easier than global liberalisation, and is therefore a necessary first step towards the latter goal. A related argument, recently advanced to extend Asean co-operation, is that in an environment of 'shrinking world markets' and of a threatened return to bilateralism, countries have little option but to follow these trends and 'go regional'.

Finally, there is the argument that, for a range of strategic and commercial issues, a regional association — in which member countries are able to subsume individual interests for a common good — will be more effective in international negotiations and forums than each country acting separately. This argument obviously has more relevance the smaller the countries concerned.

I will return to these arguments after briefly examining the Asean record. There is no need here to recount the remarkable economic success of Asean over the last two decades. Until the early 1980s the Asean economies consistently outperformed practically every other developing region in aggregate economic indicators (growth, inflation, etc) in socio-economic progress, and in managing the structural adjustment from primary commodity production to export-oriented manufacturing.

As a political and economic association Asean has without doubt been the most successful in the developing world, rapidly developing as a cohesive organisation in marked contrast to the other attempts at regional association (for instance, the East African association, the Latin American Free Trade Association, the Andean Pact) which have largely failed. Perhaps the most notable Asean successes have been in the political sphere, but Asean has also achieved much in its economic relations with its dialogue partners.

It is in the area of economic co-operation, pursued seriously only after the 1976 Bali Summit, that progress has been a good deal slower. The Preferential Trading Arrangement (PTA) scheme introduced in 1977 appears to have had only limited effect. Intra-regional trade as a percentage of the Asean total has never progressed far beyond 20 per cent. Indeed, in recent years the share has been declining because of falling prices for energy products, which still account for over half of all intra-Asean trade. It is true that successive PTAs have gradually began to bite deeper, but the concessions are still very much at the margin.

Similarly, the Asean Industrial Projects (AIPs) have not progressed as far as originally expected. Only the Indonesian and Malaysian (fertilizer) projects are in operation, and they are not profitable (admittedly in part due to unforeseen external circumstances). The Philippine project (first superphosphate, finally copper fabrication) has never got off the ground, nor has the Thai soda ash plant. Moreover, Singapore's own involvement in the AIPs has been strictly limited and its project (Hepatitis-B vaccine) very small.

Finally, the achievements of the Asean Industrial Complementation (AIC) scheme, designed to encourage private sector participation, have been very modest.

In view of this patchy record, some observers now regard Asean, as a regional association, as being at the crossroads, and they argue that bold new initiatives are required to inject new life into the organisation. The view is reinforced by two additional arguments. First, as noted above, that international markets are shrinking and that there is a return to trading blocs and bilateralism. Second, that to maintain its political clout, Asean must continue to expand its economic underpinnings, including closer co-operation. This is the argument that 'the world will not take Asean seriously unless Asean takes itself seriously' (and by implication forges stronger regional economic ties).

How valid are these arguments? What options does Asean have for closer economic co-operation? I first examine some issues related to these arguments and then consider some concrete proposals for co-operation.

CURRENT ISSUES IN
ASEAN ECONOMIC CO-OPERATION

Several issues need to be addressed in deciding future options for Asean. In this section I will argue the following:

(1) *There is little prospect of a return to the years of rapid growth, but the international economic outlook is perhaps not as gloomy as it is sometime suggested.*

It would be foolish to deny that global economic growth is patchy, and that international trading institutions — themselves impaired by damaging 'exceptions' — are in a precarious state. Nevertheless, the picture is not one of unrelieved gloom.

- While growth is subdued, lower energy prices hold out the prospect of improved OECD (Organisation for Economic Co-operation and Development) growth, and lower interest rates are offering some relief for debt-ridden economies.
- Exchange rate movements in the last 18 months have generally been in the 'right' direction. The massive appreciation of the yen offers new export opportunities for Asean (notwithstanding continued Japanese non-tariff barriers) and may lead to some relocation of Japanese manufacturing capacity. Similarly, the dollar depreciation will hopefully forestall gathering protectionist sentiments in North America.
- The Northeast Asian newly industrialised countries (NICs) (Hong Kong, Korea,

Taiwan) continue to perform very well. This has important implications for Asean. One is the benefits of proximity — new export markets for Asean, some industrial relocation to Asean, and increased services trade. The other is that these countries illustrate that it is not necessary to form economic blocs to succeed.
- Asia's two giants, China and India, are beginning to look outward and to introduce some liberal policy reforms. This development poses great challenges to Asean, as the two countries have a similar range of export specialisations. But there are also greatly expanded commercial opportunities for goods and services exports from Asean.
- Trade in services in the Western Pacific is growing rapidly, and much of this trade is less restricted than goods trade. This is an area in which some of the Asean countries are clearly internationally competitive (eg, tourism, construction, civil aviation, financial services). The Asean countries can also reap the benefits of proximity to the fast-growing Northeast Asian centres, particularly as proximity is a more important determinant of the pattern of services trade than it is of goods trade.

To repeat, these arguments do not detract from the many pressing global economic problems. However, there are important commercial opportunities which the Asean countries can seize only if they continue to look outward.

(2) *There is an urgent need for Asean to act decisively in international trade negotiations and forums in order to keep markets open.*

The Asean economies are more trade-dependent than most developing countries, and these countries therefore have a vital interest in keeping international markets open. As an increasingly influential body in world affairs, Asean should aggressively tackle international trade negotiations to ensure a return — or adherence — to fundamental Gatt (General Agreement on Tariffs and Trade) principles. This is of obvious importance in the case of the Multi-Fibre Agreement and other pernicious schemes which frustrate domestic (Asean) policy reforms aimed at increased efficiency. Asean action could also be significant in relation to market access issues for primary commodities, and in combatting a return to bilateralism among its major trading partners as a means of resolving their trade problems.

This is a clear example where joint Asean action is necessary, for the simple reason that several countries acting together are more powerful than one country. There is also considerable scope for Asean enlisting the support of neighbouring countries where common interests are at stake. Examples include Korea (textiles and other manufactures) and Australia (primary commodities).

There is an inevitable trade-off between international commercial diplomacy aimed at improving market access on the one hand, and steps towards stronger regional ties on the other. Both are extremely demanding of scarce, high-level bureaucratic resources in Asean. Negotiations over the PTA, the AIPs and AIC all proved very time-consuming. If a comprehensive new initiative is envisaged for Asean, it is likely to result in a diminution of Asean's drive for improved international market access, with potentially harmful consequences for its export industries.

(3) *Asean's access to international markets may be adversely affected by stronger regional integration measures.*

Asean's credentials — and its bargaining power — at international negotiations over market access may be weakened to the extent that it closes off its own markets to other trading partners. This was implicit in the statement last year by the United States' Secretary of State, when he asserted that if Asean wanted continued (and improved) access to the United States market it would need to 'keep its own house in order'. Reduced access to major OECD markets for Asean exporters would thus exacerbate the costs of trade diversion of a regional integration programme, even though the initial effects may not be large.

(4) *It is very difficult to reverse major changes in trade policy.*

The experience of many countries, together with the growing literature on the political economy of protection, underline the difficulties of achieving major trade liberalisation once a system of protection is deeply entrenched, even when economic analysis dictates such a change. This proposition is illustrated in the extraordinary obstacles to changing the costly EEC agricultural protection, in Australia's protection of motor vehicles and textiles, and in some of the Asean countries' experiences. The reason, simply, is that a complex network of political interests develops around the protective system, which is very difficult for governments to remove. It is much easier for governments to introduce trade barriers than to remove them.

(5) *It is by no means obvious that the benefits of trade creation in the Asean case would outweigh the costs of trade diversion.*

It is very difficult to determine 'optimum' sizes of regional associations, but in general the larger the proposed area of the union the greater the benefits from trade creation. These benefits arise, especially, from the economics of large-scale production and through intra-industry specialisation. In this context the Asean economies are still 'small' (the total Asean economy is similar in size to the combined Australian and New Zealand total), intra-industry trade within the region is limited and the export structures of most of the economies are largely competitive rather than complementary. For all these reasons the costs of trade diversion implicit in substantial Asean integration are likely to be substantial.

Although concrete measures for a Western Pacific economic union are not under active consideration, if the arguments for some kind of regional association become compelling, Asean ought perhaps to consider a broader, rather than a narrower, regional grouping.

LOOKING TO THE FUTURE

The path ahead for Asean is likely to be considerably more difficult than was the case in the last decade. Just as countries pass through the so-called 'easy phase' of import substitution to a more complex set of industrial policy choices, so has Asean completed the phase of relatively simple concessions. The challenge now is to maintain the momentum of progress, consistent with the same pragmatic orientation which brought past successes. The challenge is all the more difficult in an era of slower growth. Structural reforms inevitably result in some groups being adversely affected. In an era of rapid growth it is much easier to provide compensatory assistance for these groups.

If the political imperative in Asean dictates new initiatives to encourage economic co-operation, but these initiatives fall short of a comprehensive customs union, what measures might be considered? It is difficult for outsiders to proffer advice, but the following suggestions might be worth examining:

Maintaining the momentum for unilateral policy reform. There have been major (and largely unilateral) policy reforms in the Asean countries in recent years. Perhaps the most decisive have been in Indonesia, where a series of important measures — banking reform, a major change in the customs system and several alterations to trade policy — will produce a more outward-looking and competitive economy. Important changes have also occurred in the Philippines, in response to the current economic difficulties and in appreciation of the dangers of an intense politicisation of economic policy-making. Significant developments have also occurred in the other Asean countries.

These changes are important not only because they signal a continuation of Asean's pragmatic approach to economic policy-making,

but also because of the implications for Asean economic co-operation. Reforms which produce more resilient economies are the surest means of promoting Asean's long-term economic interests. These reforms, though unilateral in nature, will also directly lead to greater Asean economic co-operation. This is because of the effects of proximity: Intra-Asean trade is already 'intense', in the sense that regional trade volumes are much greater than would be expected on the basis of each (Asean) country's share of world trade. An expansion of each country's trade will reinforce this regional orientation.

A maintenance of the momentum towards policy reform is important because of the opportunities it provides for the Asean private sector. It is likely that the private sector will play an increasingly dominant role in Asean affairs because the financial capacity of Asean governments is diminished in an era of low commodity prices, because of increased interest in the concept of privatisation, and because over time the Asean private sector is becoming stronger.

Promoting services-led co-operation. There is a strong case for increased emphasis on co-operation in services: As an end in itself, as a means of facilitating goods trade, and perhaps also because it is politically easier. Services is a case where across-the-board liberalisation is likely to lead to stronger Asean co-operation. This is because proximity factors in 'personnel-intensive' service activities are more important in determining services trade patterns than in goods trade.

The range of services amenable to co-operative measures is very large in the case of Asean. Many of these have obvious spin-offs for merchandise trade, including shipping and civil aviation services. Much more extensive educational exchanges could be considered. Labour mobility within Asean is already considerable (although not always legally sanctioned), but perhaps more could be done to permit skilled labour movements, including extended transfers in the public and private sectors.

Financial services are another example where co-operation could be extended.

All these measures would encourage a growing awareness of the region, and open up new commercial opportunities, without imposing the potentially considerable costs of trade diversion measures.

Maintaining existing schemes. Although the current schemes of economic co-operation have not been conspicuously successful, there seems to be a strong case for their maintenance, both for their symbolic importance within and beyond Asean, and for their modest contribution to regional co-operation.

Assisting the process of structural adjustment. All governments seeking to encourage structural change confront powerful vested interests in the industries affected. Whether Asean opts for some form of economic integration, or whether unilateral policy reform is the major priority, there is a strong case for the introduction of facilitating measures to ease the difficulties of adjustment, and to compensate groups adversely affected. This is an area in which Asean could pool its resources to establish a structural adjustment facility, and perhaps in addition seek support from international agencies.

37.
THE ASEAN SUMMIT AND ASEAN ECONOMIC CO-OPERATION

FLORIAN A. ALBURO

THEORY AND TRADITION

The theoretical rationale behind regional economic integration is the notion in trade theory that a partial move towards freer trade improves welfare among the member nations. The removal or reduction of tariffs among the member countries should improve resource allocation and expand markets. In addition, there is a greater scope for improved efficiency if the countries produce similar products. Thus, whether integration is only beginning, such as in the case of a free trade area, or will move along higher forms (for example, a customs union, a common market, or an economic union), freer trade will be beneficial.

In the theory of the second-best, however, we are warned that not every move towards free trade is welfare-improving (Viner 1950; Lipsey 1960). If integration leads to trade diversion away from efficient sources under a nondiscriminatory situation to an inefficient partner source under the integration scheme, then resource misallocation takes place. If this trade diversion outweighs the trade creation, then integration may not be welfare-improving overall.

When the member countries of ASEAN are seen in this regard, it is immediately apparent that the countries are not homogenous economies. Singapore and Brunei have virtually no agriculture sector to speak of and very limited amounts of natural resources. Indonesia is a fairly large country with a size-able domestic market which enables it to reap economies of scale. In terms of trade barriers, Singapore and Brunei have lower tariff walls than the other four countries (Estanislao 1983; Saw Swee-Hock 1980; Ariff and Hill 1985).

The differing levels and paces of development among the ASEAN countries and the disparities in their protective structures and geographic sizes indicate that integration benefits may not accrue uniformly across the countries. And differences in their production structures also suggest that the benefits and efficiencies that can be captured from greater integration will differ.

What this implies is that under an integration setup, whereby the ASEAN countries reduce their protective walls against each other and at the same time retain their individual protection against the rest of the world, the benefits to each member country would not be the same geographically or temporally. In particular, countries that have a high level of

Reprinted with slight abridgement from Florian A. Alburo, "The ASEAN Summit and ASEAN Economic Cooperation", in *Economic Development in East and Southeast Asia: Essays in Honor of Professor Shinichi Ichimura*, edited by Seiji Naya and Akira Takayama (Singapore: Institute of Southeast Asian Asian Studies, and Honolulu: East-West Center, 1990), pp. 300–305, by permission of the author and the publishers.

protection in the first place may benefit more (or earlier) than those with a lower level of protection for example, Indonesia vs. Singapore. Furthermore, liberalization may not be deemed economically efficient in the longer term for infant industries that require protection in the initial stages until economies of scale are allowed to operate. That is, there is a trade-off in the sense that protection can lead to improved efficiency in the long run due to market size. Thus, integration left to itself may not yield a practical and acceptable result.

However, this does not mean that ASEAN attaches no value to integration. Indeed, schemes were put in motion more than a decade ago precisely to begin reducing barriers to intra-ASEAN trade. The countries drew up schedules of products whose existing tariff structures would be gradually reduced. In addition to these measures, specific economic cooperation agreements were entered into to promote economic interaction in ASEAN.

ASEAN EXPERIENCE IN
ECONOMIC INTEGRATION AND COOPERATION

The experience of ASEAN in economic integration and cooperation has been visible in at least two fronts: (1) in the form of direct governmental arrangements along specific economic problems, and (2) through influencing trade direction by altering the tariff structures of privately-traded goods.

ASEAN provides a plethora of symbols of economic cooperation. Thus far, economic cooperation among the ASEAN governments include a food security reserve system that provides an emergency rice reserve, joint programs for eradication of foot and mouth disease, and a training institute in the area of agriculture. There is an ASEAN Swap Arrangement that provides for US$299 million in standby credit for members with balance-of-payments problems. ASEAN also expresses a common stance on international economic issues with regards to the multilateral negotiations under the auspices

of GATT, the European Community (EC), and other international commodity agreements.

In industrial cooperation, ASEAN governments are not short on mechanisms for resource pooling or market sharing. Several upstream projects have been agreed upon, and in some cases have already begun in the different countries. Examples include a fertilizer project in Indonesia, a rock salt-soda ash project in Thailand, and a superphosphate project in the Philippines. However, apart from the visible hand of government in the implementation of these projects, several problems were encountered. For example, under the program on ASEAN Industrial Complementation (AIC), the development of an automotive industry in ASEAN encountered difficulty in product identification and country allocation since government participated in manufacturing location decisions (Chng 1985). Thus, industrial cooperation under these programs were not generally successful in accomplishing the program's goals.

It is perhaps in the area of trade liberalization, or in influencing trade direction, that the greatest achievements and potential of economic integration in ASEAN can be seen. The major mechanism in ASEAN for promoting economic integration is the Preferential Trading Arrangements (PTA). Under the PTA, the ASEAN countries agree to reduce their tariff rates through preferences. From the original margins-of-preference (MOP) of 20 to 25 percent, tariffs were cut further with the MOP being raised to 50 percent. The trade preferences were first established with voluntary offers whereby each country extended regular preferences. This was later expanded to an across-the-board approach whereby automatic preferences were given for certain levels of import values. In subsequent years, the ceiling values for imports receiving preferences were raised from $50,000 to $10 million to open up a stronger basis for integration.

Despite what appeared to be an important vehicle for pushing private trade into regional interaction, the PTA suffered from a host of of problems. First, because of the voluntary nature of the items offered for tariff preferences, products included under the PTA were those of no consequence to ASEAN trade. Thus, despite the increasing number of items that were being listed under PTA, the value of trade that was affected by the PTA was insignificant. Second, the acceptance of across-the-board items for preferences and the switch to increased ceiling values was effectively nullified by allowing member countries to put up an exclusion list for "sensitive" product imports. As a result, the value of items that were excluded from receiving preferences ranged from 2 percent in Singapore to 63 percent in Thailand. Finally, associated with the institution of the PTA is a rules-of-origin requirement, which also effectively limited the scope for increased intra-ASEAN trade as a result of the margins of preferences (Ooi 1981; Chng 1985).

In general, past ASEAN experience indicates that ASEAN has failed to fully capture what theory argues to be the potential benefits of integration. Several reasons can be offered to explain this. First, the institution of the PTA, while meaningful, was not systemic in nature. That is, the Arrangement was set up so that each member government independently decided on the list of items to be included. Moreover, the extent of the preferences for each individual item was not drawn up jointly among all members. Second, there was no clear long-term scenario envisioned for the ASEAN economic front. And third, the explicit economic cooperation efforts were dominated by government intervention and did not actively promote private sector contribution and cooperation.

Nevertheless, this does not mean there were no real achievements to speak of. If anything, work among ASEAN economic committees and discussions and exchange between bureaucrats did help to break down barriers. Indeed, this experience paved the way for the introduction of bold initiatives and a more dynamic vision for ASEAN.

ASEAN SUMMIT ECONOMIC PROPOSALS

The economic proposals that were approved at the ASEAN Summit were formulated by the countries' economic officials. The proposals were drawn from an array of schemes that were suggested by the private sector, ASEAN business groups, and studies commissioned by the different ASEAN economic committees (Naya 1987; Institute of Southeast Asian Studies 1987; Group of Fourteen 1987; Suh 1987).

The proposals ranged from the formation of a customs union to across-the-board increases in the minimum margin of preference for non-agricultural traded products. In the Institute for Southeast Asian Studies Colloquium, a hybrid system that recognizes the existence of varying tariff structures inherent of the ASEAN countries and the differing levels of development among the ASEAN members has been proposed. Under this system, a customs union would be formed among the four countries of Indonesia, Malaysia, the Philippines, and Thailand, and a free trade area would link the union with Singapore and Brunei. By reducing tariffs among the four countries toward some average figure (e.g., Malaysia), intra-ASEAN trade would be promoted. Since the common tariffs would mean a general reduction for the high-tariff countries (Indonesia, the Philippines, and Thailand), trade diversion can be reduced. On the other hand, free trade arrangements with Singapore and Brunei would likewise reduce trade diversion in as much as both countries would maintain their respective tariff levels (Institute of Southeast Asian Studies 1987).

The ASEAN Chambers of Commerce and Industry supported a proposal which urges an "ASEAN Market Liberalization Initiative." In the Initiative, a 50 percent minimum MOP on an across-the-board basis for nonagricultural products is suggested. The exclusion lists would be eliminated, and waivers would be allowed only in emergency cases and where injury is certain in some specific sectors of a country. For agriculture, there would be a continuing product-by-product approach to liberalization (Group of Fourteen 1987).

A study commissioned by the ASEAN Committee on Trade and Tourism (COTT) recommends quantifiable targets to achieve an "ASEAN Trade Area" by the year 2000 (Naya 1987). Under this proposal, 90 percent of total ASEAN trade would be under preferences by the year 2000, there would be a reduction in the exclusion list to 20 percent of import volume, and there would be differential elements for Singapore and Indonesia. The suggestion of differential elements reflects both a practiced principle of "6-X" which has been applied to rules of origin for Indonesia, and an earlier move by Singapore not to participate in the ASEAN Industrial Complementation Schemes (Chng 1985).

Other dimensions of economic cooperation were also given new initiatives. For example, in the ASEAN COTT study, greater cooperation in industrial joint ventures and the establishment of an ASEAN Development Bank were proposed as complementary measures to the reduction in trade barriers (Naya 1987). In the ASEAN Market Liberalization Initiative, strengthening of the ASEAN Industrial Joint Venture (AIJV) program, streamlining of institutional machineries through the consolidation of existing committees and the creation of new ones, and improving the infrastructure for ASEAN trade in transport, education, and financial institutions were suggested as measures supporting the overall move towards ASEAN integration. By and large, however, ASEAN spent its efforts on establishing schemes that directly encouraged greater trade and integration.

In the final analysis, the Summit's economic proposals were drawn from these various alternatives. At the same time, the proposals reflected a clear recognition of the realities of the different individual country polity, culture and level of development. In addition, the proposals took into account what is feasible and what can be achieved with the minimum amount of disturbance to the ASEAN institutional structure.

ASEAN's thrust does not seem to be in the abstract notion of integration or trade preferences, i.e., where general trade barriers are removed and market forces are allowed to determine net trade effects. Rather, the Summit proposal is anchored on strengthening the Preferential Trading Arrangement from where integration will be realized.

Specifically, the proposal entails the following:

First, one of the objectives is to increase the share of trade that is covered by PTA, both in terms of volume and value, by the turn of the century. This objective, while not cast in quantitative terms, nevertheless reflects a schedule and a timetable, and when viewed in the context of the other features that have been proposed, the objective is equally contemplative as a pronouncement for the year 2000.

Second, the Summit envisions a reduction in the exclusion list to 10 percent of traded items (using a standard intra-ASEAN trade classification scheme and integration), and 50 percent of intra-ASEAN trade value. At the same time, the countries will harmonize their exclusion lists.

Third, margins of preferences are to be deepened from its present minimum of 25 percent to 50 percent for those goods enjoying some tariff reduction under the existing PTA.

Fourth, allowance will be made for some countries for differential treatment in the enhancement of PTA. For example, ASEAN has accepted a longer time frame for both Indonesia and the Philippines as to when these countries are expected to achieve their targets. Finally, ASEAN committed itself to a standstill in the imposition of further trade barriers and a rollback in terms of nontariff barriers.

Apart from this major scheme through the PTA, the Summit also approved other supplementary schemes. Recognizing the existence of trade-investment linkages and feedbacks, the Summit also moved to strengthen the AIJV program through specific proposals, including the establishment of an automatic list, MOP on ASEAN-sourced inputs, a 90 percent MOP for AIJV products among participating countries, as well as improvement of economic machineries and other programs.

CONCLUSION

Given the Summit's economic initiatives, will integration in ASEAN be realized? Can the benefits of integration, as noted by trade theory, be achieved? And will the initiatives around PTA be superior to, say, a customs union?

A seriously pursued and strengthened PTA along the lines of the Summit's economic proposal will definitely expand the scope of intra-ASEAN trade. A harmonized and limited exclusion list to the PTA guarantees that exemptions would not be fragmented, even though their identification and determination are subject to negotiations. An agreed-upon depth in the MOP among the ASEAN members will certainly induce efficiencies in import substitution.

The fact that such PTA improvement is proposed to have a five-year schedule will also help to rationalize the incremental phasing-in process. In addition, the approved review process will allow adjustments to the more detailed aspects of the PTA. Further, because the implementation of the PTA is to be spread over time, differential speeds of liberalization for certain countries such as Indonesia and the Philippines is possible and feasible.

In short, increasing MOPs exercised through PTAs are close substitutes to a purely free trade area, and they become even closer the greater the share of intra-ASEAN trade that is affected. This is different from a collective declaration of all six countries as a free trade area or eventually a union. Indeed progressive declines in trade barriers among the ASEAN countries through the PTA will achieve similar integration potentials.

Because of the more systematic nature of the measures, signals to the private sector will be clearer and will provide the private sector and the markets with greater certainty. The increased certainty in the markets will facilitate planning by the private sector. Similarly, a specified schedule and timetable will also give the various governments the parameters needed to design domestic policies and programs in support of the Summit's proposals.

To summarize, the strengthening of the PTA will endow economic benefits to ASEAN in the same manner as indicated in some of the theoretical arrangements under economic integration. This would not of course be superior to a customs union or its primary form, a free trade area.

Yet, the Summit's economic scheme appears most feasible and acceptable and, at the same time, satisfies the character of ASEAN tradition and economic theory. Perhaps what this proposal preserves is much of the ASEAN bureaucracy that has grown over the years. In fact, the proposal can give greater meaning and direction to ASEAN itself. In particular, the various arenas for negotiations will become more focussed. For example, instead of establishing separate exclusion lists, substantive work will be focussed on harmonizing such lists across countries. A review process will proceed throughout the first five years of implementation and can provide a juncture within which the bureaucracy and ASEAN machinery are put to work.

The Summit economic schemes, minus the "free trade," "union," or related jargon, aim at the same integration vision. Only this time, there remains a certain amount of intervention within the frame of reference of much of the existing regional capacities, if not machineries.

38.

THE CHANGING ROLE OF ASEAN IN THE COMING DECADES
Post-Manila-Summit Perspectives

MOHAMED ARIFF

The third ASEAN summit held in Manila on 14–15 December 1987 has helped ASEAN not only to refurbish its image internationally but also to take a hard look at itself. The Manila Summit has acted a launching pad for a number of new initiatives, both political and economic.

The main focus of the Manila Summit was intra-regional economic cooperation especially in the realm of intra-regional trade. Some bold decisions were taken and new directions were charted. The PTA was retained as the principal instrument but significant changes were made to render it more meaningful. First, the exclusion lists of member countries are to be reduced to not more than 10% of the number of traded items and/or 50% of the value of intra-ASEAN trade. Second, new items are to be phased out of the exclusion lists into the PTA with a minimum MOP of 25%. Third, the MOP is deepened to 50% for items already included in the PTA on the basis of an across-the-board concession of 5 percentage points per year or product-by-product concessions. Fourth, the ASEAN content requirement in the Rule of Origin is to be reduced on a case-by-case basis. Fifth, an immediate "standstill" of non-tariff barriers (NTBs) is to be accompanied by a negotiation for a "rollback" of such NTBs.

It is significant to note that ASEAN, for the first time, has set for itself a definite timetable. The above measures are to be implemented over the next 5 years, with annual reviews being undertaken to monitor the progress. It is also important to note that ASEAN is looking beyond the next 5 years and several possibilities of further improvements in the PTA (i.e., smaller exclusion list, deeper MOP, better Rules of Origin and more extensive rollback of NTBs) have already been identified. The accent is clearly on increased transparency and greater predictability of the PTA scheme. The scheme has also been rendered more down-to-earth by accommodating the differences in the tariff levels and development stages of member countries so that some countries can be phased in over a period of time.

The Manila Summit also endorsed ASEAN's commitment not only to increase the flow of foreign investments into the region but also to raise intra-ASEAN investments to at least 10% of total foreign investments by the turn of the century, with manufacturing value added growing at the rate of 8% a year. The AIJV

Excerpted from Mohamed Ariff, "The Changing Role of ASEAN in the Coming Decades: Post-Manila-Summit Perspectives", in *Global Adjustment and the Future of Asian-Pacific Economy*, edited by Miyohei Shinohara and Fu-chen Lo (Tokyo: Institute of Developing Economies, and Kuala Lumpur: Asian and Pacific Development Centre, 1989), pp. 154–73, by permission of the author and the publishers.

scheme has been singled out as the most important vehicle for reaching these goals, with important changes being introduced to render the scheme more flexible, more attractive and more effective by (a) facilitating the establishment of AIJVs through a pre-approved list of products, (b) allowing non-ASEAN equity of up to 60% in AIJV projects (until 31 December 1990) subject to a minimum of 5% equity from each participating ASEAN country and (c) expanding and deepening incentives and privileges under the scheme.

In this regard, it is important to note that MOP for AIJV products is increased from a minimum of 75% to a minimum of 90%. In addition, the waiver period of MOP is extended from 4 years to a maximum of 8 years for the non-participating countries which are unable to give reciprocal MOPs. Besides, an AIJV product is granted local content accredition if it is used as a component in the production of any product in the participating countries which have local content regulations. Furthermore, AIJV products are to be protected by not lowering the participating countries' tariff rates for substitutes for 4 years from the start of commercial operations. Additional protection is to be given in the event of dumping and unfair trade practices from external sources.

Cooperation in the field of banking and finance has also received due attention at the Manila Summit. The private sector initiative to establish the ASEAN Reinsurance Corporation was endorsed by the summit. The corporation, with an authorized capital of US$10 million and a paid-up capital of $3 million, shared equally among the six-country shareholders, is to be set up by mid-1988. Other areas of cooperation underscored by the summit include the use of the intra-ASEAN modes of Double Taxation Convention as a guide in negotiations with third countries for the avoidance of double taxation, the liberalization in the use of ASEAN countries for intra-ASEAN trade and investments and cooperation in the training of ASEAN tax and customs administrators.

Cooperation in the promotion of tourism was also given due emphasis, recognizing the growing importance of tourist trade. In this regard, it is of significance to note that the year 1992, the 25th anniversary of ASEAN, has been declared as "Visit ASEAN Year."

Other areas which were singled out for closer intra-ASEAN cooperation included technology transfers, R&D and manpower training in the development of energy resources and the promotion of shipping links. The ASEAN private sector has been invited to play an active role in the promotion of intra-ASEAN shipping links by setting up a bulk pool system, broken telegraph system, freight booking and cargo consolidation centres, etc.

Regional cooperation in food, agriculture and forestry was given new direction with stronger emphasis being placed on the development of farmers fishermen and lumberers. The private sector, once again, is invited to play an active role in ASEAN undertakings in food, agriculture and forestry.

The summit also reaffirmed the importance of functional cooperation, calling for the wider involvement and increased participation by the people. In this regard, the role of ASEAN Inter-Parliamentary Organization (AIPO) ASEAN affiliated non-governmental organizations (NGOs) and inter-governmental organizations (IGOs) in ASEAN undertakings was underscored. Regional cooperation programmes in science and technology, especially in the fields of biotechnology, material science and microelectronics, are also to be strengthened. The need for Intra-ASEAN cooperation in the development of the potential of women and youth to ensure their maximum involvement in the future development of the region has also been highlighted. Other functional areas, which have been specified for further regional cooperation, include health promotion, drug abuse prevention, environmental management, social welfare programmes and cultural exchanges and, above all, human resource development.

On external relations, new directions given by the summit point towards increased market access, tourism and investment promotion, technology transfers, institutional linkages, and human resource development as areas of interest that should be pursued vigorously in ASEAN's dealings with its dialogue partners. It was also agreed that ASEAN should solicit their support for ASEAN positions in international fora such as the General Agreement on Tariffs and Trade (GATT). The summit also stressed the importance of developing relations with additional third countries, although it was cautious about giving full dialogue partner status to such relations.

It is also interesting that it was agreed in principle to hold summits every 3 to 5 years, and provisions were also made for Joint Ministerial Meeting of Foreign and Economic Ministers as and when necessary. However, ASEAN's organizational structure was left intact, although the need for continued improvement was duly recognized.

CONCLUSION

ASEAN is 20 years old, but its progress in economic cooperation lags behind its achievements in the political arena. Nonetheless, there is no denying that ASEAN countries have grown stronger both as a group and as individual nations over these years. Its very existence was an important factor that has helped member countries to concentrate on economic pursuits. By sticking together ASEAN countries have benefitted in their dealings with third countries.

Intra-regional trade is small, accounting for about 18% of the total, but this is hardly surprising, given the resource and factor endowments of the member countries whose economies are competitive and not complementary. One cannot therefore attribute the low level of intra-ASEAN trade entirely to lack of progress in terms of trade liberalization. This, however, is no argument against trade liberalization. ASEAN will certainly gain from trade liberalization as it will reduce distortions and help allocate resources more efficiently, even if it does not result in increased intra-regional

trade. Low level of intra-regional trade is not necessarily a bad thing. It is in ASEAN's interest to sell its products in a market which is most profitable and to source its imports from a country that is most price-competitive. A higher ratio of intra-ASEAN trade might imply costly trade diversion. As it is not possible to predetermine the optimum level of intra-regional trade, it will be wise for ASEAN to leave it to market forces rather than force the pace. Meanwhile, ASEAN must continue to liberalize its trade regime, preferably on non-preferential basis.

Industrial cooperation has also produced meagre results. Worse still, costly mistakes have been made in the name of industrial cooperation. The two urea projects are now saddled with excess capacity, high costs and heavy debts. Several projects were abandoned after much ado. What was missing in all this was private sector participation which is an important ingredient for successful industrial cooperation. Bureaucratic red tapes and excessive regulations seem to have hindered active private sector participation in industrial cooperation ventures. This calls for a streamlining of ASEAN bureaucracy and policies so as to encourage the private sector to play an active role.

It is in the realm of external relations that ASEAN has scored its highest credits. By staying together, ASEAN has not only put its members on the world map but also helped them get better deals with third countries. The manner in which ASEAN has conducted its external affairs contributed greatly to the emergence of a strong regional identity, unity and solidarity. However, further achievement in this front will depend mainly on ASEAN's ability to demonstrate its cohesiveness and resolve to carry out intra-regional cooperation programmes.

The third summit held in Manila has been described by some as timely, although only a few would dispute that it was extremely overdue. Be that as it may, the Manila Summit was unquestionably a major event in the history of ASEAN. Although no dramatic decisions that would influence the geopolitical and economic environment in the immediate future were taken at the summit, the summit did mark a milestone for regionalism in Southeast Asia.

The main achievement of the Manila Summit lay perhaps in the fact that it did take place at all, amidst so much political and economic uncertainties and enormous security risks. It is no exaggeration to say that ASEAN would have been written off totally, had the Manila Summit been postponed. Surprisingly, the actual summit took no more than 18 minutes, excluding the close-door sessions which lasted about an hour. The short duration, however, is no reflection of the importance of the summit or the seriousness of the deliberations. In fact, the third summit turned out to be most productive in terms of results achieved. ASEAN leaders went to the third summit better prepared than they were for the previous two. Behind the 18 minutes of actual summit lay no less than 18 months of hard homework done by ASEAN officials, businessmen and academics. At the Manila Summit, ASEAN heads of state did not rush into hasty decisions the way they did at the Bali Summit 11 years earlier.

The decisions to widen the coverage of PTA, deepen the tariff cuts, freeze the non-tariff barriers with a commitment for an eventual rollback and minimize the exclusion list were all bold in no uncertain terms. These measures may not produce immediate results in terms of a higher ratio of intra-regional trade, but will help reduce distortions and pave the way for a better resource allocation. As argued earlier, a high ratio of intra-regional trade in ASEAN's trade matrix may not be in the interest of ASEAN. Trade liberalization measures taken without setting rigid intra-ASEAN trade targets are therefore wise decisions in the direct direction. The success of the new PTA will, however, hinge critically on the progress in dismantling NTBs.

The contribution of the Manila Summit to the promotion of regional industrial cooperation also appears to be significant and pragmatic. The decisions to minimize government involvements

and maximize private sector participation seem particularly appropriate, based on the previous experience. The liberalization of the AIJV scheme with respect to equity participation and increased incentives in terms of margin of preferences all augur well for regional industrial cooperation. However, the concept of pre-approved list, which is intended to facilitate AIJVs, can be a drag. Much will depend on the contents of the list. It would be better if the private sector is allowed to nominate projects for approval, in addition to those that are pre-approved. That the AIJV scheme now requires just the participation of a minimum of two countries and only for participating countries to extend tariff preferences among themselves has no doubt rendered the scheme easier to implement. But, the danger is that regional cooperation may degenerate into mere sub-regional cooperation, unless all members are involved in one way or another in a criss-cross fashion. Something ought to be done to encourage wider participation.

New proposals announced at the Manila Summit are indeed laudable. On paper, at least, they appear sound and promising. It is one thing to make decisions and quite another to have them implemented. Much will therefore depend on the pace of follow-up actions by the governments and the extent of collaboration between the governments and the private sector.

By going ahead with the Manila Summit and by announcing the new proposals for closer regional economic cooperation, ASEAN leaders have demonstrated to the world that they mean business. The world is once again beginning to take a serious view of ASEAN. The Manila Summit has thus given a boost to ASEAN's external relations. In the years to come, ASEAN is likely to put greater emphasis on multilateral solutions to gain greater market access than it has done in the past. ASEAN seems poised to play an active role in the Uruguay Round of trade negotiations and to solicit the support of like-minded nations on several issues. This, however, does not mean that ASEAN will de-emphasize the bilateral approach. The existing format for bilateral relations with dialogue partners will probably be kept with minimum changes, as it has proved adequate in the past. Nonetheless, the private sector will be drawn increasingly into the dialogue sessions. ASEAN is not keen to extend the network of dialogue partners, although it is willing to hold talks with other countries without granting formal dialogue partner status. Internationally, ASEAN will keep a rather low, albeit active, profile, as it has neither the political leverage nor the economic clout to make it a major player in the international arena.

What is particularly disappointing about the third summit is that nothing was done about ASEAN's organizational structure, although it was agreed that it should be continually improved and that the ASEAN Standing Committee will review the structure. It is no secret that ASEAN's present regional secretariat at Jakarta is poorly manned. The Secretariat has been denied the muscles it needs in order to produce tangible results. It is clear that ASEAN members are not ready to change the basic structure of the grouping. Further expansion of the membership is not likely in the foreseeable future, although Burma and the Indochinese states are potential candidates in the geographical sense. It is significant to note Papua New Guinea was given an observer status in the Manila Summit. Similar overtures to other countries outside the region cannot be ruled out.

ASEAN heads of states are likely to meet more often than they had in the past. That they have met only 3 times during the past 20 years speaks poorly of the grouping. It was agreed in Manila that ASEAN summits will be held every 3 to 5 years, although "if necessary" caveat was thrown in. Ministerial meetings are likely to be held at more frequent intervals than was the case before.

All these notwithstanding, the long-term vision is still unclear. The textbook customs union model, the common market framework, and the economic union concept are not necessarily good for ASEAN. ASEAN is too heterogeneous a group to feel comfortable in any of these standard outfits. ASEAN member countries are of different size and at different stages of economic development. The only common denominator in this regard is that they are all market economies with a strong export orientation. Regional economic "integration" can do more harm than good as it might render the group more inward-looking. After all, regional economic cooperation is only a means and not an end in itself. The second-best theory will tell us that regional economic cooperation is not costless. And, cost might vary with the degree of regional integration aimed at. ASEAN may therefore be advised that it should continue to liberalize its trade and investment regimes and allow the market forces a freer hand to shape up things.

39.

GOVERNMENT AND PRIVATE SECTOR RELATIONS IN ASEAN ECONOMIC CO-OPERATION

NARONGCHAI AKRASANEE and SOMSAK TAMBUNLERTCHAI

INTRODUCTION

As was the common practice in the formation of almost all regional organizations, the establishment in 1967 of the Association of Southeast Asian Nations (ASEAN) was taken at the initiative of the government rather than the private sector. Consequently, the government played a very large role in shaping the policies and framework for regional cooperation in the early years of ASEAN's existence. For example, in industrial cooperation, the ASEAN Industrial Project (AIP) was largely confined to the participation of the member governments. The private sector was hardly involved at all. Not surprisingly, the AIP scheme was not successful. Subsequently ASEAN realized the need for private sector participation, resulting in the planning and implementation of the ASEAN Industrial Complementation (AIC) and ASEAN Industrial Joint Venture (AIJV) schemes. In recent years, the private sector has been increasingly drawn into ASEAN's various regional cooperation schemes, and the prospects for enhancing such cooperation look promising. The major objective of this paper is to discuss the rationale for closer government-private

sector cooperation within the framework of ASEAN regional cooperation, the institutional framework and development of such cooperation and, finally, recommendations for improving ASEAN government and private sector cooperation.

In the past, several governments in the region tended to ignore the private sector when they were formulating or implementing various development projects. They felt that they knew what was best for the country and that they had the mandate to develop the country as rapidly as possible. The private sector was generally regarded only as a source of tax revenue and not as a partner in development. Some governments were reluctant to share the decision-making process with the private sector or did not trust the private sector sufficiently to make them privy to government decisions or policies. At most, governments paid lip service to the need for cooperation with the private sector but generally ignored the potentially significant role which the private sector could play.

Over time, however, governments began to realize that without the cooperation of the

Reprinted in abridged form from "Enhancing Cooperation between the Government and the Private Sector within the Framework of ASEAN Industrial Cooperation", *Development and South-South Cooperation* 5, no. 9 (December 1989), pp. 115–30, by permission of the authors and the Centre for International Cooperation and Development, Slovenia.

private sector, attainment of economic development objectives would be difficult. At the same time, as economists learned more of the development experience of several successful countries such as Japan and the Republic of Korea, they became convinced of the need for closer government and private sector cooperation and that such cooperation is an important ingredient in the successful implementation of government projects and the efficient operation of private enterprises. Countries that have ignored the imperative for closer cooperation have failed to make much headway in their development efforts. Consequently, there has been a clear trend towards enhanced government and private sector cooperation in many countries.

In addition to the recognition of the link between private sector-based development and economic growth, the slowdown in international trade in the 1980s and growing protectionism in developed countries encouraged governments in several countries to look towards the private sector to stimulate growth and search for new sources of exports. Experiences with government monopolized projects and enterprises have generated frequent disappointment, and such projects have ended in deficit, delay, and unsatisfactory performances. At a time when many developing countries are adopting an export-oriented development strategy and as the world economic environment changes rapidly, prompt reaction to the evolving competitive environment is the key element to ensure successful export development. Government enterprises are generally ill-suited to produce for the highly competitive export market as they generally produce for a local and heavily protected market. Thus, in times of strong competition and the imperative to increase exports, the government must turn to the private sector to develop exports and boost foreign exchange earnings.

Finally, slow growth has depleted the financial resources of several countries. Lower commodity prices and the slower growth of exports have resulted in declining export revenues

and increasing balance of payments difficulties, and several countries have been adversely affected by a general scarcity of foreign capital flowing to developing countries. In the aftermath of the debt crisis, commercial banks have been reluctant to increase their loans to developing countries. Because of shortfalls in government revenues and difficulties in obtaining external financial resources from banks, governments are finding increased difficulties in adopting a "go-it-alone" policy in development. Moreover, they no longer have sufficient financial resources to subsidize inefficient state enterprises. Greater partnership with the private sector has become more urgent, and governments have been responding to this need. This trend is evident particularly in the Asia-Pacific region, not only among the market-oriented newly industrialized economies (NIEs) and ASEAN countries, but also in much more planned economies such as China and India.

GOVERNMENT AND PRIVATE SECTOR
COOPERATION IN ASEAN

Much of what has been said about government and private sector cooperation applies in particular to the ASEAN countries, where the governments have shown varying degrees of enthusiasm in cooperating with their respective private sectors. Cooperation ranges from relatively minimal in Brunei to relatively significant in Singapore. When ASEAN was first established, initiatives for industrial cooperation were taken mainly by the member governments. The private sector was largely excluded from the regional cooperation schemes. But over time, almost all ASEAN countries have come to accept the necessity of government and private sector cooperation. This development is reflected in the cooperation strategies of the organization.

The AIP was the first major industrial cooperation scheme in ASEAN. The AIP was unique in that it was entirely a government project, as each government was responsible for the identification of the appropriate project for the country and was involved in direct investment and participation and negotiation of loans. Under the AIP, the host country took 60 % of the total equity with the remaining 40 % being equally shared among the other ASEAN member governments. Enterprises in the private sector were not considered as active participants in the equity sharing arrangement. Thus, AIP was in effect an ASEAN government project. Not surprisingly the AIP scheme was not so successful. Of the original five proposed projects, only two were eventually implemented and even then after a long delay.

Dissatisfaction with the outcome of AIP convinced ASEAN policymakers to involve the private sector in formulating subsequent ASEAN industrial cooperation schemes, namely the AIC and AIJV. The AIC scheme, in effect since 1983, involves the division of different production stages of vertically integrated industries among different ASEAN countries. AIC projects can be initiated either by the private sector or by the government. Originally, some 30 AIC proposals were made by various regional clubs, but only two packages involving automobile parts and components have been formally suggested by the ASEAN Chamber of Commerce and Industry (ASEAN-CCI). The first package was started in 1983, but the project was unsuccessful as the value of trade involved was reported to be very small, representing less than one percent of the total intra-ASEAN trade. In view of the lack of success of the first AIC, the second package, which was proposed to be characterized by brand-to-brand complementation, was postponed for some time. It was finally approved at the Meeting of ASEAN Economic Ministers (AEM) in 1988, with the participation of three ASEAN members: Malaysia, the Philippines, and Thailand.

AIJV projects, on the other hand, are initiated by the private sector. The program aims to promote industrial joint ventures among ASEAN investors. The AIJV scheme seems to be the most viable among the three industrial cooperation schemes as it was initiated by

private sector actors actually making the investment, and the conditions set for the scheme have been more lenient compared to the other two cooperative schemes. More attention has been recently placed on AIJV. The key guiding principles in the AIJV, signed by the ASEAN foreign ministers in 1983, include:

1. participation in an AIJV comprises at least two ASEAN countries but is not necessarily limited only to ASEAN investors, provided that the ASEAN nationals' component is at least 51 percent;
2. an approved AIJV product will enjoy up to 50 percent;
3. other ASEAN countries can refuse preferences of AIJV but any similar product cannot enjoy special tariff preferences;
4. participating countries need not encourage new additional capacity for approved AIJV products during a certain predetermined short period;
5. whenever feasible, AIJV products are to be equitably allocated to the participating ASEAN countries; and
6. an AIJV product should be of internationally acceptable quality and its price relatively competitive.

Considering the limited number of projects, the success of AIJV was quite limited. Investors applying for AIJV projects encountered excessive delay in getting formal approval. AIJV products also have to compete with non-ASEAN suppliers. In addition, if the products produced are not supplied to the ASEAN market, the margin of preference (MOP) is of no use to the investors. There are, in fact, many intra-ASEAN joint ventures but these investment projects have not entered into the AIJV scheme.[1] The cumbersome procedure of applying for AIJV and the modest incentives granted to the investors could be the major reasons most ASEAN investors did not bother to enter into this scheme.

In addition to the private-sector orientation, the AIJV program has an advantage over AIC since the projects could be on a smaller scale and hence easier to manage. Since AIJV has a provision for non-ASEAN participation, it opens the opportunity for transnational companies (TNCs) to be involved. The provision for private sector and TNC input in AIJV enables a greater mobilization of resources and puts greater emphasis on international competitiveness.

PROBLEMS OF ASEAN GOVERNMENT AND PRIVATE SECTOR COOPERATION

It would appear that ASEAN government and private sector cooperation is flourishing and is continuing to evolve satisfactorily. However, a closer examination of the nature and extent of such cooperation reveals that improvement is needed.

First, there is no legal framework for ASEAN government and private sector cooperation. This means that such cooperation is largely dictated by the inclination of the ASEAN governments. For example, at the Fourth ASEAN-U.S. Dialogue in March 1982, the ASEAN section of the ASEAN-U.S. Business Council (AUSBC) found that its activities had been omitted from the agenda and its views completely disregarded.[2] According to one ASEAN official, AUSBC was a private sector organization and did not have sufficient standing in a meeting between governments to warrant discussion as a separate item on the agenda. On the other hand, AUSBC felt that ASEAN was a joint effort between the governments and the private sector and that the ASEAN-U.S. dialogue should not be confined purely to government matters. In another example, one businessman recalled a time when he turned up at an ASEAN ministers meeting as instructed but was kept waiting because the meeting wanted to continue discussing government matters. In any case, the private sector has grown quite wary of attending official meetings because such meetings are generally "unproductive". Thus, although ASEAN businessmen would like to work closely and on a continuing basis with the ASEAN governments on economic matters because such cooperation would bring tremendous benefits to the private sector and manufactures, they feel that their participation is subject to the whims and fancies of government officials.

Second, although all the ASEAN industrial cooperation schemes have a private sector component, the private sector is becoming disillusioned with the schemes. This is partly because some of these schemes are not financially attractive and involve bureaucratic red tape which causes excessive delay in implementing these schemes. AIC projects, for example, are first negotiated by the private sectors, after which they must obtain government commitments in terms of investment promotion and tariff preferences. The involvement of the government, in the eyes of businessmen, often means excessive political control over economic issues which inhibits more prosperous economic activities in ASEAN. In addition, some member countries' desires to protect their infant industries may also clash with the schemes.

Finally, the private sector complains that it is not adequately involved at the planning and implementation stages of ASEAN cooperation schemes. For example, the AIC guidelines were drawn up without private sector participation and have been described as inflexible and impractical by some ASEAN businessmen.

RECOMMENDATIONS TO IMPROVE ASEAN GOVERNMENT AND PRIVATE SECTOR COOPERATION

In most ASEAN countries, a market-oriented strategy has been adopted, and businessmen in the private sector are the ones who carry out trade and industrial activities. It is conceivable that any industrial cooperative scheme will not be successful without the active support of the private sector. Given the rapid changes in the economic environment as a result of rapid change in comparative advantage and keen competition among countries, and as protectionistic trade practices loom large, there is clearly a need for closer cooperation between the government and the private sector to facilitate the efficiency of policy implementation and, more importantly, to promptly respond to changing circumstances. However, such cooperation is not easy and can only function smoothly if there is mutual understanding and trust. It has taken a number of years for the ASEAN governments to cooperate among themselves; it may take just as long for ASEAN governments to cooperate with the private sector. There is, however, no doubt that such cooperation is essential, especially if ASEAN is to succeed in implementing its various regional schemes. For this reason, both the government and the private sector in ASEAN have to examine ways and means of fostering such cooperation. In this connection the recommendations made by the G-14 in this Report on ASEAN Economic Cooperation and Integration ("ASEAN: The Way Forward", 1987) may be worth reiterating.

For the private sector to perform its functions effectively, it is desirable that the private sector be given a more formal and active role in planning and implementing ASEAN projects. Without active private sector participation, economic cooperation, especially in trade and industry, is unlikely to make headway. Similarly the private sector may also invite the public sector to participate in its deliberations. This interaction must take place both at the regional and national levels.

Therefore, it is recommended that:

1. The ASEAN-CCI and its members be closely consulted in the formulation of trade and industrial cooperative programs. The President of the ASEAN-CCI and the Six Vice Presidents should be invited to attend official ASEAN meetings such as the AEM, and be allowed to participate in specific items on the agenda of which the ideas of the private sector are useful for decision making.[3]

2. There should be greater coordination of the official dialogue relations between ASEAN and the dialogue partners, and private sector consultation with their counterparts in the dialogue partner countries. At present, the two dialogue processes have their own momentum and direction. Coordination of both dialogue processes would yield greater benefit to ASEAN and, accordingly, the following are proposed:

   i. A meeting between the ASEAN-CCI and the Standing Committee be held at least once a year. This meeting can also cover other areas of ASEAN economic cooperation;

   ii. Participation of the President of the ASEAN-CCI or his representative in the ASEAN dialogue process as a member of the ASEAN delegation.

3. There is a need for a permanent secretariat of the ASEAN-CCI which should be co-located with the ASEAN Secretariat in Jakarta. This will facilitate a greater flow of information, allow closer coordination, and be in keeping with the other measures being proposed for the ASEAN machinery.

4. The private sector should be allowed to play a role in ASEAN development cooperation with third countries, which is presently confined essentially to the public sector.

5. Frequent consultations among representatives of ASEAN governments and the private sector would be helpful in sharing experiences in various matters relating to public-private cooperation. Problems arising from such cooperation could be identified, and this would facilitate efficient cooperation in the future.

In conclusion, the private sector must be viewed as an important component of ASEAN economic cooperation. Governments took the initiative in establishing ASEAN. To ensure its success the private sector has to become an active partner and make ASEAN a joint venture between the government and itself rather than a purely government organization. If ASEAN economic cooperation is to be achieved, governments cannot exclude the participation of an important section of their economic system. ASEAN bureaucrats need to cross-fertilize the ranks with businessmen who have lived in the marketplace The ASEAN economic endeavour should be viewed as 'an equal partnership between the government and the private sector' if anything significant is to emerge from the various schemes of cooperation.

NOTES

1. See Somsak Tambunlertchai und Umphon Panachet, "Foreign Direct Investment in ASEAN", paper prepared for the 13th Federation of ASEAN Economic Associations on Foreign Investment in ASEAN: Strategies and Policies, 17-19 November 1988, Penang, Malaysia.

2. New Straits Times, March 10, 1982.

3. The regional industry clubs (RICS) can also request, through the respective Working Groups and subject to the approval of the Chairman of the relevant Permanent Committees, to attend selected meetings when an issue of interest of the RIC is being discussed. Their attendance should however, be restricted to specific items on the agenda. While the private sector should be able to present its views, it would have no role in the actual decision-making. This should rest with member Governments. Similarly, there is also a need to affiliate the other nongovernmental organizations (NGOs) with the Permanent Committees or subcommittees and provision should be made for regular interaction between them. This format for regular participation by the private sector will, in addition to allowing the representation of the views of the business community, also provide an impetus for the ASEAN-CCI and the NCCI machineries to get their act together and work more efficiently with specific targets in view.

40

INTRA-ASEAN ECONOMIC CO-OPERATION
A New Perspective

MARI PANGESTU, HADI SOESASTRO, and MUBARIQ AHMAD

There are two approaches to strengthen intra-ASEAN economic co-operation. First is the encompassing idea of a free trade area, with the understanding that all else will follow. Second is the question whether the free trade area is sufficient to enhance the larger market forged through intra-ASEAN trade and investment, i.e. are specific or new programmes necessary in addition to the free trade area.

THE ASEAN FREE TRADE AREA

Before analysing the prospects of the free trade area in strengthening intra-ASEAN economic co-operation, the basic net benefits from economic integration still stands as a strong argument for having such a concept.

The static welfare gains from integration will result from net increases in production and consumption.[1] The size of the gains will depend on the size of the union, the higher the level of intra-regional trade, and the higher the differences between pre- and post-integration tariffs. In the case of ASEAN, intra-regional trade is small (lack of complementarity); present market size is small; and the differences in pre- and post-integration tariffs is substantial but narrowing due to unilateral liberalization. Differences in the level of development could also lead to unequal distribution of gains. Imada et al. (1991) estimates that reducing tariff barriers will have a positive but not substantial effect on trade and production in the region.

However, while the net static gains are likely to be small, what is more important is the potential dynamic gains from the change in production structure and more efficient resource allocation; economies of scale; scope for intra-industry trade; increased investments; and technological and innovative developments due to increased competition. Furthermore, differences in development are narrowing as each country experiences robust growth; the size of the ASEAN market in terms of population and purchasing power will become substantive; and the potential for inter-industry trade is great.

Towards a Free Trade Area

The idea of a free trade area is closer than ever to being attained. At the Manila Summit, the concept was still unacceptable, but discussions

Reprinted in abridged form from "A New Look at Intra-ASEAN Economic Co-operation", *ASEAN Economic Bulletin* 8, no. 3 (March 1992), pp. 344–52, by permission of the authors and the Institute of Southeast Asian Studies.

in anticipation of the coming summit have gone quite far in formalizing the concept.

Renewed support for the ASEAN Free Trade Area (AFTA) began in 1991. The idea was revived by Thai Prime Minister Anand Panya-rachun in early 1991 and was endorsed by Prime Minister Goh Chok Tong of Singapore.

In the ASEAN Foreign Ministers meeting in Kuala Lumpur, July 1991, the AFTA proposal received enthusiastic support. The position of various countries at the time can be sum-marized as: ". . . Singapore and Malaysia had wholly supported the FTA proposal. Indonesia and the Philippines had some reservations on how fast they should go".[2] The latter two countries point to the differences between the two countries as leading to the possibility of dumping.

Agreement over AFTA came much earlier than expected at the October 1991 ASEAN Economic Ministers Meeting (henceforth the AEM agreement). Official acceptance will only occur at the ASEAN Summit meeting, but endorsement at the ministerial level already provides a strong indication that agreement will be reached. AFTA will be the main vehicle to strengthen intra-ASEAN economic co-operation.

In considering the prospects and problems of the ASEAN free trade area (AFTA), several aspects need to be analysed. These include the transition period, the scope of the free trade area, and the mode to reduce trade barriers.

Transition Period

Prior to the AEM agreement, there was already much discussion on the need for a deadline to indicate the political commitment to the objective of a free trade area. In June 1991, the ASEAN-ISIS suggested 2007, the 40th anniversary of ASEAN.[3] At the Foreign Min-isters Meeting in July 1991, achievement of AFTA in ten years was suggested by Thailand. A shorter deadline is preferable or it may be too far away to be meaningful.

The AEM agreement settled on a fifteen-year deadline or 2007 as suggested by ASEAN ISIS. The outcome appears to be a compromise between countries which wanted a shorter deadline (mainly Thailand and Singapore) and those which wanted a longer deadline (mainly Indonesia and the Philippines).

While it is true that a shorter deadline would have been more meaningful, given the consid-erations of Indonesia and Philippines, agreeing upon a deadline in itself must already be seen as a positive development. Furthermore, the deadline is meant to be a guideline which does not preclude some countries from achieving it earlier.

The crucial push comes in the work toward achieving the deadline in a constructive and dynamic way. Experience of other integration efforts is that deadlines are often arbitrary dates chosen with practical and political con-siderations. The responses by the private sector are often unanticipated and faster than hoped for. For want of a better term, it can be termed as the "announcement effect". What often happens is that once a deadline is announced and a clear political commitment made to achieving the deadline, economic forces will take over. For instance, in the Australia-NZ free trade area and EC single market cases, the deadline led to responses by the private sector to adjust and then lobby for a faster reduction in trade barriers.

Scope of AFTA

In conceptualizing the scope of AFTA, two aspects are important: first is whether an across the board or sectoral approach is adopted, and second, which trade barriers are to be included. The first approach is more efficient and easier to administer. Each country can reduce tariffs across the board by a certain MOP for all sectors to achieve a zero tariff by the prescribed deadline. However, such an approach is not likely to be accepted by the ASEAN-4.

Once a sectoral approach is adopted, then a decision is needed regarding which sectors will be excluded from the free trade area. The decision in the AEM agreement reflects this approach. Several sectors are excluded[4] under AFTA: agriculture and services as expected and most importantly capital goods. Within the prescribed industrial sector, a subsector approach is adopted under the CEPT agreement discussed below.

A possible modification that would clarify the direction that ASEAN is going would be to keep the option of liberalization of other sectors open by providing a programme for the phasing in of the now excluded sectors over some specified time period. This will provide an important signal of political commitment to the objective.

On the type of trade barriers to be included for liberalization, the existing schemes under ASEAN focus on reducing tariff barriers with the standstill and roll back agreement on non-tariff barriers since 1987. Under the AEM agreement, the focus is only on reducing tariffs. However, goods chosen under CEPT for tariff reduction cannot be subjected to non-tariff barriers.

The CEPT Modus

As part of the AEM agreement, the Common Effective Preferential Tariff (CEPT) has been chosen as the modus to achieve AFTA, the idea being that ASEAN countries shall be given uniform preferential treatment in intra-ASEAN trade. The main difference between Preferential Trading Arrangements (PTA) and CEPT is that PTA is granted only by the nominating country and there is no reciprocity. Whereas under CEPT there is reciprocity in that once the good is accepted to be under CEPT by all countries or accepted subset of countries (other countries to follow in three years), then all countries or subset thereof must give the preferential tariff. Therefore, the CEPT is potentially more encompassing. ASEAN Senior Officials are working on a list to be included in the CEPT and the product list

at present includes furniture, fertilizers, processed foods, garments and textiles.

The eventual aim is to have zero effective tariff, but at the beginning of the scheme there will be four tariff groups: 0–5 per cent, 5–10 per cent, 10–15 per cent and 15–20 per cent. However, the existing tariff rate for that particular product will remain unchanged *vis-à-vis* non-ASEAN countries in accordance with the definition of a free trade area.[5] No exclusion list was originally proposed under the scheme.

In theory, the CEPT will lead to the realization of a free trade area once it is reduced to zero. However, in practice, several implementation problems are evident. The details of the CEPT proposal are still being negotiated, but potential problems based on the AEM agreement actually point to a less than optimistic prospect for the realization of an ASEAN free trade area.

First, contrary to the initial proposal that suggested a broad sector by sector approach with a clear timetable, the definition sectors chosen in the AEM agreement were at the six-digit Harmonized Code level, which is still too disaggregated.[6] All goods in the prescribed scope of industrial products should reach a tariff of zero to five per cent by 2007.

A second problem is that too many exclusions would render the programme ineffective. There are several exclusions to be considered. Countries which feel that goods within the six-digit classification are still "sensitive", can exclude the goods at the eight- or nine-digit level. Such exclusion lists are reminiscent of the early days of PTA and runs counter to the initial proposal of not having an exclusion list. If the exclusion cannot be eliminated, then a strict restriction will be needed to prevent the exclusions from being larger than the inclusions, and for a deadline on the exclusion.

Another exclusion is that not all countries need to agree to the goods under CEPT. The suggestion is for a 6-X approach: that is as long as there is an accepted number of countries (to be decided, three to four out of six probably), then the product will be included under CEPT for participating ASEAN countries. No deadline was given to the phasing-in of non-participating ASEAN countries.

A final important exclusion is of capital goods. This will dilute the attraction and benefits of AFTA since it will reduce the possibility of setting up integrated production networks. It would also not be possible to liberalize inputs at a faster rate than final goods.

The third issue of concern under CEPT is with regard to operationalizing it as the modus for achieving partial AFTA, especially in the light of existing PTA.

Firstly, on how to reduce the tariffs, the tendency is to go with an MOP to achieve the desired CEPT of between 0–20 per cent, much like the PTA system. This would entail looking at each nine-digit item within the suggested six-digit category and working out the MOP for each item which may have different tariff rates. Then an averaging will need to be worked out to arrive at the MOP needed at the six-digit level. However, the approach appears cumbersome and administratively complex to implement. A simpler approach would be to determine a set tariff rate in the agreed categories and apply it across the board at the six-digit level.

Secondly, on merging the PTA with the CEPT, under the AEM agreement it is not clear how this should occur. Several possibilities can be considered. Both could run parallel, that is existing items under PTA will now have the target of deepening of MOP to 95–100 per cent by the imposed deadline. New products or sectors can be added on to the PTA or CEPT list with the same requirement of achieving 95–100 per cent MOP or zero-five per cent tariff by the prescribed date. The list of products under PTA or CEPT should then also concur with the identified sectors under the free trade area and all countries must have the products under those designated sectors under PTA or CEPT.

Another possible and preferable way would be to subsume the PTA under the CEPT since the latter is potentially more encompassing. Products already under the PTA scheme would come under the CEPT scheme and this can be done in several ways.

The first step would be to cross the PTA list of each country and determine which PTA products are common to all countries and subset of countries. One possible way then is to determine that all PTA products already identified by a minimum subset of countries (the lower the better, therefore between two to four), will automatically come under CEPT and a decision made regarding the tariff category.

A gradualism approach is also possible, by saying that if x countries already picked a product under PTA, then 6-X have a specified number of years to match and the product will then be under CEPT. New sectors will then be added accordingly under the CEPT.

A final issue concerns establishing rules of origin. The ASEAN content for CEPT products to be eligible for the preferential tariff is 40 per cent. Implementing rules of origin in a timely way based on pre-approved standards and procedures will be crucial for the success of the CEPT proposal.

The Need for an ASEAN Economic Treaty

The possibility of having an ASEAN economic treaty has been suggested by Philippines, the idea being that AFTA needs to be couched in a legally binding document to indicate the strength of the political commitment. Compliance to AFTA will then be ensured. Furthermore, a treaty should help national governments deal with vested interests in their countries against AFTA since the agreement is *internationally binding*.

In the AEM agreement, it was decided that a treaty was not necessary; instead a framework for agreement, which is a less legally binding document, was chosen.

Further Steps

Most discussions on ASEAN FTA focus on liberalization of tariffs. However, further thought is still needed on the issues of reducing non-tariff barriers, government procurement policies and other policies that impose trade barriers in general. Besides standstill procedures, reduction of non-tariff barriers in a systematic way will be necessary.

Furthermore, once integration to facilitate trade of goods begins, the liberalization of services and factors of production will be a natural outcome to encourage the process of integration. Another corollary is that differences in industrial standards, customs classifications, environmental policies, investment policies, labour movements, taxes and other domestic policies that can limit intra-regional trade and investment will also need to be harmonized and standardized.

RESPONDING TO MARKET-FORGED LINKAGES

Private Sector Participation in Agenda Setting

Under the umbrella of intra-ASEAN economic co-operation, the issue of private sector participation is not a new one. Failure of government to government industrial co-operation led to this recognition in the early 1980s. Thus, under ASEAN industrial co-operation (AIC), the ASEAN Chambers of Commerce and Industry (ASEAN-CCI) would be given the task to identify appropriate products or industries to be included in the AIC package.

However, such schemes have not been effective, so the response by the private sector to intra-ASEAN economic co-operation has not been forthcoming, as was evident with the AIJV. The above discussion of the problems with the various programmes indicate that the programmes and their implementation have not been designed with facilitating private sector participation in mind. There is obviously a problem in the mechanism by which private sector input should be filtered into the process of intra-ASEAN economic co-operation. The problem exists on both sides.

The private sector feel that the government

and private sector dialogue is one way since the ASEAN-CCI only reports and is not involved in the decision making process to ASEAN programmes which are supposed to be implemented by the private sector. "... they (the private sector) felt their participation is on *ad hoc* basis and subject to the whims and fancies of officials" and this is because "at the working level, government servants have not got the right kind of perception and understanding of their role".[7] Another common criticism regarding the ASEAN-CCI input is that they often do not represent the private sector in their respective countries.

The governments, on the other hand, claim that despite efforts to communicate requests for input and including their participation, the private sector are often not prepared and do not participate fully in the meetings. Furthermore, it is difficult to deal with the private sector since they are not a homogeneous group of people; parts of the private sector will support trade liberalization, while others would like to maintain protection.

Given the importance of the private sector in forging intra-ASEAN links, now more than ever, the mechanism which relates the ASEAN-CCI to the ASEAN machinery needs to be upgraded from simple reporting to implementation.

The ASEAN-CCI is the most logical and convenient umbrella representing the private sector. However, since the issue of whether the ASEAN-CCI represents the private sector has been raised, other ways of private sector representation needs to be thought of. Regular meetings between MNCs, domestic businesses and the government officials involved with ASEAN could be one way. At the recent ASEAN-ISIS meeting (June 1991) one idea suggested is to provide a role for the ASEAN think tanks. The idea would be to have a tripartite (government, academics and business) ASEAN forum on ASEAN economic co-operation. Its effectiveness will depend very much on the participation of relevant government officials who have influence on the decision making process.

With regard to specific policies to facilitate the two market-forged links discussed above, it is our opinion that, rather than come up with new schemes, it is more pragmatic to come up with policies that would facilitate and foster increased intra-ASEAN linkages forged by the market.

Implications of the Growth Triangle for ASEAN Economic Co-operation

Can the Growth Triangle accelerate intra-ASEAN economic co-operation if it is expanded (concentric circles) or replicated (other triangles)? The 6-X approach is not a new one and is an appealing one. Expansion of the Singapore-Johore-Riau (SIJORI) growth triangle on the Indonesian side seems feasible and is already happening. The growth zone on the Indonesian side has expanded from Batam to Bintan and to another two islands. It is quite probable that more Riau islands will be developed in the same way. The logical spread effects would be for developments in Sumatra; that is Sumatra can act as the hinterland for the Riau islands and enhance the linkage and spread effects.

On the other hand it is unlikely that Johor will be expanded. The immediate problem is whether Johor should be declared duty-free or only parts of it and whether this could be done by expanding the existing export processing zones.

Replication of the triangle to other parts of the region to expand intra-ASEAN economic co-operation is not as feasible as it may first appear. There must be very strong complementarity between the different areas and preferably existing economic links such as in the case of SIJORI. Then the role of government policy is to facilitate and accelerate the process. At the AEM meeting in October 1991, the contribution of the Growth Triangle toward overall ASEAN economic co-operation was recognized, but no formal endorsement was given.

Furthermore, strong complementarity alone may not be sufficient. In the SIJORI case, despite the complementarity between Batam and Singapore, investors were hesitant until the Singapore Government provided support. Another consideration is the unique role of Singapore in providing supporting infrastructure and market access which may not be replicated in other growth areas. A final consideration is the danger that creation of sub regions of economic co-operation will detract from the main objective of regional economic co-operation — the 6-X will not sum up to six in the long run.

There is the familiar chicken and egg problem. If there is no trade and investment links to begin with, then should the government step in and provide infrastructure and facilitating policies in the hope that private sector investments will flow in? But if there had been strong enough complementarity, then the private sector would have seen the business opportunity and developed trade and investment links, as well as pressured the government to provide the necessary infrastructure and changes in policy — much like in the SIJORI case. The evaluation needs to be made on a case by case basis, but in general it would be difficult to replicate the concept without the existence of very strong complementarity.

Implications of Increased Trade due to Investment Flows

Is the FTA sufficient policy to attract MNCs with a regional production network? Or will specific policies be needed given the problems of realizing the FTA and the slowness anticipated in implementing AFTA?

It turns out that as long as the production undertaken by MNCs are exported, then the import of components and intermediate products are duty exempt. Therefore, intra-ASEAN trade in supplying components, parts, and intermediate products can run smoothly as long as the final product is exported to non-ASEAN countries. This can be achieved in all the ASEAN countries by locating in duty-free zones or applying for duty exemption or drawback. As long as the investment is export oriented, then it is difficult to think of policies that would enhance such flows.

MNCs will usually buy from the cheapest source which may not necessarily be their own affiliates or head office. However, there is often also pressure to take from within their own network because of transfer pricing and other reasons. Therefore, an important question to ask in approaching the production base type of investments is, what the benefits to the host country are.

The pattern of investment and trade are now influenced by global production strategies of MNCs. How can ASEAN economic co-operation facilitate the flow of goods and services so that MNCs and ASEAN business groups will invest in multi-plants spread throughout ASEAN and relying upon a larger market?

Some possible programmes to enhance intra-regional linkages through MNCs and ASEAN business groups include: national treatment for investment by ASEAN nationals; ASEAN content to be treated as local content; 100 per cent MOP for AIJV products; improving AIJV approval mechanism and better co-ordination of policies concerning MNCs, such as harmonization of incentives.

Chee (1988) also suggested that special incentives can be given to investors which fulfil certain objectives such as involvement in ASEAN Economic Cooperation Schemes, exports, or facilitating domestic tie-ups. The incentives suggested were obtaining the same tax treatment as locals, access to domestic credit and percentage of equity ownership. Chee also suggested that there could be co-operation over technology acquisition and information-sharing by MNCs. The latter would include monitoring MNC activities, reviewing policies on regulations affecting MNCs, assistance in seeking and selecting joint-venture partners, and providing information and expert assistance on technology.

CONCLUSIONS

The major stumbling block toward the realization of ASEAN economic co-operation has been the lack of political commitment. If investors are to take the ASEAN concept seriously and incorporate it in their long-term strategies, then it will be crucial to have a more serious level of commitment.

Given that it is now imperative, feasible and desirable to foster greater intra-ASEAN economic co-operation, the renewed push for the FTA in the coming summit is timely. Even though the net trade creation effects are likely to be small at present, the dynamic gains from increased efficiency and investments are likely to be great. Furthermore, by the time the FTA is achieved, ASEAN will be an important market to contend with. Investors will be attracted to the region not just for a production base to export from, but also as a dynamic and growing market to sell in. These tendencies are already apparent from the strategies of MNCs in the region.

Initial reactions to the FTA have been pessimistic and sceptical, even though most of the recommendations about having a deadline and utilizing CEPT were accepted. The main problem still appears to be too many exclusions reaffirming the recurring perception about the ineffectiveness of ASEAN economic co-operation programmes. However, the form will not be as important as the political commitment that underlies the decision to push for the FTA in the *post* summit implementation. Early concessions on tariff preferences on a broad basis, minimum administrative processing and clear, as well as operational, implementation of the ASEAN content rule will be needed to provide the crucial signal about the seriousness of the ASEAN governments in implementing the FTA.

To make ASEAN credible, it will be imperative to indicate the direction and timetable for strengthening intra-ASEAN economic co-operation. Indications regarding the steps in achieving FTA need to be spelled out in a clear and consistent way, which further steps will be considered and when they will be phased in will be important. This will eliminate the *ad hoc* approach that characterizes ASEAN economic co-operation to date that has discouraged investors from taking a longer term perspective.

Improvement of existing schemes much along the lines already recommended follows: maintenance of targets and deadlines, reducing the bureaucracy of implementation, increasing promotion and dissemination of information on the programmes, strengthening of the institutional set-up such as the ASEAN Secretariat and so on, should be continued.

In responding to the market-driven responses that have led to increasing intra-ASEAN economic ties, it becomes more important to rethink the role of the private sector in ASEAN economic co-operation.

However, despite the new constellation, introduction of new ASEAN economic co-operation schemes to incorporate the needs of the private sector such as the common market and harmonization of policies are not recommended at present. These types of policies should come as a corollary once the FTA programme is under way, and the success of the FTA remains the main objective. Nevertheless, some simple harmonization programme could be initiated even now such as with industrial standards, documentation and so on. A work-able area should be chosen and harmonization efforts undertaken.

Specific programmes to cater for increasing the forging of intra-ASEAN links through growth triangles and private investment flows are also not pragmatic or workable. In addition to the FTA as the main programme, each ASEAN country should continue unilateral liberalization, improvement of investment climates and removal of bottlenecks such as infrastructure. Existing policies that favour export oriented industries in all the ASEAN countries are sufficient for export base investments. If there is a problem, it is more to do with implementation and how to make the process more efficient.

In the final analysis, increased intra-ASEAN links through MNC affiliates, and linkages that will increasingly involve the domestic suppliers and companies, will probably be best served by the formation of AFTA. There is an important link between pushing for greater intra-ASEAN economic co-operation through the FTA and enhancing intra-ASEAN linkages through private investors. By the time AFTA is achieved, the size of the ASEAN market will make it very attractive for investors. Additional incentives and new programmes of economic co-operation will not be needed. What will be of paramount importance is the political commitment, certainty and increased attractiveness that ASEAN can provide with AFTA. Investment will no longer be based just on resource pooling production-base considerations but also on market sharing considerations. If this sounds very familiar, we have come full circle with the ASEAN concept after all.

NOTES
1. That is trade creation minus trade diversion effects.
2. *Straits Times*, 19 August 1991.
3. See ASEAN-ISIS (1991).
4. Including sectors excluded based on considerations of safety, security and protection toward small scale producers.
5. Recall that in the difference between a free trade area such as AFTA and EFTA, member countries do not impose a common tariff on non-member countries such as in the case of a customs union like the EC.

6. The reasoning is that at the six-digit level, there is a an internationally consistent description of goods. For higher than six digits, national description of goods prevail.
7. Chee Peng Lim, p. 107, in Noordin Sopiee et al. (1987).

41.

THE ASEAN MODEL OF REGIONAL CO-OPERATION

JOHN WONG

More than a decade after the Bali Summit, ASEAN's achievements in the major area of regional economic cooperation have been uneven and modest. Its trade liberalization program, which lacks sufficient breadth and depth, is still ineffective in terms of restructuring ASEAN's trade pattern and shifting it toward a greater regional focus, even though some nineteen thousand commodity items are now on the official list of tariff preferences. Results of industrial cooperation as embodied in the AIP and AIC programs are even more disappointing, and only a number of small joint ventures under the AIJV scheme are actually moving ahead. Is the lack of conspicuous success in ASEAN's economic cooperation endeavors tantamount to a failure for ASEAN itself, as in the case of other ill-fated Third World regional groupings?

A proper evaluation of ASEAN's progress toward regional cooperation must be made by placing it in the context of the historical circumstances under which ASEAN has evolved — that is, the geopolitical forces that have shaped it and the chronic problems that are inherent in the economic structures of the member countries. It is also not appropriate to pass judgment on ASEAN's present pace of progress without taking into account its own stated time frame. The ASEAN leaders have all along stressed that economic cooperation is to be realized as a long-term goal, and fluctuation of events in the short run is considered irrelevant to these long-term objectives. As long as the ASEAN institutional apparatus is kept in existence, the option of cooperation is open and the process continues. In any case, it does not cost much to maintain the ASEAN machinery; the ASEAN Secretariat in Jakarta is inexpensive to run compared to many huge international bureaucracies. Hence there is quite a favorable cost-benefit ratio for ASEAN members.

Furthermore, ASEAN is already reaping remarkable benefits from its extraregional cooperation activities. Over the years it has been successful in developing a unified perception of the many regional and international economic issues, such as protectionism, that affect it as a group. ASEAN has also developed a framework for regular dialogues with Australia and New Zealand, Canada, the EC, Japan, and the United States in order to improve bilateral relations. In this way, it has learned to yield some considerable external leverage in order to secure a better deal for its common interests. Gains from external cooperation

Reprinted in abridged form from "The ASEAN Model of Regional Cooperation", in *Lessons in Development: A Comparative Study of Asia and Latin America*, edited by S. Naya, M. Urrutia, S. Mark and A. Fuentes (San Francisco: International Center for Economic Growth, 1989), pp. 121–41, by permission of the author and the publisher.

can serve to increase ASEAN's internal cohesiveness. They can also provide the needed incentive for the group to maintain its operational momentum despite sluggish progress and even despite setbacks in its intraregional cooperation programs.

Ultimately, the effectiveness of ASEAN as a regional economic grouping will depend on breakthroughs in its formal areas of cooperation covering the trade and industry sectors. It is here that ASEAN's past experiences in economic cooperation will be instructive both for ASEAN itself and for other regional groupings among developing countries. It is not possible in this context to go into all the major causes and circumstances that have led to the underperformance of ASEAN's economic cooperation programs. Many of the underlying causes are well known and have been extensively discussed by ASEAN scholars and officials elsewhere. Here, ASEAN's past problems in economic cooperation will be examined in terms of two "gaps": one expectation, the other implementation.

The expectation gap. The underperformance of ASEAN's existing programs can be attributed to the existence of what may be called an expectation gap. Because of structural and policy obstacles, there has been a difference between what the existing economic cooperation programs were expected to achieve and what was actually attainable. Both the trade liberalization and the industrial cooperation programs were established to build some measure of regional economic integration. Yet neither has made much progress even though both may be theoretically sound. Apparently these programs could not overcome the structural and policy constraints.

The basic structural constraint on ASEAN's economic cooperation efforts is obvious. ASEAN is one of the world's few regional groupings that is characterized by vast disparities in the economies of its member countries in terms of size, structure, orientation, resource base, and stages of economic development. Some

member countries in ASEAN do not even enjoy physical contiguity with each other. The differences in their economic structures and orientations, as well as in their levels of economic development, are particularly unfavourable to efforts at regional economic cooperation. The less-developed members in the group are usually more inward-looking in their overall economic orientation, since they are generally preoccupied with such domestic economic and social development problems as poverty, unemployment, and inequality of income. These countries cannot depend on external economic cooperation programs to cope with these problems, at least at the initial stage; rather, they need to devise appropriate domestic policies. The governments of the less-developed members are also reluctant to fully commit themselves to regional economic activities, which are perceived as invariably operating in favor of the more-developed members. Ironically, the more-developed members (which are generally outward-looking and are supposed to capture more gains from the various regional cooperation programs in the short run) may not necessarily accord high priority to a particular regional cooperation program either. This is because regional economic cooperation in developing countries can sometimes lead to serious trade diversion, which adversely affects the economically more-efficient members.

To tackle the problem of unequal distribution of gains, some regional groupings — the Andean Pact countries, for instance — have devised special treatment for the less-developed members in the group.[1] However, ASEAN has no such provisions. The issue of distributive gains is instead dealt with indirectly, under the consensus mechanism of decision making. It is tacitly assumed that in reaching a consensus, no member country should take undue advantage of the others, and none should feel it is being exploited. Admittedly, this is an inefficient way of dealing with the equity issue, as in actual practice members tend to stall the decision-making process whenever they think their national interests are at stake. This leads to delay in the implementation of regional cooperation programs. In addition, ASEAN has introduced the five-minus-one principle, which allows for negotiations excluding one country if that country prefers to be excluded. It has rarely been applied, however, because of the strong preference for the prevailing consensus principle. Neither of these principles seeks to address the equity issue in a direct and efficient manner; it ultimately requires some kind of redistributive arrangements. The main problem in ASEAN is that its least-developed member is Indonesia, which happens to be the largest country, whereas the more-developed members like Brunei or Singapore happen to be disproportionately small. Small members are inherently limited in their capacity to satisfy the needs of large members in any redistributive exercise.

Along with these structural constraints, there are a number of self-imposed policy barriers that the ASEAN governments have chosen to erect against their regional cooperative programs. From the start, ASEAN has consciously avoided the term "integration"; all its regional activities are officially referred to as "cooperation," which is by definition a lower level of regional activity. Some ASEAN governments have expressly stated their reluctance to participate in any substantial market-sharing arrangement as opposed to types of cooperation that involve pooling resources. This not only rules out any direct moves toward a free trade area or a common market, but also sets a natural upper limit on virtually all trade and industrial co-operation activities. As a result, the actual progress of ASEAN economic cooperation has fallen short of common expectations.

The implementation gap. A survey of ASEAN's regional cooperation experience would reveal that some of the programs have had good potential for regional economic integration and yet have failed to achieve anything substantial. This points to the difference between what is achievable and what has actually been achieved, or what may be called the implementation gap. Apart from the structural and policy constraints previously discussed, the various regional economic cooperation programs have underperformed because of a number of technical and administrative problems that have arisen in the process of implementation.

To begin with, the AIP would have had greater success if the projects had been selected more carefully and sufficient technical preparation had been carried out beforehand. The first AIP package was hastily adopted after the Bali Summit without careful deliberation or a feasibility study. Sound preparatory work would have revealed the numerous practical problems inherent in Thailand's soda ash project, as well as the duplication in Indonesia of the designated diesel engine project for Singapore. Singapore had to withdraw hastily from the diesel engine project, and Thailand took years to complete its feasibility study on the soda ash project, only to abandon it later.

Proper technical preparation not only would have avoided the political embarrassment caused by the scrapping of some AIP projects but also could have reduced the many difficulties encountered at the implementation stage. To set up any new industry, a host of basic industry-specific problems pertaining to optimal location, infrastructural support, raw materials supply, labor availability, and pricing and market arrangements first have to be sorted out. It has been argued that if all these details had been dealt with at the beginning by the ASEAN leaders — who from the outset stressed that final approval would be given only to projects that were economically viable — the whole AIP package might not have been launched at all. There are many industries in the ASEAN region that could not be competitive at world market prices even if all the national markets in the region were fully integrated. None of the present AIP projects would have passed such a stringent market test. This inability to compete in world markets in many industries despite full regional integration also explains why it is so difficult for regional groupings to come up with a viable package of industries to achieve regional integration — a package that would yield optimum resource allocation on a regional basis and yet satisfy the various national objectives of the individual members. If tradeoffs must be made between economics and politics or between efficiency and equity for the sake of fostering the larger cause of regionalism, these decisions would best be made at the highest level by the political leadership. Such a procedure would be preferable by far to letting indecisive bureaucrats chip away at the problems in their endless rounds of meetings.

This leads to the second aspect of administrative constraint, which involves the critical role to be played by ASEAN's bureaucrats. It has been the practice of ASEAN political leaders to concern themselves only with the broad principles of the regional programs while leaving implementation to officials of the individual governments. These bureaucrats, though technocratically competent, tend to be overly cautious and averse to taking risks — unlike the business leaders, who have a keen sense of the market and are capable of perceiving prospective gains in the longer run. In the business world, successful new enterprises are normally launched on the basis of entrepreneurial decisions, but seldom in a bureaucratic way. Nor can bureaucrats match politicians in their ability to develop a vision and make bold decisions on larger issues and for the longer term. Not surprisingly, most ASEAN projects have been stymied in the implementation process as the bureaucrats struggle to balance the minutest costs and benefits and jealously safeguard national interests. Such a defensive approach is hardly conducive to the innovative decision making that is required to initiate a major regional project.

The bureaucratic decision-making process is intertwined with complicated institutional arrangements covering the operation of all the regional cooperation programs. Although the ASEAN Secretariat, which functions only as a coordinating body, has not yet developed into an unwieldy structure, it is already accompanied by a web of working committees, expert groups, ad hoc working groups, and other subsidiaries. The complicated institutional structure, when coupled with the bureaucratic decision-making processes, has combined to cause delays in the implementation of regional programs.

CONCLUSION

Regional economic cooperation in ASEAN, as in many other regional groupings of developing countries, is destined to be a long, laborious process. In a microeconomic sense, ASEAN's existing economic cooperation programs could considerably enhance their operational effectiveness and improve their performance standards if some of the administrative and technical constraints were removed and the key problems were properly addressed. However, the chances of substantial progress still depend critically on those of a more favorable macroeconomic environment, which in turn depend on the continuing economic growth and development of ASEAN. In the final analysis, economic development remains the most effective technique of achieving regional economic cooperation.

NOTE

1. For a more detailed discussion of the comparative experiences of ASEAN and the Andean Pact, see Wong (1986).

Section VI

INTRA-ASEAN
ECONOMIC CO-OPERATION

Introduction

Joseph L.H. Tan

Aside from the rapidly changing international economic environment, the economic growth and development of the ASEAN countries will be influenced not only by the internal dynamics within each individual economy, but also by their co-operation with one another. ASEAN's founding document, the Bangkok Declaration of 1967, calls for economic co-operation in five areas: 1) Co-operation in Trade and Tourism (COTT); 2) Co-operation in Industry, Minerals and Energy (COIME); 3) Co-operation in Food, Agriculture and Forestry (COFAF); 4) Co-operation in Finance and Banking (COFAB); and 5) Co-operation in Transport and Communications (COTAC).

The first five selections in this Section concentrate on concerns pertaining to developments and co-operation in the areas of trade, industry, energy, and agriculture. A discussion on the ASEAN Preferential Trading Arrangements (PTA) by Gerald Tan indicates that the main impediment to greater intra-ASEAN trade is rooted in the economic structures of the ASEAN countries which are competitive rather than complementary. For instance, the regional investment planning and complementary schemes have been fruitless simply because national interests overwhelm the regional interests. His pessimism on the prospect of enhancing intra-ASEAN trade was also influenced by the adverse international economic events current at the time of writing. However,

with the adoption of the ASEAN Free Trade Area (AFTA) and its operative mechanism, the Common Effective Preferential Tariff (CEPT), since the Fourth ASEAN Summit in January 1992, a more optimistic perspective on the prospect of regional trade co-operation is found in Mari Pangestu et al. (see Section V). This is followed by reviews and recommendations concerning ASEAN industrial co-operation, authored by Chee Peng Lim and Jang-Won Suh. Their proposal comprises two complementary schemes: the ASEAN Small and Medium Industries (ASMI) and ASEAN Joint Industrial Co-operation (AJIC). According to Chee and Suh, if ASEAN is serious about accelerating the present pace of industrial co-operation, it will need to incorporate various dimensions of such co-operation including non-manufacturing sectors, particularly finance and marketing. In a separate selection, Chee explains the vital importance of promoting closer economic co-operation, specifically to develop the small and medium industrial sector from which the bulk of the ASEAN population particularly in the urban areas draw benefit and livelihood. He puts forward a plea for establishing a special organization — an ASEAN Small and Medium Industry Centre — to provide the needed assistance to the numerous small industries which tend to be neglected. Moving on to the third major area of ASEAN co-operation (food, agriculture and forestry), L.S. Cabanilla reviews the performance of the ASEAN agricultural sector and assesses past efforts at regional co-operation. He makes the point that in the general pursuit of industrial development, agricultural development and co-operation should not be neglected. Indeed, the rural/agricultural population could provide the vital source of demand for the industrial output of the region. Cabanilla calls for more efficient ASEAN co-operation in the area of food and agricultural and of forestry, on the basis of the principle of comparative advantage so that their differential resource endowments and capabilities could be deployed to promote more efficient use of the region's resources. Shankar Sharma's article gives a comparative analysis of the energy policies of ASEAN member countries especially after 1973. It discusses the limited impact of various committees and programmes in their attempts to promote co-operation in this sector. Sharma concludes by providing suggestions on areas for fruitful co-operation, including the need to develop a comprehensive and standardized regional database, essential for the development of a sound and comprehensive energy policy facilitating substantive regional co-operation.

The next four selections focus on the problems and prospects for intra-ASEAN economic co-operation in the service sectors, including banking and finance; tourism; transport; and human resource development. David L. Schulze discusses financial integration in ASEAN, and makes recommendations aimed at lowering barriers presently hindering such integration. However, the continuing dilemma is how much economic sovereignty ASEAN members are willing to give up in order to attain higher levels of economic integration. Steven C.M. Wong examines various measures to further enhance ASEAN's collective efforts in promoting five

specific areas in the tourism sector: (1) planning and research; (2) institutional strengthening; (3) preferential demand and supply of tourism inputs; (4) joint promotion and marketing and (5) reducing and rationalizing travel barriers. Another services sector with potential for a regional development approach is that of transport. G. Naidu discusses various possibilities for greater ASEAN co-operation in this area.

Since the mid-1970s, human resource development (HRD) programmes have become an integral part of national development plans in ASEAN countries. In the 1980s HRD became a major area of ASEAN co-operation. C.P.F. Luhulima examines the nature and extent of that co-operation by focusing on ASEAN's experience in terms of the "structural differences" between the ASEAN-Japan HRD Programme and the ASEAN-Pacific Co-operation HRD Programmes.

The last three selections draw compelling attention to the importance of mounting regional co-operation on environmental issues, and the continuing need to focus on privatization and deregulation issues. Dhira Phantumvanit and Juliet Lamont discuss specific steps to improve the development of environmental policies and their implementation in ASEAN and in East Asia. Ng Chee Yuen and Norbert Wagner analyse the rationale for privatization in ASEAN after reviewing the proliferation of public enterprises in the region. They highlight the problems of privatization, for example, limitations of capital markets, and resistance from both management and trade unions. Peter O'Brien and Herman Muegge discuss ways of promoting joint investments, particularly in the industrial sector. These UNIDO experts analyse the advantages of various forms of joint ventures, and the prospects for greater intra-ASEAN investment.

42.

ASEAN PREFERENTIAL TRADING ARRANGEMENTS
An Overview

GERALD TAN

A BRIEF REVIEW OF THE ASEAN PTA

The Agreement on Asean Preferential Trading Arrangements was signed in Manila on Feb 24, 1977. The stated aim of the PTA was to encourage greater intra-regional trade through the use of long-term quantity contracts, preferential terms for financing imports, preferential treatment of imports by government agencies, preferential tariff rates, and the liberalisation of non-tariff barriers to regional trade. The agreement also allowed for the temporary suspension of tariff cuts where local industries or foreign exchange reserves were seriously affected, and made special supplementary arrangements for the inclusion of products arising from industrial complementation schemes.

The main instrument for trade liberalisation that has been applied to date is the granting of tariff preferences to Asean member countries. In the initial stages of the scheme, tariff preferences were granted on a product-by-product basis, with each member country committed to offer a set number of tariff preferences each year. Tariff preferences took the form either of not increasing tariff levels for a five-year period (especially when the existing tariff rate was already zero), or an actual reduction in existing tariff rates. At first tariff cuts were of the order of 10 per cent but later, tariff cuts of up to 25 per cent were made.

To ensure that intra-regional trade would benefit Asean countries, various rules of origin were implemented. These specified that products eligible for inclusion under the PTA have to be either products wholly produced or obtained in Asean countries; or products whose non-Asean content did not exceed 50 per cent in value, and whose final stage of manufacture was performed in Asean countries. There was also a cumulative rule of origin which specified that products which used imported inputs which were themselves subject to preferential tariffs must have an aggregate Asean content of not less than 60 per cent by value.

The product-by-product approach to tariff reduction was a time-consuming exercise as each product had to be discussed and examined closely before tariff preferences could be agreed upon. Moreover, the commitment to offer a set number of new tariff preferences each year led to what can only be described as 'padding' of the number of items included in the lists of products in the scheme. The end result was a proliferation of the number of items (about 6,000 by 1980) which were granted tariff preferences, without much prospect of achieving a

Reprinted in abridged form from "ASEAN Preferential Trading Arrangements: An Overview", in *ASEAN at the Crossroads*, edited by Noordin Sopiee, Chew Lay See, and Lim Siang Jin (Kuala Lumpur: Institute of Strategic and International Studies, 1987), pp. 63–69, by permission of the author and the publisher.

significant effect on the expansion of intra-regional trade. Many of the items included in the scheme were not traded by the member countries. For some product categories, up to two-thirds of the items granted preferential tariffs by some countries were not actually traded by them.

Of those that were traded, many took the form of variants of the same product at the seven-digit level of the BTN classification code (for instance, 84.21.110 Domestic sprayers [plastic], 84.21.120 Domestic sprayers [aluminium], 84.21.190 Domestic sprayers [others]). 'Others' were items which were imported from outside the region, but for which Asean member countries did not manufacture or export (presumably because they did not have any comparative advantage in doing so). For some product groups (for example, machinery), as much as three-quarters of the preference items offered by some countries fell into this latter category. For some Asean countries there were also a large number of items for which the existing tariff was already zero and for which preferential treatment took the form of a 'zero-binding' commitment for five years. For some countries, the proportion of zero-binding tariff preference items for some product groups was as high as 98 per cent.

Thus, the frequent announcements of an ever-increasing list of items included under the PTA gave an illusion of progress in the liberalisation of intra-regional trade. What started out as a serious attempt to stimulate trade between the Asean countries soon began to look more and more like a public relations exercise.

At the same time as the product-by-product approach to tariff reductions was in progress, some Asean member countries were undertaking bilateral negotiations for across-the-board tariff reductions. Early in 1977, Singapore and the Philippines (Thailand was later included) agreed on a 10 per cent reduction in tariffs on commodities traded. By 1980, all Asean countries had joined in across-the-board tariff reductions. Initially, a 20 per cent tariff cut was agreed

upon for all imports which had a value of less than US$50,000 each in 1978. This ceiling was later raised to US$500,000 and then to US$1 million.

The speed at which across-the-board tariff reductions were embraced by the Asean countries is a reflection of the less tiresome negotiations these involved, compared with the product-by-product approach. However, across-the-board tariff reduction had the danger of including items which were 'sensitive', in the sense that reduced tariffs on these items might adversely affect certain industries in member countries. In order to guard against this, the scheme allowed for the exclusion of certain sensitive items, and provided for the suspension of preferential tariffs where they threaten 'serious injury' to domestic industries, or adversely affect the balance of payments.

Although across-the-board tariff reductions on traded goods have the advantage, by their very nature, of not including goods which appear on trade classification lists but which are not traded, they did not overcome the problem of offering tariff cuts on imports from outside Asean, which member countries did not export, because they had no comparative advantage in their manufacture. Thus, a tariff cut of 20 per cent on all traded goods with a value of US$500,000 may include many items which Asean countries imported from outside the region, simply because they had no comparative advantage in their manufacture and export. The significance of this is that across-the-board tariff reductions do not necessarily lead to greater intra-regional trade. As in the product-by-product approach, the announcement of an increasing number of items included under the across-the-board tariff cuts did not necessarily mean that intra-regional trade was likely to increase.

All empirical studies on the likely impact of the PTA scheme on intra-regional trade confirm that the effects of tariff cuts would be minimal. Armas (1978) concluded that a 10 per cent across-the-board tariff cut on Philippine imports from Asean countries was likely to increase Filipino intra-Asean imports by only 2.5 per cent. Akrasanee and Koomsup (1979, p 54), in their estimate of the effects of tariff cuts on six Thai imports from Asean countries in the first batch of items agreed upon under the PTA, concluded the effect was 'very small, ranging from 0.06 to 22.2 per cent'. Naya (1980, pp 22-23) examined the likely effects of a 10 percent across-the-board tariff cut on total intra-Asean trade and found that it would be of the order of less than 2 per cent. Ooi (1981, p 20) found that a 20 per cent across-the-board tariff cut on Asean imports (whose values in 1978 were less than US$50,000) into the Philippines and Thailand would have a negligible impact on the relevant intra-Asean imports into these countries (0.06 per cent and 0.02 per cent respectively) although, for some individual products, the estimated increases were a little higher. Even if the valuation ceilings were raised to US$50,000 the estimated effect on intra-regional trade would only be about 2 per cent.

The main reason for these very low estimates were: The tariff cuts offered were relatively small; the number of products included under the PTA was relatively few in comparison with the total number of items traded by Asean countries; and estimated price elasticities of the product groups concerned were rather low. An additional reason was (as pointed out above) that the preference lists agreed upon by the Asean countries under the PTA were padded with many items which were either not traded at all, or if they were, comprised many items imported from outside the region because Asean countries did not have any comparative advantage in their manufacture. In addition, many items already had zero or close to zero tariffs so that their inclusion in the PTA was unlikely to increase intra-regional trade any further. There were also cases where tariff cuts were offered on meaningless items such as snow-ploughs and nuclear reactors which Asean countries were unlikely to use, or were unable to manufacture.

BASIC OBSTACLES TO GREATER INTRA-ASEAN TRADE

The main obstacle in the way of increased intra-regional trade through preferential tariffs is the fact that the economic structures of most of the Asean countries are competitive rather than complementary.

Leaving Singapore aside for the moment, the other Asean countries are predominantly primary producers specialising in the export of food, raw materials and minerals, and whose major markets are in advanced industrial countries. Although industrial development has progressed significantly since the formation of Asean, much of this is still inward-looking and concentrated on import replacement. Where export-oriented industries have been established, many are directed towards markets in advanced industrial countries, either in the form of components manufacture (such as electronic components) or in finished products such as textiles and garments. This lack of complementarity in economic structure, and the need to protect import-replacing industries is reflected in the kinds of items for which preferential tariffs are granted under the PTA.

Singapore is an exception in the sense that it does not have a predominantly agricultural economic base, has always been an outward-looking economy, and has few import-replacing industries protected by high tariffs. Its industries have grown from simple components-assembly and labour-intensive manufactures to middle and high technology manufactures. In many ways therefore, Singapore exhibits the complementarity of economic structure, vis-a-vis other Asean countries, that a preferential trading system could enhance. This by itself is, however, not necessarily conducive to greater intra-regional trade through preferential tariffs. The main reason for this is that Singapore has historically dominated regional trade in the Asean region. Indeed, much of the post-war period was marked by the various countries in the region making efforts to reduce this dominance. In addition, national economic priorities often emphasised the diversification of economic structure through industrial development. It is therefore unlikely that the other Asean members would acquiesce to a preferential trading system likely to result in the increasing dominance of one member country in the export of manufactured goods, even if that was allocatively efficient from a purely economic point of view.

The basic problem is that Asean member countries are at markedly different stages of economic development. This is reflected in the differences in their economic structure. Unless special measures are taken, the liberalisation of intra-regional trade is likely to benefit the more developed member countries to a greater extent than the less developed member countries. The nature and scope of the Asean PTA, as it is currently implemented, represents one way of dealing with this problem.

It should also be remembered that, historically, the major markets for the exports of Asean countries have been the advanced industrial countries. Apart from the entrepot trade and the raw-material processing activities in Singapore (which are only intermediate stages in exports eventually destined to go outside the region), Asean member countries have traditionally looked outside their region for their exports. Given that the growth prospects of these extra-regional markets are usually better than those of intra-regional markets, it is natural to see less preoccupation with intra-regional trade.

This is compounded by the fact that national, rather than regional, interests dominate Asean economic affairs. This is clearly seen in the negotiations surrounding the Asean Industrial Projects and the Asean Industrial Complementation scheme (Young, 1981, pp 118-337). In general terms, the problem first arose in the realisation that complementarity could be fostered through a form of regional industrial planning. The long-term interests of Asean as a regional entity could be enhanced by investments in complementary industrial facilities which would presumably take advantage of each member country's comparative advantage,

and which would then lead to greater intra-regional trade. This realisation was followed by a less palatable one, that regional investment planning quite often implied that some rationalisation of industrial activity was necessary in the sense that some existing (high cost) producers had to be phased out in order for more efficient producers in the same, or in some other, Asean country to reap economies of scale. This problem is compounded by the fact that, for some industrial products, economic efficiency requires that manufacturing facilities be established in a member country which has a small domestic market which would then export the product to other member countries where most of the consumers are located, but in which it is economically inefficient to locate the manufacturing facilities. The conflict between national interests and long-term regional interests that is now apparent, is usually resolved in favour of the former in preference to the latter.

An associated issue concerns the fact that regional investment schemes usually require some degree of protection from imports originating from outside the region. Insofar as some member countries are more strongly committed to free trade policies than others, this makes agreement on the appropriate level of protection for regional investment schemes difficult. The experience of the Asean Industrial Projects bears this out.

To summarise, the lack of complementarity between Asean economies is the main obstacle in the way of increased intra-regional trade through preferential tariffs. In principle, this obstacle could be eroded over time through judicious regional investment planning. In practice, however, this option is closed by the dominance of national interests over longer-term regional interests.

CONCLUSION

The Asean Preferential Trading Arrangements have not been a very effective instrument for increasing intra-regional trade because of some basic structural problems arising from the lack of complementarity of Asean economies. Thus far, efforts to overcome these through regional investment planning and complementation schemes have not been successful because national interests have taken precedence over regional interests.

The prospects of increased intra-regional trade through a change in these attitudes are not bright. The collapse of commodity markets and the general downturn in external trading conditions in recent years, coupled with internal economic difficulties, all point to the likelihood of an entrenchment rather than a relaxation of the obstacles which impede the growth of intra-Asean trade. While the problems manifest themselves in the sphere of economics, their resolution often lies in the realm of politics.

43.   ASEAN INDUSTRIAL CO-OPERATION

CHEE PENG LIM and JANG-WON SUH

OBJECTIVE AND SCOPE OF STUDY

 The major objective of this study is to review the existing form of industrial co-operation in ASEAN (Association of Southeast Asian Nations) in order to determine its weaknesses and shortcomings and on this basis, formulate a new form of co-operation which would incorporate not only the desirable features of the present form but also such desirable features as may be found in other regional schemes, especially those in the Andean Common Market (ANCOM) and European Community (EC) countries. Although the study concentrated on industrial co-operation, regional co-operation in non-manufacturing sectors which were related, such as finance and marketing, were also included within the scope of study.

ISSUE IN INDUSTRIAL CO-OPERATION

Generally, ASEAN countries give priority to the development of their manufacturing sector in their overall development strategies. Despite such priority and their intensified efforts, however, industrial development in ASEAN has not progressed significantly. Up till now, the entire

original ASEAN countries' share of world manufacturing value added is only just over 1 per cent. When ASEAN was established, it was hoped that regional co-operation could help to accelerate industrial development in the region. Unfortunately, the performances of ASEAN industrial co-operation schemes based on ASEAN Industrial Project (AIP), ASEAN Industrial Complementation (AIC) and ASEAN Industrial Joint Venture (AIJV) have been disappointing. Thus the major issue facing ASEAN policy-makers is whether to maintain the present form of industrial co-operation and expect little progress; or to adopt a new form which will help to boost industrial development in the region. The alternative of adopting a national as opposed to a regional strategy of industrial development sacrifices the potential for more rapid industrialization which regional co-operation offers.

WEAKNESSES IN EXISTING FORM

The existing form of ASEAN industrial co-operation based on AIP, AIC and AIJV have not made any significant impact on ASEAN industries for various reasons. Firstly, the present

Reprinted from the Executive Summary in *ASEAN Industrial Co-operation: Future Perspectives and an Alternative Scheme,* edited by Chee Peng Lim and Jang-Won Suh (Kuala Lumpur: Asian and Pacific Development Centre, 1988), pp. xvii–xxv, by permission of the editors and the publisher.

schemes do not take into account the lop-sided structure of the industrial sector in the ASEAN economies, especially the under development of small and medium industries (SMI). Secondly, the existing schemes place too much emphasis on market sharing, an emphasis which is at variance with the expressed reluctance of several ASEAN countries to move towards a free trade area. Co-operation in resource pooling especially in industrial finance, marketing and technology is not an important feature of the existing scheme. Thirdly, apart from preferential tariffs, other forms of incentives or assistance are excluded. Given the low level of margin of tariff preference, existing industrial co-operation schemes are not attractive enough for potential investors. Fourthly, the private sector is not given any substantive role under the existing scheme although there is a lot of emphasis on private-public sector co-operation. Finally, there are several weaknesses in the institutional and procedural framework relating to the existing form of ASEAN industrial co-operation. In view of the above shortcomings, a new form of ASEAN industrial co-operation is needed to accelerate industrial development in the region.

OBJECTIVES OF
ASEAN INDUSTRIAL CO-OPERATION

Although the objectives of ASEAN industrial co-operation were never explicitly stated, these objectives have to be specified to provide the basis for formulating a new form of industrial co-operation. We believe that in view of the aspiration and present level of industrial development in the region, the major objectives of ASEAN industrial co-operation should be:

1. to accelerate industrial development in the region so that ASEAN will account for at least 5 percent of the global manufacturing value added by the year 2000;
2. to develop a more balanced industrial

sector in the ASEAN countries by promoting the modernization of SMI and subcontracting;
3. to promote integration of the industrial sector in ASEAN which should be the long-term objective of regional co-operation.

RATIONALE OF A
NEW FORM OF CO-OPERATION

The above objectives cannot be achieved if ASEAN relies on the existing form of co-operation which is not only inadequate but also suffers from several inherent shortcomings. These include the absence of any mechanism to ensure a more even distribution of the gains from industrial co-operation, problems relating to implementation and the almost exclusive emphasis on market sharing. Apart from a lack of overall planning and consistency, the existing form fails to provide an integrated package of assistance to potential investors. Finally, a new form is needed which will take into account the realities of the ASEAN industrial sector, especially the different problems and needs of the small and medium industries and large industries (LI) sub-sectors.

CONCEPTUAL FRAMEWORK OF NEW FORM

In view of the unique characteristics and problems facing SMI and LI, the new form makes a distinction between these two sub-sectors not only to correct the lop-sided nature of the industrial structure in ASEAN but also to assist these countries develop SMI and subcontracting in order to improve industrial efficiency and achieve a faster rate of industrial development. Thus the new form is based on two basic schemes which are designed to reflect the basic differences in the two sub-sectors. The proposed ASEAN Small and Medium Industries (ASMI) and ASEAN Joint Industrial Co-operation (AJIC) schemes complement each other with the former focusing on SMI and the latter on LI. Projects approved under either scheme will be awarded on ASEAN status which will qualify them for special incentives and assistance. Apart from recognizing the distinction between SMI and LI, the conceptual framework also takes into account the various dimensions in which co-operation among ASEAN countries are required to overcome the major constraints encountered by ASEAN industrialists.

reasonable cost for LI and thus help to increase overall industrial efficiency.

The proposed form of SMI co-operation will encourage the establishment of new SMI through the ASMI scheme and the development of both new and existing SMI through the establishment of ASEAN Small and Medium Industries Centre (ASIC). SMI and ASIC will complement each other and their activities will be co-ordinated by the ASEAN Committee on Industry, Minerals and Energy (COIME).

ASEAN INDUSTRIAL CO-OPERATION IN SMI — THE ASMI SCHEME

SMI refer to manufacturing enterprises, employing less than 100 workers. They constitute a very large majority in the manufacturing sector in the ASEAN countries. Most SMI employ traditional management and production techniques and are found in the household, cottage and marginal industries producing almost mainly for a restricted local market. However, there is also a small group of SMI which produce mainly parts and components for LI. These SMI have the potential for further development because they employ modern management and production techniques and have a relatively high level of productivity. What they lack is a larger market to expand production. These are the SMI which we have targeted for development under the ASMI scheme.

Modern SMI like their traditional counterparts generally suffer from a discriminatory policy environment and have inadequate resources especially finance, marketing and technology. For example, even the present form of ASEAN industrial co-operation have an inherent bias against SMI. An ASEAN co-operation scheme on SMI may be necessary to overcome this bias and provide an integrated package of assistance to promote SMI development. The objective of such co-operation is to promote modem, self-supporting and economically viable SMI which will produce quality components at a

ASEAN JOINT INDUSTRIAL CO-OPERATION IN LI — THE AJIC SCHEME

LI employ 100 or more workers, involve large investments and generally produce on a large scale. Although LI account for a small proportion of ASEAN enterprises they produce most of the output and account for a large proportion of the export. LI may be labour-intensive such as in electronics components and textiles, capital-intensive such as in steel mills and cement plants, or technology-intensive such as genetics engineering and information technology. In ASEAN, LI predominate in petroleum refinery, chemicals, metals and metal products, textiles, motor vehicles and transport and machinery sub-sectors. Like SMI, LI confront several problems including finance, marketing and technology although the nature and magnitude of the problems may differ. Regional co-operation in LI is needed to ensure the viability of these enterprises given the large scale of their production. Such co-operation will enable the industrial sector in ASEAN to increase its export capabilities and enhance industrial development in the region. The framework for ASEAN co-operation in LI is the proposed AJIC scheme.

Like ASMI, which it complements, AJIC replaces the existing ASEAN industrial co-operation schemes but retains all its desirable features. AJIC projects will receive ASEAN *status* which will enable them to receive certain incentives and assistance.

SYSTEMS APPROACH TO
BUILDING INSTITUTIONAL FRAMEWORK FOR
NEW FORM OF ASEAN INDUSTRIAL CO-OPERATION

The design of the institutional framework for the proposed new form of ASEAN industrial co-operation is based on a review and analysis of the roles and functions of the existing institutional framework. Needless to add, the new institutional framework is developed in line with the conceptual framework for ASMI and AJIC. The main objective is not only to eliminate major problems related to the existing framework, such as delays in approval procedure but also to suggest new institutional arrangements and institutions which would help to overcome the gaps and weaknesses in the present framework. In addition, the role of the private sector and its interaction with the public sector is clearly delineated in the proposed institutional framework.

REVIEW OF EXISTING INSTITUTIONAL FRAMEWORK
FOR ASEAN INDUSTRIAL CO-OPERATION

On the government side, the major institutions directly concerned with ASEAN industrial co-operation schemes are ASEAN Economic Ministers (AEM) and COIME. In the private sector, the related institutions are Working Group on Industrial Co-operation (WGIC), Regional and National Industry Clubs, ASEAN Chambers of Commerce and Industry (ASEAN-CCI) and ASEAN Finance Corporation (AFC). In terms of present institutional arrangement, COIME invites nominations for AIJV products from ASEAN-CCI and ASEAN member countries. Nominations are considered by the Regional Industry Club (RIC), WGIC and ASEAN-CCI Council before submission to COIME. These are compiled at a COIME meeting into a tentative list of AIJV products. The list is examined by ASEAN members who then indicate their preferences, if any, to participate. The final list of AIJV products together with the participating countries is then submitted to AEM for approval and thereafter made available to ASEAN-CCI.

In terms of institutions, those which are presently established are only involved in project proposals (National Industry Club, RIC, WGIC and ASEAN-CCI) or project approvals (COIME and AEM). None of the institutions is involved in planning or monitoring of the projects. The ASEAN Secretariat as stated earlier is not directly involved in ASEAN industrial co-operation schemes. AFC does not finance any ASEAN project and there is no other supporting institution which provides any form of marketing or technological assistance. The institutional lacuna is too obvious to merit any further discussion.

PROBLEMS WITH
EXISTING INSTITUTIONAL FRAMEWORK

Under the present arrangement, the ASEAN Secretariat does not play any direct role either in identifying or approving products for ASEAN industrial co-operation schemes. The private sector, through ASEAN-CCI, has a role in nominating and considering products for ASEAN co-operation but policy-making and approval functions are exercised solely by the government institutions, namely COIME and AEM. There is little co-operation or interaction between the government and private sector institutions when it comes to formulation of policies and guidelines for ASEAN industrial co-operation schemes. More unfortunately, COIME and AEM members represent the national interests of their respective countries while ASEAN-CCI represent the interests of private sector LI. There is no institution representing either SMI or the broader ASEAN interests.

Apart from the significant gaps in representation, the existing institutional framework gives rise to bureaucratic delay. ASEAN projects have to go through unnecessary channels before they are approved. Once approved there is no systematic arrangement for monitoring or providing supportive assistance for these projects.

In view of the above shortcomings, a new

institutional arrangement may be necessary to provide a more conducive environment for the proposed new form of ASEAN industrial co-operation.

OBJECTIVES AND UNDERLYING PRINCIPLES IN DEVELOPING THE NEW INSTITUTIONAL FRAMEWORK

The principles underlying the design of the institutional arrangement and framework for the new form of co-operation are minimal government intervention, simplicity and economy. We believe that the government's role should be confined to that of providing a conducive environment for private sector investments. Its intervention should mainly take the form of providing incentives, assistance and approval for ASEAN projects. Procedures for project consideration and approval should be simple and reduced to a minimum. In the interests of economy, new institutions will be built on existing ones whenever possible. Finally, in view of ASEAN's reluctance to share markets the main instrument for co-operation will be resource pooling instead of market sharing.

PROPOSED PROCEDURES

ASEAN industrial co-operation projects may be eligible for an ASEAN status either under the ASMI or AJIC schemes. Proposals for such projects will be initiated by potential investors in the private sector. Proposals will be submitted to ASIC or WGIC for consideration in the case of ASMI and AJIC schemes respectively. They will then be transmitted to COIME for approval. Once approved, the proposed incentives will be provided by ASEAN governments, and the implementation of the project will be monitored by ASIC and WGIC in the case of ASMI and AJIC projects respectively.

For the purpose of awarding incentives and assistance, ASEAN status projects will be distinguished between those which are:

1. ASEAN market-oriented (selling 70 per cent or more of their output in ASEAN); and

2. Extra-ASEAN market-oriented (selling 30 per cent or more of their output outside ASEAN).

ASEAN market-oriented ASMI projects will be allowed duty free entry to ASEAN markets while AJIC products will enjoy 75 per cent margin of preference (MOP) and waiver privileges. Both ASMI and AJIC products which are extra-ASEAN market-oriented will enjoy 50 per cent MOP, waiver privileges and a set of fiscal incentives and preferential government procurement provided by the host government in addition to an integrated package of assistance provided by AFC, ASEAN Technology Development Centre (ATDC) and ASEAN General Trading Corporation (AGTC).

NEW INSTITUTIONS

For ASMI, two new institutions are proposed: one at government level and the other in the private sector. These are Federation of ASEAN Small and Medium Industries (FASMI) and ASIC respectively. FASMI will be the SMI counterpart of ASEAN-CCI and will represent the sector's interests in matters related to SMI. ASIC will be established to co-ordinate government assistance for SMI at the regional level. FASMI, ASIC and ASEAN-CCI will be represented at COIME meetings. This will enable the private sector to play a more meaningful role in ASEAN co-operation especially at the policy and guideline formulation level.

To assist both ASMI and AJIC projects in securing concessionary loans AFC will be expanded to take on the functions of a development bank. In the long run, an ASEAN Development Bank may be established. In addition, an ASEAN Technology Development Centre and an ASEAN General Trading Corporation will be established to provide technological and marketing assistance for ASEAN status projects.

In view of its extended responsibilities COIME will be strengthened in the short run with the help of a full-time secretariat. In the long run, however, we propose that FASMI and ASIC together with ACCI should join COIME to form ASEAN Industrial Development Corporation (AIDC) which will take over the present functions of COIME. Although the government representatives will have veto power in AIDC, the private sector will have the right to be consulted on policies and guidelines relating to industrial co-operation.

CONCLUSIONS AND RECOMMENDATIONS

If ASEAN is serious about accelerating the present pace of industrial co-operation it would have to consider a new form of such co-operation which will not only incorporate the various dimensions of such co-operation but also provide the basic framework for accelerating industrial development in the region. In view of this, a new form of industrial co-operation is proposed comprising two complementary schemes — ASMI and AJIC. For the effective implementation of these two schemes a new institutional framework with simplified procedures and supporting institutions is proposed. Among the new institutions, proposed priority should be given to the establishment of ASIC and the expansion of AFC. The major differences between the existing and the new form of co-operation are as follows. Firstly, the new form of co-operation emphasizes co-operation rather than integration, that is, the focus is on resource pooling rather than market sharing. Secondly, the new form of co-operation provides additional incentives and a new package of assistance to encourage investors to look beyond the ASEAN market. Thirdly, under the new form of co-operation the private sector is given a more meaningful role to play in formulating policies and guidelines in ASEAN industrial co-operation. Finally, the institutional framework envisaged for the new form of co-operation provides a simpler arrangement and reduces bureaucratic delays. In view of the above, we are confident that the acceptance of this proposal for a new form of industrial co-operation will enhance industrial development in ASEAN and enable the region to increase its manufacturing value added fivefold by the year 2000. Needless to add, further detailed studies may be required if the proposal is accepted in principle.

44.   SMALL ENTERPRISES IN ASEAN

CHEE PENG LIM

Most conspicuously missing from the list of ASEAN co-operation programmes and institutions to date is a programme for co-operation in the development of small enterprises and an institutional mechanism to encourage such co-operation. No doubt suggestions for such co-operation might have been made at the numerous meetings of the Committee on Industry, Minerals and Energy (COIME), but for various reasons these suggestions have neither been seriously considered nor adopted. Thus one finds that, although ASEAN co-operation has been instituted in various schemes and organizations, there is still no form of co-operation in the development of small enterprises. Consequently, the outside observer may be pardoned for thinking that small enterprises are an insignificant element in the ASEAN economies or that such enterprises do not have any vital role to play in ASEAN economic co-operation. The truth is just the reverse.

The scope of discussion in this paper will cover the ASEAN countries, with the exception of Brunei because there is no known study of small enterprises in that country. Furthermore, the discussion will be confined to small enterprises in the manufacturing sector, because non-manufacturing small enterprises are quite different in their characteristics and problems.

Moreover, the manufacturing sector is one of the fastest growing sectors in the ASEAN region, and all the ASEAN countries aspire to become industrialized by the year 2000.

IMPORTANCE OF SMALL ENTERPRISES

However, much more important than their numerical predominance in the ASEAN economies is the significant role which small enterprises play in the overall economic development of these countries. Briefly, small firms employ more workers per unit of capital; they help to increase total savings in the economy; they have a favourable impact on regional development; they serve as a "training ground" for developing the skills of industrial workers and entrepreneurs, and finally, they play an important complementary role to large firms in the economy. In short, small enterprises constitute a *vital* majority in the manufacturing sector in the ASEAN region.

The important role which small enterprises play in ASEAN has been substantiated by findings from various studies of small enterprises. (See for example, Chee 1975; Saeng et al. 1979; UP-ISSI 1979; World Bank 1982; World Bank 1979; and Lee and Tan 1981).

Reprinted in abridged form from "Small Enterprises in ASEAN: Need for Regional Co-operation", *ASEAN Economic Bulletin* 1, no. 2 (November 1984), pp. 89–114, by permission of the author and the Institute of Southeast Asian Studies.

SOME SUGGESTIONS

Although small enterprises play a significant role in the ASEAN economies, their potential has not been fully developed because of the handicaps and other problems which they face. In view of this, special policies and programmes for small enterprises are required within the framework of overall ASEAN development plans. As a first step, ASEAN countries should formulate a well-defined policy for small enterprises. The existing industrial policy tends to favour large firms. A more suitable industrial policy would ensure a more even-handed treatment of both small and large enterprises.

Furthermore, any policy for developing small enterprises should aim at promoting modern, self-supporting and economically viable manufacturing enterprises rather than a group of weak and inefficient industries which would need to be artificially sustained in their production, management, and financing. Even though some of the newly-established industrial units would need to be supported over a certain period of time, the purpose of promotion and assistance measures should be to guide and help small industrialists until they are able to stand on their own feet. After that they should not be accorded any special treatment. In fact, a national policy for small enterprise development should not be based on the assumption that small enterprises require preferential treatment to be viable. This is not the case as many studies have shown. Small enterprises are generally competitive with large enterprises and do not require preferential treatment. But the competitive base of small enterprises may be eroded if the government, deliberately or otherwise, discriminates against such enterprises (Chee 1979*a*).

Having formulated a suitable policy for small enterprises, the next step is to design a comprehensive plan for the promotion of the sector. Here priorities should be indicated in respect of industries to be encouraged and means of action to be followed. Various means exist to foster small enterprises, such as technical and financial assistance, improved supply and marketing arrangements, promotion of industrial co-operation and complementarity of industrial activities, and training of personnel. In view of their importance, we will focus on the main areas of assistance in relation to the more pressing problems facing small enterprises in the ASEAN countries. As we have seen, the most serious problem is the shortage of working and fixed capital. Many small enterprises can obtain no significant leverage through institutional borrowing and are limited to their own and family resources. As a result they find it difficult to compete with their large-scale counterparts.

It should be pointed out that small enterprises do not have sufficient capital, not because they cannot afford the cost of credit, but because in many cases it is simply not available (except outside the organized money market). In fact, many small enterprises would not mind paying a rate of interest slightly above the market rate if credit were available. The higher rate would be much less than the rate charged by non-institutional sources. More significantly, the rate would also be much less than the marginal rate of return under self-financing investment using existing techniques. Greater access to credit is especially important in view of the limited sources and type of credit available to a small enterprise in the ASEAN region, where the money market is still not fully developed.

Improving access to credit for small enterprises should begin by strengthening existing loan programmes through improvements in staffing and in project follow-up. Once this is done, there should be a substantial increase in the volume of small enterprise loans. The central banks in the ASEAN countries could do this either by authorizing commercial banks to increase their loans to small enterprises or encourage commercial banks to lend to such enterprises by providing the banks with loans at a special discount rate for re-lending to small enterprises. At the same time the commercial banks should also make a greater effort to assist small enterprises. They should adopt a development rather than a commercial orientation in processing loan applications from small entrepreneurs. A change in attitude will be beneficial to the commercial banks since small enterprise financing is going to form the basic type of commercial bank portfolio in the long run. This has been the experience in India[1] and will no doubt also be the experience in other developing countries.

In order to encourage commercial banks to lend to small enterprises, central banks should not force the banks to provide such loans at a rate of interest below the market rate. The problem facing small enterprises is access rather than the cost of bank loans. It will be difficult to improve the access and lower the cost at the same time. If it is really desirable to lower the cost of credit to small enterprise, governments should subsidize the difference and not expect the commercial banks to do so.[2] In any case, providing the loan at the market rate of interest will not deter the small borrower if he has a viable project.

We are not suggesting that removing the financial constraint would be sufficient to solve the problems of small enterprises. As a matter of fact, these enterprises also suffer from a variety of other problems such as outmoded techniques of production; ineffective marketing organization; poor quality of product; and inefficient management. Besides, the typical small ASEAN entrepreneur has no formal management training and little practical managerial experience. In view of this, a purely financial solution to small industry problems will obviously have a very limited efficacy. An effective solution will require a comprehensive programme comprising the provision of credit facilities, industrial advisory services, and other developmental aids. Any single factor approach to small enterprise development is likely to be ineffective and wasteful. An integrated programme that works on a carefully selected combination of factors simultaneously is much more likely to prove worthwhile.

Apart from providing direct assistance to small enterprises, ASEAN governments should also encourage large enterprises to help the small ones and the small enterprises to help themselves. One way of encouraging co-operation between large and small enterprises is the development of subcontracting. At the moment, subcontracting has not been fully developed in the ASEAN countries due to a number of factors. For example, the sales tax on final products involving cumulative tax payments, acts as a disincentive to subcontracting. Taxation on value added would, on the other hand, favour subcontracting. In addition, information on the possibilities of complementary relationships between large and small enterprises is lacking. To fill this gap, a subcontractor's exchange should be set up whereby demand and supply are made known and information provided. Thus on the supply side there would be information on the availability of machinery, production capacity, and specialization of small enterprises. On the demand side, information would be provided regarding parts, components, and processing of finishing operations offered by large establishments.

Government policies can also directly and immediately promote the growth of subcontracting by requiring that large firms receiving public contracts must subcontract specified portions of the work to small firms. Specifically in cases where individual contracts for supplies or services are necessarily of large size — because, for example, they call for a big volume of a uniform product, with clear-cut responsibility for quality and deliveries — the procurement agency can nevertheless substantially influence the primary bidders to subcontract part of their orders to small firms; it may, indeed, be a condition of the tender that a specified percentage, or certain components, be procured from small firms. In the absence of a subcontracting exchange, government agencies may assist prime contractors to locate eligible small firms, to help upgrade the latter's capabilities, and to establish equitable contract conditions. The potentialities depend of course not only on the nature of the goods/services being ordered, but also on the orientation and ingenuity of the procurement agency.

Public intervention in the private sector to influence large manufacturing and trading firms to subcontract with small industry can be justified on the basis of potential benefits to the economy and to participating firms. Such potential benefits include: improvements in overall capacity utilization and productivity; creation of income and employment opportunities; potential for a more efficient division of labour and allocation of resources; and the development of entrepreneurial, managerial, and technical abilities.

In the private sector, on the basis of Japanese and European experiences, one would expect that the greatest scope for subcontracting in the long run would exist in the metal products, machinery, electrical appliances and transport equipment industries. These are relatively undeveloped in many ASEAN countries at the moment. Government encouragement of subcontracting in these industries may take the forms, *inter alia*, of (a) compiling information regarding subcontracting opportunities and candidates, perhaps establishing subcontracting exchanges to match needs and capabilities; (b) assisting small industry in upgrading to meet quality and production requirements of prime contractors; (c) setting objective quality standards and specifications; and (d) assuring that subcontracting arrangements are not abused, through regulation or arbitration. Experience suggests that moral suasion and government incentives for large firms to use small industry subcontractors may also be effective.

Other possible measures to this end include reduced import duties on machinery for subcontractors; rental of government-owned equipment to subcontractors (mostly in construction); accelerated depreciation allowance on equipment to facilitate subcontractors' acquisition of capital assets; provision of industrial extension services, materials testing equipment, and industrial estate facilities; and, where opportunities exist, helping to organize joint contracting arrangements among small firms.

Given suitable encouragement there is no doubt that large enterprises will be willing to help small firms acquire new skills and technology. After all, the large enterprises realize that they will also benefit from the modernization of the small enterprise sector. In fact, the whole economy benefits because, if small and large enterprises grow together in a mutually reinforcing and complementary manner, industrialists will be able to take full advantage of all the possibilities for specialization and division of labour that exist in the industry.

ASEAN governments might also consider encouraging small enterprises to form co-operative societies. Collective action could be taken by small establishments without losing their independence. In this way they could get together to perform some functions which, because of their size, they are unable to perform individually. They could undertake joint programmes on such matters as marketing, export, and purchase of raw materials. The system could also enable the small industrialists to participate in fairs and exhibitions, something that would be difficult on an individual basis. Co-operatives are particularly useful in promoting exports of small industry.

Finally, the review and analysis of government policies towards small enterprises suggests that government policy-makers should bear in mind the interests and problems of small enterprises in the formulation of any government policy. Wherever possible, exemptions should be given to such enterprises. When that is not possible, the proposed policy should be flexible towards small enterprises. Similarly, every policy should be implemented with consideration and flexibility as far as small enterprises are concerned, and government officials should always be sympathetic to any appeal for special consideration by small firms affected by the implementation of the policy. We are not suggesting that small enterprises be exempted from all government regulations or requirements, but that such regulations and requirements do not impose a greater burden on small enterprises than on their large-scale counterparts.

PROPOSAL FOR AN ASEAN
SMALL ENTERPRISE CENTRE

At the regional level, ASEAN countries should

try to co-ordinate their policies and assistance programmes for small enterprises. Considering the important role which small enterprises play in the ASEAN economies, the governments of this region should give the same attention to co-operation in small enterprise projects that they have given to the large industrial projects. The co-operation could take the form of establishing an ASEAN Standing Group consisting of planners, small enterprise promotional officers, small enterprise trainers, academic technologists, marketing specialists, and some small entrepreneurs drawn from various ASEAN countries. This Group could meet at regular intervals and should be entrusted with the responsibility of a continuous evaluation of the policies, programmes, and role of small enterprises in ASEAN. Affiliated units may be set up in individual countries. The continuous monitoring and evaluation of small enterprise programmes in ASEAN will be useful in policy formulation, establishing an organizational network, and also undertaking long-range programmes of entrepreneurial stimulation. Eventually, the ASEAN governments should consider the establishment of an ASEAN Small Enterprise Centre to co-ordinate the development of small enterprises in the region.

At present several small enterprise institutes or agencies exist in the ASEAN countries. For example, there is the University of Philippines — Institute of Small-scale Industries in the Philippines (UP-ISSI), the Directorate-General of Small-scale Industries in Indonesia, and the Division of Small Enterprises in Malaysia. Each ASEAN country should designate one institute or agency as a focal point for a regional network of exchange of information and co-ordination of small enterprise development activities (training, research, and so on). The proposed ASEAN Small Enterprise Centre should, among other functions:

1. focus on the dissemination of existing information and research on small enterprises, especially within the ASEAN region, including the preparation of small industry profiles, information on available technology to enhance the capabilities of small entrepreneurs, and market and subcontracting opportunities for small enterprise products;
2. provide training and research facilities for personnel involved in small enterprise development such as extension service agents, bank loan officers, or other officials;
3. act as a focal point for seeking out and channelling external assistance for small enterprise development for the ASEAN region.

There is an urgent need for the establishment of the ASEAN Small Enterprise Centre for several reasons. Firstly, such a centre would encourage the mutual exchange of information and ideas and the pooling together of training and research facilities which would provide a tremendous stimulus for the development of ASEAN small enterprises. Secondly, many of the ASEAN countries have had at least fifteen years of involvement in small enterprise development programmes, but all this time each country has been working more or less in isolation from the rest. Consequently, many innovative and successful programmes which could have been adopted by other ASEAN countries remain confined to the boundaries of the country of origin. On the other hand, mistakes committed by one country are often repeated in others (Sharma 1979). All these mistakes could have been avoided and useful experiences could have been exchanged if there had been an institutional framework for ASEAN co-operation in small enterprises.

Thirdly, there is a need to change the course of ASEAN industrial co-operation. The U.N. Study Team which in 1974 was organized to look into the scope of economic co-operation for ASEAN did not appear to give adequate weight to the significance of small enterprise development in the region and opted for the implementation of large-scale projects. Unfortunately the Report's recommendations (United Nations, 1974) were closely adopted by the

ASEAN leaders in Bali who, like the U.N. Study Team, failed to realize that small and not large enterprises form the backbone of the ASEAN economies. Consequently, ASEAN has spent the last eight years in a fruitless pursuit of large-scale, grandiose projects which hardly made any impact on ASEAN industrial co-operation and which have certainly not benefited the masses in this region.

In view of this, it may be time to shift gears and reconsider a different industrial strategy. There is a great deal of scope for ASEAN co-operation in the promotion of small enterprises since, as many economists have rightly pointed out, there are bright prospects and opportunities for the development of small enterprises in the ASEAN region. (See for example, Chee 1984*b*; Falk 1983, and Laumig 1983). Possibly the first step which should be taken in this direction is the establishment of the ASEAN Small Enterprise Centre.

CONCLUSION

ASEAN industrial co-operation has not been very successful because it has been based on the development of large-scale enterprises such as the ASEAN Industrial Projects. Such projects not only require huge investments but also involve a long gestation period. More significantly, their impact on the majority of the peoples in the ASEAN countries may not be felt for a long time. On the other hand, co-operation in small enterprise development does not require a huge amount of resources and would bring immediate benefits to the vast majority of entrepreneurs in the ASEAN region. In view of this, the ASEAN Committee on Industry, Minerals, and Energy should place regional co-operation in small enterprise development at the top of the agenda at its next major meeting. Given the bright business prospects and opportunities for small enterprises in the ASEAN countries predicted by a number of economists, and given adequate regional co-operation in promoting small enterprises, we have no doubt that such enterprises in ASEAN will be able to realize their full potential and play a significant role in the economic development of the ASEAN countries. So let us hope that ASEAN leaders will have the vision to chart a new course in regional industrial co-operation.

NOTES
1. According to Mr S.V.S. Sharma, former Principal Director, Small Industry Extension Training Institute, Hyderabad, India.
2. A government subsidy to cover the differential cost of lending to small industry might be justified on the grounds of differential contribution of such industry to employment and/or entrepreneurial development.

45.
ASEAN CO-OPERATION IN FOOD, AGRICULTURE, AND FORESTRY

L.S. CABANILLA

The highs and lows in the ASEAN[1] countries' economic performance is now recognized to be mainly due to the dependency of growth on trade in primary products[2] — the international prices of which, are prone to wide, volatile changes. It is due to this experience that policy makers, generally acting for the interest of their individual countries attempted to make structural changes in their economies. More specifically, efforts have been made to diversify exports to lessen dependence on primary products.

However, despite some perceptible adjustments, the structure of the ASEAN developing economies remained essentially the same. Except for Singapore, agriculture continues to be a dominant sector. This Chapter hopes to contribute something in paving the way for a more effective cooperation in Food. Agriculture and Forestry among the ASEAN countries. It first describes very briefly, the agricultural economy of the six member countries, then reviews past cooperative undertakings from which "gaps" will be identified and used as basis for identifying future cooperative undertakings.

THE ASEAN AGRICULTURAL ECONOMIES

The agricultural sector of the ASEAN member countries, with the exception of the city state Singapore, is a vital sector of their economies. And, although there has been an observed decline in the relative share of agriculture in the total GDP of the countries, agriculture will still have profound socio-economic implications in each of the member countries in the future. For one thing, majority of the population lives in the rural/agricultural sector. For another, agriculture has proven to be a potent engine of growth for the whole economy. As in the case of the Philippines, during the most recent economic crisis of the eighties, agriculture posted positive growth rates when all the other sectors experienced negative growth. Given this, agriculture will definitely serve as a focal point in the region's pursuit of the dual objectives of growth and equity.

Among the member countries, Philippines' agriculture contributes the most (29 per cent) to real GDP in 1985 followed by Indonesia (24 per cent), Thailand (23 per cent), and Malaysia 21 per cent). Except for Singapore, more than half of the growth in GDP seems to come from the countries' agricultural sector. More than half of the total labor force in Thailand (67 per cent) and Indonesia (55 per cent); close to half in the Philippines (46 per cent)

Reprinted in abridged form from L.S. Cabanilla, "ASEAN Cooperation in Food, Agriculture and Forestry: Past and Future Directions", in *ASEAN Economic Cooperation: A New Perspective*, edited by Hendra Esmara (Singapore: Chopmen Publishers for Federation of ASEAN Economic Associations and Ikatan Sarjana Ekonomi Indonesia, 1988), pp. 55–69, by permission of the author and the publisher.

and one third in Malaysia in 1985 is employed in agriculture. Finally, it should be noted that except for the oil-rich Brunei and the city-state Singapore whose agricultural imports have been growing much faster than their exports, the agricultural sector of the member countries are net contributors to their economy's foreign exchange earnings; with Malaysia's agriculture as the highest net foreign exchange contributor from 1970–1985.

Because of this striking similarity in their economic structure, some people tend to regard the ASEAN member countries to be competitors rather than complements. It is worth noting however, that their resources base show some differences, evident in the fact that at least 3 member countries are petroleum exporters and the rest net importers.

Competitors or otherwise, cooperation in agriculture food and forestry should nonetheless be an important agenda for action within the region. Exploiting the region's comparative advantage in agriculture as a group will provide the necessary impetus to its industrial development efforts. Wage goods need to be produced efficiently as the region's land frontiers are fast closing if not already closed in some member countries. Since foreign exchange earnings from agriculture and forestry will all the more become vital as the region strives for industrial development, cooperation will be a vital factor in the continuing effort of meeting the problems of growing protectionist staunch of the industrialized countries — the traditional markets for the region's primary export products. For example, the region's vegetable oil exports is facing a formidable problem in the EEC and the US markets. Similarly, Thailand's cassava exports to the EEC for political reasons, are facing a declining trend in the mid-eighties.

The dominance of agriculture serves as the common denominator in the region. It goes without saying that agriculture will continue to be an important factor in the region's pursuit of growth and equity. Presumably, economies of scale will always be present in achieving these objectives. Logically therefore, the member

countries will be better off attaining this dual objectives collectively than individually.

In relation to world agricultural trade, ASEAN is considered to be a vital force. It exports more than half of the world's total exports of natural rubber (mostly from Malaysia, Indonesia and Thailand); palm oil (Malaysia, Indonesia and Singapore); copra and coconut oil (Philippines, Malaysia and Indonesia) and spices (Malaysia, Indonesia and Singapore). It is also worth pointing out that although ASEAN exports on rice (Thailand), sugar (Philippines and Thailand) and forest products (Malaysia, Indonesia and Philippines) are small in proportion to the world exports, they are nonetheless important sources of foreign exchange for the respective countries mentioned.

Crop Production: Agricultural crop production within the region is basically composed of two distinct subsectors — the export/commercial subsector producing cash crops mostly for exports and the subsistence subsector producing primarily food (rice) and feed (corn) grains. It is expected that both subsectors will continue to be important to the ASEAN economies in the future.

Commercial agriculture will have significant contribution to export earnings although institutional development within the region may somehow diminish this role. Likewise, since majority of the agricultural population will continue to depend on rice and to a lesser extent, corn, for subsistence, these crops will continue to be important in the ASEAN agricultural economy.

Data show that of the total regional rice output in 1985, 49 per cent was produced by Indonesia, 35 per cent by Thailand, 13 per cent the Philippines, and 3 per cent by Malaysia. It will be noted however, that except for some political exports of rice from the Philippines and some amount of exports from Indonesia during the recent years, it is only Thailand that has consistently maintained its reputation as the region's rice exporter.

The same thing is true with corn. Although

Indonesia produced most of the region's corn output, Thailand seems to be the only net corn exporter. The Philippines has gone through several corn production programs since the mid-seventies in an effort to attain corn self-sufficient and some export capability but it has remained as one among the region's biggest corn importers. Corn production in the region seems to have expanded faster than rice but with the growing demand for feed grains, the region needs to produce more in the future.

Growth in the region's crop output have come primarily from increases in area rather than yield.[3] In contrast to the relatively more successful technical improvements in commercial/plantation crop production, technical innovation in the subsistence crops subsector is very slow resulting in a chronically low farm yields. For examples, despite the introduction of the high yielding varieties (HYVs) of rice in the early sixties, yield per hectare has remained low — well below the average yields of Korea and Japan. Rice yield in the Philippines, which is supposed to have one of the largest proportion of rice areas planted to the HYVs in the region, has remained relatively stagnant and almost one third of the yield level in Japan and Korea. Significant rice yield increases are observed in Indonesia during the eighties but generally, yield performance in the region is still low — implying that there is a big room for improvement in technical innovation.

The yield story on corn is just as bad if not worse than rice. Even the yield level of Thailand, the region's corn exporter, is way below that of other corn exporting countries like the United States. Again, this is an indication that prospects of shifting the production possibility frontier of the region through technical breakthroughs are substantial.

In view of the closed land frontiers in some of the member countries, the yield constraint problems must be removed if the region hopes to produce enough food for its growing population. Similarly, socio-economic constraints must be dismantled. For example, since one of the reasons for low yield is the low levels of fertilizer application due to unfavorable fertilizer-rice price ratio, some adjustments in farm price incentives must be done.

Substantial post harvest losses reaching as much as 20–30 per cent compound the problem of low levels of productivity in the ASEAN grains subsector. This phenomenon is due mainly to the lack of post harvest facilities such as storage, transportation, drying and processing. In the rural areas for example. Drying is done mostly in concrete pavements, something that is not possible during the wet season.

The Livestock Subsector: The livestock subsector serves as an important link between the crops subsector (feeds source) and the agro-processing subsectors (meat processing and feed milling). Although it is not as yet as important as the crops subsector in terms of value added, its significance is expected to grow as demand for meat increases resulting from the increase in per capita incomes in the member countries. The prospects of this subsector become even brighter if one notes that at present, Thailand is the only net exporter of meat in the region. This brings to the fore another possibility of increasing intra-regional trade in agriculture with Singapore and Brunei remaining as the biggest meat importers.

Looking at the livestock inventory per capita in the region swine and poultry seem to show the best potential sources of increasing intra regional meat trade — with the Philippines and Thailand as best prospective candidate exporters. It should be pointed out however that ASEAN's capacity to produce more meat, especially the nonruminants, depends on its capacity of producing more feedstuffs notably corn. At present, only Thailand is blessed with excess corn production — a logical explanation to its being the region's main exporter of meat particularly chicken meat. Inevitably, the other ASEAN livestock producers like the Philippines has to import corn either from Thailand or the United States.

Corn substitutes like cassava are presently

produced in substantial quantities in the region (Indonesia and Thailand) but the use of cassava for foods has been constrained by the scarcity, hence, prohibitive price of protein supplements like soybean meal.[4] As a result, instead of being used as domestic feed ingredient, cassava produced in the region is exported to the EEC.

PAST AND FUTURE COOPERATION

In the previous section we have noted that: (a) ASEAN agriculture, particularly the food crop subsector, is characterized by low levels of productivity; (b) post harvest losses particularly on grains, are high; (c) ASEAN agricultural trade is heavily dependent on export of a few primary products which at present are facing slackening demand due to the growing protectionist mood among the importing industrial countries, and (d) Intra-ASEAN agricultural trade is low but livestock promises to be a good source of intensified intra-regional trade.

These observations serve to underscore the importance of cooperation among the member countries. Technology development to improve productivity is costly, hence, it will be less painful, budgetary-wise if the ASEAN countries solved their technological woes together. In a similar manner, the growing agricultural protectionism among the industrial countries could be more effectively counter-balanced if the member countries acted together. As a group, they would have a better leverage in the trade negotiating trade.

In this section, we try to review the past cooperation on Food, Agriculture and Forestry with the aim of determining the possible "gaps in cooperation". From this review, we identify future activities which may foster closer cooperation in the area of agricultural development among the ASEAN countries.

Operationally, ASEAN, work through committees in the identification and implementation of cooperative undertaking. For agriculture, food and forestry, the ASEAN Committee on Food, Agriculture and Forestry (COFAF) is the workhorse. This committee in turn works through a system of sub-committees and co-ordinating boards/councils.

Established in 1977 during the third ASEAN Economic Ministers' meeting in Manila on March 20–22 of the same year, COFAF has the following tasks:

1. To coordinate periodic reviews of the food, agriculture and forestry situation in the ASEAN region and to prepare studies on the short-term and long-term prospects of the food, agriculture and the forestry situation in the region as well as at the global level.
2. To develop effective methods of exchange of information among member countries pertaining to food, agriculture and forestry, with a view of facilitating cooperative undertakings in these sectors of the economy.
3. To identify specific fields of cooperation among the ASEAN member countries as well as with third countries, groups of countries, or international agencies, in order to promote sound development of the food, agriculture and forestry sectors in the ASEAN region.
4. To maintain close cooperation with other related ASEAN Committees and bodies as well as with related extra-ASEAN national and international bodies and organizations.
5. To submit to the ASEAN Economic Ministers periodic reports on the progress of work of the committee.

In the past 10 years of COFAF existence, records show that the committee has met 16 times — all (except one) of which, were held in Indonesia. Except for the sub-committee on Food Handling, all the other COFAF subsidiary bodies have met in less number of times (Table 5.1).

From these meetings, based on COFAF classification, a total of 46 cooperative projects have been identified — 6 in food, 10 in agriculture, 15 in forestry, 8 in livestock and 6 in

TABLE 5.1: Number of Meetings of COFAF Subsidiary Bodies
During the Past Ten Years

Subsidiary Body	Number of Meetings
Livestock Coordinating Group	9
Forestry Coordinating Group	10
Crops Coordinating Group	6
Fisheries Coordinating Group	8
Food Handling Sub-Committee	19
Council of ASEAN Directors of Extension (CADEX)	10
ASEAN Agriculture Research Coordinating Board (AARB)	6

SOURCE: COFAF Records.

fisheries. Of the total number of projects as of September 1985, 13 are ongoing, 4 were completed and 29 are not yet implemented. The Philippines has the most number of projects hosted followed by Malaysia, Thailand and Indonesia. Brunei, having joined the association only in 1984 hosts no project so far. Most of the projects approved are not short duration in nature with the ASEAN Food & Security Reserve, Food handling and the ASEAN Agricultural Development Planning Centre as the only undertakings that seem to be pursued on a long term basis. It should be noted also that the bulk of the funds to support the cooperative projects (either on-going, completed or proposed) come from donor countries outside the region — a phenomenon that does not speak well of regional cooperation.

The ASEAN Food Security Reserve project which establishes an ASEAN Emergency Rice Reserve to be contributed by each of the member countries to wit:

Indonesia	=	12,000 metric tons
Malaysia	=	6,000 metric tons
Philippines	=	12,000 metric tons
Singapore	=	5,000 metric tons
Thailand	=	15,000 metric tons
Total		50,000 metric tons

is a commendable undertaking. Statistics show that world rice production that enter world trade is small. This implies that the world market is not a reliable source of rice during

times of unfavourable harvest within the region, hence the necessity of establishing a regional rice reserve.

We would like to recommend, however, that since in extreme drought situations, planting materials become a problem in some of the member countries, token amounts of seed reserves must be put aside. If this is not possible, at least an explicit agreement among ASEAN members in terms of providing emergency planting materials must be made. The food handling and crops post-harvest programmes funded by Australia and IDRC respectively, are likewise worthy of praise. These efforts will go a long way in reducing post-harvest losses which in the long run, improves the regions food supply situation. It is hoped that these efforts will continue in the future.

As a whole, our inventory of ASEAN co-operative on food Agriculture and Forestry, however, show that not one among the approved projects is a serious effort to increase levels of productivity. Projects on integrated past management and irrigation system management are underway but it appears that the region as a whole, is bent on depending on International Organizations (e.g. IRRI) for the development of superior genetic crop varieties although some member countries are now allotting some budget for genetic improvement in food crops (e.g. Philippines Rice Research Institute). As a long term solution to the low productivity problem, the area of genetic materials must be considered by the ASEAN. It must be borne in mind that while the role of international organizations such as IRRI are geared towards this effort, their activities are not specifically geared for ASEAN.

It is also noted that the kinds of cooperation that are completed, on-going or are still to be implemented reflect the interests of government ministers, hence, involvement of the private sector in these cooperative undertakings is wanting. For a more effective exploitation of the region's agricultural resources, the private sector must be activity involved in the future

ASEAN cooperation. Agro-processing activities that serve to strengthen the link between agriculture and industry would be a good area to start with, and the ASEAN Chamber of Commerce and Industry could serve as the logical conduit for these kinds of cooperative undertakings.

Finally, our review does not show a strong and solid effort towards the establishment of a common agricultural policy in the region. In fact, the basic foundations upon which a common agricultural policy shall be based are not in place. Maybe a comprehensive analysis of the region's comparative advantage and economic incentives in agriculture is a good start. There have been patches of studies of this kind in the member countries but what seems to be needed at this point is an ASEAN wide study. The ASEAN Agricultural Planning and Development Centre could possibly initiate this effort but since it does not possess the necessary manpower to undertake an activity like this, the effort could be done in collaboration with other institutions like the Center for Policy and Development Studies (CPDS) at the University of the Philippines at Los Banos (UPLB) and other similar institutions in the region. And, as a long term activity, a regional center for agricultural policy studies that will undertake regional policy analysis if only for the purpose of having a more unified and coherent agricultural policy must be established.

CONCLUSION

As the member countries strive for industrial development, they should not lose sight of the fact that agriculture is an important partner in this effort. The region as a whole should not fall into the pit of neglecting the agricultural sector in the process of industrial development.

For one thing, the rural/agricultural population is a vital source of demand for the region's industrial products. For another thing, as the agro-processing sector grows, demand for raw materials from the agricultural sector rises, hence, the need to produce these materials as efficiently as possible to make our agro-processing industries competitive in the international market. Of course, it will be realized that the member countries, due to some differences in resource endowments, will have different capabilities in achieving agricultural development. This underscores the need for a strong cooperation in food, agriculture and forestry.

For food security reasons, it is understandable that each of countries will strive to achieve self sufficiency in food crops but it must be emphasized that extra effort must be directed at achieving excellence in the areas of activities where the number countries are inherently good at. To use the economic jargon, the member countries should engage only in activities where they have strong comparative advantage over the others. This way, the region's resources will be more efficiently utilized.

Our discussion on the forestry sector did not have the same space as that of agriculture. However, it is hope that this paper has shed some light in the effort of regional cooperation.

NOTES

1. Because of data problems for Brunei , most of the ASEAN data refer to those of Indonesia, Malaysia, Philippines, Singapore and Thailand.
2. John Wong, *ASEAN Economies in Perspective: A Comparative Study of Indonesia, Malaysia, The Philippines, Singapore and Thailand* (Hong Kong: The Macmillan Press Ltd., 1979).
3. *Ibid.*
4. L.S. Cabanilla, *Economic Incentives and Comparative Advantage in Livestock Production*, Ph.D. thesis; University of the Philippines at Los Banos, College, Laguna, Philippines, 1983).

46.

STRUCTURAL CHANGE AND ENERGY POLICY IN ASEAN
Towards Regional Co-operation

SHANKAR SHARMA

ASEAN as a group has a fast-growing economy. The economic performance of individual member countries — Brunei, Indonesia, Malaysia, Philippines, Singapore, and Thailand — has been impressive during the last two-and-a-half decades. The success of the economic development, in general, can be attributed to their market-oriented, outward-looking economic policies.

The region, whose economy is closely related with the energy sector, comprises both energy importers and energy exporters. Three major producers of oil and gas — Indonesia, Malaysia, and Brunei — depend heavily on oil and gas exports for foreign exchange earnings and government revenues. Singapore, the largest oil-refining and trading centre in the region, is a major exporter of petroleum products. On the other hand, the Philippines and Thailand depend overwhelmingly on imported oil. The high degree of dependence on energy has made the economy of these countries vulnerable to energy prices. Despite the impressive economic growth, the region was greatly affected by the oil crises.

Rapid price increases and vulnerability in supply in the 1970s led oil-importing countries to pursue various counter-acting policies. ASEAN countries formulated and implemented comprehensive energy policies; exploration and production activities of energy resources were intensified. Substitutions of other sources of energy for oil were sought and encouraged. Efforts were also made to increase the efficiency in energy use. Different pricing policies were adopted and macroeconomic policies were adjusted to ease the adverse impact of the oil crises. However, because of the diverse nature of the countries, the policy responses to the energy crises and the experiences were different.

After the oil crises the demand for oil as well as non-oil energy slowed down in the ASEAN countries, mainly because of higher prices, but the demand growth rates were still higher than the averages for the world and the Asian-Pacific region. The higher demand growth was the result of higher economic growth in the region. The shift in the sectoral demand does not show any pattern; the differences might be due to the level and the growth rates of economic development, availability of energy resources, level of industrialization, etc.

Another successful strategy was observed

Reprinted in abridged form from "Structural Change and Energy Policy in ASEAN", in *Energy Market and Policies in ASEAN*, edited by Shankar Sharma and Fereidun Fesharaki (Singapore: Institute of Southeast Asian Studies, 1991), pp. 26–56, by permission of the author and the publisher.

in supply management. Production of oil as well as non-oil energy was increased rapidly. Oil was substituted wherever it was commercially feasible. Since most of the substitutes for oil compete with fuel oil, the demand for fuel oil declined as the alternative sources of energy were developed. Substitution was more pronounced in the situation of faster electricity growth. About 35 per cent of the increase in demand for energy between 1973 and 1987 was met by the substitution of oil by other energy resources.

Another important factor observed was the narrowing of the wedge between domestic and international prices. During the 1970s (including the period before the first oil crisis) the pricing policies of petroleum products in most of the developing countries were affected and motivated by fiscal and distributional consideration rather than economic efficiency. Kerosene and diesel were subsidized to prevent erosion of real incomes arising from higher oil prices and was targeted to the poor people, but gasoline was taxed more heavily. The average domestic prices of petroleum products were almost four times higher than the international prices in 1973. The difference was only about 2.3 times in 1988.

There have been some attempts to conserve energy, but it seems that most of the measures were temporary regulations to reduce oil consumption. In the transportation sector the efficiency increased in most of the countries because of the development of energy-efficient vehicles. There have been some changes in energy intensity in the industrial sector but they are mainly due to structural change in industry and use of new energy resources. Data are not available on how much conservation has been achieved owing to the change in plant and equipment and new technology. This is a research question. But scant evidence shows that progress in energy conservation has been limited.

Oil-importing countries were highly successful in diversifying their source of energy supply, increasing indigenous production, and reducing the oil-import dependence. However, oil exploration activities have slowed down after 1982 in ASEAN countries because of declining oil prices. But production is increasing in all oil-producing countries in the region except Brunei. As it is rich in natural gas and oil reserves, Brunei will not have any production problem for at least 20–30 years into the future. Production of oil in Brunei was reduced to prolong the life of the petroleum reserves. Singapore is also trying to diversify its energy consumption by importing natural gas from Malaysia and Indonesia.

Among oil-exporting countries, Indonesia's oil consumption increased by more than 150 per cent between 1973 and 1987, but production in 1987 was about the same as in 1973. Similarly, total primary energy consumption increased by almost four times but production grew by only 55 per cent. Thus, energy substitution should take place at a rapid rate to prolong the present rate of oil exports.

So far as the macroeconomic effects of the oil shocks were concerned, oil price increases in general had a negative impact on the balance of payments, terms of trade, and inflation in oil-importing countries. Growth rates of real GDP were not affected immediately after the first oil crisis. The expansionary economic policies adopted by most of the ASEAN countries after the crisis and higher export growth rates helped them to maintain higher economic growth. But after the second oil crisis export growths were lower than before; most of the countries were already in heavy debt and could not borrow more. As a result, in addition to the adverse impact on balance of payment, terms of trade, and inflation, the second oil crisis also adversely affected the economic growth. The oil price decline after 1982 has had a positive impact on the economic indicators of these countries. But in general, the countries that were more outward oriented in terms of trade and foreign investment were more resilient to the oil shocks.

CONCLUSION

It is difficult to forecast the future outlook of the ASEAN energy market. But it is expected that the region's economy will grow by at least 4–5 per cent in the medium term. This will stimulate energy demand in the region. The demand for oil in the region is also forecast to be one of the highest in the world.[1]

Energy exploration and energy production will also be strengthened. The short life of oil reserves and the large natural gas deposits provide enough incentives to develop gas, which will play a major role in the development of the region's economy. The scope for substitution of fuel oil by natural gas in power generation is great.

However, production, distribution, and consumption of all commercial energy contribute negatively to the environment. Nitrogen, carbon dioxide, and sulphur oxides are the main pollutants resulting from fossil fuel (coal, oil, and natural gas) combustion. They are also the main culprits which cause the greenhouse effect and acid rain. Production and distribution also cause different safety and environmental effects. Public consensus on environment is growing in developed countries and its effect is being felt in ASEAN countries.

The growing commercial energy use and its increasing share are making the environment a more burning issue and the time has come to integrate energy and environment policies in the development of these countries. Taking into consideration the environmental effects of energy development in the formulation of energy policies will minimize the long-term environment control cost and help in the development of a healthy energy system.

The conservation measures taken in ASEAN countries are minimal. Structural change in the industrial sector and the growing use of energy-efficient vehicles raised energy efficiency in these sectors in some of the ASEAN countries. But substantial/concerted efforts for energy conservation are lacking in ASEAN countries. This could be due to resource and manpower constraints. The low energy intensity of the economy reduces the vulnerability to a sharp rise in international oil prices and supply disruption. Energy conservation efforts in the long run will improve industrial competitiveness in the international market.

Countries should try to take measures to increase efficiency in energy use. Observations show that energy intensity started increasing in the first-half of the 1980s, during which oil prices were also declining. It looks like the increase in energy intensity was due partially to the structural change in the industrial sector and partially to lower oil prices. In any case there exists sufficient scope for improvement. Similarly, energy conservation in heating/cooling and lighting systems for buildings can be made more efficient. Technology transfer from European and American experience can be useful in this sector.

In terms of transportation, the technology is transferred from the industrialized countries, but the policies adopted by Singapore to reduce traffic congestion are praiseworthy. These policies also reduce pollution and improve conservation. Other countries, wherever feasible, should follow Singapore's experience in traffic management.

Pricing policy is the most important tool of energy demand management. Governments of all countries are involved in one way or another in the price-setting process. The retail prices of petroleum products deviated from the international prices because of taxes or subsidies, and the deviations were very high. Intervention in energy pricing is made to promote conservation (to reduce demand), to generate revenue for the government, for income distribution (by subsidizing kerosene/diesel used by relatively poor consumers and taxing gasoline), and to minimize the import bill (minimize supply insecurity). But these criteria conflict with the objective of economic efficiency. Efficient pricing helps in optimal allocation of resources. Any deviation from this principle results in inefficiency in the economy. The diverse nature of the economy of different countries requires different pricing objectives, but in the long run the economic principle of efficiency should be the basis for setting prices.

Furthermore, energy pricing policy is the major issue for natural gas development in the region. The growth rate of natural gas demand in the region is expected to be the highest among the fuel categories. But none of the ASEAN gas producers has any uniform gas-pricing policy. Prices are set differently in different sectors of the economy. Moreover, the export price of gas is set by a formula that is linked with crude oil It is all right to link the price of natural gas with one of its closest substitutes, but in a situation of low oil prices (as happened in 1986), buyers will find natural gas less economical than oil owing to the high fixed-cost ratio of natural gas. Since pricing policy is the key issue for the development, consumption, and trade of natural gas, it may be worthwhile to set a policy for natural gas pricing in ASEAN countries.

It is true that the energy market is volatile and can be affected by OPEC production, technological breakthroughs, new discoveries of energy resources, environmental concerns, political turmoils and so on. But, in the final analysis, whether the countries can become more resilient in riding out crises and uncertainties depends largely on the energy policies they devise.

Addendum

ASEAN co-operation on energy in the region is being promoted by a variety of activities. Regional activities are undertaken mainly through the ASEAN Council on Petroleum (ASCOPE), the Committee on Industries, Minerals and Energy (COIME), and the Committee on Science and Technology (COST). Several technical and sectoral committees have been formed under these committees and the programme of action has been approved on coal, electricity, petroleum and natural gas, geo-thermal resources, new and renewable sources of energy, energy conservation, energy and environment, research development and demonstration and energy policy and planning. The ASEAN-EC Energy Management Training and Research Centre has also been established to launch comprehensive research and training programmes in energy. Countries are also integrated through various agreements including ASEAN Petroleum Security Agreement and Agreement on ASEAN Energy Co-operation.

Despite various committees and programmes, the impact of co-operation in the energy sector has been limited. Some of the areas where co-operation can be enhanced are as follows.

ASEAN is a net oil exporter. However, although the region has oil exporting countries, only about one-third of the regional oil is from the region itself. Trade in crude oil among the countries of the region has increased significantly especially since 1973, but less so for the products. Oil is still traded more with traditional buyers mainly outside the region. The scope for increasing intra-ASEAN trade in oil is promising.

Similarly, demand for natural gas in ASEAN is expected to increase rapidly mainly because of the short life of oil reserves, increasing dependence on the Middle East for oil imports, rising environmental concerns, and the large natural gas deposits in the region. At present, Singapore is the only country in the region which imports natural gas through a pipeline from Malaysia. Malaysia is also hoping to export piped natural gas to Thailand after the third phase of the Peninsular Gas Utilization project which is expected to be completed in 1995.

Co-operation in the natural gas sector can be expanded significantly. This will help in improving energy supply security to importing countries and in expanding exports of natural gas to exporting countries. A feasibility study of the trans-ASEAN pipeline, a project proposed to connect ASEAN countries through a natural gas pipeline, is being carried out. If this project materializes, domestic utilization as well as trade in natural gas are expected to increase significantly.

Although trade in energy in ASEAN is dominated by oil and gas the diversity of these countries in terms of other energy resource endowments like hydroelectricity and coal provides opportunities for increased interconnection in electricity and trade in coal in the region.

The growing commercial use of energy is creating greater awareness of environmental burning issues. Energy conservation, improved efficiency and recycling have become the catchwords in matters related to the environment and energy development. ASEAN countries, which are at different levels in terms of environment related problems and capabilities, should share their expertise and knowledge with each other and work closely in the area of local, regional, and global environmental issues.

Lack of comprehensive and standardized energy statistics is still one of the constraints in analysing and comparing the energy situation between countries and in examining specific problems in ASEAN. Even if the energy statistics were available, their coverage is different in different countries and vary from one publication to another. Without a database, planning and implementation of energy co-operation are not possible. Efforts to strengthen a database must be accelerated.

In addition to the areas discussed above, there are a number of other specific areas where co-operation can be extended. In this regard, initiatives aimed at improving mutual understanding and co-operation among ASEAN countries should be encouraged and supported.

Shankar Sharma
April 1992

NOTE
1. For the oil-demand growth of the Asian-Pacific region see Miyata (1990) and Fesharaki and Totto (1989).

47.

ASEAN CO-OPERATION IN BANKING AND FINANCE

DAVID L. SCHULZE

A small, but high quality, body of literature already exists on ASEAN cooperation in banking and finance. As much of it is reasonably up to date, I do not intend to review every aspect of current banking and finance cooperation.

ASEAN LITERATURE

Michael Skully's excellent study, *ASEAN Financial Cooperation: Developments in Banking, Finance and Insurance*,[1] is a comprehensive treatment of the subject. It catalogues and describes, in great detail, all aspects of financial cooperation through about mid-year 1983. Another valuable source is the proceedings of the Seventh Annual FAEA Conference,[2] particularly the papers by Nimit Nontapunthawat[3] and S.Y. Lee.[4] The first provides a general review while the second outlines the role of Singapore's offshore market in ASEAN. A rather more dated, but still valuable, source is the ASEAN Economic Research Unit Workshop Proceedings, *ASEAN Economic Cooperation*.[5] Of particular relevance are the review article by Chia S.Y.[6] and Supachai Panitchpakdi's article on investment and finance cooperation.[7] The preparation for the ASEAN Summit has

also produced a number of policy papers. Among those publically available, the Report of Group of Fourteen[8] contains ten recommendations for increasing financial cooperation.

In order to develop some general guidelines for the future of banking and finance cooperation (increased financial integration), it is necessary to have some notion of the ultimate objectives of ASEAN economic cooperation. Although the actual form of financial cooperation at any point in time will reflect changing economic and political situations, the long run thrust of financial cooperation depends on the level of economic cooperation desired. A different set of policy recommendations would emerge if the long run were the formation of a common market or economic community than if some lower level of economic cooperation were the ultimate objective. Certainly the former goal implies a higher degree of financial integration than the latter. While many financial cooperative projects would be consistent with either ultimate goal, the lower the ultimate goal of economic cooperation, the more potential projects to increase financial would be excluded.

In what follows, it is assumed that the ultimate objective is the formation of a common market. This assumption is made for descriptive

Reprinted in abridged form from "ASEAN Cooperation in Banking and Finance", in *ASEAN Economic Cooperation: A New Perspective*, edited by Hendra Esmara (Singapore: Chopmen Publishers for Federation of ASEAN Economic Associations and Ikatan Sarjana Ekonomi Indonesia, 1988), pp. 157–89, by permission of the author and the publisher.

purposes and not as an endorsement of that objective.[9] From a pragmatic point of view, given the current low degree of financial integration in ASEAN, the need to promote financial cooperation from the ground up means that new projects undertaken in the next few years would probably be consistent with most ultimate goals for economic cooperation.

With a common market as the ultimate goal, financial cooperation should focus on eliminating the disruptive effects of unexpected changes in intra-ASEAN exchange rates on economic cooperation. One way to accomplish this would be to adopt an adjustable fixed-parity system for ASEAN exchange rates. From political and, to a lesser extent, economic perspectives, such a cure may be worse than the disease. To avoid the rigidities of an adjustable fixed-parity system, financial cooperation could proceed sequentially, as follows:

1. Elimination of all barriers to intra-ASEAN currency convertibility. Removal of all currency composition requirements for settlement of intra-ASEAN trade, e.g. requirements that a portion of payment for exports to other ASEAN members be made in non-ASEAN currencies.
2. Establish a common unit of account in which any contract could be settled, at the option of the contracting parties. This would leave ASEAN currencies free to fluctuate against each other as well as the unit of account.
3. Establish a common ASEAN mention of exchange. This would be the final financial step in achieving full economic integration.

Each of these steps is controversial and their actual implementation would present many economic and political difficulties. Rather than trying to provide any more detail for this sketchy map to a hypothetical future, I turn now to the present state of financial integration in ASEAN, barriers to further cooperation, and a few, hopefully, more concrete recommendations.

First, a general point. Although much has been made about the difference between 'supply-leading' and 'demand-following' financial development[10] broad historical patterns and recent econometric studies[11] support the proposition that demand-following financial development is by far the most important. That is, financial development usually follows as a result of development in the real sector of the economy rather than leading real sector development. In our context financial integration (cooperation) in ASEAN will follow increased cooperation in the real sectors, particularly trade. In fact, the rather disappointing performance of the ASEAN Finance Corporation to date, discussed in the following section, illustrates the difficulties faced by a 'supply-leading' financial institution.

Simply put, the low level of intra ASEAN real economic activity is a major cause of the low level of financial integration and is a significant barrier to future financial cooperation. While increased financial cooperation/integration would boost the level of intra-ASEAN real economic activity, it is primarily increases in the latter that will provide the impetus for increased financial integration.

We review the barriers to financial integration and recommendations for dealing with them. The following are the major barriers to financial integration.

(1) Low Level of Real Economic Integration

Policies to foster intra-ASEAN trade and other forms of economic cooperation lay the essential groundwork for financial cooperation and increased financial integration. As real economic linkages increase, the demand for financial cooperation/integration will increase.

Recommendation 1: Government monetary authorities and the private financial sectors should support the planning and development of projects designed to bolster real economic cooperation.

(2) Widely Different Stages of Domestic Financial Development

Domestic financial development and intra-ASEAN financial integration are goals which may be both complementary and conflicting. Of the two, certainly domestic financial development has a higher priority.

Recommendations 2:
(a) Relaxation of regulatory restrictions on intra-ASEAN branch banking. ASEAN banks should be treated more favorable than other foreign banks.
(b) Strengthen the channels through which ASEAN experience and expertise on domestic financial development can be shared, including the existing training programs for management and personnel of banks and other financial institutions.
(c) Consider establishing an ASEAN fund for lending to financial development projects. AFC's lending criteria and advisory capacity could also be broadened to include this category.

(3) Exchange/Capital Controls

Recommendations 3:
(a) A task force should be formed to study these controls in depth in each ASEAN country. The task force's report should serve as a major input for multilateral negotiations to remove or rationalize these controls within ASEAN to the maximum extent compatible with domestic economic imperatives.
(b) The task force should also consider the feasibility and implementation of a standard unit of account for intra-ASEAN contracts.

(4) Exchange Rate Variability

Establishing a common unit of account would minimize the adverse impact of fluctuating exchange rates on intra-ASEAN economic integration (see 3 above). Clearly, this barrier is closely linked to the problem of exchange and capital controls. Recommendation 4 is independent of the issue of a common unit of account.

Recommendation 4: Every effort should be made to strengthen existing forward markets in ASEAN currencies. The network of markets should also be extended by formalizing (or creating) forward markets in Singapore dollars/ Ringgit, Rupiah/ringgit, etc. contracts.

(5) Unequal Tax Treatment

Recommendation 5: A task force should be established to study these barriers in each ASEAN country. The ultimate goal should be either a multilateral tax agreement or a series of bilateral tax agreements among ASEAN members to rationalize the tax treatment of domestic and foreign, i.e. other ASEAN based, income, assets, etc.

(6) Regulation of Domestic Financial Institutions

The prudential and monetary control functions of financial regulation cannot be compromised. Nevertheless, regulations on the asset and liability structures of banks and other financial institutions from significant barriers to financial integration. Widely different regulatory policies also inhibit cooperation among ASEAN banks.

Recommendations 6:
(a) Banks should be encouraged to hold intra-ASEAN trade bills, by permitting them to use a portion of their holdings to satisfy liquidity or other asset requirements.
(b) Once a common unit of account is established, financial institutions should be permitted to hold ASEAN government securities written in this unit. A portion of these holdings could be used to satisfy asset requirements.

(c) ASEAN based borrowers be given favorable treatment in the current set of regulations limiting lending in domestic currencies to nonresident borrowers.

(d) Other regulations should be harmonized to allow greater cooperation between ASEAN financial institutions. Implementation of this recommendation would require an in depth study and government negotiations.

(7) Supervision of Financial Institutions

Nonconformity with acceptable commercial practices and noncompliance with existing regulations may form a barrier to financial integration if significant loss of confidence results. Financial crises and scandals tend to undermine both domestic and international financial system.

Recommendation 7: Financial regulatory authorities should continue to upgrade the standard of their supervision of financial institutions.

(8) Information Flows

Recommendation 8: Standards of corporate reporting should be raised Reports should be issued more frequently, perhaps quarterly, and should disclose more details of the firm's operations.

CONCLUSION

While the present level of financial integration in ASEAN is not high, the prospects for increased banking and financial cooperation are bright given ASEAN's commitment to greater economic cooperation. The ultimate form of that cooperation will, to a large extent, determine the degree of financial integration and the forms of banking and financial cooperation. At the same time, increased financial integration will magnify the gains from economic cooperation.

The essential dilemma is how much economic sovereignty ASEAN members can and should give up to achieve greater economic integration. The economic answers to such a question are far from clear cut. Nevertheless in the rough and tumble process of arriving at actual answers, ASEAN stands to gain not only increased economic strength, but also greater mutual understanding and political cohesiveness.

NOTES

1. Michael Skully, *ASEAN Financial Cooperation: Development in Banking, Finance and Insurance* (London: Macmillan, 1985).
2. J. Soedradjad Djiwandono and Hendra Esmara (Editors), *International Financial Instability and ASEAN Financial Cooperation*, (Singapore: Chopmen Publishers, 1985).
3. Nimit Nontapanthawat, "Financial Cooperation in ASEAN" in J. Soedradjad Djiwandono and Hendra Esmara (Editors), *op. cit.*, pp. 101–115.
4. S.Y. Lee, "The Role of Singapore as a Financial Centre" in J. Soedradjad Djiwandono and Hendra Esmara (Editors), *op. cit.*, pp. 116–153.
5. Chia Siow Yue, (Editor), *ASEAN Economic Cooperation* (Singapore: Institute of Southeast Asian Studies), 1980.
6. Chia Siow Yue, "Survey of ASEAN Economic Cooperation: Developments and Issues", in Chia Siow Yue, (Editor), *op. cit.*, pp. 1–23.
7. Supachai Panitchpakdi, "Investment and Finance in ASEAN: Problems and Relevant Issues", in Chia Siow Yue, (Editor), *op. cit.*, pp. 139–162.
8. The Group of Fourteen, *ASEAN: The Way Forward*, (Kuala Lumpur: Institute of Strategic and International Studies, 1987). The Group is composed of prominent individuals from the private sector.

9. A discussion of the relative merits of a common market vis-a-vis other forms of economic cooperation is well beyond the scope of this paper.
10. See H.T. Patrick, "Financial Development and Economic Growth in Underdeveloped Countries", *Economic Development and Cultural Change* (January 1966), No. 14.
11. See K.L. Gupta., *Finance and Economic Growth in Developing Countries*, (London: Croom Helm, 1984), Chapter 3, for a excellent review of the literature and a variety of empirical tests.

48. ASEAN CO-OPERATION IN TOURISM

STEVEN C.M. WONG

The business of tourism in the Association of Southeast Asian Nations (Asean) is sophisticated, competitive and multi-dimensional. Sophisticated, because it is the end-product of a wide range of service activities; competitive, because whole countries, not just industries, often compete intensively for similar market segments; and multi-dimensional because, as a basically social time-space activity across national boundaries, its development can have far-reaching consequences on the whole spectrum of Asean political, economic and social relationships.

In exploring the vast unknown reaches of this territory, a definitive set of answers might not emerge over a more approximative or tentative one. Nevertheless, as in any good business enterprise, risks and uncertainties are never grounds for inaction.

STATUS OF ASEAN TOURISM CO-OPERATION

Asean co-operation in tourism has tended to be concentrated heavily in certain operational areas, viz, the promotional, marketing and research aspects of tourism. Co-operative efforts in other areas have been less forthcoming although there has been one major initiative in the form of the Asean circle and promotional fares. These and other forms of co-operation are highlighted below.

Asean Travel Information Centre. The Asean Travel Information Centre being established in Kuala Lumpur will be SCOT's permanent secretariat and act as an information centre on Asean tourism. Specifically, it will co-ordinate and manage marketing programmes and projects approved by SCOT, liaise with other world and regional tourism bodies and the private sector, conduct public relations and other activities related to the promotion of Asean travel.

Asean tourism fora. Asean tourism fora have been held on a triennial basis since 1981. Integral parts of the Asean tourism fora include the forum proper, industry workshops in the respective areas of tourism and the travel mart which brings Asean sellers of tourism services together with foreign buyers. These fora represent a unique occasion for regional and foreign private and public sectors involved in Asean tourism to interact.

Thus far, tourism fora have been organised and funded largely by Asean NTOs. Efforts to

Reprinted in abridged form "Asean Co-operation in Tourism: Looking Back and Looking Forward", in *ASEAN at the Crossroads*, edited by Noordin Sopiee, Chew Lay Lee, Lim Liang Jin (Kuala Lumpur: Institute of Strategic and International Studies, 1987), pp. 371–93, by permission of the author and the publisher.

get the Asean private sector associations — Aseanta, the Asean Hotels and Restaurants Association (AHRA) and the Federation of Asean Travel Agents (FATA) — to assume a greater role (possibly infusing a greater private sector orientation into the organisation of Asean tourism fora) have not been successful owing to organisational and financial limitations.

Asean promotional chapters. There are six Asean promotional chapters acting as SCOT's promotional arms in major tourist markets (with Asean chairmen given in parentheses): Australia-New Zealand (Malaysia), Hong Kong (the Philippines), Japan (Malaysia), United Kingdom (Singapore) and the US (the Philippines). These chapters are staffed by personnel seconded from either overseas offices of the respective Asean NTOs or tourist desks of their embassies.

Asean promotional chapters are an important communications link in ensuring that continuous information and promotion of Asean is kept channelled to major markets. The Australian-New Zealand promotional chapter, for example, has implemented AFTEL, an Asean information database accessed by Australian travel agents. The US chapter, on the other hand, is planning to conduct a series of Asean travel schools to give first-hand education to US travel agents on Asean tourist destinations. For these and other activities, the Asean promotional chapters have been allocated US$62,000 in 1987.

Collective representation. Asean NTOs have collectively attended world travel markets and fora to project a common Asean image. For example, Asean NTOs jointly promoted the region through an 'Asean Village' exhibition stand at the ITB 1987 in Berlin, West Germany from March 7-12.

Asean travel films and brochures. Asean countries have combined resources to produce a travel film entitled *Asean Mosaic* and an 'Asean Welcome' brochure.

Research and manpower training. This is still a relatively new field of tourism co-operation with the major programmes undertaken being: The First Workshop on Tourism for Research Officials of SCOT in Kuala Lumpur in 1986, where it was agreed that a set of common tourism terminologies for data collection be drawn up to facilitate information exchange among Asean countries; and the First Asean SCOT Workshop on Tourism Manpower Planning in Indonesia in 1986 where the needs and problems faced in training and the mechanisms for effective co-ordination on a regional level were discussed.

Third party technical assistance and dialogue. In this area SCOT has been involved in:

- UNDP foreign market study for Asean: Asean has collectively benefitted from financial and technical assistance provided by the United Nations Development Programme (UNDP) in the form of tourist market studies of Hong Kong and Australia. The UNDP has further agreed to use the balance of the Third Cycle Inter-Country Programme Fund to finance additional studies of the Scandinavian and West German markets for Asean.
- Asean-European Community co-operation in tourism: Avenues for greater Asean-European Community co-operation in market research, training and marketing are currently being explored. So far this year, four project proposals in the field of research have emerged and are being implemented.
- Asean-New Zealand co-operation in tourism: In recent Asean-New Zealand dialogue, tourism emerged as one of the new areas where co-operation could be strengthened. SCOT is currently preparing submissions to be forwarded to COTT in the area of a tourism trade and consumer survey of the New Zealand market.

Asean circle and promotional fares. The one significant initiative outside the field has been Asean circle and promotional fares. Air transportation constitutes the main mode of transportation for all Asean countries. Thus, Asean circle and promotional fares were aimed at providing inexpensive travel within Asean. Since introduction, however, these fares have suffered from insufficient publicity and overly strict conditions attached to their availability. There is also doubt as to whether these fares are really cost-effective for intra-Asean travel, especially when compared to the minimum selling price of first-tier air carriers and the under-counter pricing practised by the private sector. Efforts are currently under way to investigate the problems associated with the present fare structure and, if necessary, consider add-on fares as a substitute.

POSSIBLE DIRECTIONS FOR ASEAN TOURISM

Co-operation in planning and research

Among Asean NTOS, there is a perceived need to properly define and market the tourism products of the region. The fact that Asean has already forged ahead with a marketing plan targetting joint promotion in major travel fora without doing so makes the need for co-ordinated planning an especially critical one.

Short-term market intelligence is now the prime concern of Asean countries. This is understandable in view of the weaknesses certain countries in the region currently face in generating visitor arrivals and receipts. It is pointless, however, to invest heavily in obtaining an accurate picture of a target market without having the tangible products to offer or the means to exploit it. If, on the other hand, on obtaining the necessary information individual countries then decide to capture market share independently of one another, the fragmented market may not be able to sustain or justify the heavy promotional costs put in by individual countries. This is eventually also self-defeating.

A 'plan-to-plan' approach, comprising three

phases as outlined below, may be in order under these circumstances.

First, an Asean tourism audit. A major study of the region's tourism resources can be considered a starting point. Optimally, the services of a group of experts may be called on to perform a country-by-country analysis of the strengths and weaknesses of existing products. Problem areas detected could be the basis of an agenda for priority attention by both the Asean public and private sectors. The audit may also survey the competitive world environment to identify where opportunities may lie and what threats lie ahead.

Second, a tourism forecasting and impact study. Forecasts are invaluable aids for planning purposes so long as they are revised regularly. At the same time, an attempt to evaluate the impact of different tourism scenarios on Asean economies could be made. This information would be invaluable in supporting the case made by Asean NTOs for the greater government assistance which would inevitably be entailed.

Third, a long-range tourism plan. With the preceding two inputs, NTOs could begin to start the process of formulating long-range goals, objectives and strategies on a quantitative, as well as qualitative, basis. It should be stressed that the very act of planning itself calls for the greatest degree of co-operation. This would become evident when the different aspirations and ideas of six individual member countries are expressed and have to be combined into one integrated framework. Research to support this effort would be required but, since most NTOs already have quite sizeable divisions of their own and a move to standardise data collection has been initiated, few problems are foreseen.

Funding for the three programmes may ultimately run into hundreds of thousands of dollars and many hundreds of man-months of labour. It is imperative that the costs be fairly shared among NTOs and between the public and the private sectors. Technical assistance grants from Asean's dialogue partners or international agencies should also be solicited.

Co-operation in institutional strengthening

Since tourism is not the product of one but many businesses, each self-seeking, there are possibly more divergent interests than synergies in Asean tourism at present. In a sense, although NTOs by virtue of their public office and funding currently spearhead the thrust in regional co-operation as image-builders, it is the NFCs, hoteliers, travel agents and others in the private sector who are the real movers of tourism co-operation in Asean.

Upgrade Aseanta. A very significant strengthening of the private sector's involvement in Asean tourism may have to be one of the top priorities in improving the framework for co-operation. Having said this, one is quickly conscious of the many organisations set up on a regional and world level to champion members' interests in the field of tourism. The proliferation of even more institutions in Asean could very well lead to effects which are opposite to those intended. It is therefore suggested that existing Asean associations be upgraded and expanded to reflect the vital role of the private sector in developing regional business.

A substantial increase in the coherence of private sector participation in tourism can be envisaged by widening Aseanta's role and functions in a way that can better serve the objectives of regional tourism development. Aseanta could be shaped into a more operationally facilitative umbrella body representing all components of the tourism trade. In this way, it would emerge as a single, influential industry association. Its functions could be expanded to include liaison and consultation work (a role it already plays to some extent at present); setting up of various technical committees to initiate research into problems and practices pertaining to Asean tourism; arbitration insofar as it is able to obtain agreement from members on basic guidelines and procedures; information dissemination; and self-regulation by formulating acceptable guidelines and monitoring the quality and price levels of tourism services provided in the region.

As a regional trade association, it would be helpful if the organisation could be equipped with fulltime, professional secretariat and administrative staff to assist in the efforts of its part-time members. Funding and manpower are both critical aspects of Aseanta's upgrading and it is not clear if increased contributions by its members will be sufficient. Funding from independent third party sources may be necessary and Asean NTOs could actively support the fundraising measures in a joint public-private sector exercise.

Amalgamate SCOT into COTAC. The costs of travel into Asean clearly shape the potential the region holds as a tourist destination. Any country or region wishing to expand its share of tourism needs to make realistic assessments not only of the absolute cost of travel, both present and future, but also costs relative to competing destinations. From an economic perspective, transport policies should be based on securing the maximum benefits to the region as a whole, rather than maximising air carrier revenues alone. In value-pricing supply decisions, it is the total tourist budget spent on both air and ground activities that should be taken into account. It is therefore important to reiterate the need for a significant degree of policy co-ordination among tourism servicing components if real progress is to be made in developing the industry.

The case for amalgamating SCOT into COTAC can be argued to be a positive step in forging these necessary alliances. From the view of administrative efficiency, such a step would lead to better, more effective decision-making and resource allocation. SCOT does not, by and large, address critical issues of transport as they are outside of its organisational domain. Nor does COTAC place a high priority on initiating transport co-operation around tourist needs. A second, related point is that the alliance can bring a more comprehensive focus and balance in areas where there are potentially divisive policy conflicts and trade-offs. Thirdly, because transport and tourism benefit mutually and synergistically, there has to be close investment co-ordination to ensure that no bottlenecks result. An Asean economic committee responsible for both tourism and transport would be a concrete measure providing the necessary channels of communication and co-ordination.

Co-operation in the preferential purchase and supply of tourism inputs

With import leakages as high as they are, Asean countries could stand to gain in financial terms with greater co-operation in the purchase of goods and services needed in tourism. However, it is not easy to 'plug' such leakages: Many items, especially highly capital-intensive ones, are sourced outside the region only because there is no readily available and competitive regional source. However, countless other items (foodstuffs, beverages, building supplies, etc) can be substituted at little or no sacrifice to price and quality. It will be recalled that one of the main objectives underlying the Asean Preferential Trading Arrangements is to use resources available in Asean as far as possible. Tourism, it may be argued has special relevance insofar as the PTA instruments — long-term quantity contracts, purchase finance support, extension of tariff preferences and liberalisation of non-tariff measures — are concerned. Local importers can be encouraged to shift their sourcing from foreign multinationals through differential tariffs thus increasing the amount of intra-Asean trade.

A regional sourcing policy of this kind can be implemented at a number of levels. At the first level, Asean countries could agree on a rather benign policy through the usual process and promise to exercise 'best efforts' in promoting the regional sourcing of goods. At the second level, Asean countries could more actively encourage the purchase of these inputs by deepening the margins of tariff preferences and/or incentives of their respective countries.

At the third level, on adoption of a set of financial incentives, a timetable could be set for a gradual managed substitution process to take place. A study could then be undertaken to determine where Asean countries could clearly benefit, if not immediately then in the longer term.

It should be added that regional sourcing of inputs can help cultivate a more Asean image and character among tourism services. This can constitute a large advantage in differentiating the Asean region from others.

Co-operation in promotion and marketing

Although Asean co-operation has been strongest in this area, additional refinements are possible to make the region a more attractive and appealing destination. The suggestion in this area stems from the fact that although tourists into the region may at first be attracted by an 'Asean image', in the final analysis a choice has to be made between or among one or more countries within it. If this is the case, there may be benefits in further subdividing the region into what can be known as Asean travel areas.

Asean bilateral/trilateral promotion and package travel programmes. Each of the Asean travel areas may constitute two or more countries which can be promoted and/or packaged and sold in foreign markets. The Northern Asean Travel Area, for example, may include Thailand and Malaysia. A package tour comprising Bangkok-Phuket-Penang/Kuala Lumpur may be offered as this would be a viable one-week holiday for a long-haul traveller. The Southern Asean Travel Area could include Singapore-Jakarta-Bandung/Bali as a possible itinerary. Similarly, the Eastern Asean Travel Area could include the Philippines, Brunei and East Malaysia.

In order to put the Asean travel area concept into effect, the respective countries would have to formulate separate agreements to jointly promote and market their destinations overseas under the auspices of Asean. Malaysian and Singaporean authorities have agreed to jointly promote the two countries and discussions have reportedly been held to draw up plans to offer a travel package to these destinations overseas.[1]

Co-operation in rationalizing travel barriers

This is probably the most difficult area in which to foster tourism co-operation, largely because the problems concern issues which are not strictly confined to the realm of tourism. Owing to controversy on the subject, Asean would have already made significant progress in tourism co-operation if it were able to get the issue onto the discussion table.

Inter-committee approach. The COTT-SCOT combination is only one element of a wider coalition of committees which will have to take a common stand acceptable to all member countries. In particular, the Committee on Finance and Banking (COFAB) and the Committee on Transport and Communications (COTAC) must become integral parts of the efforts to recommend that appropriate measures be taken with respect to the travel barriers.

Rationalization of travel barriers. Three options could generally be adopted. *Option One:* All countries could agree to maintain the status quo. This would be significant in maintaining the harmony within Asean although the issue would be left unresolved. Tourism co-operation in this area would therefore reach a stalemate. *Option Two:* Member countries could seek rationalization and/or exemptions to the various travel taxes imposed. This would make it less burdensome for Asean citizens to travel within the region. This would be the conceptual equivalent to the application of 'averaging tariffs' or an 'exclusions list' in the Asean trade arena. *Option Three:* Countries

could seek total elimination of travel barriers within a specified time frame. This would be the path of greatest resistance given that there is already strong opposition to the dismantlement of travel barriers but this would have the greatest effect in liberalising intra-Asean tourism.

As a rule, Asean economic co-operation can only be enhanced if the sovereign interests of member countries are respected. While the practice of consensus-seeking has undoubtedly contributed to the slow progress to date, this has meant that whatever decisions taken have been strongly supported by all countries. In this situation, it may be preferable to discuss ways in which member countries could co-operate in finding a compromise. To negate fears that exemptions could lead to international gateway problems (that is, nationals leaving the region from other Asean countries), one solution would be for the countries now imposing travel taxes based on departure to switch to taxes based on entry. Tax computation could in fact be made more flexible and equitable if based on length of stay since it could be designed to permit more short-haul tourism among Asean countries while discriminating against long-haul tourism to other destinations.[2] COTT could study the feasibility of such a tax and, if found desirable, recommend it in lieu of taxes now being imposed.

CONCLUDING REMARKS

In Asean, an often-used cliche is that governments must have a certain amount of political will in order to promote economic co-operation. In tourism, political will is not the only necessary factor — the private sector must also have the will to co-operate. Private sector will is based on the fact that through co-operation, tourism development can increase at a much faster pace than would otherwise be the case. By taking advantage of long-term tourism synergies, each component industry would be better off as would the country in which it is operating. To advance Asean economic co-operation, five areas of possible co-operation in tourism have been suggested. These in no way constitute the only or necessarily the best proposals that can be made. But they do seek to identify more feasible areas of co-operation which can be of mutual benefit to member countries. With more thought and attention given to the subject, more innovative and effective ways can certainly be devised.

NOTES
1. *NST* (July 26, 1985).
2. Wong (1987).

49.

ASEAN CO-OPERATION IN TRANSPORT

G. NAIDU

This article attempts to evaluate regional cooperation in transport in ASEAN. For a number of reasons the discussion is less than comprehensive. First, ASEAN cooperation in communications is excluded largely on account of my own limitations in this particular area. Second, it suffers from being the first effort to evaluate regional cooperation in transport among ASEAN member countries. There has been no attempt thus far to scrutinise ASEAN's attempts at cooperation in transport, upon which a study of this nature can build on. The reason for this is simple: the deliberations and decisions of the agencies responsible for initiating and implementing regional cooperation in transport are generally shielded from public view. Consequently, except to those directly involved in the decision-making process, the status of regional cooperation in transport is largely unknown.

Cooperation in transport among the ASEAN member states is guided by the Integrated Work Programme in Transportation and Communications (IWPTC). The Committee on Transportation and Communications (COTAC) has formulated 2 work programmes *viz.* IWPTC 1982–86 and IWPTC 1987–1991. The discussion here is confined to IWPTC 1982–86 though many of the observations are applicable to IWPTC 1987–1991.

The first point worth noting is that it took COTAC almost five years to draw up its Work Programme. This does not indicate any urgency on the part of COTAC to foster regional cooperation in transport especially since the IWPTC 1982–86 was little more than a reproduction of the projects already identified by the Permanent Committees.

Fifty-nine projects in the transport sector are listed in the IWPTC 1982–86. The majority of them (27) are in the maritime sector, civil aviation and land transport each has 16 projects.

Over the period 1982–86 only eight of the fifty-nine projects were completed (and those not implemented have been included in the IWPTC 1987–91). Bearing in mind that a large number of the IWPTC projects were actually initiated during the era of the Permanent Committees, ASEAN's achievement in regional cooperation in transport is by any reckoning far from impressive. Moreover, more project were withdrawn (11) than completed.

REGIONAL COOPERATION
IN TRANSPORT: AN EVALUATION

A closer analysis of the projects in the IWPTC

Reprinted in abridged form from "ASEAN Cooperation in Transport", in *ASEAN Economic Cooperation: A New Perspective*, edited by Hendra Esmara (Singapore: Chopmen Publishers for Federation of ASEAN Economic Associations and Ikatan Sarjana Ekonomi Indonesia, 1988), pp. 191–204, by permission of the author and the publisher.

1982–1986 reveals some striking features. A number of projects involve the creation of ASEAN-wide organisations with no particular economic impact. An even larger number of projects listed in the IWPTC are technical in nature whose economic impact, if any, is only marginal. A third category of projects involves either a compilation of a data base or exchange of information and expertise among ASEAN countries. The economic potential of these projects is greater but frequently these projects are either not implemented or have not been pursued to the point where the economic benefits are actually reaped. Finally there are projects that are ostensibly intended to effect economic cooperation in the transport sector of ASEAN. But invariably these projects take the form of economic studies. While it is only proper to undertake feasibility studies before embarking on a project, it is equally reasonable to expect that viable projects will be implemented. But this seldom happens in the case of the IWPTC projects. The present system is almost farcical in that the completion of a study or a technical report is taken to mean the end of the project. That no implementation measures are devised for project execution and hence no substantive regional cooperation materialises from the study is apparently of no particular importance. An example should illustrate the point. The project on the "Development of Maritime Legislation" was completed but none of the ASEAN countries have revised their maritime legislation to incorporate the recommendations of the study.

Overall, and despite the priority accorded to regional cooperation in transport, the record is dismal. There has certainly been no lack of project proposals or activity: meetings of the non-governmental organisations such as FASC and FASA, the Sub-Committees and COTAC continue unabated and the official records of COTAC proceedings get bulkier every year. But a realistic assessment of ASEAN's efforts at regional cooperation in transport must necessarily be pessimistic.

There are many plausible explanations for ASEAN's failure to achieve a substantial measure of regional economic cooperation in transport:

(1) A major explanation for ASEAN's failure to foster regional cooperation in transport lies in the absence of a coherent set of objectives for such cooperation. To put simply: what is it that ASEAN wishes to achieve from cooperation in transport? COTAC's terms of reference merely specify its role but fall short of establishing the purpose of regional cooperation in transport. This failure to establish clear objectives partly explains the biases in the IWPTC projects and in the lack of progress in many of them.

(2) National priorities are dominant in the transport policies of ASEAN governments. Regional cooperation can and usually does mean intensified competition for the transport sector of the member states of ASEAN. And ASEAN governments are not always prepared for this. The alleged lack of commitment and enthusiasm on the part of ASEAN governments towards regional cooperation in transport is not unrelated to national priorities superceding regional considerations. For instance, protectionism in the shipping sector of ASEAN (which can take the form of cabotage restrictions, bilateral shipping agreements and similar cargo reservations or preference schemes) is widespread in ASEAN and constitutes a formidable impediment to regional cooperation in shipping.

(3) Part of the problem of regional cooperation in transport arises at the stage of project identification and formulation. Currently projects for regional cooperation emanate from the Sub-Committees and the non-governmental organisations. Both the NGOs and the Sub-Committees lack the expertise to formulate substantial projects of a regional character. Additionally it has been asserted that they have lost enthusiasm.[1] COTAC too is in no position to assess the potential of projects for regional implementation, no doubt in part because of the lack of expertise at COTAC, and partly because in the absence of an unambiguous set of objectives COTAC is in no position to evaluate projects effectively.

(4) There are also problems at this level of project implementation. In the first place there is an over-reliance on external sources for project funding. Such assistance has not always been forthcoming. SEATAC, one of the principal implementing agencies of the IWPTC, not only faces problems of funding the projects, it frequently does not possess the technical expertise required for project implementation. Where project implementation is left to the NGOs the lack of technical expertise frequently prevents the projects from being implemented. One additional factor that impedes project implementation is the practice of rotating the Chairmanship of the Sub-Committees on an annual basis. Such a practice clearly impedes the Sub-Committee from monitoring the projects from the time they are formulated to the stage where projects are completed.

REGIONAL COOPERATION
IN TRANSPORT: THE WAY AHEAD

The lack of progress up to this point should not be construed to mean that there is no scope for regional cooperation in transport. Nor should it be presumed that the scope of cooperation is limitless as it is sometimes assumed. ASEAN member states would do well to recognise this and to lower their expectations, at least for the forseeable future.

Notwithstanding what has been said above, there is significant potential for regional cooperation in some areas:

(i) ASEAN countries should promote a more extensive exchange of information and expertise in the transport sector;

(ii) In the area of training there is scope for adopting regional programmes and for establishing regional training institutions especially if there are sufficient economies to be obtained from such arrangements;

(iii) Standardisation in many areas of transport operations can confer benefits to member states; and

(iv) In areas where the practices or policies of third countries affect ASEAN, there is some benefit to be gained by adopting a regional response. In fact ASEAN has had some measure of success in this area as evidenced by ASEAN's united response to Australia International Civil Aviation Policy.

But when ASEAN goes beyond the above-mentioned obvious areas and into economic cooperation in transport there are obvious limits to regional cooperation. In what follows a number of suggestions are put forward to help ascertain the extent to which cooperation is feasible and the mechanism to promote such cooperation more effectively.

(1) Arising from what has been said before, there is an urgent need to establish as clearly as possible the objectives of regional cooperation in transport. The principal objectives should include the following:

(a) to promote and facilitate the exchange of information and personnel between ASEAN countries if such measures help to raise the level of efficiency in the transport sector of ASEAN member states;

(b) Wherever possible to conduct training programmes at the regional rather than at the national level. (Training for seafarers and for container terminal operations are good cases for implementation at the regional level). The purpose of a regional approach would be to minimize the cost of manpower development and to avoid the costly duplication of facilities by member countries; and

(c) To promote all forms of cooperation in the transport sector that will reduce the cost of transport between ASEAN countries, both of goods and passengers. The specification of the objective of regional cooperation in this form underlines the fact that regional cooperation in transport is not an end in itself but a means to an end i.e. the promotion of trade and the facilitation of movement of people between member states. It would also provide the criteria for the evaluation of project proposals.

(2) For each project selected for implementation COTAC should identify those national policies or practices of member countries that can obstruct the project's execution. (An example is the bilateral shipping agreements between ASEAN member states that impede the implementation of an ASEAN liner service). Where strongly entrenched national priorities threaten to undermine regional cooperation, COTAC can adopt one of two courses of action. COTAC could strive via a superior body to eliminate these obstacles by persuading member countries to subscribe to general principles. (In this regard ASEAN could benefit from the EEC experience where the transport policies of member countries are required to conform to the free and fair competition articles of the Treaty of Rome). Alternatively if the implementation of a regional transport project conflicts with the national policies of a member state, COTAC should adopt the principle of "6-X" (but leave the option for those excluded to join in at a later stage). Such a practice will overcome a constraint now impeding regional cooperation i.e. the agreement of all six member states before a project is implemented.

(3) There should be a comprehensive review of all IWPTC projects in the context of (1) above. It might be preferable to limit the number of projects to be submitted by each Sub-Committee to a fixed, small member and to require them to be ranked according to priority. COTAC should then determine the time-span over which the projects should be implemented. This contrasts with the prevailing system where

projects appear to go on indefinitely. To ensure effective project implementation, and since the Chairman of the Sub-Committees would be frequently responsible for project implementation, it is necessary to extend the Chairmanship of Sub-Committees to more than the present one-year term.

(4) There is nothing inherently wrong in the present organisational structure. But two improvements are likely to contribute to more effective regional cooperation in transport. First there is a need for COTAC to have a technical arm. The ASEAN Secretariat has proposed the creation of an ASEAN Development Centre for Transport and Communications (ADCTC).[2] Such an agency would not only be responsible for evaluation of project proposals, it should also undertake the necessary studies that may be required for the project concerned. Second, ASEAN ministers of transport should meet on an annual basis to review the progress of regional cooperation and in the process inject some urgency into the whole exercise. (In the EEC the European ministers of transport meet annually to discuss and resolve matters of mutual concern). Of greater importance is that such a gathering provides an avenue to overcome obstacles to regional cooperation arising from the policies of individual member countries.

(5) Finally it is suggested that the proceedings of COTAC and its Sub-Committees be made available to researchers and the public at large. In the long-run this would provide useful feed-back to COTAC and could even constitute a form of pressure on COTAC and the ASEAN ministers of transport to meet forward in fostering regional cooperation in transport.

NOTES
1. See R.V. Navaratnam, "ASEAN Cooperation in Transportation: Looking Back/Looking Forward", First ASEAN Economic Congress, Kuala Lumpur, March 1987, p. 11.
2. See ASEAN Secretariat Paper: *Brief Review of Transport and Communication Cooperation Efforts in ASEAN*, Annex R, Report of the Meeting of Issues Committee (VI) COTAC, June 1987.

50. DEVELOPMENT CO-OPERATION IN HUMAN RESOURCES
The ASEAN Experience

C.P.F. LUHULIMA

If the trend towards the development of human resources had become an integral part of national development plans in ASEAN member countries by the late 1970's, it was in the beginning of the 1980's that it became a major area in ASEAN cooperation. Yet the development of human resources itself needs capital input. It is here that the Japanese Government stepped in to provide the sum of US$100 million to finance such a project on a regional scale.

ASEAN-Japanese Human Resources Development Cooperation

Although the development of human resources has formed an integral part of the national development plans of each ASEAN member country since the middle of the 1970's, ASEAN's regional human resources development programme was essentially a Japanese initiative. ASEAN's first project for human resources development was announced by the former prime minister of Japan, Zenko Suzuki, on the occasion of his visit to the region from 8-20 January 1981.

The Japanese idea of developing human resources is that it is a basic ingredient of the process of nation-building in the developing countries. There is in the Japanese government's view a functional relationship between human resources development on the one hand and nation-building on the other. The development of "those nations' human resources, the people who will formulate and carry out development programs," is of vital importance if nation-building is to be implemented efficiently and effectively. It is for this reason "that we attach so much importance to cooperation for developing human resources in the developing countries in the framework of Japan's aid policy, and are making every effort to expand our cooperation in that area." The development of human resources is perceived by the Japanese side as essentially developing the immense potential of the next generation. "It is the duty of the present generation to develop that potential. I am totally convinced that it is of the utmost importance to promote our work related to human resources, that is, to promote international cooperation in a global context, in the last two decades of this century."[1]

The fields of development the Japanese proposed are essentially rural and agricultural development, energy resources development

Reprinted in abridged form from "Human Resources of ASEAN Development and the ASEAN Countries", in *Regional Cooperation in the Pacific Era*, edited by Dalchoong Kim and Noordin Sopiee (Seoul: Institute of East and West Studies, 1988), pp. 281–98, by permission of the author.

(in accordance with the sentiments at the time) and promotion of small and medium industries. The project will be sustained by establishing centres in each of the ASEAN member nations, either by setting up new institutions or by strengthening existing institutions in the fields to be agreed upon with the objective of achieving full implementation of human resources development projects "in harmony with the values, customs and needs of each country."[2] The Japanese government also established a centre in Okinawa affiliated with the Japan International Cooperation Agency (JICA). There will, however, be no organic linkage between the national centres in the ASEAN countries and the international centre in Japan. This does not preclude the possibility of establishing appropriate linkages at the programme level as a networking arrangement among the centres. This strong sentiment is primarily voiced to avoid the international centre in Japan acting as the dominating center of the network. A total amount of US$100 million (US$20 million for each ASEAN country) will be disbursed to cover the construction cost of the buildings and related facilities, purchase of equipment and materials, as well as technical assistance, including the operational cost of the five ASEAN human resources development centres. The duration of the Japanese sponsored HRD project was determined to be 5-7 years, leaving each member country to decide for itself the starting date for the implementation of its project.

ASEAN-Pacific Cooperation in Human Resources Development (APC/HRD)

Developments since the early 1980's also indicate the growing importance of the Pacific region in the world economy. Although the world economic situation continued to be adversely affected by the prolonged recession, the economies of many Pacific countries have grown remarkably in comparison with other regions in the world. A great economic interaction and interdependence has developed among the Asia-Pacific countries, including the ASEAN countries.

The ASEAN Post-Ministerial Meeting of six ASEAN countries and five Pacific dialogue partners (i.e. Australia, Canada, Japan, New Zealand and the United States of America) is an excellent forum for regular exchanges of views on current developments and the future of the Pacific region. It contributes to the creation of a better understanding of the region. It was envisaged that the dialogue with the countries in the Pacific region be conducted on two levels. One is on the general trends for the future of the Pacific region which will become a permanent feature of future Post-Ministerial conferences and the other is on specific themes for possible cooperation in the region.

The first activity Indonesia's foreign minister proposed was the human resources development programmes and the five Pacific dialogue partners have agreed to support the idea. This programme would not entail, as in the case of the ASEAN-Japan human resources development cooperation, the establishment of new institutions but utilisation of existing establishments. It was also emphasised that the programme should not be confined to ASEAN but should include citizens from the developing countries of the South Pacific and South Asia as well.

The brief overview of the ASEAN human resources development shows the structural differences between the two programmes. The ASEAN-Japan HRD programmes started with institution-building whereas the ASEAN-Pacific cooperation in human resources development started with programmes in existing institutions. However, the purpose of both HRD programmes is essentially to develop the necessary knowledge and skill to catalyse and promote economic growth in the member countries in line with the evolving requirements and modernisation of their societies. The development of skills which are geared to the requirements of the Pacific economy, i.e. from the most basic skills to the most advanced and sophisticated areas of HRD was considered most appropriate and urgent in the framework of the overall development of the Asia-Pacific region. Thus it is of no use to classify technology into divisions such as "elementary technology," "intermediate technology," "high technology" or "sophisticated technology" as is still frequently being done. It is far more instructive to determine which technology can solve what specific problem without concern for whether such technology is primitive, intermediate, advanced or sophisticated. "Appropriate technology" in the sense that it is useful to solve a concrete problem stretches from the most elementary technology to the most sophisticated one. Thus, it is far more important to assume that with painstaking and thorough preparation and development of its human resources, the capability of any ASEAN society can be magnified to master the sophisticated science and technological achievements for the solutions of the concrete problems it faces and to improve upon its added value processes. Japan and Korea have demonstrated that without possessing significant natural resources a country can continuously raise its welfare by relying on skilled human resources and appropriate technologies.

This is the reason why the scope of the ASEAN HRD programmes is so vast, because the needs of its societies are so vast. Prioritisation is indeed a catch-word for narrowing-down the scope of the HRD programmes. Yet the determination of the areas of concentration of HRD which have been agreed upon remain vast. Management and entrepreneurship, science and technology, agriculture, forestry and fisheries, industry, transport and communications, trade and services, and research and planning are indeed vast areas of cooperation. Any subdivision is possible and as a consequence any priority setting.

A second reason for the vast array of HRD programmes is the specific character of ASEAN as a loose organisation, with a highly decentralised nature and, particularly, a weak Secretariat. National priorities in HRD have equal weight which means that regional priorities are the sum total of national priorities. Prioritisation on an ASEAN scale could indeed be better achieved by the establishment of a more centralised management. If prioritisation on an ASEAN scale is already extremely difficult, prioritisation on a wider scale of ASEAN-Pacific cooperation is close to impossible.

Another reason for the broad areas of priority is the dependence or rather over-dependence of ASEAN on donor countries for organising and financing its HRD programmes. Such a dependence involuntarily leads to "impositions" in the field of training and its management. The expression of such sentiments from the ASEAN side is understandable: both sides operated from different perspectives. As the ASEAN committees, representing six nations, went through the mechanics of project choice, many political, socio-economic and cultural considerations entered into the process. Nevertheless, there was no dominant strategy which determined final project selection or a proposition of what was best for the region or what purpose was to be achieved. The lack of an overriding conviction in the absolute necessity of making choices or setting priorities on the part of ASEAN allowed its Pacific partners to insert their own principles for project determination. Devising a strategy essentially means the systematic identification of future opportunities and challenges which, in combination with other relevant data, provide the basis for making better decisions. The key element in planning an ASEAN strategy is to agree on priorities and to be willing to finance the programme. Otherwise, pressures of the donor government to act on behalf of other interests are indeed unavoidable.

Thus, these shortcomings have made it close to impossible to calculate human resources requirements on the projections of future output by the economic sector as is suggested in the beginning of this paper. The listing of the number of workers, by occupation, which will be required in the future will remain an impossibility as long as ASEAN remains a loose organisation and as long as ASEAN is reluctant

to utilise its own funds to finance such programmes. Neither are health and nutrition
brought into the equation. Although there is
a Sub-Committee on Health and Nutrition, a
subsidiary body of the ASEAN Committee on
Social Development (COSD), the projects are
not aligned to human resources development
programmes. Coordination of programmes and
projects is indeed ASEAN's major flaw.

HUMAN RESOURCES DEVELOPMENT AND THE FUTURE OF ASEAN

In a rapidly changing and highly competitive
world, the ASEAN policy makers realised that
science and technology (S & T) will continue
to determine the pace and magnitude of developments in the region. They decided that
ASEAN should focus its attention on developing
an intelligent and highly professional and
productive work force to grapple with the
progressive increase in the sophistication of
future work demands. The scientific and technological leapfrogging advances the world over
demand a parallel growth of a trained pool
of workers in the ASEAN member countries,
particularly through research and development
(R & D), the development of scientific and
technical manpower and management systems.

The funds for R & D which are needed
to further technology development have now
become too large for developed countries
alone to provide. The developing countries,
in this case the ASEAN countries, have to
be included in the technology development
process. Their purchases of high technology
products will provide significant contributions
to the funding of the R & D of sophisticated
technology industries. Thus, the population of
ASEAN, as well as that of other developing
countries, can become a big market and an
important donor of high technology industry
R & D funds only if its income and purchasing
power increase. This increase cannot be sufficiently stepped up through the provision of

commercial or soft loans, but should be obtained
by way of improving added value processes.
This improvement can only take place with
the progressive enhancement of technology
and of human resources.

From this perspective it is thus not only
developing countries that are interested in
technology transfer.[3] For their market's sake,
advanced countries themselves have an interest
in transferring their technologies to developing
countries, including ASEAN. The increase in
living standards of the societies of the ASEAN
countries is not only in the interest of the
developing countries, but that of the developed
countries as well. Even the most sophisticated
technology cannot anymore be the exclusive
property of the advanced countries.

It is by way of transferring technologies
that people can be developed into high-value
renewable resources for value-added processes.
For technology transfer to be successful it is
imperative to harmonise and match the interests of the technology transferer and the
technology receiver. Technology receivers
should realise that the biggest incentive for
technology transfer is the widening of the
market, the increase of sales volume and the
raising of R & D funds to further improve the
technologies. This can be promoted by R & D
cooperation programmes on both sides.

It is here that the difficulty comes in for
the technology receiver. A major constraint
which is faced by the technology receiver is
the absence of an experienced work force.
Moreover, the added value processes undertaken by the receiver lack the integrative
network available in the organisation of the
technology transfer. Because of these constraints, factories in developing countries have
to make additional investments in infrastructure,
plant facilities, education and training, in systems and work procedures in the effort to
change themselves into what is now generally
called "technology carries."

ASEAN HRD programmes should take cog-
nisance of these structural changes. To cater to
this, ASEAN's education and training programmes

should be further geared towards the development of a core of highly motivated and trained manpower in scientific, technological and managerial skills.

NOTES

1. Kazuo Aichi, Parliamentary Vice-Minister for Foreign Affairs, at the prepatory meeting on the ASEAN Human Resources Development Project, March 31, 1981, p. 2.
2. *Ibid.*, p. 3.
3. For this section I am indebted to B.J. Habibie, "Sharing Responsibility over the Less Fortunate," in *Jakarta Post*, November 16, 17, 18, 1987.

REGIONAL CO-OPERATION IN ENVIRONMENTAL ACTIVITIES

DHIRA PHANTUMVANIT and JULIET LAMONT

THE GLOBAL PERSPECTIVE

Sustainable development is now a household phrase, and its underlying concept is rapidly acquiring priority status as a pivotal challenge for the global community. The "environment" has moved to center stage, evidenced by continuous media coverage of environmental issues which highlight concerns about environmental integrity at both the local and international levels. Spurred by milestone events — in particular, publication of the report, *Our Common Future*, in 1987 — the concept of sustainable development has entered the local and international consciousness, affecting government as well as the private and public sectors. Significantly, the trend to incorporate environmental management and planning policy into mainstream economic development strategies is now viewed as a necessary prerequisite for successfully achieving sustainable development. Acknowledgement of this requirement has resulted in a substantial evolution in the characteristics of environmental philosophy.

First, it is recognized that environmental concerns must become a trans-boundary, global responsibility. "Think globally but act locally" is now a universal motto. This characteristic has been highlighted by issues such as global climate change, ocean dumping, hazardous waste disposal, and the depletion of stratospheric ozone. The response has been accelerating global and regional momentum for resolving environmental concerns, evidenced by the expanding array of international conferences addressing environmental issues, including recent gatherings such as the Montreal Protocol (1988), the Basel Convention on the Control of Transboundary Movement of Hazardous Wastes And Their Disposal (1989), and the Netherlands Climate Change Conference (1989), as well as the upcoming United Nations World Conference on Environment and Development in Brazil (1992). Several conference outcomes have proved remarkable in setting precedents for voluntary, international cooperation on environmental issues, most notably the Montreal Protocol. In addition, actions such as the formation of the Intergovernmental Panel on Climate Change (IPCC), which is developing a series of specific recommendations to address global climate change concerns, indicate that global momentum and cooperation in tackling environmental concerns is gaining strength.

A second distinct characteristic of the emerging environmental philosophy is that the

Reprinted in abridged form from *Regional Network on Sustainable Development* (Bangkok: Thailand Development Research Institute, 1990), pp. 1–35, by permission of the authors and the publisher.

diverse impacts of environmental decisions, and consequent increase in the number of players involved in environmental policy issues — from high-level government administrators to local village residents — requires increasingly co-operative approaches to resolving environmental problems. Government, business, and public interests must all be considered integral to determining a final decision.

Finally, the emerging environmental ethos demands that simple cause-and-effect explanations — and responses — to environmental policy issues must give way to an acknowledgment of the complex economical, political, and social relationships embedded in environmental policy problems and decisions. Approaches to problem resolutions must therefore be multidisciplinary, encompassing the numerous and diverse facets of environmental issues, if policy strategies are to be effective.

In sum, the severity and complexity of current environmental problems, and their noticeable impacts on the global community, have required the evolution of a new environmental management ethos. The new outlook is transboundary, cooperative, and multidisciplinary in nature, to encompass the diverse array and complexity of environmental issues currently being addressed.

RESPONSES IN THE DEVELOPING COUNTRIES

In developing nations, interest in the environment is only beginning to emerge, and is often offset by the daily realities of poverty, urbanization pressures, or on a national level, the need for continued economic expansion. Ironically, it is in these younger economies, which are often resource-based, that the need for environment-economic integration is the greatest, in order to avert depletion of the vital resource base that sustains economic viability.

Pushing intellectual acceptance of the environmental 'ethos' towards pragmatic policy implementation in developing nations is a difficult, but crucial, step. It requires, at the outset, demonstrating that the change is clearly beneficial to the common people, which may in turn necessitate national actions that support and encourage the benefits of the change. It also requires global recognition of the large disparities between various countries and regions in their ability to address environmental problems.

Developing nations will view global environmental management efforts as being clearly hypocritical if there is no parallel indication of leadership from their industrialized counterparts, showing that they are willing to make sacrifices for the global good. Likewise, developing nations cannot be expected to forego their own individual economic progress for the benefit of the global community if they receive neither support nor benefit for their actions, or guarantees that they can continue to move towards an equitable standard of living. Cooperation and exchange of information must occur between developed and developing nations as well as between countries with similar concerns, to ensure more effective and efficient development of policy strategy which bypasses needless replication of effort, while building on knowledge already available elsewhere to tackle new environmental issues.

In focusing on specific steps to improve environmental policy development and implementation in developing countries of ASEAN and East Asia, this paper will first examine achievements and progress in the environmental policy field thus far. It will then explore the feasibility of establishing a mechanism to facilitate regional policy formulation among developing nations. The ultimate goal is to enable equitable dialogue between North and South countries in order to identify and address those environmental issues which will require resolution through concerted global effort.

ENVIRONMENTAL ACTIVITIES OF REGIONAL
AND INTERNATIONAL ORGANIZATIONS

The past five years have marked distinct growth and progress in the environmental field, particularly with respect to achievements encouraging sustainable development. From government legislation to public awareness, environmental concerns are attracting notable, increased attention, while stimulating attempts to develop both short term and long term solutions to environmental problems.

At the international and regional level, leading institutes directly involved in environmental policy promotion include ESCAP, UNEP and ASEAN, along with specialized agencies of the UN such as FAO, WHO and UNESCO.

Aside from UN agencies, several regional bodies are actively involved with environmental concerns. Foremost among them is the Association of Southeast Asian Nations (ASEAN), which initiated a collaborative ASEAN Environment Program (ASEP) in 1978. Now in its third five-year phase, ASEP is serving the six nations of Brunei, Indonesia, Malaysia, Philippines, Singapore and Thailand. ASEP was originally supervised by the ASEAN Expert Group on the Environment (AEGE). In 1981, environmental management and natural resource conservation concerns were highlighted as part of ASEAN's cooperative efforts in the First Minister's Meeting on the Environment, held in Manila. Environmental emphasis has intensified over the last decade, as evidenced by progressively more action-oriented ASEP strategies, and increased focus on the need for improved education and public awareness campaigns about environmental issues throughout the ASEAN region.

In 1987, ASEAN's general environmental concerns coalesced in the adoption of the Jakarta Resolution on Sustainable Development, which targeted sustainable development as the over-riding objective for all future ASEP activities (Jakarta Resolution, 1987). Commitment to the Resolution was confirmed by the framework of ASEP III (planning period 1988-1992). The evolution culminated in June 1989 with the upgrading of the AEGE supervising body to the ASEAN Senior Officials on the Environment (ASOEAN), in essence a full incorporation of the environmental facet into the ASEAN structure.

Another focal point for regional cooperation is the Pacific Economic Cooperation Conference (PECC), and its more recent outgrowth, the

Asia-Pacific Economic Cooperation (APEC)*. PECC and APEC are part of a tri-partite regional grouping whose aim is "enhancing economic cooperation in the region" (PECC, 1990), by addressing regional economic and trade issues. PECC, whose members come from governments, the private sector, and academia, is the non-governmental arm of the group. It functions through task forces set up to study various economic-related topics in the region. PECC has been instrumental in coordinating members in the business and economics sector. At present, environmental concerns are considered integral to several of the projects operating under PECC task forces, particularly Fisheries and Forestry. The attempt to establish a "PECC Integrating Group on the Environment" has not yet received the endorsement of PECC's Steering Committee, which met in Singapore in May 1990.

APEC is PECC's government counterpart. Its objective is to review regional trade and economic issues through the perspective of the government sector. Conclusions of APEC's first meeting in March 1990 indicate that the body will function through work projects targeting specific regional economic issues. Of the first six projects agreed upon, two could have direct relevance to the development of environmental policy strategies in the Pacific Rim, namely, Marine Resource Conservation and Regional Energy Cooperation (APEC, 1990). Within its overall economic scope, APEC is undertaking these projects to examine the "interaction between environment and economic decision-making" (APEC, 1990). At this stage, however, environmental considerations are still an appendage to the body's central mandate, and are therefore likely to receive less emphasis and in-depth analysis than other economic issues.

PRIVATE SECTOR'S NETWORK

A recent initiative of the private sector is noteworthy. Nomura Research Institute, established by the Japanese brokerage firm, Nomura

Securities Corporation, has formed a network of policy research institutes, informally called the "Asia Think-tank 9" (AT9), from nine countries of the Pacific Rim region. AT9 was officially launched in April 1990. and consists of members from Hong Kong, Indonesia, Japan, Malaysia, Philippines, Republic of Korea, Singapore, Taiwan and Thailand.

The rationale behind the formation of the AT9 was that due to the numerous and rapid economic changes occurring in the Asian region, and to a more complex and competitive global economy, "the Asian countries face many challenges in sustaining their growth and prosperity." Therefore they would benefit from pooling their resources "to learn from each other for the development of each country's economy, and thereby contribute to global prosperity, by enhancing the exchange of studies and free discussion with each other" (Asia Club, 1990).

It is expected that concentration areas for joint cooperative research will soon be identified. The challenge is to link environmental issues with the work of the AT9, which would encourage and facilitate the environment-economic integration that is essential for the successful implementation of sustainable development strategies. Given that dialogue about economic issues is already underway among premier regional policy research institutes through the AT9, it would appear to be a natural extension to add the equally necessary environmental facet.

NATIONAL GOVERNMENT ACTIONS

While high-level environmental activities in the region are often publicized by international agencies, national governments in the region have carried the bulk of the work at the field level.

In the area of forestry, Thailand brought about the most dramatic legislative change through an unprecedented ban on logging activities, announced by the government in February of 1989. The ban was imposed in response to severe flooding and mudslides in the southern provinces, a consequence of extensive deforestation throughout the country. The governments of China and the Republic of Korea are also recognized for their large-scale reforestation programs to rehabilitate deforested tracts and watershed areas.

Newly-industrializing-countries of the region, facing severe environmental quality deterioration in urban centers, have introduced legislation to curb and regulate pollution. The government of Hong Kong recently passed a round of new laws aimed at reducing air pollution, including a partial ban on the use of fuels containing high sulfur concentrations, in order to reduce sulfur dioxide emissions. In early 1990, the government of Singapore, known for its stringent anti-pollution legislation and enforcement, more than doubled user fees on cars entering the city as a method to control increasing traffic congestion and air pollution problems.

Actions have not been limited to the past few years. As early as 1980, the government of Malaysia established effluent limitations for industrial dischargers, directed mainly at regulating discharges from the palm-oil industry, at that time the single largest source of industrial effluents (Lan, 1980). The Indonesian government has promoted extensive environmental education programs over the last decade, in order to increase public awareness of environmental issues.

In fact, while extensive environmental legislation is still absent in many nations, governments throughout the region have initiated serious attempts to remedy this yap in the past ten years, and have intensified these efforts considerably over the course of that period. These actions indicate that receptiveness to new environmental action exists at the national government level, and should provide an advantageous base for the development and implementation of future environmental policy strategies.

NGO ACTIVITIES

NGOs constitute perhaps the fastest growing

sector of influence in the environmental field. In developing countries such as Thailand, Malaysia and Indonesia, NGOs have acted as a mobilizing force for local communities and the public, initiating and supporting action at the ground level. Indonesia has further strengthened NGO impacts through the formation of WALHI, a national coordinating body for the country's NGOs. NGOs in Thailand have intensified efforts to encourage cohesiveness within the NGO movement through the organization of such events as the "Environment 1990" conference, the first nation-wide gathering of NGOs in the country, organized in early 1990 in Bangkok by the Society for the Conservation of National Treasures and Environment (SCONTE).

A fundamental feature of NGO activities is public education, which is used as a means to build awareness of environmental concerns, and thus to motivate ground-level action. NGOs produce a wide range of publications on environmental issues, such as Sahabat Alam Malaysia's "Environment News Digest," and the "Asia-Pacific Environment Newsletter," published by the Asia-Pacific Peoples Environment Network. Community action programs launched by NGOs have also had a large impact in raising public consciousness, and could serve as models for future campaigns throughout the region.

A second significant feature of environmental NGOs is their increasing influence on government and policy through active lobbying, and through their extensive expertise in specialized issues. The Wildlife Fund of Thailand, for example, was instrumental in the implementation of the recent ban on marketing ivory, which comes from elephant tusks. Its projects in elephant conservation in northeast Thailand provided concrete data to support recommendations for the ban.

In the past, environmental NGOs have been viewed by many governments as a purely oppositional force in the policy development process. However, the realities of their growing influence, as well as their rising input to international environmental fora such as the recent Bergen Convention (May 1990), indicate that they will be an integral element in future policy development. Their access to and acceptance by the public, and their down-to-earth nature, should be addressed as a complementary and positive component of environmental strategy development.

ESTABLISHMENT OF A REGIONAL ENVIRONMENT CENTER — A NEW OPTION FOR ENVIRONMENTAL MANAGEMENT?

Environmental management policy in the developing countries of East Asia and ASEAN is at a turning point. Building on their economic achievements, governments in the region are, by now, aware of the significance of environmental issues. Policy measures such as the ban on logging in Thailand to reduce deforestation rates and consequent flooding suggest that governments will respond quickly and decisively to environmental crises. Yet the incorporation of effective environmental management into mainstream development policies has just begun throughout the region.

Individual sectors have made significant impacts both in promoting environmental consciousness and in translating that momentum into pragmatic action. International organizations such as ESCAP, UNEP, FAO and WHO have organized numerous conferences aimed at high-level government officials to promote environmental management. Government agencies at the national level are adjusting their organizational structures to address current natural resource and environmental management concerns, as well as implementing reforms in natural resource policies to reflect the changing socio-economic conditions of individual countries. Technical research institutes, both university-affiliated and independent, are placing greater emphasis on natural resources and environmental curricula. NGOs throughout the region are becoming increasingly effective at disseminating information, and building up grass-roots support, and have accumulated extensive field knowledge and contacts with local communities in their areas of operation over the years. Finally, the media and the public are evolving as a significant, influential force in pressuring governments and the private sector to incorporate environmental management into development strategies.

However, these contributions have remained relatively independent of one another, or are often the products of specific, isolated events. In fact, a noticeable, and substantial gap in the nature of regional achievements thus far is the lack of any coordinated effort to develop effective regional policy strategies for long term sustainable development. One response to this absence has been a proposal to establish a regional center for environment, which would act as a regional hub for technical assistance, information dissemination, and policy coordination. However, after careful analysis, such a proposal may not be justified.

Establishing a regional center can be time-consuming, duplicative, costly, and ineffective. Firstly, environmental issues are multidisciplinary in nature, ranging from deforestation to fisheries development to hazardous waste management, to name just a few. Unless financial resources are limitless, it is not possible for a single center to possess adequate manpower and expertise to respond to all environmental needs of its member states.

Secondly, at the policy coordination level, United Nations agencies such as ESCAP have already been performing a catalytic role, helping countries to cooperate on regional environmental programs. More specific technical issues are already handled effectively by specialized international agencies such as FAO and WHO, and by other regional bodies, including the International Board for Soil Research and Management (IBSRAM), which specializes in land resources; the International Center for Living Aquatic Resources Management (ICLARM), for marine resources; and the Committee for Coordination of Joint Prospecting for Minerals in Asian Offshore Areas (CCOP), which promotes offshore mineral resources development. In addition, there are numerous regional projects on forest resources, such as the ASEAN Institute of Forest Management and the ASEAN Timber Technology Centre, both in Kuala Lumpur.

Given these factors, and the financial pressures already faced by developing nations, the establishment of another regional center for the environment does not appear to be a cost-effective or logical option. A more realistic and effective approach to filling this regional need is to focus on policy development itself, and on a modus operandi which enhances the formulation of effective environmental policies throughout the region, while drawing upon existing institutes at both the national and international level.

THE ROLE OF POLICY RESEARCH INSTITUTES

Policy research institutes, by definition, are required to conduct technical and policy analysis across a range of policy issues to support the formulation of long term strategies for sustainable social and economic development. Individual institutes vary in their degree of specialization; however, the underlying objective of producing and disseminating reliable policy research is a distinguishing feature of all such organizations.

Policy research institutes throughout ASEAN and East Asia are often consulted by national governments, as sources of information about critical policy issues, and as initiators of new policy strategies.

Their contributions to policy development throughout the region have been further shaped by current regional trends. The Pacific Rim is in the midst of rapid economic development. Excluding the developed countries, the Republic of Korea, Hong Kong, and Singapore are already strong members of the international economic community, with solid industrial, import and export bases. The emergence of younger, expanding economies such as Malaysia, Thailand and Indonesia, has accorded the region a status of that with the world's fastest economic growth rate. Policy research institutes have been linked to this economic development, providing analysis and synthesis of complex and rapidly changing economic trends, while evaluating and modifying various policy options to meet the demands of intensifying international economic competition.

Rapid economic advances have brought about significant social and political changes as well. As a result, development issues in the Pacific Rim are of a tremendously complex nature. Environmental issues, in particular, encompass a wide range of social, ecological, political, and economic components. Individual policy strategies thus have ramifications across other sectors and interests, and must address and integrate these diverse components to ensure effective policy implementation. If the objective is to formulate regional environmental strategies, then more thorough understanding of common regional issues must be undertaken. Policy research institutes have found a niche by proving themselves effective at analysing complex, multi-faceted policy issues, and at synthesizing results to produce appropriate policy strategies.

The trans-boundary nature of policy issues in the Pacific Rim has been a final element in heightening the impact of policy research. Economic policies are heavily dependent on inter-regional trade and development, as well as on economic developments in other regions of the world. Social issues such as immigration and emigration between neighboring countries require dialogue and common understanding. Environmental issues such as marine exploration and fishing rights, deforestation and timber supply, and transnational river management require policy solutions that transcend traditional national borders. Essentially, what is ultimately required is the ability to integrate all these issues together into cohesive regional development plans.

ISSUES

The concept of the regional network, is to

harness the strengths of existing policy research institutes for the following purposes: to exchange existing information and research on natural resources and the environment; to coordinate and prioritize regional environmental policy concerns so as to identify appropriate areas in which to initiate collaborative research efforts; and finally, to strengthen the Asian position in environmental policy strategy with respect to the global community, through the preparation of regional "position" papers.

The nature and quality of network output is fundamental to the network's long term success, as it will be the visible product of network activities. The output, which is proposed to consist of regional position papers based on collaborative research efforts, will only have value and impact if it addresses critical issues now facing the region. Therefore, a central objective in interviewing potential network members was to identify environmental concerns of common interest, and of high priority, throughout the region.

The results of the interviews with policy research institutes in the Pacific Rim confirmed that there are several environmental issues of immediate relevance and concern to the region. The environmental concerns appeared to fall into two categories: broader "macro-policy" environmental issues that are relevant across a range of specific environmental concerns; and the more specific topical issues themselves.

The macro-policy issues commonly identified by potential network members included: the integration of economics and environment; the future state of natural resources and environment in the Pacific Rim, alias, a "Pacific Rim 2010 Study"; and development assistance and cooperative strategies between developed and developing nations, i.e., addressing the "North" — "South" differential.

TOPICAL ENVIRONMENTAL ISSUES
OF REGIONAL CONCERN ARE NUMEROUS

While there are a variety of environmental problems throughout the Pacific Rim, interviews conducted in the region indicated that current policy priorities fell into five specific concerns: global climate change, tropical deforestation, urbanization and environment, energy and environment, and hazardous and solid waste disposal. Rankings among these issues tended to vary according to the nation's stage of development, the resource base upon which it drew, population size, and other factors. However, each of the five issues were targeted as priority concerns by at least three or more institutes from different countries, and thereby were considered to warrant full attention as over-riding regional concerns.

NOTE

* APEC: 12 members — ASEAN plus US, Canada, Japan, Australia, New Zealand, and South Korea.

52. PRIVATIZATION AND DEREGULATION IN ASEAN

NG CHEE YUEN and NORBERT WAGNER

Privatization and deregulation have attracted increasing attention in Southeast Asia, especially among ASEAN countries in recent years. In 1985, the Asian Development Bank (ADB) held a conference in Manila, Philippines, on "Privatization Policies, Methods and Procedures". Meanwhile all ASEAN countries have, in varying degrees, studied the necessities and possibilities of privatization and deregulation.[1] Some countries are already carrying out several privatization and deregulation attempts, while others are lagging behind. Even countries like Vietnam are considering if not privatization, then deregulation of parts of their economies.

In developed countries like France and Japan where government intervention, regulation, and manipulation have been dominant measures in economic policy-making in the past, privatization and deregulation are considered key instruments to restructure the economies and promote economic growth. Even in China and the Soviet Union where the most dominant and pervasive role has always been assigned to the state, leaders have seriously reviewed the continued appropriateness of such policies and have been striving for a larger role for the private sector and the market mechanism.

The recent emphasis on privatization and deregulation can also be seen in an ethical context as a manifestation of the spreading of democracy and individual freedom throughout the world. To a large extent, one is the corollary of the other since privatization and deregulation leave additional areas for individual decision-making, whereas democracy and individual freedom inevitably demand a predominant role being given to market forces.

THE MEANING OF PRIVATIZATION

Privatization as it is used here and throughout this volume is defined in a rather broad sense and includes deregulation as well. Thus, it comprises

— the *transfer of ownership* from the public to the private sector,
— the *transfer of production* previously produced by the public sector to the private sector,
— the *financial privatization* where the government charges market prices instead of fees for goods and services supplied,
— the *deregulation* of the economy, i.e., liberalization and relaxation or removal of government regulations interfering with market forces.

However, the focus of privatization clearly is

Reprinted in abridged form from "Privatization and Deregulation in ASEAN", *ASEAN Economic Bulletin* 5, no. 3 (March 1989), pp. 209–223, by permission of the authors and the Institute of Southeast Asian Studies.

the investment of public enterprises in favour of private investors and, consequently the transfer of ownership and decision-making from the public to the private sector. This reduces the role of the state and enlarges the scope of the market forces.

PERCEPTIONS OF PRIVATIZATION AND DEREGULATION IN ASEAN

Privatization and deregulation are complex concepts which may embrace many different policies and measures. In ASEAN countries, where not only the socio-economic objectives, but also the extent of the involvement of public enterprises in economic activities differ considerably, there are varying views on the degree to which privatization and deregulation are desirable or feasible. These varying perceptions are to a large extent influenced by the respective socio-economic objectives and policies towards public enterprises of countries in the region. These views range from an emphasis on a continued role for public enterprises but with improved efficiency to the belief that total privatization is the panacea to cure the ills of the economy being constricted by many inefficient public enterprises.

Whatever the pros and cons of privatization and deregulation in the ASEAN region, the interest in the process has grown considerably. The governments of the ASEAN countries are increasingly committed to privatization and to reduced interference in the economy.

PUBLIC ENTERPRISES IN ASEAN COUNTRIES

Public enterprises have increasingly played an important role in most national economies of Southeast Asia. This phenomenon coincided with rapid industrialization in the region and to a great extent was aided by growing government revenue resulting from high commodity prices and economic growth. The tendency of increasing government involvement in the national economy has, to a large extent, been supported and driven by:

— the underdevelopment of capital markets and their inability to mobilize the necessary financial resources;

— the reluctance or inability of the private sector to invest in those sectors or industries with unusually high commercial and non-commercial risks and to implement investment projects which require large amounts of investment; and

— the general conviction prevailing among development economists, development agencies, and governments of industrial as well as developing countries throughout the fifties, sixties, and even early seventies that only governments can undertake the steps necessary to promote and guide the development process.

However, the more specific rationale for establishing public enterprises and the philosophy under which these enterprises were run differed among the countries.

THE CASE FOR PRIVATIZATION IN ASEAN

Public enterprises in all ASEAN countries are, as noted earlier, not confined to activities with characteristics of increasing returns, indivisibility, and positive externalities — such as justice and security — where optimal outcomes are unlikely to be achieved through private markets; or activities such as services of public utilities and housing, where state intervention has the possibility of reducing transaction costs. All states are also involved in activities that were or could have been the domain of private enterprise. However, control measures, orientation, and attitudes towards public enterprise differ among the ASEAN states and these factors directly or indirectly determine its nature, orientation, and structure.

In Singapore, public enterprises are run strictly on a commercial basis, especially those involved with activities that could have been the domain of private enterprise. Public enterprises are expected to make profits and expand where feasible. If they lose money, they are supposed to be permitted to go bankrupt. For that matter, it is also the stated policy of the government not to buy failing private companies just to secure jobs. In fact, public enterprises in Singapore are obviously more efficient than other local companies. In this manner, Singapore has been able to avoid a number of major pitfalls so prevalent in other developing countries.

For the other ASEAN states, though they may have professed some or all of these same policies, the results have not been the same mainly because the implementation and aims have been rather different. Generally, public enterprises are characterised by:

— operating deficits, causing a drain on public budgets;
— over-staffing, in many cases with politicians, relatives, friends, and ex-generals who have little concern or real incentives for efficient management;
— heavy dependence on domestic and foreign credit, leading to serious indebtedness; and
— sub-optimal use of resources, further lowering labour productivity.

Public enterprises are run with inadequate attention to profitability, cost control, and efficiency. These enterprises receive privileges from the government, and in turn are used for blatantly political purposes, regardless of their qualifications. Even in some cases where enterprises are honestly run, they have often displayed a lack of initiative and arrogance towards the public they served. These and other factors contributed to the huge losses sustained by public enterprises and the burgeoning external debt of many ASEAN countries.

THE PROGRESS OF PRIVATIZATION IN ASEAN

Modes of Privatization

The predominant modes of privatization in ASEAN countries comprise:

— new listing in the stock market;
— secondary offer to the public at large or to existing shareholders;
— management buy-out;
— sale to original promoters;
— negotiated sale; and
— selective tender.

The appropriateness of the mode of privatization depends on the respective circumstances. But, in the interest of an open and clean implementation of privatization, public enterprises should seek random allocation through listing or secondary offer to the public. This mode of disposal will not only add to the needed depth and breadth of the fledgling stock markets in the region, but also, improve absorptive capacity.

However, with the exception of Singapore, capital markets are not well developed and this imposes serious limits to their absorptive capacities. In order to broaden the scope of possible shareholders, foreign investors may be invited to buy shares. However, due to strong nationalistic feelings many countries may be reluctant to open their capital markets to a considerable extent to foreign shareholders.

PROBLEMS OF PRIVATIZATION IN ASEAN

As in other countries or regions, privatization in ASEAN faces, many obstacles, hurdles, and problems which are hard to overcome. In some instances these problems are country-specific. Most of them, however, appear to be common to many other countries carrying out similar privatization programmes.

Nationalistic Sentiments

A major obstruction to privatization can come from increased nationalism and the suspicion of foreign influence into or even dominance of the economy. These sentiments played a major role when in August 1988 President Aquino announced the indefinite postponement of plans to privatize the Philippines National Oil Corporation (PNOC). The arguments of national independence and national security serve in many countries as the ultimate resort to stop the discussion on privatization and to prevent any further privatization attempts.

However, it needs to be emphasized that foreign investors have been invited to participate in several instances. Thus, for example, Singapore has allowed foreign ownership of shares of Singapore Airlines. The Philippine Government has explicitly stated that in view of the limited internal capital market it is inevitable that foreign ownership be allowed in order to raise the maximum amount of funds.

Management Resistance

A very serious threat to any privatization effort may stem from resistance of the managers (bureaucrats) of those public enterprises which are to be privatized as they stand to lose their jobs, perks, fringe benefits, influence, and decision-making power. The government needs to persuade, cajole, and at times even pressure managers of public enterprises to co-operate in the national effort to privatize.

Admittedly, countries like Indonesia and Malaysia face immense problems because of vested interests of managers of public enterprises as well as because of resistance of politicians concerned. For example, there was a flurry of activity and news concerning privatization in Indonesia during the first half of 1987. Ministers were told to report to the President, within a month, the performance of companies under their respective portfolios. At the same time, President Soeharto ordered the establishment of high-powered ministerial and official teams to study the feasibility of privatizing public enterprises. Subsequent public discussions showed that there was a general reluctance to privatize. Various ministers pointed out that most of the companies under them were profitable; in cases

where they were making losses, they were classified as essential areas vital to national security (see above).

The resistance of managers heading public enterprises also hampered the privatization progress in Thailand and the Philippines.

On the other hand privatization is often opposed because of an alleged shortage of capable and efficient managers to run the companies after they are privatized. However, this argument is hardly convincing. On the contrary, one could argue that the previous reliance of many governments upon public enterprises and interference into the economy prevented the emergence of indigenous private entrepreneurship and management skills. Furthermore, given the poor performance of public enterprises in almost all ASEAN countries, the lack of efficient managers in the public sectors appears to be at least as prevalent.

Employees Resistance

Privatization is also opposed by employees and trade union leaders because of fears that it might result in job losses and thus contribute to an even larger unemployment problem within the country concerned. Employees of public enterprises may fear, too, that they may lose their benefits and perks after privatization. Trade unionists may also perceive privatization as the government's stick to tame the trade union movement. As the predominant objectives of privatization are to ease the budgetary burden of public enterprises and to improve the overall efficiency of the economy, the reduction or abolition of some of the worker's previous benefits and the lay off of part of the work force seem almost inevitable. Apart from these short-term effects however, privatization may rather improve the employees situation in the long term as it contributes to the improvement of the economy's growth prospects and, thus, generates additional job opportunities.

The position of employees and trade unions towards privatization in ASEAN countries is rather mixed. The Singapore trade union hardly comments on privatization, whereas trade unions in Thailand strongly oppose the government's endeavour towards privatization. Trade union leaders of Thai state enterprises have even set up a "watch-dog" committee in order to monitor any move to privatize state enterprises. In the Philippines the guidelines of the privatization programme state that the disposition entities are to give due consideration to the impact of privatization on employment. However, the number of employees affected by privatization has been minimal so far. Some firms have even increased their work-force after privatization. In Malaysia, the government has required that there should be no layoffs for a certain period after privatization, and that employees of privatized companies should not lose any benefit they would be entitled to in government service. In general, trade union opposition towards privatization in Malaysia has not been very strong.

Legal Problems

In some countries privatization faces some legal problems, too. In Thailand only companies established under certain legal acts can be privatized without requiring approval of the parliament which might be either time consuming or render privatization unfeasible because of vested interests. The privatization programme in the Philippines is severely hampered by objections of previous owners who dispute the authority of the Asset Privatization Trust to sell the assets.

Capital Markets

The capital market plays a crucial role in any divestment process. The better developed the capital market the easier it is to sell the shares to the public or to find a suitable owner through auctioning. On the other hand, privatization may also contribute to develop and to strengthen the capital market by attracting new capital and new participants, either from within the country or from abroad. The participation of foreign investors may enhance the possibilities of raising maximum revenue, but may also cause nationalistic sentiments to increase (see above).

The capital markets in Singapore and Malaysia are developed well enough to facilitate the privatization process whereas in the case of Indonesia and the Philippines the limitations and weaknesses of the capital markets may imply a serious constraint on privatization. Even in Singapore with total investable funds amounting to S$30.8 billion (which far exceeds the value of shares to be divested, amounting to S$20.8 billion) disruption in the market is likely to happen if the divestment is too rapid (Public Sector Divestment Committee 1987, p. 53). As to Indonesia, it needs to be seen whether the recently announced liberalization of the Indonesian capital market can improve the absorptive capacity of the capital market.

Distribution Effects

The privatization of public enterprises may have some repercussions on the distribution of income and wealth. First, privatization implies a transfer of ownership and control of assets from the public to individuals. Second, the mode of privatization and the valuation of the assets transferred can result in a substantial distributional effect. The problem of these distributional effects is particularly sensitive as the distribution problem is in many cases linked to ethnic groups.

Thus, for instance, Indonesia seems to face a dilemma. On the one hand, the transfer of ownership of public enterprises to Chinese Indonesian entrepreneurs could cause serious political problems. On the other hand, businessmen with the entrepreneurial skills and resources to take over the public enterprises belong mostly to the Chinese Indonesian ethnic group. Even foreign ownership would be more acceptable than privatization that primarily favours this ethnic group (see also *Indonesia Business Digest*, 1987).

Malaysia's solution to this problem is quite unique. Public enterprises were initially promoted to rectify the economic wealth of the Malays who hold political power. Privatization is, therefore, politically not feasible, unless it serves the same purpose. Consequently, the government nowadays considers it to be advantageous for the Malay community to privatize those public enterprises which have previously been established for the benefit of the same community.

> Privatization is also expected to contribute towards meeting the objectives of the New Economic Policy (NEP), especially as Bumiputera entrepreneurship and presence have improved greatly since the early days of the NEP and they are therefore capable of taking up their share of the privatized services (Hassan Abdul Karim, in Jomo 1988, p. 122).

The linking of privatization and the New Economic Policy will, however, make the progress of the privatization programme even more difficult, as it reduces the chances of finding entrepreneurs with the capital as well as the managerial and technical skills to run the privatized companies.

Moreover, this approach may cause additional problems. Privatization may favour the Malay community but may also contribute to further skew the distribution among this ethnic group. It is likely that political influence and connections will increasingly become decisive. One example is the privatization of the North-South Highway. The contract to build this highway was awarded to the company United Engineers Malaysia (UEM) which not only tendered at a price (M\$3.4 billion) that was much higher than many others, but was also known to be insolvent and suspended by the Kuala Lumpur Stock Exchange with reported losses of more than M\$100 million. This company, it is alleged by Mr Lim Kit Siang, an Opposition Member of Parliament, is 50 per cent owned by Hatibudi Sdn. Bhd., the investment arm of UMNO, the main component party of the ruling National Front. The trustees of the company include the Prime Minister himself and a number of other ministers. Therefore, Mr Lim alleges conflict of interest and applied for an injunction in the Supreme Court which has prevented the signing of the contract for the time being; but before the Supreme Court could hear the case, both Mr Lim and his counsel, Karpal Singh, were detained under the country's Internal Security Act ("UEM: Political time-bomb ticking away". In *Business Times*, 12 January, 1988).

In other cases, privatization has not even been implemented by the open tender system. Rather, it appears, that beneficiaries are chosen on the basis of political and personal connections (see Hassan Abdul Karim, in Jomo 1988, p. 123.). Cases of contracts without open tender include the M\$1.4 billion worth of 174 water supply projects that have been awarded to Antah Biwater which is a joint venture between a British company, Biwater PLC, and Antah Holding Sdn. Bhd. which is owned and controlled by the Negeri Sembilan Royal Family.

Another considerable impact of privatization on the distribution may evolve from the under-valuation of shares sold to the public. For example, in Malaysia the subscription price of some shares was substantially lower than the price after these shares were traded at the stock exchange, thus indicating a considerable under-pricing. Under-pricing is likewise a serious problem in Singapore and a number of initial public issues were grossly oversubscribed. These include Jurong Shipyard Ltd (145.7 times), Development Corporation Pte Ltd (14.2 times), Singapore National Printers (118.7 times), and Sembawang Maritime Ltd (93.3 times). This implies that the government collected far less revenue than would have been possible. Such a policy, however, whether deliberate or not, results in a transfer of wealth from the public to those who are lucky enough to get these shares. The argument that under-pricing may encourage a wider share ownership appears to be not valid, as especially smaller shareholders obviously sold their shares almost immediately in order to realize the gain.

Privatization and Efficiency

The most crucial aspect of the privatization progress is, however, to what extent it leads to improved efficiency and thus contributes to the further economic development of the countries concerned. It is, of course, premature to thoroughly assess the impact of privatization on efficiency in the ASEAN context given the only recently emerging endeavour for privatization and the thus far rather limited progress of privatization in the region. Yet, some general remarks may already be possible.

In order to improve efficiency, privatization must meet two basic requirements. First, the control of a company must really be transferred from the government to the private sector, thus making the private owner fully responsible and accountable for all management decisions as well as the consequences (e.g., losses) of these decisions. Only if control is fully transferred will the private owner be forced to achieve efficiency at the firm level by producing at minimum costs at a given market price. If the public sector continues to maintain a stake in a company (for instance, in the case of partial divestment) the government is most likely to continuously interfere, directly or indirectly, with the management decisions and, thus, will also be responsible for the consequences of these decisions. Moreover, in the case of partial divestment the companies concerned are most likely to maintain certain advantages and privileges over their competitors, like a better standing in the capital market and easier access to government contracts.

The problem of a reduced impact of privatization upon efficiency on the firm level is particularly relevant in the ASEAN context. There are several examples (in Singapore, Malaysia, and Thailand) where previously publicly-owned companies are only partially divested or transformed into a private company, but the shares of this company are held by the government.

Furthermore, in the case of Singapore, it appears that overall government control is not reduced even in those instances where previously publicly-owned companies are fully privatized as some of the funds raised are invested into new industries and sectors which the government considers to be promising in the future. Hence, the government uses these funds to implement a policy of industrial restructuring but by no means reduces the level of control over the economy and its interference with the market forces.

Abolition of government control and interference is necessary but not sufficient to increase overall efficiency. A second condition must be met, too, namely increased competition. If monopoly power is merely transferred from the public to the private sector only, there will hardly be any effect on overall efficiency. This problem is particularly relevant in the case of telecommunication services, electricity and water supply, postal services, highways, and public transport. These industries usually enjoy economies of large scale and, consequently, a lack of competition.

The danger of a mere substitution of private for public monopoly power, however, is prevalent not only in the case of more or less "natural" monopolies. Yet, examples from Malaysia and the Philippines suggest that privatization, as it is implemented there, may lead to an even higher concentration of wealth in the hands of a few rich families and cronies. In such cases, not only is the objective of increased efficiency not met, but a worsening distribution of income and wealth is the consequence of privatization.

Prospects

Privatization can only be a gradual and difficult process in the ASEAN region. The prospects of privatization may vary markedly among the ASEAN countries. Privatization is unlikely to be significant in Indonesia. At best, a few enterprises may be privatized and the main focus is on areas related to deregulation and liberalization of the Indonesian economy. The other countries of ASEAN may achieve partial privatization with varying degrees of success. Singapore may be able to privatize most of the identified enterprises. This, however, does not imply that state control would be reduced. In fact, if the Singapore Government continues to reinvest the revenue generated into new industries such as those identified by the Economic Development Board, the government's control over the economy may be further strengthened. Privatization in Malaysia, Thailand, and the Philippines is likely to encourage greater foreign participation. For Malaysia in particular, if the present methods of privatization are not altered, fiscal problems may be further exacerbated.

Addendum

The committed move towards privatization and deregulation in ASEAN effectively implies a greater role for the private sector in the region. This trend has important implications for regional co-operation in a number of ways. Priority is given to the market mechanism and private initiatives with profit maximization as the main motivation force. The trend also reflects greater political maturity and a sense of confidence in the region — replacing nationalistic sentiments with the more practical business approach to regional co-operation.

Should the privatization and deregulation exercise prove successful in some of these countries, which seems to be the case, it will have significant demonstration effects and will encourage the rest of the countries to further liberalize, deregulate and privatize their economies. Such a trend will shift previously obstructive political objectives such as those related to nationalistic considerations to that of the predominant economic objective of profit optimization — effectively a depolitization of business activities in the region. Although this trend necessarily implies greater competition among the ASEAN countries in the economic arena which will nurture competitive and efficient ASEAN industries, at the international level, it is also necessary to foster closer co-operation among the ASEAN states *vis-à-vis* industries from other parts of the globe.

With the down-play of nationalistic sentiments, a more open and deregulated economic environment and a larger role for the private sector, there will be greater feasibility and opportunities for a better division of labour among ASEAN states. Off-shore production in other ASEAN states motivated by comparative advantage and profit objective will forge a stronger economic linkage among the states. Politicians will be left with the less onerous task of smoothening the process in terms of legal and bureaucratic discrepancies. These private sector initiated economic activities are more likely to succeed compared to the previous joint ASEAN projects forged through political compromises. One significant manifestation of this new co-operation is the growth triangle comprising Singapore, Johore in Malaysia, and Riau in Indonesia.

Ng Chee Yuen and Norbert Wagner
May 1992

NOTE

1. Indonesia Business Digest, *State Enterprise and Privatization* 1, no. 5 (June 1987); "A Few Facts About Privatization in the Philippines", *IPP Bulletin* 1, no. 2 (February 1987); Government of Malaysia, *Guidelines on Privatization* (Kuala Lumpur: Economic Planning Unit, Prime Minister's Department, 1985); Government of Singapore, *Report of the Public Sector Divestment Committee*, February 1987; Vuthiphong Priebjrivat, *Financial Picture of the Thai Public Sector* (May 1987).

53.

PROSPECTS FOR INTRA-ASEAN INVESTMENT

PETER O'BRIEN and HERMAN MUEGGE

THE CHALLENGE FACING ASEAN

The ASEAN countries are looking for ways to increase economic growth at a time of much slower progress in the world economy and when significant and rapid changes in technology, industrial organization, and industrial location are taking place. ASEAN industrial co-operation is therefore seen as a means of accomplishing two aims: stimulating economic growth and reinforcing economic unity among the members. At no time in the past, nor indeed now, do ASEAN members view these two aims as anything other than complementary — there is no question of sacrificing overall national growth in order to increase co-operation. The apparently limited extent of industrial co-operation achieved so far and its contribution to economic expansion in the region nevertheless needs to be put in perspective. On many economic indicators, including changes in income per head, increase in industrial exports, capacity to manage foreign debt, or attraction and absorption of foreign investment, the ASEAN countries have performed well in relation to developing countries as a whole. It is when applying their own ambitious yardstick of comparison — which is with some other countries in the region, particularly the Republic of Korea and Japan — that ASEAN performance seems less satisfactory. The frequent exhortations to improving co-operation have to be seen in this context. It is thus not correct to argue that ASEAN economic expansion has been below average; quite the contrary, it has been good against any comparisons save those with a few of its neighbours.

Admittedly, the progress has been achieved largely as a function of co-operation with third countries, e.g., Japan and the United States, rather than with each other. On the particular issue of intra-ASEAN industrial co-operation it is, however, by no means clear that ASEAN performance has been weak compared with that of other developing country groupings. Several schemes have been tried in Latin America over the past quarter of a century, ranging from endeavours to expand intra-trade through the Latin American Free Trade Association (LAFTA) and Latin American Integration Association (LAIA); explicit attempts to create joint investments and allocate production among members through the Andean Pact; and on to significant bilateral arrangements of which the 1986 accord between Argentina and Brazil is the most substantial. However, the actual results of these schemes, in contrast to the declared objectives, have so far been quite insignificant. Intra-trade

Reproduced from "Prospects for Intra-ASEAN Investment", *ASEAN Economic Bulletin* 4, no. 2 (November 1987), pp. 190–96, by permission of the authors and the Institute of Southeast Asian Studies.

in industrial products has not gone beyond a tiny proportion of aggregate trade for the larger member countries and even for the small ones the shares of items receiving preferential treatment have rarely approached more than about one-sixth of the total. Industrial investment among Latin American countries has also attained much lower levels than the attention given to this issue would seem to warrant. Most of the Andean Pact schemes, which relied heavily on commitment of public funds, have failed to materialize or, where they did, to survive. The burst of private investment observed, particularly from Argentina and Brazil, towards the end of the last decade and the beginning of this, also has to be put in its proper setting. In aggregate terms the proportion of total foreign investment accounted for by these transactions did not for any recipient country reach as much as 5 per cent; the investments were not carried out, except in a handful of cases, under the aegis of bilateral or multilateral co-operation agreements; and in any case the latest information suggests that a by no means negligible number of these investment projects have subsequently been discontinued.

It is correct to argue that ASEAN co-operation has been much more limited than that of the EEC. Yet the different circumstances have to be kept in mind. The EEC was committed from the beginning to a timed creation of a customs union heading on towards a common market — this has been exactly three decades in the making and even now further steps to establish the Common Market are still required.[1] The question concerning joint investments was not explicitly considered by the EEC countries, since they believed that the expansion of trade would itself be sufficient for production and industrial specialization to increase along with the growth of individual firms in the Community. Thus, although there could admittedly be some debate over the appropriate figures to employ in any comparison, it is almost certainly correct to assert that intra-EEC industrial investment, at least in the sense in which ASEAN countries understand the term, is but

a minor and probably only a tiny proportion of aggregate industrial investments in the European countries.

One final initial remark needs to be made on the circumstances in which ASEAN countries are trying to expand joint industrial investments. Their economies are closely bound to the fortunes of others whose presence in the Pacific is extremely powerful, viz., Japan, China, the Republic of Korea, and the United States. These countries are now in a phase when the economic links among them seem to be growing much faster than their overall economies and when each of them is paying progressively more attention to other countries in the Pacific, above all the ASEAN members. It is scarcely surprising that ASEAN feels not only that such expansion may create new opportunities for it but also, and in a contrary sense, that there is a real danger of being overwhelmed by fast-growing, technologically powerful, and overseas-oriented industrial and industrial service economies. Undoubtedly joint investments, even if they also involve some non-ASEAN participation, are seen as a means of preserving industrial identity in the face of such a challenge.

THE RATIONALE FOR
INTRA-ASEAN INDUSTRIAL INVESTMENTS

Intra-ASEAN industrial investment (IAII) is subject to both general and specific conditions. Like any other form of foreign investment it will respond primarily to economic conditions and be based on various entrepreneurial determinants within the country concerned such as the comparative attractiveness of the production sites (in terms of labour costs, infrastructure, proximity to markets, etc.) and the availability of financial resources for expansion. A secondary set of considerations is connected with the legal and institutional framework for foreign investment in the host country. Surveys on the behaviour of foreign investors over the past twenty years have, however, repeatedly shown that, notwithstanding the vociferous petitions made by foreign investors for greater liberalization of the legal requirements they must meet, actual investment decisions appear to be affected only to a limited extent by the various incentives provided for in the institutional and legal environment. The critical determinants are thus long-term market potentials and production factor costs.

A variety of characteristics distinguishes the form of actual and potential IAII. Capital participation can be any mix of public and private, may involve just two as well as more ASEAN member countries, and may be with or without involvement of third parties. The investments usually result in the formation of new ventures but may well be offshoots of enterprises already in operation; there seem to be few if any examples of joint investments which have come about from purchases of already established firms. The enterprises vary in terms of size, market orientation and level of technology, and cover many subsectors.

What then would be the prevailing or potential advantages for entrepreneurs in the ASEAN countries with regard to investing in the region? On the face of it, and although the concerned product groups are not easy to identify, private entrepreneurs in the ASEAN region may indeed enjoy some real competitive edge over external investors. That edge stems primarily from greater knowledge of the region. It can take several forms including intimate knowledge of product markets and distribution systems (valuable on the assumption that production is destined mainly for ASEAN consumption), greater understanding of management of local labour, familiarity with administrative systems, and quite possibly a fairly similar business history which permits entrepreneurs to operate from similar perspectives. There is, furthermore, an advantage which by now has been acquired as a result of the operation of ASEAN itself, viz., through the ASEAN business associations functioning at branch level. As a result, entrepreneurs in the region have established close contacts with each other and an awareness

of common problems and potentials. These advantages are not, however, necessarily exclusive. In particular those transnational corporations (TNCs) which have operated in ASEAN member countries for many years, and indeed which are themselves represented in ASEAN-wide industrial associations, may also possess some of these advantages. Nevertheless, the linkage which the affiliates must perforce retain with overseas headquarters does put them in a somewhat different category.

To the extent that these advantages can be translated into production terms, it would be expected that local private entrepreneurs would utilize them even in the absence of specific incentives from member governments (the same argument would not apply to public sector investments of a joint character since the legislative restrictions on such activities would need explicit handling). As has often been indicated in economic policy discussions however, the deficiencies of information across countries along with a certain degree of risk aversion by relatively new entrepreneurs may warrant some type of special support. Those incentives could take the following forms: national treatment of fellow ASEAN investors within member countries; trade preferences for products manufactured by firms with IAII; various devices to reserve markets within ASEAN for such firms, e.g., through preferential public procurement; and incentives in specific branches linked to R&D efforts by the firms concerned.

Thus far ASEAN has tackled the question of incentives only in an *ad hoc* and perfunctory fashion. Explicit national treatment has not been established on a solid basis; trade preferences have been granted partially but not fully; the reservation of markets, which was certainly envisaged in the early days of ASEAN industrial corporation (AIC) schemes, has not in fact been practised, and there is little evidence of the R&D connection. Indeed, those advantages which have been legislated have also been extended in various instances to all enterprises legally established in the region without regard to who really controls them — in this sense, just as has frequently occurred in Latin America, the benefits can also be captured by TNC affiliates.

In short, the present position seems roughly as follows. Local capital may possess some advantages based primarily upon knowledge of local markets and production problems but it is not in exclusive possession of those advantages. Such incentives as have been established are not yet clear-cut and certainly do not aim sharply at local entrepreneurs as compared with foreign-controlled enterprises. It is, then, not surprising that the number of IAII, of whatever form, remains small (it appears that only nine ASEAN industrial joint ventures currently operate and there are even fewer ASEAN industrial complementation arrangements). Those entrepreneurial groups in the region which are eager to penetrate markets of member countries currently place heavy emphasis on trade liberalization measures by ASEAN such as preferential access. From this fact it could be deduced that they would be more ready to export directly from their own countries rather than set up production facilities in collaboration with local capital in the recipient country. There is unquestionably a strong interest in expanding sales but it is not obvious that a commensurate interest exists in expanding investment. Moreover, there is some evidence to suggest that entrepreneurial groups in Singapore and the Philippines have been directing attention abroad towards one or two developed countries, especially the United States. Intra-ASEAN investments may in fact have taken more of a back place as compared with investments abroad made from the region.

POSSIBILITIES FOR INTRA-ASEAN INDUSTRIAL INVESTMENT

The picture sketched in the preceding section suggests that under current circumstances the prospects for achieving substantially larger intra-ASEAN investment are not very promising. First, within the region itself the advantages possessed by and incentives offered to local entrepreneurs have not been exclusive to them nor have they been very strong. Second, the absence of more open trading possibilities has created a situation where joint investments could easily mean sales in just one member country rather than several. Third, so far public sector investments of a collaborative character have mostly been unsuccessful. Fourth, the experience of other regions, especially Latin America, indicates that the scope for securing joint investments is constrained by various factors. Specifically, where joint ventures of the public sector have occurred in Latin America, the partners have often been very unequal in the sense that big companies from the bigger countries operating in fairly large-scale and heavy industry branches have been providing some equity along with much technology and loan capital to create production in smaller countries. Where private investors have been involved, again entities from the bigger countries have been by far the most active and much of their investment behaviour has been connected with defensive strategies against highly uncertain conditions in their own countries. Admittedly, it is necessary not to lose sight of the very different environment and approach to industrial development in ASEAN and Latin American countries respectively. ASEAN has been concerned, by and large, to follow the trends on international markets and to pursue integration with them; this approach has been in a context of quite rapid overall growth, an acceptable degree of price stability, and the avoidance of chronic debt problems. In Latin America the perspective has been different, particularly for the three largest countries and the members of the Andean Pact. Their aims have been explicitly to build integrated industrial structures with promotion of capital goods industries being a constant theme. Although actual performance, particularly in the present decade, has often been disappointing in relation to those objectives, the accent has nevertheless been on creating industrial systems which are self-sustaining.

All in all, expectations for IAII cannot be great given prevailing conditions. Even the establishment of a handful of such ventures within the next year or two would have to be counted as real progress compared with performance in the past. If such investment flows are to be encouraged to increase more significantly a number of measures, both general and specific, would seem necessary to be considered:

— ASEAN would have to provide clear evidence to investors that it is indeed committed to creating an economic area where trade and investment among partners is given strong preferential treatment at least in some key branches;

— this commitment would have to include an explicit time schedule of measures to be introduced so as to make investment planning an easier activity;

— a striking example of joint public sector investments could act as a strong catalyst for actions by private entrepreneurs;

— encouragement in the form of funding by ASEAN of pre-investment studies could be a helpful first step to overcoming reticence, especially by medium-size firms in the region;

— some form of promotion of particular branches, and not just ASEAN investors, may well be required. This could be through the establishment of priority subsectors to which additional support would be given or some form of market reservation could be arranged;

— the provision of capital may itself be a problem given the limited scope of capital markets in the member countries. ASEAN may therefore have to establish much larger funding sources on a regional basis to which would-be local investors can apply in their attempts to establish IAII;[2]

— given the current pressures on ASEAN by the main investor countries in the

OECD to liberalize legislation it may be necessary/appropriate to retain the possibility of non-ASEAN participation in some of these joint ventures;

— since both the satisfaction of regional demand and the expansion of exports are key elements of existing industrial strategies, it may be necessary to give equal treatment to joint ventures irrespective of their market orientation;

— it would be important for ASEAN countries jointly to single out a few key industrial subsectors in which they wish to make an innovative effort, then the provision of additional incentives for joint ventures in those subsectors could well be justified.

The above conditions add up to the need for clear policy decisions in the areas of protection, investment legislation, public sector commitments, and innovation. They mean that IAII is likely to respond much more to improved overall organization within ASEAN than to minor adjustments of existing schemes, which in any case are reasonably flexible. Thus the point made earlier in this paper resurfaces: the problem up to now has not been an absence of flexibility in ASEAN but rather the absence of a clear-cut commitment to some form of economic integration.

The experience in both Latin America and the EEC in this regard has been instructive. Foreign firms, especially from the United States, managed to take full advantage of the integration schemes. In Latin America this was to an important extent at the expense of local enterprises, while in Europe, despite the fears which were strongly debated some twenty years ago, the outward orientation of European investors themselves meant that there was a readiness to allow all firms to utilize the integration schemes. For ASEAN the situation differs in that Japan is clearly the strongest foreign investor (data on foreign investment in ASEAN over the period 1980–85 show that Japan was the largest investor in the region every year except 1982, that it is the only country not to have recorded any net disinvestment, and these trends have been recently reinforced by new measures announced by the Japanese Government). Accordingly, the fear of too much foreign participation does exist. Against this there are only two possible directions which can be followed, i.e., for individual members to encourage national investment and/or for ASEAN countries as a whole to encourage joint investments. The latter will unquestionably remain only a small proportion of the former for quite some time to come. This paper argues that the relative weight of each factor would change only if ASEAN entrepreneurs were genuinely encouraged to adopt an ASEAN perspective in their thinking. That perspective is best served by setting up a broader market, by establishing financial facilities for conducting pre-investment studies and raising loan capital, and by an indication that the public sector in member states is likewise interested in the same goals. If those conditions can be met, then IAII may become a more powerful stimulus both to co-operation and regional economic growth than it has been during the past few years.

Several remarks have been made in this paper regarding experiences of, and co-operation with, other countries and institutions. It is only appropriate, therefore, that three areas of such co-operation be underlined. To begin with, the references to co-operative arrangements among firms can be looked at in the light of the recent (1985) programme in the EEC for co-operation in R&D, the so-called EUREKA programme. The member states include the EEC, EFTA, and Turkey. The aim of the programme is to increase competitiveness of European firms in the field of high technology. The focus is strongly towards the development of marketable products, most of the participants are firms rather than universities and research centres, more than half of the funding comes from the entities themselves, and they do most of their co-ordination themselves, i.e., EUREKA has only a small secretariat. Up till now 109 projects covering a wide range of products have been approved and it would seem that this kind of flexible approach could fit well within the perspective usually adopted by ASEAN. In the ASEAN context both parts of the electronics industry and of the bio-technology industry would seem to qualify as prime candidates for a joint ASEAN R&D programme.

The second area of explicit co-operation could be through the joint venture approach in which also foreign participants are welcomed. As noted earlier, Japanese investors are the leaders within ASEAN and the data so far point strongly towards the joint venture approach as the preferred form of Japanese involvement. Moreover, although the EEC countries account for a far smaller proportion of total foreign direct investment in the region, they too have recently placed much greater emphasis on joint ventures as a preferred form of collaboration. Under existing provisions for intra-ASEAN joint ventures these linkages with abroad are permitted; what may be necessary now is to integrate them more clearly with any changes in investment policies towards the OECD countries.

Finally attempts to improve methods for raising capital in the region and encouraging cross-country investments may well receive support from international financial bodies. Thus, some ASEAN member countries have received structural adjustment loans from the World Bank in recent years; and during the past two or three years a scheme was proposed for offering investment guarantees. Since joint investments by ASEAN entrepreneurs are also foreign investments, it may be worthwhile for ASEAN to explore the possibility of World Bank back-up for such investments. This could include both methods of raising capital and the provision of guarantees against certain non-commercial risks. By the same token, the European Investment Bank (EIB) can, according to Article 18 of its Constitution, assist EEC member states in investments outside the EEC itself. ASEAN could explore with EIB ways in which this provision could be effectively utilized in the context of collaborative arrangements where two or more ASEAN countries were involved together with EEC country entities. Under these circumstances IAII could be stimulated by being linked more closely with the encouragement of investments from outside the region.

NOTES
1. On present schedules this will be accomplished by 1992.
2. A prime objective of World Bank policies in the region is the rapid expansion of local capital markets.

Section *VII*

ASEAN EXTERNAL ECONOMIC RELATIONS

Introduction

Joseph L.H. Tan

There are two obvious approaches to organizing the selection of literature on ASEAN external economic relations. One approach would be to focus on major thematic issues. The other approach, and the one adopted in this Section, is to present ASEAN external economic relations systematically in terms of its bilateral relations with various trading partners including the United States, Japan, and the EC; China, South Asia, Indochina, and Myanmar; and finally, in the steps of Ferdinand Magellan, across the Pacific to Latin America.

Tan Kong Yam, Toh Mun Heng, and Linda Low review ASEAN's involvement in Pacific economic initiatives, and provide a prognosis of trends in foreign direct investment and trade in the Asia-Pacific. Various regional economic groupings are discussed: APEC (Asian Pacific Economic Co-operation); PECC (Pacific Economic Co-operation Conference); and the EAEC (East Asian Economic Caucus). The authors highlight the policy implications by calling for "an active and strategic positioning" of ASEAN within the wider Asian Pacific configurations. They argue that ASEAN should work within a larger group(s) to advance the benefits of economies of scale and division of labour, and push for a freer multi-lateral trading system. Finally, they call for ASEAN to be more assertive by taking an active rather than a passive role in evolving open regionalism, particularly within APEC.

A notable milestone in ASEAN-U.S. relations is recorded in the influential report — submitted to the Joint Steering Committee of the ASEAN and U.S. governments — prepared by Seiji Naya, Kernial S. Sandhu, Michael Plummer, and Narongchai Akrasanee. The authors review substantive issues, including trade in goods and services between the United States and ASEAN; the contentious intellectual property rights issue; and U.S. investment in ASEAN. The authors advocate an ASEAN-U.S. Trade and Investment "umbrella agreement" incorporating features of other successful pacts which favour trade and investment liberalization, and promote economic efficiency and welfare. Such an "umbrella agreement" could also be a model for similar arrangements with other nations in the Asia-Pacific.

Chng Meng Kng and Royokichi Hirono cover both trade and investment relations between Japan and ASEAN. They examine dimensions of Japan's reliance on ASEAN for its supply of strategic raw materials; ASEAN as a market for Japan's industrial exports; and ASEAN's dependence on Japan for investment funds, capital, intermediate and final products, as well as industrial technology. These facets of bilateral relations are reviewed in the context of economic restructuring and policy implications for promoting economic co-operation. The authors recommend that Japan's overseas development assistance (ODA) should be on a longer-term basis to stimulate more effective development of domestic resources in ASEAN as well as to alleviate problems of unemployment, energy shortage, and food production in the region.

Hans Christoph Rieger provides a critical and realistic appraisal of the status of ASEAN-EC co-operation. By applying an innovative game theory approach, he identifies possibilities for further improvements in bilateral relations. He makes the salient conclusion that Europe is primarily preoccupied with its own internal problems and challenges and ASEAN seems to be relatively much less important for Europe than vice versa. However, he underlines the importance if not the imperative for ASEAN to continue its external economic/trade liberalization process, which will help in its bilateral as well as its multilateral relations with the EC.

China's economic relations with the ASEAN countries is examined by Chia Siow Yue. She makes a comparative analysis of the efforts of ASEAN and China in promoting international investments as a background to assess the bilateral flows of investment between ASEAN and China, and she applies a similar approach to the study of trade relations. Chia concludes by drawing attention to important complementary and competitive aspects of ASEAN-China trade and investment relations.

Mya Than calls for closer economic co-operation between ASEAN and Indochina and Myanmar. He argues that there are increasing complementarities amongst the ASEAN-6, the Indochina-3, and Myanmar, both in trade and investment relations. Mukul G. Asher and Charan D. Wadhva discuss ASEAN-South Asian economic relations. They review not only trade and investment, but also bilateral relations, including labour and tourist flows as well as the possibility of financial institutional linkages. At the time of writing, the economic recession did not allow for an optimistic trend towards a substantive increase in ASEAN-South Asia economic interaction. However, in the early 1990s — with the largest of the South Asian countries, that is, India, becoming a sectoral partner to ASEAN and with India's perceptible and growing external economic/trade liberalization — the prospects of greater economic interaction and co-operation between ASEAN and India/South Asia became more promising.

Finally, Francisco Orrego Vicuña focuses on trade issues and prospects for developing institutional linkages to foster co-operation across the Pacific — between Latin America and the ASEAN countries. He makes a visionary call for developing countries of the Pacific Basin to establish the foundations for trans-Pacific co-operation involving ASEAN, the South Pacific, and Latin America.

54.

ASEAN AND PACIFIC ECONOMIC CO-OPERATION

TAN KONG YAM, TOH MUN HENG, and LINDA LOW

The trend of rising economic linkages among the ASEAN countries and between ASEAN and the other Asia-Pacific economies, based on a web of production, sourcing and distribution network system, is likely to accelerate. ASEAN economies will be drawn deeper and deeper into the division of labour rapidly emerging in the Asia-Pacific region. Consequently, ASEAN countries' economic growth and political legitimacy would increasingly be tied to their interests in these Asia-Pacific economic linkages and the open investment and trading system that sustained them.

With the decline of U.S. hegemonic power, the rise of multipolarity, and the increasing trend towards regional economic groupings, it is pertinent for ASEAN to evaluate the costs and benefits of participation in these groupings and their impact on ASEAN cohesiveness, collective bargaining power and leverage with other economic groupings.

Asia Pacific Economic Cooperation (APEC)

The APEC process, which ushered in a new stage in the evolution of wider Asia-Pacific economic co-operation, was launched in November 1989 with its first Ministerial meeting in Canberra. Prior to this inter-governmental forum, the only one initiated by ASEAN was in 1984 through the convening of its annual ministerial level consultations with its Pacific dialogue partners in the context of the ASEAN Post-Ministerial Conferences (ASEAN PMC). At private sector or tripartite levels, that is involving the private sectors, governments and academia, are organizations such as the Pacific Business Economic Council (PBEC) and the Pacific Economic Cooperation Conference (PECC) respectively.

APEC was articulated by Australian Prime Minister, Mr Bob Hawke in January 1989. An idea like APEC is not new and its successful inauguration can be attributed to a number of factors.[1] One is its pragmatic approach on substantive areas of clear common interest. Second is its sensitive approach with regard to the possible operational modalities. Third is the careful and extensive consultations undertaken by Australia in developing and preparing the concept. However, more significantly, over and above these fundamental ingredients is the confluence of new trends and developments

Reprinted in abridged form from "ASEAN and Pacific Economic Co-operation", *ASEAN Economic Bulletin* 8, no. 3 (March 1992), pp. 309–31, by permission of the authors and the Institute of Southeast Asian Studies.

in the regional and global economies which made it increasingly imperative for the establishment of more formal inter-governmental arrangements for consultation and co-operation on economic issues.

The existing 12 APEC members are the United States, Canada, Australia, New Zealand, Japan, South Korea and the ASEAN six. In time to come, APEC cannot avoid the issue of membership of the two Chinas and Hong Kong, among others. These were discussed at the Second Ministerial Meeting in Singapore in July 1990.

At the Singapore meeting, the APEC Ministers endorsed seven working groups which identify its areas of interest for co-operation. These are to review trade and investment data, trade promotion, expansion of investments and technology transfer, human resource development, regional energy co-operation, marine resource conservation and telecommunications. Preliminary work on three other areas in fisheries, transportation and tourism have also been initiated.

At the outset, ASEAN has understandably been cautious about APEC. In view of the vast disparities in income, technology and skill level among the APEC economies, there was genuine concern that discrepancies in national capacities to benefit from joint regional development and co-operation could lead to asymmetrical dependence, heightened tension and North-South polarization within APEC. However, the reality of rising economic interdependence between ASEAN and the other Asia-Pacific economies, particularly after the active pursuit of outward oriented strategy by ASEAN since the mid 1980s, have persuaded ASEAN to recognize the need to participate in a wider forum to enhance economic co-operation among the Asia-Pacific economies.

Consequently, despite earlier ASEAN fears of dilution in a wider regional organization, the concern of being dominated and overshadowed by the much larger economies in APEC and the insistence on the informal arrangement and non-institutionalization of APEC, ASEAN

had expressed its preparedness to participate in APEC and to contribute constructively to the consultative process. This is a pragmatic posture as, with less than two per cent of the world GDP, it is unrealistic for ASEAN to hold back APEC. Propelled by powerful market forces and under the onslaught of direct foreign investment from the larger Asia-Pacific economies in linking their industrial structure, ASEAN economies will continue to be drawn deeper and deeper into the complex web of division of labour fast emerging in the Asia-Pacific region. A hesitant rather than an active approach towards APEC would still lead to ASEAN being subsumed as part of the global production and sourcing network of Japanese and NIEs firms, without any channel or forum for effective representation of collective ASEAN interests.

Thus ASEAN supports the APEC process on six caveats. One is that ASEAN's identity and cohesion should not be eroded and all its co-operative efforts be preserved. Second, as APEC includes developing and developed countries, it should be based on the principle of equality, equity and mutual benefit. Third is that APEC should not be an inward looking trade bloc but serve to strengthen the multilateral economic and trading system instead. In this context, a fourth consideration is for APEC to be a forum for consultations and constructive discussions of economic issues through dialogues rather than through unilateral or bilateral measures. As a self reliant process, a fifth point envisaged by ASEAN for APEC is for it to enhance individual and collective capacity of participants and articulate them in multilateral forums. Finally, a gradual and pragmatic approach with regard to its eventual institutional structure and membership problems is recommended.

The eventual active participation of ASEAN in APEC represented a fundamental rise in confidence as a result of the success of their outward oriented development strategy since the mid 1980s. It is noteworthy that ASEAN could collectively use APEC for greater influence, somewhat analogous to the occasional dispro-portionate impact of smaller states within the EC. More significantly, ASEAN is at the stage of pending takeoff in their industrialization process and the next 10–15 years of a con-ducive free trading multilateral system would be crucial. To achieve this, ASEAN need to help ensure a stable, free and open trading and investment system, preferably globally and if not, at least in the Asia-Pacific region. APEC could be an effective forum for promoting this critical ASEAN interests. In particular, APEC could be an effective counter-balance to the potential inward looking tendency of EC. In addition, ASEAN could use APEC to channel Japan and NIEs' capital flows to develop the region rather than allow them to be diverted to Eastern Europe.

The incorporation of the two largest eco-nomies, United States and Japan in APEC, while potentially able to subsume ASEAN into insignificance, could also be managed to ASEAN's long term advantage. ASEAN's support of the United States in engaging in the APEC process could be used to counter the superior bargaining and dominant position of Japan. This anchoring of the United States to the Western Pacific is particularly necessary in light of extraordinary changes in Europe and the Soviet Union, and the gathering mo-mentum in North America towards a free trade area. In addition, ASEAN could exploit the inevitable rivalry of the United States and Japan in using ASEAN countries as low cost production bases and the rising importance of ASEAN markets for their final products, to gain advantages in technology transfer, human resource development and other concessions.

East Asian Economic Group (EAEG)

The idea of the EAEG[2] came from the Malay-sian Prime Minister, Dr Mahathir, when he suggested that Malaysia would take the lead to set up an East Asian trade group to counter the single market concept of the European Community and the North American Free Trade Area. The EAEG concept was to embrace other countries including ASEAN, Hong Kong, China, South Korea, Taiwan, Japan and other countries in the Indochina region though there was no firm list of countries made out. The rationale is that co-operation and speaking in one voice was necessary among the Asia-Pacific countries especially in the face of the failure of the talks in the General Agreement on Tariffs and Trade (GATT) at Brussels, amidst the unsettled farm issues between the United States and the EC. While it is appreciated that some countries, particularly Japan, would come under pressure to reject Malaysia's proposal, the membership of Japan is considered crucial to the success of the EAEG. Malaysia may particularly want to anchor Japan to East Asia, arguing that East Asia should be Japan's natural constituency rather than have it uproot industries away to Europe or the United States.

Dr Mahathir chose the occasion of the visit of the Chinese premier to launch his idea in the hope that China would play an important role in the face of trade blocs springing up in Europe. Besides the EC, the reunification of Germany, the possibility of countries of Eastern Europe joining the EC and the United States forming joint markets with Canada fol-lowed by Mexico and possibly more Latin American countries, are his perceived threats. In Mahathir's own words,

> It is paradoxical that even as the centrally planned Eastern bloc economies espouse the free market systems as a solution to their economic problem, the erstwhile free traders of the west are opting for a controlled inter-national marketing system. But the fact is that with the formation of the European Union and the American free trading zone, that is what is happening.

> The question is what do we in this region do to rescue the free trading system of the world? Do we refuse to acknowledge the gloomy facts? Do we hush up things? Do we look the other way? Do we accept them without a

whimper? Or do we confront them: the reality of those trade blocs, that is, not the nations.

Two wrongs do not make one right. We in East Asia must not form a trading bloc of our own. But we know that alone and singly we cannot stop the slide towards controlled and regulated international commerce; which in fact is no different from the command economies of the socialist Soviets, only the scale is international; which is obviously going to replace free trade if the EC and the American Union are allowed to rewrite the rules. To stop the slide and to preserve free trade the countries of East Asia, which contain some of the most dynamic economies in the world today, must at least speak with one voice.

It will be impossible to do this unless we can consult each other, unless we can have some form of grouping which is recognizable. A free trade arrangement between us is impossible at this point in time. There is too much disparity in our development. An Economic Community after the EC pattern is far too structured and is well nigh impossible to achieve. But a formal grouping intended to facilitate consultation and consensus prior to negotiating with Europe or America or in multilateral fora such as the GATT is not too far-fetched an idea. It is also not against the GATT principle, nor will it run contrary to membership in such organisations as the APEC, in which the United States and Canada are members while having an economic union with each other.[3]

The EAEG would also ease off pressures by countries of the Organisation for Economic Co-operation and Development (OECD) on ASEAN to move toward premature membership in the OECD. It is reckoned that affinity with Japan within the EAEG could achieve this easing-off effect. As a more consolidated group, the EAEG would be able to face the new challenges confronting the Asia-Pacific region.

In particular, from the ASEAN perspective, the EAEG would strengthen and complement in a similar fashion like the Cairns Group, in the EAEG being a loose group to look into

trade matters. The EAEG is not envisaged as a trade bloc but a low level economic alliance, a mutual protection society, a pressure group or a "megaphone to magnify" the group's voice at the Uruguay Round for instance.[4] The group would thus strengthen ASEAN with dialogue partners such as APEC and the G-7. The EAEG would also have to be consistent with prevailing principles under GATT, ASEAN and APEC.

The steps toward such a group, which would a priori exclude no country in East Asia, would take two stages. First, a formation of like-minded countries which have or share common interests in specific areas of trade *vis-à-vis* GATT and the Uruguay Round would be formed. The EAEG, however, is not dependent on the success or failure of the Uruguay Round. The second stage envisages a formalization of trade and economic links which would spur trade and investment in the East Asian region. Any formal arrangements, however, would be based on GATT principles, particularly Article XXIV and/or the enabling clause, not create unnecessary barriers to third countries' imports, not divert trade and should be trade and investment enhancing.

The Malaysian proposal may be viewed from both Malaysia's domestic development and the external conditions. An ardent nationalist, Dr Mahathir has set his sights on accelerating the economic growth of Malaysia to become a developed country by 2020.[5] He has chosen to lay aside political ideals in pursuit of economic growth which may explain his implicit support of the Growth Triangle. On a broader level, Malaysia's own economic problems and attainment of aspirations may be better addressed in a more regional framework such as the EAEG to promote free flow of trade and investment. In addition, Dr Mahathir may have reckoned that Malaysia has come of age to take a higher international profile to escape the narrowness of its outlook and options.

Following the proposal, Malaysia sought the views of its ASEAN partners individually when Minister of International Trade and Industry Dato' Seri Rafidah Aziz visited Indonesia,

Singapore, the Philippines, Thailand and Brunei following letters from Dr Mahathir to the respective heads of government. It later decided that heads of government outside ASEAN would also have to be wooed though the ASEAN core was the most crucial.

Just before the Malaysian mission first came to Singapore, the initial response from Singapore was a cool one from the Minister of State for Trade and Industry, Mr Mah Bow Tan, who went on radio and stated that Singapore will not be happy to join a trade bloc suggested by Malaysia. Given Singapore's policy to be a free trader and be as non-aligned as possible when it comes to trade blocs, this initial reaction was not surprising. However, it quickly recognized the political sensitivities and gave in-principle endorsement based on three criteria. It reiterated that the EAEG should neither compromise nor dilute GATT principles nor ASEAN solidarity. Also, it would not affect the APEC initiative which has a wider scope and coverage. In fact, the Prime Minister, Mr Goh Chok Tong, went further to comment on the possibility of a crescent of prosperity linking East Asia, Indochina and ASEAN.

Singapore turned out to be Malaysia's strongest supporter when it offered to help to expand the idea. The Senior Minister, Mr Lee Kuan Yew, also endorsed the idea when he put forth the view that the EAEG is complementary to APEC and useful to ASEAN to the U.S. Secretary of State and the U.S. Trade Representative during his U.S. visit.[6]

Thailand was, however, more distant towards the idea. It prefers to see intra-ASEAN co-operation strengthened before any other trade groups are to be formed. It appears less confident that a larger East Asia would do better than ASEAN. Even current ASEAN projects aimed at smoothing trade by removing barriers have not materialized in a way that facilitated intra-ASEAN trade. On the other hand, it is more in favour of the APEC framework, partly because extra-ASEAN relations with countries like the United States, Canada, Japan, Australia and others are more crucial and direct. It was,

however, willing to have the proposal raised as an item for the next ASEAN summit though it was not as directly supportive as Singapore or the Philippines.[7]

Indonesia was also less receptive to the EAEG concept though it called for an ASEAN meeting to discuss the proposal. It was sceptical that a protectionist stance under such a trade bloc would be the appropriate medicine to fight protectionism.

Japan appears in two minds with respect to the EAEG proposal. On one hand, it argues that EAEG is against the APEC philosophy.[8] The chairman of Keidanren (Japan Federation of Economic Organization) was uncomfortable that the EAEG left out the United States, Canada and Australia. The Japanese were of the view that more efforts should be made to complete the Uruguay Round rather than form regional trade blocs which would escalate friction and protectionism. Malaysia assured Japan that nothing prescriptive at the moment was contemplated and it would proceed on a step-by-step basis. On the other hand, given Japan's extensive investment and trade involvement in ASEAN and the East Asian region, it does not want to be left out of a concept like the EAEG.

The United States also commented that the EAEG would not help the cause of liberalization.[9] While the objectives of the EAEG and APEC are similar, i.e. to maintain free trade and economic co-operation, EAEG is more restrictive. The United States felt that it was illogical to have any concern that trade liberalization throughout the Americas would result in arrangements that shut out others. While it acknowledged the concern, the answer appears to be a redoubled effort towards multilateral trade liberalization within the Uruguay Round and towards greater efforts in APEC, rather than in creating a new regional economic co-operation body that excludes the United States. A more cryptic response, considered arrogant by the Malaysian Government, was the U.S. perception that the EAEG would not succeed without the United States.[10]

Malaysian Minister for International Trade and Industry Dato' Seri Rafidah Aziz, addressing the eighth general meeting of the Pacific Economic Cooperation Conference (PECC) in May 1991 in Singapore, added further thoughts and discussion on the EAEG. Dato' Seri Rafidah Aziz assured participants that the EAEG would not be a threat to others outside the group when its membership can be defined more rigorously. The EAEG also cannot work in isolation and is considered another platform, forum and conduit for ASEAN and other members to interact with other entities like the United States and the EC. It does not imply the need to discard the strong traditional trade ties that individual East Asian economies have with other Asia-Pacific partners.

When ASEAN trade ministers met in Kuala Lumpur in October 1991, the EAEG was supported as an ASEAN initiative after Indonesia was successful in getting the name changed to East Asian Economic Caucus (EAEC). This was to defuse allegations that it was intended as a trading bloc. Malaysia will seek full endorsement for EAEC at the Fourth ASEAN Summit Meeting in Singapore in January 1992 when the subject will be discussed.

It is somewhat unfortunate that the EAEG concept, in excluding key Asia-Pacific players like the United States, Canada and Australia at its inception, has faced significant opposition from them. Their opposition further resulted in the cautious attitude of Japan and some ASEAN countries towards the idea. In addition, the insufficient consultation among the ASEAN countries before floating the concept, has made it more difficult for Malaysia to sell the EAEG as an ASEAN idea. On the other hand, Malaysia has clearly perceived the overall trend. Economic linkages among countries in the EAEG would, through natural forces of the market, create a de facto trading group with significant common shared interests in the next 20 years. However, when Northeast and Southeast Asia have not yet collectively achieved self sustaining growth and continue to require the huge North American market and the support

of the United States in upholding the free multilateral system for trade and investment, at least for the next 10 years, it is not clear that an early and somewhat antagonistic (at least as perceived by some quarters) articulation of collective East Asian interests could not turn out to be somewhat premature.

On the other hand, the gradual evolution of the EAEG idea from an economic bloc to that of a forum for ASEAN and East Asia to interact with EC and the United States could pave the way for it to metamorphosize into an East Asian caucus within the APEC framework.

Pacific Economic Cooperation Conference

The Pacific Economic Cooperation Conference was set up in September 1980 in Canberra. By 1990, the membership consisted of the six ASEAN countries, Australia, New Zealand, Canada, the United States, China, Japan, South Korea and Taiwan. In 1991, four new members, namely Hong Kong, Chile, Peru and Mexico, were admitted.[11] The tripartite representation of the PECC, consisting of government officials, businessmen and academics, all in their private capacities, provides an ideal forum for its task forces, working groups and fora. Activities of these groups are varied, including agriculture and fisheries, minerals and energy, trade, transportation, telecommunication and tourism, science and technology, human resource development and economic forecasting.

There is a close relationship developing between the PECC and APEC as the latter has sought the expertise and resources of the former in areas of mutual interest. Thus, the PECC task forces and working groups in fisheries, Pacific economic forecasting and human resource development have been requested by APEC to undertake similar studies for mutual use. Such non-governmental organizations like the PECC can serve as brokers as well as testing grounds for ideas on co-operation to be launched which might otherwise be bogged down by administrative and bureaucratic bargaining in a governmental forum.

The increasing web of investment flow and trade linkages between the Northeast Asian economies and ASEAN would lead increasingly to a closer East Asian economic grouping. Moreover, as a significant component of Northeast Asian direct investments into ASEAN is to take advantage of ASEAN as production bases for exports to the North American and EC markets, the inevitable consequence is the spreading of Japan and NIE bilateral imbalances and eventual trade conflicts with the United States and EC to ASEAN. The resulting U.S. and EC pressure on ASEAN could lead further to a closer nexus between Northeast and Southeast Asia.

It is probably not in the long-term collective interests of ASEAN to allow existing market forces to draw them too close to the Northeast Asian economies, thus creating overwhelming centrifugal forces among themselves in economic co-operation, as well as trade conflicts between them and the United States and EC. It is in this context that an active and strategic positioning of ASEAN within the wider Asia-Pacific configurations should be conceived.

It is clear that in the coming decade, ASEAN needs to work within a larger context or group to realize better the benefits of economies of scale and division of labour as well as collectively help to promote the free multilateral trading system. In such a context, it is better for ASEAN to take an active rather than passive role in evolving groupings such as APEC. In any case, even if ASEAN chooses to remain passive or adopts a "do nothing" policy, market forces that are fast spinning the web of economic linkages within the Asia-Pacific region would operate to subsume it under a wider framework, possibly as a part of the regional production and distribution structure with Japan as its core. It would thus be better for ASEAN to be prepared with the right institutions and policies to interact with other groupings in the manner that it has selected, and better if by its own terms as a group.

In this context, the ASEAN Post-Ministerial Conference (PMC) could conceivably evolve into a more cohesive grouping of ASEAN against the other trading partners. While it has been generally acknowledged, even by participants, that the dialogue process had not achieved meaningful results, this is a forum where the cohesive force of ASEAN presenting a common front to dialogue partners could counter the centrifugal forces generated by the increasing economic linkages between each individual ASEAN country and the other economies. The solidarity cannot but give ASEAN far greater clout in negotiating with other parties than they would have individually. Past PMC successes included Cambodian and the Indochinese refugee problem, Australia's backing down on an aviation quarrel with Singapore in the late 1970s and New Zealand decision not to drop Singapore and Brunei from its GSP programme in 1985. In particular, the ASEAN-PMC framework could become a more effective forum for defending ASEAN's collective interest in expanding trade by expanding market access and obtaining preferential treatment for ASEAN products, promoting the inflow of direct foreign investments, technology transfer, funding and other assistance to ASEAN in technical training, energy conservation and help in adapting ASEAN products to partners' market. In recent years, with the involvement of the private sector in business councils and in the official joint co-operation committee meetings, the effectiveness of the ASEAN-PMC forum could be more fully exploited.

In addition, in view of the significance of the United States as the major trading partner for all the ASEAN countries and the fact that a significant proportion of the direct foreign investment inflows from Northeast Asia into ASEAN are targeted at the vast U.S. market, the ASEAN-U.S. Initiative takes on a significant role. Unlike the idea of a U.S.-Japan Free Trade Area, a closer U.S.-ASEAN economic relationship is politically popular in the U.S. Congress as the complementarity of the economic structure and different stage of development would result in substantive economic gains for both sides arising from greater liberalization in the trading relationship. The Philippines and Thailand already have a bilateral agreement to enhance trade and investment with the United States. Singapore and the United States have recently agreed to negotiate a similar framework agreement. These could constitute the building blocks leading to closer economic relationships between the United States and ASEAN. In view of the momentum of the North American Free Trade Area to encompass Mexico, it is imperative for ASEAN to foster a closer linkage with the U.S. economy, not only to counterbalance the dominance of the Northeast Asian economies but also to ensure free access to the U.S. market in competition with Mexico and other Latin American countries who are at a similar stage of development.

NOTES

1. "Asia Pacific Economic Cooperation (APEC): Implications for ASEAN" by Ali Alatas, speech presented in Bali, Indonesia, 5 March 1991, p. 2.
2. The EAEG has since changed to East Asian Economic Caucus (EAEC) in 1992.
3. Speech by Prime Minister Mahathir bin Mohamed in Bali, Indonesia on 4 March 1991.
4. Noordin Sopiee, "Misunderstanding and the East Asian Economic Group". The *New Straits Times*, 19 January 1991.
5. An economic council comprising 10 cabinet ministers, eight senior members from the public sector and 44 top leaders from business would meet three times a year under the chairmanship of Dr Mahathir. This 62-member Malaysian Business Council need to ensure that the economic aspiration of a developed country by 2020 would not conflict with post-1990 policies to ensure a more balanced growth among the races (*Straits Times*, 1 March 1991 and *Business Times*, 7 March 1991).
6. *Business Times*, 24 January 1991.
7. *Straits Times*, 19 January 1991.
8. *Business Times*, 28 January 1991.
9. *Straits Times*, 6 March 1991.
10. *Straits Times*, 19 May 1991.
11. Russia is the latest member in 1992.

55.

ASEAN-U.S. INITIATIVE

SEIJI NAYA, KERNIAL S. SANDHU, MICHAEL PLUMMER, and NARONGCHAI AKRASANEE

As part of their development effort, the ASEAN countries place increasing emphasis on intra-regional economic co-operation. They also act as an economic bloc in multilateral negotiations. ASEAN has seven dialogue partners: the United States, Japan, the European Communities (EC), New Zealand, Australia, Canada, and the United Nations Development Program. The ASEAN-U.S. Initiative (AUI) stems from the economic dialogue and is designed to enhance bilateral economic co-operation. This study on the AUI was commissioned in July 1988.

Both the ASEAN countries and the United States have achieved solid rates of economic growth in recent years. Singapore, Malaysia, and Thailand have exhibited high growth rates; Indonesia has coped well with the fall in oil prices, diversifying its economy away from nearly exclusive reliance on oil, as Brunei Darussalam is beginning to do. The Philippines has rebounded from the slump of the 1983–86 period. The United States is experiencing its longest peace-time economic expansion, now into its seventh year.

The relationship between the United States and ASEAN is growing in importance. In the past ten years, ASEAN trade with the United States more than doubled. The United States is now ASEAN's largest export market and its second largest source of imports, after Japan. At the same time, the composition of this bilateral trade is changing. Although ASEAN remains a major supplier of primary products, over 36 per cent of U.S. imports from ASEAN are manufactured goods. The growing trade relationship is paralleled by expanded U.S. investment in the region The rate of increase in U.S. direct investment to ASEAN over the past decade has been double that to any other country, with the stock reaching more than US$10 billion in 1987. There is evidence that actual direct foreign investment (DFI) is substantially larger than the reported figures indicate.

TRADE IN GOODS

Most ASEAN members depend on exports as a major source of income, ranging from more

Excerpted from Seiji Naya, Kernial S. Sandhu, Michael Plummer, and Narongchai Akrasanee, co-ordinators, *ASEAN-U.S. Initiative: Assessment and Recommendations for Improved Economic Relations; Joint Final Report* (Singapore: Institute of Southeast Asian Studies and Honolulu: East-West Center 1989), pp. 1–11, by permission of the co-ordinators and the publishers.

than 130 per cent of GNP for Singapore to 23 per cent for the Philippines. And the most important destination of these exports is the U.S. market The increased reliance on trade is the outcome of outward-looking development strategies, involving structural changes based on the countries' comparative advantage. As a result of industrial restructuring, the commodity structure of ASEAN-U.S. trade has changed in recent years. The promotion of manufacturing as an essential ingredient in the development strategy plays an important role in this change. Though labour-intensive manufactures and food processing remain large, the ASEAN countries are starting to turn towards industries with higher value added. The decline of world primary commodity prices also intensifies the structural change.

The United States ranks first in bilateral trade with Singapore and the Philippines while Japan ranks first with other ASEAN members. U.S. imports from Brunei Darussalam, Indonesia, and Thailand have increased significantly in recent years. The relatively free access to the U.S. market, compared with that in Japan and the EC, coupled with the increased export orientation of the ASEAN economies, has underlined the importance of the United States for the economic future of ASEAN. This dependence is especially pronounced in the case of manufactured exports. The United States is not dependent on ASEAN to the same degree, but it is seeking to expand its exports to this fast-growing market with which it currently has a US$8 billion trade deficit.

The U.S. and ASEAN economies are complementary in nature. ASEAN is a large exporter of petroleum, rubber, sugar, and tin, while the United States is a net importer of these goods. The trade patterns for manufactures reflect the factor and technology endowments of the respective countries. The ASEAN countries are competitive exporters of labour-intensive manufactures such as textiles, garments, handbags, and other light consumer manufactures. The United States is a large net importer of these goods. In turn, the United States is a

large producer of capital- and technology-intensive goods such as chemicals, electrical and non-electrical machinery, and transportation equipment, while the ASEAN countries are primarily net importers of these items. The exception is electrical machinery where a significant amount of intra-industry trade takes place, as many U.S. multinational corporations (MNCs) have subsidiary plants in the region. While there is a potential for significant increases in U.S.-ASEAN trade, Japan and increasingly the Asian Newly Industrialized Economies (NIEs) are strong competitors in most products of interest to U.S. exporters.

There is a danger that the intensified trade relations could be halted by rising U.S. protectionism or inward-looking policies in ASEAN. While tariffs in the United States are low and the U.S. market continues to be one of the most open in the world, it has used in recent years voluntary export restraints to protect certain (mainly labour-intensive) industries. High trade deficits, coupled with the perception that the United States is fighting with "one hand tied behind its back", have encouraged protectionist sentiments. The U.S. Government has been largely successful in resisting demands for increased protection, but this stand is losing popularity. The U.S. trade deficit should not be addressed by trade barriers, which lead to decreases in domestic and global welfare; it should be reduced through rational macroeconomic policies at home, increased competitiveness of U.S. exports abroad, and more rapid opening of foreign markets to U.S. exports. Trade barriers in ASEAN are significantly greater than in the United States, and much work remains in further liberalization. These barriers include high tariff levels in most ASEAN countries, import licensing, and various quantitative restrictions. Yet, the ASEAN countries have undertaken unilateral trade liberalization in the 1970s and 1980s. It is desirable for domestic and international reasons that these policies be continued and trade liberalization carried further.

Both the United States and ASEAN are

dedicated to the success of the Uruguay Round of GATT negotiations. Both have already demonstrated a potential to work together, especially on agricultural trade issues.

Despite more than ten years of negotiations, the trade impact of ASEAN economic cooperation has not been substantial. The high economic and export growth rates in the region in the 1970s cannot be directly attributable to the ASEAN Preferential Trading Arrangements (PTA). In fact, it is estimated that only 5 per cent of the trade within ASEAN is covered under the PTA. None the less, significant improvements in the PTA were made at the Third ASEAN Summit, including a programme to place 50 per cent of the total intra-ASEAN trade under the PTA within five years. The ASEAN Industrial Joint Ventures (AIJV) programme was also expanded; it now allows for 60 per cent foreign participation.

In sum, the ASEAN-U.S. economic relationship in trade in goods is strong and strengthening. However, there remains much work to be done before it reaches its vast potential. Liberalization of trade barriers, promotion of efficient production, greater information on export opportunities in each other's markets, and expanded participation at the Uruguay Round of GATT to reduce direct and indirect barriers to global trade are in the interest of all.

TRADE IN SERVICES

Services trade now accounts for about a third of world trade. U.S. exports of private services (travel, transportation, royalties and fees, banking, and other miscellaneous private services) increased more than fivefold since the early 1970s to more than US$57 billion in 1987. A similar increase took place in U.S. imports of services, which amounted to US$56 billion in 1987.

ASEAN's service-sector trade has been growing as well. Since 1976 ASEAN exports of service have quadrupled to over US$11 billion. The Philippines, Thailand, and especially Singapore had surpluses in service transactions in the 1980s. There are, however, many problems involved in addressing trade in this sector. Most fundamentally, there is no clear definition of what the service sector is and data are very difficult to obtain. In addition, trade in services is closely tied to investment in services. In most service industries, including banking, production and consumption occur at the same time and place. Therefore any discussion of service-trade liberalization must include some liberalization of investment in this sector as well. This has been an extremely contentious issue to most developing countries, which worry about domestic sovereignty, national security, and protecting fledgeling service-sector industries.

Important barriers to services in ASEAN include (1) restricted access to markets in services; (2) leasing restrictions; (3) motion picture limitations; (4) limited foreign ownership of banking; (5) advertising restrictions; and (6) preferential treatment of domestic transportation. Many of these barriers are investment-related in the sense that they constitute obstacles to establishing and operating affiliates in host countries. Significant efficiency gains have been realized in the United States from deregulating certain service industries, and ASEAN could benefit from a similar action, especially in the information sector. Moreover, ASEAN would increase efficiency and attract larger amounts of foreign investment by relaxing foreign equity controls. Services in the United States are generally free of barriers at the federal level, although there are some restrictions at the state level. The United States has been criticized for certain antitrust laws which inhibit international trade, as well as a lack of U.S. export consciousness. Improvements in these areas would facilitate trade in services as well as goods.

We recommend that ASEAN liberalize the service sector to facilitate export-oriented growth. Liberalization and deregulation would also enhance market incentives and allocative efficiency, thereby strengthening the dynamism of the ASEAN economies.

INTELLECTUAL PROPERTY RIGHTS

Protection of copyrights, trademarks, patents, and trade secrets has been a contentious issue in the Uruguay Round. The United States has pressured several ASEAN countries to tighten their intellectual property laws and to increase their enforcement efforts, and threatened retaliatory measures against developing countries that fail to do this. Moreover, it has emphasized the long-run benefits of increasing intellectual property protection to encourage domestically generated innovations. For their part, some ASEAN members believe that in demanding intellectual property rights protection, the United States is intruding on their sovereignty and is not sensitive enough to their development needs. Others insist that they have already legislated sufficient protection. The ASEAN countries have responded differentially to American pressure in terms of *de jure* laws and actual enforcement, reflecting the diverse nature of ASEAN. All of them have improved protection of intellectual property to conform more closely to international standards. Indonesia made major improvements in protecting trademarks and copyrights, is considering joining one of the two international copyright conventions, and is negotiating with the United States on a bilateral copyright agreement. Malaysia has greatly strengthened legislation protecting intellectual property and is negotiating a bilateral copyright agreement with the United States. The Philippines is a signatory of both the Paris and the Berne Conventions. Thailand is in the process of changing its laws to conform to modern commercial practices world-wide; it is already a signatory of the Berne Convention. Singapore strengthened comprehensive laws protecting intellectual property. However, the enforcement of intellectual property rights has been inadequate in some ASEAN countries.

In sum, the ASEAN countries' protection of intellectual property has improved considerably. Nevertheless, the United States continues to be dissatisfied with some aspects of ASEAN intellectual property protection, for example, in pharmaceuticals and computer software.

As ASEAN improves its protection of intellectual property, it will benefit from increased foreign investment and technology transfer, as well as greater incentives to indigenous technological development. If intellectual property is not adequately protected, the country will be deprived of cutting-edge technologies, products and techniques, as well as risking continued frictions with innovation-exporting countries.

For its part, the United States should concentrate its efforts on developing broader international standards and should continue to improve its own system of enforcing intellectual property rights. U.S. accession to the Berne Convention was a step forward.

INVESTMENT

The chapter on investment in this report concentrates on direct foreign investment (DFI), even though DFI constitutes a relatively small share of total capital flows. This is because DFI is important in the development process. Along with Japan, the United States is the most significant source of DFI in ASEAN. U.S. DFI is concentrated in petroleum and electronics. High rates of return to DFI in ASEAN, stable political environments, economic robustness, low-cost of indigenous labour, large markets, and an atmosphere conducive to foreign business are the attractions for U.S. investment U.S. firms have not been found to have responded significantly to investment incentives. An area in which U.S. capital may be able to play a somewhat greater role in the future is in service industries such as trade, banking, and finance.

In any case, U.S. DFI in ASEAN has become increasingly important in the 1980s, accounting for more than 3–5 per cent of total U.S. investment. But Japanese investment in the region, as elsewhere, has been growing more rapidly. This trend is also likely to continue given the large Japanese trade surplus. The Japanese have been very successful at their attempts to blend official development assistance with private-sector projects in a way in which the United States has not attempted.

U.S. DFI in ASEAN has obviously been of benefit to U.S. terms and contributes to the U.S. economy. At the same time, it benefits ASEAN nations in a number of ways, by (1) providing access to modern and efficient management techniques; (2) facilitating the transfer of technology in production, management, marketing, and other intangible assets; (3) training the indigenous labour force for high-skill jobs; (4) providing needed foreign exchange; (5) providing jobs, especially in manufactures; and (6) engaging significantly in international trade. The dynamics of industrial restructuring (along the lines dictated by comparative advantage) attendant upon DFI may be the most important beneficial consequence for ASEAN in the long run. On the other hand, DFI in ASEAN that depends on tariff barriers erected for sectors with comparative disadvantage can inhibit long-run economic growth by drawing resources into inefficient industries.

Aspects of U.S. policy that might be promoted to increase DFI to ASEAN, include (1) more rational taxation measures; (2) relaxation of international trade and strategic trade controls; (3) more comprehensive information on DFI opportunities, especially for small- and medium-sized firms; and (4) further revision of the Foreign Corrupt Practices Act.

At the same time, ASEAN can reduce certain impediments to DFI including (1) lack of infrastructure; (2) performance requirements; (3) bureaucratic red tape; (4) trade restrictions; and (5) equity restrictions.

ASEAN governments should provide more business infrastructure. This is an important consideration in a firm's plans to invest in a particular country. In some cases, it may even be possible to solicit foreign involvement in the infrastructure development projects themselves. Moreover, the achievement of a more regional ASEAN market through improvements in the ASEAN PTA, and the possibility

of greater foreign involvement in AIJVs should also increase the flow of foreign investment.

Complicated and restrictive performance requirements, equity restrictions, and extensive bureaucracy are widely acknowledged to be the greatest barriers to DFI in ASEAN. In addition, because these requirements vary considerably within ASEAN, many U.S. firms, particularly small- and medium-sized enterprises, find it difficult to take a regional approach to investment in ASEAN. A common set of general DFI guidelines would greatly facilitate this process. A Bilateral Investment Treaty between the United States and ASEAN would be an effective way of achieving this goal.

The United States and ASEAN could jointly implement a number of measures to promote greater flows of DFI as well as increase benefits from existing investments. For example, the United States and ASEAN should work together to increase the supply of information. Although the U.S. Government supplies a considerable amount of information on investment opportunities in ASEAN, it appears that the use of such information is limited. The government or business organizations, such as the Chamber of Commerce, could expand efforts to disseminate information on ASEAN investment opportunities. Furthermore, ASEAN governments also provide a substantial amount of information, but accessibility could be improved. Governments will have to bear partial responsibility in making improvements in the distribution of this public good, although it is clearly in the interest of business organizations to assist such efforts wherever possible since their members will be the primary beneficiaries. Hence, the establishment of an institution, initiated through public action but financed through private means, that could provide information dissemination and a channel for co-ordination of U.S. investors, especially for small- and medium-sized firms, could be an important catalyst in shifting the orientation of American firms towards the Asia-Pacific in general and ASEAN in particular.

The growth in importance of the U.S. Overseas

Private Investment Corporation (OPIC) in the mid-1980s is impressive and increased OPIC activity is likely to assist in the advancement of DFI as well as forge a closer relationship between the U.S. Government and U.S. private firms interested in making foreign investments. It is also possible that special incentives designed to redirect factors of production away from inefficient industries could be beneficial. If well conceived, such schemes could promote more efficient rationalization of production capacity in activities where the United States is clearly losing comparative advantage. This principle extends to the ASEAN economies as well.

RECOMMENDATIONS FOR AN ASEAN-U.S.
TRADE AND INVESTMENT AGREEMENT

Based on our findings and arguments, it is desirable that ASEAN and the United States consider entering into an economic co-operation agreement. It should consist of a general umbrella agreement which would have provisions for more specific bilateral arrangements. Within the scope of such an agreement, the United States and ASEAN would be able to negotiate a wide range of formal agreements, ranging from formal comprehensive treaties to sector- and issue-specific arrangements. The umbrella agreement would become an important catalyst for increased trade and investment between the two parties, and would also provide for negotiations between the United States and individual ASEAN nations.

Recommendations for an Umbrella Agreement

The umbrella agreement should include characteristics of other successful bilateral pacts by focusing on trade and investment liberalization and promoting economic welfare and efficiency, and should serve as a model for similar arrangements with other nations in the Asia-Pacific region. Yet, an ASEAN-U.S. agreement would be unique, as the ASEAN-U.S. economic relationship is unique. The complementary nature of the U.S. and ASEAN economies and the extensive economic interchange suggest that bilateral agreements under the umbrella designed to resolve any disagreements or seize important opportunities would be welfare-enhancing, without contradicting multilateralist ideals. Indeed, all actions would be consistent with GATT.

The initial umbrella should consist of the following components. First, it should establish a set of basic guiding principles for the conduct of trade and other economic relations between the United States and ASEAN, based on GATT compatibility and affirming the primacy of multilateral liberalization. It should be grounded on the presumption that trade and investment flows are determined by market forces as much as possible, the nature of government intervention should be strictly defined and temporary. Most basically, the United States and ASEAN should commit themselves to the principle of "stand-still and roll-back" of trade barriers. Moreover, measures harming other trading partners should be avoided.

Second, the umbrella should establish the administrative and implementing guidelines for the United States and ASEAN negotiating a series of subsidiary agreements on subjects such as subsidies, double taxation, intellectual property rights, investment, services, non-tariff barriers, and safeguards, supplemented by more detailed accords where needed.

Third, the umbrella should delineate effective procedures to administer the agreement and resolve disputes in a timely and efficient manner.

Fourth, it should create a Consultative Committee, composed of government representatives at the level of trade minister and advised by experts and private-sector representatives, which should meet at least on an annual basis. The Consultative Committee would have several important tasks. It should be responsible for considering trade and investment disputes in a manner defined by the umbrella agreement.

Also it should oversee the negotiations of the subsidiary agreements, and should serve as a forum for moulding joint ASEAN-U.S. positions on these issues at the current and subsequent GATT rounds. Moreover, the Consultative Committee should authorize the preparation of studies, formation of working groups, and other vehicles for improving understanding of and co-operation in bilateral economic relations.

Fifth, the umbrella agreement should lay the foundation for further bilateral and multilateral co-operation.

Possible Trade and Investment Pacts under the Umbrella

After the establishment of the umbrella agreement, the United States and ASEAN could negotiate a series of bilateral pacts, from a formal free-trade agreement (FTA) to sector-specific agreements. In this section, we assess some of the available options which the Consultative Committee should consider. However, the list is not exhaustive. Many of the issue-specific topics are being considered at the Uruguay Round. Nevertheless, bilateral ASEAN-U.S. trade and investment agreements could complement the GATT talks and, perhaps, provide an exemplary framework in certain areas.

ASEAN-U.S. Free-Trade Agreement. We believe that an ASEAN-U.S. FTA should be the ultimate goal of the Framework Agreement. An ASEAN-U.S. FTA would be very complex and is likely to take a long time to negotiate. However, there is great potential for improved trade and investment relations in such a pact. Commissioning a comprehensive study should be among the first inquiries the Consultative Committee should launch.

The conformity of an FTA with GATT rules is clearer than with any other option. Free-trade agreements have come to mean far more than merely reducing internal tariffs on trade in merchandise. As in the U.S.-Canada agreement and the Closer Economic Relations pact between New Zealand and Australia, trade in services,

investment liberalization, protection of intellectual property, and so forth, are often included. Similarly, an FTA between the United States and ASEAN should include an entire range of issues. A U.S.-ASEAN FTA could also serve as a forerunner to a wider accord in the Asia-Pacific region.

Because of the complicated nature of negotiating something as complex as an FTA, we recommend that the technical details of such an arrangement be studied in depth by a bilateral commission under the supervision of the Consultative Committee. Questions such as the net effect on global efficiency (for example, trade creation and diversion), the impact on third countries, implications for multilateralism, rules of origin provisions, and the polarization of industrial production should be addressed. In addition, the complicated question of how and in what sequence tariff barriers should be reduced must be addressed. The possibility of FTAs with various Asia-Pacific nations or groups has already received attention in Washington. The U.S. International Trade Commission (ITC) has released a report summarizing the views of recognized experts on the pros and cons of entering into an FTA with Japan. Similar inquiries are being made with respect to other Pacific Rim nations, including Taiwan, South Korea, members of ASEAN, and countries in the Asia-Pacific region.

The complementary nature of the U.S. and ASEAN economies suggests that such a trading bloc would significantly expand bilateral trade. In addition, increased DFI flows, trade in services, technology transfer, economies of scale in production and other dynamic benefits would serve to promote the goals of both parties without negating their respective commitments under GATT. Moreover, an effective formal dispute-settlement process is more easily established in the context of a comprehensive accord because there is a larger and more detailed base of jointly agreed disciplines.

Other issues. At the sectoral level, the Consultative Committee should investigate several issues concerning bilateral trade and invest-ment, including subsidies, double taxation and tax-sparing provision, intellectual property rights, investment, services, tariff and non-tariff barriers, and safeguard provisions. Most of the issues are currently being examined in various Committees at the Uruguay Round. Being committed to multilateralist ideals, the United States and ASEAN should negotiate subsidiary agreements in these areas only where they are complementary to the GATT process. Never-theless, the United States and ASEAN have and should continue to work together to take a common position on these issues, a process which will be improved with increased eco-nomic consultation under the umbrella.

56.

ASEAN-JAPAN ECONOMIC CO-OPERATION

CHNG MENG KNG and RYOKICHI HIRONO

ASEAN-JAPAN TRADE

Existing trade relations. In practice, trade relations are not made up of economic factors alone but are combinations of economic, social, political, and international relations. The basic setting of Japan-ASEAN trade relations can be described as follows: Japan depends on ASEAN for its supply of strategic raw materials, as a market for its industrial exports, and for political support in the Southeast Asian region. ASEAN, on the other hand, depends on Japan for its supply of industrial goods, investment funds, and industrial technology. ASEAN also relies on Japan for political support in the international diplomatic arena. The differences in the economic structure and policies of the ASEAN countries and Japan, especially in the context of industrial restructuring, form the basis for ASEAN-Japan trade links and reveal the extent to which such links may be further developed in future.

Japan is the most important trading partner of ASEAN. Statistics on the direction of trade show that in 1980 Japan accounted for 27 per cent of ASEAN exports and 22 per cent of ASEAN imports. No other single country comes close to Japan in terms of the volume of trade with ASEAN. The next most important trading partner of ASEAN, the United States, accounted for only 17 per cent and 15 per cent of ASEAN's exports and imports respectively in 1980. The European Economic Community (EEC) is third with a figure of 13 per cent for both exports and imports. Intra-ASEAN trade itself averaged about 15 per cent of total ASEAN trade.

The relative importance of Japan as a trade partner varies among the individual ASEAN countries. For Indonesia and Malaysia, Japan is the most important export market as well as import source. Japan was also Thailand's biggest export market until 1979 when it was displaced from that position by the EEC; however, Japan still remains as Thailand's largest import supplier. The Philippines trade more with the United States because of their historical links but the relative importance of Japan in the Philippines' trade has been growing rapidly. The direction of Singapore's exports are more diversified but Japan is the main supplier of Singapore's imports.

Future Trade Relations

The future trend of ASEAN-Japan trade relations will not only depend on the narrow

Excerpted from M.K. Chng and R. Hirono, editors, *ASEAN-Japan Industrial Co-operation: An Overview* (Singapore: Institute of Southeast Asian Studies, in collaboration with the ASEAN Secretariat and the Japan Institute of International Affairs, 1984), by permission of the editors and the Institute of Southeast Asian Studies.

specifics of each ASEAN country's bilateral trade relations with Japan but also be much influenced by developments in ASEAN's trade policy as regards, among others, three main issues: intra-ASEAN economic co-operation, intra-Pacific Basin economic relations, and global trade practices.

Firstly, intra-ASEAN trade is not expected to grow at the expense of ASEAN's trade with third countries. While intra-ASEAN trade liberalization will promote intra-ASEAN trade in the long run, most ASEAN economies are basically competitive with one another, with similar comparative advantage in resource-based and labour-intensive industries. Furthermore, all the ASEAN economies follow outward-looking market-oriented policies, and the extent of intra-ASEAN trade preference is as yet very small. Thus, development in intra-ASEAN economic co-operation is not likely to have an adverse effect on ASEAN's trade with Japan in the foreseeable future. It may, in fact, have a positive effect if ASEAN industrial co-operation, based on the establishment of joint ASEAN projects, succeed in accelerating the rate of ASEAN's industrial growth, for Japan is a natural supplier of capital goods for ASEAN projects and a potential market for the products of such projects.

Likewise, as the ASEAN countries' industrial structure widens with the pursuit of export-oriented manufactures, and deepens with the progress of import substitution to an intermediate level of fabrication and industrial processing and the development of resource-based industries, the scope for Japanese export of capital goods to ASEAN, to feed the latter's industrialization, will greatly increase. In the context of ASEAN co-operation, the member countries' common pursuit will mean that Japan, which usually has to deal with five different countries with different economic structures and different priorities in economic policies has from now on to deal increasingly with ASEAN as an integrated economic bloc with common industrial policies.

Secondly, it is expected that the countries in the Pacific Basin will not only grow faster than other parts of the world but greatly increase in economic interdependence. Since Japan is an integral and central member of the Pacific Basin, it can be expected that it will benefit from, as well as contribute to, such developments. Bilateral trade will probably become less relevant as an issue of trade relations, and multilateral trade issues involving groups of Pacific countries will become increasingly important. ASEAN-Japan trade relations will increasingly have to take into account the Pacific Basin multilateral economic framework.

Thirdly, the present world economic recession, especially in the United States and the EEC, has depressed the world market for primary commodities and created resistance to ASEAN's exports of labour-intensive manufactured goods. This has caused severe balance of payments problems in several ASEAN countries. Under the circumstances, the ASEAN countries are likely to demand greater access to the Japanese market in order to boost their export earnings. At the same time, however, Japan is likely to find it harder to increase or expand its market share in the ASEAN countries because of keener international competition brought about by the global recession.

DIRECT INVESTMENT

Foreign investment. The ASEAN region has traditionally been dependent on foreign investment and aid. Under colonial rule or until the 1950s, most foreign capital was invested in the primary sector. It was only after the early 1960s that foreign investment began to shift towards the industrial sector and the ASEAN countries generally give preferential treatment to private foreign investment in manufacturing over that in primary export production. Consequently, during the 1970s, the share of foreign investment declined in the primary sector (excluding petroleum), and increased in the manufacturing sector.

The following points may be considered

characteristic of foreign investment in the industrial sector of the ASEAN economies.

Firstly, foreign investment in the industrial sector accelerated from the 1960s with the conscious efforts of governments to foster import-substitution and later export-led industrial growth. In Indonesia, the aggregate amount of approved foreign investment since 1967 was US$1.6 billion at the end of 1971. This almost quadrupled to US$5.4 billion at the end of 1978. The share of foreign investment in the manufacturing sector increased from 25 per cent in 1971 to almost 60 per cent in 1978. In the case of Malaysia, foreign investment in pioneer industries (that is, paid-up capital plus loan) increased from M$395 million in 1971 to M$1,032 million in 1979 and M$2,151 million in 1980. At the end of the 1970s, foreign investment in pioneer industries accounted for about 46 per cent of total foreign investment in manufacturing. In the Philippines, the aggregate foreign investment registered at the BOI since 1968 was 3.8 billion pesos in 1970, and 4.2 billion pesos by the end of 1977. Nearly half of the investments was in manufacturing. Singapore registered S$1.2 billion worth of foreign investment in the industrial sector in 1971 and this figure increased by almost four times to S$4.1 billion in 1977. The Thai aggregate foreign investment in promoted firms approved by the BOI increased more slowly from 2.0 billion baht in 1971 to 3.8 billion baht in 1977. Almost 60 per cent of these investments was in manufacturing.

Secondly, in terms of industry groups, most new foreign investments are found in textiles, electrical, and chemical goods. These three branches accounted for 40 per cent of foreign investment in manufacturing in Indonesia, 37 per cent in Malaysia, about 60 per cent in the Philippines, 23 per cent in Singapore, and about 70 per cent in Thailand by the end of the 1970s. .

Textile and electrical (especially electronics assembly) industries are typically export-oriented and labour-intensive in production technology. In fact, the low cost of labour in the ASEAN countries, at least during the 1970s, has been one of the major factors behind their success in attracting overseas investors to this part of the world. From the host countries' point of view, these industries provide great potential for employment creation. In one study, it was estimated that one-sixth of the projects established by foreign firms, especially American electronics companies, have been due to the need to develop low-cost export bases (Allen 1979).

The present structure of foreign investment is different from that of earlier years when the emphasis was on metal and resource-based (including petroleum) industries. The local market and the supply of raw materials were then the dominant considerations for investing in the ASEAN countries. This was especially so for Japanese enterprises because of the lack of natural resources in their home country.

Thirdly, in terms of the country of origin of foreign capital, Japan and the United States are the two major investors in the ASEAN region. Together, they account for about half of the total foreign investment in manufacturing. Other important investors include the United Kingdom, Germany, Australia, and the Netherlands among the developed countries, and Hong Kong and Taiwan, among the Asian countries. Intra-ASEAN investment is negligible except for Singapore's investment in Malaysia.

Investments from Japan increased substantially in the 1970s. In Indonesia and Malaysia, Japanese industrial investment, which ranked second and third respectively in the early 1970s, rose to the leading position by the end of the decade. Japanese investment has always dominated in Thailand. In Singapore and the Philippines, Japan remains the second largest investor after the United States.

Japanese direct investments in ASEAN. Direct overseas investments by Japanese businesses have increased sharply since 1970 although there have been slow-downs during the oil crises of 1973/74 and 1979/80. From just US$3.6 billion in the early seventies, Japanese foreign investment world-wide soared to well over US$50 billion by the end of 1982. The major areas of Japanese foreign investments are North America, East and Southeast Asia and Central and South America. A breakdown of foreign investments in the developed countries by types of activity indicates that they are mostly in commercial and financial activities.

The developing Asian countries constitute the next major region for Japanese foreign investments. But its investments in the Asian countries (excluding Near and Middle East) tend to be concentrated on mining and manufacturing, which accounted for 32.6 and 45.5 per cent respectively of the total of US$8,643 million invested in 1979. Of these manufacturing investments, the leading ones are in textiles (23 per cent), metals (19 per cent), chemicals (14 per cent), and electrical goods (12 per cent).

Almost 20 per cent of cumulated Japanese direct overseas investments, or 70 per cent of the investments in the Asian region, are directed to the five members of ASEAN. Indonesia is, in fact, the second largest recipient country, next only to the United States. By 1979 the total value of Japanese investments in Indonesia was US$3,888 million, accounting for about 12 per cent of the total amount of Japan's overseas investments. In comparison, investments in Singapore amounted to US$800 million, in the Philippines US$537 million, in Malaysia US$506 million, and in Thailand US$363 million. In terms of the number of investments, Singapore led the list among the ASEAN countries in 1979 with 924, followed by Indonesia with 794, Thailand with 677, Malaysia with 556, and the Philippines with 500. Evidently, the average size of investments is highest in Indonesia, followed by the Philippines. In these two countries, investments in mining (particularly oil in Indonesia and copper in the Philippines) are very important. In other ASEAN countries, especially Singapore and Thailand, investments are mainly in the manufacturing sector.

The total amount of Japanese investments in the manufacturing industries of ASEAN at the end of 1977 was US$1,614 million, or 22.6 per cent of Japan's total overseas investments in manufacturing. Textiles was the leading industry, accounting for US$505 million, of which 56 per cent was in Indonesia, 23 per cent in Thailand, and 15 per cent in Malaysia. This amount of investment in textiles in the ASEAN countries should be regarded as large as it accounts for almost 40 per cent of the total value of Japanese overseas investments in textiles. The next important Japanese industry in ASEAN is iron and non-ferrous metals, the value of which was US$206 million in 1977, or 20 per cent of total Japanese overseas investment in that sector. About two-thirds of this is in Indonesia. The other important Japanese industries in the ASEAN region are chemicals (mainly in Malaysia and Indonesia), transport equipment (mainly in Singapore and Indonesia), and electrical machinery (mainly in Singapore and Malaysia).

The major considerations that have attracted Japanese investment to the manufacturing sector of the ASEAN countries may be summarized as: a) availability of cheap labour; b) abundance of raw materials and mineral supply; c) geographical proximity and close trade/economic relations; and d) political and social stability in the region. Typically, then, Japan invests heavily in the ASEAN region to take advantage of the availability of natural resources and to utilize the plentiful supply of labour in the manufacturing activities.

These developments are in line with Japan's strategy of shifting declining industries, which have become uncompetitive as a result of shortage of labour, rising wages, and limited industrial sites at home, to overseas locations. It is also prompted by the need to conserve resources and energy, to increase imports and to concentrate on knowledge-intensive industries.

The following points have been considered characteristic of the "Japanese-type direct foreign investment" in ASEAN (or, for that matter, in all developing countries) at least up to the mid-seventies:

1. Japanese investment is "low-cost oriented" or "offshore sourcing";

2. there is a strong linkage between parent companies at home and their overseas affiliates;

3. by international standards, the average size of investments is small;

4. equity investment accounts for the bulk of Japanese investment;

5. the investment is typically a joint-venture type, concerned with "control" rather than majority equity participation;

6. many Japanese companies often invest jointly with other Japanese companies;

7. the investment in manufacturing is mostly of an import-substituting type; and

8. the plants are often located in or around major population centres of host countries (see *inter alia* Hirono 1971; Yoshihara 1978; Yamada 1978).

The shortage of capital, technology, and management resources are major reasons for the need to promote foreign investment in the ASEAN countries. The premise seems to be that direct foreign investment benefits *both* the investing and host countries, promoting their economic diversification and the upgrading of their industrial structures, thus contributing to mutual long-term prosperity. From the Japanese point of view, this has been interpreted to mean that Japan undertakes direct foreign investment in industries in which it is losing, or has lost, comparative advantage and locates them in countries that seem to have such a comparative advantage. This is what has been termed as the "Japanese-type, trade-oriented direct foreign investment" (Kojima 1978), which in fact typifies a general strategy of Japan to create dependent industries in ASEAN for the purpose of "exporting" the goods produced back to Japan. In market terms, Japan has penetrated ASEAN to such an extent that it has become virtually indispensable to the member countries although the converse is by no means true (Saravanamuttu 1983).

Chew Soon Beng and Pushpa Thambipillai (1981) have summarized some of the major findings regarding the effects of Japanese investment in the ASEAN countries as follows: the

Thai economy has been found to have gained in terms of employment, linkage effects, and possibly foreign exchange earnings. Japanese firms have also made significant contributions to Singapore's foreign exchange earnings, although in terms of linkage effects and technology transfer, the contributions may be modest. The contribution of Japanese investment, like other foreign investments, to the Indonesian economy in terms of employment, technology transfer, and linkage effects has not been very impressive either. However, it has provided good training programmes for local workers and contributed to economic growth. In Malaysia, Japanese firms have not made a significant contribution to employment creation in manufacturing although they provide excellent training programmes for their employees. The production technology that has been brought in is not adapted to the Malaysian condition. Although Japanese capital involvement may be far less than 50 per cent of the total investment, they have effective management control. Through a package deal, they provide the technology, machines, technical expertise, and even the administrative know-how (*New Straits Times*, 28 July 1982).

Japanese foreign investment is generally concentrated in the major urban areas. Thus, it does not help to narrow regional inequality in the countries. Japanese transfer of technology is more pronounced in domestic resource-based industries than in domestic market and export-oriented industries, although, generally, Japanese firms are not noted for liberal technology transfer policies. However, local R & D activity on product design tends to be significant in domestic-market-oriented industries if the domestic market is substantial. But, in so far as basic research in the host country is concerned, it is practically non-existent.

JAPANESE GOVERNMENT'S
ECONOMIC ASSISTANCE TO ASEAN

Japan has extensive economic assistance programmes on a world-wide basis. However, as it has a stake in the maintenance of peace and stability in the region, a high percentage of Japanese economic assistance goes to Asia. It has been speculated that Asia's share of Japanese economic assistance might rise significantly in view of the fact that Japan has been actively involved in the "Four Modernization Programmes" of China.

Most of the ASEAN countries have been receiving substantial official assistance from Japan. ASEAN's share of Japanese economic assistance was 36.2 per cent in 1980, and the average during 1954–80 was 34.5 per cent. However, the ASEAN countries might get a smaller share of Japanese economic assistance as Japan's economic ties with China improve.

Indonesia is the biggest recipient but gratuitous co-operation accounts for only 12 per cent of Japanese economic assistance to Indonesia. The Philippines is the second largest recipient of Japanese economic assistance and most of its share is in the form of gratuitous co-operation (51 per cent). As expected, Singapore has received the smallest amount of assistance from Japan.

Almost all financial assistance is geared towards economic activity. Japan has also committed itself for up to US$1 billion to help finance the following ASEAN Industrial Projects:

urea fertilizer project in Malaysia and Indonesia; copper fabrication plant in the Philippines; and soda ash plant in Thailand.

Besides financial assistance, Japan has also provided technical assistance to the ASEAN countries. This includes accepting local students and workers for training in Japan, and dispatching Japanese experts to conduct training programmes in the ASEAN countries. Technical assistance is generally directed towards agriculture, manufacturing, and administration. The Japan International Co-operation Agency (JICA) and the Association for Overseas Technical Scholarship (AOTS) are the two most important organizations extending technical assistance to the ASEAN countries. As expected, Indonesia is again the largest, and Singapore the smallest, recipient of Japanese technical assistance in the region.

Japanese economic assistance has been well received by the ASEAN countries. However, they have been urging Japan to provide more economic assistance on a long-term basis. In order to make the most effective use of domestic resources, foreign investment and economic assistance should be geared towards projects which ensure sufficient food, jobs, and energy for the ASEAN countries.

57.   ASEAN-EC ECONOMIC CO-OPERATION

HANS CHRISTOPH RIEGER

INTRODUCTION

The purpose of this paper is to look from an academic point of view critically and realistically at the present state of cooperation between ASEAN and the EC and to identify avenues for further improvement in the future. Before looking at the record, I would like to make some remarks about a number of concepts that we tend to use in the discussion of international cooperation without really thinking about them. What is meant by cooperation? What significance should be attached to agreements to cooperate?

BASIC IDEAS ABOUT COOPERATION

Since one cannot cooperate alone, two or more players are required in cooperation. Although this is obvious, by focusing on this aspect we are reminded that an analysis of a given or potential cooperation situation must include an analysis of the players. In ASEAN we can say that it is the ASEAN member countries that cooperate with each other, while in the EC it is the EC member countries, and that ASEAN-EC cooperation consequently takes place between ASEAN and the EC. But this is a loose kind of shorthand to express the fact that it is the governments of the countries concerned that are the players who enter into agreements to cooperate. At other levels, cooperation may take place between governmental and/or non-governmental organizations and institutions such as ministries, enterprises or even individuals from either side. When analyzing cooperation and cooperation agreements, it is important to bear in mind who the players in the game are.

In the ASEAN region as well as in Europe one frequently hears of the need to make national sacrifices in the interests of a regional gain. This approach imputes an element of supranational rationality to the member countries of a regional grouping that clearly does not exist in ASEAN, in Europe or, for that matter, in any other regions of the world. While altruism is a trait not totally lacking in human intercourse, it is extremely rare — if not absent — in the relations between sovereign nations. It would be naive to build a regional cooperation model on the expectation that such altruism exists in Europe or in ASEAN. Fortunately, the existence of non-zero-sum situations makes such unrealistic approaches unnecessary. Cooperation can enhance the

Reprinted in abridged form from "ASEAN-EC Cooperation: Some Concluding Remarks", in *Experiences in Regional Co-operation*, edited by Rita Beuter and Panos Tsakaloyannis (Maastricht: European Institute of Public Administration, 1987), pp. 243–55, by permission of the author and the publisher.

national interest, and if it does — and only if it does — it should be undertaken.

Let us look at a non-zero-sum game from the case book of ASEAN cooperation. Each ASEAN country has to maintain some food reserves for cases of emergency. By pooling resources the group can limit the amount each country has to stockpile for this purpose. On 4 October 1979 the (then) five ASEAN countries signed the ASEAN Food Security Reserve Agreement in New York. This specifies the amounts of rice to be held by each ASEAN country, namely (in thousand metric tons) 12 by Indonesia, 6 by Malaysia, 12 by the Philippines, 5 by Singapore and 15 by Thailand. Assuming that 50 thousand metric tons of rice is the reserve required by each of the countries in time of need, the gains in terms of stockpile holdings to each participating country are (again in thousand metric tons): 38 for Indonesia, 44 for Malaysia, 38 for the Philippines, 45 for Singapore and 35 for Thailand, that is a total of 200 thousand metric tons for the grouping as a whole.

Of course, the amount of security stockpile required by each country will differ but, whatever it is, 50 thousand metric tons of it is available from the ASEAN scheme, permitting a substantial reduction in individual stockpiles. The savings made through cooperation at the same level of security are quite remarkable. Although the amounts vary from country to country, each participant obtains substantial benefits vis-à-vis the situation before cooperation.

It can be seen that non-zero-sum games offer possibilities of cooperation and, from an economic point of view, if a given situation conforms to a non-zero-sum game, it can be said that cooperation in that situation can in fact increase the size of the pie in such a way that all participants can benefit in terms of improving their position in comparison to what it would be without cooperation.

When summarizing this in the realm of game theory, the following points should be noted:

— Zero-sum games have little relevance for cooperation among players.
— Non-zero-sum games offer possibilities of cooperation among players from which all of them can benefit.
— From a rational point of view, there is no room for altruism. The name of the game is: maximizing personal satisfaction, players' utility, institutional outcome and national interest.
— There is no need for benefits to be equal. Rational players should not compare each other's gains but their own gain in relation to what they would have without cooperation.

ASEAN-EC COOPERATION: THE RECORD

The development of interregional relations between the EC and ASEAN began in 1972 when ASEAN established a Special Coordinating Committee of ASEAN Nations (SSCAN) to conduct an institutionalized joint ASEAN dialogue with the EC. To facilitate the Committee's work, ASEAN also established the ASEAN Brussels Committee (ABC) comprising ASEAN diplomatic representatives accredited to the EC. Since 1972, ASEAN enjoys the EC's Generalized System of Preferences (GSP), which has been extended for another ten years. While not all of ASEAN's requests for GSP improvement have been met, the improved market access extended to ASEAN under the EC's GSP has been seen as a positive factor in ASEAN-EC trade relations. By 1975, a more formal series of consultations was established in the form of a Joint Study Group comprising ASEAN and EC officials. In 1977 another step was taken with the initiation of a dialogue between the ASEAN ambassadors in Brussels and the Committee of Permanent Representatives of the EC Council of Ministers. Their discussion laid the groundwork for a ministerial meeting. The first ASEAN-EC Ministerial Meeting was held in Brussels in November 1978 during which the ministers agreed on the desirability of placing relations between the two groups on a firmer basis through a formal cooperation agreement. As an indication of its growing interest in ASEAN, the EC established a Commission of the European Community for South and Southeast Asia in Bangkok in late 1979. Finally, after extensive preparatory work, the ASEAN-EC Cooperation Agreement was signed at the Second ASEAN-EC Ministerial Meeting in Kuala Lumpur on 7 March 1980 and it came into force on 1 October 1980. Amongst others it provided for the creation of a Joint Cooperation Committee comprising ASEAN and EC officials to monitor and assess cooperation.

In October 1985 a meeting of the ASEAN-EC economic ministers (AEEMM) was held in Bangkok. A high-level working group was set up to study the impediments to EC investments in ASEAN. Its report was submitted to a further ministerial meeting which was held in Jakarta in October 1586. In the meantime the recommendation to set up Joint Investment Committees in each of the ASEAN capitals has been implemented. Another ministerial meeting is scheduled to be held in Bonn in May 1988.

Besides trade, the EC has given financial and technical assistance to ASEAN to help promote industrial and development cooperation in the region. The aim of this assistance is to foster the resilience of the ASEAN economy and to enhance the stability of the region. By helping ASEAN to become stable and prosperous, the EC hopes that ASEAN will one day become one of the EC's major trading partners.

EVALUATION OF ASEAN-EC COOPERATION

It is worth asking whether the special relationship between the EC and ASEAN has benefited the individual ASEAN countries. According to a recent study by Rolf J. Langhammer, the cooperation agreement has provided an exclusive bargaining window — over and above those provided by UNCTAD and GATT — for ASEAN countries to negotiate with the EC (Langhammer 1985). There is some evidence of successes that may not have been so easily come by in the absence of the agreement.

However, others have been more critical. This is what Jean-Pierre Lehmann had to say about the European attitude towards Southeast Asia:

> The fact that the potential for a mutually rewarding and dynamic relationship has not been adequately tapped can be explained by a number of factors so far as the European perspective is concerned. Since the process of decolonization occurred between four to three decades ago, Europe has tended to retreat from Southeast Asia. In the course of the 1960s it was perceived by Europeans as a primarily American sphere of influence because of the Vietnam war, while since the 1970s it tends to be shrugged off as a Japanese economic sphere of influence. Furthermore, the potential for a mature, dynamic, rewarding relationship has, paradoxically, failed to be developed because of the region's comparative political stability. Africa, the Middle East, even Latin America, have been much higher on the European policy agenda. A major problem in this respect is that European foreign policy makers, in stark contrast especially to their Japanese counterparts, have been for the most part fairly illiterate in international economic affairs. This point is further illustrated in European policies towards Asia in that currently far more attention is being focused on the People's Republic of China (PRC), even though the PRC is a smaller market (in terms of purchasing power) than ASEAN, is far less developed, has fewer resources to offer and is far less interesting in terms of foreign investment. But, because 'All is quiet on the ASEAN front', Southeast Asia tends to be ignored. (Lehmann 1985)

I may add that I do not entirely share Lehmann's pessimism because there have been genuine efforts at many levels, both official and private, to overcome Europe's historically founded abstinence from greater involvement in the region. However, the point of the quotation is to show that different views of ASEAN-EC relations can be taken, depending on one's standard of comparison, one's expectations and ideals. Compared to the potential of ASEAN-EC cooperation, present achievements can be viewed as unsatisfactory. Compared with the situation in the early seventies, quite a lot has been achieved.

THE WAY AHEAD

What are the prospects for EC-ASEAN relations in the future? One thing has become clear: Europe is primarily concerned with its own internal problems, and ASEAN is relatively less important for Europe than Europe is for ASEAN. I would like to draw the following conclusions for the way ahead in EC-ASEAN cooperation.

First, one should not expect too much from ASEAN-EC cooperation but be realistic about what can be achieved given the wide differences in emphasis placed by both groupings on each other's problems.

Second, study not only your own gains from potential cooperation measures, but study your partner's goals as well. Only by seeing what the EC can gain from ASEAN, will ASEAN be able to negotiate gains for itself.

Third, become strong in ASEAN, because only by being strong will ASEAN be able to gain larger benefits from interregional cooperation. For ASEAN countries this means putting their individual houses in order first. Indonesia should continue and, if possible, intensify its drive towards the deregulation of its economy, the dismantling of market distorting monopolies and the liberalization of its trade. It should be noted that every country has a comparative advantage in something and should therefore not fear the loss of inefficient industries through liberalization. The political leadership in Malaysia should listen more to its own economists, not to common sense alone. Economics has shown again and again that well-meant common-sense solutions often have the opposite effect of what one wants to

achieve. In the Philippines the new constitution has set the stage for an economic recovery, and one would hope that the political stability needed for a new phase of economic growth will eventually return. Once the politics are out of the way and some form of land reform has been implemented, the prospects for the Philippines will again look bright. Singapore, in my view, should continue to privatize government-run industries and generally reduce government involvement in what should be private decision-making — including marriage and procreation! Thailand has done remarkably well during the recent recession and will doubtless continue to do so by listening to its excellent economists. As far as Brunei is concerned, little is to be said except that diversification should continue, in both the economic as well as the social sphere.

Fourth, ASEAN countries should continue and if possible intensify their efforts to gain economic strength by integrating their individual markets. Just as the EC feels it will be better able to compete in the world arena after the completion of the internal market, so ASEAN can become a far more potent economic force in the Southeast Asian region by closer economic cooperation. Creating the ASEAN market will attract investment not only from the EC but from other economic powers as well. At the same time it will conserve capital within the region that at present seeks investment opportunities outside ASEAN.

Fifth, if for some reason ASEAN integration does not proceed quickly enough, unilateral liberalization will help. The point is that international competitiveness can only be achieved through specialization, and specialization requires trade as a concomitant. If closer ASEAN cooperation succeeds, it should not be at the expense of external liberalization either. An ASEAN trade area should, in the long run, be a step towards further global liberalization.

Sixth, one has to bear in mind that at present ASEAN is growing much faster than Europe — in GDP, not in number of members. ASEAN's negotiating strength with the EC will therefore tend to grow over time.

Seventh, ASEAN countries should get together to plan development assistance from the EC and to concentrate on regional infrastructure projects which will give the private sector greater scope to unfold its dynamic vitality. There does not seem to be much point in industrialization projects or government-run complementation schemes in ASEAN, nor should it be necessary to teach Thai farmers how to grow rice. On the other hand, EC officials complain — no doubt with at least some justification — of the lack of ASEAN coordination in planning and implementing the EC's development assistance.

Eighth, ASEAN countries should utilize the opportunity of learning from the mistakes made by the EC. The CAP is a case in point. The lesson to learn is that well-meant policies that ignore the economic forces acting in society not only lead astray but can be extremely costly and are invariably extremely difficult to reverse.

Finally, the channels of communication to Europe should be kept open for a fruitful dialogue.

58. CHINA'S ECONOMIC RELATIONS WITH ASEAN COUNTRIES

CHIA SIOW YUE

The focus of this chapter is on economic relations between China and the member states of the Association of Southeast Asian Nations (ASEAN)—Brunei, Indonesia, Malaysia, the Philippines, Singapore, and Thailand. They form the market-oriented economies of Southeast Asia. Although the focus is on economics, it is recognized that politics played a key role in the evolution of bilateral economic relationships.

BILATERAL TRADE AND INVESTMENT

Although bilateral economic relations are generally multifaceted, trade and investment are the most important avenues for such relations. In addition, the trade relation is the most readily quantifiable. The ways by which the ASEAN and China economies interact are manifested in their respective trade patterns and in their cross-investments.

ASEAN-China Bilateral Trade

Before the normalization of diplomatic relations between China and most of the ASEAN states in the mid-1970s, bilateral trade, except for Singapore, was executed largely via Hong Kong and Singapore. Because of different political systems, direct trade with China was carefully controlled by the government in most ASEAN countries. Also, since China has a different economic system, much of the bilateral trade is handled by state and quasi-state trading corporations. In absolute levels, total two-way trade with China rose rapidly from only US$0.2 billion in 1970 to US$4.2 billion in 1985, a twenty-four-fold increase, faster than either the growth of ASEAN's global trade or of China's global trade. Exports to China grew from $45 million to $989 million, or 22 times, while imports from China grew from $131 million to $3.2 billion, or 25 times.

Looking at bilateral trade from the ASEAN perspective, China remains a small trading partner of ASEAN countries, even though the share of China in ASEAN's total direct trade increased from 1.3 percent in 1970 to 3.1 percent in 1985. ASEAN is more dependent on China as a source of imports than as a market for exports, with the import share rising from 1.8 percent to 5.1 percent and the export share rising from 0.7 percent to 1.4 percent in the

Reprinted in abridged form from "China's Economic Relations with ASEAN Countries", in *ASEAN and China: An Evolving Relationship*, edited by Joyce K. Kallgren, Noordin Sopiee, and Soedjati Djiwandono (Berkeley: Institute of East Asian Studies, University of California, 1988), pp. 189–214, by permission of the author and the Institute of East Asian Studies, University of California.

same period. However, the shares would be higher if the indirect trade via Hong Kong is fully taken into consideration. Also China can play a potentially larger role in helping ASEAN countries diversify the highly concentrated market structure of their foreign trade and reduce the heavy dependence on trade with the developed market economies.

Among the ASEAN countries, Singapore is China's largest trading partner, followed by Thailand, Malaysia, the Philippines, Indonesia, and Brunei. In fact, Singapore accounts for the bulk of the ASEAN-China trade. Singapore's share of the two-way trade rose from 26.1 percent in 1970 to 61.6 percent in 1985; while Singapore's export share declined from 51.1 percent in 1970 to 33.7 percent, its import share rose sharply from 17.6 percent to 70.2 percent. In value terms, Singapore's trade with China grew very rapidly in recent years, from US$0.4 billion in 1978 to US$2.6 billion by 1985. In 1985 alone, the bilateral trade grew by 64 percent over the preceding year. Singapore became China's fifth largest trade partner, and China ranked sixth in Singapore's foreign trade.

Now looking at the bilateral trade from the China side, the share of ASEAN in China's total trade is larger but shows wide fluctuations over time, ranging from 7.4 percent in 1970, falling to 4.2 percent in 1983, and recovering to 5.6 percent in 1985. Even excluding the indirect trade via Hong Kong, the direct trade alone is quite important for China, especially since the balance of this trade is invariably in China's favor. The ASEAN share of China's exports declined from 12.8 percent in 1970 to 5.2 percent in 1983, and recovered to 10.3 percent in 1985. The ASEAN share of China's total imports rose from 2.6 percent in 1970 to 4.7 percent in 1982, but declined to 2.7 percent in 1985. Thus, ASEAN is more important as a market than as a source of supply to China. The ASEAN market has always been a significant outlet for Chinese merchandise, from traditional foodstuffs to various kinds of low-priced textiles and garments, and household goods and tools. ASEAN, after Hong Kong,

has been an important source of foreign exchange for China.

ASEAN-China trade shows a chronic deficit for ASEAN as a whole and for every ASEAN country, with the exception of Thailand in 1982 and 1985. The deficit has widened rapidly in recent years in spite of some attempts by China to secure balanced trade. By and large, the trade imbalance is caused by the strong demand for a wide variety of Chinese goods while China has a low demand for the limited range of commodities exported by ASEAN. The predominant imports of China from ASEAN are primary products, largely natural rubber, palm oil, copper concentrates, timber, and rice. In recent years, China has been under mounting pressure from individual ASEAN countries to balance bilateral trade. The bilateral deficit is largest for Singapore; however, Singapore to some extent balances its deficit in merchandise trade with its surplus from service exports to China.

ASEAN-China Investment Ventures

Since the 1960s, the ASEAN countries have been actively promoting the inflow of foreign investments to accelerate the pace of economic development. All the ASEAN countries have very active foreign investment promotion programs. The major sources of foreign investments are the industrial market economies of Japan, the United States, and Western Europe. However, sizable investments are originated from developing countries, particularly from the Asian NICs. Traditionally, foreign investments have moved into resource development. Since the 1960s sizable investments have moved into manufacturing activities to assist in the industrialization programs. Except for Singapore, foreign investments in the services sectors of ASEAN are still somewhat limited. There are also sizable outward investments by ASEAN countries, much of it occurring within the Asian region, with cross-investments between ASEAN countries. Thus, Singapore investments are fairly large in Malaysia and Indonesia, while Malaysia is also a significant investor in Singapore. In recent years, outward investments have also gone to China in response to the open-door policy.

For China, the promotion of inward foreign investment is a much more recent phenomenon. Opened at the first level are the special economic zones (SEZs). Foreign investors can now benefit from a much-improved infrastructure and industrial facilities, preferential taxation treatment, eased restrictions on entry of foreign personnel, and better access to foreign exchange and working capital. Export-oriented industries are foremost to be developed and complemented by import-substituting ones. Opened at the second level are fourteen coastal cities, where infrastructural facilities and preferential treatment have likewise been accorded foreign investors.

China's attraction for foreign investors lies in its vast home market and labor reservoir and its potential for growth. There are now Chinese-foreign joint ventures, as well as Chinese-foreign cooperative enterprises and wholly owned foreign enterprises in various economic productive lines. The Ministry of Foreign Economic Relations and Trade (MOFERT) statistics show that there was a total of US$16,200 million of agreed foreign investment that had been made in China in the 1979–85 period. Foreign banks have also established business operations in China. By December 1985 there were 155 branch offices of foreign banks stationed in China. China has also invested abroad since 1980. By the end of 1984, US$150 million was invested in more than 100 noncommercial cooperative undertakings in more than 30 countries. These ranged from the exploitation of natural resources, manufacturing, construction, to shipping, finance, insurance and consultancy services, as well as restaurants.[1]

Chinese data also show that ASEAN investments in China reached over US$250 million up to September 1985.[2] Most are concentrated in infrastructure and hotel construction, and in medium-technology manufacturing. ASEAN investors lack the financial and technological capability to compete with Japan and Western countries in large-scale projects. As China's investment climate improves and ASEAN businessmen develop a greater capacity for outward investments, the ASEAN countries may be expected to increase the level of their investments in China.

Among the ASEAN countries, Singapore has the largest number of investment projects in China, undertaken by both the private and public sectors in Singapore. The Singapore investments are spread thinly over a large number of projects, ranging from oil exploration to hotel management. Geographically, they are spread out over more than a dozen provinces. China has encouraged Singaporeans to negotiate investment projects directly with the provincial governments. The two countries also signed an investment protection agreement in November 1985. Businessmen from Thailand have also been quite assertive in investing in China. It is estimated that there are about twenty-five investment projects with Thai involvement. In contrast to investments from Singapore which are more diverse and technologically more sophisticated, Thai investments are in consumer durables, light machinery products, and construction.

China's investments in the ASEAN countries are still on a limited scale, and very minor when compared to the extent of foreign investments in the region. So far the investments have been mainly in Singapore and Thailand, while investments in Malaysia and Philippines are in the pipeline. China is not permitted to invest in Indonesia.

ISSUES AND PROSPECTS

There are a number of issues in the new phase of ASEAN-China economic relations which slow the development of bilateral economic relations. Some are long-standing and political, while others are newer economic issues.

On the economic front, the euphoria of ASEAN political leaders and businessmen, following the implementation of economic reforms and the open-door policy in China, has given way to a more realistic assessment of the challenge in developing economic relations with a country with a different political and economic system. China has to grapple with the political and economic problems arising from a system of partial economic liberalization. The ASEAN countries are concerned with the ability of China to maintain its present course of economic liberalization and open-door policy, the need for ASEAN countries to develop a more diversified export capacity and economic complementarity with China, and mutual solutions to problems of trade imbalance, inefficient trade practices, and the regulatory and bureaucratic controls on foreign investors in China.

ASEAN's trade with China is more subject to political influences than is its trade with other similar market-oriented economies. Any abrupt change in China's domestic political and economic scenario can affect the amount of foreign exchange allocated for foreign trade, or the reintroduction of state controls to regulate the volume of trade. Will there be a halt or reversal of China's present economic policies? In addition, will China be tempted to use foreign trade and investment as a political weapon in the future? There are no certain answers. Hence, the bilateral relations of ASEAN countries with China are in a state of flux, rather than in one of stable continuity.

China's trade with ASEAN countries has grown rapidly in recent years, but not as rapidly as trade between China and the developed market economies. The further growth of bilateral trade is somewhat restricted by the underdeveloped institutional framework supporting trade as well as by the basic lack of complementarity of the ASEAN (excepting Singapore) and Chinese economies.

The institutional support for ASEAN-China trade has to be strengthened. This would involve greater official support for the development of two-way trade, and the removal of physical, bureaucratic, and financial restrictions inhibiting the freer flow of goods and people. Trade practices (such as countertrade) and trade

protocols that emphasize balanced trade are also inhibiting factors, but given the current foreign exchange problem faced by China and ASEAN countries, these practices cannot easily be replaced by more efficient trade practices.

To accelerate the pace of development of bilateral trade in goods and services between ASEAN countries and China, greater areas of economic complementarity have to be identified. Traditional complementarity arises from the differences in resource endowment between tropical and subtropical countries, giving rise to an exchange of agricultural products. But competitive elements also exist in such resource-based trade. Both China and ASEAN are major producers of rice. In addition, it is possible to grow a number of tropical crops such as rubber and palm oil in Southern China, particularly on Hainan Island. China and ASEAN also share a number of common nonrenewable energy and mineral resources, with possible competition in export markets.

Among countries at different levels of development, complementarity exists in the vertical division of labor, while among countries at advanced levels of development, complementarity exists in the horizontal division of labor. Among countries at low levels of development, there is limited complementarity. Industrialization is based on specialization not in technologies but in resource-based and labor-intensive goods. Being at similar levels of development, China and the ASEAN countries share similar trade structures, importing technology, machinery and equipment, as well as intermediate goods from the developed market economies, and exporting resource-based goods and labor-intensive goods to the markets of the advanced countries. There is limited absorptive capacity in China for ASEAN products and vice versa.

ASEAN countries are faced with the challenge to diversify the composition of their exports to China, so that the export momentum can be sustained and the bilateral trade deficits contained. They also face a potential competitive threat from China in third country markets. In particular, China is already a large producer and exporter of labor-intensive manufactures such as textiles and garments. To earn the necessary foreign exchange to support its import requirements, as well as to provide employment for its huge labor force, China will have to accelerate its exports of labor-intensive manufactures in the years to come. China has a competitive edge from an abundant labor supply and low labor costs. But ASEAN countries have the advantage of greater economic and managerial flexibility and better infrastructural support. So it is unlikely that China will have a comparative advantage over the whole spectrum of labor-intensive manufactures. The task is for ASEAN countries to find their own niches. In the final analysis, competition is the engine of growth of capitalist economies. The ASEAN countries will inevitably face competition in exports, if not from China then from other countries.

Of the six ASEAN economies, Singapore's tends to complement China the most. In the present and medium term, Singapore has a demand for China's resource-based exports, that is, foodstuffs, energy and industrial raw materials, as well as basic manufactures for which Singapore has no comparative advantage because of land scarcity and resource poverty. China has, in turn, a demand for the high value-added and medium- and high-technology goods and services that Singapore can provide with advantage. Singapore's present phase of economic development places priority on high value-added and capital- (human and physical) and technology-intensive goods and services, which places it in a good position to supply part of China's vast needs. In addition, in view of its role as a regional entrepôt and as a transportation and financial center, its well-developed physical and human resources, and the cultural and linguistic affinity of its population with China, Singapore is well placed to act as a conduit for the movement of people, goods, services, and technology to and from China.

Like the trade relations, the ASEAN-China investment relations have complementary and competitive angles. Complementarity arises from investments in each other's economy, to take advantage of country-specific as well as industry- and firm-specific advantages. Thus, Singapore businessmen have invested in China in hotel development, shipbuilding and ship repair, and oil exploration, while both the government and private companies have set up consultancy services. Despite disenchantment with the efficiency of China's economic institutions and the associated investment risks, ASEAN businessmen cannot afford to ignore the huge potential of the China market. However, China is not only competing for ASEAN investments, but also to some extent competing with the ASEAN countries for the same pool of international investments, in particular investments from Japan, the United States, Western Europe, and the Asian NICs. The ASEAN countries will therefore have to ensure that their investment climates remain attractive.

In spite of the problems that exist in the bilateral economic relations between ASEAN countries and China, and in the potential negative spillover effects of China's open-door policy on ASEAN export and investment competitiveness, the economic benefits for ASEAN from a prosperous and economically vibrant China far outweigh the costs. As Japan has done in the last two decades, China can also become the engine of growth in the Asia-Pacific region, with beneficial direct and indirect spillover effects on the ASEAN economies. This assessment, however, is valid only to the extent that China continues to move along the path of nonideological development and contributes to the peace and security of the Asia-Pacific region.

NOTES

1. Cheng and Zhang, in *ASEAN-China Economic Relations*, p. 27.
2. Ibid.

59.

ASEAN, INDOCHINA, AND MYANMAR

MYA THAN

INTRODUCTION

The geopolitical situation in the world has changed dramatically in the last few years. Recent developments in Southeast Asia are no less significant. The Association of South East Asian Nations (ASEAN), an "economic grouping" which became politically united as a result of the threat posed by the Vietnamese invasion to Cambodia, is now faced with new challenges. Member countries are developing new strategies to meet these new challenges; Thailand, for example, pursued the policy of "turning battle field into market place", at least in practice and proposed a Suvanna Bumi (Golden Land or Peninsular) concept, in a bid to form an economic co-operation ring including the Indo-Chinese nations and Myanmar. On the other hand, there is a trend of forming regional and subregional groupings which have a clear common interest based on security, culture, geography, trade or economic development. One of these groupings is the East Asian Economic Grouping (EAEG) mooted by Dr Mahathir Mohamad, the Malaysian Prime Minister. It is the outcome of the failure of the GATT meeting in Brussels in 1990. Its aim, according to Mahathir, is "to speak with one voice to stop the slide towards protectionism and to preserve free trade". It is ". . . intended to facilitate constitution and consensus prior to negotiation with Europe or America or in multilateral fora such as GATT" (*Straits Times*, 5 March 1991). Japan, NICs, the Indo-Chinese nations (namely, Vietnam, Laos, and Cambodia) and Myanmar would be included in this grouping. Thus, Indo-Chinese nations and Myanmar came into the limelight in regional fora and it is therefore timely to examine their relations with ASEAN member countries.

In addition, since there are growing complementarities between ASEAN and these four nations, especially as ASEAN industries and services begin to move into the capital intensive stage, these less developed states from mainland Southeast Asia could fill up the gap being vacated by ASEAN economies. This calls for closer economic relations among these four countries and ASEAN.

Moreover, recent changes in developmental policies in these countries attract potential investors and traders not only from the region but also from outside the region. In addition, there are suggestions that these nations sign the Treaty of Amity and Cooperation, and that a loose, consultative forum between ASEAN and these countries be established to facilitate more dialogue, and better understanding and goodwill.

Reprinted in abridged form from "ASEAN, Indo-China and Myanmar: Towards Economic Co-operation?", *ASEAN Economic Bulletin* 8, no. 2 (November 1991), pp. 173–93, by permission of the author and the Institute of Southeast Asian Studies.

ECONOMIC RELATIONS BETWEEN ASEAN AND
INDO-CHINA AND MYANMAR

Trade Relations With ASEAN

Although informal trade plays a very important
role in the countries of mainland Southeast Asia
(it is estimated at 50 to 100 per cent of official
trade), there is no reliable data. However, since
1989–90, Myanmar, Laos, and recently, Cambodia, regularized border trade, and trade
statistics from 1990/91 onwards would be
nearer to the actual figure. For the purpose
of this section, IMF data from the *Direction of
Trade Statistics* (DOTS) Yearbook will be used.

The level of ASEAN's export and import
trade with Vietnam, Laos and Myanmar between 1979 and 1989 is shown in Table 1.
Based on that data, it was found that ASEAN's
exports to the region increased 6.5 per cent
annually from 1979 to 1989 whereas its imports
from the region increased 4.5 per cent during
the same period. At the same time, ASEAN's
total exports to the world grew 8.9 per cent
annually while its total imports from the world
grew 9.6 per cent. That is to say that although
ASEAN's export and import trade with Vietnam, Laos and Myanmar was increasing, its
foreign trade with the rest of the world was
increasing more rapidly.

On the other hand, ASEAN's total exports
to these countries as a percentage of its total
exports to the world was very insignificant

with less than 1 per cent and it declined from
0.25 in 1979 to 0.19 in 1989. Similarly, the ratio
of ASEAN's imports from these countries of
mainland Southeast Asia as a percentage of
its total imports from the world was also less
than 1 per cent and it decreased from 0.36 per
cent in 1979 to 0.21 per cent in 1989. (It should
be noted that these low trade figures were
probably because informal trade, sometimes
as high as about 50 to 100 per cent of the
official trade, was unaccounted for.) However,
trade with ASEAN is still significant for Vietnam, Laos and Myanmar; their annual exports
to ASEAN as a percentage of their exports to
the world for the last 11 years averaged about
18 per cent while their imports from ASEAN
as percentage of their total imports from the
world averaged about 23 per cent.

In sum, as far as trade between Vietnam,
Laos and Myanmar and ASEAN countries is
concerned, the level by international standards
is low. In other words, Indo-Chinese countries
and Myanmar are not major trading partners
for ASEAN but they are alternative or additional sources of imports. However, for Vietnam,
Laos and Myanmar, ASEAN is one of the major
trading partners and the volume of trade among
them is increasing. Moreover, for ASEAN the
countries of mainland Southeast Asia with over
100 million people are attractive markets for
their made-in-ASEAN goods.

TABLE 1: ASEAN's Export and Import Trade with Vietnam, Laos and Myanmar, 1979 and 1989

Country	Export To		Import From	
	1979	1989	1979	1989
Myanmar*	23.2	99.5	139.68	109.84
Vietnam*	54.3	65.6	21.2	105.6
Laos*	47.07	67.24	4.12	36.99
Group Total*	124.57	232.34	165.00	247.43
World Total*	50,798	119,536	46,488	116,158
Group Total/World Total (%)	0.25	0.19	0.36	0.21
Myanmar/World Total (%)	0.05	0.01	0.30	0.09
Vietnam/World Total (%)	0.11	0.01	0.01	0.09
Laos/World Total (%)	0.09	0.01	—	0.03

* In millions of US$.

TABLE 2: Exports and Imports of Southeast Asian Countries, 1979¢89 (In US$ millions)

	1979	1980	1981	1982	1983	1984	1985	1986	1987	1988	1989	Growth Rate (1979–1989)
Exports												
ASEAN												
Indonesia	15,579	21,909	23,810	22,329	21,146	21,881	18,597	14,809	17,170	19,376	21,936	3.5
Malaysia	11,077	12,960	11,773	12,044	14,128	16,563	15,408	13,977	17,934	21,125	25,049	8.1
Philippines	4,602	5,787	5,721	5,020	4,932	5,343	4,614	4,807	5,696	7,034	7,754	0.4
Singapore	14,239	19,377	20,970	20,787	21,832	24,070	22,812	22,501	28,703	39,322	44,769	12.1
Thailand	5,301	6,501	7,027	6,935	6,368	7,414	7,123	8,864	11,564	15,992	20,028	14.1
Indo-China												
Laos	17	23	17	26	27	11	16	14	64.3	95.8	98	19.1
Vietnam	156	155	156	210	206	269	238	296	366	458	740	14.3
Myanmar	389	415	446	391	378	301	303	288	211	147	250	4.7
Imports												
ASEAN												
Indonesia	7,226	10,837	13,270	16,859	16,351	13,880	10,275	10,724	12,850	13,489	16,467	8.9
Malaysia	7,842	10,821	11,550	12,409	13,241	14,057	12,301	10,828	12,701	16,567	16,513	7.7
Philippines	6,613	8,295	8,477	8,263	7,863	6,262	5,351	5,211	6,937	8,662	11,165	5.4
Singapore	17,643	24,013	27,571	28,178	28,158	28.667	26,237	25,513	32,626	43,869	49,694	10.9
Thailand	7,164	9,215	9,954	8,532	10,283	10,415	9,260	9,166	13,003	16,292	25,296	13.5
Indo-China												
Laos	123	85	87	80	36	51	56	83	111	122	85	−8.5
Vietnam	980	883	631	509	413	509	554	534	541	642	741	−8.2
Myanmar	573	786	823	895	268	239	783	304	260	244	311	−8.9

SOURCE: IMF, *Direction of Trade Statistics Yearbook*, various issues.

Table 2 shows time series data of exports and imports of Southeast Asian countries from 1979 to 1989 taken from the various issues of the *Direction of Trade Statistics Yearbook*.

Unlike ASEAN nations, the economies of the Indo-Chinese nations are organized in Marxist socialist form: large-scale means of production are public-owned and all main economic activities are centrally planned. However, the private sector accounts for a fairly large part of production and trade since their economies are based on agriculture. Both Laos and Vietnam, along with Myanmar, belong to the' world's twenty poorest nations and according to T. Kimura (1986), Vietnam's economy is at the same level as Myanmar, is two-thirds that of China and one-fifth that of Thailand (p. 1040). However, *Asiaweek*

(21 June 1991) mentioned that per capita GNP of Laos and Vietnam for 1991 were US$180 and US$200 respectively compared with Myanmar's US$278.

As for items of trade, Laos exports timber and forestry products, tin, gypsum, handicraft and electricity (especially to Laos). On the other hand it imports machinery and raw materials, petroleum products, rice and food stuffs. Exports of Vietnam are natural rubber, vegetables and fruits, coal, chromium, and footwear whereas its imports are machinery and equipment, petroleum, fertilizer, rice, corn, maize, sugar, wool, and cotton fabrics. Their imports of rice make trade relations complementary to trade with Myanmar and Thailand.

The foreign trade of Indo-Chinese nations were concentrated mainly with the CMEA group comprising socialist countries, better known as COMECON. According to London-based EIU (Country Report, *Indochina* 3 [1988], 61 per cent of total exports and 54 per cent of total imports of Laos were traded with CMEA, while Vietnam's 44 per cent of total exports and 40 per cent of total imports were traded with CMEA. Table 3 shows that Laos has had more trade with developing countries (i.e. 85 per cent of exports and 61 per cent of imports were traded with developing countries). Similarly, Vietnam exported 44 per cent of its total exports to developing countries and 33 per cent of its imports came from those

countries during 1988. The majority of the trading partners from developing countries are from Asia.

Similar to the Indo-Chinese economies, Myanmar's economy until 1988 was a command-controlled economy and since 1987 the country was officially listed as a "Least Developed Country", at its own request to alleviate the debt problem. It used to be one of the largest exporters of rice and teak. At present, Myanmar's exports consist mainly of agricultural produce such as beans and pulses, oil cakes, maize, rubber, jute forestry products such as teak and hardwood; base metals and ores; animal

TABLE 3: Trade Pattern of Southeast Asian Countries (% Distribution) in 1988

	Total US$ mil.	%	Industrialized Countries	Countries	Africa	Asia	Europe	Middle East	Western Hemisphere	East Europe
Exports										
Burma	588	100	12.9	79.2	24.1	50.2	—	1.9	3.0	6.4
ASEAN										
Indonesia	19,376	100	71.4	28.0	0.9	24.1	0.5	2.2	0.2	0.4
Malaysia	21,125	100	52.5	46.7	0.6	41.8	1.0	2.5	0.8	0.8
Philippines	7,034	100	77.0	22.3	0.2	19.7	0.1	1.4	0.7	0.3
Singapore	39,322	100	50.6	48.8	2.0	41.4	1.0	2.8	1.5	0.6
Thailand	15,992	100	62.4	36.5	3.3	25.7	0.6	6.0	0.7	0.7
Indo-China										
Laos	88	100	13.5	85.3	0.1	37.4	47.1	0.6	—	—
Vietnam	518	100	47.1	44.1	1.0	32.7	10.3	—	—	—
Imports										
Burma	741	100	45.7	32.7	0.3	38.1	1.2	—	—	14.0
ASEAN										
Indonesia	13,489	100	67.8	31.0	1.3	22.6	0.5	5.0	1.6	0.6
Malaysia	16,567	100	62.2	37.1	0.7	32.7	0.4	1.7	1.7	0.5
Philippines	8,662	100	57.4	42.1	1.1	28.9	4.7	9.6	2.0	0.5
Singapore	43,869	100	54.4	45.1	0.6	33.7	0.5	9.2	1.1	0.5
Thailand	16,292	100	55.5	42.3	2.0	32.0	1.1	4.9	2.4	1.6
Indo-China										
Laos	132	100	24.8	61.3	0.2	48.3	12.8	—	—	—
Vietnam	804	100	50.3	33.0	0.8	23.4	8.2	0.7	—	—

SOURCE: IMF, *Direction of Trade Statistics Yearbook*, 1990; Country Report, EIU, no. 3, 1988 (for 1986).

hides and skin; and fish and fish products. As far as imports are concerned, Myanmar gives priority to capital goods (machinery, equipment, etc.), raw materials, and spares for inter-industry use at the expense of consumer goods (mostly pharmaceutical products, edible oils, and milk products).

Its external trade partners are mainly from Asia, such as China, India, Japan, and ASEAN nations. Up to 1988, more than 80 per cent of its exports went to developing countries whereas about 40 per cent of its imports were from the developing areas. After border trade was formalized in 1989, trade with neighbouring countries like China, Thailand, Bangladesh and India has increased significantly.

In sum, it can be said that the low share of these countries' trade in ASEAN's total trade itself and growing complementaries between them indicate that there is large potential for expansion of trade between these four and ASEAN.

Investments by ASEAN Countries in Indo-China and Myanmar

Recently, Vietnam, Laos, Cambodia and Myanmar stressed the significance of foreign direct investment in the development of their respective countries. Each launched its own foreign investment law almost at the same time in 1987 and 1988 to tap foreign capital, technology and management expertise. Lower labour costs and an abundance of natural resources are the main attractions for foreign investment in these countries.

However, political uncertainties (the still unresolved Cambodian issue and the possibility of a return to hard line economic policies in Indo-China and political disquiet in Myanmar), economic disincentives (lack of banking facilities and inadequate business infrastructure), and a difficult operating environment (lingering bureaucratic hurdles, ill-trained workforce) on the domestic front, and the trade and aid embargo imposed by the United States, the European Countries, and Japan, on the international front, make attraction of foreign investment difficult.

Notwithstanding these difficulties, it was found in the cases of Vietnam and Myanmar that investments from private "Western" firms in these two countries have the lion's share of total foreign investment. Although the United States has not lifted its embargo, it was found that there were already many investors from the United States in these countries. Probably some investments from Taiwan and Hong Kong are from the U.S. firms. It was also found that although ASEAN investments in these countries of the mainland Southeast Asia are small, they are increasing year after year.

CONCLUSION

Findings from the previous sections would lead us to the following conclusions:

1. Impoverished for many decades by their pursuit of socialist policies, the Indo-Chinese countries and Myanmar have decided to transform their command-controlled economies to market-oriented ones. Modest recovery has been registered in their economic performances since the adoption of new economic policies. In doing so, they have sought their own models since each country has its own political, social, economic and cultural characteristics. However, it seems that these countries' models of development are closer to China's model of *perestroika* without *glasnost* or *perestroika* with a little glasnost rather than to the Eastern European model of *perestroika* with *glasnost*.

2. Political, social, economic, and cultural relations between the countries of mainland Southeast Asia and ASEAN are improving although the degree of interaction is still low by international standards. There are many indications that the Cambodian issue will be resolved more easily than seemed possible a few years ago. More importantly, a number of

moves are under way to promote better and increased political, diplomatic, military and economic links between the individual ASEAN nations and Vietnam, Laos, and Myanmar.

3. Economic relations between ASEAN and the nations of mainland Southeast Asia are improving although, here again, the level by international standards, is very low. This low level of trade itself indicates that there is enough potential for further expansion of trade between ASEAN and the four from mainland Southeast Asia. We found that Indo-Chinese nations and Myanmar are not major trading partners for ASEAN. However, ASEAN member nations are the major trading partners for Indo-Chinese countries and Myanmar. At the same time this group's imports from, and exports, to ASEAN are increasing at the annual average rate of about 5 per cent during the last 11 years.

Recently, Vietnam, Laos, Cambodia and Myanmar stressed the significance of foreign direct investment in the development of their respective countries. However, due to trade and aid embargoes imposed by the United States, the European Community, Australia and Japan, attracting foreign capital was not easy. Notwithstanding this, it was found that FDI from "private" Western firms in these countries have the lion's share in the total FDI. It was also found that although ASEAN's investment in this part of the region is small, it is increasing year after year. Expansion of trade and investment activities depend on the resolution of the Cambodian issue, political stability, realistic foreign exchange rate, and improvement in infrastructure, bureaucratic machinery and banking facilities in this region.

In short, the diversification in these two groups of nations in terms of the levels of development, resource availability, and consumption pattern indicate the large potential for expansion of intraregional trade in Southeast Asia.

4. Finally, concerning prospects for close co-operation between individual countries of ASEAN and Vietnam, Laos, and Myanmar, all seem to be included in ASEAN or EAEG or any other regional forum, at least in spirit. Vietnam has openly shown its interest for affiliation in ASEAN. Some ASEAN leaders had also mentioned the possibilities of including these countries in ASEAN or in EAEG. By joining these regional fora, Vietnam, Laos, Cambodia and Myanmar would have political and economic gains by means of a demonstration effect, bandwagon effect, or spillover effect. Similarly, ASEAN could gain politically as well as economically by expanding co-operation with these countries since they legitimately belong to Southeast Asia. They are ASEAN's neighbours and therefore it is in the interest of ASEAN that these four countries succeed in their transition from command economies to market-oriented economies.

On the other hand, these countries are preoccupied with their domestic problems and at the same time they are enjoying the benefits from the present bilateral relations with ASEAN countries. They also know that ASEAN is more successful in political affairs than in economic co-operation and that intra-ASEAN trade in not as successful as expected. In the case of Myanmar, one of the reasons why it did not wish to join ASEAN in the late 1960s was because some of the ASEAN member countries had foreign military bases. This reason is still valid unless the military government revises its previous policy. On the other hand, ASEAN leaders would like to see these countries "cleaning their homes" first before they apply for membership. Furthermore, the gap between the levels of development of these two groups is quite large and their political systems are also quite different. Therefore, for exogenous and endogenous reasons, it is unlikely that Vietnam, Laos, Cambodia and Myanmar would become full-fledged members of ASEAN in the immediate future.

However, there are suggestions that these countries can, as a token of their goodwill and as a first step toward co-operation, make a move to accede to the ASEAN Treaty of Amity and Co-operation. Thus, over time, as there are more and more economic linkages and commonalities, the comfort level will increase between ASEAN and these four countries. As a result,

> The gap will diminish, the commonalities will expand, and in time their admission to an expanding ASEAN would not be disruptive of what ASEAN wishes to accomplish but would add to an expanding ASEAN pie. In the not too distant future these four countries — Vietnam, Laos, Cambodia, and Myanmar — could become members of the ASEAN community (Joint IPS-ISEAS ASEAN Roundtable 1991).

60.

ASEAN-SOUTH ASIA ECONOMIC RELATIONS

MUKUL G. ASHER and CHARAN D. WADHVA

Broad trends and features of ASEAN-South Asia economic relations are presented here. This would be of assistance in assessing problems and prospects concerning their economic relations.

Trade Relations

Some of the indicators concerning ASEAN-South Asia trade for the year 1981 are presented in Table 1. With the aid of the data in the table, and on the basis of the country papers, broad features of ASEAN-South Asia trade may be summarized as follows.

1. As far as total exports are concerned, each region is not of overwhelming importance to the other. This, of course, need not hold for a particular group of commodities. The ASEAN market is, however, of somewhat greater importance to South Asian countries than vice versa. Even among the ASEAN countries, the South Asian market is of some importance to Singapore and Malaysia. Between them, they account for 85 per cent of total ASEAN exports to South Asia. Among the countries of South Asia, India and Pakistan together account for

three-quarters of total South Asian exports to ASEAN. Thus, with respect to exports, these four countries are of overwhelming importance in the present ASEAN-South Asia trade.

2. As far as imports are concerned, those from ASEAN are of moderate importance to South Asia. South Asian imports, however, are of negligible importance to ASEAN. The ASEAN imports from South Asia are somewhat less unevenly spread, though Singapore and Malaysia still account for a little more than two-thirds of the total ASEAN imports. India and Pakistan account for roughly the same proportion of total ASEAN imports as their share in exports to ASEAN. Imports by both Bangladesh and Sri Lanka from ASEAN have increased rapidly in recent years.

3. The trade balance was generally in favour of South Asia in the early 1970s, but it is now substantially in ASEAN's favour. Each of the ASEAN countries has a favourable trade balance with South Asia as a whole. This is all the more noteworthy in view of the trade deficits experienced by countries such as Singapore, the Philippines and Thailand. So far, such imbalance in ASEAN's favour has not been a source of friction between the countries of the

Reprinted in abridged form from "An Overview: ASEAN-South Asia Economic Relations", in *ASEAN-South Asia Economic Relations*, edited by Charan Wadhva and Mukul Asher (Singapore: Institute of Southeast Asian Studies, in collaboration with the Indian Council for Research on International Economic Relations and the Marga Institute, 1985), pp. 1–26, by permission of the Institute of Southeast Asian Studies.

TABLE 1: Some Summary Indicators of ASEAN-South Asia Trade, 1981

	ASEAN[a]				
Country/Region	*Share in Exports to South Asia*	*Exports to South Asia as % of Total*	*Share in Imports from South Asia*	*Imports from South Asia as % of Total*	*Balance of Trade (US$ million)*
ASEAN	100.0	2.87	100.0	0.72	1405.1
Indonesia	6.1	0.53	13.2	0.50	49.0
Malaysia	25.8	4.42	23.7	1.05	373.0
Philippines	3.2	1.08	2.7	0.16	48.8
Singapore	59.7	5.46	45.7	0.85	911.0
Thailand	5.2	1.46	14.7	0.73	23.3
	SOUTH ASIA[b]				
Country/Region	*Share in Exports to ASEAN*	*Exports to ASEAN as % of Total*[a]	*Share in Imports from ASEAN*	*Imports from ASEAN as % of Total*	*Balance of Trade (US$ million)*
SOUTH ASIA	100.0	3.70	100.0	6.59	− 1470.5
Bangladesh	15.3	9.97[c]	13.3	10.41	− 185.3
India	56.7	3.75	63.1	6.73	− 961.0
Nepal	0.5	4.26	0.7	7.01	− 11.0
Pakistan	19.3	3.47	15.1	5.54	− 200.0
Sri Lanka	8.1	4.13	7.8	8.01	− 113.2

NOTES: [a] based on ASEAN countries' data
[b] based on South Asian countries' data
[c] substantial discrepancy between Singapore country data and Bangladesh country data.
SOURCE: IMF, Direction of Trade, 1982, various country tables.

two regions. This may be due to the importance of energy and cooking oil imports by South Asia from ASEAN, both of which are essential items. If invisibles are added, especially the tourist flows, the balance is even more favourable to ASEAN, especially to Singapore.

4. As noted, energy and cooking oil dominate ASEAN's exports to South Asia. Manufacturing items (SITC 5 to 8) are also of major importance in both ASEAN's exports to and imports from South Asia. In general, ASEAN countries' exports to South Asia do not compete with one another. A similar pattern is found for South Asian exports to ASEAN. This may imply that an export push by a particular country to the countries in the other region is unlikely to harm the exports of its regional partners.

5. The extent of intra-industry trade is quite low, both in terms of coverage and values for particular industries. As may be expected, intra-industry trade is more important in Singapore's and Malaysia's trade with India, and to a lesser extent with Pakistan.

The above discussion suggests that South Asia has become not an insignificant customer of the ASEAN countries, especially of Singapore and Malaysia. Therefore, these two countries may want to nurture and cultivate the South Asian market. South Asian countries rely on ASEAN for many of their essential imports.

Investment Relations

Among the South Asian countries, only India, and among the ASEAN countries, only

Singapore have substantial equity investment in joint ventures in the countries of the other region. Sri Lanka and, to a considerably smaller extent, Pakistan also have some equity investments in ASEAN. However, in all cases, the equity investment in relation to the total in a given country is quite small. A major portion of India's global investments are in the ASEAN region. India has investments in all five ASEAN countries in a wide range of areas, such as computers, cement, textiles, paper and pulp, precision tools, office furniture, and so forth. The sophistication of the technology employed also varies considerably from the most sophisticated (such as the Tata-Elxsi computer operation in Singapore) to quite labour-intensive operations on a smaller scale. There appears to be a recent trend among the Indian joint ventures to also include a third party, usually a multinational firm. Indian joint ventures, however, have had their share of problems in ASEAN, especially in Malaysia and Indonesia. The more open environment of ASEAN demands different business strategies from the less open South Asian environment. These difficulties have been aggravated by the currency devaluation in Indonesia and by the recent slow-down in the world economy. While many Indian ventures appear to be domestic-market oriented, several newer ones have been attempting to broaden their market to regional and world level. In the joint ventures, the Indian partners generally have a minority share. This may be partly due to the fact that they have less "proprietory assets" which they need to protect. It appears that the Indian joint ventures, especially those in manufacturing, have reached a consolidation phase; and the newer ventures are likely to be larger, more diversified and more professionally managed than was generally the case in the 1970s. There also appears to be an increase in recent years in non-industrial joint ventures, such as consultancy services, and hotels.

Singapore has recently become an important investor in Sri Lanka and Bangladesh, concentrating on textiles and jewellery. However, as Singapore does not keep data on overseas investments, it is not possible to separate firms which are Singaporean from those which were or are based in Singapore but whose ownership is non-Singaporean.

Since the discussion of investment relations in the following papers is not based on a survey of joint ventures, it is difficult to provide answers to important questions such as their financial performance, management style, whether "appropriate technology" has been employed, whether there is transfer of technology, whether they are based on "know-how" or "know-why", their marketing strategies, and so forth. This is an obvious area for further research.

Other Relations

These consist mainly of manpower and tourist flows between the two regions and the operations of financial institutions. While manpower flows cannot be precisely quantified, sizable communities of South Asian nationals in all the ASEAN countries indicate that these flows are not unimportant. In countries such as Singapore and to a lesser extent Malaysia, which have deliberately imported professional and skilled and semi-skilled manpower to fuel their growth, the contribution of South Asian nationals appears to be significant, deserving wider recognition than has been the case so far.

The tourist flows from South Asia to ASEAN are also significant, especially when account is taken of the length of stay and the per capita expenditure. Both these are, paradoxically, higher for an average South Asian visitor, compared to the average for all visitors. This may be explained by the greater availability of consumer durables in ASEAN, especially in Singapore, as compared to South Asia. Sri Lanka's attempt to provide attractive shopping opportunities to its visitors is too recent to indicate the degree of success. On the other hand, ASEAN visitors have shown relatively less preference for South Asia as a destination. Thus, the flow of visitors is substantially balanced in ASEAN's favour.

Financial institutions from only India and Pakistan have operations in the ASEAN countries. There are no ASEAN financial institutions operating in South Asia. Given Singapore's importance as a financial centre, the presence of financial institutions from India and Pakistan is not surprising. The Indian institutions mainly finance third-country trade, but have also financed many Indian joint ventures in the region. They have also used the Asian dollar market to raise funds for Indian and other firms, and have participated in syndicated loans. They have also been attempting to broaden the deposit base and loan portfolio.

While impossible to demonstrate or quantify, it appears that there is a close connection between the operations of money-lenders in ASEAN, and foreign exchange transactions in the grey markets in South Asia. Many of the money-lenders, especially in Singapore and Malaysia, are of South Asian origin.

The precise contribution of financial institutions, both formal and informal, to ASEAN's growth, however, remains to be investigated. Since the Indian financial institutions have financed many of the Indian joint ventures, problems faced by these ventures in Indonesia and in Malaysia have spilled over to these institutions as well. How these problems are resolved would significantly influence the future role of the Indian financial institutions in ASEAN.

The discussion in this section suggests that the economic relations between ASEAN and South Asia are multifaceted. They are also not unimportant, especially when non-trade relations are taken into account. But what are the prospects for these relations? It is this question to which we turn next.

PROBLEMS AND PROSPECTS

If the present levels of economic relations between the two regions are to be expanded, attention would have to be devoted to several areas.

1. Differences in Business Cultures and Environment: There are many important differences between the South Asian and ASEAN regions concerning business culture and environment. ASEAN has generally adopted an outward-orientation development strategy. This strategy has meant a broad acceptance of the present division of labour among the countries; concentration of efforts towards ways and means of benefiting from this division of labour; and seeking to increase international competitiveness. South Asia's strategy, at least until very recently, has been much more of the import-substitution type. As a consequence, the ASEAN market is much more of a buyer's market than that of South Asia. Moreover, industries in South Asia, once established, can look forward to government protection to a much greater extent than is the case in ASEAN. Multinational firms also play a proportionately larger role in ASEAN than they do in South Asia. While in both regions, the role of government is extensive, it would appear that the approach of the ASEAN governments has been somewhat more technocratic and result-oriented than has been the case in South Asia. The recent privatization drives in Malaysia and Thailand seem to have fewer counterparts in South Asia.

Given these differences, it would be surprising if each side did not have problems operating in the other region. Since it is South Asia which has a substantial current account deficit with ASEAN, it is the South Asian countries which would need to make the greater effort to understand and adapt to the business environment of ASEAN. While there have been some signs that this is being done, the success of the South Asian countries is far from assured in this respect. South Asia may need to rely less on their State organizations and more on the private sector. The State, however, can play an important role in ensuring quality and creating awareness of the need for an export culture. The State in South Asia may also need to become more technocratic and result-oriented.

It would appear that ASEAN firms also need

to make greater attempts to adapt to the South Asian domestic environment, especially if joint-ventures are contemplated.

2. Problems of infrastructure: The above problems of adjustment are made somewhat more difficult by inadequate, and relatively expensive shipping and other infrastructural services between the two regions. This is even more relevant when perishable commodities, such as fruits, vegetables, and other such items, are involved. The efficiency of infrastructure within many South Asian countries also needs to be improved.

3. Political and Psychological Factors: While a paper concerning these factors is not included in this volume, given their importance, a brief mention of these factors is necessary here.[1] ASEAN, since its inception, has evolved into a politically cohesive organization. In recent years, political differences have appeared between ASEAN and India on the issue of Kampuchea. The other South Asian states, such as Pakistan, Bangladesh, and Sri Lanka,[2] have generally leaned towards the ASEAN position on this issue. These political differences, combined with ASEAN's psychological orientation towards the West and Japan (for example, Malaysia's "Look-east Policy") seem to have affected to a certain extent economic relations between ASEAN and South Asia, especially India.[3] With the setting up of the South Asian regional grouping in August 1983, it is hoped that such bilateral differences will not unduly affect the economic relations between the two regions. Political differences among the South Asian countries themselves also hamper economic relations. In both intra-South Asia trade and that between ASEAN and South Asia, political will would be necessary to expand economic relations, the benefits of which are generally conceded. Much would also depend on how political relations between the United States, China, Japan, India, the rest of South Asia, and ASEAN develop, as both the sub-regions are subject to great power rivalry.

4. Financing Facilities: Many exporters in South Asia, especially India, have long complained of inadequate specialized export-financing which has made their exports, especially capital goods exports, less competitive. Recently, India has set up an Export-Import (EXIM) bank with an authorized capital of US$225 million, and a paid-up capital of US$84.4 million. The EXIM bank is also authorized to raise loans in international money markets.[4] The existence of such an institution is likely to mitigate the export-financing problem somewhat.

The above discussion, along with the current economic recession, would suggest that no sharp increase in the economic relations between the two regions is likely to take place in the near future. There are, however, several steps, in addition to those mentioned earlier which may be taken to improve these relations.

Some Suggestions for Improving ASEAN-South Asia Relations

1. It appears that in trade relations between the two regions, almost exclusive attention is being paid to the export (or re-export of) finished or intermediate goods. Such a preoccupation leaves at least two areas relatively unexplored. The first is the possibility of a division of labour between the two regions based on the various stages of production. As an example, Singapore which aspires to be a publishing centre, may undertake to have certain skilled, labour-intensive, earlier stages of production, such as editing, done in South Asian countries such as Sri Lanka or India. Such a division of labour would be mutually beneficial, as high value-added stages, such as marketing, could still be done in Singapore, and at the same time the South Asian countries would better utilize their labour resources. Similar situations may exist in other areas, such as in standardized goods and in computer software. The second area is the relative neglect of trade in services, such as in hotels, restaurants, consultancy, entertainment, and so forth.

2. There may also be potential for the exchange of professional manpower between

the two regions. Thus, a multinational firm operating in one or both regions may utilize the services of professional manpower from the other region. This may prove to be more cost-effective than importation from the West. Furthermore, as the ASEAN countries, besides Singapore, implement ambitious rural development plans, and as South Asian countries try to develop energy plans, an exchange of experts between the two regions may prove cost-effective.

3. There appears to be areas in the two regions where trade and other links are negligible. For example, there are few, if any, economic links between Sabah and Sarawak and South Asia. The economic relationships between the Philippines and South Asia especially Sri Lanka and Pakistan, are also negligible. Therefore, some attention needs to be paid to these areas.

4. There also appears to be some scope for unorthodox ways of engaging in trade between the two regions. These include barter trade, counter-purchase policy and its variations, non-convertible currency trade on a multilateral basis, and other such schemes. These schemes can well supplement the conventional trade in hard currencies. Malaysia is already reported to be discussing barter trade with India.[5] These unorthodox schemes may also prove attractive, for different reasons, to Indonesia and the Philippines. Both these countries need to curb their hard currency imports. Given the large balance of payments deficits of South Asian countries, these schemes may also prove beneficial to them.

5. The ASEAN and South Asian countries may also devise a joint strategy to increase the procurement shares of United Nations contracts and those of multilateral development banks going to the developing countries.

6. There may also be scope for sharing ways and means of increasing the productivity of primary products, such as rubber, copra, tea, cocoa, etc., and to devise joint marketing strategies for these products.

7. It appears that there is an absence of firms specializing in finding joint-venture partners in the other region. This is especially important, given the different business environments in the two regions, and in view of the general difficulty in finding suitable joint-venture partners. Perhaps such a firm could be set up as a joint venture between the two regions. As the ASEAN region moves to higher levels of technology, South Asia may provide a base for its labour-intensive operations.

8. There has been a recent tendency of diplomatic missions of some countries to devote a substantial proportion of their energies to commercial and market intelligence efforts. However, this tendency does not seem to have been prominent in the diplomatic missions of some of the countries of the two regions. These countries need to attach much greater importance to commercial and economic diplomacy than has been the case so far.

9. Mention has already been made of a need to overcome infrastructural bottle-necks in the two regions.

That expansion of economic relations between ASEAN and South Asia is likely to be mutually beneficial is generally conceded. While there are impediments to the expansion of these relations, it is our hope that sustained efforts will be made by countries of both regions to expand these relations, thereby providing impetus to South-South economic co-operation.

NOTES

1. See, however, Leo E. Rose, "India and ASEAN: Much Ado About Not Much", in Economic, Political, and Security Issues in Southeast Asia in the 1980s, edited by Robert A. Scalapino and Jusuf Wanandi (Berkeley: Institute of East Asian Studies, 1982), pp. 93-107.

2. Sri Lanka has applied for membership of ASEAN, but the application is unlikely to be favourably considered.

3. See Barry Wain, "Kampuchea Hampers Ties Between India and ASEAN", Asian Wall Street Journal, 8 August 1983. Wain quotes an Indian consultant in Malaysia as complaining that since 1980, their competitive offers are being passed over in favour of others. This is in contrast to the period up to 1979, during which Indian consultants' expertise was valued highly. Recently, however, Malaysia has shown an interest in setting up a training centre of the type run by the Tata conglomorate of India in Singapore.
4. For more information, see EXIM Bank: India (Bombay: Export-Import Bank of India, October 1982).
5. Straits Times (Singapore), 27 July 1983.

61

LATIN AMERICA AND THE ASEAN COUNTRIES

FRANCISCO ORREGO VICUÑA

INTRODUCTION*

Relations between the Latin American countries and the members of the Association of Southeast Asian Nations (ASEAN) have been gradually intensifying in recent years, giving rise to a trend which now seems to be of considerable significance. Not all the Latin American countries are taking part in this process, however, and for this reason the present article will be confined to the most important cases, outstanding among which is the policy of linkage pursued by Chile, the country that has made the greatest progress in this field. In some instances, it will also be necessary to include references to other Asian countries, especially Korea, Hong Kong and Taiwan, which have similarly come to the fore among Latin America's trade partners.

It is important to point out that this co-operation process is not restricted to the field of trade alone, since it is also signally manifested in matters of finance, in resource policy, in functional areas and in respect of specific contemporary political situations. Its main aspects will be analysed below, with the inclusion of some of the salient features of its historical background.

ECONOMIC MODELS AND
CO-OPERATION PROSPECTS

One of the factors that has contributed significantly towards co-operation between Latin America and the member countries of ASEAN has been the similarity of the economic development models adopted by several countries in each region. In this connection the other more advanced developing countries in Asia should also be included.[1] While it is true that in this regard some differences in emphasis appear, both between the two regions and within each of them, the incorporation of certain common basic principles has determined an orientation which is substantially comparable. Some authors, however, have questioned the comparability of the Asian and Latin American policies in this respect.[2]

The chief characteristic of these models is that of basing the economies concerned on the operation of the market, reducing the extent of State intervention in the economy or else subjecting it to clearly defined norms of competition and efficiency. The elimination of price controls is one of the direct consequences of this policy, the market being allowed to determine price levels. Encouragement of the

Reprinted in abridged form from "Prospects of Co-operation between Latin America and the ASEAN Countries", *Contemporary Southeast Asia* 4, no. 1 (June 1982), pp. 19–34, by permission of the author and the Institute of Southeast Asian Studies.

private sector's role is also one of the most typical manifestations of the policy in question and makes for satisfactory mobilization of productive resources.

Similarly, many of these economies are characterized by a marked degree of openness to international trade, as a result of which they have in some cases been typified as "small open economies"On this basis, a general liberalization of international financial operations has taken place and a policy of non-discrimination has been adopted in relation to foreign investment. Monetary and exchange policies, in their turn, have in some cases been liberalized, or else have taken the form of alignment with hard currencies in world-wide circulation, in particular the United States dollar.

Within the sphere of ASEAN, policies of this nature can be identified in the case of Singapore — which is one of the most typical examples in this respect — and to some extent in that of Malaysia. Other ASEAN countries share some aspects of this liberal approach, but not the whole of it. Hong Kong, Taiwan and Korea also have typically liberal economies.

In the Latin American region, policies of this kind are found, with some variants, mainly in the Southern Cone of the continent. Argentina, Chile and Uruguay have adopted liberal policies. Brazil pursued such a policy for a period but has reverted in some respects to a State-interventionist economy. Bolivia, Colombia and Peru have also begun a gradual approach towards a liberal economic policy.

TRADE BETWEEN
LATIN AMERICA AND ASEAN

According to the figures available for 1980, trade between Latin America and ASEAN totalled approximately US$1,000 million. In that year exports from ASEAN to the Latin American region totalled US$663 million, or 1 per cent of its total exports. Latin America, in its turn, exported US$342 million worth of goods to ASEAN, equivalent to 0.4 per cent

of its total exports. If these figures seem low in percentage terms — as this trade has been developed only recently — the total volumes are by no means insignificant. Moreover, a rising trend is shown, so that yet higher figures may be expected in the near future.[3]

A point to note, of course, is that in respect of its foreign trade each of these regional groups is highly dependent upon Japan and the United States, a fact which has also set limits to the expansion of their reciprocal trade. Argentina, Brazil, Chile and Cuba have been the biggest exporters of Latin American products to ASEAN, while Singapore accounts for 77 per cent of ASEAN's exports to Latin America. Malaysia too has begun to emerge as a country of some importance, with a share of 17 per cent of ASEAN's exports to Latin America. The total exports of the two regions are thus comparable, with that of Latin America totalling US$82,392 million in 1980 while that of ASEAN, US$67,063 million.

Another aspect of the trade situation that should be borne in mind is that between the more advanced developing countries of Asia, such as Taiwan, Korea and Hong Kong, and Latin America, which also opens up interesting prospects.[4] Exports from this Asian group to Latin America expanded by 23.8 per cent per annum in 1969–78 and by 13.8 per cent per annum in 1974–78, which is the latest period for which complete figures are available. In this connection, attention should be drawn to the special case of Chile, which, during the latter period, increased its imports from this Asian group by 66 per cent annually.

The leading Latin American importers from this Asian group are: Panama (35 per cent), particularly in terms of services; Brazil (9 per cent); Mexico and Chile (7 per cent). In turn, the chief Latin American exporters to the group are Brazil (45 per cent), Argentina (18 per cent), and Chile (8 per cent), all in terms of the figures given for 1978. This same comparison shows that Taiwan absorbs 42 per cent of the imports from Latin America, Singapore 25 per cent and Korea 15 per cent. The main exporters in the Asian group are Taiwan (34 per cent) and Singapore (24 per cent).

The principal exports of the group of Asian countries under discussion are clothing, petroleum products, rubber, electrical machinery, vegetable oils, communication equipment, crude petroleum, tin and other less important items. In the case of Latin America, the staple export items are crude petroleum, sugar, iron, coffee, copper, nuts and oilseeds, animal feeds, maize and other agricultural and mining products.

IMPORTANCE OF TRADE PROSPECTS

The effect that is being produced by the trade relations described is a *rapprochement* between the more advanced developing countries in each region, which includes in Singapore, Malaysia, Taiwan, Hong Kong and Korea on the one hand, and Argentina, Brazil, Chile and Mexico on the other. This is the first time that such a thing has happened, and some of its consequences are of the greatest international importance. This group of developing countries, characterized by their economic dynamism, today accounts for more than one-third of the total exports of developing countries in the entire world. By the end of the present decade their share will reach approximately 45 per cent of the total exports, with 27 per cent attributed to the Asian group, although it is estimated that the exports of the Latin American group will also expand at a rapid rate.[5]

The situation will confer on the group of ten more advanced developing countries a role of great significance in international economic negotiations, enabling them to gain an influence which hitherto has been somewhat nebulous. Furthermore, these are rapidly growing countries, with average annual increases of about 8 per cent in their gross national product, and with an annual export growth rate of 12 per cent. These same characteristics will help to step up the reciprocal trade between these two groups, including of course that of

ASEAN itself. The growth of national income and the opening up of some Latin American countries to free trade will also contribute to the expansion of trade flows between the two regions.

From this point of view it is interesting to examine the composition of reciprocal trade, an aspect of the question which brings to light certain factors that also exert a positive influence on the expansion of trade. The exports of Asian countries to Latin America consist mainly of manufactures and only secondarily of primary commodities. In 1977 the corresponding figures were US$298 million and US$193 million respectively, according to studies carried out in relation to a group of representative Asian countries. In contrast, if the composition of Latin American exports to Asia is analysed, an inverse ratio will be observable; they consist mainly of primary commodities and only secondarily of manufactures. The figures for the same year were US$512 and US$66 million respectively. The incidence of manufactures in the external sales of the Asian countries is four times greater than in the case of the Latin American countries.

As mentioned above, Latin America's most important export items are wheat, meat, sugar, animal feeds, vegetables, pulp and paper and fertilizers. The Asian countries export chiefly boats, clothing, telecommunication equipment and electrical machinery.

Thus, a significant complementarity between the economies of the more advanced countries in each group is discernible, and this too encourages the expansion of trade. As far as ASEAN is concerned, however, it is chiefly with respect to Singapore and Malaysia that one can speak of complementarity, since the lines of production of the other members are, in general, competitive with those of Latin America, especially as regards petroleum, footwear, coffee and some mineral products. But even in this case, Chile and Argentina must be singled out from the rest of Latin America, since they are countries whose temperate-zone products are also complementary to the products of the Philippines, Indonesia and Thailand. Thus, the complementarity factor can be seen to exist in a good many situations, although of course instances of competition cannot be entirely ruled out.[6]

ASEAN, LATIN AMERICA AND THE PROSPECTS FOR CO-OPERATION IN THE PACIFIC

The Government of Japan has recently sponsored initiatives directed to exploring the idea of the creation of a Pacific Community, a concept which subsequently aroused special interest in some Australian circles.[7] This idea has been carefully considered by some of the Latin American countries, inasmuch as it might imply an increase in co-operation in the Pacific, but subject, of course, to certain indispensable clarifications. In this sense, the region's reaction has been a mixture of interest and caution. Similar approaches have emanated from the academic institutions of the ASEAN countries.[8]

On this level, an interchange of opinions among the ASEAN countries, the South Pacific and Latin America — the nucleus of developing countries which might be called upon to participate in a trans-Pacific co-operation scheme — might prove of decisive importance in ensuring that any initiative in this field should take into account the basic interests of the group in question. At the same time, it would forestall attempts to divide opinion among the countries concerned.

The co-ordination postulated in this article concerning the developing countries of the Pacific Basin might establish the bases for firm trans-Pacific co-operation, founded on the trilogy represented by ASEAN, the South Pacific

and Latin America. This trans-Pacific bridge of action would exert a positive influence on the stability of a Pacific Community, inasmuch as it would ensure that participation would be fuller, more equitable from the standpoint of economic development needs and, in the final analysis, represent a more balanced concept. Furthermore, a co-operation scheme of this kind would certainly not affect the co-operation patterns that each region might wish to develop among its member countries, nor would it obstruct whatever relations it desired to maintain with any other country or region in the world. Co-operation in the Pacific would thus complement rather than replace the currently prevailing approaches.

Latin America made its first appearance on the scene of trans-Pacific co-operation only a decade ago, when in 1970 the Institute of International Studies of the University of Chile convened an international conference on the subject of "Latin America returns to the Pacific".[9] The distinguished personalities participating in this conference included Mr. S. Rajaratnam, the then Foreign Minister of Singapore. In October 1981, the Institute received a visit from another eminent figure in ASEAN, Mr. Siddhi Savetsila, the Minister for Foreign Affairs of Thailand. This afforded an opportunity for retrospective appraisal of the progress achieved during the 1970s in this field, where a steady increase in reciprocal knowledge, co-operation and interchange was observable. This is a reality which will find expression in more specific steps with every passing day. To that end, the outlook and interrelationships of the two regions' more important academic institutions can be a decisive factor in the future progress of trans-Pacific co-operation.

NOTES

* This article is based on a lecture given by the author at the National University of Singapore, at the invitation of the Institute of Southeast Asian Studies and the Institute of International Affairs of Singapore, on 10 November 1981.
1. In this connexion see the paper presented at the Conferencia sobre Experiencias y Lecciones de las

Economias Pequenas y Abiertas [Conference on Experience and Lessons of Small Open Economies], Institute of Economics of the Catholic University of Chile, 1981, in particular the studies by Dr. Pang Eng Fong and Professor Lim Chong-Yah (Singapore).

2. See for example, Fernando Fajnzylber, "Some Reflections on South-East Asian Export Industrialization", *CEPAL Review* (December 1981).

3. See Francisco Orrego Vicuna and Juan Reutter, "Economic Co-operation and Conflict in the Pacific Basin: a South American View", Pacific Forum Symposium, Bangkok, 14–15 November 1981.

4. See Ernesto Tironi, "Trade Relations between Latin America and the Asian Advanced Developing Countries", Eleventh Pacific Trade and Development Conference, Seoul, 1–4 September 1980, mimeographed.

5. Ibid.

6. A periodic analysis of trade relations can be found in *Chile Report for ASEAN Countries*, published by the Chilean Embassy in Singapore, no. 1 (November-December 1981), and subsequent issues.

7. See Sir John Crawford, ed., *Pacific Economic Cooperation* (Singapore: Heinemann Educational Books, 1981).

8. See Narongchai Akrasanee et al., *ASEAN and the Pacific Community* (Jakarta: Centre for Strategic and International Studies, May 1981).

9. For a report on the activities of the Institute of International Studies of the University of Chile in relation to the Pacific, see *Project on the Pacific, 1982* (Institute of International Studies of the University of Chile, 1982).

Section VIII

DEFENCE AND SECURITY

Introduction

Chandran Jeshurun

One of the great truisms of the character of ASEAN has been its avowed desire to remain as a prime example of regional co-operation in Southeast Asia without being in the least suspected of serving the covert security needs of either the individual member countries or its own collectively. This deeply-felt conviction among its leaders ever since its formation at a time when the region was in the throes of great power rivalry and domestic insurgencies has been the subject of much debate among students of Southeast Asian international history. To some extent it is, of course, understandable that the predominant pattern of regional conflict during the post-World War II period reflected the alliances between client Southeast Asian states and their great power patrons who provided the necessary security cover.

This, in turn, resulted in the creation of a system of military and defence pacts such as the well-known Southeast Asia Treaty Organization (SEATO) of 1954, the Anglo-Malaysian Defence Agreement (AMDA) of 1957, the Five Power Defence Arrangements (FPDA) of 1971 and the Soviet-Vietnamese Treaty of Friendship and Co-operation of 1978. Only Indonesia and Burma were successful in remaining free of such alliances with external powers. But it is open to question whether they too have not, at various points in their history as independent nations, been put in a compromising diplomatic or strategic position as a consequence of the Cold War.

Nevertheless, the founders of ASEAN were so insistent that their intention was only to foster co-operation in the economic, social and cultural spheres that there has always been fairly wide speculation of more covert forms of security relations within the organization. The communist bloc in particular was never convinced that ASEAN was anything other than a West-inspired military alliance directed primarily against China and the Indochina countries. At the same time, most regional security specialists have invariably focused their attention on the practice of some of the ASEAN member countries in conducting bilateral defence and military co-operation and tended to deduce from the web of criss-crossing security relationships among them the existence of a *de facto* pact. The end of the Cold War has, if anything, rather ironically triggered off even more discussion and debate about ASEAN's alleged defence and security role. Recent indications by its leaders that the organization should address the question of regional security more directly in its dealings with dialogue partners will no doubt fuel even more speculation about its past record.

The literature on the defence and security aspects of ASEAN is, in view of the circumstances described above, somewhat uneven. Both the intellectual quality and the veracity of much of the details that are to be found in it are intrinsically flawed. In any case, information about military matters is generally quite limited in the region as a whole. Scholars have naturally found it somewhat trying to piece together a sufficiently authoritative account of how ASEAN has dealt with the complex issue of regional security all these years. In the event, much of the earlier writing about the defence policies of individual countries and the discussion of regional security issues as they pertained to ASEAN in the initial years after its formation have not been particularly illuminating. This is well reflected in the selection that is offered here as only three of the eleven items pre-date the 1980s when more serious and focused work on this vital but sensitive subject began to be undertaken, especially by scholars indigenous to ASEAN.

Thus, the pioneering efforts of outside specialists who tended to understand the broader context of ASEAN's defence and security dilemma are followed by four examples of the new approaches that were attempted by scholars from within the region. The 1990s are now recognized as a decade of openness in the region and nowhere more so than in the field of security studies where much more hitherto inaccessible information became available to the serious analyst. Again, the selection attempts to highlight the important new advances that were made in the study of the hardware aspects of defence and security issues. There are also some examples of the much more candid assessments of the future directions in ASEAN's prospects for security co-operation. It is recognized that not all the views and conclusions that have been included in this Section may meet with unanimous approbation. However, the individuals whose writings are cited here are the leading spokesmen for the region on this often tricky subject.

62.

REGIONAL SECURITY IN SOUTHEAST ASIA

J.L.S. GIRLING

In Southeast Asia the need for external protection and the striving for independence lie contradictorily at the heart of the various conflicting or overlapping security movements or associations which have been erected from within or inspired from outside the region. National and ideological tensions are both reflected in the most recent category of rival Indochina 'fronts', one officially backed, if not promoted, by Peking, the other also without a formal alliance structure but materially dependent on the United States. The second category comprises old-style military pacts with outside participation: SEATO, ANZUS and the 5-power British Commonwealth arrangement. The third type is the hoped-for new emerging force in the region, ASEAN, which so far has avoided an explicit defence commitment.

The spilling-over of the Vietnam struggle into Laos and Cambodia has created the two Indochina fronts, one largely of governments, the other mostly of dissidents, divided (more or less) along ideological lines. The Summit Conference of Indochinese Peoples held in April 1970 grouped together North Vietnam, the National Liberation Front and Provisional Revolutionary Government of South Vietnam, the Pathet Lao and 'patriotic neutralists' of Laos, along with Prince Sihanouk and his camp followers.[1] In contrast, President Thieu of South Vietnam appealed for a 'joint anti-communist fight by Vietnam, Cambodia, Laos and Thailand to shorten the (Vietnam) war'.[2] But the Laotian Prime Minister, Prince Souvanna Phouma, rejected any plan for a military pact because it would be contrary to the Geneva agreements and would aggravate the present situation;[3] while the Thai Foreign Minister advised that 'a plan of such magnitude' could only be adopted and carried out 'after much deliberation'.[4] President Thieu then conceded that an Indochina alliance was not feasible.[5]

Divergent national interests were chiefly responsible for this fiasco. The neutralist Prime Minister of Laos is seeking to negotiate a settlement with the Pathet Lao, not to get further embroiled in the Vietnam conflict. The Thai leaders, military and civilian, are aware of their own insurgency difficulties, divided on the issue of fighting in Cambodia and worried about the effects of American withdrawal. In any case a formal alliance structure is irrelevant when the armed strength of the United States provides the major *de facto* support of the governments of Laos, Thailand and South Vietnam. Just as America is still the main partner on the one side, so North Vietnam undoubtedly plays the dominant military role (with China providing

Reprinted in abridged form from "Regional Security in Southeast Asia", *Journal of Southeast Asian Studies* II, no. 1, (March 1971), pp. 56–65, by permission of the author and the National University of Singapore.

political guidance) as regards the Pathet Lao, the N.L.F. and Sihanouk's 'National United Front of Kampuchea'. The Indochina question, which is the crux of the issue, will be resolved, not in Bangkok, Phnom-Penh or Vientiane, but — to repeat — by the success or failure of 'Vietnamisation' and by the determination or exhaustion of Hanoi.

In this struggle, old-style pacts like SEATO have been by-passed by events. SEATO's chief objective, from its founding in 1954, was to guard its members against conventional armed attacks; but the danger turned out to be, not a North Vietnamese Korean-type invasion across the 17th parallel or the 'downward thrust' of communism directed by Peking, but internal cleavages, governmental instability, political subversion (i.e. illegal opposition) and rural-based insurgency. SEATO nevertheless had a certain utility: it bolstered Thailand and it gave legal cover to America's intervention in South Vietnam, a protocol state.[6] SEATO is not so much an autonomous security organisation as an instrument serving great power purposes, which have sometimes been swayed or distorted by the diplomatic persistence, febrile emotions or bargaining skill of smaller states. But this has been exceptional.

There were, for example, inspired comments from Bangkok that the SEATO Council meeting in July 1970 would legalize Thai intervention on behalf of Lon Nol in Cambodia. Thanat Khoman himself urged SEATO to provide 'full scale' military aid to Cambodia.[7] This was just one day after a member of a Thai parliamentary delegation to Phnom-Penh announced he had informed the Cambodian Foreign Minister that the 'proper thing' to do was to 'approach SEATO with an appeal as a protocol state'; for only as SEATO partners could the United States and Thailand 'properly and legally go to the assistance of Cambodia'.[8] However U.S. Secretary of State Rogers reportedly dissuaded Lon Nol from making any such appeal[9] and the SEATO Council of Ministers obediently favoured a 'political solution' based on Cambodian neutrality.[10] Ironically, America's 'insistence' on

neutrality for Cambodia brings to mind the British and French refusal to accept SEATO intervention in Laos, on behalf of the right-wing Government in Vientiane, a decade before. The European powers were urging a political solution; the United States, backing Marshal Sarit of Thailand, was on the other side.

Differing national interests were (and are) a characteristic of SEATO. In mainland Southeast Asia only Thailand became a member. The Philippines, isolated by geography and its 350-year colonial past, lauded SEATO's anti-communist posture but was all the time aware that the islands' defence rested on a bilateral treaty with the United States. Pakistan joined SEATO as a safeguard against India: but this aim was jeopardised by Washington's decision to act only against 'communist aggression'.[11] France dropped out in disapproval of American intervention in Vietnam. Britain's reduced role East of Suez focussed on Malaysia and Singapore. Australia and New Zealand, conservatively governed, increasingly followed America as Britain's declining interest, with the end of Confrontation, became obvious. The Australian and New Zealand administrations of course welcomed SEATO from the point of view of their own 'forward defence' and as a means of 'engaging' America in Asia; but their main reliance, naturally enough, is on the ANZUS treaty.[12]

Even member states of ASEAN — the Association of South East Asian Nations — which are geographically close-knit, have very different preoccupations. Despite a common need for 'stability', a realisation of the benefits of co-operation, a common awareness that internal weaknesses can be readily exploited by outside powers, a certain shared resentment of Japan's economic pre-eminence and a fear of China's domination, despite all these factors making for a sense of community, the divisive colonial past and diversity of current circumstances so far have prevented any effective combination for political purposes.

Unlike ASPAC — the Asian and Pacific Council — which has anti-communist origins emphasised by the presence of the partitioned trio of South Korea, Taiwan and South Vietnam, ASEAN is explicitly 'non-communist'. ASPAC, wider in area and looser in scope, includes Australia and New Zealand and especially Japan, all of which play a moderating role;[13] yet Indonesia is not a member. ASEAN, in the absence of Australia, New Zealand and Japan, reflects Indonesia's foreign policy of non-alignment — hence the omission of a defence structure: but it is also influenced, somewhat contradictorily, by the anti-Chinese suspicions of the Indonesian military.

NOTES

1. 'Joint Declaration of Summit Conference of Indochinese Peoples', *Peking Review*, 8 May 1970.
2. Speech at Vung Tau, *The Australian*, 14 May 1970. Vice President Ky also proposed an 'anti-communist front line' on 22 May 1970, to include the same countries.
3. Report to the National Assembly, 8 June 1970. However the Assembly Vice-President, Chao Sopsaisana, took a contrary line urging that 'all countries within the Indochinese peninsula, including South Vietnam, Cambodia, Laos and Thailand, should form an economic, political and social bloc for survival'. He added that there was 'even more reason for a military bloc'. *Bangkok World*, 30 July 1970.
4. Thanat Khoman, 22 May 1970.
5. Speech in Cambodia, 17 July 1970.
6. Cambodia, Laos and South Vietnam were designated in the 'protocol' to the South-East Asia Collective Defence Treaty as subject to its articles, provided this was at their invitation or with their consent.
7. *Bangkok Post*, 14 June 1970.
8. Representative Panit Sampavakoop. *Bangkok Post*, 13 June 1970.
9. Neil Jillett reporting from Manila. *Canberra Times*, 6 July 1970.
10. Rogers told the SEATO Council: 'We concur in the position taken by the Cambodian Government which does not favour Cambodia's military association with SEATO.' This speech and Council communique are reported in *SEATO Record*, Bangkok, August 1970.
11. 'Understanding of the United States of America': Manila, 8 September 1954.
12. Sir Alan Watt, "The ANZUS Treaty: Past, Present and Future", *Australian Outlook*, April 1970.
13. ASPAC members are: Australia, Taiwan, Japan, South Korea, Malaysia, New Zealand, Philippines, Thailand, South Vietnam. Laos sent an observer to the fifth Ministerial meeting at Wellington in June 1970. The meeting reported 'concern and apprehension' over the tense situation in the region, discussed the implications of the changing policies of the major powers' and urged the need for regional cooperation on the widest possible basis. ASPAC's economic, cultural and technical projects are listed in *Current Notes on International Affairs*, Department of External Affairs, Canberra, June 1970.

63.

THE STRATEGIC BALANCE IN SOUTHEAST ASIA

BRUCE GRANT

SECURITY ARRANGEMENTS IN SOUTH-EAST ASIA

Remnants of earlier security arrangements remain, without cohesion or, indeed, coherence. The South-East Asia Collective Defence Treaty (1954) remains on paper, but the South-East Asia Treaty Organization (SEATO), its military component, has been disbanded. Its membership has collapsed and its anti-Communist objectives, always confusing, have now become irrelevant.[1] The Asian and Pacific Council (ASPAC), formed in 1966, was political in conception, and some hoped it might be the beginning of a wider regional security arrangement. It is now dormant and, because it includes Taiwan, is unlikely to be revived.

The ANZUS Treaty (1951) remains active, but as its members comprise only Australia, New Zealand and the United States, and as its vaguely defined theatre ('the Pacific area') has tended at least in the United States' interpretation, to exclude South-east Asia, it has no direct regional influence. The so-called five-power defence arrangement (1971) between Malaysia, Singapore, Britain, Australia and New Zealand remains in being, but both Britain and Australia have withdrawn their ground forces, and the arrangement's purely Commonwealth nature and its stopgap character severely limit its

regional application. Indeed, it has sometimes seemed pre-occupied with keeping Singapore and Malaysia on sensible terms. It is notable that Britain maintains forces in Brunei. The United States has almost completely withdrawn her forces from Thailand and is in the process of negotiating terms for retaining her bases in the Philippines, with whom she has a bilateral security treaty, the only one in South-east Asia.

The Association of South-East Asian Nations (ASEAN), formed in 1967, is the most substantial regional grouping which offers some kind of counter to Vietnam. It has been slow to develop, but it includes five important states (Thailand, Malaysia, Singapore, Indonesia and the Philippines) and has shown some skill in creating a consensus on foreign-policy issues. Its economic and cultural co-operation remains low-key, however, its regional organization has little status or authority, and it has deliberately avoided security decisions itself, although it has encouraged security co-operation among its members. The ASEAN states have taken the view that economic development is the most effective form of security, and the biggest and most important of them — Indonesia — has deliberately starved her armed forces, especially her navy and air force, of scarce foreign exchange. While its potential is strong, ASEAN

Excerpted from *The Security of South-East Asia*, Adelphi Papers, no. 142 (London: International Institute for Strategic Studies, 1978), pp. 2–4 and 29–31, by permission of the publisher.

is still in two minds about its future as a security arrangement.

The security arrangements that remain in South-east Asia today are the left-overs of the Anglo-American ascendancy; they are ineffectual, yet give rise to the suspicion that they could be revived.

THE EXAMPLE OF VIETNAM:
A PATTERN FOR THE FUTURE?

There is also a symbolic aspect to Vietnam's strength, which is that the Vietnamese are heroes of history. Every nation has its heroes, but the Vietnamese in power today in Hanoi must rank high on any list of heroes, especially in South-east Asia where, with the exception of the Indonesians who removed the Dutch by a combination of armed resistance and active diplomacy, the existing nation states had a comparatively easy road to independence. The Vietnam War, the longest and bloodiest of all wars of national independence since the colonial era began to crumble after World War II, resulted not only in the success of the Vietnamese Communists, but in the first military defeat of the United States and in a major reversal of American foreign policy. The consequences of this are still not clear. To some extent the rethinking of American foreign policy since 1969, when the commitment in Vietnam began to be reversed, was prolonged by the discrediting of President Nixon and the interim leadership of President Ford, and it is only since the installation of a new President in 1977 that the future outline of American policy in the Asian–Pacific region has begun to emerge. It is possible that the heroic stature of Vietnam may act as a source of national fulfilment, rather than as a spur to further demonstrations of her prowess. But for the other states of South-east Asia, which had been growing accustomed to the long, slow, pragmatic process of consolidating independence after the transfer of sovereign political power, the emergence of a vital, confident, new state, freshly successful from a classic colonial war, has caused apprehension and self-examination. In addition, it may be that the profounder effects of the defeat in Vietnam on United States policy have not yet emerged.

There is a widespread view that South-east Asia will 'settle down' or 'right itself' in time. It is held that the region is capable, with its porous borders, passive populations and strong governments, of absorbing shocks and accommodating itself to conditions of not-too-efficient survival. One should not think of South-east Asians as constituting nation states. Rather, their ties are more strongly with race, family and commerce. They are fated (doomed or privileged, according to taste) to have a low profile in international affairs because they acquiesce willingly to international forces, whether religious, political or commercial. This view, however, puts too low a value on nationalism to provide a useful guide to future events. For the state is no less powerful in South-east Asian countries than elsewhere and, whether in the policing of internal security or in the protection of territorial integrity, it has shown itself to be as self-conscious as any. In the last ten years South-east Asian nationalism has indeed been low-key. The Vietnam War was the dominant issue of those ten years, and political nationalism in the region was subdued, not only by the determining strategic effect of the war but also by the profits which flowed from it. But the arrival of a united Vietnam on the scene will (with other factors) stimulate the latent nationalism, which never lies very far beneath the surface in South-east Asian politics.

The shift of power to Vietnam has raised afresh the problem of Communist insurgency in South-east Asia. In both Thailand and Malaysia Communist insurgency has been increasing recently, and the success of the Vietnamese troops in guerrilla warfare (like that of the Chinese Communists before them) will no doubt inspire confidence in the strategy of insurgency. Yet the assumption that Vietnam is the model for revolutionary guerrilla warfare in other countries of South-east Asia would be just as much a mistake now as it was in the 1960s.

As will be seen, her problems are different. Moreover, it is worth recalling that, so far, Communist insurgency in South-east Asia has not been successful, with the exception of Vietnam. The uniqueness of Vietnam, which made her a model of successful defiance of all the arts of counter-insurgency that money could buy, lay in the distinctive combination of nationalism and Communism which gave her revolution particular force. The Viet Minh were the patriots, Ho Chi Minh was the father of the nation, and France and the United States, trying to build an alternative nationalism around other leaders in the south, were opposing Vietnamese nationalism. In the rest of South-east Asia the situation was reversed. The departing colonial powers gave authority to the nationalists, and the Communists had to attempt to seize power from nationalist leaders, which they failed to do. It is, therefore, unlikely that the brilliant Vietnamese victory will be repeated elsewhere in South-east Asia, always provided that the performance of nationalist governments can be maintained.

EQUILIBRIUM: PRACTICAL ALTERNATIVE
TO HEGEMONY?

The notion of a shift of power to Vietnam may seem to pre-suppose that a balance of power should be brought into existence to correct it. However, the concept of a balance of power does not readily fit the known dispositions of either the states within the region or the powers external to it.[2] If history is a guide, petty rivalry within the region and external hegemony or pervasive penetration from outside is a more likely pattern. The famous balance-of-power system which maintained conditions of relative peace in nineteenth-century Europe (even if it did not preserve internal peace, as witness the uprisings of 1848 and 1870) was upheld by resident actors who were not themselves subject to major pressures from outside Europe. In South-east Asia the resident states, such as they are, have not traditionally been the objects of a power balance in the region, let alone the focus of a concert of powers. To the extent that they have been subject to the exigencies of their foreign relations, they have been rivals skirmishing for minor advantages under the broad influence of outside forces, whether the cultural and trading stimulus of India, the tributary system of China, the domination of the European colonial powers, the Japanese 'Co-Prosperity Sphere' or the United States' strategy of containing Communism.

Strategic power can change the course of history. The long period of colonialism did not, however, for it merely divided South-east Asia along different lines, so that the Asian states become proxy rivals for their metropolitan powers: Indonesia looking to Holland; Indo-China to France; Singapore, Malaysia and Burma to Britain; and the Philippines to Spain and then to the United States. The later attempts of the United States to fuse the regional states into a bloc united in opposition to China (and to Communism) failed because some of the most significant states — Indonesia, Malaysia and Singapore (not to mention India, if we go as far afield as Pakistan for one new nation which *did* respond) — declined to join. The result was that no tradition of regional response has emerged to replace the waning, discredited tradition of hegemony.

Nor is there an external balance of power which might hover benevolently over South-east Asia, while the connective tissues of regional co-operation were formed. The great powers are disengaged at present, but their interests are so divergent that it is difficult to be confident that there exists between them a 'field' of unity which could be exploited to create equilibrium. The prospect of a balance of power in South-east Asia has intrigued observers, since in proclaiming the Guam Doctrine in 1969, subsequently refined as the Nixon Doctrine in 1971, the United States has indicated that, while honouring her existing treaties and continuing to provide a nuclear shield, she could not be expected to support her allies with manpower in the event of conventional aggression or internal subversion. Writers have imaginatively constructed intersecting triangles of different qualities of power and have suspended mobiles with forces interacting at different levels and angles to demonstrate the variety of power and influence available in the major states concerned: the United States, the Soviet Union, China and Japan. However, while diplomatic unity is emerging among these four powers, in the sense that they perceive and treat each other more or less as equals, this consensus reflects, as yet, only a phase in their relations. The apparent abandonment of hostility between the United States and China, for example, has not yet been tested by new positions. In the absence of new policies or strategies, the four powers have adopted a wait-and-see attitude, without quite abandoning old policies or proposing new ones. What we have, in other words, is not so much a balance as a 'pause' or 'hiatus'.

It would seem unlikely, therefore, that the strategy of containment, as practised by the United States against China, can be transferred somehow to a lower gear for use against Vietnam, or that a regional balance of power, based on the shifting weight of a group of countries consciously rectifying imbalance, will emerge from the present circumstances of South-east Asia. The problem is one of relating an external balance, or the lack of it, to an internal balance, or the lack of it, bearing in mind also that security alliances in Southeast Asia must deal more with political instability, subversion and territorial attrition than with identifying adversaries and offering a credible deterrent to them.

Some general observations about South-east Asian security can be stated more explicitly:

(1) No power or group of powers, whether the combination is external or regional or both, can expect to dominate South-east Asia in peacetime. This is partly the result of the present divided nature of the area — a power or combination of powers that might expect to dominate mainland South-east Asia would be resisted by another power or combination of powers in the archipelago states — but it is also an effect of the checks and balances applied by the external powers to each other. None of them is disposed to allow others to dominate South-east Asia. It sometimes appears that China and Japan would be prepared to allow the United States to do so, and in the case of Japan this is probably true at present. However, it may be true only so far as the conservatives continue to hold power in Tokyo, and even in conservative circles there is a wariness about relying on the United States. In addition, enticements for the United States to 'stay' in South-east Asia must be assessed against a background of American unwillingness, after Vietnam, to give South-east Asia a high priority. A plea for the United States not to go too far away is different from asking her to take a dominant role.

It is sometimes said that Japan and China, because they are Asian powers, have 'natural' rights in South-east Asia. This is not the view of the region itself. Japan's right to a 'sphere of influence' in South-east Asia is not taken seriously, even in Japan, while she has no external military capability. Economic dominance is possible but, as already noted, this would expose Japan's political and military weakness. A view that Chinese influence is more acceptable now in South-east Asia than that of other external powers is not borne out by the attitudes of Djakarta and Hanoi, nor by the suspicion of Chinese minorities by South-east Asia's ethnic majorities. The commercial nature of South-east Asia's links with the outside world and its importance as an international thoroughfare would make Chinese dominance difficult, although a slow growth of benign Chinese influence can be expected.

(2) The position of Singapore and Malaysia as the pivots of the former British security arrangements, and of Thailand and the Philippines as mainstays of an American presence, can no longer be maintained. The two most important countries, which were excluded from the security arrangements for the region in the 1950s and 1960s, are Indonesia and Vietnam.

These are stronger and more ambitious states than the four which provided the basis for Anglo-American hegemony, with a correspondingly less pliant attitude to outsiders.

(3) The main guarantee of peace in South-east Asia, as in the Asia–Pacific region generally, lies in the absence of conflict between the four powers, the United States, the Soviet Union, China and Japan. If conflict or rivalry between these four powers becomes intense, South-east Asia will suffer as the great powers move and manoeuvre in the pursuit of major interests to which South-east Asia is peripheral. On the other hand, conflict between South-east Asian states, if unattended by the great powers, is unlikely to affect the stability of the region as a whole. South-east Asia thus has a stake in the success of detente between the United States and the Soviet Union, in accommodation between the United States and China, and in the satisfaction of Japan's economic and political interests without conflict. On the evidence of its history and its geopolitical situation, South-east Asia cannot insulate itself from great-power relationships.

These observations point to continued great-power involvement in South-east Asia without, however, indicating how this will or can contribute to its security. It is difficult at present to see how new forms of security can emerge, if these would require military arrangements with the great powers, yet it is also plain that the dream of some South-east Asian nationalists, that everything would be fine if the external powers were removed, is not about to be realized either. The essence of the security question is that no counter exists to the power, actual and potential, of Vietnam, which is indisputably South-east Asian and nationalist. A counter is needed because her fellow South-east Asians have based themselves on non-Communist, even anti-Communist, forms of society which they fear, in the absence of their protectors, they will not now be able to sustain.

Time is needed for the ASEAN states, especially Indonesia, to become accustomed to the shift of power to Vietnam and to make more precise assessments of the kind of threat, if any, Vietnam offers to the stability of South-east Asia. If an organization for Asia existed on the model of the Organization of African Unity (OAU) or the Organization of American States (OAS) it would no doubt be the forum for discussion of ways of reconciling the new Vietnam with the old South-east Asia but, significantly, no such organization exists. There are probably too many powers in Asia. The OAU works because it excludes only a few African states whereas many important Asian states might have to be excluded from any Asian organization. The OAS works because there is only one dominating power (the United States) whereas there might be too many states of the second rank attempting to dominate any Asian organization. Proposals for something even as loose as an Asia–Pacific forum by leaders like Mr Whitlam and Mrs Gandhi have foundered on the issue of who, indeed, is in Asia, let alone 'Asian', and Mr Brezhnev's collective security proposal for Asia has been coolly received, partly because of suspicion of Soviet motives, but partly because it is being promoted by a power whose claim to be 'Asian' is no greater than that, say, of the United States.

Time may be available. Vietnam has a long task of rehabilitation and reconstruction ahead and has problems to attend to in her relations with the Soviet Union, China and Cambodia. The future of Thailand could severely test relations between Vietnam and the ASEAN states but the issue has been raised too soon after the Vietnam War to stimulate genuine interest in an anti-Communist common front on Thailand's behalf. The process of disintegration in Thailand is likely to be slow. While the case for a classic neutrality is hard to make in present circumstances in South-east Asia, a mixture of the two options — to divide the region into its mainland and archipelago components, the mainland group comprising the states of former Indo-China, and the archipelago group comprising the ASEAN countries or regional neutrality as in the Malaysian proposal for a zone of peace, freedom and neutrality

(ZOPFAN) — could emerge in time, as the ASEAN states become more confident that, in the absence of external powers, they can reach a *modus vivendi* with Vietnam. The outcome could be a novel form of detente.

European detente began as the essentially strategic concept of two super-powers, whose armed forces, with those of their allies, divide Europe. South-east Asian detente would be more complex. It would be intra-regional, requiring an understanding essentially between Vietnam and Indonesia, but it would also require a form of detente between the four external powers, either formal or tacit, that they would not interfere militarily within the region. A model could be the Chinese anti-hegemony clause, which is directed against the Soviet Union but could be adapted by the South-east Asians for use against all the external powers. Probably, however, a process will emerge by trial and error, as it did in Europe, requiring pressures from within (such as the efforts of Willy Brandt) as well as calculations from without. South-east Asia is well sited for the test, as it is an area where the four powers have almost equal status, although differing widely in their respective economic, political and military weight. This gives a kind of unity, if largely diplomatic, to their presence and to their acknowledgment of each other. It is also an area where local diversity is strong. The popular slogan 'unity in diversity', which is useful to cover situations where an enforced unity would mean no unity at all, would apply, in the sense that if the external powers were unified in their disposition not to take up dominant positions in the region — and the analysis of this paper suggests that their interests do not stand in the way of such consensus — variety and diversity in South-east Asia, as well as stability, could be maintained. But it is, admittedly, a sophisticated idea and statesmanship, both inside and outside the region, is not noticeably active on its behalf at the present moment.

However, the absence of immediate answers may be reassuring, if we recall the lack of success of instant solutions in the past. The conditions for spectacular diplomacy are not present, and forcing the issue could be harmful. Although diplomacy could have an important role to play in the security of South-east Asia in the future, it must first encourage the right conditions — a 'balance of confidence' in the region, so that the states of South-east Asia do not fear each other, and a more deliberate appreciation by the external powers of the benefits of peaceful relations between themselves. The argument for time is not, therefore, an argument for leaving things alone. It is an argument for consciously encouraging a relaxation of tension in the belief that, calmly examined, the interests of states in the region and the powers outside it can be harmonized.

Other trouble spots are pre-occupying the great powers. Europe itself, the Middle East and southern Africa are more pressing, as are Korean and Taiwan in the Asia–Pacific region. Indeed, after a couple of decades on the front burner, South-east Asia sometimes seems to have been removed by many governments not to the back burner, but into cold storage. We can be sure, however, that it will not remain there indefinitely: both history and geography will see to that.

NOTES

1. SEATO was dismantled on 30 June 1977, but signatories used the occasion to note that they remained parties to the Manila Treaty, which would continue. The Australian Government, for example, said the Treaty remained 'an expression of the determination of member states that the countries of this region should be free to determine their own destinies and plan their own futures free from outside interference'. The Manila Treaty is important to Thailand which, unlike the Philippines, has no other security treaty with the United States. Article IV, Paragraph 1, states that each party will, in the event of aggression by means of armed attack in the treaty area, 'act to meet the common danger in accordance with its

constitutional processes'. Paragraph 2 states that the parties 'shall consult immediately in order to agree on the measures which should be taken for the common defence'.

2. The difficulties in applying 'balance of power' concepts to Asia are examined by Coral Bell in *The Asian Balance of Power: A Comparison with European Precedents*, Adelphi Paper No. 44 (London: IISS, 1968). See also Michio Royama, *The Asian Balance of Power: A Japanese View*, Adelphi Paper No. 42 (London: IISS, 1967).

64.

IS ASEAN A SECURITY ORGANIZATION?

MICHAEL LEIFER

The Association of South East Asian Nations was conceived as a means of promoting intra-regional reconciliation in the wake of Indonesia's confrontation of Malaysia. Its founders exhibited also an interest in the management of regional order. At the formation of ASEAN in August 1967, the Governments of Thailand, Malaysia, Singapore, Indonesia and the Philippines committed themselves "to accelerate the economic growth, social progress and cultural development in the region". This commitment assumed greater initial prominence than the promotion of "regional peace and stability". But the underlying concern intensified concurrently with changes in the balance of external influences bearing on South East Asia exemplified above all by the direction of American policy. In consequence, ASEAN is best contemplated as a security organization even though it does not possess the form or the structure of an alliance and its corporate activity has been devoted in the main to regional economic cooperation. This paradox is a function of the perceptions of threat held by the individual governments of the association and of other limits to the degree of cooperation between them. It is the intention of this article to explore the paradox and to explain why

ASEAN cannot assume alliance form or undertake activities which are normally associated with security organizations.

SIGNIFICANCE OF THE BALI SUMMIT

It is some indication of the limited measure of progress on the part of ASEAN that more than eight years elapsed from its advent before the heads of government of its member states deemed it appropriate to convene a common meeting. This meeting took place in February 1976 on the island of Bali in Indonesia and was prompted by the shared sense of anxiety at the radical political changes which had occurred throughout Indo-China in the preceding year. At the Bali Summit, the prime common interest of the members of the association was articulated explicitly within a joint Declaration of ASEAN Concord. The five heads of government maintained that:

> The stability of each member state and of the ASEAN region is an essential contribution to international peace and security. Each member state resolves to eliminate threats posed by subversion to its stability, thus strengthening national and ASEAN resilience.

Reprinted in abridged form from "The Paradox of ASEAN: A Security Organisation without the Structure of an Alliance", *The Round Table*, no. 271 (July 1978), pp. 261–68, by permission of the author and *The Round Table*, London.

The significance of this statement was that it demonstrated the common perception of threat held by the five governments. Thus, although an earlier commitment by ASEAN Foreign Ministers in Kuala Lumpur in November 1971 "to secure the recognition of South-East Asia as a Zone of Peace, Freedom and Neutrality" was reaffirmed, provision for security through the exclusion of extra-regional involvement had become a secondary consideration to containing internal challenge of an ideological kind. Indeed, much of what the ASEAN states have striven to achieve in economic cooperation has been justified in terms of security. Thus, although its members have engaged in cooperative enterprise directed against protectionist practice by industrialized states, a common denominator of interest has been a desire for mutual protection on the part of conservative governments which wish to uphold the political status quo. This close link between economic and social advance and political stability in the region was enunciated in the final communiqué of the second meeting of ASEAN heads of government which convened in Kuala Lumpur in August 1977 to commemorate the tenth anniversary of the formation of the association.

The *raison d'etre* of ASEAN has been well indicated by a Yugoslav observer who has maintained that "The identity and closeness of many political and economic interests of these countries stemming from the similarity of their socio-political orders as well as their more or less outspoken hostility towards the national-liberation movements in Vietnam, Laos and Cambodia provided the cohesive element and basis for their association".[1] This observation requires some qualification because from the advent of the communist governments in Indonesia, the ASEAN states ceased their "out-spoken hostility" and welcomed the new administrations in Vietnam, Laos and Cambodia. This attempt to face up to political facts has, however, not changed the sense of common identity and outlook of the ASEAN states or the common concerns from which they derive.

Paradoxically, the nature of perceived threats as well as of the capability of the ASEAN states has meant that there are major obstacles to cooperation to serve common interests. One such obstacle arises from the fact that the security threat is posed in such a way that it is neither practical nor politic for the members of ASEAN to contemplate an alliance role. A significant impediment to alliance formation is that while the five governments share a sense of common uncertainty arising from regional circumstances, they have been unable to engender a prerequisite consensus by identifying a tangible external threat against which it might be possible to concert and mobilize countervailing military power. For example, one might contrast the front line outlook displayed by the government of Thailand with the sense of maritime insulation of its counterpart in the Philippines, despite the current dispute with Vietnam and China over the possession of islands in the Spratly Archipelago. Indeed, this divergence in perspective was very marked during the tenure of office of the former Prime Minister of Thailand, Thanin Kraivichien, who was obliged to take account of alternative attitudes to security when he visited the capitals of the member states. On his departure from the Philippines in January 1977 after a tour of these capitals, President Marcos maintained, "We pinpointed insurgency and not external aggression as the principal problem confronting our respective countries in the immediate future".

COPING WITH BORDER PROBLEMS

Given the obstacles to multilateral military cooperation within ASEAN, the members of the association seek to meet their individual security needs on *ad hoc* bases outside of its formal structure. Apart from exchanges of information between intelligence communities and occasional joint military exercises between two and at the most three member states, substantive military cooperation has taken place along common borders straddled by insurgent activity. Indeed, bilateral military cooperation to this end between Malaysia and Thailand, and Malaysia and Indonesia, preceded the establishment of ASEAN in August 1967. Cooperation has taken the form of combined operations such as those launched from January 1977 by Malaysian and Thai security forces against the fractured military wing of the Malayan Communist Party. But provision for security of this kind is not an identifiable function of ASEAN. Nor is the association linked in any way with those security arrangements of a formal kind distinguished by external powers' participation which involve Malaysia, Singapore and the Philippines. Nonetheless, ASEAN is best regarded as a security organization, given the shared sense of priorities of its member governments. But they are only able to give attention to apprehensions which they hold in common through displays of political solidarity and attempts at harmonization of policy as well as through economic cooperation. Alliance association is out of the question.

PREVENTING RADICAL INTERNAL POLITICAL CHANGE

The nature of ASEAN has been discussed in terms of the limitations placed on the fulfilment of its unstated function as a security organization. Any such organization based on an intergovernmental structure will tend to be less than cohesive in the absence of an identifiable common threat to its members. Such a common threat does not manifest itself in external form in South East Asia and in internal form varies very much with individual circumstances which do not necessarily lend themselves to joint military action. In this respect, the limitations of ASEAN as a security organization are an essential product of its nature and it would be unreasonable to expect spectacular success in regional cooperation from such an association.

ASEAN is nonetheless a security organization because its members share a common interest in preventing radical internal political change. Indeed, the five governments which established the association in August 1967 bear a resemblance in outlook and priorities to those which adhered to the Act of the Holy Alliance drafted by Tzar Alexander I at the Congress of Vienna in 1815. The ASEAN governments seek to promote mutual security by consultation and cooperation wherever practical and also to engage where possible in conflict avoidance, exemplified by the statement by President Marcos in Kuala Lumpur in August 1977 that he would be taking steps to withdraw the territorial claim of the Philippines to Sabah.

The rationale of the collective exercise is that by promoting harmony within the walls of ASEAN, the member states will be more able to devote their energies to the cause of internal economic development, while external powers will be prevented from exploiting regional tensions to their own advantage. The association is moved by a belief that political instability is indivisible among its members and that political stability attained in one state will contribute to the attainment of such a circumstance in the others. Its goal is the realization of a condition described by the Indonesian Government as national resilience which, in aggregate form, is expressed as regional resilience. The progress of ASEAN towards this end has been limited rather than outstanding and has come about primarily from individual rather than collective endeavour. The very nature of the association and of the problems which confront it serve to ensure only modest achievement.

NOTE

1. M. Zarkovic "The Revival of ASEAN", *Review of International Affairs*, October 5, 1977.

65.

ASEAN AND THE INDOCHINA CONFLICT

CHAN HENG CHEE

With the outbreak of the triangular war between Vietnam, Kampuchea and China, the inherently unstable post-Vietnam regional strategic context has been charged with even greater tension as the 'ominous' was seen to have taken place. The changing balance of big power presence thrust the Soviet Union and the PRC into a prominence that was not traditional in the region, in the wake of a US strategic retreat in Asia; and each is seeking to extend its influence by backing an antagonist in the Vietnam-Kampuchean conflict. The non-communist states of ASEAN, which courageously attempted to normalize relations with Vietnam to derive mutually beneficial ties, now respond with greater cynicism and caution; this mood is reflected in the hardening of position towards Vietnam since her army invaded Kampuchean soil. The easing of the crises and the return of trust to relations between ideologically opposed systems, seem a long way from realization and it would appear Southeast Asia faces a period of continued destabilisation for the short and possibly middle term prospect.

In the unfolding post-war situation of 1975, ASEAN has not found it easy to define a satisfactory relationship with Vietnam. Just as the communist state is critically evaluating the sincerity of the overtures of ASEAN, the non-communist states fear the intransigence and duplicity of the communists. In any case, a revolutionary regime ideologically committed at least in rhetoric, to advancing a change in the conservative status quo, possessing the largest and best military forces in Southeast Asia, not to mention the five billion dollars-worth of captured US weapons and equipment, is a strong candidate for regional domination and an uneasy prospect to abide. But ASEAN's response to and relations with Vietnam have been restrained by the fact she does not speak with one voice or one mind on how to deal with questions of regional stability or security. As a regional organization, it is perhaps understandable that there are areas of differences and areas of divergence in foreign policy outlooks arising from diverse cultures, history, geography and internal political dynamics. Collective decision-making in ASEAN understandably is a tentative and cautious matter.

The Philippines, geographically distant from the Indochina sub-continent, does not share the same degree of involvement in or anxiety about security threats posed by the newly established communist power as the adjacent

Reprinted in abridged form from "The Interests and Role of ASEAN in the Indochina Conflict", in *Indochina and Problems of Security and Stability in Southeast Asia*, edited by Khien Theeravit and MacAlister Brown (Bangkok: Chulalongkorn University Press, 1981), pp. 184–96, by permission of the author and the Institute of Asian Studies, Chulalongkorn University.

mainland and peninsular states. Furthermore, her security has been for the past three decades ensured by the presence of two major US bases at Clark Air Field and at Subic Bay, and though there is today some doubt over the commitment of interests, the bases nevertheless provide the psychological and symbolic assurances that can dull perceptions of threat.

Indonesia, to a lesser extent than the Philippines, is also not imminently affected by developments in Indochina, insulated as she is by her archipelagic status, but the populous, resource rich and politically ambitious nation whose independence struggle has been one of the most chequered and heroic in recent Southeast Asian history, apart from the Vietnamese, nurtures aspirations to regional leadership and undoubtedly views Vietnam as the closest rival. Her view of Vietnam can best be paraphrased as ambivalent with different views emanating from different political quarters in the country. Ideologically, she has proudly maintained through Sukarno's era an independent and active foreign policy independent of great power alliance and active in the struggle against neocolonialism.[1] Her most radical phase was when Sukarno sought to establish a Jakarta-Peking-Pyongyang-Hanoi axis and a front of NEFOS against OLDEFOS when he pulled out of the UN. Her Foreign Minister, Dr. Mochtar Kusumaatmadja in an interview with *Far Eastern Economic Review* in December 1978 expressed the sense of affinity and admiration that Indonesia bore towards Vietnam because of their similar long struggles for independence.[2] Under the New Order, the 'independent and active' credo has still been upheld as policy though the interpretation is now elastic. Since 1975 the Indonesians have leaned heavily on US military aid and purchases, although their view of security publicly is one which emphasises 'national resilience: which is the condition of ensuring domestic political stability through economic development and military preparation. In Indonesian eyes the major source of destabilisation in the region in the long term is in fact posed by the PRC and not Vietnam,

and the military regime's involvement with the PKI and GESTAPU has coloured its view of the Chinese role in the internal politics of the country and therefore of their aims. The latent ethnic antagonisms are further buttressed by contact with the domestic minority and it is not remarkable that the government should hold a more benign view of Vietnam, seeing the latter as a check on future Chinese ambitions.

Malaysia has been the forward strategist for improved relations between ASEAN and Vietnam. Her anti-communist stand internally did not prevent her initiation of a proposal for a zone of peace, freedom and neutrality to be underwritten by the US, the Soviet Union and the PRC as a means to reduce external interference in the peace and stability of the region. Her response to Vietnam after April 1975 has been consistently one of conciliation and in line with her new orientation towards neutrality and her lately acquired self-perception as an innovator in foreign policy. She casts herself as the bridge between Vietnam and ASEAN. It would appear that Malaysia's underlying distrust of Chinese intentions fed by her domestic experience with an insurgent communist movement backed by the CCP and the competition of ethnic forces for political and economic power has predisposed her to favour Vietnam as the counterweight to an active Chinese role in the long term.

Singapore, the smallest of the ASEAN states, sees the answer to regional order in a multipolar presence, relying on the self interests of each big power to check the expanding tendencies of the other. She has been the most articulate advocate in ASEAN to counsel a return of US presence to Southeast Asia following the American retreat after the Vietnam war; but even Singapore has not clarified within what treaty or alliance framework she requests this presence. Currently, the Singapore leadership views the greatest threat to international peace and security in the region to be the Soviet Union, which, it argues, possesses both the will and the means to seek world domination.[3] It is as a Soviet surrogate that

Vietnam is considered an imminent threat to the region. Her attitude towards Vietnam at the end of the war was cautious, awaiting signals on the kinds of policies Vietnam would adopt economically and militarily, reserving judgement on Vietnamese intentions. The Vietnamese propaganda war against ASEAN was not as generously overlooked as it was in the other ASEAN capitals and the Vietnamese invasion of Kampuchea in Singapore's view vindicated her hardline position. Singapore's assessment of the threat to regional peace, whilst it nails Vietnam and the Soviet union at the moment, does not altogether dismiss China's potential for destabilisation. In an interview with *Asiaweek (March 28 1980)*, S. Dhanabalan, the Minister for Foreign Affairs, in answer to a question, whether ASEAN saw China as a long term threat, replied, "in the sense that we don't want to be dominated by anyone. China is also communist. I don't think we can forget that. And we cannot forget what the long term interest of the communist philosophy is . . . . It just happens that at this present juncture we happen to be on the same side . . . . It doesn't mean we're on China's side or that they are on our side."

Without a doubt, Thailand lies in the most vulnerable position after Kampuchea, should Vietnam's ambitions vault beyond her national boundaries. Thai suspicions and even antagonisms towards Vietnam have their roots in history. The competition for domination among the myriad of succeeding kingdoms and empires over mainland Southeast Asia eventually left Vietnam and Thailand the major contestants for power and influence. This competition continued with each side competing for buffer states and each side supporting dissident groups to subvert the security and political control of the other. When the Thais assisted the US war effort against Hanoi she was not simply fighting an ideological war to preserve a way of life, she was also holding a traditional rival at bay. When it became clear that the Vietnamese victory could not be denied, Thailand turned to cultivate the

PRC as the countervailing power to check Vietnamese influence. However, her sensitive geopolitical position enforces a complicated and more subtle set of policies towards Vietnam and initially Kampuchea, than is found in other ASEAN states. The Thai approach to her communist neighbours has shown a mixture of restraint, conciliation and toughness, though conciliation and accommodation were postures more obviously identified with her civilian politicians. The time-tested response of increased militarisation and reliance on US backing is the military regime's approach to security problems.

These differences aside, ASEAN clearly shares a common concern with security even though the members are not totally agreed on what constitutes the main threats to the peace and stability of the region; and the regional body seeks to realise the same objective which is the maintenance of a non-communist, free-market conservative socio-political order. It is committed to deny prospects of growth to insurgent communist movements, within their respective national territories and within the region, through economic cooperation which its member states believe will enhance individual state resilience and consequently regional resilience. It can also be said that collectively ASEAN does not want to see the region dominated by any external power and is most anxiously concerned not to be caught in the vortex of a Sino-Soviet conflict, both of which conditions would destroy the prospects of building stable independent political systems.

Between the second and third Indochina wars, ASEAN/Vietnam relations improved when Deputy Foreign Minister Phan Hien visited four of the five ASEAN countries in 1976 and paved the way to dialogue. Mutual suspicions were not dispelled by the initiative, for shortly after the visit Vietnamese-ASEAN interests crossed at the Fifth Non-Aligned Summit Conference in Colombo. Laos supported by Vietnam succeeded in blocking any reference in the political declaration of the summit conference to the Kuala Lumpur version of the

Southeast Asia Zone of Peace, Freedom and Neutrality. Instead, Laos called upon the conference to support the struggle of the people of Southeast Asia against neo-colonialism and to assist the region to become "truly independent, pacific and neutral", and thereby provoked a strong reaction from the Singapore Prime Minister, Lee Kuan Yew, who wondered which countries of Southeast Asia did not enjoy "genuine" independence and whether the communist powers intended to assist them to become 'genuine'. In hindsight, it can be said that the new Vietnamese policy to open dialogue with ASEAN was prompted by the brewing competition between China and Vietnam, and, in anticipation of a major showdown, each side launched a diplomatic offensive to line up support for her cause.

In January 1978, the Vietnamese Foreign Minister, Nguyen Duy Trinh, visited all the ASEAN states except Singapore (to demonstrate displeasure with the republic for her refusal to return the hijackers of an Air Vietnam DC-3 who had killed 2 crew members), and by the middle of the year Vietnam clearly dropped her hostility to the regional grouping. In July, Phan Hien in Tokyo recognised ASEAN as a 'genuine regional organisation for economic cooperation' dropping the charge that ASEAN was a militaristic tool of US imperialism.[4] Pham Van Dong's visit to all the ASEAN states in August and September 1978 marked the high point of ASEAN-Vietnam relations, although his offer to sign non-aggression treaties with ASEAN-states met with a cool response. Again in hindsight, the Vietnamese obviously wished to reassure ASEAN of her peaceful intentions in view of her decisions to enter into a treaty alliance with the Soviet Union and to invade Kampuchea. Indeed, Pham Van Dong expressedly gave assurance to Thailand and Malaysia that Vietnam would not support insurgent movements to overthrow the established governments. With the signing of the Soviet-Vietnamese Treaty of Friendship and Cooperation followed by the December-January lightning strike across the border on Kampuchea, the incipient trend towards accommodation between the communist and the non-communist states of Southeast Asia halted.

NOTES

1. Franklin B. Weinstein, *Indonesian Foreign Policy and the Dilemma of Dependence. From Sukarno to Soeharto.* (Ithaca: Cornell University Press, 1976).
2. *Far Eastern Economic Review*, Vol. 102, No. 50, December 17, 1978.
3. The Singapore position has been eloquently put by S. Rajaratnam on a number of occasions. For a sample see *The Mirror*, Vol. 14, No. 33, August 14, 1978; *The Mirror*, Vol. 15, No. 18, April 30, 1979; *The Mirror*, Vol. 16, No. 8, April 15, 1980; *Far Eastern Economic Review*, Vol. 105, No. 34, June 24, 1977.
4. *Far Eastern Economic Review*, Vol. 96, No. 25, June 24, 1977.

66.

THE LIMITS OF
CONFLICT RESOLUTION IN
SOUTHEAST ASIA

JUWONO SUDARSONO

THE MATRIX OF CONFLICT

From both the theoretical and practical points of view Southeast Asia ranks as one of the more complex regions, resulting in difficulty in establishing conceptual, much less policy-relevant, security arrangements. Neither the United States nor the Soviet Union regards the entire region as an area of vital security interest. Their marginal economic and military involvements absolve them from pursuing any sustained, concerted, or coherent effort in the manner that Central Europe provides a stabilizing framework, leading to the institutionalized security interests through NATO and the Warsaw Pact forces. Of the two other major powers, neither Japan nor China possesses overwhelming political *and* economic preponderance over the entire region, a preponderance essential in devising a durable security framework commensurate with its short-term and long-term interests.

It is this marginality and asymmetry of major power interest in the region that makes attempts at regional or comprehensive solutions difficult at best. A distribution of relative indifference among major powers can, to some extent, work to the advantage of regional powers that are seeking an autonomous solution to the security of the indigenous states. But this presumes that the regional states themselves see some commonality in extraregional sources of security threats.

Indeed, the very fragility of most of the Southeast Asian states (and, no less importantly, of their governments) in turn often calls for periodic interventions by extraregional powers to secure the survival of assorted regimes within the region. Coupled with attendant problems of socioeconomic development and of domestic political management, a circle of conflict arises and creates a momentum of its own, one which neither major power nor the indigenous states themselves are able to control.

The asymmetry of relationships among the major powers is compounded by a balance of weakness within regional states. Not one of the Southeast Asian states is likely to be able to bear its full imprint on the entire region. Vietnam since 1975 and particularly since 1979 may have achieved de facto primacy over the Indochina region, and the ASEAN states after the Bali Summit of early 1976 may claim to some semblance of influence to determine the parameters of international politics in the

Reprinted from Juwono Sudarsono, "Security in Southeast Asia: The Circle of Conflict", in *Economic, Political and Security Issues in Southeast Asia in the 1980s*, edited by Robert A. Scalapino and Jusuf Wanandi (Berkeley, Calif.: Institute of East Asian Studies, University of California, 1982), pp. 63–68, by permission of the Institute of East Asian Studies, University of California.

maritime portion of the region. But neither the Indochinese nor the ASEAN grouping is likely to be able to claim full authority over the entire area.

The conflicting ebb and flow of major power involvement, the diverse strategic outlook of the Southeast Asian states in regard to the form and source of extraregional threats, and, not least, the differing priorities in economic development efforts defy attempts to achieve an immediate and practical solution to the current crises in the region.

The *fait accompli* which the Vietnamese presented to the region in 1978-1979 heightens the complexity of the regional security situation at present. In addition to the interplay of major power involvement, regional security interests are defined by individual countries of the region according to varying levels of perception and interpretation. At times even a single country's security perception changes markedly with the reshuffling of the composition of its government. Often the style of a particular leader or of an important faction can substantially change previously agreed understandings, necessitating perhaps a fundamental reexamination of past initiatives and commitments.

THE REGIONAL APPROACH

First attempts at unraveling the crisis precipitated by the Vietnamese occupation of Kampuchea were inspired by a common diplomatic perception among the ASEAN states that the *fait accompli* in Kampuchea was unacceptable on grounds of principle. Throughout most of 1979 the ASEAN states, with the support of the United States, Australia, and New Zealand, condemned Vietnam for its invasion of Kampuchea and its attendant policy of evicting mainly ethnic Chinese nationals from the country. Diplomatic victory was achieved in November 1979 when the U.N. General Assembly called for the withdrawal of foreign troops in Kampuchea. Indonesian perceptions of the nature of the problem (and to the manner of its resolution)

changed in early 1980. Apart from its empathy toward Vietnamese revolutionary achievements, the Indonesian government began to emphasize the need to reevaluate the main source of threat to the region in the long term.

Despite outward appearances of ASEAN solidarity or common outlook, it was clear that Indonesia saw China as the greater threat to regional order. While Thailand and Singapore regard Vietnam as nothing more than a proxy for the Soviet Union, Indonesia (and to some extent Malaysia) tended to accept some of the more political as well as military justifications for the Vietnamese intervention in Kampuchea. In effect, this was the beginning not only of a reconsideration of past events in Indochina of the 1977-1978 period (particularly as regards Chinese provocations toward Hanoi through the Pol Pot government) but, more importantly, of the desirable course of diplomatic action to break out of the Kampuchean logjam.

The Kuantan principle, while admonishing the Vietnamese for their action in Kampuchea, in effect constituted an attempt by the Indonesian and Malaysian governments to seek a more regional approach in resolving the crisis. Perhaps it may have inadvertently inspired later counterproposals by the Indochinese governments to construct a dialogue between ASEAN and the three Indochinese states rather than to broaden the issue by encompassing extraregional powers.

Apart from differences regarding the main source of threat to the region, the Indonesians and Malaysians also differed with the Thais and Singaporeans in respect to resisting the Heng Samrin government in Phnom Penh. While Singapore often spoke openly of a strategy of attrition to bleed the Vietnamese, Indonesia and Malaysia felt inclined to consider with sympathy Vietnam's fears in respect to Chinese threats toward it from three sources: the Sino-Vietnam border, the Kampuchean-Vietnam border during the Pol Pot regime's control over Kampuchea, and the role of the ethnic Chinese in the Vietnamese economy.

The Kuantan principle almost immediately

lost its luster in the wake of the Vietnamese incursion into Thailand in June 1980. Indonesia and Malaysia were subsequently put into a defensive position, and ASEAN's diplomatic unity was regained with the repeated call for the withdrawal of foreign troops from Kampuchea at the U.N. General Assembly meeting in October 1980. The meeting also called for the holding of an international conference as part of a continuous effort to achieve a comprehensive solution to the Kampuchean crisis. In effect, the holding of the conference in July 1981 marked the formal end on the part of the Indonesians to seek a more regional-centered solution.

THE COMPREHENSIVE APPROACH

Despite the failure of the Indonesians and Malaysians to convince their ASEAN colleagues of their more sympathetic approach toward Vietnam and despite their acquiescence to the formal declaration of the U.N. Conference on Kampuchea, the Indonesians continued to maintain sporadic dialogue with the government in Hanoi. The decision to continue the dialogue with Hanoi in part reflects the previous emphasis on the nature of the long-term threat to Southeast Asia from China. But in part it also stems from a growing realization that a comprehensive and internationalized (as opposed to a region-based) approach to the Kampuchean question brings more complications to the issue in question. By recognizing the legitimate interests of all parties concerned, the conference approach institutionalizes the essentially extraregional character of the Sino-Soviet conflict as a substantially more impelling issue than the presence of Vietnamese troops in Kampuchea.

While recognizing the fact that one of the more important reasons for Vietnamese intervention in Kampuchea was its growing enmity with China, Indonesians believe that two extraregional dimensions were too difficult a task to handle by all conflicting parties concerned. In addition, resort to a comprehensive approach, even if it places priority on an understanding reached among Southeast Asian nations, necessarily reduces the prime responsibility of the Southeast Asian states in initiating breakthroughs involving matters of concern to the region. To the Indonesians and Malaysians, the comprehensive effort smacks of a great power imposition of a security arrangement that serves primarily the interests of the United States, China, and Japan.

In deference to Thailand, however, both Indonesia and Malaysia for the moment seem to be willing to give the comprehensive approach a chance. In the meantime, both governments (or at least elements within the respective governments) out of choice and opportunity will be eager for a more propitious moment for another round of an intraregional-centered understanding.

The Malaysian foreign minister recently warned China that its strategy of attempting to bleed the Vietnamese into submission was foolish and bound to fail. Coming as it did prior to deliberations at the United Nations on the Kampuchean question, it may portend further evidence of a two-track diplomatic-cum-military approach evidently pursued by Indonesia and Malaysia, on the one hand, and the unified ASEAN stand, on the other.

INDONESIAN VIEWS ON THE CONFLICT

Indonesia's clear preference for a regional approach rests on three premises, which differ distinctly from the underlying principles governing the objectives of the conference approach. First, Indonesia's view on the motives of Vietnamese intervention into Kampuchea differs from that of Thailand and Singapore. Although it cannot openly endorse the installation of a government through the use of armed force in a neighboring country, most Indonesian observers view the Pol Pot-Ieng Sary government as having been overtly provocative toward a nation which, from an Indonesian point of view, has strong claims and a legitimate position of dominance within the Indochina region.

In addition, whatever misgivings China may have over Vietnam's treatment of its ethnic Chinese minority, Indonesians view with sympathy Vietnamese apprehension over the degree of control that the ethnic Chinese have over the commercial economy. Finally, in strategic terms a strong Vietnam within a consolidated Indochinese front would act as an important buffer against Chinese expansionism in the long term. Indeed, concern over the future of Chinese conventional and nuclear capability, helped by current U.S. and Japanese diplomatic and economic support (particularly after the August 1978 Sino-Japanese Treaty of Peace and Friendship and the recognition of the Beijing government in January 1979), has underscored Indonesian concerns over the future of regional resilience, one of Indonesia's principal tenets of national defense.

Viewed from Indonesia's defense perspective of concentric circles emanating outward against extraregional threats, a convergence of interests between ASEAN and the Indochinese states would constitute a formidable bulwark against China as well as insurance against potential domestic fifth columnists.

Understandably, the Indonesian perspective is viewed with strong suspicion and alarm in Thailand. Thailand's traditional rivalry with Vietnam for influence over Laos and Kampuchea has in the past aligned it with China for precisely these reasons. Thailand was also fully aware that ASEAN unity could only go as far as concerted diplomatic efforts; the combined forces of the ASEAN countries remain no match for the battled-hardened Vietnamese army.

Whereas Indonesia had strong reservations about China's punitive action toward Vietnam in February-March 1979, Thailand was relieved that China's limited attack forced the Vietnamese to think twice about possible consequences of a second front should it contemplate moving its troops well beyond Indochina. Thailand was also relieved to note that there were limits

to the Soviet support of Vietnamese regional ambitions when the Soviet Union only provided verbal support to Vietnam during the Chinese attack.

Since in the view of Thailand only China retains any semblance of effective deterrent against Vietnamese aggression westward, there are also important discrepancies in respect to Thai and Indonesian tactics in regard to the Thai-Kampuchean border area. Thai units are known to resupply Khmer Rouge forces who cross the border and then return to fight Vietnamese and Heng Samrin forces. Thailand has also permitted movement of Chinese military supplies for the anti-Heng Samrin resistence forces. The Indonesians view such tactics as not only perpetuating the border area conflict but, more importantly, as exacerbating the Sino-Vietnamese conflict. Also, the Indonesian and Malaysian view of a strong Indochina acting as a buffer zone against China is in direct conflict with the Thai view that it is only Vietnam that poses an imminent threat to the rest of mainland Southeast Asia.

The second point of contention between Indonesia and Thailand in regard to extraregional dimensions involves the role of the Soviet Union. The Soviet Union recognizes the different perceptions among the ASEAN states concerning the sources of instability to the region. As the Chinese and U.S. governments gradually moved toward normalization of diplomatic relations and the Vietnamese hope of diversifying its major power relationships were constricted by Chinese pressure and U.S. vengeance, the Soviet Union successfully persuaded Vietnam that a Soviet-Vietnam alliance was a firm guarantee in securing economic and military assistance.

From the Thai perspective, Vietnamese dependence on Soviet support enhanced its perception of an increased Vietnamese capability to strike across the border toward a wider regional dominance. The Indonesian view, on the other hand, was that the Soviet-Vietnamese alliance came as a result of U.S. failure to give the Hanoi "Titoists" a fair chance to embark upon a more flexible and independent foreign policy stance. That this U.S. failure was perpetuated in tandem with the Carter administration's obsession with its strategic understanding with China was all the more reason for Indonesian empathy for the Vietnamese predicament. More importantly for the Indonesians, the U.S. obsession to reach a strategic understanding with China, subordinating Hanoi's concern with the larger perceived threat of Soviet naval power, served to confirm the belief that the sooner ASEAN and the Indochinese grouping agreed to a region-based and region-centered security arrangement, the better it would serve the long-term interests of all the states concerned.

In the eyes of the Indonesians, what has transpired in the past five years in the broader spectrum of East Asia has not been favorable to Southeast Asian regional stability. A system of quasi-alliances has polarized the East Asian setting in the six months between July 1978 and January 1979, one of which only served to aggravate the intraregional nature of the conflict centering on Kampuchea.

First, Japan concluded with China (at the active encouragement of the Carter administration) the Sino-Japanese Peace and Friendship Treaty. It was immediately viewed by Moscow as a major breakthrough as part of an effort to establish an East Asian anti-Soviet alliance.

When the deteriorating Sino-Vietnamese and U.S.-Vietnamese relations finally brought about the Soviet-Vietnam Treaty of Friendship and Cooperation, the Chinese in turn foresaw the prospect of a Vietnamese invasion into Kampuchea. China then normalized diplomatic relations with the United States, hoping that it would deter Vietnam from overturning the Pol Pot government. When it failed to do so, the U.S. connection seemed sufficient to deter Soviet military reaction to China's subsequent military action into northern Vietnam in February-March 1979.

The crisis in Kampuchea, initially a conflict among fraternal Communist states within Indochina, has thrust itself into three layers of extraregional conflict: the Sino-Vietnamese dispute, with strong implications for both intra-ASEAN and ASEAN-Indochina relationships; the hardening of Sino-Soviet competition with respect to their secondary security relationships in Southeast Asia; and Soviet-American rivalry at the global level, specifically at "periphery areas."

Given the intricacies of the issues involved, it is doubtful whether a comprehensive solution as envisaged through the U.N. conference system can ever have a chance to succeed. Indeed, the long-term and internationalized nature of the comprehensive approach serves to confirm Indonesian fears that the circle of conflict in Southeast Asia is beyond the capacity and political willingness of the Southeast Asian states to break.

67.   ASEAN AND REGIONAL SECURITY

NOORDIN SOPIEE

The ASEAN experience has been one filled with paradox. Intended by its founding fathers to be an organization for primarily economic and cultural co-operation, it has developed only in the field of politics. Judged from the perspective of 'economic integration' EEC-style, it has been a substantial disappointment and arguably an abysmal failure. In overall organization terms, its level of integration is extremely low — it still decides on the basis of the lowest common denominator (euphemistically called a system of 'consensus'); there has been little in the way of sacrifice of sovereignty on the part of its members; its institutional structure is more rudimentary than modest. The machine works because it is not asked to do too much work; because not too much is demanded of it or of its members; because it is not pushed to the limit or overloaded. It might be interesting to note also that in the entire 17 years of its existence, there has possibly never been one instant when integration has been seriously elevated to the status of being an end in itself as opposed to being a means to other ends. It may be unfair to judge ASEAN on the basis of criteria borrowed from some other geographical area and on the basis of yardsticks that are inapplicable in the context of ASEAN's ambitions and intentions. Most certainly, when it comes to producing security, stability and sub-regional order, it has been a resounding success, whose record is possibly unmatched in the contemporary experience of the Third World.

This paper is an attempt to look at the ASEAN contribution to the security of the ASEAN community and to regional security in Southeast Asia. It has no polemical purpose and no theoretical pretensions. It will not suggest that regionalism is a panacea (a clearly preposterous idea), or that it is easy to make it work or that if it works it will at all times and in all contexts make a major contribution to peace and security. It merely contends that one regional organization, an association of five (now six) Southeast Asian nations founded in August 1967, has made a substantial difference not only to the ASEAN sub-region but also to Southeast Asia as a whole.

One way to demonstrate this is to imagine what it would have been like if the beast had not been born. If ASEAN had not existed it is possible that there would have been substantial turbulence in the relationship between Malaysia and the Philippines with regard to the Sabah territorial claim, with regard to the southern

Reprinted from Noordin Sopiee, "ASEAN and Regional Security", in *Regional Security in the Third World: Case Studies from Southeast Asia and the Middle East*, edited by Mohammed Ayoob (London: Croom Helm Ltd., 1986), pp. 221–31, by permission of the author and the editor.

Philippines Muslim problem and possibly the mutual interventions and verbal altercations which would have been *de rigueur* in the tense relations between countries that are adversaries. Without the psychological cushion that was provided by ASEAN and if Thailand had felt alone and isolated, might it not have panicked — not once but twice in the last dozen years? Would it have been pushed into finding solace in the dragon's den in order to ensure its security from the ancient enemies of the East, even before they themselves went into the warm embrace of the northern bear? If in the mid-1970s, Thailand did not succeed in making an alliance with Beijing, would it not have been intimidated by Vietnam? Would the whirlwind events of ten years ago not have hurled it from pillar to post? If it had succeeded in making a military alliance with the only available and functionable partner, China, what would have been the repercussions on Thai-Malaysian relations, indeed on Indonesia, Malaysia and even Singapore? Assume bad Malaysian-Thai relations and one can imagine the southern Thai Muslim problem and the problem of Thai refuge for the remnants of the Malayan Communist Party blowing up into something more than peripheral irritations.

If Indonesian foreign policy had not been conceived within the ASEAN parameter, would it be what it is today? Indeed, what would have been the shape and substance of the foreign policies of each of the ASEAN states had they been evolved separately instead of in a context of co-operation and full consultation? Not an academic question given that there have been and there are different strategic perspectives, ambitions, emotions and historical experiences. Indonesia is a large far-flung country of islands twice removed from Indochina. Thailand is in Southeast Asian terms a medium land power at the very doorstep of confrontation. It is clear beyond any doubt that the existence of the ASEAN system has worked for the harmonization, moderation and accommodation of interests and policies among the ASEAN states.

If ASEAN had not been there, would Singapore have become an armed citadel, surrounded by an antagonistic Malay world, living in dread of the 'Brown Peril' and arming itself to the teeth in order to fend off its real or imagined enemies? Could Singapore have become an 'Israel'? What would have been the consequences to the region? Would the ASEAN community have become a cockpit for the big powers in the same way that the Indochinese states have been and continue to be?

What would have been the consequences of general panic in 1975? What would Southeast Asia be like today if the nations of ASEAN, instead of finding solidarity and confidence and generating dynamic and developing societies, had instead been living in fear, in isolation, with a sense of immense insecurity and vulnerability, quarrelling among themselves and tempting all sorts of intervention from powers, big and not so big, Communist and non-Communist? Would the ASEAN states have been able (in the end) to dismiss the domino theory with such aplomb and arrogance? What would have been the effect of diverting precious resources to economically unproductive military tasks? What would have been the political and security consequences (never mind the economic and social repercussions) if the ASEAN community had failed to attract foreign expertise, technology, investments and markets, if the ASEAN states (without exception) had not been able to chalk up impressive growth rates which have made the community as a whole one of the most dynamic areas of the world? Throughout the ASEAN community, the political and security consequences would have been serious, whilst in a country like Malaysia the ramifications would have been grave. Would the community (save the Philippines) be facing the future as it does now, with so much confidence, hope and expectation?

It is absolutely true that if the overall configuration of ambitions and correlation of forces had been substantially different, if other crucial cards had fallen in other ways, the ASEAN community today might be in different shape. But this only means that ASEAN has not been the sole determinant. There is no gainsaying that as a variable it has had a crucial impact as a producer of security for each and all of the member states, for the ASEAN community and for the Southeast Asian region.

First, the Association has played a critical role in banishing that psychological sense of isolation which can often lead to panic or ill-advised action. ASEAN has given its member states that psychological sense of confidence and security without which mature responses and policies would have been less likely. Over the years, the psychological shield that ASEAN was seen to provide and the confidence in dealing with the external environment that it engendered, allowed the ASEAN states to concentrate their primary attention on domestic, not external, concerns, as important a factor as any in explaining the security success of the community, given that the greatest threats to each of the ASEAN states lay within rather than without.

Second, it has succeeded over the years in preventing a sense of powerlessness on the part of the member states. If power corrupts, so too does weakness and powerlessness. Over the years, ASEAN has given its member nations a sense of power and capability which has allowed them to behave not as objects but as subjects of the international political system. It has allowed the ASEAN states to adopt active foreign policies, to seek solutions rather than to have them imposed, to attempt to shape their environment and their future. ASEAN has worked for the realization that one's destiny is not to be decided by others and that the helping hand one needs is at the end of one's right arm. In the ASEAN community, there is little of the psychology of dependence that is found in many other parts of the world; there is much of the psychology of self-help, assertive self-help. When the Americans left, the political vacuum in the ASEAN sub-region was filled by the constituent states themselves, acting nationally and through the ASEAN concert. The process has made the entire community the stronger for it.

Third, ASEAN has provided the community with a sturdy policy 'meat grinder'. What has often been referred to as the ASEAN process has resulted in continuous and repeated discussions and deliberation — talk, talk and more talk — and multilateral decision-making. The process subjects the most persuasive arguments, ideas, and proposals to the test of open debate and criticism; it subjects the strongest of personalities to peer pressure. By the time proposals, ideas and initiatives come out of the meat grinder they will have been given the works. Some important foreign policies do not go through the meat grinder of course. And there must have been many great ideas that have been reduced to sausage. But in the main, the principal strands of ASEAN foreign policy have been unusually sophisticated and mature. To give just two examples: immediately after the fall of South Vietnam, the general line was conciliatory but not weak; again, despite the fact that the ASEAN states generally felt that they had been taken in by the Hanoi peace offensive of mid-1978, whether there had been a deliberate intention to do so or not, there was no immature emotional response following the Vietnamese Christmas Day invasion which led to the conquest of Kampuchea.

It is suggested here that the confidence and security, the assertiveness and feeling that one does not have to play the role of spectator or victim and the process of consultation and deliberation that are the rotating blades of the meat grinder (that are there because ASEAN is there) have contributed most substantially to a broad range of common policies which have in turn contributed most substantially to the security of the ASEAN community and, at least indirectly, to the peace and security of Southeast Asia.

Historically, without the confidence and psychological crutch that ASEAN provided to Thailand especially and to the others in general it is possible to perceive of response fluctuating from crass defiance to cringing appeasement. Without the confidence that ASEAN helped so substantially to generate there would have been a rush either to arms, which would have meant arming oneself to the point of bankruptcy or economic disaster; the alternative would have been a clutching at the straw of military alliance with some big power guarantor, which would have been provocative and which would have intensified their rivalry. Because there was good sense and confidence, the ASEAN states adopted a policy of big power equidistance, a policy and a process that was dynamic, differential but never deferential.

Meat grinder wisdom and confidence lay behind the common position that the main guarantee of national security lay in national resilience, making sure that one has the capacity to deal with one's internal problems, that one provides no strategic opportunity or cause for external intervention and that one has the capacity to bounce back after the most serious setbacks. These factors lay behind the recognition that the legitimate interests of all the big powers, even of Vietnam, ought to be accommodated by the ASEAN states and within the ASEAN community. They also underpinned the common stand that one must act in such a way as to maximize non-provocation, that the ASEAN states should be above involvement in the Soviet Collective Security System, above involvement in China's anti-hegemonism drives, and not as far as is possible involved in the Sino-Soviet conflict. Meat grinder wisdom and confidence have also played a major part in ensuring the enduring common stand that for the long-term peace, security and stability of the region as a whole it is necessary to prevent the permanent division of Southeast Asia into two confrontationist blocs, one determinedly anti-ASEAN and the other determinedly anti-Communist.

Fourth, the ASEAN process, less productive in the first ten years, much more productive in the last seven, has created an ASEAN sense of community. Anyone who underrates what has been achieved on this score should go back to the situation of the ASEAN area before the advent of ASEAN. Before the birth of the Association, the sub-region had no sense whatever

of unity, solidarity, oneness of any sort. There was a pan-Malay feeling which to Jakarta and Kuala Lumpur embraced Indonesia and Malaysia, but not the Philippines. There was, at times, a paraded pan-Malay feeling on the part of the Filipinos that generally meant little beyond the dictates, attractions and exigencies of the moment. Certainly, in the pan-Malayism, Singapore merited a footnote and Thailand was not in the book at all. As Arnfinn Jorgensen-Dahl notes in his study on *Regional Organisation and Order in Southeast Asia*, 'there existed in Southeast Asia no indigenous tradition of thinking which conceived of the . . . states that came to form . . . ASEAN . . . as a political, economic and cultural entity which could serve as an ideal alternative to traditional interstate politics and to which appeal could be made and from which inspiration could be received'.[1] Outside the handful of diplomatic technocrats, Thailand and Indonesia, Thailand and the Philippines, Malaysia and the Philippines, the Philippines *vis-à-vis* all the others, were as strangers. Worse than strangers, many of the relationships were relationships of enmity. Malaysia, the only country sharing a common border with all its ASEAN partners, had endured a period of undeclared war with Indonesia called *Konfrontasi*. Relations between Kuala Lumpur and Singapore were tense in the aftermath of separation in 1965. Diplomatic ties had been broken with the Philippines as a result of the Sabah claim. There were tensions between Singapore and Indonesia as a result of the execution of Indonesian marines. The ASEAN states are strangers no more (except perhaps in the case of the newest ASEAN member, Brunei) and, more important, they are enemies no more.

It might well be asked how an ASEAN sense of community contributes to the security of the ASEAN community. It does so in a myriad of ways. Members of the same family are more open to give and take, are not so fast in flying off the handle with each other. Without ASEAN, there would not today be the level and intimacy of bilateral intelligence and military co-operation. There would be less probability of joint naval patrols. There would be less co-operation with regard to sea lanes. There would be more problems arising out of the delineation of territorial seas, the division of economic zones. There would be more conflict in quantitative as well as qualitative terms. There would not be quite the same motivational impetus to bury hatchets, to resolve conflicts, to work for consensus and agreement.

There is a fifth way in which ASEAN has contributed most substantially to the security of the ASEAN community. There can be no doubt that as a result of reasoning together, talking together, quarrelling together, the ASEAN process has created a sturdy structure of trust, confidence and goodwill between the member states. Most international organizations are generally preceded by such a structure. In the case of ASEAN, trust, confidence and goodwill have been the result rather than the cause.

The contribution that confidence in each other, the reduction of unpredictability on the part of member states, trust and goodwill make to the structure of peace, security and stability requires little elucidation. How the ASEAN states have been able to put these things in the place of suspicion and animosity over the years is of more than academic interest.

There have been four basic methods used to strengthen trust, confidence and goodwill. There has, first, been the most liberal use of loosely structured, non-crisis ridden, non-problem-solving summitry at the topmost level. Taking the Philippines out of the reckoning, it has become a convention for every new ASEAN head of government to touch base with his counterparts at the earliest opportunity. Secondly, there has been a seemingly endless number of meetings between ministers and between officials at the less elevated plane. The number of non-governmental, basically ASEAN-wide meetings on matters ranging from body-building to librarianship is legion. In 1982, the Thai Foreign Ministry is said to have counted more than 400 such meetings.

The third method of strengthening the structure of confidence, goodwill and trust has been intense problem- and issue-oriented diplomatic consultation with all partners with regard to new initiatives or new responses to external events. Thus, Malaysia, which for domestic election reasons felt it had to pioneer the opening of diplomatic relations with the PRC, briefed every ASEAN capital fully before it proceeded. Since 1971, all ASEAN countries have adopted the practice of exchanging notes on their individual dialogues with China, Vietnam, the Soviet Union, Kampuchea, the EEC, Japan and the United States. It is not rare to find several ASEAN states issuing similar if not identical communiqués at the end of a visit by a common visitor.

The fourth activity which has contributed to the building of a substantial structure of goodwill, trust and confidence in the ASEAN community has been joint diplomatic-political action and co-operation in pursuit of goals that are of salience to one or two member states but not to all. As examples it is possible to point to the joint action against Japanese synthetic rubber production, the joint confrontation of Australia over its airline policy.

The sixth contribution that ASEAN has made to the security of the ASEAN community has been in the area of actual conflict resolution, the most serious of which, the conflict between Malaysia and the Philippines over Sabah destroyed ASA (the Association of Southeast Asia) and virtually put ASEAN in cold storage in the first two years of its existence. The second Sabah crisis broke out when the Manila press reported in March 1968 the Philippine government's training of Filipino soldiers for possible use in Sabah. In August of that year diplomatic relations were once again severed between Manila and Kuala Lumpur. A Thai initiative in December to resolve the crisis failed. The process of political and diplomatic de-escalation only started as a result of the Indonesian initiative of May 1969. And it took another seven months to re-establish diplomatic relations between the two member states. Interestingly, it was not until the Kuala Lumpur

ASEAN Summit of 1977 that President Marcos announced that 'the Government of the Republic to the Philippines . . . is taking definite steps to eliminate one of the burdens of ASEAN, the claim of the Philippine Republic to Sabah'. As, interestingly, these definitive steps (repeal of the Bill passed by the Philippine Congress on 20 August 1968) have not yet been taken although the claim has not since been resurrected, the conflict has been completely de-escalated and the issue swept under the carpet (a technique for dealing with conflicts that has all too often been underrated).

There have been cases of other less serious conflicts being resolved, which might not have been so easily or quickly resolved had the ASEAN process and the pressures and the intangible but real 'spirit' of ASEAN not existed. It might be argued that as important a role has been played by ASEAN in sublimating and defusing conflicts as in actually resolving them.

If that counts as ASEAN's seventh major contribution to security in the ASEAN community, number eight is the role that ASEAN has played in laying down the rules of the peace game within the sub-region and in getting system-wide acceptance of these rules. Through a combination of the process of deliberate 'legislative' action (laid out in such documents as the 1976 Treaty of Amity and Co-operation in Southeast Asia signed in Bali) and implicit acceptance and espousal over the years, the ASEAN process has established at least four ground rules of inter-state relations within the ASEAN community with regard to conflict and its termination. The first rule of the game is system-wide acceptance of the principle of the pacific settlement of disputes. The second is non-interference and non-intervention in the domestic affairs of member states. The third is respect for each others' territorial integrity and independence. The fourth is the principle of not inviting external intervention on one's behalf in the pursuit of disputes.

The sum total of all these contributions has been to bring the ASEAN area to the brink of what Karl Deutsch has called a pluralistic security community. Such a system is one at peace, where no nation continues to accept war or violence as an instrument of policy against another community member and where no actor seriously prepares for war or violence against another. There is no guarantee that such a situation will be sustained in the future. Peace is always a constant struggle. But to come close to being a security community from a starting point so distant within a time span so comparatively short is no mean achievement. Admittedly the ASEAN security community has in part been the result of other factors, not the least of which was the perception of extra-ASEAN threats. But without the existence of ASEAN there would today be no such quasi-security community. And history tells us that common external threats can lead to division as well as unity.

Given that the ASEAN contributions noted above have almost exclusively been to the ASEAN community, might it not be argued that whilst ASEAN has played a central role with regard to the sub-region, it has not played a significant role in the context of the wider region? Though it is patently clear that the Association's contribution outside the ASEAN community has been of a different order, there are two reasons why that proposition is incorrect.

First, the ASEAN community is the core of the Southeast Asian region and the Indochina states and Burma are its periphery. Such is the attention that war attracts, such has been the perceptual neglect of those parts where the guns are silent that it will be a surprise even to scholars of Southeast Asia that the ASEAN area constitutes five-sixths of the region's land area, and more than 90 per cent of its total GNP. Just about four out of every five Southeast Asians are residents of the ASEAN community. An organization that contributes so substantially to the security of so much Southeast Asian real estate cannot be said to contribute insignificantly.

Secondly, the existence of ASEAN and the activities of ASEAN have contributed significantly also to the periphery of Southeast Asia and to the entire region. In the same way that a peaceful, stable and unaggressive Indochina would contribute to the security of the ASEAN sub-region and the region as a whole, a peaceful, stable and unaggressive ASEAN community has contributed to Indochina and to Southeast Asian security. By denying to the big powers any vacuum in the ASEAN community and giving them no opportunity to propel themselves into any void and by sanitizing the sub-region from high-profile big power rivalry too a contribution is made. It is also arguable that the existence, solidarity and strength of ASEAN provides a balance of political power to Hanoi and imposes a psychological check and counter to Vietnam, thus contributing to the security of the entire region (including that of Kampuchea and Laos in the future).

History may yet prove the ASEAN states right in their belief that Vietnamese aggression in Kampuchea has to be punished and not rewarded — because it is aggression, and the punishment of aggression perpetrated by any state in the region must be part of the rules of the game in Southeast Asia. ASEAN's posture, policies and actions with regard to the Kampuchean question cannot be divorced from the endeavour of every ASEAN state to seek to impose upon the region as a whole the rules which they have legislated for the ASEAN community: the pacific resolution of conflict, non-interference and non-intervention in the domestic affairs of other states, respect for each state's territorial integrity and independence, commitment to the principle of non-invitation of external big power intervention on one's behalf. They are unlikely to succeed in the foreseeable future in their endeavour. But it is perhaps not wrong for them to try.

NOTE

1. Arnfinn Jorgensen-Dahl, *Regional Organisation and Order in South-East Asia* (Macmillan, London, 1982), p. 70.

68.

THE U.S. AND ASEAN'S APPROACH TO SECURITY IN SOUTHEAST ASIA*

MUTHIAH ALAGAPPA

Almost every ASEAN joint communiqué and ASEAN-sponsored United Nations Resolution on Cambodia has identified the Cambodian conflict as the major stumbling block to the realization of ZOPFAN. In fact, frustration issuing from the lack of progress in settling the Cambodian conflict prompted some ASEAN members to pursue the nuclear-weapons-free-zone proposal to keep ZOPFAN alive. As such, it is logical to expect that a political settlement in Cambodia would provide fresh momentum to ASEAN's proposals to make Southeast Asia a Zone of Peace, Freedom and Neutrality and to create a nuclear-weapons-free zone (SEANWFZ) in the region. Indonesian and Malaysian concerns over the evolving Sino–Thai military relations may add to the urgency attached to the realization of ZOPFAN, with the positive changes in the security environment in the Asia-Pacific region being viewed as propitious for such an undertaking.

A comprehensive discussion of the concepts of ZOPFAN and SEANWFZ is beyond the scope of this paper.[1] In essence, the ZOPFAN proposal seeks to progressively create a new regional order in Southeast Asia that would eschew the use of force in the conduct of international relations. States in the region would be required to endorse and abide by certain basic principles in their international relations, and external power involvement in the region would have to be "legitimate and constructive". The latter is, in fact, the primary concern of the 1971 Kuala Lumpur Declaration which seeks to make Southeast Asia "free from any form or manner of interference by outside powers" — the underlying assumption being that great power rivalry was the root cause of instability in Southeast Asia and that, left to themselves, the Southeast Asian states can amicably resolve their differences. Not all the ASEAN states concur with this diagnosis and prescription but different calculations converged to support the adoption of the proposal in 1971.

In pursuit of the "neutrality" goal, the states in the region are required to be impartial and to refrain from direct involvement in ideological, political, economic, armed or other forms of conflict between extra-regional powers. The latter are required to refrain from interfering in the domestic and regional affairs of the states in Southeast Asia. In operational terms, this would entail the eventual removal of foreign military bases from the region; prohibition of the use, storage, passage and testing of nuclear weapons in the zone; and the phasing out of security arrangements with external powers.

Reprinted in abridged form from "U.S.–ASEAN Security Relations: Challenges and Prospects", *Contemporary Southeast Asia* 11, no. 1 (June 1989), pp. 1–39, by permission of the author and the Institute of Southeast Asian Studies.

The United States has all along accorded a cool reception to ZOPFAN. The U.S. view has been that, while it is an acceptable long-term goal, conditions are not appropriate enough for the implementation of the concept. In the early 1970s, the U.S. argument against ZOPFAN focused on:[2] a) the impact it will have on neo-isolationist forces in the United States which will make it difficult for the United States to discharge its obligations in the region; b) inappropriate timing as the Vietnam war was still far from conclusion; c) the security of the countries in the region was in jeopardy and US. assistance was still essential; and d) the difficulties surrounding the neutralization of an entire region. Uppermost in U.S. considerations was perhaps the loss it would incur through the implementation of the proposal. The United States had treaties with the Philippines, Thailand, South Vietnam, and Lon Nol's Cambodia, and had bases in Thailand and the Philippines. Malaysia and Singapore were members of the Five-Power Defence Arrangements. All these would be jeopardized and the USSR and the PRC would be allowed legitimate entry into Southeast Asia. ZOPFAN was generally perceived as undercutting U.S. interests and strategy in the region.

This perception has not changed, as witnessed by the recent U.S. objection to the SEANWFZ proposal. The United States takes a dim view of it and has indicated firmly that it will not support such a proposal. American presence in the region is viewed as part of a global deterrence posture and the creation of a NWFZ in Southeast Asia is perceived as undermining U.S. deterrence capability. It is argued that the United States is primarily a maritime power and restrictions issuing from the creation of a NWFZ in Southeast Asia are, therefore, likely to have unequal effects on the United States and the Soviet Union, favouring the latter at the expense of the former. It is also argued that the Soviet Union may not abide by its commitment and that the countries in the region do not have the means to verify and to take appropriate actions in the event of violations. In the American view, Southeast Asia, unlike Latin America and the South Pacific, is too close to the Soviet Union and China. Its denuclearization, therefore, cannot be approached in a manner similar to the other two regions. The United States has informed ASEAN that it cannot support a NWFZ in Southeast Asia and that a negotiated bilateral reduction of nuclear weapons is the most effective approach to international security.

The U.S. decision not to support any new NWFZ proposals appears to be a product of two concerns.[3] The first is the fear of setting a precedent. An acceptance by the United States of a ban on stationing nuclear weapons or port calls may be cited by other treaty allies and would have a snowballing effect. The United States is concerned with the growing number of proposals for regional nuclear free zones in the "free world" that is unmatched in the Soviet bloc. This is considered as undermining Western security. Secondly, because of the reliance on nuclear deterrence and the crucial importance of nuclear testing in ensuring effective deterrence, the United States is unwilling to oppose nuclear testing by its NATO (North Atlantic Treaty Organization) allies such as France in the South Pacific. In the face of U.S. opposition, ASEAN soft-pedalled the SEANWFZ proposal.[4] Renewed urgency on the part of ASEAN in pursuing the ZOPFAN and SEANWFZ proposals has the potential to create tensions in U.S.–ASEAN relations especially if it were to coincide with the negotiation of a new bases agreement with the Philippines.

NOTES

* As ASEAN is not a security organization and because of the differences in threat perception among its member states, it may appear inappropriate to discuss U.S. security relations with ASEAN as an entity.

Furthermore, the major part of security relations with ASEAN is, in fact, with individual countries on a bilateral basis. However, U.S.–ASEAN co-operation over the Cambodia conflict in which ASEAN has acted in unison, is informed by and in turn influences the tempo of U.S. bilateral security relations with individual member countries. Moreover, ASEAN would have to act collectively on its ZOPFAN and SEANWFZ proposals and these would have an impact on bilateral security relations with the United States. The phrase "U.S.–ASEAN security relations" as used in this paper, therefore, covers U.S. relations with ASEAN as an entity, where appropriate, and bilateral relations with individual ASEAN countries.

1. For a discussion of the early U.S. response to the ZOPFAN proposal, see Dick Wilson, *The Neutralization of Southeast Asia* (New York: Praeger Publishers, 1975), pp. 103–8.
2. Muthiah Alagappa, "A Nuclear Weapons Free Zone in Southeast Asia: Problems and Prospects", *Australian Outlook*, December 1987, pp. 178–79.
3. Ibid., p. 180.
4. Stanley Roth, "Issues in Future US Policy: Negotiations over Military Base Rights", *The United States–Philippines Relationship in the New Administration and Beyond*, Report prepared for the use of the Committee on Foreign Relations, United States Senate (Congressional Research Service, Library of Congress, Washington, 1988), pp. 86–87.

69

THE PATTERN OF MILITARY MODERNIZATION IN SOUTHEAST ASIA

AARON KARP

Purchases of major weapon systems are important political events in Southeast Asia, where arms transfers are heavily discussed in the regional press and easily become sources of controversy. Yet, these purchases are usually moderate by international standards. As they have gone through the transitions in their military procurement policies from reliance on aid, to purchasing second-hand weaponry, then buying new systems, costs have risen dramatically while military budgets have risen much more slowly, forcing procurement quantities to drop sharply. The multi-billion dollar transactions that distinguished the international arms market in the 1980s have not become routine in Southeast Asia, where only two individual "arms packages" worth more than US$500 million have been negotiated since the fall of South Vietnam (Soviet resupply of Hanoi after its 1979 China war, and Britain's 1988 Memorandum of Understanding [MOU] with Malaysia).

The modest size of Southeast Asian major weapons contracts does not make them less controversial. Indeed, the region is unusually sensitive to the introduction of a new system such as an advanced fighter aircraft, air-defence system or frigate. The impact of a US$380 million order for a new squadron of advanced fighters on the regional balance of power may be slight, but the changing balance of prestige between nations and individual services within a nation usually demands that a countervailing purchase follow quickly. The sequential orders for U.S. F-16 fighters placed by Singapore (8 ordered in 1984), Thailand (12 in 1985), and Indonesia (12 in 1986) illustrate a procurement pattern visible in ship-to-ship missiles, surface-to-surface missiles, 155 mm artillery, ASW (anti-submarine warfare) frigates and jet trainers.[1] The situation barely qualifies as an arms race since these countries have no intention of using their recent purchases against each other and procurement quantities are kept within understood limits dictated as much by respect for stable budgets as by tacit rules of neighbourly competition.

It is also characteristic of these procurement decisions that they are made by a small group of decision-makers, sometimes by a single official acting alone.[2] In most countries in the region, the head of state, defence minister or relevant service chief has the power to make binding agreements, to extend letters of offer and acceptance in consultation with a few close colleagues. Once announced, such decisions may be subjected to heated debate and severe criticism. Their precise terms may be altered,

Reprinted in abridged form from "Military Procurement and Regional Security in Southeast Asia", *Contemporary Southeast Asia* 11, no. 4 (March 1990), pp. 334–61, by permission of the author and the Institute of Southeast Asian Studies.

but an outright reversal is rarely possible. This situation is not unique to Southeast Asia — defence decision-making is similar throughout most of the Third World and "closed politics" are not unknown in Western Europe. The situation may reveal more about a nation's constitutional order than anything unique about its military procurement decision-making.

How Large is the Southeast Asian Arms Trade?

Statistical data on arms transfers to Southeast Asia are elusive and problematic. Although several governments in the region release extensive reports on their military budgets, these generally do not break spending data down into individual procurement categories. Other countries release virtually no military spending data at all. Consequently, analysis must rely on arms trade figures from outside sources, notably from the U.S. Arms Control and Disarmament Agency's (ACDA's) annual *World Military Expenditures and Arms Transfers* and the independent Stockholm International Peace Research Institute's (SIPRI's) annual *Yearbook*.[3] There are difficulties with both of these sources which tend to underestimate the true value of Southeast Asian arms imports.

The size of the Southeast Asian arms market is usually submerged within arms trade statistics for East Asia as a whole. Combining all of East Asia into a single annual figure is a geographical simplification that probably confuses more than it illuminates; Northeast and Southeast Asia are distinct regional sub-systems with separate strategic concerns and arms trade patterns.[4] Arms shipments to Northeast Asian countries such as Japan or North and South Korea have little or no direct impact on the strategic balance in Southeast Asia. Even the deployment of new conventional weapons in China and Taiwan only weakly affect procurement decisions in, for example, Malaysia and the Philippines, and certainly no more so than new weapons purchases by India or Saudi Arabia.

Disaggregating arms import data for the ten Southeast Asian countries gives a more accurate impression of the region's global standing (Figure 1). Using either data source shown, the value of arms imports to Southeast Asia equals approximately half (41 to 68 per cent depending on the year) of the arms transfers to all of East Asia combined. At the levels of the mid-1980s, the Southeast Asian arms market by itself was about one-fifth the size of the Middle East market, half as large as that of Africa, and roughly comparable to the arms markets in Latin America, South Asia or Northeast Asia.

Southeast Asian regional arms import statistics are heavily dominated by Vietnam. This was most profound in 1978 to 1981 when Vietnam's invasion of Kampuchea, followed by the brief but intense war with China, led to a large-scale build-up and subsequent re-arming. Vietnamese arms imports peaked in 1979–80, constituting 60 to 82 per cent of all arms received in the region, depending on whether ACDA or SIPRI is consulted. For the ten-year period 1977–86, Vietnam received 57.6 per cent of all arms sent to Southeast Asia according to ACDA figures, and 26.4 per cent according to SIPRI.

There are reasons to believe, however, that the actual level of regional arms transfers is significantly higher than an immediate acquaintance with the two traditional data sources leads one to conclude. ACDA figures, in particular, may err substantially by missing much of the arms trade to the region. While ACDA arms trade values for Vietnam appear to be reasonably accurate, values for the other nine Southeast Asian countries probably need to be raised considerably. This can be seen by comparing the methodologies employed by the two data sources with the discrepancies between their published arms trade values.

ACDA arms trade statistics are not comprehensive but attempt to include as much of the global arms trade as possible, excluding only dual-use items such as food and petroleum products, and manufacturing equipment purchased through civilian contracts. Most ACDA

FIGURE 1: Arms Transfers to Southeast Asia
(In US$ billion)*

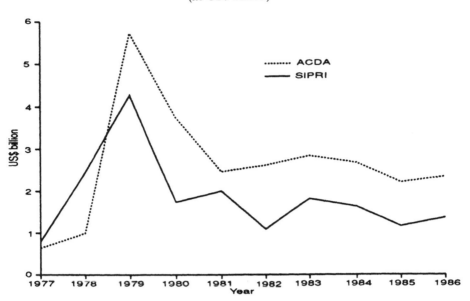

* ACDA data is in constant 1984 U.S. dollars; SIPRI data is in constant
1985 U.S. dollars.

arms trade data are based on reports from U.S. military attaches abroad, compiled by the U.S. Defense Intelligence Agency. By comparison, SIPRI arms trade data do not attempt to be equally comprehensive. Working from published sources of information, SIPRI covers only transfers of major weapons systems — such as aircraft, armoured vehicles, guided missiles and naval vessels over 100 tons — and support items and training included as part of the contracts for these items. SIPRI's methodology precludes covering transfers of small arms, ammunition, quartermaster supplies, communications equipment, logistic and combat engineering vehicles, spare parts, military construction or any of the other myriad elements that modern military forces require. As a result, SIPRI arms trade values should be considerably less than ACDA figures, typically by a ratio of 2–3:1.[5]

The data on arms transfers to Southeast Asia do not correspond fully to this expectation. ACDA and SIPRI data display an orthodox ratio

for Vietnamese arms transfers, with ACDA values 2.5 times as great as SIPRI values (Figure 2). This corresponds to the ACDA's greater comprehensiveness. But figures for the other nine Southeast Asian countries reveal that SIPRI values are equal to, and sometimes higher, than the ACDA's. This discrepancy suggests that ACDA arms trade data for Southeast Asia are seriously incomplete or under-priced. Since

FIGURE 2: Southeast Asian Arms Imports, 1977–86
(In US$ million)

Source	All Southeast Asia	Vietnam	9 Other Southeast Asian Countries
ACDA*	26,671	16,321	10,350
SIPRI**	16,865	6,486	10,379
Ratio ACDA/SIPRI	1.6 / 1	2.5 / 1	1 / 1

* Includes all arms transfers. In constant 1984 U.S. dollars.
** Includes transfers of major weapons only. In constant 1985 U.S. dollars.

SIPRI data use published reports on weapons deliveries and commercial pricing, it is unlikely that its figures for the rest of the region are exaggerated.

The discrepancy between ACDA and SIPRI arms trade figures points to the conclusion that, unless there is a major and unknown flaw in SIPRI data, the total value of the arms trade to the nine countries of Southeast Asia other than Vietnam is significantly greater than previously thought. Assuming that the orthodox ratios apply here and SIPRI data cover one-third to one-half the total arms trade, their arms imports are probably two to three times higher than the ACDA figures. For the years 1977–86, arms transfers to the eight countries of Southeast Asia other than Vietnam would not be US$10.3 billion, but approximately US$20.6 to US$31.2 billion. Including Vietnam, the ten-year value of Southeast Asian arms imports would not be US$26.7 billion, but US$37 to US$47.4 billion (in 1985 U.S. dollars). While Vietnam remains the region's largest military consumer by far, the shares of other Southeast Asian countries in the regional arms market are probably higher than widely thought. Correspondingly, the place of arms transfers in their domestic economies and government spending is probably greater as well.

MILITARY CAPABILITY, POLICY AND REQUIREMENTS

All Southeast Asian countries face distinctive military problems to which they bring their own blends of historical disposition, economic resources and expectations. As arms importers, they fall into three categories: Vietnam, whose huge forces and reliance on Soviet aid put it in a category by itself; Indonesia, Malaysia, Singapore and Thailand with comparable levels of military spending, arms import policies and defence industries; and Brunei, Burma, Kampuchea, Laos and the Philippines, with very little in common except their low military budgets and reliance on foreign assistance.

Their military procurement and arms import policies are reviewed here, emphasizing their force planning and development, the role of alignments and foreign assistance, the significance of individual arms deals, and their future military requirements.

Despite its combat experience with China and in Kampuchea, Vietnam's People's Army remains much as it was at the time of the surrender of Saigon in April 1975, with a large air force (330 fighters) and a huge radar network and surface-to-air missile system (over 200 batteries) designed to shoot down United States bombers, and a fleet of about 70 small naval vessels intended to guard its coasts from the United States Navy.[6] Having withdrawn its technically less sophisticated ground forces out of Kampuchea, Vietnam must support an enormous military equipped for missions unlikely to be needed again, all of which it can ill afford to maintain.

The Vietnam situation is complicated further by the country's almost total reliance on the Soviet Union for equipment. Since the deterioration in relations with China, 1969–71, Hanoi has had no choice but to seek continued Soviet assistance. Moscow was a generous patron, completely rebuilding and enlarging Vietnamese forces in 1979–81. But as the Soviet Union tries to reduce its obligations to regional allies under President Gorbachev, it seems unlikely that it will continue to support Vietnam's present force levels. Since the early 1980s, the Soviet Union has been parsimonious in its transfers of advanced weapons to Vietnam, offering single squadrons of MiG-23BN fighters, Mi-24 helicopters, an SA-6 surface-to-air missile battalion, but refusing to fully re-equip the rest of Vietnam's forces.[7] It is reasonable to expect the Soviet Union to transfer small quantities of recent-vintage items such as MiG-29 fighters, T-72 tanks and BMP APCs (armoured personnel carriers) in the foreseeable future. Sales of *Scud* 300-km range ballistic missiles are also feasible. Most of the Vietnamese units, with the exception of its navy, will continue to operate vintage equipment of the early 1960s.

Vietnamese reliance on Soviet assistance is too extensive to give way to other forms of military procurement in the near future. Soviet transfers of second-hand weaponry could even increase following the completion of the treaty on Conventional Forces in Europe (CFE) which will force Moscow to transfer or destroy thousands of armoured vehicles and artillery tubes, as well as hundreds of tactical aircraft and helicopters. Other Soviet clients are interested in this prospect, including India, Iraq, Libya and Syria, which may compel Vietnamese officials to offer market prices to acquire them. As Vietnam is gradually drawn into cash payments for military equipment, purchases of limited amounts of Western technology could be especially helpful in upgrading aging Soviet and Chinese armaments which Vietnam cannot afford to replace outright. This will depend on improvements in diplomatic relations with the West and changing strategic circumstances.

The second category of Southeast Asian arms importers includes four countries with significant arsenals. Like Vietnam, they face the question of how to update inventories composed largely of early-1960s vintage equipment. But as leaders in Asian economic expansion, they are better positioned to adapt to the economic and technological realities of new military equipment. Having made the third transition from aid and purchases of second-hand armaments to procurement of highly advanced weaponry, they also have much higher expectations. Indonesia, Malaysia, Singapore and Thailand are able to invest several hundred million dollars annually in military procurement, with purchases of major weapon systems alone averaging US$325 million, US$207 million, US$144 million and US$224 million respectively during the years 1977–86 (in constant 1985 U.S. dollars).[8] This gives them substantial flexibility in composing their forces, but still imposes severe limitations overall.

For a nation of its size, Indonesia is modestly armed. The world's fifth most populous nation has the twenty-fourth largest military establishment and ranks 121st in military personnel per 1,000 people, although with 280,000 men in uniform its armed forces are not unimpressive.[9] With 88 combat aircraft, 130 light tanks and no artillery over 105mm, its air force and army are not as well equipped as their counterparts in Singapore. Appropriately for an archipelagic nation, the navy is better equipped, although its leading force of seven missile-armed frigates and three West German submarines supported by many older vessels display a growing preference for quality over quantity.[10]

This low level of armaments is made possible by a relatively benign security environment. Indonesia has fought no major wars since independence. The 1963–65 confrontation in Borneo with Malaysia was limited and counter-insurgency operations in the South Moluccas and later in East Timor found little role for major weaponry. While geography and stability enable the nation's leadership to restrain military requirements, procurement is also heavily influenced by memories of Indonesia's large arms deals in the mid-1960s, when Moscow provided about 130 MiG fighters, 25 Tu-16 bombers, support aircraft and a complete navy including a cruiser, 14 submarines, 7 destroyers, 7 frigates, 62 smaller combatants and many auxiliary vessels. Much of the equipment was beyond Indonesian abilities to operate and service and soon deteriorated. The rest needed Soviet parts and support which were difficult to acquire after relations deteriorated in the late 1960s.[11] Today, only a few of the naval vessels, light tanks and APCs remain operational. Since then, Indonesian leaders have kept major arms purchases much smaller, tailoring purchases to clear requirements, and avoiding over-reliance on any single supplier.

After purchasing substantial quantities of second-hand U.S. A-4 fighters, French AMX-13 light tanks and training systems, in the 1980s Indonesia generally bought small quantities of new equipment, including 12 U.S. F-16 fighters, separate orders for 3 and 4 Dutch frigates, 2 West German submarines, British jet trainers and air-defence systems, and anti-ship missiles from France and the United States. This has resulted in very uneven forces. The navy is well-equipped but small. The air force consists largely of smaller and older tactical aircraft except for the F-16s. The army remains more a *gendarme* for internal order than an international fighting force.[12] Unless the defence budget can grow consistently through the 1990s, it will be extremely difficult to change this force structure. Re-equipping the entire air force with advanced fighters is out of the question, while navy expansion is equally prohibitive. Nor is there great interest in building up the army. Instead, Jakarta may find it easiest to invest in individual defence projects which enable the armed forces to maintain cadres proficient in the latest technology as a reserve for mobilization in times of national emergency. The F-16 squadron is such a cadre, a basis for familiarization and expansion, even if it does not improve national military strength decisively.[13]

Malaysia's armed forces were expanded in the 1970s and 1980s to cope with internal security concerns, doubling in strength from 60,000 in the mid-1970s to 113,000 today.[14] Arms purchases were primarily in support of this mission, leading to large contracts for low-technology systems. Since 1971, for example, Malaysia has purchased more than 1,100 light armoured vehicles from suppliers in five countries. Investments in major weapons systems such as helicopters, artillery and missiles tended to be small, reflecting the lack of firm requirements for more sophisticated and demanding systems.[15]

This situation began to change in the late 1970s as tentative measures were undertaken to build up the air force and navy. An initial order for one squadron of U.S. F-5 fighters in 1972 led to the establishment of the country's first fully capable air combat unit in 1976. In 1981 the air force was expanded greatly with an order for 88 second-hand U.S. A-4 *Skyhawk* fighters, half of which were cannibalized for parts. The navy was strengthened for long-range patrol duties with a vessel from South Korea and low-cost frigates from West

Germany. Naval striking power was fortified with missile-armed fast attack craft from France and Sweden.[16]

Throughout this gradual build-up, Malaysia was exceptionally careful to divide its orders into several small purchases from diverse suppliers. This kept individual contracts small and easy to finance, while preventing any single supplier from accumulating undue influence. This approach created logistic problems of supplying forces with endless special parts and made co-ordination difficult but it enabled the Malaysian Armed Forces to develop expertise with a wide array of military systems.

In September 1988 Malaysia signed a Memorandum of Understanding with the British Government which represented its largest defence contract ever. The deal was reported to involve the acquisition of twelve *Tornado* interdiction bombers (later reduced to eight *Tornados*), one refurbished *Oberon*-Class submarine, nine 155mm howitzers, *Rapier* air defence systems and surveillance radars.[17] The deal was striking not only for its size — at US$1.6 billion the largest single arms deal in the region except for U.S. and Soviet shipments to Vietnam — but also as the first fully integrated defence contract signed by Malaysia. Each service received something in an area where it was especially lacking. The deal painted a clear image of the direction in which Malaysia and its armed forces would prefer to evolve. The small quantities of weapons involved (nine howitzers?) also show how far Malaysia has to travel to accomplish this goal of military modernization. Re-building its armed forces around the kinds of systems included in the *Tornado* deal is economically prohibitive. Meanwhile, other requirements remain unsatisfied, including requirements for destroyer-size naval vessels, tanks for the army, air superiority fighters, and replacements for the aging F-5 and A-4 ground attack fighters.

Singapore has a reputation for being the "most heavily armed country on earth", with sizeable armed forces crowded into its exiguous territory. These are the only armed forces in the region fully oriented for conventional, as opposed to counter-insurgency, warfare. Singapore's armed forces also stand out by virtue of the government's willingness to invest not only in equipment, but also in advanced basing, support structures, and especially training to keep its forces combat ready.

Starting with British military traditions and preferences left from its colonial period, Singapore made a swift transition from aid to domestically-financed procurement in the mid-1970s. Contracts initially went mostly to the United States. While a preference for U.S. equipment remains, especially within the air force and the army to a lesser extent, diversification has led to large contracts with most Western European arms exporting countries, as well as Israel and several Arab countries.[18]

Large purchases of second-hand items, such as some 300 AMX-13 light tanks, 80 U.S. A-4 *Skyhawks* (plus others for cannibalization) and low-cost items such as U.S. F-5 fighters and M-113 APCs, have led to rapid force expansion. But this leaves Singapore with the problem of matching quantity with quality. The problem is eased through selective investments in force multipliers — equipment enabling other systems to perform more effectively. Two prominent examples are the four U.S. E-2C *Hawkeye* advanced early warning aircraft purchased for US$600 million in 1983, and four C-130B transports converted for aerial refuelling. A second approach is refurbishment and modernization of aging weapons platforms. A well-publicized programme to update about fifty A-4 *Skyhawks* with new General Electric F404 turbofan engines, avionics and controls is one of the most prominent retrofit projects anywhere. Singapore's AMX-13 tanks have been modernized similarly.[19] These efforts can help to preserve an aging weapon's military usefulness for another decade or so, delaying the point at which painful choices must be made. Finally, Singapore trains its troops to maximize the effectiveness of its military investments. But training opportunities are limited by its lack of space, often necessitating diplomatic

arrangements with neighbouring governments to permit training overseas.[20]

An order for eight U.S. F-16 fighters in 1984 (updated in 1985) worth US$280 million symbolized Singapore's intention to maintain forces second to none in Southeast Asia.[21] With its other major weapons systems updated, it faces fewer problems maintaining credible inventories than most other countries in the region. With no need to mount operations far beyond its territory and the additional support of the Five-Power Defence Arrangements with Britain, Australia, Malaysia and New Zealand, Singapore's armaments policy would seem to complete a system of security that other Southeast Asian countries still strive to equal.

Thailand finds its security needs influenced largely by its proximity to Vietnam. Although it faces domestic insurgencies, problems of border control, and the danger of incursions from Kampuchea and Laos, Thai military capabilities are naturally measured through comparison with Vietnam. There is no small degree of resemblance between the two countries' military procurement. Despite their size, both continue to rely extensively on foreign military assistance. Moreover, their forces are not oriented around their air forces or navies, nor are their armies configured for maintaining domestic order, as is the case elsewhere in the region. Rather, they deploy disproportionately large ground forces configured for conventional mechanized operations.

At this point the similarity ends. Thailand is wealthier and in no sense isolated diplomatically. It has access to all major arms exporters except for the Soviet Union and much greater freedom to design its own forces. Through a combination of aid and commercial purchases, Thailand has acquired the best equipped army in Southeast Asia.

Thai forces received their most important impetus for expansion from the United States, which provided large-scale assistance starting in the mid-1960s to balance the North Vietnamese presence in Laos and Cambodia, and in exchange for basing privileges for the U.S.

Air Force. Consistent with the development of Thai air bases and its own doctrine in Vietnam, U.S. aid especially favoured Thai air power. By 1974 the Thai Air Force possessed a squadron of F-5 fighters, an A-37 ground attack squadron and two squadrons of OV-10 counter-insurgency fighters, as well as several dozen transport, observation and training aircraft. Army aviation received about 200 Bell helicopters of various models. The navy received a few small warships for coastal patrol, while army ground forces were built around a nucleus of 300 M-41 light tanks and about 300 M-113 APCS.[22]

After the fall of South Vietnam and the rapid decline of U.S. assistance, Thailand gradually emerged as a major buyer on the international arms market. At this point domestic politics intervened to favour the army, the only service able to lead successful *coups d'etat* such as those in 1973 and 1976. Army-dominated governments gave the service virtually complete autonomy over its budget, enabling it to acquire 65 M-48A5 medium tanks, 170 155mm towed guns, 100 self-propelled guns, over 200 more M-113 APCs and numerous other items from the United States. Britain supplied 144 *Scorpion* light tanks, while other army equipment was purchased from Austria, Brazil, Israel, the Netherlands and Sweden. The air force was not ignored, receiving at least 54 additional F-5 fighters from 1978 to 1988. Transport aircraft and jet trainers generally were purchased second-hand. In 1985 Thailand completed a contract for twelve U.S. F-16 fighters for US$380 million, its most expensive single military order to date.[23] The navy has been the least favoured service, receiving no ships larger than corvettes and fast attack craft since 1973. Its lack of capital ships is compensated to some degree by orders for anti-ship missiles from France, Israel and the United States.

The second impetus for army expansion came from China, which provided massive supplies of armoured vehicles in the mid-1980s to counter Vietnam's presence in Kampuchea. At special "friendship prices", the Thai army received 53 Type-69 tanks, 779 APCs and token quantities of artillery. The navy was able to purchase four Chinese frigates and two submarines for US$272 million. The air force was offered Chinese copies of Soviet MiG-21 fighters but turned them down.[24] The sudden influx of Chinese arms augmented Thai forces but did not replace more expensive Western armaments. A 1987 order for 108 *Stingray* light tanks from the United States worth US$160 million continued unaffected by the Chinese assistance.[25] Small naval vessels from Italy and West Germany continued to arrive, as did anti-aircraft weapons from several European suppliers.

This expansion of its forces did not abruptly improve Thai fighting abilities. In the winter of 1987–88 the Thai army suffered an embarrassing defeat at the hands of a small Laotian force staking out a border claim. The defeat was attributed to poor leadership and distant command. It also revealed crippling logistic shortfalls and a general lack of training. Since then, steps have been taken to correct some of these problems, such as investing US$100 million in badly needed trucks.[26]

On paper, Thailand has forces adequate to cope with any likely Vietnamese threat. Much of its equipment is of early-1960s vintage design, but so is most of Vietnam's. The navy is comparable to other navies in the region. The air force remains weak, however, with no clear role or mission to guide its expansion. The F-16s are important symbolically, but too costly to form a basis for growth. Modernization of the F-5 fleet will keep it operational, but cannot overcome the fundamental weaknesses of its design — inadequate range, payload and capability in poor weather. Indeed, the air force's transport and liaison roles often receive more emphasis and the army's helicopter fleet is stronger in many respects.

The final category of Southeast Asian nations covers those with low defence budgets and limited military requirements. These five nations, Brunei, Burma, Kampuchea, Laos and the Philippines, have very different domestic political orders and economic endowments.

They share some common military characteristics: heavy reliance on foreign military assistance, their armed forces are oriented around counter-insurgency and domestic order missions exclusively, and arms transfers are received only intermittently and then in small quantities. Despite their limited military capabilities, they often have small pockets of surprising sophistication within their armed services.

Brunei Darusalam has one of the most unique armed forces in the world. The brigade-sized force with a total of 4,000 troops under the personal authority of Sultan Hassanal Bolkiah began to expand in the 1970s in anticipation of independence which came in 1984. The Sultan's vast oil revenues permit large purchases of arms, but his forces are constrained by lack of personnel. Mostly consisting of transports, the armed forces' lethal weapons systems include three missile-armed fast attack craft purchased from Singapore and a few dozen light armoured vehicles from Britain. These small purchases kept Brunei's average annual bill for major weapons down to US$18 million annually for 1977–86. Heavy reliance on British expatriates for training and management is another major expense, as is the 1,000-man British Army Gurkha Garrison.[27]

Brunei has no apparent external threats from other Southeast Asian countries, but there is concern about covert attacks on its oil installations, the rise of Islamic fundamentalism, and the possibility of antagonisms with neighbouring governments. These concerns culminated in October 1989 in an unprecedented arms contract with Britain worth US$400 million, including sixteen *Hawk* light fighters, missiles, trainers, and three missile-armed corvettes.[28] While this contract will not eliminate the risk of violent conflict, it will help to ensure that Brunei can cope with any foreseeable contingency without extensive foreign help.

Burma's armed forces were established with British assistance in the 1950s. Its 200,000 troops are armed exclusively for counter-insurgency operations against guerrillas and drug smuggling in the North, and they have been used to suppress political dissent, as was seen in 1988. Its armed forces operate virtually without major weapons systems. Fifteen AT-33A jet trainers acquired from the United States in the late-1960s are used for ground attack, as are three dozen propeller trainers purchased from Italy and Switzerland since 1975.[29] The lack of further military requirements enables Burma to keep its transfers of major weapons down to an average of US$5 million annually, the lowest in the region by far.

Kampuchea's armed forces, built up to substantial proportions by the United States by 1974, lost all their major weaponry in the chaos of the Khmer Rouge rule and the subsequent Vietnamese invasion. China responded to the Vietnamese action by arming guerrilla groups with small arms and anti-tank missiles. Not until 1983–84 did Vietnam and the Soviet Union begin to re-establish government forces, at first with small quantities of armoured vehicles and a total of nine helicopters. In 1986 a squadron of MiG-21 fighters was received from the Soviet Union and about five aging MiG-19s originally given to Vietnam by China. Pilots were sent to the Soviet Union for training.[30] As insurgent activity accelerated in the late 1980s, two non-communist guerrilla groups began to receive small arms and anti-tank missiles manufactured in Sweden and West Germany, apparently with the assistance of some ASEAN members.[31] Arms shipments to guerrilla factions could easily have surpassed the value of arms transfers to the Vietnamese-backed government in Phnom Penh, although reliable figures for Kampuchea are difficult to ascertain.

Laos has seen its small inventory of U.S.-furnished equipment from the Vietnam war era gradually replaced with Soviet-made systems, much of it supplied by Hanoi. Regular shipments of Soviet-made major weapons systems since the late 1970s, worth an average of US$46 million annually, have permitted the Laotians to accumulate two squadrons of MiG-21 fighters with a total of approximately forty aircraft. Small quantities of armoured vehicles, artillery, anti-aircraft missiles and transport aircraft also appear to have been received. Deliveries of Mi-8 and Mi-6 helicopters in the 1980s have been confirmed.[32] More detailed reports about the Laotian armed forces remain speculative.

Finally, the Philippines displays contradictory impulses regarding armaments. On the one hand, the country faces several strategic concerns including the active communist and Muslim rebellions, disputes over South China Sea islands, control over shipping, fishing and piracy within its 200-mile Exclusive Economic Zone, and serious questions regarding the long-term strategic impact of closing the U.S. bases on its territory. On the other hand, domestic political priorities make large-scale re-armament unacceptable. Having come to power with the assistance of rebellious soldiers in 1986, and having narrowly escaped attacks by her own armed forces in 1987 and 1989, President Cory Aquino can have no confidence that new weaponry will not be used against her. Civilian distrust of the armed forces, combined with economic pressure, makes major new defence expenditures unappealing. The declining popularity of defence spending has pushed military spending down by 40 per cent since the mid-1970s, leaving little room in the budget for replacing existing armaments.[33]

The result of this situation is most visible in the air force and navy, neither of which has undergone major weapons modernization since the late 1970s, when the air force received 25 second-hand U.S. F-8H fighters and the navy acquired three refurbished *Cannon*-Class frigates. Both services operate at the minimal level made possible by United State assistance.

The F-8H fighters were withdrawn in 1986 because of chronic maintenance problems.[34] The navy and coast guard, with a combined strength of about 250 vessels (most of them under 100 tons), can only put about one-tenth of these to sea regularly. Both operate principally with secondary systems: a dozen F-5A jet fighters and OV-10, T-28, T-34 and SF-260 propeller aircraft for the air force, minesweepers, patrol craft and landing craft for the navy.[35]

The army is only marginally better off, largely because of the priorities of counter-insurgency warfare, with about 200 tracked armoured vehicles of various types and 135 armoured cars, mostly provided by the United States. The army also controls some 100 helicopters operated by the air force.[36]

Rebuilding its armed forces into credible instruments against foreign as well as domestic threats will require large sustained investments. This is unlikely to happen under present political circumstances. A contract for eighteen Italian S.211 jet trainers costing US$73 million was signed in March 1989. The Philippine's most costly military contract, it aroused passionate debate about economic priorities.[37] The contract is militarily important if the country is to have jet pilots and hopes to maintain or expand its air force. The navy has proposed purchases of fast attack craft, minesweepers and patrol vessels, but has received no response. For all three armed services, rebuilding will mean virtually starting from scratch, and modernization will mean replacing virtually everything.

NOTES

1. J.N. Mak and Brian Wanstall, "Improving ASEAN Air Force Links", *Interavia* 7 (July 1989): 711–14.
2. An exceptionally frank account of this decision-making process based on Thailand's F-16 decision is Randall J. Larsen, "The Modernization of the Royal Thai Air Force", *Asian Defence Journal* 5 (May 1987): 4–10.
3. U.S. Arms Control and Disarmament Agency, *World Military Expenditures and Arms Transfers* (hereafter referred to as WMEAT) (Washington D.C.: U.S. Government Printing Office, various issues); and Stockholm International Peace Research Institute (SIPRI), *SIPRI Yearbook* (Oxford: Oxford University Press, annual). Throughout this paper the 1987 volume of *WMEAT* is used because of its presentation

of arms trade values in constant 1984 U.S. dollars, making its data roughly comparable to SIPRI arms trade data presented in constant 1985 U.S. dollars.

4. The concept of regional sub-systems used here is derived from Louis J. Cantori and Steven L. Spiegel, *The International Politics of Regions: A Comparative Approach* (Englewood Cliffs: Prentice Hall, 1970).

5. Methodologies of the two arms trade data sources are described in *WMEAT*, pp. 144–45; and SIPRI, *SIPRI Yearbook 1988*, "Appendix 7D. Sources and Methods", pp. 256–60.

6. John Moore, ed., "Vietnam", *Jane's Fighting Ships, 1987–88* (Coulsdon, Surrey: Jane's Publishing, 1987); and Douglas Pike, *PAVN: People's Army of Vietnam* (London: Brassey's, 1986).

7. Various annual volumes of the *SIPRI Yearbook*.

8. Data compiled directly from the SIPRI Arms Trade Data Base in Stockholm.

9. *WMEAT*, pp. 38, 62.

10. Bradley Hahn, "South-East Asia's Miniature Naval Arms Race", *Pacific Defence Reporter*, September 1985, pp. 21–24; and A.Z. Grazebrook, "Indonesia Builds for its Needs", *Pacific Defence Reporter*, October 1986, pp. 15–17.

11. Wynfred Joshua and Stephen P. Gibert, *Arms for the Third World: Soviet Military Aid Diplomacy* (Baltimore: John Hopkins Press, 1969), pp. 57–58, 64–68, 73–75.

12. John P. Holdridge, "Indonesia has neither Disposition nor Resources to Act in Aggressive Manner", *Pacific Defence Reporter*, June 1986, pp. 6–7.

13. Andrew MacIntyre, "Don't Worry About Those Indonesian F-16s", *Pacific Defence Reporter*, August 1986, pp 9–10.

14. "Malaysia: Preparing for Change", *Jane's Defence Weekly*, 29 July 1989, p. 159.

15. Michael Brzoska and Thomas Ohlson, *Arms Transfers to the Third World, 1971–85* (London: Oxford University Press, 1987), pp. 216–18, and interview with Malaysian Army Chief of Staff Gen. Yaacob Mohd Zain in *Asian Defence Journal* 3 (March 1988): 16–23.

16. "Malaysia's Hand-Me-Down Air Strategy", *Newsweek* (International Edition), 27 May 1985, p. 49; and R.J.L. Dicker, "HDW's FS 1500: The Bargain Basement Frigate", *International Defence Review* 11 (November 1984): 1667–69.

17. Tai Ming Cheung, "Enemy Spotting: Malaysia buys Military Muscle at Last to Defend Itself", *Far Eastern Economic Review*, 24 November 1988, p. 23; Michael Richardson, "Huge Malay Arms Deal Signals Determination to Upgrade Defenses", *International Herald Tribune*, 4 October 1988, p. 7; and David White, "UK, Malaysia Sign £1bn Arms Deal", *Financial Times*, 28 September 1988, p. 8.

18. R.S. Sassheen, 'The Singapore Armed Forces", *Asian Defence Journal* 4 (April 1989): 4–21.

19. Brian Cloughley, "Singapore Fortifies Defence Stance", *Jane's Defence Weekly*, 27 August 1988, p. 368; and Michael Richardson, "Singapore's A-4 Update", *Pacific Defence Reporter*, March 1988, p. 16.

20. Peter Kien-Hong Yu, "Singapore Faces Training Dilemma", *Jane's Defence Weekly*, 30 September 1989, p. 655; and M. Shuhud Saaid, "The Singapore Army", *Asian Defence Journal* 6 (June 1987): 4–18.

21. The original contract for limited performance F-16/J-79 versions is described in "Singapore to Buy Eight F-16s in $280m Deal", *Jane's Defence Weekly*, 7 April 1984, p. 514. After the Thai Government received U.S. permission to buy regular F-16As, Singapore upgraded its order. "F-16/79 Purchase Deferred", *Milavnews*, no. 272 (June 1984), p. 19.

22. R.S. Shassheen, "Thai Armed Forces: Modernisation to Meet New Challenges", *Asian Defence Journal* 12 (December 1988): 9–31.

23. Brzoska and Ohlson, *Arms Transfers*, pp. 259–62; Rodney Tasker, "Diplomatic Dog Fight", *Far Eastern Economic Review*, 2 February 1984, p. 32; and John McBeth, "F16 Counter-Attacked", *Far Eastern Economic Review*, 25 October 1984, p. 50.

24. Paisal Sricharatchanya, "The Chinese Firecracker", *Far Eastern Economic Review*, 8 December 1988, p. 34; Michael Richardson, "Thailand's Bargain Buy, But Indonesian's Wonder Why", *Pacific Defence Reporter*, August 1987, pp. 5–7; and "Thailand: Chinese Fighter Interest", *Milavnews*, no. 328 (February 1989), pp. 20–21.

25. Frank Lombard, "Thai Army Chief Denies Tank Buy 'Irregularities'", *Jane's Defence Weekly*, 28 November 1987, p. 1251; and "Gen. Wanchai Says 'Arms Dealers' Behind Criticism of Stingray Purchase", *Asian Defence Journal* 1 (January 1989), pp. 14–16.

26. Frank Lombard, "Royal Thai Army: Politics of Reform", *Jane's Defence Review*, 7 January 1989, pp. 14–16.
27. Shuhud Saaid, "The Royal Brunei Armed Forces", *Asian Defence Journal* 1 (January 1988): 13–23. The figure of US$18 million in average annual imports of major weapons is derived from SIPRI data.
28. Mark Urban, "Brunei to Buy Arms for £250 m from UK", *The Independent*, 21 October 1989, p. 14; and Mike Wells, "Brunei's Armed Forces Set for $400m Boost", *Jane's Defence Weekly*, 4 November 1989, p. 962.
29. Tin Maung Maung Than, "Burma's National Security and Defence Posture", *Contemporary Southeast Asia* 11, no. 1 (June 1989): 40–60.
30. "Air Force of Kampuchea Liberation Army", *International Air Forces and Military Aircraft Directory* (Stapleford, Essex: Aviation Advisory Services, 1988), p. 179; and *SIPRI Yearbook*, various annual volumes.
31. Steven Erlanger, "Aid to Cambodian Non-Communists is Detailed", *New York Times*, 16 November 1989, p. A16.
32. "Laos: Air Force of the People's Liberation Army", *Flight International*, 29 November–5 December 1989, p. 74; and *SIPRI Yearbook*, various annual volumes.
33. *WMEAT*, p. 73.
34. Frank B. Mormillo, "No More Crusaders", *Proceedings of the U.S. Naval Institute*, August 1987, p. 80.
35. *The Military Balance, 1989–1990* (London: International Institute for Strategic Studies, 1989); "The Philippine Air Force", *International Air Forces*, pp. 225–26.
36. "Unsuitably Equipped", *Far Eastern Economic Review*, 26 November 1987, pp. 37–38.
37. Robert Karniol, "Rebuilding the Philippines' Forces", *Jane's Defence Weekly*, 7 October 1989, p. 709; and Rodney Tasker, "Purchasing Power", *Far Eastern Economic Review*, 23 March 1989, pp. 30–31.

70. ASEAN AND THE FUTURE OF REGIONAL SECURITY

SHELDON N. SIMON

If superpower détente translates into a reduction of forward deployed forces in Southeast Asia during the 1990's, are the ASEAN states considering an alternative security posture? Although a formal ASEAN defense arrangement is unlikely, the association's membership has developed norms and a structure for the management of disputes sufficiently successful that military budgets have been restrained. Moreover, through annual meetings with the world's major economic powers as dialogue partners, ASEAN has advanced its members' mutual interests in a global setting.

Militarily, two developments can be anticipated for the 1990's: a movement toward regional arms control and confidence-building measures (including the normalization of relations between ASEAN and Indochina); and efforts to effect higher forms of military cooperation within ASEAN. In 1989, Malaysian, Indonesian and Singaporean officials discussed prospects for ASEAN-wide maritime defense, including trilateral exercises. The establishment of a Thai-Chinese arms stockpile also points toward innovative security arrangements as a reduced United States presence seems probable, despite Malaysian and Indonesian objections to China as a long-term security threat.

However, the possibility of a United States exit from Southeast Asia apparently exacerbates the differences among ASEAN states' regional security views. Indonesia sees a great power withdrawal as the best opportunity to become the region's primary maritime power. Thailand, in contrast, believes that a relationship with China remains essential to balance Vietnam. Malaysia and Singapore seem to be leaning toward Indonesia if Indonesia agrees to develop a cooperative defense arrangement for the Malacca Straits. The Philippines is too weak militarily and economically to make a regional defense contribution.[1]

Other clouds on the ASEAN-United States horizon cover economic relations. The United States is either the first or the second largest trading partner with every ASEAN state except Brunei. All, except Brunei, are in trade surplus with the United States; and all have benefited in the past decade from America's open market and insatiable appetite for foreign products. As Washington tries to put its economic house in order, however, efforts to expand United States overseas markets are regarded in Southeast Asia as attacks on ASEAN's economic growth. Pressures on Singapore, Malaysia and Thailand to revalue their currencies and remove

Reprinted in abridged form from "United States Security Policy and ASEAN", *Current History* 89, no. 545 (March 1990), pp. 97–132, by permission of the author.

restrictions on the entry of foreign goods as well as the need for local legislation to protect American intellectual property rights (patents and copyrights, particularly for computer software and pharmaceuticals) have led to charges that the United States is undermining its friends' prosperity.[2]

NOTES

1. These prospects are discussed by Donald E. Weatherbee, *ASEAN after Cambodia: Reordering Southeast Asia* (New York: The Asia Society, June 1989), pp. 17–24.
2. Karen Elliott House, "Mahathir Charges U.S. Is Trying To Hold Back Asian Growth," *The Asian Wall Street Journal Weekly (AWSJ)*, November 6, 1989.

71.

PROSPECTS OF TRILATERAL SECURITY CO-OPERATION IN ASEAN

MOCHTAR KUSUMA-ATMADJA

If we are thinking of building up ASEAN military capability, using the existing co-operation between the Indonesian, Malaysian and Singaporean armed forces as a nucleus, what are we to do with existing defence alliances, arrangements, or understandings?

The question of the Manila Pact and the U.S. bases in the Philippines will not be discussed here because, in the context of global security, these bases may still have a reason to be there for some time to come, perhaps in another form more acceptable to the Philippine body politic. It is assumed that the nationalistic sentiments expressed are an accurate reflection of the people's feelings and aspirations, and that the politicians can reach an agreement among themselves as to what the Philippines as a nation precisely wants.

The prospect of converting these facilities into huge repair and shipbuilding or manufacturing facilities for (commercial) aircraft or other civilian items, thus turning them into giant economic power houses for the Philippine economy fuelled by the United States, Japan, Taiwan, Hong Kong and Korea seems to be remote. This idea would fit in well with the Japanese concept of comprehensive security but not with the U.S. concept of security which is almost exclusively military and defence-oriented.

The Five-Power Defence Arrangements between Malaysia, Singapore, Australia, New Zealand and the United Kingdom are more relevant. In Indonesia it is understood that this arrangement is an insurance against a possible reversion of Indonesia to its old ways, exemplified by its Confrontation campaign against Malaysia in the early 1960s.

It is questionable whether the continuation of this defence arrangement is advisable if the three-power ASEAN defence co-operation between Indonesia, Malaysia and Singapore is expected to continue to grow. The three ASEAN member states not only share military training facilities, with more possibly in the pipeline, but are increasingly becoming economically interdependent as Singapore is pushing ahead with the Singapore-Johor-Batam growth triangle project, with plans to expand it in the near future.

The abandonment of the Five-Power Defence Arrangements by Malaysia and Singapore would *immeasurably* strengthen the political and psychological basis for the continued growth of a three-power ASEAN military co-operation, as the elements of suspicion and

Reprinted in abridged form from "Some Thoughts on ASEAN Security Co-operation: An Indonesian Perspective", *Contemporary Southeast Asia* 12, no. 3 (December 1990), pp. 161–71, by permission of the author and the Institute of Southeast Asian Studies.

distrust would be removed. There is no reason why three ASEAN countries could then no longer have joint exercises in the future with Australia as a friendly neighbouring power. This process of abandonment of the Five-Power Defence Arrangements could be done gradually over, say, the next five years, with the maturing process of a Three-Power Defence Arrangement.

Some permanence could be given to the existing practice of joint exercises conducted periodically by ASEAN member countries besides the other forms of military co-operation, if ASEAN established a military or defence committee.

This embryo of an organized or institutionalized form of co-operation could be started by the three Malacca Strait countries, Indonesia, Malaysia and Singapore, which have the closest kind of military co-operation in ASEAN, thus avoiding the opprobrium of it being an ASEAN body.

The advantages of setting up such a *three-country military committee* are several:

1. It establishes a formal link with the government and policy-making establishment;
2. It ensures continuity of co-operation and working together at the staff level and the ability to defuse potential conflict that may arise in the field; and
3. A permanent committee will make it possible for proper planning, programming and budgeting for a reasonably long period of, say, three to five years.

Such a gradual approach to the institutionalization of the *de facto* situation of military co-operation existing at present between the three Malacca Straits countries should be acceptable even to those most allergic to ASEAN military co-operation.

If the term "military cooperation committee" is unacceptable we might call it "defence cooperation committee". Surely no one can deny Indonesia, Malaysia and Singapore the right to co-operate in defending themselves?

This author agrees that the approach outlined above seems to be a *minimalist* one, but in his opinion this is what is attainable at present, given the low level of institutional integration within ASEAN. Legally speaking, ASEAN is not even an organization but merely an association of states.

Considering the reversals ASEAN has endured since Chatichai's single-minded pursuit of Thailand's national interests, the question can legitimately be asked are the members of ASEAN still committed to the ideals, aims and objectives of ASEAN or do they think it no longer necessary? That is the basic question which we have to ask ourselves. Indonesia, Malaysia and Singapore seem to be more firmly committed than some of the other members.

That fact or impression plus the close co-operation the armed forces of the three countries have been engaged in during the last five to ten years are the basis for the above proposal for an embryonic organizational framework for military defence co-operation, linking it with the respective governments rather than remaining a series of bilateral military exercises.

This modest proposal is based on the assumption that the answer to the basic question posed above is in the affirmative. As for the basic question on the need for ASEAN to continue to exist, the choice is ours to make, with each government making up its mind as to what is best for its people and the future of the region. The fact is that some member countries need ASEAN more than others, but this writer submits that we all need a stronger ASEAN and will be better served by it in the longer term. Time is running out and will not wait, the time to take the decision is now. Let us hope that the decision taken is the right one.

72.

ASEAN SECURITY CO-OPERATION IN THE POST-COLD WAR ERA

JUSUF WANANDI

In any case, ASEAN has to begin to prepare itself for the possibility that, as history has shown, any vacuum created by the withdrawal of one power will be filled in by other great powers. Given the uncertainties, ASEAN needs to enhance its cooperation in the defense field. ASEAN members should strengthen the existing bilateral and trilateral defense cooperation among its members so that they become a web of defense relations which eventually could transform into more formal defense coordination among the countries concerned. ASEAN could also develop closer defense cooperation with Australia, but this cannot be based on the Five Power Defense Arrangement (FPDA) which was originally formed against Indonesia.

If the US decides to totally withdraw from the Western Pacific, however a remote possibility, ASEAN might consider a more formal defense arrangement with the countries in the Southwest Pacific (Australia, New Zealand, and Papua New Guinea). In addition, it should seek cooperation with Japan in the area of technology transfer and the supply of equipments that could assist ASEAN in safeguarding the SLOCs in Southeast Asia which are vital to Japan's security interests. ASEAN will oppose any Japanese attempt to police the SLOCs in Southeast Asia but it is ready to cooperate with Japan since it cannot carry the financial burden of this task by itself. ASEAN could also examine future US capabilities to supply the necessary technologies and equipments to ASEAN.

A formal ASEAN cooperation in defense cannot come about overnight. As a prerequisite, ASEAN needs to resolve many of the prevailing problems between its members, which thus far are simply swept under the carpet. These include among other things the Sabah problem between Malaysia and the Philippines, as well as Thailand's ambivalence towards ASEAN and its greater interest to play a leadership role in continental Southeast Asia. Of equal importance to ASEAN defense cooperation is the development of a common perception of threat, in particular in assessing the roles of China and Vietnam in Southeast Asia, as well as on the relations with the other great powers. This will require more precise formulation and adaption on the implementation of the ZOPFAN (Zone of peace, freedom, and neutrality) concept.

In addition to their security implications, the recent changes in the global environment

Excerpted from Jusuf Wanandi, *ASEAN and Security Cooperation in Southeast Asia* (Jakarta: Centre for Strategic and International Studies, 1990), by permission of the author and the publisher.

also have political and economic implications for the region. The political implications of the dramatic developments in Eastern Europe are to be seen in a greater awareness globally of the concepts of freedom, democracy, political pluralism, the rule of law, and human rights. These influences are immediately felt by the socialist countries in the region, namely China, Vietnam, and North Korea, whose political leaders continue to resist the necessity to change. Mongolia, Myanmar, and Nepal have also been affected, and the influence will also be felt in the other countries in the Asia Pacific region although not immediately. In fact, popular movements in South Korea, the Philippines, and Taiwan have begun much earlier than in Eastern Europe. A cursory examination of the developments in these different countries suggests that change will be more rapid when a country faces grave economic difficulties.

The implications of global economic changes have been widely discussed. In the Asia Pacific region, these changes have led to greater economic interdependence among the Western Pacific countries. This has brought about new economic opportunities for the countries in the region, especially the developing countries, but it also is a major source of political frictions. In recent years, the region has also seen a dramatic increase in Japanese direct investment in manufacturing into Asia. This has led to greater intra-industry trade among the countries in East Asia and Japan. This development can also be beneficial to the ASEAN countries, but it is also a source of potential political discontent, especially if the resulting regional production structure is overly dominated by Japanese companies. In addition, the region continues to witness economic and trade frictions between the two major regional economies, the US and Japan. This development has de-stabilizing effects upon the entire region.

All these developments suggest the necessity for ASEAN to strengthen cooperation amongst itself and to take an active part in the promotion of Pacific economic cooperation.

A CONCLUDING NOTE

The preceding discussion clearly shows the importance of a strong and cohesive ASEAN to cope with the major changes that are taking place in the various fields, in the security and strategic fields as well as in the international economy. In fact ASEAN has recognized this necessity in the last AMM. Strong proposals were made to take bold initiatives in enhancing regional economic cooperation and to strengthen the mechanisms for cooperation, including the ASEAN Secretariat, the Joint Ministerial Meeting, and the involvement of ASEAN economic ministers in the ASEAN PMC. In addition, the need to have a dialogue on politico-security matters was also recognized.

Cooperation among the armed forces of the ASEAN countries in the defence field has been undertaken bilaterally or trilaterally for some time now, and they are outside the framework of ASEAN in accordance with the ASEAN Concord of 1976. This cooperation in defence includes regular meetings of commanders in chief and the chiefs of staff of the various forces, intelligence exchanges, joint exercises, exchanges of officers to participate in each other's staff colleges, joint seminars on defense and security matters, development of ideas and concepts about procurement procedures, the possibility of co-production of military equipments and spareparts, cooperation in repair and maintenance of military hardware, including aircrafts.

The possibility of transforming this "web of bilateral defense relations" into a multilateral framework for cooperation will need time. A pre-requisite for this is the development of a common perception of threat, a common interpretation of ZOPFAN and its implementation, and resolution of bilateral problems that still exist among various ASEAN countries. Thus far, many of these problems have been swept under the carpet. Most of them are historical in origin and have resulted in some deepseated mistrust among some ASEAN member countries. This already has been the subject of discussions in the AMM process, and these discussions and exchange of opinion in the AMM is supporting the efforts in defence cooperation although it is being implemented outside the ASEAN context. Because common perceptions of threat is the prerequisite of a sound and stable defence arrangement and cooperation in the future for ASEAN.

A web of bilateral defense relations between ASEAN member countries and their neighbors in the Southwest Pacific (Australia, New Zealand, and PNG) should also be promoted in the future.

The pressures and fundamental changes at the international level and in the Asia Pacific region, as examined earlier, might accelerate the development of a multilateral framework for defense cooperation among the ASEAN countries. It is likely, however, that this multilateral cooperation would still be outside ASEAN and will be undertaken by the armed forces of the ASEAN member countries. In fact, the abolition of military blocs and alliances, as the cold war has come to an end, would make it easier for the ASEAN countries to engage in multilateral defense cooperation.

Another important item in ASEAN's agenda is normalization of relations and cooperation with other countries in Southeast Asia, particularly Vietnam, as soon as the Cambodian conflict is resolved. It is important that ASEAN could find the modality to involve non-ASEAN countries in Southeast Asia in the implementation of the ZOPFAN idea. A step in this direction is to invite those countries to participate in ASEAN's Treaty of Amity and Cooperation, such as was the case with Papua New Guinea. This implicitly means that they accept the peaceful settlement of conflicts in the region.

In the end, ZOPFAN can be realized only on the bases of national and regional resilience. Therefore, it is imperative that the ASEAN countries continue to give the highest priority to economic and national development. ZOPFAN also implies that relations between the ASEAN countries and the Indochina countries are harmonious and peaceful, and based on mutual trust. The other important element of ZOPFAN is the development of a structure of relations between ASEAN and the major powers. In this connection, it is in ASEAN's primary interest that the region would not be dominated or come under the hegemony of any major power, although the legitimate presence of the major powers is recognized. The immediate issue facing ASEAN and other countries in the Asia Pacific region today is how to prevent a withdrawal of the US from the region in order that a balanced presence of the major powers could be maintained. It is important that US economic presence be continued and increased, and a forum such as APEC could help focus US economic attention to this region. The intensity of the US military presence in the region is likely to be influenced by the outcome of the negotiations on the use of the bases in the Philippines.

Japan's increased role and presence in the Asia Pacific region can be beneficial and will not be perceived as a threat so long as its alliance with the US is intact. The US-Japan alliance is vital to the maintenance of peace, stability and prosperity in the region. It is also in ASEAN's interest to prevent an overdependence on Japan, and this can be assured so long as the US presence in the region is adequate.

The PRC's importance to ASEAN is due to its adjacent location to Southeast Asia and due to the existence of territorial problems in the South China Sea. A forum to discuss these problems needs to be established, and this forum could for instance take up the recent proposal by Prime Minister Li Peng during his visit to Singapore in August 1990, namely to develop schemes for joint exploration and exploitation of resources in that area.

The Soviet Union should be invited to participate in the economic activities and development of the region. A main item in Soviet's agenda should be to find a peaceful resolution with Japan on the problem of the Northern Islands.

ASEAN should examine whether it can play some role to contribute to such a peaceful resolution.

In the final analysis, ASEAN will be able to undertake all the above tasks if it has the will and capabilities to enhance its cooperation in all fields. The institutional development of ASEAN is one of its most urgent tasks.

Section IX

ASEAN EXTERNAL RELATIONS

Introduction

Chandran Jeshurun

The very *raison d'être* of ASEAN's formation was to make the region's relations with external powers more manageable at a time when the level of conflict between the two sides in the Cold War was escalating rapidly. Nevertheless, the different ways in which each of its individual members handled their own external relations was not conducive to the emergence of a more corporate approach in the formulation of an ASEAN foreign policy as such. Indeed, it is, perhaps, one of ASEAN's unique characteristics that it has been able to accommodate the varied international preferences of its individual members in the world of diplomacy with the minimum of strain on the established consensus within the region. This Section, then, offers some notable viewpoints on the way in which ASEAN has responded to international issues particularly in relation to the policies of the great powers. It is also a sort of quick summary of the main bilateral links that ASEAN has developed since its formation.

In any survey of the literature of ASEAN's external relations it is necessary to determine a certain periodization and the selection here is roughly divided between the initial years up to the late 1970s, followed by the critical decade of the 1980s and finally looking into the future from the vantage point of the last decade of the twentieth century. Although Chin Kin Wah is primarily concerned with the new strategies of international diplomacy that

ASEAN was forced to resort to after the brazen Vietnamese invasion of Cambodia in 1978, he nevertheless provides an insightful account of the background of regional politics that preceded it. Likhit Diravegin, on the other hand, examines the complicated nature of ASEAN's interaction with the major powers during the troublesome period of the debate over the future of the region in the context of growing U.S.-Soviet confrontation. Both Leszek Buszynski and Lau Teik Soon offer some interesting ideas of the likely trends in the future with particular reference to the new concerns that have begun to dominate the diplomatic agenda of regional organizations such as ASEAN.

Of all the external powers with which ASEAN has had dealings in the past twenty-five years, none has been as fundamental to its overall diplomatic stance than the United States. Although this was as much due to the massive American military involvement in the region as it was the result of a lack of choice due to the internal communist threats that the member countries faced, bilateral relations have not always been on an even keel. The contributions of Jusuf Wanandi and the late Robert O. Tilman bear excellent testimony to this somewhat peculiar feature of ASEAN's ongoing relations with the only superpower left in the post-Cold War era. China has also consistently loomed large on the horizon of

ASEAN's external relations and it is important to have some perspectives on the historical background of its involvement with the region. At the same time it is useful to have some idea of the prospects for change that have emerged with the new policy of opening up to its neighbours. These are expertly dealt with in the analyses of Sarasin Viraphol and Lee Lai To with some additional insights from Julius Caesar Parreñas.

If one moves away from the strictly political and security dimension of ASEAN's external relations, then it is inevitable that Japan appears as the most significant influence on ASEAN's economic well-being. Given the fact that it is in the sphere of economic co-operation that

ASEAN has been viewed by many as having not lived up to expectations, it is certainly informative to study the evolution of ASEAN-Japan relations over the years. Two interesting viewpoints on this vital aspect of ASEAN's external relations are provided in the extracts from the writings of Shibusawa Masahide and Chaiwat Khamchoo and J.C. Parreñas offers a useful historical survey. All the remaining contributions that have been included in this Section are intended to reflect as fairly as possible the evolving external links of ASEAN with countries such as the former Soviet Union, Vietnam and Australia and some other partners such as the European Community.

73. ASEAN AND THE GREAT POWERS AFTER 1978

CHIN KIN WAH

The ASEAN sector, while taking a neutral stand towards the crises in the Indochina sector, was not insulated from the diplomatic reverberations of those events. However, one positive consequence of the two tier conflict and diplomatic rivalries between the extra-regional and intraregional communist powers was that ASEAN in the course of 1978 was transformed in communist rhetoric from an appendage of U.S. imperialism and an object of disapprobation to one of respectability whose members were to be ardently lobbied. Of these communist powers, China had been quite consistent in its support for ASEAN since 1975. ASEAN's neutralization proposal had a definite appeal to Peking if it also meant exclusion of the USSR. As the Viet-Kampuchean conflict erupted, China also sought to promote a Kampuchean interest before ASEAN. In November 1977, Vice Premier Li Hsien-nien, through a visiting Singapore press delegation, urged ASEAN to improve relations with Kampuchea, which, among the three Indochinese countries, was not to be feared. Chinese support for ASEAN was reiterated during Li's visit to Manila in April and Thai Prime Minister Kriangsak Chomanand's visit to Peking in the same month.

The official Soviet attitude towards ASEAN had tended to keep pace with the Vietnamese stance. At the beginning of 1978, Moscow was still continuing to label ASEAN a potential and hostile military alliance although Vietnam was slowly beginning to broaden contacts in the region. This was indicated by Vietnamese Foreign Minister Nguyen Duy Trinh's visit to the four ASEAN capitals between 28 December and 12 January — Singapore being omitted as an intended snub, following its refusal to return the skyjackers of a Vietnamese airliner. Each visit ended with mutual assurances of peaceful co-existence, the only expression of difference being made in Manila where Vo Dong Giang, Trinh's deputy, declared that the U.S bases should be banished. However, a formal acceptance of the regional organization was bypassed. Similarly, when Soviet Deputy Foreign Minister Nikolai Firyubin visited Thailand, Singapore and Malaysia in March, ASEAN was only mentioned obliquely while Malaysia impressed upon him the nonaggressive nature of the organization.

The clearest indication of a change of Vietnamese attitude towards ASEAN came in early July (when confrontation with China was steadily mounting) with Phan Hien's statement in Tokyo that Vietnam no longer regarded ASEAN

Reprinted in abridged form from "The Great Powers and Southeast Asia: A Year of Diplomatic Effervescence", *Southeast Asian Affairs 1979* (Singapore: Institute of Southeast Asian Studies, 1979), pp. 45–60, by permission of the author and the publisher.

as a military organization and was willing to have talks with it — a position he repeated later in the month when he toured the ASEAN states. For the first time, too, Vietnam openly indicated preparedness to discuss the wording of the proposal for a zone of peace and neutrality — it having publicized a slightly different wording (including "genuine independence") for such a zone when the ASEAN Foreign Ministers were holding their eleventh annual meeting in Pattaya in June. By August, the Soviet Union in turn began to make overtures to ASEAN to have a dialogue on the neutralization concept.

In real terms, this shift of Soviet (keeping pace with Vietnam's regional diplomacy) posture enabled Moscow to move to a more positive gear to counter Chinese and Kampuchean moves vis-à-vis ASEAN while allowing for a reservation of positions. This kind of bridge-building to ASEAN was also facilitating a kind of *de facto* neutralization among countervailing and rival communist influences.

One important result of the intense diplomatic rivalry between China, Vietnam and the Soviet Union was the visit which Teng Hsiao Ping undertook to three ASEAN states (Thailand, Malaysia and Singapore) in November — close on the heels of Pham Van Dong who toured the ASEAN area between September and October. If Teng's visit was mainly derived from conflicts with Vietnam and the Soviet Union, there were also two derived problems which complicated his diplomatic offensive. Competition with Moscow (and Vietnam) made it difficult for China to disavow support for Southeast Asian insurgent movements; conflict with Vietnam had thrown up the issue of Chinese protection of overseas Chinese. In his talks with the Malaysian Prime Minister, Teng unlike Pham Van Dong before him, was unable to publicly disclaim support for the Malayan Communist Party (a similar Chinese attitude towards the Communist Party of Thailand was expressed during Kriangsak's visit to Peking). The immediate spillover effect of this in intra-ASEAN terms was the setback to efforts to resume Sino-Indonesian relations, broken off after the abortive 1965 communist attempted coup in Indonesia. Prospects had seemed good in mid October when the Indonesian Foreign Minister disclosed that Indonesia was finalizing preparations to normalize relations with China — a statement soon enhanced by a meeting (for the first time) between President Suharto and a Chinese official leading a delegation to a forestry conference in Jakarta. Such a diplomatic setback also affected prospects of establishing relations with Singapore, which had indicated a desire to let Jakarta take precedence on the matter.

To Indonesia, whose apprehension of its overseas Chinese threat was disproportionate to the size of that population, China's claim to a protective interest over the overseas Chinese added concern and provided a further obstacle to normalization. The Chinese reassurance in July (in rejection of a Soviet charge that the overseas Chinese were being organized by Peking as a fifth column) that ethnic Chinese who became citizens of another country were no longer overseas Chinese or Chinese citizens did not seem to touch on the problem of the stateless Chinese — an issue that was not resolved during Teng's tour of Malaysia.

If China sought to forge a "joint front" with ASEAN to oppose the interests of the big powers (a point made by Huang Hua during the Chinese visits to Manila in April), Teng's tour did not realize such hopes. None of the three ASEAN states was drawn into one camp or another although Thailand, with its special frontline concerns with Kampuchea and Vietnam, was more inclined towards greater cordiality with China (for want of a restraining and balancing factor). In substantive form, this cordiality was expressed in the opening of the air corridor for the Chinese through Thai air space — the effect of which was to permit Chinese supplies to reach Kampuchea via Burma and Thailand.

The general concern among the ASEAN states not to be embroiled in the great power contest also led to a certain detachment in their reaction to the Soviet Union, although the latter had established diplomatic relations with all of them. While trade between the Soviet Union and the ASEAN countries had more than doubled between 1971 and 1976, Moscow had no major development project in the area. (Malaysia, for example, for domestic reasons had earlier rejected a Soviet aid offer for a multimillion dollar dam and hydroelectric project in Pahang.) The large Soviet profile in Vietnam contrasted with its low diplomatic stance in the ASEAN sector. Firyubin's second visit to three ASEAN states was postponed at their request, possibly to avoid too close an association with Pham Van Dong's tour. Firyubin's visit in late October was kept on a low key both by himself and his hosts and he departed from Manila without the usual press conference to avoid close questioning of Soviet policy in the region.

While maintaining equidistance from the communist rivalries, the ASEAN states had also seen a much closer co-operation in the politico-economic spheres with the U.S. and Japan. During 1978, the U.S. continually reaffirmed its strategic interests with the Southeast Asian region (underlined by close military assistance to the ASEAN states on a bilateral basis). Such interests were still formally enshrined through the Manila treaty (despite the demise of the Southeast Asia Treaty Organization or SEATO) in the case of Thailand and the Philippines.

To the latter, Vice President Mondale had emphasized, during his visit in early May, the U.S. commitment to a flexible military presence in the region and assistance to maintain the existing balance of power. He also promised the retention in the Western Pacific of an existing force level, amounting to 140,000 servicemen, mostly in the Subic Bay and Clark air base. Whatever the U.S. official posturings and public controversy over human rights in the Philippines, the importance of those bases to the U.S. was never seriously undermined. Indeed, Holbrooke had in March reiterated the indispensability of those bases to the maintenance of a peaceful equilibrium in Asia and to America's friends in that region, in his support for the Administration's request for US$300 million, for development and food aid for Indonesia, US$41 million for Thailand and US$13.5 million for Malaysia. The sale of a squadron of F-5E fighter aircraft to Indonesia was approved by Congress while Mondale was able to promise eighteen similar aircraft to Thailand. The co-operative aspect of U.S. military relations with the Philippines culminated towards the end of August, after protracted negotiations, in an announcement (while the war in Kampuchea reached a climax) of a new military bases agreement which conceded to Philippine sovereignty while reserving the right to "unhampered military operations". New economic and military assistance over the next five years was also promised.

74.

ASEAN'S VIEW OF THE ROLE OF THE UNITED STATES IN SOUTHEAST ASIA

JUSUF WANANDI

The U.S. has recently regained its credibility in the eyes of ASEAN. It is a fact that the U.S. presence in Southeast Asia remains minimal, but perhaps this is what ASEAN desires, since it may better ensure the kind of relationship the Association wants with the U.S. — a relationship based on an equal footing.

The decline of U.S. interest in the Southeast Asian region since the end of the 1960s reflected the mood of the U.S. public at large, in particular the mass media, the academic circles and Congress, who wanted their country to disinvolve itself in the region. A disinvolvement in military terms was most pronounced, exhibited by a withdrawal from Thailand, a reduction in military sales to the ASEAN countries and a decrease in the capability of the Seventh Fleet. However, basically, there was the impression among ASEAN leaders that U.S. policies toward the region were very uncertain and that the U.S. as a leading world power was, in a sense, adrift. This was observed with regard to not only the Southeast Asian region but also the Asia-Pacific region as a whole and even globally. In fact, the U.S.'s uncertain policies toward other regions had had considerable psychological effects on Southeast Asia. This was shown by the reactions to Carter's plan in early 1977 to unilaterally withdraw troops from South Korea. Also, with a worsening in trade and economic relations between Japan and the U.S., there was a real concern that this deterioration in relations might spill over into the field of security, which in turn could create instabilities throughout the Asia-Pacific region.

Uncertainties in U.S. policies resulted from the constitutional crises of the political system in the U.S.; this system was severely tested as a result of the debacle in Vietnam and the Watergate affair. It was rather fortunate that within the Administration there was a group of middle-level officials who militantly endorsed a minimal presence of the U.S. in the region. Similarly, the Subcommittee on Asia and the Pacific of the International Relations Committee in Congress could be credited with keeping a modest Congressional interest in the region alive.

Early 1979 marked the beginning of a change in policies by the Carter Administration. ASEAN leaders and those of the Asia-Pacific region as a whole saw encouraging trends in U.S. policies toward the region: greater realism, clearer directions, and more co-ordination. Of importance to the region were the following trends:

Reprinted in abridged form from "A View from ASEAN on the Interest and Role of the United States in Southeast Asia", in *Regional Security Developments and Stability in Southeast Asia* (Singapore: Institute of Southeast Asian Studies, 1980), pp. 35–41, by permission of the author and the publisher.

a. Greater understanding on the side of the U.S. about the necessity to overcome its difficulties in economic and trade relations with Japan in order not to endanger their politico-security relations, which remained the pillar of regional stability;

b. The more realistic approach of the U.S. toward the PRC had lessened the concerns and the psychological impact created by the sudden normalization of relations and the euphoric mood in the U.S. with the PRC. It was hoped that the Carter Administration would maintain a balance in its relationships with the Soviet Union and the PRC;

c. The greater flexibility adopted by the Carter Administration with regard to the withdrawal of troops from South Korea had restored the credibility of the U.S. in the region. Also, new legislations in the U.S. regarding its relations with Taiwan were widely seen as a clear indication of continued commitment to Taiwan;

d. In the military field, the U.S. took concrete steps to enhance the capabilities of the Seventh Fleet. Also, the successful completion of new arrangements with the Philippines regarding facilities at Subic and Clark Field came at a time when it was clear that the Soviet Union was increasing its presence in Southeast Asia;

e. Following the Vietnamese invasion of Kampuchea, the U.S. gave full political support to ASEAN's efforts to reduce the conflict in Indochina and to strive for a political solution on Kampuchea. It also attempted to ensure Thailand's security by supplying defensive armaments to Thailand. In addition the U.S. gave positive support to help resolve the refugee problems of the ASEAN countries;

f. More concrete actions were taken by the U.S. to increase relations with ASEAN through bilateral and multilateral consultative forums; attempts were also made to increase its economic relations with and presence in ASEAN countries, and to improve co-operation in research and technology between them, for example, in the field of energy and forestry. The recognition by the U.S. of its economic stakes in the Asia-Pacific region was followed by intensified efforts by the Administration to formulate a more clearly directed economic policy toward the region.

The above changes do not mean that the presence of the U.S. would return to the levels prevailing during 1965-1973; at the most, the commitment of its troops abroad would be limited to areas considered most vital to U.S. interest. In any case, an over-presence of the U.S. in this region is not desired by ASEAN, because such an over-presence tends to create an undesirable "superpower-client" relationship and it would also encourage other great powers to increase their presence in this region, thus resulting in new instabilities.

In summing up, it can be said that the U.S. presently has laid the foundation for a more healthy relationship with the countries in the Asia-Pacific region — a "mosaic" type of relationship, involving a minimal or modest level of presence which, for the time being, is considered sufficient by the countries in the region, including ASEAN. It should be noted, however, that in its relations with the countries in the Asia-Pacific region the U.S. needs to involve itself in more consultations, in order to become more appreciative of natural differences that could arise because of differing geographical, historical, and cultural backgrounds. The U.S. also has to recognize that its understanding of nuances and complexities of situations in the region is minimal and that, consequently, its attitude often tends to be naive and very impatient.

What is needed in the not too distant future is for the U.S. to formulate a comprehensive foreign policy with a longer-term perspective, so as to reduce the propensity to adopt ad hoc and reactive policies, currently shown in the way it handles the situation in the Middle East and South Asia. Short of such a comprehensive foreign policy, the U.S. would create unnecessary backlashes which would revive doubts about its credibility.

There are two issues which the U.S. must consider in formulating the future direction of its policies toward the region. First, as a result of the events in Iran and Afghanistan, there seem to be developing strong pressures within the Carter Administration to establish a new military alliance comprising the U.S., the PRC, Japan and the European Economic Community (EEC). The PRC has been granted "Most Favoured Nation" (MFN) status and military technologies will be sold to it. It cannot be denied that a normalization of relations between the U.S. and the PRC would have some stabilizing effects in the sense that it would affirm a balanced relationship among the great powers in this region. It would also have beneficial effects for both the U.S. and the PRC. In fact, the *idea* of a potential alliance between these two countries could become an effective deterrent to any adventurous actions by the Soviet Union in the Asia-Pacific region. However, if the alliance becomes a reality, it would eliminate the deterrent value of the idea and could even inflate the Soviets' already intense paranoia vis-à-vis the PRC. This would stimulate greater Soviet reactions, essentially military in nature, for its army is the only effective instrument the Soviet Union has at its disposal. Such a reaction by the Soviet Union would leave no country unharmed, ASEAN included.

Moreover, it remains questionable whether the PRC itself intends to perform the role of a partner in alliance with the U.S., as contemplated by the latter, primarily because of the PRC's limited military capabilities. On the contrary, it is more likely that the PRC intends to use the U.S. in its struggle against the Soviet Union. In the long run, a militarily strong PRC could become a problem to the U.S., similar to the problem created by the Soviet Union in the post-World War II era despite the military support given to it by the U.S. during the war.

Secondly, the U.S. has no clear policies as yet with regard to Vietnam, and it has even given one the impression of merely following the PRC's policies. This attitude could push Vietnam further into the Soviet camp. It seems clear that the U.S. cannot normalize its relations with Vietnam before the elections at the end of this year. However, a more flexible attitude can be adopted, for example, by sending signals of the possibility of partially lifting the embargo, applying diplomatic pressures on the PRC to accept a political compromise on Kampuchea, and supporting ASEAN's diplomatic initiative towards resolving the conflict in Indochina.

It is important to note that the Southeast Asian region has been relatively stable even with the outbreak of the conflict in Indochina and the various spillovers of the conflict, such as the refugee problem. This is largely because each of the ASEAN countries has reached a certain maturity and self-confidence. Co-operation among them has been effective, because ASEAN has become a state of mind, not only among the leaders but also among a considerable portion of the population. The conflict in Indochina, which is potentially a very destabilizing factor in the region, has not created panic, but instead has given additional impetus to the strengthening of ASEAN's unity. Thailand, for example, does not have to resort to its traditional "bamboo philosophy" in its foreign policy now because of increasing confidence that it can cope with the implications of the conflict in Indochina, mainly in view of ASEAN's solidarity.

Therefore, a strong ASEAN would be in the interests of the U.S. and its support in this respect would greatly contribute to the stability and security of Southeast Asia. The ASEAN countries have clearly identified their major task as strengthening both national and regional resilience, and the U.S. can play an important role in this regard.

It is clear that the presence of the U.S. in Southeast Asia is necessary to maintain the balance of power and eliminate any attempts by the other superpowers to expand their spheres of influence to this region. It is imperative that the U.S. increase the capabilities of the Seventh Fleet to counter the Soviet naval presence in the region. At the same time, the U.S. should maintain a balanced relationship with the Soviet Union and the PRC, and should adopt a flexible attitude and policy towards Vietnam. The presence of the U.S. in this fashion would contribute to bringing about a regional order in Southeast Asia.

75.

ASEAN-U.S. RELATIONS

ROBERT O. TILMAN

In fact, Southeast Asia itself began to be viewed in the larger context of the Middle East and Pacific Basin.[1] Southeast Asia was seen as a vital link in a strategic chain of American national interests that extended from the Persian Gulf to America's eastern seaboard. Besides being a supplier of some vital raw materials, and a potential producer of considerable amounts of petroleum, much of insular-peninsular Southeast Asia sits astride the waterways that are important to America and crucial to America's most important Asian ally, Japan.[2] It was in this context that America "discovered" ASEAN.

That this took a decade might seem surprising, but in context the lateness of the discovery is understandable. America had no time to search for the attractive qualities of ASEAN when it was obsessed with Vietnam. On the other hand, for almost a decade of its existence ASEAN's attractive qualities were not readily apparent. ASEAN developed very slowly from the time of its inception in 1967, and for almost a decade few observers took it very seriously.[3] It was avowedly economic but it recorded few successes in the economic sphere. ASEAN leaders met and talked at an almost non-stop pace, but the concrete results that were forthcoming rarely if ever seemed commensurate with the level of activity that generated them. In short, ASEAN seemed very inefficient: it took a large effort to deliver a very modest product. It stood for a common market, but it could not agree on any significant reductions in tariffs on items produced by its members and distributed within the region. By 1977, however, ASEAN was coming of age, not so much as an economic grouping, which it still claimed to be, but as a forum for political discussions.[4] The many miles travelled by ASEAN leaders at all levels — heads of governments, ministers, lawmakers, and technocrats — were beginning to pay off as some Southeast Asians were at last getting to know each other and to know how to deal with their friends as well as their enemies. ASEAN may have been discovered by the world in mid- to late-seventies, but without a decade of slow evolution there would have been nothing to discover.[5] It was in this setting that first ASEAN-U.S. discussions began in Manila in 1977, the first of many such "dialogues" (as they were officially termed by ASEAN) between the Association and the major powers.

As the ASEAN-U.S. dialogues progressed, the Southeast Asian policy alternatives open to both America and ASEAN began and continued to narrow. In June 1978 Vietnam sought

Reprinted in abridged form from "Asia, ASEAN and America in the Eighties: The Agonies of Maturing Relationships", *Contemporary Southeast Asia* 2, no. 4 (March 1981), pp. 308–22, by permission of the Institute of Southeast Asian Studies.

and attained affiliation with the Council for Mutual Economic Aid (CEMA or COMECON), thereby linking the Socialist Republic of Vietnam (SRV) with the Russian wing of the socialist bloc. At the same time, the People's Republic of China was pursuing its carefully orchestrated drive towards the "four modernizations" and thereby positioning itself much closer to the Western bloc of nations. The Japanese-Chinese Friendship Treaty of August 1978, itself a by-product of the Chinese modernization movement, brought Japan, China, and, increasingly, America into a relationship that would eventually come as close to a political alliance as the three had ever had. As China, Japan, and the United States were reaching their understanding, the SRV sought further reassurance through the Soviet-Vietnam Treaty of Friendship and Cooperation of November 1978. The "China card", played by President Carter on 15 December 1978, represented the culmination of a series of developments that began with President Nixon's visit to Peking in 1972. Carter's dramatic China announcement was followed ten days later by the Vietnamese invasion of Kampuchea, and less than two months later the Chinese, perhaps reassured by their new detente with America,[6] sought to teach the Vietnamese a lesson by sending their armed forces south into Vietnamese territory, where they remained until withdrawn on 16 March 1979. By default more than design, ASEAN and America found themselves steering very much parallel courses in Southeast Asia throughout most of the Carter administration.

ASEAN Southeast Asia continues to be viewed holistically as a significant but smaller part of a larger international system, though ASEAN-Vietnamese tensions, channelled through Kampuchea and Thailand, are again tending to blur the focus of the larger picture. While some of the importance attached to ASEAN Southeast Asia continues to be derived from its direct strategic significance to the United States (the "lifeline" argument) much stems from the importance to Japan of the international waterways that pass through the ASEAN

region. As one of America's most important trading partners and America's major Asian allys Japan's well-being is crucial to American national interests. In this sense, as in others as well, America, Japan, and the states of ASEAN are inextricably intertwined in a web of American and Japanese interests.

Many of these interests also parallel the national interests of the ASEAN states as expressed by the current generation of political leadership in the region. While the United States and some of the ASEAN membership may differ considerably in political practices and styles, in the perspective of comparisons of America and other third world nations the similarities stand out more than the differences. The Philippines has received the most criticism for its violations of human rights and for the continuation of martial law rule, but, whatever its faults, the Martial Law regime is not an El Salvadorian junta and Ferdinand Marcos is not an Idi Amin. The American government can, and at least under the Carter administration it did, protest against human rights violations in the Philippines, but in the end keeping company with the Philippines is far less uncomfortable than with many third world states. Indeed, despite some well-publicized political abuses, the same can be said for all of the ASEAN states.[7]

The United States and ASEAN also share fairly similar economic philosophies, and partly because of these shared philosophies trading links between the countries of ASEAN and the United States have grown to significant proportions. Grouped together, the countries of ASEAN constitute the fifth largest trading partner of the United States (following behind the European Economic Community, Canada, Japan, and Mexico). ASEAN captures 17.2 per cent of America's East Asian trade, 10.4 per cent of all trade between the United States and the developing countries, and 4.2 per cent of America's total world trade. In direct investment, America has US$3.5 billion invested in the ASEAN states, and this represents 21 per cent of all East Asian direct investment and 2.3 per cent of America's total world investment.[8]

Given the perceived parallels in the political, economic, and social philosophies of ASEAN and America, given the realities of their patterns of trade and investment, and given the contrasts in both areas between America and the states of Indochina, it is not surprising that the United States came to distinguish between the "two Southeast Asias". Although Vietnam, and today Vietnamese-controlled Kampuchea and Laos, have not achieved the arch-enemy status held by Vietnam in the sixties and early seventies, it is clear that America regards the Vietnamese as the perpetrators and instigators of most of the troubles that confront Southeast Asia today. It is highly unlikely that the United States and the SRV are on a collision course similar to the one that characterized their relations after the fall of Dienbienphu; but it is equally clear that Washington, after some hesitation during 1975–77, now shows no reluctance to distinguish between friends and non-friends in Southeast Asia.

While discovering and embracing ASEAN, the United States thus far has been able to avoid the frequent American mistake of trying, at worst, to take over or, at best, to push a friend faster and farther than it wishes or needs to go. ASEAN operates in its own indigenous Southeast Asian idiom; and while American policy-makers must frequently have been frustrated by its more traditional style of decision-making (discussion and consensus), particularly during the early years of the Carter administration, American policy-makers generally have been willing to follow more than lead ASEAN in regional policies. A tendency to become impatient has not been unusual, but the temptation to take over, the temptation to demonstrate a more efficient American way to get things done, has been resisted. This may eventually be recorded as one of the major accomplishments of the Carter administration in Southeast Asia.[9]

The United States has cautiously reappeared on the Southeast Asian scene following its hasty withdrawal in 1975, but there have been fairly well-defined limits to its presence and power. The memories of the post-Vietnam anguish in America are fading, but there is still little sentiment that would support an American military presence on mainland Asia outside Korea. Even under the new Republican administration it is very unlikely that American public opinion would support the stationing of armed forces anywhere in Asia except in Japan, Korea, the Philippines, and perhaps other island bases such as Diego Garcia. Similarly, unless the situation erodes significantly and precipitously, it is not likely that the countries of the ASEAN region would look favourably upon the return of American forces; and if the situation did deteriorate dramatically and quickly enough to tempt the ASEAN states to invite the United States in, it is not certain that American forces could be deployed fast enough to make any real difference. In short, the limits on American power faced by the Carter administration in Southeast Asia were real, though not always well understood.

U.S.–ASEAN RELATIONS: LEGACIES AND PROBLEMS

The Carter administration inherited some problem-creating legacies from previous years, and it has left for President-elect Reagan some problems of its own making. In some areas reasonably satisfying solutions may be possible, but in others the only choice seems to be the least worst of a number of almost equally unattractive alternatives.

In the eyes of some Southeast Asians, the United States defaulted once, and may be expected to do it again if domestic politics should so dictate. Some Southeast Asians, often a younger generation of students, equally convinced that disengagement was forced on an unwilling American government by a disenchanted public, disagree with their elders and argue that the coalition of American military and multinational corporations is ready and eager to return as soon as the American domestic situation permits it. These doubts about American motives in Southeast Asia, however they may be interpreted by persons of differing political persuasions, are part of a larger problem involving the image of American leadership in the world today. While Mr. Carter has received most of the blame in recent years, the American system is often identified as the real culprit. The humorous quip of Derek Davies during the American election campaign — "if God had meant the Americans to have a President he'd have given them a candidate"[10] — says much about the image problem America faces in Southeast Asia. Even if American motives are noble, and sometimes they are more naively noble than they should be, they are rarely accepted as such. And even when American policy is rational and effective, and much rationality and effectiveness can be claimed for American policy in Southeast Asia between 1977 and 1980, the subjective image of policy continues to be shaped by the larger vision of America on a random walk through history.

In fact, how far can and will the United States go in support of its ASEAN friends? Or, put in the form of a dilemma, how can a government profess unqualified support for a friend when political realities dictate that all such support must be qualified? At the time of the Vietnamese incursions into Thailand in June 1980, Thais from many walks of life seemed to want reassurances from almost any American they encountered that the United States would stand squarely behind Thailand in its dispute with its new neighbour. The American government repeatedly gave such assurances but carefully qualified its otherwise unqualified professions of support by only discussing the initial form of reaction — the acceleration of delivery of military hardware. But, as many less diplomatically minded students were prone to ask, suppose Vietnam chose to launch a major invasion, as they had done in Kampuchea — would American support remain unqualified? The response to

this question seemed obvious — "unqualified" American support is in fact very much qualified, and most astute political leaders already recognize this political reality.[11]

On the other hand, there is a genuine ambiguity on the part of many of ASEAN's leaders and opinion-makers about the desire for an American presence in the region. Many want, and some expect, America to have a credible presence in the area, but they do not want American forces or bases on their own territory. As it is sometimes put rather indelicately in private, many Indonesians, Malaysians, Singaporeans, or Thais are likely to express the view that they welcome American bases in the ASEAN region, but they are equally pleased that they are in the Philippines rather than in their own countries. It is not unusual to hear complaints about America's low profile followed quickly by the comment that basing American aircraft or home-porting American warships in their own countries would not be in their national interests. Such ambivalence is a legacy of the era of the Vietnam war, and it will doubtlessly continue to trouble policy-makers for many years to come.

China presents the United States with two dilemmas in Southeast Asia. The first of these can best be expressed by referring to the Indian classic on statecraft, Kautilya's *Arthasastra*. According to Kautilya, "my friend's friend is my friend; my friend's enemy is my enemy; my enemy's enemy is my friend". Despite the current honeymoon between China and ASEAN, some members view China as the major short-range threat, and almost all agree that the "Middle Kingdom" constitutes a long-range threat. Despite Kautilya's commonsense proposition, China — the friend of their American friend — is viewed by many in the ASEAN region as their potential enemy. Given the pendulous history of Sino-American relations, and given a plethora of recent evidence that the pendulum is swinging quickly and decisively towards vastly improved relations between the two recent adversaries, there is a real fear in some ASEAN countries that America's love affair with China will influence its perceptions of Southeast Asia and its policies towards the region.[12]

In the second dilemma involving China, the view is sometimes heard in the ASEAN countries that in so far as the four modernizations are unsuccessful, an unstable China will result, and an unstable China poses a short-term threat to the region. In so far as they are successful, the result will be strong and stable China, and a strong and stable China presents a long-term threat. Neither statement may be correct, but both are believed by many opinion leaders in the ASEAN region. And in so far as they are believed, they constitute a problem for American policy-makers.

The "domino theory" of Southeast Asian international politics — first expounded by President Eisenhower at a press conference in 1954 — held that each state in the region was propped up by the mutually reinforcing independence of the others, and that like a row of dominoes standing on end the toppling of one would start a chain reaction ending in the fall of all. At the time the Republic of Vietnam was the first domino, but the failure of the chain reaction to occur after the spring of 1975 did not entirely discredit the model. That there is some commonsense validity to the model is obvious — it is far easier to live next to a friendly rather than a hostile neighbour — but the underlying assumptions were simplistic, if not faulty. More important, the disproportionate attention the domino theory focused on the influence of the external threat obscured some fundamental and potentially debilitating internal problems that each state in Southeast Asia also faces. In the long run, the termites inside the dominoes might prove to be far more destructive than the forces threatening to topple the dominoes. To be realistic one has to recognize that any national domino, in Southeast Asia or elsewhere, might disintegrate under the weight of its own superstructure if it is not adequately supported by its own foundations.

Whether it is the "middle-kingdom" syndrome of Vietnam, the absence of an over-arching sense of civic responsibility in Thailand and the Philippines, the Java-centric nature of Indonesia, communalism and religion in Malaysia, or success in Singapore — each Southeast Asian domino contains its own termites. It is almost as if each state were a Shakespearean tragic hero — each containing within itself the seeds of a "fatal flaw" that early in the drama appeared to be harmless and indeed served to set the hero apart from the rest of the cast as a person who is unique, perhaps amusing or fascinating, and certainly interesting to watch. However, as the drama unfolds, the fatal flaw develops and is eventually exposed for what it is — a force driving the hero towards a destruction of his own making. When the hero — or national domino — falls to outside forces, the outcome evokes pathos; when he, or it, succumbs to internal flaws it is a tragedy. Few dominoes have toppled since April 1975, and future collapses purely pathetic in nature are unlikely. Yet there is considerable potential for tragedy in Southeast Asia, and in the real world of international politics external forces are often ready and eager to serve as catalytic agents to hasten the growth of internal tragic flaws. However, unlike a Shakespearean tragic hero, corrections are possible, prophecies are not necessarily self-fulfilling, and tragic outcomes are therefore not inevitable. But they are possible, and therein lie problems not of America's making.

NOTES

1. Holbrooke seems to have been the person most responsible for the frequent State Department statements (often Holbrooke's speeches) that viewed Southeast Asia holistically. Occasional criticism could even be heard in Washington and in U.S. missions abroad that Holbrooke sometimes had difficulty seeing

the Southeast Asian trees for the total forest, but most nevertheless agreed that this was a distinct improvement over thinking in previous years that reversed the formulation.

2. More than 80% of Japan's energy supplies and 60% of all its raw material requirements pass through Southeast Asia. Jusuf Wanandi, "Politico-Security Dimensions of Southeast Asia", *Asian Survey* 17, no. 8 (1977): 779–80. Three Southeast Asian straits are of prime strategic importance to the United States and Japan. The Straits of Malacca, the second busiest waterway in the world, is 500 nautical miles in length, has an average depth of 75 feet, and a minimum width of eight nautical miles. Traffic forced to bypass Malacca (e.g., supertankers) must pass through the Sunda and Lombok straits, both of which are deeper and wider, but the northern passage out of the latter is long (700–1,000 miles) and constricted. Bypassing the Malacca Straits also adds 1,400 miles to the passage to Japan from the Middle East. See Lawrence E. Grinter, *The Philippine Bases: Continuing Utility in a Changing Strategic Context* (Washington, D.C.: National Defense University, 1980), pp. 23, 27, 28.

3. For a brief contemporary history of ASEAN's failings and accomplishments during the first decade, see Shee Poon-Kim, "A Decade of ASEAN, 1967–1977", *Asian Survey* 17, no. 8 (1977): 753–70.

4. Shee Poon-Kim (see no. 3 above) cites several examples in which ASEAN flexed its political muscle to gain economic concessions from countries outside the region, but actual evidence of economic co-operation at the time was scant. James Wong, *ASEAN Economies in Perspective* (Philadelphia: Institute for the Study of Human Issues, 1979), working with data confined chiefly to the first decade of ASEAN, deals to some extent with accomplishments and failures of ASEAN as an economic organization, but he is more concerned with a comparative study of the national economies of the five member states. The first Preferential Trading List was drawn up in Bali in 1976, but by early 1978 the membership had agreed on only 71 items on the List. However, in September 1978, 755 items were added; 500 more were added in March 1979; and 1,001 more in December 1979. *Far Eastern Economic Review*, 7 Dec. 1979, pp. 73, 74. ASEAN, acting collectively, was of prime importance in negotiating international air fares with Australia; ASEAN members diverted the course of the Havana Non-Aligned Conference; and ASEAN members have very effectively steered the Cambodian resolution through the United Nations General Assembly in 1979 and 1980.

5. This theme is developed in the author's "Mutual Predictability of Elite Behaviour: The Probable Contributions of the ASEAN Framework" (Paper presented at a symposium on "The Malay World in Transition", Ohio University, May 1979).

6. Sheldon W. Simon, "China, Vietnam, and ASEAN: The Politics of Polarization", *Asian Survey* 19, no. 12 (1979): 1171–88, makes this point. During the visit of Deng Xiaoping to the United States, the Vice-Premier dropped some hints about a possible invasion. When this actually occurred very soon thereafter, it seemed that the United States had at least not discouraged the Chinese, and perhaps the Chinese had Washington's tacit approval (pp. 1177, 1178).

7. Robert A. Packenham, *Liberal America and The Third World* (Princeton, N.J.: Princeton University Press, 1973) makes the now frequently heard argument that America's liberal constitutionalism is often not exportable into an environment where similar historical, social, and economic conditions do not exist. In a number of passages particularly pertinent to ASEAN-U.S. relations, Packenham argues, not that the United States must be blind to real political abuses, but that America must be more realistic in dealing with the world as it is, rather than a world as Americans would like it to be. Donald Weatherbee has observed that not every political prisoner in an ASEAN jail is "a defender of democracy or a bearer of the torch of liberty". Without overstating his case, Weatherbee makes the valid points that no rights are absolute, that we live in a world with many injustices, and that in the context of this world citizens of the ASEAN states enjoy relatively liberal social and political freedom. "U.S. Policy and the Two Southeast Asias", *Asian Survey* 18, no. 4 (1978): 420.

8. United States Department of Commerce, "U.S. Trade with East Asian Countries", typescript, dated 30 Jan. 1980.

9. This is the author's assessment, of course, and many observers, in Washington and in the ASEAN capitals, regarded this more as a weakness than a strength. One articulate ASEAN leader commented that in dealing with the Carter administration, "assertiveness, the desire to take over — these are the

least of our problems". Nevertheless, the willingness to follow another's lead is very uncharacteristic of American policy, but in the ASEAN area it is likely in the long run to have been the most fruitful policy for all concerned.

10. *Far Eastern Economic Review*, 24–30 Oct. 1980, p. 31.

11. Prime Minister Lee Kuan Yew of Singapore, probably ASEAN's most perceptive (and often most critical) student of American political behaviour, put it succinctly when he is reported to have said that "America's posture is well understood by her friends and adversaries. Repeating . . . assurances to friends and allies is not as affective as a visible and credible American capacity to respond to crises anywhere in the region." See Mr. Lee's interview with the *Far Eastern Economic Review*, 26 Oct. 1979, p. 19. Although Mr. Lee's confidence may have been shaken by the abortive American attempt to rescue the Iranian hostages, he has sometimes expressed the view that he is more concerned about American "will" than its "capacity".

12. When the author once referred to a South and Southeast Asian proverb — "when elephants fight it is the grass that suffers" — he was reminded by a fellow panel member, an Indian, that "whether elephants fight or make love it is still the grass that suffers". Many Southeast Asians are as concerned about the future of Sino-American love-making as they were about potential Sino-American conflicts.

76

ASEAN-CHINA RELATIONS

LEE LAI TO

From Deng's visit to the ASEAN states, it was apparent that the previous days of Sino-Vietnamese solidarity have been replaced by a growing emphasis on non-communist ASEAN in China's fight against Soviet "strategic encirclement". China apparently wants to lobby non-communist ASEAN to its side or at least to ask the ASEAN nations to remain neutral in the Sino-Soviet struggle. In addition, what China wants from ASEAN is raw materials from the region and a market for China's products. Seen in this light, Deng's visit to ASEAN was another effort to win the support of ASEAN. Deng was probably satisfied that, as a result of the visit, Sino-ASEAN trade would continue to benefit China, that his case was heard, and that the three ASEAN states would not side with the Soviet Union or with Vietnam. His success varied, however, with the three ASEAN states. Thailand, because of its fear of Vietnam as a result of strategic and geographical consideration, was more receptive to Chinese influence. Its success in assimilating the Chinese and its confidence that China is giving a low level of support to the CPT may further encourage Thailand to make use of China to counteract Vietnam. Malaysia and Singapore, though concerned with Vietnam, were more concerned during Deng's visit with communal

problems and the insurgency movement for the former and the fear of Beijing's influence on the Chinese populations for the latter. These two factors, namely, China's connections with communist insurgency movements and the overseas Chinese problem, have proven to be two of China's major liabilities in approaching ASEAN, especially in the case of Malaysia and Singapore. The former factor was obviously one of the major conflicts between Malaysia and China. It may be that the Malaysians did not feel offended when Deng reiterated China's wish to have party-to-party ties with the MCP, as China had long been saying this. What irritated the Malaysians most was that Deng reiterated China's support for the MCP even in private. This support for the MCP strained China's relations not only with Malaysia but also with Indonesia, as evidenced by the attacks on Deng by Indonesian newspapers. Thus the resumption of diplomatic ties between Peking and Jakarta suffered another major blow (*ST,* 14–16 Nov. 1978). It must be added that there seems to be a re-examination and reformulation of Beijing's policy towards communists in Southeast Asia after Deng's visit. This was disclosed by Lee in his visit to China in 1980 when he suggested that while Peking would not abandon the people whom they had

Reprinted in abridged form from "Deng Xiaoping's ASEAN Tour: A Perspective on Sino-Southeast Asian Relations", *Contemporary Southeast Asia* 3, no. 1 (June 1981), pp. 58–75, by permission of the author and the Institute of Southeast Asian Studies.

instigated and incited to revolution, it would none the less tone down its support to these people as much as possible so as not to strain its relations with the ASEAN states in the future (*ST,* 15 Nov. 1978). In the case of the MCP, the return of Musa Ahmad, chairman of the party, from Beijing to Kuala Lumpur to give himself up in November 1980, was evidently a concrete measure of the PRC to cooperate with Southeast Asian governments to resolve their insurgent problems (*ST,* 13 Jan. 1981). As for the overseas Chinese problem, ASEAN states with large numbers of Chinese are very apprehensive of the possible emotional ties by their Chinese population with China. Moreover, the reactivation of China's policy to cultivate the support of the overseas Chinese in recent years definitely will cause concern for some Southeast Asian governments. However, as far as Singapore is concerned, it seems to have more confidence in the loyalty of its citizens recently. This is demonstrated by the fact that it has relaxed visits to the PRC for Singaporeans and the import of more published materials from the PRC. But as admitted by Lee himself in an interview during his 1980 trip to the PRC, although a separate identity was discernible and that the process of building a separate identity for Singapore had already gone some way, it would require time for this identity to take a definite and distinctive shape (*ST,* 15 Nov. 1980).

Generally speaking, ASEAN states are quite pleased that Russia and China are wooing them, but they do not want to become too close to any of these countries. They would like to remain non-communist and cultivate closer ties with the United States, Japan, and other countries. However, they are aware that they cannot keep these two communist countries away and maintain the interest of these communist countries in the region. With the fall of Phnom Penh in January 1979 and the subsequent establishment of the Heng Samrin regime in Kampuchea, it seems that ASEAN states began to share the Chinese view on the threat posed by Vietnam to Southeast Asia. This was subsequently demonstrated vividly by the U.N. recognition of Democratic Kampuchea in 1979, the resolution to have an international conference on Kampuchea and call for a total pull-out of all foreign forces from that country by the United Nations in 1980 through the efforts of the ASEAN states. However, in view of the different geographical positions of each of the ASEAN states, their different needs and concerns, including different positions on the question of whether China is a threat to the peace of the region and to the security of each of the ASEAN states, ASEAN solidarity will be tested by the ability of the ASEAN nations to agree on the identification of the major threat facing them and by their ability to take concerted action.

77.

CHINA'S POLICY TOWARDS SOUTHEAST ASIA

SARASIN VIRAPHOL

Notwithstanding the favorable conditions for a positive Chinese posture in Southeast Asia, Beijing has to cope with some basic problems in the manifestations of indigenous sensitivity as well as limited physical capabilities. The most relevant issues that arouse widespread Southeast Asian suspicion are the overseas Chinese and Communist insurgency. In every single state of Southeast Asia, these two issues exist in varying degrees of gravity. The Chinese attempt to allay the local suspicion has so far proved only partially successful. The inherent difficulty is that Beijing more often than not tries to justify them as "historical and ideological problems," to which appropriate solutions will understandably require patience and effort. This approach, which allows the Chinese to escape ultimate responsibilities and commitments, is viewed consequently as unsatisfactory. As many see it, while professing interests and intentions to resolve the anomalies, the Chinese are simply indulging in double standards. It remains true that, in the final analysis, despite certain initial measures taken by Beijing over the two issues, the Chinese government has not severed its links with the overseas Chinese and the various local outlawed Communist parties. This provides ground for the argument that Beijing's recent warming up to the region's legitimate governments is nothing more than a Leninist tactic aimed at forging a convenient alliance against a more immediate foe. Obviously, this is inconsistent with Beijing's pronouncement that it does not export revolution but that it supports anticolonialist, antihegemonist revolutionary struggle — which remains vague and open to varied interpretations. Finally, there is also genuine concern expressed for the heightening of tension in the region, and here China is naturally regarded as contributing to the disequilibrium of the regional power balance.

Beijing's physical limitation affects its projection of power beyond the Chinese boundary. China's huge armed forces are essentially defensive in nature, but nevertheless are capable of undertaking limited offensives like the punitive war against Vietnam in 1979. Beijing's military capabilities are growing, but the emphasis continues to be defensive, geared toward the Soviet Union. As far as the rest of Southeast Asia in concerned, direct long-range military engagements are not anticipated, with Chinese involvements concentrated on subversion.

Reprinted in abridged form from "The People's Republic of China and Southeast Asia: A Security Consideration for the 1980s", in *Economic, Political and Security Issues in Southeast Asia in the 1980s*, edited by Robert A. Scalapino and Jusuf Wanandi (Berkeley, Calif.: Institute of East Asian Studies, University of California, 1982), pp. 147–55, by permission of the Institute of East Asian Studies, University of California.

Thailand is considered an important outpost in the current Chinese strategy. As the frontline state bordering the Communist states in Indochina, Thailand fits in with Beijing's objective of checking Soviet and Vietnamese expansionism, especially in Kampuchea and Laos. Thailand's national security is a crucial factor, which allows for the existence of a strategic symbiotic arrangement. In this respect, China and Thailand are interested that Laos and especially Kampuchea be free of Vietnamese military domination. But although Beijing is still hopeful that eventually the Khmer Rouge will return to power and that Vietnam will succumb militarily, it cannot ignore the fact that Thailand places its priority on a comprehensive political settlement of the Kampuchean question in order to restore the balance of power through the emergence of an independent and neutral Kampuchea. This awareness on the part of China is essential if Thailand is to form a link for China to the other ASEAN countries, a function Beijing realizes Thailand can serve quite effectively. The Kampuchean problem has brought about a consensus of views among the ASEAN states on the threat of Vietnam and the Soviet Union but has also highlighted basic differences in approaches and modalities regarding its solution, as well as perceptions about China's stakes in Southeast Asia which include the question of the Chinese influence in Kampuchea and Indochina. After all, it is generally regarded that China's support of the Khmer Rouge resistance keeps the Kampuchean conflict alive — but it is seldom thought the other way round, that it is the Vietnamese, with the support of the Soviet Union, who are primarily responsible for the existing violence and tension. Nevertheless, to state the obvious, Beijing will continue to support ASEAN's position so long as their interests coincide, though the status of the Khmer Rouge will ultimately remain a major difference between China and ASEAN.

It was left to Vice-Premier Deng Xiaoping to plan swift retribution against Hanoi. The final decision to teach Vietnam a lesson was approved five weeks following the Vietnamese capture of Phnom Penh. This Chinese action has set the course of Beijing's Southeast Asian policy ever since.

Given an alternative, Beijing would probably have chosen to enter into the region in a more unobtrusive manner though the growing concern of a hegemonistic Vietnam collaborating with the Soviet Union would still have figured importantly. Pushing the Four Modernizations program at home, Deng Xiaoping was arguably following Chairman Mao Zedong's and Premier Zhou Enlai's advocacies of befriending the non-Communist ASEAN countries as part of the overall effort to forge a broad alliance against hegemonism, with a complementary tactical readiness to downplay its supportive role vis-à-vis the China-supported insurgencies in the region. Deng invariably injected the element of incisiveness in this Chinese policy, with the clear-cut retributive course of action against Vietnam.

Thus, it was unlikely that China had from the beginning deliberately and actively sought to precipitate the armed confrontation with Vietnam over Kampuchea; it was more the case of China having been forced into such a circumstance. It would seem that Deng's long-term view was to promote better relations with the non-Communist ASEAN states in order to shore up China's position in the face of a deteriorating relationship with Vietnam. (For a while it did seem that ASEAN would enjoy the best of both worlds when it was actively courted by both China and Vietnam.)

In the foreseeable future, Beijing has no cause to modify or abandon the current confrontational posture against Vietnam, irrespective of what ASEAN ultimately chooses to do. To Beijing, Vietnam has staunchly allied itself with the Soviet Union and must therefore be opposed at all cost. The present Chinese leadership believes it is possible to destroy the recalcitrant Vietnamese will. In the meantime, though Beijing would certainly like to foster good relationships with the ASEAN countries — as this is a strategic gain for China — it would be prepared to resist any attempt to undermine or adversely affect the present Chinese position against the Vietnamese. Hence, an open antagonism against China by ASEAN would serve no purpose for the latter. On the contrary, because of its favored position, ASEAN could strengthen its position and bargaining power by maintaining its own principled opposition against Hanoi's aggression and occupation of Kampuchea and perhaps also by consolidating its diplomatic stature vis-à-vis Beijing, with Indonesia and Singapore maintaining official ties with China. It would influence the Chinese leadership to think and act more positively in Southeast Asia in general and help resolve the current Kampuchean problem, which is crucial in shaping the future political trend of Southeast Asia.

78

ASEAN-AUSTRALIA RELATIONS*

RHONDDA M. NICHOLAS

In general terms, each nation's policy-makers approach dealings with other countries imbued with their own ideas of what constitutes proper conduct, of right and wrong in foreign relations and with a conception of their particular nation's interests. In other words, each national group of policy-makers will come to the negotiating table with its own set of values or standards. It is the application, or rather the misapplication, of these values to other nations that may contribute to the raising of tensions in foreign relations. This study of élite perceptions of the Australian-ASEAN relationship reveals this clash of political values at work.

The political values issue may be viewed analytically on two levels, which may be termed, *systemic political values* and *moral political values*. Systemic values encompass those perceptions and attitudes derived from the individual policy-maker's experience of his/her national institutions and political culture. Due to the normative element implicit in such values, they may raise expectations with regard to the nature of the environment in which other national policy-makers implement decisions. The present study illustrates this process at work: for example, when ASEAN policy-makers

claim that the Australian Government gives too much credence to domestic electoral considerations in formulating foreign policy, they are, in fact, judging Australian policy through a lens coloured by the way in which their own domestic institutions operate. The point is not that ASEAN policy-makers are ignorant of the workings of the Australian system of government; rather, that they are bringing their understanding of the conduct of foreign policy, derived from their domestic political experience, to bear on interstate relations. When a particular state behaves in a manner inconsistent with these values or preconceptions, feelings of impatience and frustration, such as those expressed by some ASEAN interviewees in this study, may arise. If a nation does not possess an especially favourable record from past exchanges, this clash of values may lead to a temporary souring of relations or to the reinforcement of a negative image. It is not altogether clear that greater knowledge of the different system of government and culture could ameliorate these tensions, given the normative element present in such values.

The clash of moral political values produces a similar effect. Political rights, in the Western sense, define the position of the individual in

---

Reprinted in abridged form from "Misperception and Muddled Thinking in Australia-ASEAN Relations", *Contemporary Southeast Asia* 5, no. 2 (September 1983), pp. 153–71, by permission of the Institute of Southeast Asian Studies.

relation to the coercive power of the state. In liberal democracies, rights accrue to the individual, whether they are in codified form or not, which protect that person's freedom to engage in political activity unmolested. The absence of similar provisions in the ASEAN nations has attracted criticism in Australia, as outlined previously. It has been argued by some observers that the "social justice" issues which concern the ASEAN governments and societies differ only in emphasis from these liberal-democratic "rights": that it is the *collective* aspect of notions of equality that concern Southeast Asian policy-makers, rather than *individualist* notions.[1] This clash has been explained as the classical tension between liberalism and democracy writ large.[2] Hence, Third World claims for a redistribution of global economic power represent a demand for social justice on the collective level.

Regardless of whether one adheres to the view that certain political rights are immutable or not, the clash of moral political values on the interstate level has increased tensions in Australia-ASEAN relations and has had the effect of reinforcing negative perceptions on both sides, as the interview material illustrates. The clash of values on this level has been remarkable for the way in which non-governmental opinion on the Australian side has confronted government attitudes in the ASEAN states. At this point, the two levels of political values may be seen to merge: the Australian Government professes impotence to resolve this clash of moral political values, because of the way the Australian system of government operates, while ASEAN officials believe that the tension has been instigated by Australian nationals over whom the Australian Government *should* exercise influence, if not, control. This has the effect of reinforcing the dispute at the systemic level, that is, between Australian policy-makers and their counterparts in ASEAN. Thus, the political values dispute has operated on two levels and has involved two sets of actors on the Australian side, governmental and non-governmental, while ASEAN policy-makers remain the sole actors on the Southeast Asian part.

The question remains, however, why this clash of political values came to a head in the late 1970s. Many aspects of the changing strategic alignments in regional affairs such as the varying importance of alliances and changing patterns of trade, and dynamics within the ASEAN countries and within Australia, are pertinent. Nevertheless, several factors in particular appear to have presaged the manner in which these tensions arose. The first was the assertion by the member nations of ASEAN of an active stand on regional issues. The revitalization of the Association and the success its member governments achieved in attaining international recognition presented the Australian Government with a new dimension in the conduct of its foreign relations with the region. Secondly, the "irritants" in the relationship arose at a time when Australian foreign policy was in a state of flux. Tentative steps towards greater regional involvement were being made and yet an effort was also being undertaken to preserve and strengthen ties with traditional allies. Thirdly, there was a drift of diplomatic influence away from Australia and towards the ASEAN states in regional affairs, as Australia is lower in ASEAN's diplomatic priorities than the ASEAN nations are to Australia. This imbalance of power worked to place the onus on Australia to take initiatives to effect closer co-operation. However, there was, and arguably remains, no consensus within Australia on what degree of co-operation *should* be pursued with the ASEAN countries.

Finally, the very nature of some of the issues issues that caused controversy in the relationship contributed to the prominence of the political-values question. The trade dispute, for example, highlighted the increasing domestic content of foreign policy in Australia, and systemic and moral political values were brought into play by a powerful domestic constituency on the question of trade protection. In contrast, policies for closer defence co-operation do not usually arouse such a response due to the lower visibility of the issue since the defence constituency is very limited in comparison. Indeed, now that the policy issues of contention have died down, the road to closer co-operation between Australia and ASEAN may lie in the latter direction, given the continued paramountcy of security concerns in Australia's foreign policy.

NOTES

* Much of the material presented in this article was obtained through interviews which the author conducted with government officials and specialists in the five ASEAN countries during October–December 1981, and in Australia during 1982. ASEAN interviewees ranged from a deputy prime minister to academics, with the majority being upper-level public servants. Australian interviewees were, for the most part, middle to upper-level public servants from the Departments of Foreign Affairs, Trade and Resources, Aviation, and Industry and Commerce. Information was given on the basis that statements should not be attributed to individuals, and in some cases, their departments. Wherever possible, such statements have been substantiated from the public record. It is not claimed that these interviewees constitute a representative sample and hence, the mode of analysis is qualitative rather than quantitative. The author would like to thank Dr Nancy Viviani and Gerald Chan for their comments on an earlier draft of this paper.

1. Peter McCawley, "Australia's Misconceptions of ASEAN" (Paper presented at the Conference on Australia's External Relations, Australian National University, 1–4 September 1982); Hedley Bull, "Human Rights and World Politics", in Ralph Pettman, *Moral Claims in World Affairs* (London: Croom Helm, 1979), pp. 86–88. However, see J.L.S. Girling, *The Bureaucratic Polity in Modernizing Societies*, Institute of Southeast Asian Studies Occasional Paper No. 64 (Singapore, 1981), esp. pp. 53–56; and Ralph Pettman, "Moral Claims in World Politics", in Pettman, op. cit.

2. Ramesh Thakur, "Liberalism, Democracy and Development: Philosophical Dilemmas in Third World Politics", *Political Studies* 30, no. 3 (September 1982): 333–49.

79.

ASEAN AND THE
NORTH-SOUTH DIALOGUE

ALI ALATAS

What relevance do North-South issues have for ASEAN and what is ASEAN's stake in the North-South negotiations? I submit that not only has ASEAN a vital stake in them, but it has also a crucial role to play both in the North-South dialogue and in the recovery of the world economy.

ASEAN's direct interest is involved in at least four areas central to the New International Economic Order, namely, primary commodities, international trade, transfer of technology, and money and finance, with a fifth area, energy, being of particular concern to Indonesia.

First, let us consider the field of primary commodities and commodity trade. ASEAN's natural resource endowment is a cornucopia of strategically important commodities and minerals. It is the world's principal supplier of natural rubber, palm oil, and coconut oil. It is a major producer and exporter of oil and natural gas, tin, tropical timber, coffee, copper, tungsten, sugar, rice, and tobacco.

In the field of international trade ASEAN's performance is no less spectacular. It enjoys an increasing share of international trade with a steady growth rate averaging 24 percent per annum (in the period 1975–1980) as compared with a world rate of about 18 percent (in the same period). It has emerged as Japan's second largest trading partner and the fifth largest trading partner of the United States. Though its trade with the European Economic Community is of a more modest nature, it has exhibited a phenomenal growth rate of over 30 percent per annum between 1975 and 1980. Export trade alone constitutes a significant source of foreign exchange and accounted for 42 percent of ASEAN's total gross national product in 1980.

Turning now to technology, ASEAN's current vigorous level of development and its surging industrial drive inevitably create essential needs. It requires large quantities of technological imports and capital goods to sustain that development. Apart from access to and availability of technology, the enhancement of indigenous technological capability will henceforth be a crucial determinant not only for ASEAN's further growth but also for its capacity to grow.

Financing and access to financial markets have assumed a central importance for ASEAN. Adequate financing is essential to facilitate rapid industrialization and large-scale international trading. Singapore has become a financial center of growing importance for the

Reprinted in abridged form from "North-South Issues and Their Relevance to ASEAN", in *ASEAN Security and Economic Development*, edited by Karl D. Jackson and M. Hadi Soesastro (Berkeley, Calif.: Institute of East Asian Studies, University of California, 1984), pp. 10–15, by permission of the author and the Institute of East Asian Studies, University of California.

entire Asian-Pacific region. The need to assure adequate financing flows on a continuous and more predictable basis is paramount to ASEAN's continued successful growth.

Given ASEAN's heavy stake in each of these vital areas, it should come as no surprise to anyone that the ASEAN countries have assumed an active and highly visible part in the North-South negotiations since their inception.

First, because of its concentration on commodities and its predominant position in commodity trade, ASEAN has always fully supported the call for remunerative and equitable price and earnings stabilization arrangements. Thus, ASEAN countries were in the forefront in the negotiations for the Common Fund and for UNCTAD's Integrated Program for Commodities, including the establishment of new international commodity agreements for individual commodities. Of the ten core commodities of the Integrated Program for Commodities, almost all are of direct importance for ASEAN At present, ASEAN's attention is directed to the next area for negotiations, namely, the establishment of new frameworks of cooperation with a view to increasing the participation of developing countries in the processing, marketing, and transport of their commodities. The recent collapse of commodity prices has had a particularly severe impact on the ASEAN economies, and it is obvious that the existing international economic relationships continue to operate to the inherent economic disadvantage of the developing countries.

Second, the heavy dependence of ASEAN countries on international trade compels it to play a major role in restructuring trade relations. A key issue for ASEAN in world trade is that of access to markets. The current trading system tends to discriminate against imports from developing countries, especially those labor-intensive manufactures, agricultural products, and processed commodities so vital to their further industrialization. Moreover, there has been a marked rise in nontariff barriers and various new measures of contingent protection. Unlike tariffs, many of these measures fall

outside the purview of the General Agreement on Tariffs and Trade system. Their application and implications are very much dependent on the unilateral interpretation of the importing country or on bilateral arrangements between the affected parties. They appear to be directed mainly against a small number of dynamic exporting developing countries, and the ASEAN countries, due to their success in industrialization, have absorbed the full impact of such protectionism. ASEAN, therefore, has vigorously called for the redress of tariff and nontariff barriers erected against their manufactures, as well as for better regulation of the more insidious forms of protectionism.

Similarly, ASEAN places a strong emphasis on the fashioning of a more equitable and viable monetary and financial system. The dangerous contraction in international liquidity has to be effectively and comprehensively addressed. The growing deficits in the balance of payments of developing countries and the drying up of flows of multilateral concessional and semi-concessional assistance must be reversed. There also exists an objective need to develop a more effective multilateral framework for the restructuring of the debt burden of developing countries in order to provide an orderly and timely international response to the emergence of serious debt crises.

It is undeniable that the ASEAN region has become a dynamic element in the international economy. Economically, it is one of the fastest growing regions of the world. Despite the current recession, it has shown its resilience by maintaining an average real growth rate of about 7 percent per annum over the last decade. In short, it has the resources, potential, and political will to sustain its present momentum for rapid economic development.

But in the world in which we live today, sustained economic progress at the national level can be made only if it can be assured at the global level as well. As Albert Bressand rightly pointed out in the spring 1983 issue of *Foreign Affairs* magazine, the world economy can no longer be defined as and limited to the interaction of national economies. Rather, it is now the national economies that can be seen as the extension of a global and integrated system, with a logic and dynamics of their own.

This explains why the ASEAN countries, even with their proven capacity and determination to forge ahead under adverse conditions, have a vital stake in and indeed must contribute actively to the solution of North-South issues in order to secure a global environment conducive to its continued progress.

I would like to stress that while ASEAN has always been vocal and firm in its support of the New International Economic Order, its approach has always been a rational one. We do not seek a zero-sum outcome in the North-South negotiations but a global economic order of mutual and equitable benefit to all countries. While our position is inseparable from that of the Group of 77, we believe that because of particular strengths, traditions, and temperaments we can and should play a substantial, constructive, and moderating role, both within our own group as well as vis-à-vis the countries of the North. We are determined to continue to play that role in our own enlightened self-interest as well as, we would hope, in the interest of greater stability, security, and progress for the region and for the world.

80.

JAPAN'S CHANGING POLICY TOWARDS ASEAN

SHIBUSAWA MASAHIDE

The relationship with ASEAN is by and large cordial and productive. Japan has developed institutional arrangements such as the Japan-ASEAN Forum to accommodate the special multilateral character of the relationship. Moreover, the government has been successful in developing domestic consensus on ASEAN's importance for Japan and the need to extend assistance to its member countries; ASEAN, being a multilateral organization, has been helpful in pre-empting the kind of domestic opposition which frequently arises in the case of bilateral relations. Finally, ASEAN's neutralist and self-reliant stand is well adapted to the mood and leanings of Japan.

Japan's over-presence in the region causes difficulties, but there is little that can be done about this. The problem is exacerbated by the trade imbalance which Japan carries with a number of ASEAN countries. The latest attitude survey made in Thailand reveals that the public at large suspects Japan of being out for itself, and that there is a fear of economic domination.[1] Among policy-makers, too, there is a lingering suspicion that Japan is merely out to exploit the region's resources and that, when these are exhausted, it may abandon ASEAN.[2] Some ASEAN countries feel wary of Japan's involvement in the defence of sea-lanes up to 1,000 miles south of Japan, which shows that, four decades after the war, there are still misgivings about Japan's rearmament. However, the fear of the re-emergence of Japan's militarism seems to be on the wane. Thanks to a greatly increased knowledge of Japan and the workings of its political system, few in ASEAN see anything threatening in its current military build-up. Rather, they tend to regard it as a necessary step towards sharing the burden carried by the United States in the region, and towards meeting its own security needs.[3]

On the other hand, ASEAN countries are afraid that Japan may capitulate to the Soviet Union, under either pressure or intimidation, because of its lack of a defence capability. The economic and political implications of a 'Finlandization' of Japan obviously defy prediction. For nations which have so long been used to taking the healthy performance of the Japanese economy for granted, a sudden shift in Japan's orientation would spell serious problems. A Thai political scientist commented that ASEAN wants Japan to rearm to a point, but cannot agree on where that point should be.[4]

It is possible that the people and cultures of

Excerpted from Shibusawa Masahide, *Japan and the Asian Pacific Region: Profile of Change* (London: Croom Helm for the Royal Institute of International Affairs, 1984), pp. 174–85, by permission of the author and Croom Helm.

Southeast Asia touch a psychological soft spot in Japan. Although there are so many differences, there are also distinct similarities between Japan and the Southeast Asian countries — in their attitude to life, their cultural and religious tolerance, and their unique pragmatism and flexibility. After all, it was ASEAN that prodded Japan away from its hitherto omnidirectional orientation to 'special' and 'heart-to-heart' relations. Since the end of the war, the Japanese have adhered faithfully to their omnidirectional stance, partly because of the global stretch of their economy, but partly because they were afraid of reviving in themselves the pre-war Asianism which was solidly identified with the right-wing militarism of the past. The relationship with ASEAN may yet give an impetus to Japan's further tilt towards Asia, although the fear of alienating its Western and other partners may prevent it from moving too fast or too far in a regionalist direction.

In all likelihood, Japan will adhere to its economistic stance for the foreseeable future. Despite pressure from the United States, it will increase its military power sparingly, with caution. The Japanese are conscious that this choice entails continued dependence on the United States, and hence less status for their nation, which is not a comfortable position for a country of Japan's size and influence. However, the results of successive elections seem to show that, barring an unexpected shift in the international scene, the Japanese will prefer to remain economistic rather than go political, let alone military. For all the criticism of Japan being politically passive or reactive, the people seem to approve their government's reluctance to take any action which might precipitate a crisis or instability in the region. They seem to prefer the country to err on the side of inaction.

Japan certainly has more influence today than it had a decade ago, if only because of its economic strength. However, by and large, it chooses to use this influence discreetly. It is known that it has frequently offered advice or suggestions, and has counselled caution to its partners on a variety of questions, including Sino-US relations, the future of Hong Kong and Kampuchean problems, and that the results have been quite effective.[5] Undoubtedly these can be called political initiatives, and they are largely welcomed by the countries in the region. However, Japan prefers to exert its influence behind the scenes, without stating its position publicly. It is a mode of behaviour which seems to suit its current position as a primarily economic power.

Admittedly, the persistent emphasis on economism has taken its toll. For one thing, when such a stance is adopted as the central premise of national policy, it generates a tendency to evaluate every issue on its economic merits. In particular, it blurs the basic purpose of foreign policy issues, and exposes every option to pressure from various internal economic constituencies, whose motives may be largely self-interested. In other words, it makes the country's behaviour materialistic and egocentric. What Japan needs, therefore, is to develop a policy framework which is based upon a concept of a new responsibility for Japan — a responsibility which, as a big economy, it ought to embrace. In this way, it would be able to evaluate its policy options in terms of long-range and even 'moral' goals.

However, it would be difficult for Japan to make such a shift because it would entail a consensus on an overall national goal, in the context of an agreed interpretation of the world, something which the Japanese are loath to see happen. In fact, the economistic orientation developed out of a deep-seated fear that the country might one day take up another kind of goal or perception — of a kind that once brought disaster to the whole region. Therefore, any overall national objective, even if it sounds harmless, tends to be looked upon with suspicion in case it, too, might have an ugly side.

It is this state of mind that has bred the 'immobilism' of Japan's policy process, a trait that has provoked different reactions from different quarters. For example, the South

Koreans, who have been conditioned to believe that everything should be sacrificed for the sake of political freedom, regard Japan's indecisiveness as a cover-up for selfishness. The United States, too, tends to think that Japan is shirking its responsibility as a member of the free world. However, the ASEAN countries seem to find reassurance in an apolitical Japan, because this fits in with their wish to be free from the interference of outside powers, including Japan, as expressed in the ZOPFAN concept. China also seems to realize that an economistic Japan serves its current interests better than a politicized one.

The likely course which Japan will pursue is an economistic road with modifications and fine-tuning. In view of its already considerable economic involvement in the region, a modified and improved economism, if applied cohesively, might alter its relationship with the region greatly. Prime Minister Mahathir of Malaysia commented recently that the role of Japan in the region should be as 'a guide and a teacher; a transferer of technology; a role to make these countries richer and more stable, which would benefit in turn not only the region but also Japan and the world'.[6] If that is what the other countries in the region expect, there would be ample ground for Japan to continue its involvement primarily in an economic context. After all, one can contribute best by doing what one is most experienced at and has an aptitude for. The fact that, in the super-austere 1984 budget, ODA expenditure received an allocation of $2.6 billion, an increase of 9.7 per cent over the previous year (the only other increase being in the allocation to defence — 6.5 per cent over 1983), attests to the government's determination, backed by a political consensus, that the nation should try to fulfil its overseas responsibilities.[7]

There are promising signs in the private sector, too, that the country is nearly ready to make the fine-tuning that is necessary. The overwhelming response to the appeals which were made by various philanthropic organizations for assistance for the Kampuchean refugees, or for medical and educational help for the villages in Southeast Asia, indicates that people are conscious of the need to take the region to their hearts. The media coverage of the region, and the amount of regional literature that is translated into Japanese, have expanded substantially in the last few years. The increasing number of Japanese who are engaged in relief operations, or who study the languages and culture of the region, coupled with a steady exchange of professors, students, artists and young people, is beginning to create a new infrastructure in Japan for productive interchange with the region. This may well be a sign of Japan's maturing as a nation.

NOTES
1. Sukhumband Paribatra, 'Political and Security Dimensions in ASEAN-Japan Relations: Thailand's Perspectives', unpublished paper presented at Asia Dialogue Workshop, Bangkok, 23–24 January 1984, p. 12.
2. A senior Thai diplomat, in conversation with the author, November 1983.
3. Magenda Bruhan, "Political and Security Dimensions in ASEAN-Japan Relations: Perspective from Indonesia", unpublished paper presented at Asia Dialogue Workshop, Bangkok, 23–24 January 1984; Sukhumband Paribatra, "Thailand's Perspectives", *op. cit.*; Zakaria Haji Ahmad, "Political and Security Dimensions in ASEAN-Japan Relations: A Malaysian Perspective", unpublished paper presented at Asia Dialogue Workshop, Bangkok, 23–24 January 1984.
4. Likit Dherawegin, in conversation with the author, in Bangkok, March 1983.
5. A senior Japanese diplomat, in conversation with the author, Kuala Lumpur March 1983.
6. In an interview with the author, Kuala Lumpur, March 1983.
7. *Nihon Keizai Shimbun*, 25 January 1983.

81. ASEAN AND THE MAJOR POWERS IN THE 1980s

LIKHIT DHIRAVEGIN

ASEAN's perception of and attitude toward the countries who have been actors in regional politics is generally inimical to the socialist states and friendly to countries with an open-market economy. The economy of ASEAN can be broadly classified as open with an authoritarian or semiauthoritarian polity. In the final analysis, ASEAN is anti-Communist. In fact, the creation of ASEAN was in a sense an attempt to bring about collective security among the states involved against the Communist threat, with the concern initially being the People's Republic of China. Over time, however, with changing circumstances, the socialist states of the region came into sharper conflict, leading to a shift in alliances and alignments. We witness the ironical situation where two former enemies, the PRC and the U.S., now stand on the same side with regard to the Cambodia issue, while two erstwhile socialist comrades, the PRC and Vietnam, have become foes. ASEAN has also found its image undergoing a change especially in certain quarters. Initially, the PRC and the USSR viewed ASEAN as a re-creation of SEATO, with the U.S. pulling the strings behind the scene. But because of political developments, the PRC, up to then an enemy of ASEAN, has sided with

ASEAN on the Cambodia issue and cultivated ASEAN generally.

Japan sees ASEAN as a viable regional cooperation organization with indigenous roots. This is because Japan, as an economic power whose main interest is in trade and in the acquisition of raw materials, sees ASEAN as a market and a source of raw materials; but of equal importance is the fact that if ASEAN becomes a viable entity and contributes toward stability in the region, it can serve to contain the Communists, defying the domino theory.

The U.S., on the other hand, sees ASEAN as a group of countries of similar political systems with a distinctive anti-Communist outlook, and thus has given it support. The U.S. also sees ASEAN as a development in line with the Nixon or Guam Doctrine of 1969, with its key theme that indigenous forces should bear the primary responsibility for the preservation of "freedom and democracy" against the Communists with the U.S. providing material and moral support, and if essential, using its sea and air power.

ASEAN as a collective body has the following salient features. It is a new entity, a collective body initially of five countries — Indonesia, Malaysia, Singapore, the Philippines,

Reprinted in abridged form from "ASEAN and the Major Powers: Today and Tomorrow", in *Internal and External Security Issues in Asia*, edited by Robert A. Scalapino, Seizaburo Sato and Jusuf Wanandi (Berkeley, Calif.: Institute of East Asian Studies, University of California, 1986), pp. 169–94, by permission of the author and the Institute of East Asian Studies, University of California.

and Thailand. In January 1984, Brunei joined, becoming the sixth member state. ASEAN is an organization of economic cooperation and cultural exchange. It has a common anti-Communist political ideology, not in the sense of struggling against existing Communist states, but in its aversion to a Communist movement taking over state power. ASEAN would like to stay free of entanglements in the power struggle among the major powers and free from political conflicts that do not concern its members. This policy is summarized in the 1971 declaration in Kuala Lumpur known as ZOPFAN (Zone of Peace, Freedom and Neutrality).[1] There is also a policy of "national resilience,"[2] meaning the ability to turn the individual countries into viable economic units with equitable income distribution largely by each state's individual efforts in order to thwart the Communist threat, especially the insurgency movements then supported by the PRC. ASEAN at present seeks to present an image of unity and solidarity; its common goal is peace and stability in the region, and an end to the Cambodia problem.

Despite partial disengagement from the region after the Vietnam War, the U.S. cannot afford to abandon the region, if only for its own security. However, the new situation has called for a new alignment. The U.S. hopes to maintain stability in Asia and contain the Communists, especially the Soviet Union, by having the People's Republic of China (with its animosity against the USSR), Japan, and ASEAN serve as a counterbalance to the Soviet Union and Vietnam. At the moment one sees a four-pronged "alliance" consisting of the U.S., the PRC, Japan,[3] and ASEAN against the Soviet Union and its ally, Vietnam.

Thus, despite a close relationship between ASEAN and the U.S., ASEAN does not wish to appear too close to the U.S. Indeed, ASEAN was put on the defensive when it was accused of being a new SEATO in disguise. As a result, ASEAN steers clear of statements that have the appearance of deriving from U.S. policy. ASEAN has been trying to present an image of an independent organization with its own policy. However, given a political situation that would require an alliance, it is inevitable that ASEAN would become an ally of the U.S.

ASEAN and the United States

As a generalization, one can say that the U.S. supports ASEAN as a group and also as individual countries. Since ASEAN is anti-Communist, the U.S. and ASEAN have a common political interest. The U.S. is seen as a major power, which can be relied on for the supply of military needs. In the event of a crisis, ASEAN as a group would certainly appeal for assistance from the U.S. government. Two ASEAN members, Thailand and the Philippines, can still rely on the Manila Pact. Although SEATO has closed its headquarters, the Manila Pact is still binding, as has been clearly expressed by U.S. authorities. In the Philippines, Subic Bay is still the naval base of the U.S. Seventh Fleet, with Clark Airfield providing quarters for U.S. fighter bombers. And the U.S. still supplies Thailand with annual military aid.

ASEAN and the Soviet Union

The USSR is geographically remote from ASEAN. Unless its presence can be made to be felt by its naval forces, it is a country situated on the periphery. For this reason, the People's Republic of China could be seen as posing a greater threat for ASEAN in the future. But ASEAN's attitude toward the USSR has changed since Vietnam's invasion of Cambodia, when Hanoi overthrew the Pol Pot regime and installed Heng Samrin as head of a puppet government. The invasion, which took place immediately after the Soviet Union and Vietnam had concluded a treaty of alliance, was seen as a Russo-Vietnamese scheme to get a stronghold in Southeast Asia. Indeed, the invasion of Kampuchea by Vietnam is a twin of the invasion of Afghanistan by the Soviet Union, although the two events were not directly connected.[4] The Soviet Union now has access to the facilities at Cam Ranh Bay, thus enabling the USSR to connect with its fleet in the Indian Ocean and giving it a "backdoor" to the Pacific Ocean. The buildup of Cam Ranh Bay as a naval base for the Soviet Union is a destabilizing factor for the region and may raise the tension between the U.S. and the USSR. ASEAN has begun to feel the threat posed by the Soviet Union's expansion policy. The Russian-Vietnamese alliance can be seen as a plan to counterbalance the four-pronged "alliance" of the U.S., Japan, the PRC, and ASEAN.

The Soviet Union views ASEAN as a group of capitalist countries allied with the U.S. and Japan, having an expedient relationship with the PRC in order to contain Soviet influence, although, at times, the USSR has changed its attitude toward ASEAN because of the latter's regional self-awareness and independent policy.[5] In view of ASEAN's performance, the accusation of ASEAN being SEATO in disguise is now hardly tenable. Recently, for example, the Russian ambassador to Thailand, after paying his respects to ASEAN as an independent organization, accused the U.S. of trying to turn ASEAN into a military alliance,[6] taking the line of ASEAN being a U.S. creation. In fact, the Soviet Union, after changing its attitude toward ASEAN, has attempted to win ASEAN to its side by diplomatic means.[7]

Before giving support to Vietnam, the Soviet Union must have weighed the pros and cons. On one side of the scale was ASEAN, which the Soviet Union decided to trade off for its more promising ally, Vietnam. This choice was realistic because, for the time being at least, it would be difficult for the Soviet Union to compete with the PRC to win ASEAN to its side. To ASEAN, the Russians, unlike the Americans and the Chinese, are strangers, greatly alien to the region. The Russians are also different from other Europeans with whom ASEAN has been familiar, such as the British, the French, the Dutch, and the Spanish. Despite the Soviets' attempt to compete with the PRC in the region,

it is difficult for them to step into the Chinese backyard, historically an area constituting China's sphere of influence. The presence of a large number of overseas Chinese, many of whom have been holding high positions in the indigenous government bureaucracy, also sometimes serves as a positive factor for the PRC, although the overseas Chinese constitute a liability as well, raising fears of Chinese dominance.

Since ASEAN considers the USSR an outsider with whom it has to deal but wishes to keep at arm's length and the PRC is a major power and a potential problem in the long run, ASEAN hopes that the present Sino-Soviet rift will continue. As long as the two giant socialist states confront each other without the confrontation erupting into warfare, Asia — and ASEAN — will benefit.

ASEAN and the People's Republic of China

The People's Republic of China, ironically, was one of the major factors that motivated the Southeast Asian countries to form ASEAN as a collective body to reinforce, if not to serve as a substitute for, support from the West against communism. The aggressive policy of the PRC during the zenith of Mao and the material as well as verbal support given to the insurgency movements in Asia through the party-to-party relations were of deep concern. The policy of supporting Asian insurgency movements stemmed from the PRC's ideological commitment and the belief in "wars of national liberation," which were to take place one by one, a thesis not dissimilar to the domino theory. But of equal importance was the fact that in this earlier period, the PRC saw the U.S. as its enemy, entrenched in Asia with its military bases in various places, from Korea, Japan, and the Philippines to Thailand. Moreover, the Asian countries allied with the U.S. had been strongly opposed to communism, especially to Communist China. To have leverage against these countries, the PRC gave support to various Communist movements, providing arms, military training, and an opportunity to direct radio broadcasts at their targets. Although the insurgency movements were unsuccessful, they drained off the material and manpower of these countries. They also created a sense of insecurity and psychological strain for the governments of the Asian countries. The PRC has supported the insurgency movements of four ASEAN countries (excepting the fifth, Singapore). The closest link between the Communist party of China and the Communist parties in Asia was that with the Communist party in Indonesia (PKI). But the PKI's failure in the coup of 1965 brought about its destruction by the army, and since then its remnants have gone underground.[8]

The improvement of Sino-U.S. relations was given concrete impetus by the Nixon visit to China in February 1972. The subsequent diplomatic victories scored by the PRC against the Republic of China on Taiwan led to a shift of PRC policy. With its entry into the U.S. and its improved relations with other Asian countries, the PRC has greatly scaled down its support for the insurgency movements. Thailand is a clear-cut example; support for the Communist party of Thailand by the Chinese Communist party has been drastically reduced. Most notable was the closing of the clandestine radio broadcasting station, an act that played a significant role in improving the relations between the two countries.[9]

What brought ASEAN and the PRC closer, however, was the Sino-Vietnam conflict and the problem of Cambodia. The deteriorating relations between Vietnam and the PRC triggered the intervention of the Soviets, who superseded the Chinese, becoming the sole ally of Vietnam. The Chinese viewed with distaste the close Russian-Vietnamese relationship and Vietnam's occupation of Cambodia, regarding it as a plot to extend Vietnam's influence in Indochina and Soviet influence in Southeast Asia. ASEAN's view on the situation was similar to that of the Chinese. Thus, the PRC's and ASEAN's

interpretations of the present situation have generally concurred. For this reason the PRC accepted ASEAN as an "ally" conveniently placed to confront Vietnamese and Soviet expansion. Likewise, ASEAN takes the relationship with the PRC on the issue of Cambodia as a convenient alliance. Meanwhile, the need of the PRC to have "friends" to contain Vietnam and its ally, the Soviet Union, necessitated a softening of policy regarding the Chinese Communist party's support for insurgency movements The reduction of support was not clearly made in public statements, but was real, especially for Thailand, as already mentioned.

The PRC has repeatedly emphasized that it supports ASEAN as a regional organization, and it has cooperated with ASEAN on the issue of Cambodia,[10] although some differences exist. It has pledged its support if Thailand, which is a frontline state of ASEAN, were to be frontally attacked by Vietnam. ASEAN, on its part, has maintained its present relations with the PRC because of the concurrence of interest. There is still doubt about the PRC's policy, however. The pressing question is whether the present policy of the PRC and its wooing of ASEAN is only a tactical change resulting from the emergence of a new situation with the ultimate aim of increasing Chinese influence or control remaining intact in the minds of the Chinese leaders. Is the ultimate aim the communization of the area and thereby the creation of states looking to China politically and for purposes of security? Although the policy question is legitimate, it is also a reflection of the inordinate fears of the ASEAN leaders. After all, one could argue, the Communist movement would stand little chance if the domestic situation, especially the questions of equity of income distribution and political participation in an open system, were efficiently handled.

ASEAN and Japan

As mentioned earlier, Japan has taken a great interest in ASEAN because of its role as a market and because of its raw materials and energy (especially, oil and natural gas from Indonesia.) As a result of its positive attitude toward ASEAN, Japan has been greatly involved with the ASEAN countries in trade, investment, aid, technological cooperation, and cultural exchange.[11] Indeed, of the four powers critically involved with ASEAN, Japan has the greatest influence on the economic development of ASEAN and its future. ASEAN greatly needs Japan's assistance to achieve economic modernization. Trade between Japan and ASEAN is substantial, and Japanese investments in the ASEAN countries are extensive.[12] It is not the purpose of this presentation to discuss the economic transactions between ASEAN and Japan in detail. Suffice it to state that neither Japan nor ASEAN can afford a breach in their economic relations because any cleavage would disrupt the development underway.

But the relationship between ASEAN and Japan has not been entirely smooth. There have been growing complaints about Japan's insensitivity to ASEAN's needs and Japan's failure to rectify the trade imbalance that a majority of ASEAN countries suffer.[13] Anti-Japanese feelings erupted into demonstrations against Prime Minister Tanaka during his visit to ASEAN countries in 1974, starting in Bangkok, spreading to other ASEAN countries, and leading to riots in Indonesia. This episode served as a warning that an asymmetrical relationship and an unwillingness to redress grievances (such as the nontariff barriers imposed by Japan on imports from ASEAN) can lead to resentment and demonstrations. Since the 1974 events, Japan and the ASEAN countries have been trying to sort out their differences, and the ASEAN community has hoped that Japan would achieve a better understanding of ASEAN needs. With some gains on this matter, anti-Japanese sentiments have been reduced. However, ill feelings are merely dormant and can still be activated given the requisite political and economic catalysts.[14]

ASEAN was relatively complacent about Japan's role in the economic arena until the changing situation produced a demand on Japan to increase its political role. It was argued (in American circles) that as a power with enormous economic leverage, Japan should assume a political role in the maintenance of stability in the region.[15] The response from the Japanese leadership was epitomized by Prime Minister Fukuda who made a statement in Manila in August 1977 during his ASEAN tour. He made these points: (1) Japan will not become a major military power; (2) Japan will cooperate with ASEAN countries to help them attain solidarity and resilience (including the pledge of U.S. $1 billion assistance to ASEAN industrial projects); and (3) Japan will endeavor to help create a Southeast Asia in which ASEAN and the Indochinese countries co-exist peacefully.[16]

The Fukuda Doctrine was positively received, but complaints about Japan's slow action and its failure to rectify some basic problems such as the trade imbalance are still heard. Japan has also been criticized for its policy of not helping to alleviate the refugee problem. Although Japan contributed a large sum for relief purposes, it has not been willing to receive Indochinese refugees, except a tiny number, for settlement in Japan. On the positive side, Prime Minister Yasuhiro Nakasone has been supporting the political stand of ASEAN on the issue of Cambodia, that is, the demand for the withdrawal of all foreign forces from that country.[17]

ASEAN-Japan relations have thus been fairly smooth since 1974 and this trend is likely to continue. However, public outcry against Japan's domination in the economy of the region and the intrusion of Japanese culture[18] in the form of cartoon movies, large numbers of Japanese residents, and Japanese-type bars, serve to warn Japan of possible anti-Japanese resentment and to warn the host governments of the danger of losing economic independence. Yet ASEAN has only limited choices. There is need for technological know-how and grants as well as capital inflow from Japan to assist in the process of industrialization of Indonesia, Malaysia, the Philippines, and Thailand. These countries

are anxious to join the club of newly industrialized countries (NICs) applying the pattern
of Singapore; thus it is necessary for them
to maintain the present relationship. In sum,
ASEAN needs Japan.[19]

Japan, on her part, views ASEAN as an
important grouping from a political as well as
an economic standpoint. ASEAN constitutes
a vast area with a population of more than
250 million and rich resources. If ASEAN is
successful in its economic development and
the political changes that follow underwrite
national resilience, it can play an important role
in maintaining stability throughout Southeast
Asia, thereby containing communism. Like
the PRC, which would like to see the present
stable situation in the region continue so that

it can proceed with its four modernizations,[20]
Japan also desires a stable Asia, to support its
economic programs. If the equilibrium in the
region is upset by internal struggles or war, as
in Cambodia, it is detrimental for every country
concerned, including Japan — perhaps more
so for Japan because of its status as a rich,
industrial power with great dependence on
trade. Thus, the peace and prosperity of ASEAN
is to the advantage of Japan, and there is every
reason to expect Japan to continue its support
for ASEAN. The significance Japan attaches
to ASEAN can be seen from the ASEAN tours
that each new Japanese prime minister takes,
a ritual which has been now practiced for
almost a decade.

NOTES

1. See Edward Janner Sinaga, "ASEAN: Economic, Political and Defense Problems: Progress and Prospects in Regional Cooperation with Reference to the Role of Major Powers in Southeast Asia," Ph.D.
   dissertation, Graduate School of Arts and Sciences, George Washington University, 1974, pp. 249–259.
   Russel H. Fifield, *National and Regional Interests in ASEAN: Competition and Cooperation in International Politics* (Occasional Paper No. 57), (Singapore: Institute of Southeast Asian Studies, 1979),
   pp. 13–17.
2. Sinaga, "ASEAN...Problems," pp. 249–254.
3. The visit by Premier Zhao Ziyang to the United States in January 1984 has been viewed as progress
   in China-U.S.-Japan relations. An editorial in *Yomiuri* commented: "Friendly cooperative relations
   between the U.S. and China and Japan and China are indispensable for Asian peace and security.
   We hope that Zhao's U.S. visit will produce many constructive results considering that the deterioration
   of U.S.-Soviet relations heightened global tension." *Yomiuri*, January 9, 1984.
4. Cf. Likhit Dhiravegin, "Karn Patiroop Lae Karn Patiwat" [Reform and Revolution], *The Journal of
   Political Science*, vol. 8, no. 1 (January–April 1982), pp. 157–158.
5. Cf. Justus M. van der Kroef, *Communism in Southeast Asia* (London: Macmillan, 1981), p. 243.
6. Yuri Kuznetsov, the Soviet Ambassador to Bangkok, charged that the U.S. is trying to turn ASEAN
   into a military alliance. *Bangkok Post*, September 22, 1983.
7. In 1978, Soviet Deputy Foreign Minister Firubyin visited the region. For a discussion, see Lau Teik
   Soon, "Uncertain Prospects," pp. 12–13.
8. The PRC allegedly was involved in the abortive coup of 1965 in which half a million people were
   killed and the PKI was crushed. After the coup, relations between the PRC and Indonesia deteriorated.
   In 1967, Indonesia suspended diplomatic relations with the PRC.
9. *ASEAN Forecast*, vol. 3, no. 11 (November 1983), p. 136.
10. This has been repeatedly stated by the Chinese authorities. This policy was confirmed by the counselor
    of the embassy of the People's Republic of China in Thailand, Zhang Qing, in a talk at the Thai-Chinese
    Friendship Association, November 25, 1983.
11. See, for example, Sueo Sekiguchi, ed., *ASEAN-Japan Relations: Investment* (Singapore: Institute of
    Southeast Asian Studies, 1983), and Narongchai Akrasanee, ed., *ASEAN-Japan Relations: Trade and
    Development* (Singapore: Institute of Southeast Asian Studies), 1983.

12. Akrasanee, *ASEAN-Japan Relations*.
13. Ibid.
14. This statement was made by Dr Toru Yano, Center for Southeast Asian Studies, Kyoto University, at the seminar Japanese Studies in ASEAN: A Survey of Strengths and Weaknesses, organized by the Japanese Studies Center, Thammasat University, Pattaya, January 14–15, 1984. Cf. Narongchai Akrasanee and Likhit Dhiravegin, "Trade and Development in Thai-Japanese Relations," in Akrasanee, ed., *ASEAN-Japan Relations*, pp. 157–159.
15. The Japanese responded to this demand; see, for example, "Japan Prepared to Play International Roles, Government Says," *Yomiuri*, April 24, 1981; and "Japan's Political Role in Asia Stressed by Suzuki," *Asahi Evening News*, September 4, 1981. A similar policy has been pursued by other Japanese leaders including the present prime minister, Yasuhiro Nakasone.
16. Koji Watanabe, "Japan and Southeast Asia: 1980," *Asia Pacific Community*, no. 10 (Fall, 1980), pp. 88–89.
17. See speech by Prime Minister Yasuhiro Nakasone at the dinner in his honor given by Prime Minister Prem Tinasulanonda, Bangkok, May 2, 1983, in which he said: "Japan has consistently maintained that a comprehensive political settlement of the Cambodian problem, based upon the withdrawal of foreign forces from Cambodia and the self-determination of the Cambodian people, is the indispensable first step toward peace and stability in this region" (Press Release, Japan Information Service, Bangkok).
18. Toru Yano, Center for Southeast Asian Studies, Kyoto University. Special lecture given at the Faculty of Political Science, Thammasat University, January 13, 1984.
19. ASEAN will need Japan for its industrialization policy. It also needs Japanese investment, aid, and technology for its domestic development. The only alternative in Asia is probably South Korea. However, South Korea is still not comparable to Japan in its economic capacity.
20. Charles W. Freeman, Jr., Deputy Chief of Mission, American Embassy, Beijing, special lecture given at the Institute of Asian Studies, Chulalongkorn University, Bangkok, November 10, 1983.

SUKHUMBHAND PARIBATRA

Southeast Asia as a region may be on the threshold of a period of uncertainty. An era of more complex but uncertain changes and challenges, brought about by developments which have been taking place since the mid-1980s, are now strongly in prospect as the end of the present decade approaches. There seem to be three clusters of such developments relevant to the issue of ASEAN's future relations with Vietnam.

The first is the transformation of the relationships between the United States, the Soviet Union and the PRC. The bitter, cold war-like tensions existing in the late 1970s and the early 1980s, both between the United States and the Soviets and between the latter and the PRC, as well as the anti-Soviet Sino-American alignment that these tensions generated, have given way to attempts to bring about *rapprochement* in the mid-1980s.

In this respect, the improvements in the relations between Moscow and Beijing have been most dramatic. Propelled by their respective concerns with the domestic economic situation and fears of isolation in the uncertain game of great power politics, the two have adopted a lower-risk, lower-cost foreign policy,

initiated frequent bilateral political exchanges, put forward concrete proposals to resolve their differences — including the highly contentious border problems, and rapidly increased their bilateral trade. The recently held border talks, the first in almost a decade, and the agreement that there should be another in 1988, seem to indicate that the process of dialogue and negotiation between the two socialist rivals will be maintained in the years ahead.

However, this process of transformation is still evolving, and its directions and implications are by no means clear at this juncture. This uncertainty is likely to remain at least until the position of the present Soviet leadership becomes much more secure and the imminent leadership changes in the United States and the PRC have been completed.

The three great powers are to some degree involved closely in the affairs of Southeast Asia. This evolving process of transformation inevitably raises a number of questions pertaining to the future of the region:

— Will the U.S.-Soviet *rapprochement* lead to another round of *détente*? If so, what will be its impact, particularly on the American role in Southeast Asia?

Reprinted in abridged form from "The Challenge of Co-existence: ASEAN's Relations with Vietnam in the 1990s", *Contemporary Southeast Asia* 9, no. 2 (September 1987), pp. 140–56, by permission of the author and the Institute of Southeast Asian Studies.

— How far will the Sino-Soviet *rapprochement* develop? Will it ultimately fail to produce a concrete settlement because the differences are too vast? Or will it lead to a series of agreements, including one which brings about a significant reduction or cessation of Moscow's support for Hanoi, as demanded by Beijing? Or will the process of *rapprochement* lead to an "agreement to disagree" where the Kampuchean conflict is concerned, leaving the two sides to pursue their present policies while their other differences are settled? If China and the Soviet Union are able to reach an understanding on a wide range of issues, will Beijing tilt towards Moscow once more? If so, what will be the impact, especially on Hanoi and its relations with the United States and the ASEAN states?

— How will the Sino-American co-operation evolve? Will the two develop a significant security relationship, and if so, what will be the impact on ASEAN and Vietnam? Or will the two great powers be unable to maintain the present level of understanding and co-operation, and if this is the case, what will be the consequences for the region?

The second cluster of developments is the growth of protectionist sentiments, particularly in the United States, both caused by and further contributing towards the continuing malaise in the world economic system. If the present trends continue, it is certain that the open economies of the ASEAN countries will be adversely affected. The questions are: "How far?" and "With what implications?" For ASEAN, the economic ties that truly bind are with the non-communist industrialized nations, but it is not difficult to envisage a situation in which the ASEAN countries become so exasperated with protectionism in the West and Japan, that serious conflicts arise between the two sides and they become much more responsive to the Soviet Union's economic overtures,

which seem to have increased considerably since the Gorbachev initiative in Vladivostock in August 1986. It is not inconceivable also that the ASEAN countries may seek to enhance the trade relationship with Vietnam and Laos for the same reason. It is significant that Thailand, which along with Singapore is the most hardline ASEAN member in the Kampuchean issue, in recent months has strongly criticized its U.S. ally, increased trade with Moscow, initiated moves which would open up trade with Laos, and considered the option of trading with Vietnam.[1] The question is: If ASEAN enhances its economic exchanges with the countries on the other side of the Kampuchean divide, will such a process in the long term lead to changes in the political and diplomatic relations between the two sides?

Moreover, the protectionist trends in the world economy, signifying as they do decreased market opportunities and increased competition among producers of similar goods, may have an adverse impact on ASEAN's solidarity. Despite its professed intentions, economic co-operation has never been the regional organization's forte, and in a restrictive economic climate the members may find themselves competing for the same markets, especially where commodities are concerned. In such a situation the ASEAN countries' own considerable protectionist sentiments may be unleashed upon one another. If so, the crucial question is whether or how far intra-ASEAN economic competition will have spillover effects on the group's political and diplomatic co-operation, particularly in the Kampuchean question.

The third cluster of developments is concerned with the issue of political succession in the regional states. Where ASEAN is concerned, it is likely that the next five years or so will see leadership changes in all the member countries, with the exception of Brunei. The questions relevant to the present discussion are numerous. Will such leadership changes generate domestic instability and, if so, what impact will it have on regional security in general, and on ASEAN's relations with Vietnam in particular? Will the Philippines' domestic conflicts, for example, make the U.S. position in that country untenable and reduce the American role in the region? Will Thailand's internal problems, that are certain to arise out of succession questions, induce a more hardline policy as a means of unifying the country and enhancing the legitimacy of the new leaders, or will they force Bangkok to become more pliant and accept Vietnam's position in Indochina? Will the new ASEAN leaders have the same level of commitment to the regional organization and its policy towards the Indochinese neighbours as their predecessors? Will the post-Suharto regime, for example, try to forge what for long has been feared in other ASEAN capitals, namely, a Jakarta-Hanoi axis? Will the post-Prem leadership in Thailand attempt to develop an extensive and overt security relationship with the PRC, thus creating a competing Bangkok-Beijing axis, or will it try to come to a sort of *modus vivendi* with Hanoi?

The issue of political succession in the ASEAN countries is rendered more complicated by another aspect of generational change, the growing role of "technocrats". The increasing complexity of the regional economies requires the art and science of management of the manifold functional problems that arise as part and parcel of the development process. This in turn has helped to precipitate the rise of a class of highly educated, often highly motivated "professionals" whose main shared concern is to apply their acquired knowledge, skills and experience in the pursuit of excellence in their respective fields of competence. The growing role of technocrats does not mean that all decisions, political or otherwise, will be taken by them; indeed in "key" questions affecting national security, these technocrats may exert little or no influence. But it does mean that in the ASEAN countries there exist groups of influential individuals whose propensity is to devalue both the ideological and the political contents of major policies, and to stress the need for pragmatic, functional approaches to policy formulation. In the context of ASEAN's

relations with the Indochinese countries, it is not inconceivable that such groups may argue and press for more economic interactions in the near future. In this sense, the efforts of the Electricity Generating Authority of Thailand (EGAT) to purchase more electricity from Laos' Nam Ngum Dam in recent months may be but a forerunner of things to come. If greater economic exchanges between ASEAN and the Indochinese countries take place, the question is whether this economic process will have political and diplomatic consequences in the long term.

However, it is on the Vietnamese side that the issue of political succession is one of greater immediacy. Age and human mortality, years of economic mismanagement, and the existence of mass poverty were factors which precipitated economic reforms in Vietnam, beginning in mid-1985, and changes in the top leadership of Hanoi, both in the party and government structures, between July 1986 and February 1987. Although some old faces remain and there still exist differences concerning how and to what extent these reforms should be implemented, the replacement of the ideological old guard with the more progressive, younger leaders indicates that Vietnam is now committed to the task of reforming its ailing economy.

Unclear, however, are the implications of these leadership changes in Hanoi, paralleled by similar but less extensive reshuffles in Vientiane and Phnom Penh, for the former's policy towards the Kampuchean conflict. Again numerous questions arise: Will Vietnam's economic pragmatism, in combination with Gorbachev's preference for a lower cost, lower risk foreign policy, lead to a more flexible, more compromising Kampuchean policy? Or are the Vietnamese attempting to introduce economic reforms *and* simultaneously maintain their hardline posture *vis-à-vis* the Kampuchean question? Is the promotion of General Le Duc Anh, generally thought to be the main architect of the present policy, a confirmation that the policy will not change, or is it but a first, disguised step towards a more flexible position? If Hanoi does not change its Kampuchean policy and continues to be denied access to Western markets, technology and capital can its economic reforms ever succeed, and if these reforms cannot succeed, will the failure in the end bring about a more realistic appraisal of the costs of the military occupation of Kampuchea? If the Vietnamese leaders wish to change their policy, how can they do so without a) endangering their positions in the power structure of the country, b) losing "face" internationally, and c) diminishing Vietnam's security. Furthermore, how can they convince their adversaries of their good intentions at a time when faith in Vietnamese goodwill is a fast diminishing, if not exhausted, commodity?

The foregoing developments, and the questions that they raise, make the task of predicting ASEAN's relations with Vietnam in the next decade an almost impossible one.

NOTE

1. This issue is being discussed, for example, by the Thai House of Representatives Standing Committee for Foreign Affairs.

83

ASEAN'S RELATIONS WITH CHINA AND JAPAN

JULIUS CAESAR PARREÑAS

The ASEAN states have responded to changes which have increased their external threat perceptions by strengthening their co-operation. The different stages in the development of ASEAN co-operation have followed events that have forced the ASEAN states to seek greater security.

The announcement of the Nixon Doctrine, the withdrawal of British troops from Southeast Asia and the thaw in Sino–American relations have served as the background for ASEAN's formulation of the concept of the Zone of Peace, Freedom and Neutrality in Southeast Asia, which defined a commonly-accepted objective for a future political order in Southeast Asia. While ZOPFAN has often been dismissed as a goal too ideal to be realized, and while differences in interpretation between member countries (Malaysia and Singapore) had been stressed, it must be pointed out that it had provided the ASEAN states with the basic framework or constitution necessary for subsequent diplomatic, political and security co-operation. The ZOPFAN Declaration itself was a bold move that underscored the ASEAN countries' willingness, at least in principle, to place the goal of Southeast Asian unity above their particular relations with extra-regional powers.

The communist takeovers in Indochina and the perception of an eventual withdrawal of U.S. military forces from Southeast Asia spurred the ASEAN governments to bolster the organization by holding the first ASEAN summit meeting in Bali in 1976, where economic co-operation was given a big push. Although ASEAN has failed in successfully implementing the plans for greater economic co-operation, it had provided a forum for the co-ordination of foreign policy that intensified as events in Indochina headed ever closer to a conflict.

The Vietnamese invasion of Kampuchea in 1979 further cemented ASEAN co-operation in foreign policy, which became successful, especially in the United Nations, in pressuring Vietnam to agree to most of the conditions that ASEAN had set at the start. Security co-operation among the ASEAN member states, while having been faithfully kept outside the organizational framework, was quietly intensified in the mid-1970s and continued to progress throughout the years, involving consultations, joint exercises and exchanges for military education and training.[1]

The ASEAN states have also promoted co-operation in external economic relations since the mid-1970s. ASEAN became a forum for

Reprinted in abridged form from "China and Japan in ASEAN's Strategic Perceptions", *Contemporary Southeast Asia* 12, no. 3 (December 1990), pp. 198–224, by permission of the author and the Institute of Southeast Asian Studies.

adopting common approaches in negotiations with other countries and groups involving economic issues. As a result, ASEAN became a significant grouping in international organizations such as the United Nations and the UNCTAD.[2] The ASEAN Post-Ministerial Conferences have also become a venue for leading industrial countries to discuss economic issues with the ASEAN member states as a group.

The growing Chinese and Japanese roles in the region have been among the major factors that led the ASEAN states to intensify their co-operation. The prospect of China playing a larger role in Southeast Asia through its influence over communist Vietnam immediately after 1975 while uncertainty over the future U.S. security role in the region persisted created apprehensions in the ASEAN countries about Chinese and Vietnamese ties with local communist insurgents and the destabilizing effects of growing Chinese influence on the internal security and external relations of some ASEAN countries. The U.S. withdrawal from mainland Southeast Asia had left the ASEAN states with no alternative but to increase co-operation and unity to obtain greater security.

Japan was an important factor in the forging of the ASEAN states' co-operation in the area of external economic relations. The fear of Japan's economic dominance stimulated the ASEAN governments to increase their political leverage in negotiations by adopting a common stand and harmonizing their approaches towards their economic partners. However, this did not exclusively refer to Japan, but was also relevant to the ASEAN countries' other major economic partners.

It is difficult to ascertain the more or less exact direction of the ASEAN countries' policies towards China and Japan in the coming decade because of the continuing uncertainty specifically over Japan's security role and over the future direction of China's economic and security policies at this stage. However, it would be expected that the ASEAN states' policies would be influenced by their strategic perceptions of China and Japan, as the examination of their policies throughout the last two decades has shown.

For different reasons, China is perceived by the various ASEAN countries as the main long-term threat to regional stability and, either directly or indirectly, to their external security. The ASEAN countries' perception of Japan is much more positive. This is tied to the condition that Japan does not totally dominate their economies and does not extend its military role to Southeast Asia.

ASEAN's future relations with China and Japan will be affected by the direction of internal and international political changes currently taking place. The USSR's and Vietnam's past policies in Indochina have forced ASEAN (and Thailand in particular) to move closer to Beijing, despite ASEAN's perceptions of a long-term threat emanating from China.

However, an improvement in the USSR's image among Southeast Asians, improvement in Thai–Vietnamese and ASEAN–Vietnamese relations, and China's increasing political isolation would intensify ASEAN's perception of the Chinese threat.[3] Continued expansion of the PRC's naval capabilities and activities in the South China Sea could put China and ASEAN in an adversarial relationship. This could be avoided if China refrains from exerting too much influence on events in Indochina (once Thai–Vietnamese relations have improved) and from actively pursuing its claims to the South China Sea.

The future of the U.S. military facilities in the Philippines could affect ASEAN's relations with Japan, depending on Japan's response to changes regarding this issue. A reduced U.S. military presence in Southeast Asia could put pressure on Japan to take steps leading to the continued security of the sea lanes in the region. If Japan responds by further increasing its military role and extending this to Southeast Asia, its relations with ASEAN would be strained. However, if Japan responds by massively helping ASEAN enhance its economic and military capability to gradually take over responsibility for the security of the sea lanes in the region, ASEAN and Japan would move closer to each other and possibly form a political partnership in the Western Pacific.

Another factor that would affect Japan–ASEAN relations would be the international economic environment. ASEAN's success in diversifying its economic relations by building up investment and trade ties with the European Community, the United States, Taiwan, South Korea and others to balance the growing Japanese economic overdependence on Japan would ensure a positive perception of Japan within the ASEAN countries. Furthermore, the integrating effect of Japanese foreign investments on the ASEAN economies would have a positive effect on their perception of Japan as a contributor to ASEAN co-operation.

The effects of the ongoing political and economic developments on ASEAN co-operation would be vital to the ASEAN countries' individual responses to China's and Japan's changing roles in the region. The desire on the part of the individual member countries to preserve ASEAN unity has led them to modify their foreign and security policies, which could have

been different had there been little interest to co-operate their policies and forge a common stand. The Indochina issue could already have split ASEAN had it not been for the desire to preserve regional unity. There are many other issues that lie ahead which could become divisive factors.

However, ASEAN has been successful so far not only in preserving, but even in promoting its unity. Judging from its development over the last two decades, it appears that the member states' interest in ASEAN unity is greater than other interests which tend to have a divisive effect on the organization. There have been suggestions that the solution of the Indochina problem would leave the ASEAN countries with no more significant cause to rally around. These suggestions evidently do not take into consideration that the future could present even greater threats to these countries' external security. If only for the strategic uncertainties that would follow the Cold War's demise, the pressure for co-operation among these weaker states in a region dominated by several major powers could be expected to mount.

NOTES

1. Mak gives a description of the ASEAN countries' defence co-operation in the fields of joint exercises, training, C³I, joint surveillance and patrols, joint facilities, rationalization of equipment and logistics, arms and equipment production and commanders' conferences; see J.N. Mak, *Directions for Greater Defence Cooperation*, ISIS ASEAN Series (Kuala Lumpur: Institute of Strategic and International Studies, 1986), pp. 10–22. "According to Asian officials, defence co-operation arrangements between non-communist countries in Southeast Asia are being strengthened in order to reduce the U.S burden and discourage powers outside the region from filling any gaps caused by a diminished American presence. This strengthening includes more and larger bilateral military exercises, intelligence exchanges, and acquisition of advanced weapons and technology from the United States and other Western suppliers". Michael Richardson, "US is Relocating Forces as End of Manila Pact Nears", *International Herald Tribune*, 19 September 1989, p. 7.

2. Francoise Cayrac-Blanchard, "L'ASEAN et la crise indochinoise: de la diversité dans l'unité", *Revue francaise de science politique* 32, no. 3 (June 1982): 383.

3. Keith Richburg, "Cambodian Pullout: The Implications", *International Herald Tribune*, 19 September 1989, p. 6.

84

ASEAN'S CHANGING EXTERNAL RELATIONS

LESZEK BUSZYNSKI

Superpower rivalry during the Cold War had the effect of suppressing potential areas of conflict between states based upon ethnic or territorial disputes previously regarded as dormant. Similarly, the regional ambitions of the stronger powers were either repressed or subordinated to the dominant axis of East-West conflict. The removal of the Cold War framework for confrontation would eliminate a major source of conflict but would permit tensions to surface, many of which have remained quiescent during the colonial era. Other tensions would arise as products of modernization as Asian states adapt themselves to a great power role in terms of the status symbols of contemporary international politics. Such symbols can include a sphere of influence with a group of subordinate states, a naval capability and nuclear weapons. The effect of superpower decline would provide opportunities for Asian great powers as well as middle powers to realize their ambitions in this respect with uncertain consequences for the smaller states. Such great powers include Japan and China while India aspires to the status of a great power.

JAPAN has been through a destructive and abortive period of imperialism during which great power ambitions have been dissipated by the experience of defeat and compensated by economic achievements. To some extent, United States leaders expect Japan to assume a greater role in Northeast Asia in defence of the sea lanes and as a means of containing the Soviet Pacific fleet. The Japanese government has specified that Japan needs to develop a minimum deterrent for a limited defence role but there is no assurance that under changing strategic conditions Japan's defence interests would remain limited. The concept of a minimum deterrent is one that was a product of a situation in which the United States maintained its position as the stabilizing hegemon. The removal of the United States in this role would place pressure upon the Japanese to protect their oil lifeline to the Middle East or trading routes through Southeast Asia and the key sea straits.

The prime minister, Toshiki Kaifu, has floated the idea of despatching Japanese troops abroad for certain contingencies involving international peacekeeping, anti-terrorist operations and rescue missions for the protection of Japanese citizens. The defence agency has similarly advocated that Japanese warships escort vessels carrying plutonium waste from Europe to Japan for treatment. Without the assurance of a protective American role in areas considered vital

Reprinted in abridged form from "Declining Superpowers: The Impact on ASEAN", *Pacific Review* 3, no. 3 (1990), pp. 257–61, by permission of the author and Oxford University Press.

for the shipment of resources and energy to Japan the very real domestic political constraints that prevented Japan from developing an extensive military role in the region may be eroded. Southeast Asian concerns in relation to Japan have generally focused upon the danger of Japanese economic hegemony in the region. More recently, however, the Malaysian foreign minister, Abu Hassan Omar, in May 1989 noted that Japan would be the most important single factor affecting ASEAN's future.

CHINA has always regarded itself as a great power and with an indisputable sense of its own status has demanded corresponding recognition from its Asian neighbours. China's leaders have now been released from the obsessive concern with the Soviet Union over the Sino-Soviet frontier since Gorbachev has made an effort to improve relations which culminated in his visit to Beijing in May 1989. The focus of China's defence planning has moved away from the possibility of conflict along the northern border towards contingencies along China's southern borders, including the border with India, the South China Sea, and the Taiwan Straits. In particular, China has been developing a modernized navy that would enable it to prosecute its claims in the South China Sea which the Chinese regard as their sovereign territory. China's navy is still basically a submarine force with 93 submarines, 19 destroyers, and no air cover which severely restricts any effort to venture beyond the range of land-based air forces. The Chinese have been, nonetheless, constructing an air base in the Paracel Islands south of Hainan which are some 600 km from the northern Spratly Islands in the South China Sea. The basing of long-range naval aviation in the Paracels would certainly bolster China's ability to enforce its claims in relation to the Spratly Islands by providing its navy with air cover.

Southeast Asian concerns in relation to China's intentions in the South China Sea have been stimulated by the Chinese-Vietnamese clash of 14 March 1988 as a consequence of which the Chinese were able to occupy seven islands in the Spratly Islands group. Malaysia and the Philippines occupy islands in the South China Sea claimed by China and any decision by the Chinese to apply military pressure against them would have devastating consequences for the rest of ASEAN. The chief of Malaysian strategic intelligence, Major General Datuk Abdul Raja Rashid, publicly alluded to this danger when he stated that China could become more aggressive if the United States reduced its role in the region.[1]

Southeast Asian countries have expressed concern over the vaulting ambitions of **INDIA** to assume the role of a great power. Indian-Southeast Asian relations have never been close even in the era of non-alignment and Third World solidarity. From the Southeast Asian perspective, there is an Indian tendency to regard the region as a former colony of Indian civilization, a view based on a distorted understanding of the spread of Indian culture in that area in pre-modern times. Such assumptions of pride and arrogance were of little consequence for Southeast Asia while India remained distant but the expansion of an existing naval capability and the development of missile delivery systems has removed the comfort of distance. India has 2 aircraft carriers, 5 Soviet Kashin class destroyers, and 21 frigates; this limited capability enables it to extend its ambitions up to the Andaman Islands and the Malacca Straits in pursuit of what Rajiv Gandhi claimed was an effort not to lose control again over the sea approaches to the Indian Ocean.

In addition, India has developed an airlift capability which was demonstrated when two battalions were airlifted to the Maldives in response to the *coup* of November 1988. India tested an ICBM (2,400 km) called Agni in May 1989, as well as a surface-to-surface short-range missile called Prithvi in February 1989. The *Bangkok Post* claimed that India had come of age as a military power and wanted 'international recognition as a world player'.[2] Other Southeast Asian assessments in countries bordering the Indian Ocean have been considerably more suspicious of Indian intentions.

Raja Rashid feared that India may want to play a larger role in Southeast Asia to balance China in recognition that the Indian-Chinese conflict would spread without the balancing role of the United States.[3] In Indonesia there is a view amongst a minority that India may become a more direct threat than China which at the present time lacks a naval air capability, of the kind possessed by India, necessary to enforce its claims within the region.

Japan, China, and India are not the only security concerns for the Southeast Asian states. Reports about **NORTH KOREA's** attempts to develop atomic weapons are troubling and raise the spectre of nuclear proliferation amongst parties to major regional conflicts. **VIETNAM's** relationship with the rest of Southeast Asia has yet to be resolved, including its claims to the Spratly Islands. Moreover, within ASEAN, concerns have been expressed over **INDONESIA's** regional role after Suharto leaves the political scene. A more nationalistic or assertive Indonesia may be the consequence of an internal power struggle in which a faction could, as did Sukarno in a previous era, resort to aggrandisement in foreign affairs to bolster a fragile domestic position. Indonesian attitudes in this respect will be tested by problems of political stability in Papua New Guinea and, specifically, the issue of the Irian Jaya separatists and the problem of Bougainville.

APPROACHES TO ASEAN SECURITY

Previously, security attitudes in Southeast Asia could be grouped into two broad approaches according to whether security was regarded as a product of indigenous effort or a consequence of external support. The Malaysian and Indonesian foreign ministries, in particular, have propagated the idea that security could be a product of collective political agreement amongst the ASEAN countries which was enshrined in the Zone of Peace. Freedom and Neutrality Concept (ZOPFAN) of November 1971. ZOPFAN was never really defined but it expressed the desire within the region for autonomy in the face of great power intrusion and in this sense it was closely linked with the idea of nonalignment. The spirit or ZOPFAN motivated an effort on the part of the region to insulate itself from the deleterious effects of great power rivalry. Tun Razak, the Malaysian prime minister from 1968 to 1976, had attempted to give literal definition to this aspiration by negotiating the neutralization of the region with the great powers. At a later stage variant solutions were devised such as negotiating the removal of the military presences of the superpowers, or the notion of equilibrium in which no great power would have an advantage. Nonetheless, despite its impractability, ZOPFAN has continued to grip the popular political consciousness in both Indonesia and Malaysia.

The second approach adopted by Thailand, Singapore, and the Philippines entailed a reliance upon external security support against a specified external threat, or as a consequence of the realization that the state could not adequately cope with its own defence. While this latter consideration motivated Philippine thinking in relation to the American bases, which were regarded as a means of obtaining increased levels of United States aid, Thailand and Singapore were both concerned about external threats and were acutely suspicious of ZOPFAN. Security for these two ASEAN countries was very much linked to the American military presence in the Philippines, not only as a restraint upon Vietnam as the Thais would have it, but against any state that would undermine or threaten regional stability. From the Singaporean perspective, regional stability as well as the high growth rates achieved by ASEAN economies over the previous seven years were attributable to the American military presence.

These categories have become blurred in the past year given the realization that the regional security context to which they relate is changing. Security thinking amongst the ASEAN states is adjusting in anticipation of the military disengagement of the superpowers.

Policy-formulators within the ASEAN countries generally believe that the American bases in the Philippines will be eventually phased out over a five-ten-year period. That assessment is based upon an understanding of the anti-bases focus of Philippine nationalism since Cory Aquino was thrown into power in February 1986, and the realization that forward bases will become progressively less important for American policy in future decades. Philippine demands for increases in 'rent' are regarded as exorbitant by an American administration that is in the process of reducing the defence budget. The specific demand that annual payments of $1–2 billion should be enshrined in a treaty governing the bases after the expiration of the present agreement in 1991 was regarded as 'crazy' by Patricia Schroder, chairperson of the House Armed Services Subcommittee on Military Installations.[4] Congressional resistance to Philippine demands is likely to stimulate further outbursts of anti-bases nationalism and it is unlikely that the country will provide a conducive political environment for the retention of the bases over the long term.

SINGAPORE SHUFFLES THE CARDS

An event which illustrated the extent to which security thinking within ASEAN was changing occurred when Singapore, on 4 August 1989, offered to host United States military facilities in order to retain the benefits of American protection. The offer was made by minister of state for foreign affairs and finance, George Yeo, to parliament in a statement in which it was claimed that Singapore would host 'some U.S. facilities' to make it easier for the Philippines to continue to maintain the American bases at Clark Field and Subic Bay. Singapore's prime minister, Lee Kuan Yew, revealed his motivations in his National Day speech of 20 August 1989 in which he noted the rise of new regional powers, India and Vietnam, and predicted that the military capabilities of Asia's existing great powers, Japan and China, would expand in

future years.[5] Singapore's action precipitated a public debate amongst ASEAN leaders over the future of regional security.

While Singapore feared that United States withdrawal from Southeast Asia would leave it vulnerable before larger neighbours, attitudes within Malaysia and Indonesia differed considerably. Within these two countries views have been expressed that superpower decline presents the region with an opportunity to implement ZOPFAN. Such views were found amongst academics, journalists, the political parties, and within the foreign ministries of both countries. Nonetheless, the views of the defence and security establishments of these countries are closer to the Singaporean position and in conflict with the official orthodoxy of ZOPFAN. The Singapore offer revealed that security thinking within the ASEAN countries had become more complex than conventional wisdom had assumed and that divisions along institutional lines were as significant as the expected differences between the individual countries. Opinion groups in Malaysia and Indonesia emerged in these institutional areas which may not question ZOPFAN as an aim but which certainly regard the present time as unpropitious for its implementation.

Yeo's speech to parliament made no mention of the form of the United States presence, though reference was made to 'greater military use of some facilities in Singapore' with the stipulation that 'this would not be unprecedented'.[6] United States military aircraft have been using Tengah air base in Singapore for transit purposes while American naval vessels have been making regular port calls. No mention was made of a permanent presence and, indeed, subsequent American statements confirm that the intention was to establish a rotational military presence which would take advantage of Singapore's repair and maintenance facilities.[7] A United States survey team headed by the deputy chief of staff of CINCPAC, Rear Admiral David Bennett, visited Singapore in June 1989 to examine the possible use of naval facilities at Sembawang and the use of the airfield at Paya Lebar. The Americans looked for accommodation for one to two squadrons of F-16s and 200 service personnel. The report of the survey team was subsequently submitted to the joint chiefs of staff. Singapore was careful at this stage to notify its neighbours as to the purpose of the survey team's visit.

Within Indonesia, reactions to Singapore's proposal were subdued which reflected the competing perceptions of the country's security needs.

- First, there was the understanding within the defence ministry and the military that the American military presence was still required to maintain regional security and those associated with the defence minister, Benny Murdani, have adopted this view. The governor of the National Defence College, Major-General Soebijakto, publicly called for the retention of the American bases in the Philippines because of fears of China and the Soviet presence in Cam Ranh Bay.[8]
- Secondly, Indonesian officials carefully distinguished between a rotational military presence involving repair and supply facilities and a permanent military base.

A rotational presence would meet immediate Indonesian security demands for the retention of an American presence while its transient character would not be incompatible with the orthodoxy of ZOPFAN. As Benny Murdani noted, American naval vessels might take advantage of the repair facilities of Singapore but they would still be given security cover.[9] In this sense, even a repair facility can have symbolic value as an American commitment to the region.

The major concern in Indonesia was whether Singapore would present the region with a *fait accompli* in the urgent desire to enhance its own security. In response to the Singapore offer, the armed forces commander, Try Sutrisno, counselled restraint and claimed that what was at stake was 'a garage and not a base'.[10] Suharto met Lee Kuan Yew in Brunei on 3 August when

the Singaporean prime minister stressed that the offer would relate to repair and maintenance facilities. Suharto reportedly remarked that if the facilities turned out to be more than discussed problems would arise for Singapore.[11] The foreign minister, Ali Alatas, in the Indonesian parliament noted that the Singapore offer contained two key points which were repair and servicing facilities and the enhancement of existing facilities. 'Quietly we told them, there is a line. You cross that line and we speak out.'[12] The editorial of the *Jakarta Post* went further in stating that 'it would be most helpful from the outset to free ourselves of the entrenched notion that the US military presence in the region is by definition beneficial'.[13]

The Singapore offer provoked considerable hostility from Malaysia which in its intensity went beyond a reaction to the possible presence of American forces in Singapore. The issue from the Malaysian perspective involved the relationship between Singapore and Malaysia and the conviction that Malaysia has consultative rights over Singaporean foreign policy which derive from history and proximity. The defence minister, Tengku Rithauddeen, on 6 August called for the phasing in of ZOPFAN with the phasing out of foreign military bases, pending which the *status quo* should be respected.[14] The secretary-general of the Malaysian foreign ministry, Datuk Kamil Jaafar, on 8 August stressed that the Singapore offer would undermine the process of negotiating peace by involving the region in great power rivalry.[15] In this sense, the Malaysian hope was that the Soviet Union under Gorbachev might be persuaded to withdraw entirely from Cam Ranh Bay, if the American military presence in the region were withdrawn. The foreign minister, Abu Hassan Omar, claimed that Soviet objections constituted one reason why Malaysia opposed the Singapore offer adding that ZOPFAN will not be achieved with a superpower presence.[16] The prime minister, Mahathir Mohamad, was careful to distinguish between repair services which he accepted and a permanent base which he resolutely condemned: 'Our stand is that we do not agree if Singapore is to be turned into a permanent military base.' At the same time, however, the Malaysian prime minister called for a continued United States military presence in the Philippines. He emphasized that it would be premature for the United States to withdraw and that any reduction in the American presence should be introduced gradually in response to specific Soviet steps such as withdrawal from Cam Ranh Bay.[17]

In Thailand, the responses to Singapore's offer were divided which indicated how Thai security thinking was adjusting to the prospect of a reduced American presence in the region. Previously, the Thais had been assertive advocates of the American military presence but their need for American support had eased when the Vietnamese agreed to withdraw their forces from Cambodia. The greater confidence that Thailand has felt in regard to its security predicament has been expressed in the intention of the prime minister, Chatichai Choonhavan, to develop trading relationships with both Vietnam and the Phnom Penh regime. The traditional Thai desire for external security support was articulated by the foreign minister, Siddhi Savetsila, who has clashed with Chatichai's optimism in regard to the Cambodian issue in the past. Siddhi's comment on Singapore's offer reflected the foreign ministry's standard view, that American use of facilities in Singapore would enhance regional security and would maintain the strategic power balance in Southeast Asia.[18] The National Security Council chief, Suvit Suthanukul, similarly expressed concern over the 'dangerous power vacuum' that could emerge in the region without the United States military presence.[19] The prime minister himself avoided direct comment, claiming that the issue was a bilateral affair for the United States and Singapore, but his views in favour of the United States presence in the Philippines were reported nonetheless.[20] Chatichai as well as the army commander, Chaovalit Yongchaiyut, avoided the issue which revealed a prudent concern over the negative Soviet and Chinese responses. Nonetheless,

the former head of the Social Action Party, Kukrit Pramoj, opposed the Singapore offer as being divisive for ASEAN. The editorial of the *Bangkok Post* opined that 'there is no better timing for ASEAN to start seriously working towards ZOPFAN now that the prospect of a Cambodian settlement is gaining momentum'.[21]

The contentious issue of a prospective American military presence in Singapore was defused by clarifying statements on the part of Singaporean and American leaders. Lee Kuan Yew reassured his neighbours that his intention was not to go beyond repair and supply facilities. In Jakarta on 6 October, Singapore's prime minister consulted with Suharto again and affirmed that 'I can tell you there will be no American military base in Singapore'.[22] In Kuala Lumpur on 20 October, Lee Kuan Yew explained to Mahathir that no American base was intended. The Singapore offer was temporary, he claimed, as developments in military technology would minimize the need for forward bases over the next fifteen to twenty years.[23] The United States vice-president, Dan Quayle, in Kuala Lumpur attempted to calm the atmosphere by stating that the United States had no desire to establish a base in Singapore but required services for its aircraft on a rotational basis and bunkering facilities for its navy.[24] Accordingly, the Singaporean government on 18 October announced increased use of Singapore's maintenance and repair facilities by United States aircraft and more short-term visits on a rotational basis in early 1990. American service personnel in Singapore were to be increased from ten to around 170.[25]

Singapore has been obliged to modify its previously strident demand for external security support and will probably cooperate more closely with its neighbours in the future. Within Indonesia and Malaysia, government officials have identified some value in a rotating American military presence in Singapore as long as it could be seen to be compatible with non-alignment and ZOPFAN. Those ASEAN countries associated with the ZOPFAN approach to security are compelled to examine the future and to ask whether ZOPFAN would be an appropriate response in coping with Japan, China, or India. Those ASEAN countries which have advocated relying upon United States security support have doubts about the extent to which the Americans will be able to retain a military presence in the region and, moreover, need to take cognizance of the views of neighbours for whom ZOPFAN is an article of faith. If ASEAN is to reach a consensus over approaches to regional security in the age of superpower decline it will not be adequately expressed in the familiar terms of ZOPFAN, or in terms of permanent military bases. The ASEAN countries may be required to expand security cooperation among themselves in what Try Sutrisno has called a 'spider's web' of bilateral security relationships. Such bilateral security cooperation may be linked with a rotating United States military presence which may permit the region to adapt to the withdrawal of the American bases from the Philippines.

NOTES
1. *Straits Times*, 15 February 1990.
2. 'New Delhi flexes its muscles', editorial, *Bangkok Post*, 23 May 1989.
3. *Straits Times*, 15 February 1990.
4. *Ibid.*, 15 August 1989.
5. *Ibid.*, 21 August 1989.
6. George Yeo's statement in *Singapore Government Press Release*, 16 August 1989.
7. See CINCPAC Admiral Huntington Hardisty's statement in *The New Straits Times*, 11 August 1989.
8. *Straits Times*. 3 March 1989.
9. *Ibid.*, 19 September 1989.
10. *Sunday Times* (Singapore), 13 August 1989.
11. *Jakarta Post*, 10 August 1989.
12. *Straits Times*, 23 September 1989.
13. 'U.S. bases debate goes on', editorial, *Jakarta Post*, 22 August 1989.
14. *New Straits Times*, 7 August 1989.
15. *Ibid.*, 9 August 1989.
16. *Straits Times*, 18 August 1989.
17. *New Straits Times*, 16 August 1989.
18. *Bangkok Post*, 7 August 1989.
19. *Straits Times*, 13 August 1989.
20. See report by Admiral Siri Sirirangsee, Chairman of the Thai Parliament's Committee on Military Affairs, *Bangkok Post*, 19 August 1989.
21. 'Ill advised timing by Singapore', editorial, *Bangkok Post*, 7 August 1989.
22. *Straits Times*, 7 October 1989.
23. *Ibid.*, 20 September 1989.
24. *Ibid.*, 29 September 1989.
25. Singapore Government Press Statement, 18 October 1989.

85.   ASEAN AND JAPAN'S NEW ROLE IN SOUTHEAST ASIA*

CHAIWAT KHAMCHOO

Japan has a special interest in the Indochina conflict since it has potentially worrying implications for the future economic development of Southeast Asia and, therefore, for Japan's own economic security. The third Indochina war also exposed other dangers to the stability and security of the area as it not only heightened tensions between the non-Communist ASEAN states and Vietnam-dominated Indochina but also exacerbated Sino-Soviet rivalry in the region.

Japan's role in the conflict has generally conformed to ASEAN's stance. ASEAN members urged Tokyo to use its considerable economic power to dissuade Vietnam from aggression. Japan gradually took a firm stand of not resuming economic aid to Vietnam until the latter withdrew its troops from Cambodia, and until a comprehensive settlement could be achieved. Many Japanese disagreed with their government's support of the ASEAN stance on the Cambodia issue, especially that of Japan's freeze of economic aid to Hanoi. For example, the Japan-Vietnam Trade Association (*Nichietsu Boeki Kai*), formed in 1955 by Japanese traders, bankers, and manufacturers involved in trade with Vietnam, requested the resumption of economic aid as soon as possible.[1] In the end, these views did not prevail.

It was not difficult for Japan to decide whether to support ASEAN or Vietnam in the Indochina conflict. ASEAN was clearly more important to Japan than Vietnam, both economically and politically. In economic terms, ASEAN accounts for about 10 percent of Japan's total trade while Vietnam together with the other two Communist Indochina states represents less than one percent. Politically, as one Southeast Asia scholar has perceptively commented:

> The ASEAN countries are important to Japan mainly in the larger context of the Asia-Pacific region and global strategy. With their basically anti-communist governments and with economies well integrated with the non-communist nations, the five ASEAN countries are likely allies of Japan in the regional balance of power. Their support and cooperation would definitely enhance Japan's position in the international community while their political stability and friendly disposition would guarantee Japan the accessibility to its most vital lifeline, the Straits of Malacca.[2]

Japan was under international pressure, particularly from the United States, to increase its aid to countries adjacent to areas of international conflict and deemed strategically important to the west.[3] The one country within

Reprinted in abridged form from "Japan's Role in Southeast Asian Security: 'Plus ça change...'", *Pacific Affairs* 64, no. 1 (Spring 1991), pp. 10–19, by permission of the author and the University of British Columbia.

ASEAN that meets these criteria is Thailand which hosts the world's third largest Japanese embassy. While suspending aid to Vietnam and providing diplomatic support for ASEAN's stance on the Cambodia conflict, Japan increased its economic aid to Thailand to strengthen the local economy and ensure stability. Thailand was the seventh largest recipient of Japanese ODA contributions in 1960–79, but it moved up to second place in cumulative terms between 1979 and 1986.[4]

In addition, in order to demonstrate its willingness to play an active role in promoting peace and stability in the region and thereby mitigate the criticism often leveled against it for its tendency to remain on the sidelines of international conflicts, Japan has worked with ASEAN to help resolve the Cambodia issue. Tokyo has made several proposals regarding a peaceful solution to the Cambodian conflict, all closely linked with ASEAN positions. During his visit to the ASEAN region in May 1989, Prime Minister Takeshita Noboru stated that Japan stood ready to strengthen its cooperation with the ASEAN countries to settle the decade-long conflict in Cambodia. Japan would consider offering financial help, contribute personnel to a peacekeeping force, and provide non-military material to help the peace process.[5]

Japan hosted a meeting in Tokyo between Prince Sihanouk, leader of the anti-Vietnamese resistance, and the Vietnamese-backed Premier Hun Sen in early June 1990 at the urging of Thai Prime Minister Chatichai Choonhavan. The outcome of the meeting could not be considered a success, since the Khmer Rouge, the strongest of the tripartite coalition resistance, rejected the Tokyo accord signed between Sihanouk and Hun Sen. However, Japan was able to demonstrate that it did its utmost to promote the peace process. The Tokyo meeting thus served to enhance Japan's political stature in the region.

SECURITY RELATIONS WITH ASEAN

For over a decade, there have been contacts between the Japanese defense establishment and its ASEAN counterparts. Japan, however, has steadfastly refused to enter into formal military cooperation agreements with these countries. Some ASEAN countries, especially Indonesia and Thailand, have shown interest in receiving arms and military technology from Japan in order to bolster their own defense capabilities and to enhance regional security,[6] but Japan refused to sell military hardware to any nation.

Although Japan has declined to supply arms and other military hardware, it has complied with requests for education and training of military personnel from the region. Of the 128 foreigners who attended Japan's military school between 1975 and 1985, 80 came from Singapore and Thailand.[7] In early July 1988, Prime Minister Lee Kuan Yew of Singapore told Tsutomu Kawara, then Japan's self-defense director general, that his country appreciated Japan's acceptance of its students at the Japanese Defense Academy and expressed the view that it was important for Japan and ASEAN to strengthen defense cooperation through the exchange of personnel.[8] Kawara's visit to Southeast Asia was widely regarded as the beginning of a thaw between Japan and ASEAN in defense matters, the visit being the first ever by a Japanese defense minister. Kawara said in Jakarta that greater understanding on defense issues between ASEAN and Japan "would be useful." He was nevertheless vague about the possibility of closer defense cooperation in areas such as exchange of military personnel and the transfer of military technology.[9]

Important, too, is the fact that some Japanese strategic analysts have called for the abandonment of "the unrealistic policy of 'armed forces' separated from other areas," and the promotion of "all-round linkages of politics, economics and military." Writing in the *Liberal Star*, the ruling LDP official newspaper, Makoto Momoi commented that "as long as we are afraid of such linkages, contradictions in technical transfer policy will arise due to the change in *de facto* policy. Indeed, if the ability of Asian countries to defend their territorial waters improves thanks to Japanese technical help, Japan can spend less money defending itself."[10] Hozumi Toshihiko, former Japanese Marine Self-Defense Forces officer and currently director of the Japanese Center for Strategic Studies, recommended in 1984 that Japan "improve on the policies which have limited the deployment of its forces to exclusively defense purposes" and prevented a more realistic collective defense in cooperation with other countries which would allow Japan to assume direct defense of the sea line of communication in collaboration with the Southeast Asian nations.[11]

Successive Japanese governments have nevertheless insisted that Japan engage in "security-related cooperation" with ASEAN countries only in the economic field. They have repeatedly emphasized the importance of Japan's contribution to stability in Southeast Asia through its economic role, rather than by means of direct military assistance.

One could argue that Japan's economic aid has the same effect as military aid since such assistance, especially in the form of program loans, allows recipient states to allocate a greater proportion of their own resources for military purposes. Japan can thereby play a significant, albeit indirect, role in regional security without pledging direct military support.[12] A senior Japanese defense official has in fact agreed that Japanese policy might be assessed in this way, but he also maintained that this did not reflect Japan's intention.[13]

Japan's refusal to assume a military role does not of course mean that it has not been concerned about military security in the region. Indeed, since 1980, every White Paper on defense has mentioned the military situation in Southeast Asia as a matter of serious concern. A typical statement notes that "the ASEAN countries occupy important geopolitical positions along routes [used] for the supply of raw materials to Japan and have strong economic ties with Japan. Therefore, the security of

ASEAN countries is essential to the security of Japan and Japan is watching developments there with great concern."[14] This is the primary reason why Japan wants the United States to remain involved in the region. It is hardly surprising, then, that Japan was gratified when U.S. leaders and officials reaffirmed the U.S. commitment to east and Southeast Asian security. Commenting on Japan's role in the Cambodia conflict, Watanabe Koji, a senior official at *Gaimusho*, wrote that "among the encouraging factors in the regional scene is the revival of U.S. interest in Southeast Asia."[15] The Japanese are concerned in particular about the erosion of U.S. influence in the Philippines, which has immediate implications for the preservation of U.S. bases in that country. Japan, in the words of one American critic, "was (and is) ready, willing, and able to root for the strategic team as long as all the game players were Americans."[16] Japan desires continued U.S. involvement not only for strategic reasons, but for economic reasons as well. The idea and hope is that the U.S. military as well as economic presence will reduce the appearance of the "overpresence" of Japan's economic activities in the area.

While attempting to encourage the United States to continue to provide a military deterrent, successive Japanese governments, as noted, have continued to insist that Japan would play an economic role only in helping to stabilize Southeast Asia. Prime Minister Suzuki said back in January 1981:

> I do not believe that military power is the only solution to peace and stability. It is necessary for a country to prosper economically so that the people's living standards improve and the society stabilizes. That will both reduce the seeds of conflict in the society and the possibility of invasion or domestic upheaval. Japan intends to contribute to the goal of peace and stability through economic cooperation.[17]

The Japanese economic approach to regional security is based on the assumption, valid or not, that the promotion of economic and technological cooperation will create the basis for political and economic stability in the whole of Southeast Asia. Hence, from Japan's perspective, the best Japan can do to enhance regional peace and security is to further its economic development by means of aid, trade, and investment. It is further assumed that there is less chance of domestic or international disturbance if *each* country achieves economic progress. Hosomi Takashi, then president of the Overseas Economic Co-operation Fund (OECF), an organization for the promotion of economic cooperation between Japan and developing countries, has argued that unchecked economic instability in the region would promote political upheaval and, ultimately, military involvement by Communist countries in the area. Therefore, Japan's aid in resolving economic pressures could effectively "help maintain a resilient government in office." Non-military aid to ASEAN countries "would solidify internal political bases and stabilize both the political and the military balance in the area." Such aid, it was felt, would serve to alleviate "regional tensions and establish a cohesive, viable political stability."[18]

These official views are shared by many leading Japanese experts on Southeast Asia who likewise accept the assumption underlying Japan's approach to the problem of stability and security in the area.[19] These experts are generally of the view that Japan playing only an economic role can strengthen ASEAN governments, thereby promoting regional stability. They believe that Japan must not exert any military pressure in regional conflicts as in Cambodia and that Japan's influence should be restricted to the economic and diplomatic arenas, avoiding direct participation in the Southeast Asian balance of power. They also believe other countries should maintain the balance of power in the region, lending support to the idea that the United States and Japan should engage in a division of labour in maintaining peace in Southeast Asia, with Japan handling economics and the United States

handling military defense. There is a general consensus that it would be "a most unwise, a most incredible, and a most irrational approach" for Japan to resort to military means to secure its national interests. These would be better served, it is argued, by the continued development of strong, sustained, and mutually beneficial trade relations with the regional countries. In short, the Japanese experts believe that continued emphasis on a purely economic role is more consistent with Japan's real interests as well as its self-perception. "After all," wrote Shibusawa Masahide, "one can contribute best by doing what one is most experienced at and has an aptitude for."[20]

The prevailing attitude within and outside the government seems to be: "Our present policy works well, so why change it?" The past policy of maintaining a dichotomy between economics on the one hand and politics on the other appears to have been extraordinarily successful. The Japanese policy of political and military non-involvement in line with the tenets of the post-war "Peace Constitution" has certainly facilitated Japanese penetration of both developed and developing world markets.

To be sure, there is a sector both in and outside the establishment that believes Japan should participate more actively in world affairs, even though this would entail a controversial role for the military.[21] This is presumably the opinion in support of a bill recently proposed by Prime Minister Kaifu Toshiki that would allow the prime minister to dispatch Japanese troops on peacekeeping missions in cooperation with the United Nations. However, every public opinion poll has shown that a large majority is against sending troops overseas. Newspaper polls of Japanese legislators have shown that a solid majority of Diet members, including the ruling LDP party members, oppose the bill.[22] The law was apparently proposed under heavy pressure from the United States who wanted Japan not only to provide funds but also to send Japanese personnel to join the multinational forces arrayed against Iraq in the Persian Gulf.[23] With strongly adverse public reaction, however, Prime Minister Kaifu decided to scrap the troop proposal.[24]

JAPAN'S MILITARY SECURITY POSTURE

While Japan has yet to play a direct security role through military means, it has continued to boost its own military capabilities. Changes in Japan's external environment, especially since the U.S. retreat from Vietnam in 1975, have forced reassessment of its security situation. The relative decline of U.S. military power affects the very premise on which Japan's defense and security has rested. In the past, the assumption has been that Japan could almost totally depend on the United States for its defense. This has now been called into question. The July 1980 report of the Comprehensive National Security Study Group reflects the general decline of Japanese confidence in American strength and leadership, both globally and regionally.

> In considering the question of Japan's security, the most fundamental change in the international situation that took place in the 1970s is the termination of clear American supremacy in both military and the economic spheres.
>
> The military balance between the U.S. and the Soviet Union has changed globally and regionally as the United States has held back on strengthening its military arsenals since the mid 1960s while the Soviet Union has continued to build up its military force. As a result, the U.S. military is no longer able to provide its allies and friends with nearly full security.[25]

In the light of these fundamental changes in Japan's external security environment and U.S. demands for larger contributions to defense efforts, Japanese governments have steadily, if slowly, increased defense spending. Over the past five years, Japan has increased military spending by 6 percent per annum on average. Between 1982 and 1989, the annual rate of increase in defense spending alongside that of

official development assistance spending has exceeded the rate of growth in total budget spending. In terms of GNP however, Japanese defense spending remains small: its ratio to GNP of about 1 percent is among the lowest in the world. But, bearing in mind that Japan's GNP is second only to that of the U.S., Japan's defense outlay still ranks fifth in the world (or the third largest in the world if personnel and pension costs are included).

Despite the recent dramatic improvements in east-west relations, Japan plans to continue to strengthen its military power. In his testimony before the Foreign Affairs Committee of the Upper House in early December 1989, Foreign Minister Nakayama Taro said the political environment in the Asian region makes it unlikely that Japan will reduce the size of its military forces. To justify Japan's position he cited continuing tension on the Korean Peninsula, the conflict in Cambodia, and the Soviet threat in Asia, diminished though this may be.[26]

Japanese government leaders have vowed that Japan will continue to maintain an exclusively defensive military capability. Even if the U.S. bases in the Philippines were to be closed, Prime Minister Kaifu has said in an interview that Japan would not attempt to develop an offensive capability.[27] In this connection, a Japanese diplomat has remarked: "Bitter experience has taught us not to fill any superpower vacuum."[28]

It is noteworthy that since the end of the Vietnam War and particularly after the Soviet-supported Vietnamese invasion and occupation of Cambodia, the non-Communist ASEAN countries have no longer opposed the gradual military buildup of Japan and its enlarged security role within the framework of the U.S.-Japanese security arrangement. Given the lingering memory of Japan's past military aggression, none of the countries in the region expect Japan to step into the military shoes of the Americans to ensure the security of Southeast Asia. Instead ASEAN hopes that Japan will be inclined "to take up some of the slack in the American presence in Asia,"[29] and that a "strong" Japan will serve as a deterrent against Soviet "expansionism." In other words, ASEAN has no objection to a strengthening of Japan's military capability as long as a stronger Japan would contribute directly to ASEAN security.

Some ASEAN leaders initially expressed concern about U.S. pressures on Japan to expand its navy so that it would be capable of defending sea lanes of up to 1,000 miles. After the Soviet Union began to use Vietnam's air and naval bases, ASEAN countries began to perceive that an expanded Japanese navy which could share defense tasks with the U.S. would be necessary in order to help prolong U.S. naval presence in the region. As their leaders told Prime Minister Nakasone during the latter's April-May 1983 tour of Southeast Asia,[30] each ASEAN country finally came to approve the plan.

Thus, ASEAN was not unconditionally opposed to a wider Japanese security role in the region. Some ASEAN leaders believe that if smooth relations between ASEAN and Japan are established, Japan's enlarged security role would not pose a threat. As General Suryohadiprojo Sayidiman, Indonesia's Ambassador to Japan, has said, "As long as relations with ASEAN are smooth, ASEAN would not be threatened even if [Japan's] Self Defense Forces advanced into sea areas close to Southeast Asia and even if they undertook escort operations for U.S. aircraft carriers. Whether or not the strengthening of Japan's self defense power will pose a threat to ASEAN depends ultimately upon whether or not relations between Japan and ASEAN are stable."[31]

However, more recently, with the lessening of the Soviet threat and new U.S. plans to reduce its military personnel, ASEAN has become wary of the possibility of Japan taking on an expanded military role. The views expressed by Singaporean Prime Minister Lee Kuan Yew probably reflect sentiments common to all these countries. He openly supports the U.S. military presence in Asia as a means to restrain not only Soviet power but also *Japanese* power.[32]

NOTES

* This is a revised version of a paper presented at the conference on "The Changing Context of Security Relations in Southeast Asia: Implications for Conflict Management in the 1990s," Montebello, Quebec, Canada, 1–4 May 1990. I would like to thank the conference participants, Paul Evans in particular, as well as the reviewers of this journal for their helpful comments. I remain, however, solely responsible for the argument.

1. *Japan Economic Journal*, March 15, 1980; Nichictsu Boeki Kai, *1983 nen nichietsu boeki nempyo* [A chronological table or 1983 Japan-Vietnam Trade] (Tokyo: Nichietsu Boekikai, 1983), p. 1. It was the prevailing belief among trading circles that if Japan decided to lift the freeze on economic assistance to Vietnam, trade between the two countries would drastically increase. *Yomiuri Shimbun*, June 24, 1982.

2. Fung-wai Frances Lai, *Without a Vision: Japan's Relations with ASEAN* (Singapore: Chopmen, 1981), p. 3.

3. See Takubo Tadae, *"Senryaku naki kaigai enjo no kyoko"* [Fallacy of foreign aid without strategy], *Voice*, November 1981, pp. 120–30.

4. Gaimusho, *Waga gaiko no kinkyo* [The recent state of Japanese diplomacy] (Tokyo: Okurasho Insatsukyoku), various years.

5. *The Nation*, May 6, 1989.

6. See Dennis Yasutomo, *The Manner of Giving: Strategic Aid and Japan's Foreign Policy* (Lexington: D.C. Heath, 1986), p. 64; *Manichi Daily News*, July 24, 1984; and *Sankei Shimbun*, October 31, 1981.

7. See Japan Defense Agency, *Defense of Japan 1985* (Tokyo: The Japan Times, Ltd., 1985), p. 312.

8. *Nihon Keizai Shimbun*, July 3, 1989.

9. *Far East Economic Review*, July 14, 1989, p. 34.

10. Makoto Momoi, "Japan's Defense and Realism," *Liberal Star*, September 10, 1984, p. 11.

11. Toshihiko Hozumi, "SLOC Security Problems in Southeast Asian and the Southeast Pacific," in Tunhewa Ko and Yuming Shaw, eds., *Pacific Sealane Security: Tokyo Conference, 1983*, The Asia and World Monograph Series, no 34 (Taipei, ROC: The Asia and World Institute, 1985), p. 83.

12. For example, see Tsuchiya Takeo, *"Nihon no keizai 'enjo' shin dai toa kyoeiken enjo kiso tsukuri"* [Japan's foreign "aid" paves the way for a new Greater East Asia Co-Prosperity Sphere], *Sekai kara*, special edition vol. 18 (Winter 1984), p. 45; and a panel discussion of Asian intellectuals, "New Political Trends in Asia," *The Seventh Asian Roundtable Proceedings*, October 10–11, 1980 (Tokyo: The Asian Club, 1981), p. 18.

13. Interview with an official of the Japan Defense Agency, July 11, 1984.

14. Japan Defense Agency, *Defense of Japan 1980* (Tokyo: The Japan Times, Ltd., 1981), p. 78. See also *Defense of Japan 1981–1989*.

15. Koji Watanabe, "Japan and Southeast Asia, 1980," *Asia Pacific Community*, vol. 10 (Fall 1980), p. 86.

16. Edward Olsen, *U.S.-Japan Strategic Reciprocity: A Neo-Internationalist View* (Stanford: Hoover Institution Press, 1985), p. 22.

17. *Japan Insight*, January 23, 1981. He reiterated this point at the fifth Shimoda Conference, held in early September 1981. *Japan Times Weekly*, September 12, 1981.

18. Takashi Hosami, "Economic Aid and Japan's Security," *Roundtable Reports*, no. 6 (New York: East Asian Institute, Columbia University, 1983), pp. 8–11.

19. See, for example, Toru Yano, "Toward a Reorientation of Asian Policy: The Fukuda Doctrine and Japanese-U.S. Cooperation," in Herbert Passin and Akira Iriye, eds., *Encounter at Shimoda: Search for a New Pacific Partner* (Boulder, Colorado: Westview Press, 1979), pp. 127–45; Okabe Tatsumi, *"Hachijunendai ni okeru Nihon no Tonan Ajia seisaku"* [Japan's Southeast Asian policy in the 1980s], in Nihon Kokusai Mondai Kenkyusho, *1980 nendai Nihon no shinro* [The direction of Japanese foreign policy in the 1980s] (Tokyo: Nihon Kokusai Mondai Kenkyusho, 1980), pp. 226–53; Masashi Nishihara, *East Asian Security and the Trilateral Countries*, A Report to the Trilateral Commission, no. 30 (New York and London: New York University Press, 1985); Imagawa Eiichi, *"Tonan Ajai ga haramu shomon-dai: towareru nihon no seijiteki yakuwari to taio"* [Some problems of Southeast Asia and Japan's political role], *Komei*, no. 231 (April 1981), pp. 46–54; Masahide Shibusawa, *Japan and the Asian Pacific Region* (London & Sydney: Croom Helm, 1984).

20. Shibusawa, *Japan and the Asian Pacific Region*, p. 117.

21. For an insightful analysis of various Japanese views of Japan's role in international affairs, see Kenneth B. Pyle, "Japan, the World, and the Twenty-First Century," in Takashi Inoguchi and Daniel I. Okimoto, eds., *The Political Economy of Japan*, vol. 2, *The Changing International Context* (Palo Alto, Calif.: Stanford University Press, 1988), pp. 446–86.

22. *The Nation*, November 4, 1990. According to a poll taken by *Asahi Shimbun*, barely half (49.2 percent) of the ruling LDP members of the lower house agreed to the UN Peace Cooperation Law unconditionally; 56.2 percent of members of all parties opposed the bill against only 29 percent in favour, 59.9 percent of the lower house said they were against Japanese military playing a noncombat role in any future UN force; and 72.8 percent said they would oppose using them in a combat role (*Asahi Shimbun*, November 1, 1990).

23. Initially, Prime Minister Kaifu publicly ruled out sending Japanese troops to the Gulf. But after being pressed by President Bush, he decided to include troops in the proposed peacekeeping corps. A Japanese senior official was quoted as saying that Bush called Kaifu to urge him to contribute personnel to the Gulf. *The Nation*, October 18, 1990.

24. *Asahi Shimbun*, November 6, 1990.

25. Summary of the report by "The Comprehensive National Security Study Group," *Economic Eye*, vol. 1, no. 2 (December 1980), p. 15.

26. *Japan Times Weekly*, December 23, 1989.

27. *The Nation*, March 20, 1990.
28. Quoted in *Bangkok Post*, March 12, 1990.
29. K.S. Sandhu, "The ASEAN Equation," *Intersect*, vol. 1, no. 4 (April 1985), p. 11.
30. See Tade Takubo, "First Round of Nakasone's Diplomacy," *Asia Pacific Community*, vol. 2 (Summer 1983), pp. 7–8.
31. An interview with *Mainichi Shimbun* on April 9, 1983.
32. *Japan Times Weekly*, March 19–25, 1990.

86

ASEAN AND GLOBAL ISSUES

LAU TEIK SOON

Asean has achieved a remarkable degree of unity. This unity is a strength which Asean should use to express its views and initiate policies in the international arena. This unity must not be undermined in any way, otherwise Asean's credibility will be questioned and its influence will be diminished in global affairs.

Critics of Asean have often referred to its fragile foundation. They point to the main differences as well as the major problems in intra-Asean relations. However, it is significant that such differences and problems have not retarded the growth of Asean's unity since its foundation 24 years ago.

In the post Cold War situation, no matter how limited its influence in the Asia-Pacific region, Asean's unity should be the basis for initiatives on various global issues. Already, Asean's collective strength has been demonstrated in the United Nations and other international forums. Its initiatives on the Cambodian problem and the neutralisation of Southeast Asia can be cited as examples.

Asean must stand for certain ideals in international relations. More than that, it should strive to achieve these ideals. In this brief presentation, I shall mention some global issues which Asean should give more attention to and if possible provide the lead in the international community.

The most basic issue which Asean should stand for is the defence of the independence, sovereignty and territorial integrity of a state. In a hostile situation, either a weak state may be threatened and even agressed by a powerful neighbour, or an external power to the region may use a 'proxy state' to undermine another state's independence, sovereignty and territorial integrity.

Asean has stood up for this ideal, for example, the cases of the Vietnamese aggression against Cambodia and Iraqi invasion against Kuwait. Asean with other countries have stood firm without compromise on the principle that a state must maintain its independence, sovereignty and territorial integrity. As a result, the aggressors in these two cases, namely Vietnam and Iraq respectively, have succumbed to international pressures and withdrawn their occupation forces.

This is not to say that there are no differences among the Asean governments on these issues. In view of different national characteristics, the governments have to respond to their domestic constituents. Hence, for example, Malaysia has been less vocal in its condemnation of Iraq's

Reprinted from "Asean and Global Issues", *Asean-ISIS Monitor*, Issue No. 1 (July 1991), pp. 14–15, by permission of the author and the Institute of Strategic and International Studies, Malaysia.

invasion of Kuwait. But reservation has not prevented Malaysia, together with other Asean countries, from calling for the withdrawal of the Iraqi troops from Kuwait.

The next issue which Asean should stand firm is the self determination for viable nationalities in various parts of the world. In this day and age, it is anachronistic and untenable for groups of people to be subjected to various forms of colonialism, imperialism and hegemonism. Additionally, a people should not be denied sovereignty over a territory in which they have ancient and traditional claims.

The case of the Arab Palestinian people comes immediately to mind. Asean should stand firm in support of Resolution 242. The Palestinians must be given the right of self determination and a state of their own. The Israelis must withdraw immediately from occupied territories in West Bank and Gaza strip. Also, it must be conceded that Israel must be recognised as an independent and sovereign state.

OCCUPIED TERRITORIES

On this issue, there had been some misunderstanding on the part of some Asean countries. For example, when President Herzog of Israel visited Singapore, there were criticisms and even demonstrations in Malaysia aimed against the Singapore government. These were understandable. But it was not well publicised in Malaysia that Singapore had and still has taken a firm stand calling for the creation of the Arab Palestinian state and the withdrawal of the Israelis from occupied territories.

Another major issue is arms control and disarmament, particularly the non-proliferation of nuclear weapons. On this issue, Asean should not hesitate in exerting its views calling for arms control and disarmament and in particular, the creation of nuclear weapon free zone (NWFZ) in various parts of the world. No doubt, there have been some difficulties among Asean concerning the creation of the NWFZ in Southeast Asia in line with Asean's proposal for Zopfan (Zone of Peace, Freedom and Neutrality). This should be achieved as soon as possible.

It may be that the Philippines has some difficulties going along with the NWFZ in Southeast Asia. But if the Philippines can come to an agreement with the United States concerning the storage and transit of nuclear materials and weapons on its territory, then Asean can stand united on this issue.

All Asean governments have agreed on the non-proliferation of nuclear weapons. In this regard Asean should take a firm stand against the production of nuclear weapons in North Korea.

Since the end of the Cold War, the United Nations particularly its Security Council, has played an active role in managing peace and security in certain regions of the world. Asean should promote the role of the United Nations in peacekeeping operations as well as in the resolution of regional conflicts.

ENVIRONMENTAL PROTECTION

Asean governments should contribute in whatever way they can to the United Nations' efforts. In this connection, the contributions of small contingents of various Asean states to the United Nations Peacekeeping Force in the Gulf is a significant action. Other opportunities should be explored for Asean's contribution in UN peacekeeping operations.

There are other global issues like the protection of the environment and the problem of famine and hunger in various regions. The role of Asean countries in these issues in the United Nations and other international forums should be highlighted. For example, some Asean countries, for example, Malaysia, as reflected in the Langkawi Declaration and Singapore as the Chairman of the United Nations Committee on the Environment, are taking the lead on environmental issues.

Last but not least, Asean must provide the

initiative for the creation of regional organisations aimed at cooperation in the economic and security fields in the Asia-Pacific region. Asean is regarded as a fast growing economic entity and any proposal to establish a regional body cannot be successful without the participation of Asean countries. It is axiomatic that Asean's agreement and even initiative must be a precondition before any proposal for the establishment of a regional body can be implemented. This can be manifested in the process concerning the formation of the APEC forum. Although Australia initiated the proposal, yet it could not be realised without Asean's concurrence.

An immediate concern of Asean is Malaysia's proposal for the East Asian Economic Grouping (EAEG). Asean must stand firm in supporting this proposal. This assertion is based on the following grounds:

1) East Asian countries should come together to discuss economic issues. By East, we mean the Asean countries, Indochina, China, Japan and the Koreas.

2) East Asian countries together will provide the collective strength for negotiations with other countries on economic matters.

3) The EAEG is an intermediate organisation between Asean and APEC, and it is proposed that it should be compatible with free trading arrangements.

4) in other regions, there are sub-regional groupings in existence. For example, in North America, the United States, Canada and Mexico are involved in free trading arrangements (FTAs). There is, of course, the European Common Market (ECM) due to be established in 1992.

Asean governments individually or collectively should promote the EAEG proposal. Countries like Japan and China should be encouraged to join the organisation. It will be useful for East Asian countries to consult and if possible coordinate their positions so that there will be a successful conclusion of the Uruguay Round.

In conclusion, it is time for Asean to be more assertive in global affairs. For about a quarter of a century, Asean has built up its unity. It is now well recognised internationally. But it should be used as a force for peace, cooperation and security in the international community.

Section X

THE FUTURE OF REGIONALISM
IN SOUTHEAST ASIA

Introduction

Sharon Siddique

Section I argued for the relevance of placing ASEAN within the context of Southeast Asia's past. Section X will discuss scenarios which speculate on ASEAN's place in Southeast Asia's future. To continue the past-future analogy, it is indeed striking to reflect on parallels between the post World War II period and the post-Cold War period with reference to Southeast Asia. The former we could analyse with the benefit of almost fifty years of "hindsight". The latter we are currently living through, and therefore the insights which are brought to bear on our present condition, and our immediate future, quite quickly become superceded by unfolding events.

There is a fluidity to our present historical moment (late 1992) which is as exhilarating as it is bewildering — and both these emotions are reflected in the contributions to this Section. How appropriate that, in the face of such uncertainty, the ASEAN states themselves have chosen to cap the first twenty-five years of their organization by setting a fifteen-year timetable for the next stage of ASEAN's evolution. The implementation of AFTA (ASEAN Free Trade Area), which was agreed upon at the January 1992 Singapore Summit, provides ASEAN with a guide and a purpose to help propel it into the new century.

Several criteria were used in the selection of articles in this Section. First, there is an attempt to reflect a continuity in the two main themes which emerged as definitive in our treatment of ASEAN's twenty-five year history. Our picture of ASEAN has emerged largely as a portrait of the key political and economic developments of the region. And thus we feel it is appropriate to extend this discussion of political and economic trends into the future. What will be the impact of the so-called New World Order on security arrangements in the region? How will the development of other regional players, particularly Japan, China and the NIEs affect ASEAN? What will be the impact of the changing world economic order? How will the emergence of trade areas such as SEM and NAFTA affect GATT negotiations? How will ASEAN as an organization be affected by the perceptions of individual members with regard to their own national destinies?

Second, there is obviously no "one" opinion of the future, and so some effort has been taken to assemble a diversity of opinions, some highly optimistic, others tempered by pessimism; some more practical in their concerns, others quite general and visionary.

Third, we have attempted to move from various views on how the complex global changes of the late 1980s and early 1990s are affecting the Asia-Pacific region in general, to the more specific question of how ASEAN as a regional grouping will fit into this larger region. Of particular interest in this context is ASEAN's position *vis-à-vis* the parallel development of a number of other regional groupings, such as APEC (Asia Pacific Economic Co-operation); PECC (Pacific Economic Co-operation Conference); and the EAEC (East Asian Economic Caucus). Narrowing the focus even further, some attention has been given to exploring how ASEAN itself will evolve from within, particularly in terms of the implementation of AFTA (ASEAN Free Trade Area) and its impact on ASEAN's overall direction and internal organization.

Finally, the authors themselves serve to reflect the fact that scholarly interest in analysing the unfolding events in the ASEAN region has become more and more of an international effort. Thus we have attempted to provide a sample of diverse opinions from regional scholars, as well as from scholars from the CIS, UK, United States, Canada, and Japan. In so doing we are certainly not suggesting that these scholars are representing "national" perspectives on the region. Rather we are seeking to illustrate the increasing interest of the international research community in one of the most exciting regions of the world — a region with a future.

87.

GLOBAL TRENDS AND THE ASIA–PACIFIC

CHIN KIN WAH

SHIFTS IN THE ORDER OF POWER

It could be claimed with some exaggeration that at the "end of history"[1] the world is finally left with one superpower. However, the United States is no longer the economic hegemon it once was, with the capability and confidence to restructure an international economic order after its own design. Indeed, the United States is still overburdened by its budget and trade deficits. Nuclear power itself is no longer fungible politically in a post-cold war era, while economic constraints (and domestic questioning about overseas embroilment) have undermined a previous willingness to unilaterally uphold regional and world order.[2] Nevertheless, the 1991 Gulf War did show that the use of overwhelming and concentrated conventional "high-tech" power was a crucial (newly industrializing economies), in order to defend its own national interest.[13]

American role was exercised also highlighted the importance of broad international consensus and burden-sharing (financial, political, and to a lesser extent, military). In the Asia–Pacific, the major focus of burden-sharing is Japan, although as demonstrated by Japanese reactions to the Gulf War, its attempts to define a role beyond that of an economic power continued

to be hampered by domestic ambivalence, ambiguity and immobilism.

Along with the decline of bipolarity is the emergence of new power-centres in Asia and Europe. In the Asia–Pacific, Japan is already an economic superpower by any measurement (gross national product, level of technology, foreign trade, international financial power, innovation in research and technology, and quality of human resources and organization). These are also assets and attributes which can readily be converted to military power. As Lee Kuan Yew put it during a visit to Europe in 1990, the possibility of Japan as an independent military power at the turn of the twentieth century is a horrendous one, such a possibility being real given the Japanese propensity to be "Number One" in whatever they seek to accomplish.[3] So far Japan continues to move with caution and ambiguity towards defining a regional security role (preferring to rely excessively on financial diplomacy in fulfilment of an economic security role) despite increasing pressures to shoulder a greater burden.[4] This is a reflection of the continuing lack of national consensus as well as regional reservations (most loudly articulated by Japan's Northeast Asian neighbours). Most recently, this was evidenced by the domestic public furore over the issue of

Reprinted in abridged form from "Changing Global Trends and Their Effects on the Asia–Pacific", *Contemporary Southeast Asia* 13, no. 1 (June 1991), pp. 1–16, by permission of the author and the Institute of Southeast Asian Studies.

despatching Japanese military personnel to the Gulf during the 1990–91 crisis. Yet, Japan has been taking incremental steps to expand and improve its self-defence forces which will have a bearing on the regional balance of power should future strains in the U.S.-Japanese security relationship result in a more independent and assertive Japan. Such a development would have very disturbing implications for China and a future reunified Korea.

China is the one major power in the Asia–Pacific to have left the longest historical imprint on the security equation of the region, which, of course, includes Southeast Asia. Whether an economically weak, unstable and factionalized China, or a modernized, economically strong, politically cohesive and assertive China, its impact on the security concerns of others in the region is inescapable. Currently, China's domestic economic preoccupations point to a renewed stake in peace and a stable regional environment, which has led it to mend fences with Vietnam. Interestingly, the Chinese Prime Minister Li Peng has found it necessary to reassure that this would not work against ASEAN's interest. China also made the final efforts necessary to normalize relations with Indonesia. These developments create a certain expectation that China is preparing itself to play a more stabilizing role in the management of regional conflict. Yet, China is also proceeding with the modernization of its conventional military force and will in time be able to project its naval power into the Southeast Asian part of the Asia–Pacific. While its historical reliance on support for local insurgencies as a means to project its political influence may fade away, China is acquiring a wider and more effective range of conventional capabilities which would enable it to advance and protect its interests in the region even more effectively.

Over the horizon we can expect India to play a role too, as a major Asian power in its own right. Although for the moment its security role is most clearly focused on the South Asian subcontinent, its future naval reach and the modernization of its force structure may well reflect an interest that goes beyond the Indian Ocean. Within Southeast Asia, Vietnam and Indonesia can be regarded as local powers of major importance. Their roles in the management of regional security relationships with China will have important consequences for others in the region.[5] Further beyond the Asia–Pacific, a new power-centre is emerging in a unified Western Europe which incorporates a reunified Germany that is likely to be inwardly preoccupied in the near future. Nevertheless, even an inward-looking Germany, or a wider "Eurocentricism", will generate effects that cannot be overlooked in the Asia–Pacific.

Looking at the shifting balance of power, one could speculate that with the end of the cold war, the waning of bipolarity and the scaling down of Soviet and American forces, the security balance in the Asia–Pacific will become multipolar, and thus make the interactive process more complex. The end of the cold war may have brought "peace", but it may also unleash new competitive forces on the economic plane that could result in new sources of international instability.

SHIFTS FROM GEOPOLITICS TO GEOECONOMICS?

Three European trends, namely, the "freeing" of Eastern Europe, the reunification of Germany and the European Community becoming a single European market by 1992, are well entrenched. However, the effects of these developments on the Asia–Pacific are not altogether clear. At one level, there is concern that Western Europe is likely to divert much of its investments to Eastern Europe and, given that the total amount that the West can invest is finite, the flow of funds to one region will mean less for another.[6]

At another level, there is concern that these Euro-centric developments might add to the shaping of an economically trilateral world in which economic competition (or "geoeconomics") among the European Community, the United States, and an economically resurgent Japan will be the main theme that would displace cold war issues from the centre stage. In this new "geoeconomics", the competition for influence through capital flows rather than troop deployments will be the order of the day.[7] Already, at their 1989 meeting in Malaysia, the Commonwealth Heads of Government had warned of the possible dangers of growing regionalism of trade through the creation of new trading blocs.[8]

This theme was amplified by the then Singapore Prime Minister, Lee Kuan Yew, at the opening of the Asia–Pacific Economic Cooperation (APEC) group meeting in July 1990, when he spoke of the world becoming divided into three separate trading blocs, dominated respectively by the dollar, the yen, and the deutschmark. As he saw it, a *de facto* emergence of such blocs would mean a world fraught with conflicts: "Asians will feel that they have been quarantined into the Japanese Yen bloc so that they can be excluded from the markets of prosperous Europeans and Americans, that the Whites have changed the rules just as Asians have learnt to compete and win under those rules".[9] In Lee Kuan Yew's opinion, such an economic division of the world on racial lines would create bitterness and animosity, adding to the normal conflicts of interest between states. Behind such a warning lies a hope that through the APEC co-operative process (which includes the United States and Canada, though not the EC) and other multilateral processes, such as the Uruguay Round of multilateral trade negotiations within the General Agreement on Tariffs and Trade (GATT), such conflicts may be moderated if not averted.

After the failure of the latest Uruguay Round of multilateral trade talks in December 1990, Malaysia's Prime Minister Mahathir Mohamad proposed an East Asian Economic Grouping (EAEG) to promote co-ordination of regional policies towards the Uruguay Round and foster trade liberalization and economic co-operation within the region. As envisaged, the group would initially comprise the ASEAN countries, and eventually, it would be extended to China, Japan, South Korea, Taiwan, Hong Kong and the Indochinese countries. The proposal reflects an underlying concern about the economic union between the United States and Canada and the forthcoming single market in Europe which could turn into trading blocs. The United States has so far opposed the idea, given its exclusion from the EAEG, while Japan and Indonesia continue to have reservations about the proposal. Singapore gave support to the idea during Prime Minister Goh Chok Tong's visit to Kuala Lumpur in January 1991 but it has also highlighted the three underlying conditions of the proposal — namely, that it should be GATT-consistent, complementary to APEC, and not diminish ASEAN.[10]

DECLINE OF IDEOLOGICAL CONCERNS AND THE NEW REALISM

The decline of ideological concerns in domestic, but more importantly, foreign policy formulation, is an inevitable consequence of the end of the cold war (it can also be seen as its cause). In practical terms, a new realism based on profitability rather than ideological affinities now determines economic transactions between states across the old cold war divide. The growing contacts and transactions between Eastern European states and South Korea are a reflection of this trend, which is cold comfort, as it were, for North Korea. Even the largesse from former fraternal countries can no longer be taken for granted by North Korea. The collapse of European communism and the withering away of COMECON (Council for Mutual Economic Assistance) have led East European countries to reconsider their aid to Vietnam and Cambodia. One Hungarian diplomat in Hanoi reportedly said: "We want a relationship with Vietnam similar to that of any other Western European country, based on clear mutual and commercial interests".[11] The concern of the Indochinese states must be that they are being considerably downgraded in the order of priorities of Moscow and other

East European states. According to a Soviet diplomat in Hanoi, in January 1991, the Soviet Union entered into new agreements with Vietnam which sharply reduced Soviet aid and placed trade relations with Vietnam on the basis of hard currency payments at world market prices. The two countries are also expected to recalculate all payments in hard currency and reach agreement on debt servicing by Vietnam.[12]

The emerging new realism could mean the erosion of a U.S. *noblesse oblige* which could in turn see the United States becoming tougher and more demanding on its allies — principally the Japanese — with regard to the Asia–Pacific on trade and other "rice-bowl" issues. Indeed, if the Asia–Pacific no longer needs to be underpinned economically as a strategic bulwark against Soviet expansionism, then the United States might perhaps consider it necessary to take a tougher stance to deal with the economic challenge from Japan or other East Asian NIEs (newly industrializing economies), in order to defend its own national interest.[13]

THE TREND TOWARDS DEMOCRATIZATION AND ECONOMIC LIBERALIZATION

The democratization process within the Soviet Union, but more importantly, within Eastern Europe has had its effects on other communist and non-communist countries. In the Asia–Pacific, communist regimes in China, Vietnam and even Outer Mongolia have had to cope with or react to the rising demands for economic liberalization, political participation and *glasnost*. Although there is no indication yet of domestic unrest in North Korea, in response to changes in Eastern Europe, Pyongyang has found itself increasingly isolated, as

its one-time East European allies hasten to develop ties with Seoul.[14] China will find it particularly hard to forget that the early stirring of the 1989 Tiananmen incident coincided with Gorbachev's visit to Beijing, although as the crisis unfolded, the pro-Democracy Movement turned to American democratic values and political symbolism. Transnational influences from the United States and Hong Kong, facilitated by the new communications and information technology, fuelled the movement subsequently — leading to a temporary closing up of China to the outside world.

In contrast to the East European regimes, the hardline regimes stretching from China, North Korea, and Vietnam, to non-communist Myanmar (Burma), are reacting with a general hardening of political posture, while some like China and Vietnam are publicly maintaining at the same time a commitment to economic reform. Both China and Vietnam have also sought to differentiate their political conditions and even ideological purity from the current Soviet or East European conditions.[15] In the long run, however, it may well be that Asian communist political systems will also have to adapt and evolve, though perhaps not into the Western democratic variety which may not be suited to their political cultures and political styles.

Even the non-communist regimes of Southeast Asia may have felt the pressure for political openness and participation, although many have made adjustments (even before the East European phenomenon) to pre-empt such pressures from arising at the grassroots level. If they need no conversion to the virtues of the free-market economy, they are at least confirmed in the wisdom of economic growth led by the private sector.

NOTES

1. Francis Fukuyama has sought (in a manner that proved controversial) to theorize about the flood of events that marked the end of the cold war. As he sees it: "What we may be witnessing is not just the end of the Cold War — but the end of history as such: that is, the end point of mankind's

ideological evolution and the universalization of Western liberal democracy as the final form of human government". See Francis Fukuyama, "The End of History?", *The National Interest* (Summer 1989), p. 4.

2. For a discussion of the changing nature of U.S. power, see Catherine McArdle Kelleher, "The Changing Currency of Power: Paper I — The Future Nature of US Influence in Western Europe and North-East Asia", *Adelphi Papers No. 256* (IISS, Winter 1990/91).

3. Lee Kuan Yew, interview with *World Link*, reproduced in *Straits Times*, 2 May 1990.

4. Kwan Weng Kin, "Japan in dilemma over role of defence forces", *Straits Times*, 24 November 1989.

5. See Philip Bowring, "Middle Power Rivalry", *Far Eastern Economic Review*, 12 April 1990, pp. 20–21.

6. Addressing the World Economic Forum at Davos, Switzerland, in February 1990, Lee Kuan Yew pointedly cautioned the Western Europeans against neglecting the Pacific Basin for Eastern Europe (*Straits Times*, 7 February 1990). The Malaysian Prime Minister Dato Seri Dr Mahathir Mohamad expressed similar concerns during the Eighth ASEAN-EC Ministerial Meeting held in the same month (FBM, No. 39/90, 17 February 1990).

7. Thomas Omstead, "Iraq is Distracting America from Serious Problems", *International Herald Tribune*, 22–23 September 1990.

8. *FBM*, No. 246/89, 25 October 1989.

9. *FBM*, No. 174/90, 31 July 1990. See also "A Region at the Crossroads", *Asiaweek*, 10 August 1990, pp. 24–25.

10. *Straits Times*, 12 January 1991.

11. Ibid., 7 April 1990.

12. Ibid., 8 February 1991. According to one East European diplomat, Vietnam owed the Soviet Union more than 8 billion roubles, representing about 85 per cent of its total foreign debt (*Straits Times*, 12 January 1991).

13. See Asad Latif, "U.S. will lose clout in Asia with dwindling military presence", *Straits Times*, 10 October 1990.

14. In February 1990, Hungary, Yugoslavia, Poland and Bulgaria had established diplomatic relations with South Korea. The Soviet Union itself had agreed in December 1990 to establish diplomatic relations with South Korea.

15. Writing in *The Independent*, Andrew Hinggins has noted that a Chinese Party document being circulated after the upheaval in Romania contained pages on the internal crisis in Eastern European countries and the Soviet Union. It concluded that China alone had followed the correct path (article reproduced in *Straits Times*, 16 January 1991). Interestingly, the Deputy Editor of *Nhan Dan* has in a critical essay commented that the Vietnamese Communist Party "is stressing that it has a mission to safeguard Marxism-Leninism . . . . This way of interpreting events in Europe amounts to a kind of panic . . . which is blocking the moves towards democratization . . . " (Bui Tin, "A Dramatic Reversal", *Far Eastern Economic Review*, 14 March 1991, p. 5).

88.

FROM THE USSR TO RUSSIA ON THE PACIFIC

VLADIMIR I. IVANOV

IN SEARCH OF A NEW IDENTITY

There has always been a debate in Russia as to whether it is a European or an Asian country. The "Eastern Question" was reviewed by Feodor Dostoevski who came to the conclusion that compared to Europe, Russia is Eastern, but compared to Asia, it is a Western country. In the 1990s the problem of identity reemerges, and the question of Russia's future on the Pacific could be as difficult as the problem of its integration into the European Community. Now, when socialism is abandoned as the national identity, and the East-West division is gradually losing its importance, a new and real identity can be found only in relation to the existing division between North and South, advanced industrial democracies and developing societies. Russia, for its own sake, has to go through the process of coming to terms with itself as a developing country but with nuclear weapons and modern military forces, a relatively high level of education, and a strong egalitarian tradition.

Russia needs a competent government and an efficient and internationalized bureaucracy capable of managing the long-term economic priorities of the nation. It has to learn how to make maximum use of its human capital. After all this is the factor, which, in less than 30 years, has fuelled the economic and social progress of the countries and economies of East Asia, in the process of which Russia's geo-strategic environment and position in Asia and on the Pacific has been substantially altered. Economically, Russia has become not just a backyard of Europe, but a relatively underdeveloped part of the whole "northern belt" of the industrialized world, including East Asia.

A new generation of politicians, mostly well educated and with access to information, is now trying to solve Russian problems accumulated over the years. They continue to look West, but they cannot ignore the experience of newly industrialized societies, which serve as recent examples of dynamic economic growth and rapid modernization. They are thinking about potential partners and probably understand that it is Japan and the NIEs, more than others, that can provide large scale capital investment, modern industrial technology, and new managerial expertise to Russia. On the other hand, culturally, psychologically and emotionally they are more comfortable in relations with Europe and North America. The Russian system of education is almost entirely Europe oriented in terms of foreign languages, history and literature. Hundreds of thousands of school and

Reprinted in abridged form from "From the USSR to Russia on the Pacific", *Southeast Asian Affairs 1992* (Singapore: Institute of Southeast Asian Studies, 1992), pp. 71–87, by permission of the author and the publisher.

university graduates can read and write English, but very few can read and write Chinese, Japanese or Korean. In addition, recently, the most capable teachers of oriental languages have been leaving language schools and universities for private businesses, and oriental studies programmes are financed even more poorly than before 1985.

Russia has to plan for the long term and make a very careful assessment of both Western and East Asian experiences with the capitalist production system, organization of society and role of the government in the modernization process. The economies of East Asia pose challenges even for the most advanced powers like the United States and the leading Western European states. Russia, as the smallest and weakest nation bordering the North Pacific, has to decide whether it is going to be a mere economic annex of Asia-Pacific economic growth, or a genuine part of it, making full use of its geography, resources, and traditional and modern values. It also has to deal with the problem of an entirely new geo-strategic environment and new priorities both in foreign policy and strategic posture.

IMPLICATIONS FOR SOUTHEAST ASIA

The end of the Cold War opens up tremendous opportunities in the North Pacific. Post-communist Russia will play an important catalyst role in the transition to a new order, and if helped politically and economically, has good prospects for becoming a valuable member of the Pacific Community. The market economy in Russia, when it becomes fully operational, will generate further economic growth, co-operation and competition. It is likely that the countries of Southeast Asia, in particular the more advanced economies of ASEAN, will find both new market opportunities and scope for a horizontal division of labour with Russia, and not only the Russian Far East, as a partner.

The political reintegration of the North Pacific, like the political reintegration of Southeast Asia, will require co-operation and readjustments in defence postures and military doctrines, deployments and other sensitive matters. There is good reason to expect that Russia will proceed with unilateral cuts in its forces on the Pacific, in particular strategic nuclear weapons. That alone can lead to a substantial reduction of tensions in the North Pacific. It will allow for a build-down of Russian naval presence in the North Pacific, which currently is strongly linked to the deployment of Submarine-Launched Ballistic Missiles (SLBMs) in the Sea of Okhotsk. A complete Russian withdrawal from Camranh Bay, which will be good for Southeast Asia, could be a good indicator of movement in this direction. A Russian nuclear build-down in the North Pacific can eventually lead to the creation of a Nuclear-Weapons-Free Zone in the North Pacific, which most probably will cover the territory of the Russian Far East, and in combination with the NWFZ on the Korean peninsula, will discourage Japan from going nuclear in the future. Hopefully, it may also constitute a disincentive for China's nuclear programmes and its nuclear forces deployments in the region, including the South China Sea. The NWFZ in the North Pacific, in combination with the South Pacific NFZ, could create a momentum for similar moves in Southeast Asia, and the Indian Ocean and Indian subcontinent. This will be one way of preventing nuclear proliferation.

A nuclear-free North Pacific is likely to facilitate the improvement of Russian-Japanese relations, and decreased military tension in the Sea of Okhotsk and Sea of Japan will eventually lead to the solution of the territorial dispute, hopefully on the basis of compromise and through involvement of the United Nations. If this happens, it will serve as a model and precedent for the settlement of territorial disputes in the South China Sea, with UN involvement. The economic co-operation with Japan and the United States could make Russia a competitor of ASEAN and Southeast Asia for capital investments, especially from Japan.

These developments, in combination with

other factors, will inevitably lead to a declining American military profile in the Asia-Pacific region. For the North Pacific, this will require major rearrangements for the United States in the field of security relations with Japan, China, Korea and Russia. The multilateral political-security arrangements can in the future supplement the existing security alliances. Under it, every country in the North Pacific, including China, will be required to keep its defence posture and military programmes within certain limits. Hopefully, something similar could take place in the Southeast Asian and Indian Ocean regions, thus covering the whole Asia-Pacific region with the new-type multilateral security relations. Today all this may sound like wishful thinking. But after the collapse of communism in Eastern Europe, nobody even thought that the same could happen in Russia so soon, and without violence.

89.

THE REGIONAL SECURITY ENVIRONMENT

RICHARD STUBBS

The collapse of the Soviet Union, the concomitant decline in the appeal of communism around the world, and the widespread recognition in the Asia Pacific region—underscored most recently by the news that the United States will begin its withdrawal from its bases in the Philippines earlier than expected—that the U.S. is adopting a lower regional military profile has set in motion a number of significant trends in Southeast Asia. But these trends have not impinged upon the region's security environment in a uniform way. The fact that Thailand is very much part of mainland Southeast Asia has been an important factor in its assessment of the changes that are taking place within the region. Despite indications that the threat has diminished somewhat, the Philippines government continues to be preoccupied with the domestic security problems posed by communist guerrillas and Muslim secessionists, and hence, the newly emerging trends have had a relatively limited influence on the government's thinking about defense issues.[1] For Malaysia, Singapore, and Indonesia, their common location in archipelago Southeast Asia has produced similar perceptions of the consequences of the trends for their own security and defense needs. In other words some of the key security changes that are taking place in the region are tending to divide the ASEAN members in terms of their differential impact, how they are being perceived, and what they mean for regional cooperation.

Changes in the ASEAN region's security environment are taking place on three broad fronts. First, the land-based threat to the region's stability, which was thought to be posed by the expansionist aims of Vietnam, was removed for most of the countries of the region when the bulk of the Vietnamese occupying forces were withdrawn from Cambodia in September 1989. Once it became clear that the Vietnamese government had been prompted to get out of Cambodia, not only by pressure from Moscow but, most importantly, by the virtual collapse of its economy and the consequent need to develop good trading relations with its neighbors, potential donors, and investors, it was obvious that the chances of the ASEAN members being caught up in a land war had been markedly reduced if not eliminated.[2]

There has been one exception, however, and that is Thailand. With the departure of the Vietnamese troops came a resurgence of the guerrilla opposition groups, especially the Khmer Rouge. The increased instability, the use

---

Reprinted in abridged form from "Subregional Security Cooperation in ASEAN: Military and Economic Imperatives and Political Obstacles", *Asian Survey* XXXII, no. 5 (May 1992), pp. 397–410, by permission of the author and the Regents of the University of California.

made by the Khmer Rouge of the camps along the Thai-Cambodian border as bases for attacks on the Cambodian government's forces, and the ever-present threat of a new flood of refugees crossing into Thailand if the fighting spread meant that the Thai military made the border with Cambodia its top priority. And while the recent agreement to implement the United Nations peace plan holds the prospects of a peaceful settlement to the long-standing conflict, the Thai government cannot afford to let down its guard given the fragility of the current lull in hostilities.

Second, while the potential for a recrudescence of insurrectionary activity should not be underestimated, it has to be noted that over the last few years the internal threats to the security of ASEAN members have diminished appreciably. This change in the security environment of the region was best symbolized by the signing in December 1989 of agreements between the Communist Party of Malaysia (CPM) and the Thai government and the CPM and the Malaysian government that formally ended the 41-year armed struggle against the Malaysian government. The demise of communism in the former Soviet Union and Eastern Europe, the defensive posture of the Chinese after the events of Tiananmen, and the general sense of prosperity that has overtaken much of the ASEAN region have combined to reduce the perceived threat from internal subversion.

Again, however, there is one clear exception. The Philippines continues to be absorbed by its own internal instability. Although the fortunes of the major guerrilla organization, the New People's Army (NPA), is thought to have declined somewhat in recent years, it still represents a major threat to the government, particularly in Manila. The Moro National Liberation Front, which is based in the southern island of Mindanao and favors the creation of a Muslim secessionist state, also produces sporadic encounters with the Armed Forces of the Philippines (AFP). The AFP itself is not a united organization. There have been a number of attempted coups since President Aquino

took office in March 1986, and key elements of the AFP, most notably the Reform the Armed Forces Movement and the Young Officers Union, are clearly opposed not only to particular government policies but also to individual senior AFP officers and the president. Given these circumstances and the U.S. security shield provided by the Mutual Defense Treaty of 1951, it is not surprising that the government has paid relatively little attention to external security issues.

Third, while land-based threats have diminished for most members of ASEAN, maritime-based threats have been on the increase. The extent to which the Spratly Islands have emerged as a potential regional flash point serves to highlight this particular trend. Situated in the South China Sea, they are claimed in whole or in part by the People's Republic of China (PRC), the Republic of China (Taiwan), Vietnam, the Philippines, and Malaysia. The problem, of course, is that none of these claimants accepts the claims of the others and each has gone some way toward militarizing the archipelago. Relatively rich fishing grounds, the possibility of commercially viable undersea deposits of hydrocarbons and phosphates, and the territorial imperative make the contest for the islands, islets, reefs, and sandy cays of the Spratly group a matter of increasing security interest even for countries in the region such as Indonesia, which are not directly involved in the territorial dispute. Most particularly the armed clashes between the PRC and Vietnam during 1988 and the takeover by the PRC in May 1989 of an atoll claimed by Vietnam have raised the specter of an open conflict escalating to involve others in the region.

This concern has been spurred by the expansion of the Chinese navy and the widespread perception that, as one analyst has noted, the long-term priority of the Chinese government "is to establish China as a major regional sea power with an expanded sphere of influence."[3] The South Sea Fleet currently includes two submarine squadrons, five destroyers, and twelve frigates and is still growing as the PRC government puts an increasingly greater share of its defense spending into the navy.[4] These trends clearly have security implications for the littoral states of the South China Sea. The most directly affected are the archipelago states of the ASEAN region, especially Brunei, Indonesia, Malaysia, and Singapore, all of which must be concerned about their ability to safeguard territorial seas and the neighboring sea lanes of communication on which they rely for their rapidly expanding trade links.

On top of this there are other maritime security issues that the archipelago states must face. The recent establishment of Exclusive Economic Zones (EEZ) by the countries of the region has created overlapping claims, not just in the area of the Spratly group. The responsibilities that go along with this increased jurisdiction are numerous and include dealing with polluting vessels, foreign fishing craft, pirates, smugglers, and boatloads of illegal immigrants and refugees. In addition, there is always the issue of securing drilling and production activities in the offshore oil and gas fields.

As with the two previous trends that have been discussed, the ASEAN states have reacted rather differently to the growing number of maritime-based threats to regional security interests. Thailand is the one country that has shown the least interest. Preoccupied with settling its border dispute with Laos and the border problems associated with instability in Cambodia and Burma, the Thai government has not been able to put maritime security issues high on its list of priorities. Moreover, Thailand has built up strong links to Beijing as a result of the Thai army helping the Chinese supply the Khmer Rouge guerrillas in their campaign against the Vietnamese-supported Cambodian government. Hence, while the Malaysian and Indonesian governments have been very wary of the recent growth in the PRC's naval force projection in the South China Sea, the Thais have expanded their defense links with China, buying more than US$400 million worth of armaments from Beijing between 1980 and 1988, including four Jianghu class frigates.

Overall, then, the trends in the ASEAN region's security environment have generally served to emphasize the common interests of Malaysia, Indonesia, and Singapore, and to a lesser extent Brunei, while at the same time taking Thailand and the Philippines in directions that isolate them from the security interests of their fellow ASEAN members. This turn of events is, of course, interesting in itself but it becomes more so when it is evaluated in conjunction with recent economic trends in the region.

NOTES

1. Interestingly, at the ceremony to mark his appointment as Philippine Armed Forces Chief of Staff, Lieutenant General Rodolfo Biazon said that "the armed forces will shift from that of an organisation fitted for internal security operations to that of external defence mode and plans for this must be made." *Straits Times* (weekly overseas edition), January 26, 1991. The important point here is that it will take a good many years for the Philippines to shift its defense orientation.

2. See the discussion in Paul M. Evans, "Vietnam in the Changing System of Economic and Security Relations in Eastern Asia," in Richard Stubbs, comp., *Vietnam: Facing the 1990s* (Toronto: Joint Centre for Asia Pacific Studies, 1989), pp. 43–60.

3. Tai Ming Cheung, *Growth of Chinese Naval Power: Priorities, Goals, Missions, and Regional Implications* (Singapore: Institute of Southeast Asian Studies, 1990), p. 9.

4. Ibid., pp. 58–59 and 64.

90.   DEVELOPING THE ASIA-PACIFIC REGION

SABURO OKITA

Historically, economic development in the Asia-Pacific region centering on East and Southeast Asia has occurred in successive and overlapping waves, with Japan taking off in the 1960s, the Asian NIEs in the 1970s, and the ASEAN countries and China in the 1980s. This type of regional economic development is best characterized as the flying-geese pattern of development, which essentially refers to the inverted-V pattern of development in which one country after another takes off toward industrialization. As such, it provides a snapshot of the dynamics of the relationship among the countries as they shift from vertical to horizontal integration, the less developed countries catching up with the front-runners. In this process, the geese (countries) that take off later benefit from access to the others' capital and technology, which enables them to bypass some historical steps and to grow very quickly, thus enabling them to catch up with the others and to gradually establish horizontal relationships.

There are many factors that have made this flying-geese pattern of development possible. First is the success of export-oriented industrial development strategies. Expanding exports have given this region a larger share of world trade. Accounting for 14.3% of world exports in 1980, total exports from Japan, the Asian NIEs, the ASEAN countries, and China were up to 21.5% by 1987. Among the ASEAN countries, Thailand, Malaysia, and Indonesia all had strong export growth in 1989, Thai exports up 25.5%, Malaysian up 18.6%, and Indonesian up 13.2% over the previous year. Likewise, the Asian NIEs' share of world exports expanded from 1.6% in 1965 to 7.6% in 1987 and their share of world imports rose from 2.1% in 1965 to 6.5% in 1987. While some of this export expansion has been in competition with the Western industrial countries, it should be noted that the enhanced import capability that their export earnings have given them has generated new markets and created complementary relationships.

The region-wide spread of export-oriented industrial development strategies has worked through the resultant competition and complementarity to create greater consecutivity and acceleration in East and Southeast Asian economic development. Thus it is misleading to claim that export promotion policies only increase exports. Rather, the enhanced purchasing power and greater economic interdependence that results also increases imports. At the same

Reprinted in abridged form from "Perspectives for the Asia-Pacific Region in the 21st Century", *ASIEN*, no. 42 (1992), pp. 5–10, by permission of the author and the German Association for Asian Studies, Hamburg.

time, these countries' export structures are also changing. In Thailand, for example, manufactured goods' share of exports was 23.8% in 1975 but had increased to 57.5% in 1988. As a result, Thailand has a more stable economy than it did when it had to rely upon primary commodity exports.

The second factor that has made this flying-geese pattern of development possible is the overall expansionary trend in the world economy, which has proved hospitable to export-oriented industrial development strategies. World trade volume expanded 35% in 1980-88, far ahead of the 23% growth in world production for the same period. Among the reasons for this are the progress made in trade liberalization during the 1964-67 Kennedy Round and the 1973-79 Tokyo Round of multilateral trade talks, the dollar's exchange strength and the booming U.S. economy in the first half of the 1980s, and the yen's exchange strength and strong Japanese domestic demand in the second half of the decade. All of these factors have meant sharply expanded trade and investment for the region. This economic vitality has in turn generated greater intra-regional trade as seen in the fact that intra-regional exports by the 15 member countries of the Pacific Economic Cooperation Conference (the ASEAN countries, the Asian NIEs, Australia, Canada, China, Japan, New Zealand, and the United States) increased from 54.4% of their total exports in 1970 to 65.8% in 1988. Extra-regional trade also thrived. The Asian NIEs exports to the EC grew an average of 37.8% per year in 1985-88, out-performing Japan's 34.6% and the United States' 20.8%. It is clear that expanding world trade and the existence of an international free-trade system that makes such expansion possible is crucial not only for intra-regional but also for extra-regional trade. Accordingly, the Asia-Pacific countries have a vital interest in rebuffing protectionism and ensuring that the GATT Uruguay Round is a success.

East and Southeast Asia are still heavily dependent upon the U.S. market, and a recession sparked by economic adjustments there would have a deflationary impact on this region. This export dependence, however, has been gradually diminishing over the last few years. Japan's dependence has shrunk from 38% in 1986 to 37% in 1987, 34% in 1988, 34% in 1989, and 31% in 1990; and the Asian NIEs from 37% in 1986 to 35% in 1987, 31% in 1988, 30% in 1989, and 25% in 1990. As the Asian NIEs and the ASEAN countries expand their exports of manufactured goods, it is imperative that Japan become better able to absorb more imports from them by expanding domestic demand and making its markets more accessible, both to lower their dependence upon the U.S. market and to maintain this region's economic vitality. Japan's ratio of manufactured goods to total imports has risen from 31% in 1985 to over 50.4% in 1989. Furthermore, as of August 1991, the Japanese economy entered the 57th month of a long-term economic expansion marked by real economic growth of 6.2% in 1988, 4.7% in 1989, and 5.6% in 1990. This growth continued to be domestic-demand-led. Japan is also a major supplier of capital goods to the other countries in the region, and access to the latest capital goods can have basically the same favorable impact on local productivity that technology transfer and domestic development do.

The third factor making this flying-geese pattern possible is that the less developed countries have adopted catch-up industrial and trade policies supplementing market mechanisms to take advantage of the comparative advantage provided by their large pools of inexpensive labor. These policies rely on the government's skillfully mixing market mechanisms and government planning and guidance techniques and are particularly attractive when the private sector is still in the infant stages. Albeit with some differences of emphasis, such policy thinking is central not only in the Asian NIEs and the ASEAN countries but also in socialist China, Vietnam, and the East European countries and the Soviet Union as these countries have recently expressed considerable interest in the "Japanese model" as they make the transition from centrally planned to market-oriented economies. More than import substitution strategies, export-oriented industrial development strategies heighten cost consciousness and encourage the efficient use of management and productive resources. This in turn makes the entire economy more efficient. Accordingly, cost considerations have to be included even in central economic planning and there is a need to develop plans that reflect effective market forces. Benefiting from economic reform and openness, the Chinese economy recorded impressive average per-annum growth of 9% in 1980.

The fourth factor facilitating this flying-geese pattern is that the countries of East and Southeast Asia have, even in the initial stages, received aid that encouraged bootstrap efforts. Japanese aid has long been criticized for its low grant element, but, Asia's impressive development is arguably an eloquent vindication of aid policies firmly anchored in the idea of economic efficiency, given that Japanese aid has expanded considerably over the last few decades and that Asia received more than 90% of Japanese bilateral official development assistance in the 1960s and early 1970s and nearly 70% since the mid-1970s. Also attracted by high rates of return on capital because of the comparatively low production costs, the relaxation of regulations governing direct investment, and the adoption of preferential treatment for investment, foreign capital infusions to the ASEAN countries have recently shifted to direct investment, and the resultant increase in intra-company transactions has contributed to the expansion of intra-regional trade. Japan's overseas direct investment flow has grown sharply since the appreciation of the yen after the 1985 Plaza Accord. In the latter half of fiscal 1987, the flow of direct investment from Japan to the ASEAN countries picked up. In fiscal 1988, this Japanese investment flow was $13.6 billion to the ASEAN countries compared to $7.7 billion to the Asian NIEs. Japanese total overseas direct investment

increased sharply from $12.12 billion for fiscal 1985 to $67.54 billion for fiscal 1989 and $56.91 billion for fiscal 1990.

Another interesting development for the region is the increase in direct investment by the Asian NIEs in the ASEAN countries, as reflected in the way the Asian NIEs' share of direct investment in Thailand jumped from 17.7% in 1987 to 27.7% in 1989, in Malaysia from 37.9% in 1987 to 43.0% in 1989, and in Indonesia from 11.6% in 1987 to 20.7% in 1989. On the other hand, the confluence of the worldwide savings shortage, the bloating of the U.S. net foreign debt outstanding to $663 billion as of the end of 1989, and the flow of capital to Eastern Europe and the Soviet Union to aid economic reform there has fueled fears that the developing countries of Asia may no longer have sufficient access to the capital they need. In turn, this has made it all the more imperative that the OECD countries maintain or raise their domestic savings rates. In particular, the United States must raise its domestic savings rate, rein in its massive budget deficit, and reduce its trade deficit by improving its export competitiveness, and thus once again become a capital exporter.

The final point is that the Asia-Pacific region contains a multifaceted and diverse mix of disparate elements in an intricate weave of competition and complementarity. The difference between the European economic integration scheduled for 1992 and Asia-Pacific economic cooperation is the difference between integration among relatively homogeneous political and economic systems and the gradual creation of a cooperative relationship premised upon diversity among countries at different stages of development. Another difference is that while EC integration was promoted by government policies and treaties, regional economic cooperation in the Asia-Pacific was promoted mainly by private enterprises motivated by market forces. Organizations promoting this regional cooperation, including the PECC with its distinctive tripartite structure of government officials, business people, and academics since

1980 and the ministerial-level meeting for Asia Pacific Economic Cooperation (APEC) formed in 1989, are well aware of the need to maintain the dynamism of this region while reconciling the different and at times conflicting interests of the various countries and are discussing strategies to prevent protectionist policies and to support the global free trade system while respecting the potential of the region's developing countries. Economic cooperation grounded in liberalization is prerequisite to sustaining regional activity in a region with the kind of multifaceted character that makes the flying-geese pattern of development possible. Accordingly, this regional cooperation is non-discriminatory toward extra-regional countries and is an effective means of promoting global free trade.

91. GLOBAL RESTRUCTURING AND SOUTHEAST ASIA

CHRIS DIXON

SOUTH EAST ASIAN STATES AND THE RESTRUCTURING OF THE WORLD-ECONOMY

In all the South East Asian economies the state has played a major role in the development of capitalist production. The relative weakness of the indigenous capitalist classes is reflected in the extent to which the military and the bureaucracy have come to exert decisive control over the state apparatuses. In general the policies of repression of labour organisations, subsidies on food and fuel, protectionism and investment in infra-structure and production have fostered the growth of the previously weakly developed indigenous capitalist class. In certain periods some of the states have been able to defend the interests of domestic capital against those of international capital. Complex inter-relationships have been built up between international and domestic capital, the bureaucracy and the military. This is perhaps most apparent in Indonesia and the Philippines. However, Robison's (1986: 374) description of the Indonesian situation could, with limited modification, be applied to much of the region:

> The state played its key role in the development of the capitalist class, not only providing the political conditions for capital accumulation, including the political repression of labour and the subsidisation of food and fuel

prices, but actively investing in infrastructure and production. At another level it was active in resolving the conflicts internal to the class alliance, intervening decisively on behalf of domestic capital in the mid- and late 1970s. However, the very fragmentation of the capitalist class enabled the state to play a relatively autonomous role in its relations with capital. The relative weakness of indigenous elements within the capitalist class meant that no powerful bourgeois party emerged to challenge the formal hegemony over the state apparatus by military and, to a lesser extent, civilian politico-bureaucrats, whose political power grew out of the state apparatus itself. In this separation of political and economic power, the capitalist class, particularly international capital, financed the state and centres of politico-bureaucrat power which exercised hegemony over it, through formal revenues (oil taxes) and informal funding. The relationships between state, politico-bureaucrat and capital were further complicated by the bonds between individual politico-bureaucrats and capitalists, not to mention the fact that an increasing number of politico-bureaucrats were themselves also capitalists.

During the 1980s these complex interrelationships have been placed under increasing strain. Those that control the state apparatus

---

Excerpted from Chris Dixon, *South East Asia in the World-Economy* (Cambridge: Cambridge University Press, 1991), pp. 223–26, by permission of the author and the publisher.

have come to occupy a highly compromised position between the conflicting interests of domestic and international capital. Further compliance with the increasing demands of international capital threatens not only the political power base of the politico-bureaucratic group but also the stability of the state. Indeed there is an inherent contradiction between the policies pressed on the region's states by the IMF and the consequences of their implication for the interests of international capital.

These conflicts of interest are apparent in both the resistance by individual states to 'restructuring' and the 'softening' of the IMF demands. The latter has been most clearly apparent in the negotiations with the Philippines during 1988 and 1989.

Paradoxically those economies most attractive to international capital because of their relative political stability, resources, economic growth and market potential were often those which were best able to defend the interests of domestic capital. This was perhaps most clearly seen in Indonesia during the 1970s.

During the 1980s all the states have at various times and to different degrees compromised their domestic policy in favour of the interests of international capital. The situations that enabled countries to resist the pressure to abandon ISI in favour of EOI no longer prevail. In general, a combination of changed international circumstances and pressure from the international agencies has resulted in a sharp reduction in state-led development. The notable exceptions to this are Indonesia and Singapore.

State expenditure and budget deficits have been sharply curtailed, most spectacularly in Malaysia. There has been a general retreat from regional planning and controls over the economy. The 'buzz-words' of development are 'private sector', 'privatisation', 'allocative efficiency', 'free market' and 'comparative advantage'.

However, the rhetoric of development frequently remains separate from reality. Government and international agency statements cannot be taken at face value. The structures built up during the 1960s and 1970s have not and indeed cannot be removed at a stroke. Indeed as Robison *et al.* (1987, 11–12) have said, some states are 'caught in a bind' and, whatever the pressures, can realistically only engage in a very limited degree of restructuring. While it is tempting to compare the present partial adoption of the newest 'orthodoxy' to the transition from ISI to EOI, the situation in which this is taking place is a radically different one. For the South East Asian states the situation is much more precarious, their positions, internationally and internally, are weaker; the conflicts and contradictions of the development process are sharper; and the prospects of major political upheaval throughout the region greater perhaps than ever before.

Out of the process of global restructuring and the associated recurrent crisis of the 1970s and 1980s a new pattern of world production is beginning to emerge (Thrift, 1986a: 12). It may be still too early to infer the outcome of present trends. However, the world-economy is becoming more integrated at all scales. Most significant is the integration of international production and finance. As a result changes in the global pattern of capitalist production take place even more rapidly.

The key element in the emergent pattern is a new and more intense cycle of the internationalisation of capital. This process has operated extremely unevenly. The NIDL has only had a major impact on a small number of Third World countries and industries (Thrift, 1986a: 46–7). South East Asia is among the more significant to be so affected.

The new and intensified penetration of South East Asia was spearheaded by the influx of financial resources of which direct foreign investment is only the most obvious. The South East Asian states have been major recipients of the rapid expansion in foreign investment which has taken place since the early 1970s. Initially this was encouraged by their high levels of tariff protection. However, during the 1970s barriers to the operation of foreign investment began to emerge, most significantly in Indonesia and Malaysia. Restrictions on the free movement of foreign investment and MNC are now seen as barriers to the intensification of capitalist production in the region. Thus governments are under increasing pressure to dismantle the apparatus that was instrumental in the establishment of many of the region's manufacturing sectors.

Further development of South East Asia's position in the NIDL depends, of course, on the continuation of the trends giving rise to this new global pattern. As Jenkins (1984) has suggested the NIDL as we currently recognise it may prove to be a very temporary phenomenon. Moves towards automation of labour-intensive processes, reinforced by increased political uncertainty in South East Asia and increased protection of developed world markets, may well result in a movement of MNC activity and foreign investment back to the USA and Western Europe. The major American-based electronics MNCs, such as Motorola and Fairchild, are beginning to repatriate assembly and testing work back to the USA (Henderson, 1986: 104).[1] Indeed a study by OECD (1988) suggests that this may become a major trend as the NICs as a whole lose their cost advantages over the developed economies.

The growing tendency for Japanese manufacturing investment to flow to developed rather than less-developed locations is principally a reflection of growing protectionism. With the prospects of the world-economy moving towards 'highly managed regional trading blocs' (GATT, 1988), Hongkong, Singapore, South Korea and Taiwan are beginning to follow the Japanese lead. It is likely that these flows will increase with, for example, the prospect of increased EC protection after 1992 (Wilson, 1988).

If the currently rapid opening of China to international capital continues it is likely that much activity will be diverted away from South East Asia. The increasing likelihood of opportunities opening up in the USSR and Eastern Europe can be viewed in a similar way.

This concluding discussion highlights the need for an international perspective. The degree of integration and speed of change exhibited by the world-economy make it increasingly difficult to produce a meaningful analysis of individual countries or regions such as South East Asia in isolation. Rather they must be studied as interacting parts of the world-economy.

NOTE

1. Similar moves are taking place in the printing industry.

OPTIONS FOR ASEAN

LEE POH PING

[I]t can be seen that ASEAN faces two developments of great significance to it, that of a world economy moving against the producers of commodities, and that of the diminishing need for cheap labour on the part of the advanced countries. There is yet another challenge, that of the fall-out from the strained Japanese-American relations, as expressed in the huge deficit Americans suffer in bilateral trade relations with Japan. These strained relations may be the result of the more successful adjustment of Japan to high technology or to other reasons.[1] Whatever they may be, it behoves the ASEAN countries to consider the possible scenarios and outcome as these two giants wrestle with each other.

The existence today of a huge American deficit in the balance of trade between the United States and Japan (about US$60 billion in 1986) and an even bigger global deficit has led many Americans to question the wisdom of maintaining a free trade policy and the concomitant open American market. It may be that the root cause of this deficit lies in declining American competitiveness and not alleged unfair Japanese trading practices. It may be that other countries such as West Germany, Taiwan and Korea are also contributory. But the country which has been most

salient in American eyes is Japan, particularly as the Americans who have been most vocal are those in industries most affected by Japanese competition. And such voices have in no way been stilled by the continuing huge deficit despite Japanese market-opening measures and the rise of the yen. The danger exists, as exemplified by the Jenkin's Bill over which Congress only narrowly failed to override the presidential veto, and the Gephardt Bill which sought to legislate against Japanese and other imports, that American law-makers may come to the conclusion that the only way to reduce this deficit and save American jobs is to shut out Japanese imports. The consequence of this would be disastrous. Japan and other affected countries will retaliate. The casualty will be the post-war economic order, with the likely scenario of ensuing trading blocs with Japan dominating East and Southeast Asia, the Americas under the United States, and Africa under Western Europe. We may see the resurrection of what was thought obsolete: imperialism and spheres of influence.

Such a scenario, however, is not a foregone conclusion because of a very keen awareness among the Japanese and many others that something must be done to prevent this, and because the United States has not lost out in

Reprinted in abridged form from "ASEAN and the Asia-Pacific in the 1990s", *Contemporary Southeast Asia* 9, no. 2 (September 1987), pp. 157–66, by permission of the author and the Institute of Southeast Asian Studies.

everything. It is still strong in commercial aviation and services, for example, and not everyone will bet that Japan will beat the United States in the high technology race. What is more likely and is now already happening to some extent, is a United States pursuing narrow economic interests irrespective of whether the interests of other countries which may be allies or friends are hurt in the process. Recent examples come to mind, such as the subsidized sale of American rice in the world market, estimated by some to affect possibly as many as one million Thai farmers, and the subsidized sale of sugar and wheat to communist countries which has been perceived in Australia as damaging to its national interests. There is also the generally hard-nosed attitude in American negotiations with Korea and Taiwan, where the United States is taking a tough stand on textile import limitations, intellectual copyright, market-opening measures, insistence on the removal of export clauses in joint-venture agreements between these countries and Japan, and so on. The United States may have a case in many of these steps and may have to respond to domestic political exigencies. But such an attitude contrasts sharply with the attitude of the 1950s and 1960s when the United States would not only not resort to such steps where allies and friends were concerned but would probably not even have contemplated them. We remember then the American encouragement of economic development among its friends and allies, not to mention the existence of all manner of economic aid. That probably is a bygone age, while it is likely this tough American attitude will continue for some time.

Another likely scenario is a realization on both sides that Japan and America are so intertwined that there is a limit to which either side can push the other without bringing the whole house down. In order to prevent this, both sides may find it expedient to arrive at mutual agreements that may pay very little heed to the interests of other countries, and attempt to overcome protectionist pressure by acting against countries of lesser global economic consequence. Already there is talk in certain circles of an American-Japanese condominium in managing the global economy. A recent article in the influential journal *Foreign Affairs* coined the term "bigemony" to describe this joint condominium.[2] This is not to suggest that such "bigemony" already exists, but the situation is best described by the Asian proverb that when elephants fight or make love, the grass beneath them are trampled upon.

Keeping in mind such scenarios, how should ASEAN respond? One option proposed is to emphasize self-reliance, to depend less on foreigners to produce the needed goods and services. Exactly how this can be done, given the present limited economic co-operation and the competitive nature of many of the ASEAN economic activities, is often not spelt out. A logical extreme of this will be an autarchic economy or the delinking of the ASEAN economies from the international economy. Given the fundamental nature of the challenge to the ASEAN economies and the purpose of this conference to consider broad ASEAN paths in the 1990s, a discussion of this theoretical possibility is not out of order

The attraction of an autarchic economy is that ASEAN will be master of its own economic destiny, and not be subject to outside powers which may have little concern for the interests of ASEAN. Yet, is it realistic? It will be instructive first to consider two near Asian examples, Burma and China. In the decades after World War II, Burma decided to isolate itself from the world economy, choosing a path called the "Burmese Road to Socialism". This policy was further made possible as the geopolitical designs of the two most important powers to Burma, China and the United States, fitted well with this isolation. Yet, the cost has been an extremely low standard of living (Burma recently declared it was one of the poorest countries in the world) despite the possession of abundant natural resources. There are now increasing doubts within Burma itself of the wisdom of this policy.

The failure of the Chinese autarchic experiment is even more evident. China detached itself from the international capitalist economy when the communists took over, and, with the advent of the Sino-Soviet conflict, also from the international socialist economy dominated by the Soviet Union. This autarchy found its extreme expression in the Cultural Revolution. It was thought that with its immense population and resources together with its strategic weight, the Chinese could pull this off. It was therefore a most spectacular turnabout when Deng Xiaoping in 1979 made the decision to open the Chinese economy to the West and Japan. This decision was brought about not least by a realization that the Maoist self-reliant policy had not brought China anywhere near the economies of the advanced countries, and that countries with some racial and cultural affinity to China, such as Korea, Hong Kong, Taiwan and, of course, Japan, are streaking ahead economically because they do not have autarchic economies.

The second problem is whether it is strategically possible, given that Southeast Asia possesses abundant natural resources which, despite the changed world economy, may still be needed by the advanced economies. A good example is oil, a fuel which is unlikely to be obsolete by the 1990s and for which there might even be a shortage then. Moreover, Southeast Asia is not unimportant geopolitically to the big powers now present. For example, the Straits of Malacca, through which more than 80 per cent of Japanese oil needs derived from the Persian Gulf pass through, is important to Japan while the American bases in Clark Field and Subic Bay in the Philippines are integral to the present American Asian-Pacific strategy. In addition, the Chinese may fear that Southeast Asia, particularly Indochina, could be used by a hostile superpower, such as the Soviet Union against it. By the same token, the Soviet Union may find Southeast Asia, and especially Indochina, useful against China. All these do not mean that the big powers may not change their strategies in the 1990s or that they may not be able to achieve their geopolitical designs with an autarchic ASEAN economy. This latter is, however, extremely unlikely as far as the United States and, even more so, Japan are concerned.

Even if the strategic circumstances were not unfavourable, an autarchic economy would necessitate massive involvement by the state apparatus. Quite apart from the possible political problems which might arise, it is questionable whether the state has the will and capacity to do so in the present age. There is a worldwide trend to reduce state involvement in the economy — privatization is the catchword here. And this is happening in countries of varying ideological colour. In the ASEAN countries, where the state has been involved, it is with the purpose of "restructuring", that is, to enable certain disadvantaged economic groups to participate more fully in the modern international economy, not shut themselves from it. Moreover, the present globalization of many national economies, wild currency fluctuations and so on make it difficult for any state to control its own economy even if it wanted to. In this connection, it is relevant to note that one of the conclusions of a recent discussion between Henry Kissinger and ASEAN leaders was that the world economy is going out of control.[3]

The second option for ASEAN is to embark on industrialization (taking a "hard" path) and rely less on commodities. This will make ASEAN less subject to the violent fluctuations of the prices of commodities. However, quite apart from the internal problem of ASEAN's ability to industrialize, the export of manufactured goods will likely encounter protectionism in America as posited in the foregoing second scenario. Nor will Japan act as a significant market in the 1990s. The other alternative is the ASEAN market. Quite apart from the fact that it is not as rich as either Japan or the United States, the ASEAN countries are still in the process of discussing about further economic co-operation. It remains to be seen whether a common market or even a free trade zone can be achieved by the 1990s.

The third option is to go into the high technology or the softnomics path. Then ASEAN will be with the wave of the future. However, the problem will be even more difficult for ASEAN than in the second option. It first involves a double leap, from a pre-industrial economy to a high-technology one, which will probably also be costlier. It is also not likely that ASEAN, with the possible exception of Singapore, can attract the kind of Japanese and American investment that can lead to a high technological economy.

Finally, the ASEAN countries can remain as they are, relying again on their commodities, and try to ride the present recession through. But, if the Drucker argument is right, this will not work in the long term.

Given such, it is quite likely that the ASEAN countries will adopt a mixture of the last three options in the 1990s, a mixture of the "hard" path, softnomics and continued reliance on commodities. Thus, all the ASEAN states will try to industrialize, with Malaysia and Singapore in the forefront, while Singapore will also attempt to go into high technology. All but Singapore will probably continue producing commodities. Where the emphasis will be or how it is mixed will depend very much on the paths the two Pacific giants take. It is thus appropriate now to consider ASEAN's relations with them in the Asian-Pacific context. To do so, one should distinguish between explicit attempts to create an Asian-Pacific organizational structure after the fashion of the United Nations, EEC or whatever, from that of the initiation of steps through dialogues and meetings to influence Japanese-American relations for the profit of ASEAN, or to limit damage.

The former path is unlikely to be fruitful at this juncture. Any attempt at organization creation carries with it a definition of membership. This is somewhat undesirable to ASEAN at present as it could take on a narrow political and economic colouration which may clash with ASEAN's professed aim of neutrality or with ASEAN's relations with other economic groups such as the EEC. It might also pose problems for ASEAN itself whether it should enter as a group or individually — a formal statement either way may not harmonize with the spirit of ASEAN cohesion which rests less on formal criteria than on consensus building. In addition, the distribution of power, realistically speaking, would likely be weighted towards Japan and the United States in any formal organization.

The latter path may be more desirable. In this respect, ASEAN should work with and encourage as many of the non-governmental Asian-Pacific dialogues as possible and also engage itself governmentally, as in the ASEAN Plus Five. What viewpoint should ASEAN convey in such dialogues?

ASEAN should first make both powers aware of the crisis in its economy brought about by the structural decline of commodity prices, the recession this has induced and the possible eruption of social and other tensions which have been kept under control by high economic growth. It may be too much to ask for price stabilization schemes, but awareness should at least be stimulated.

Secondly, in the movement towards high technology both countries, especially Japan, will find many of their "hard" industries uncompetitive. Such industries could be relocated in the ASEAN countries. Of course, the ASEAN countries themselves should undertake the kind of economic reforms conducive to the receipt of such and other investment.

Thirdly, the ASEAN countries should aim at some damage limitation. Efforts should be made to persuade the Americans that it is to their long-term interest and also ASEAN's to allow the continual access of ASEAN manufactured goods, for while protectionism may be the short-term answer to political exigencies, the ultimate victim will be the international trading system. It should also urge the United States not to undertake the kind of rice subsidy which will have a tremendous negative impact on rice farmers in Thailand. In addition, continued efforts should be made to persuade Japan to open its market further.

And fourthly, efforts should be made to persuade Japan to divert some of its funds now floating in the international economy or used for the purchase of American treasury bonds together with American and Japanese real estate, to some kind of a Marshall Plan for ASEAN.[4]

Finally, what cards can ASEAN play? Probably not too many. Two may, however, be considered. The advent of high technology notwithstanding, ASEAN still has a population of about 300 million people who constitute a market of not inconsiderable significance, particularly as they have the purchasing power of medium income countries. Natural resources will still be abundant, with many still needed for the international economy of the 1990s. In addition, ASEAN has a reasonably cheap skilled labour force which will still be needed despite high technology. For example, we are told that robots and computers have taken over many of the functions of humans in manufacturing but exactly in what functions and in what ways they affect labour cost have not been adequately spelt out. Thus, in the manufacture of cars, for example, robots can probably do welding and painting more efficiently than human labour. Yet, there are many sophisticated functions such as the insertion of the fuel pump that robots cannot adequately handle. Human labour is still needed. In addition, the differential in the wage rate may be so great in some cases (for example, the average wage for labour in Japan is about ten times the average wage in Thailand) that manufacturers can be quite easily influenced by this to postpone further computerization and robotization. Moreover, developments in international finance, specifically changes in the exchange rate of relevant currencies, can further reinforce the importance of cheap labour. The striking example is the revaluation of the yen (or *endaka* as the Japanese call it). Since the G-5 meeting in September 1985 in New York, the yen has appreciated more

than 40 per cent to the American dollar. This has put a tremendous strain on the Japanese economy and has almost played havoc with its small and medium industries. These industries are finding it difficult to cope and have rushed to invest in South Korea, Taiwan and other suitable ASEAN countries.

In addition, the participation of ASEAN gives the community a "developmental" aspect.[5] For any community or international organization to have global significance, those advanced countries which advocate this should not only invite some developing countries as members for window dressing but should set aims that are of some meaning to the latter. It is for this reason that the original proposal of a Pacific community of the five advanced countries, the United States, Japan, Canada, Australia and New Zealand, did not go very far as it would then be a grouping of rich countries only. Moreover, the smaller advanced countries, such as Australia and New Zealand, together with Korea will be most keen to have ASEAN as members or participants, for then they will not be so overwhelmed by Japan and the United States. It may be that the "development" theme is holding less enchantment in America than was the case in the 1950s and 1960s, but for Japan it may have some effect. And this may be in two ways. Japan is now fighting a battle to maintain free trade or at least free trade according to GATT (General Agreement on Tariffs and Trade) rules. Any support it can get from ASEAN will be helpful. Secondly, Japan will soon emerge as a great power not only in the economic sense but also in the sense of one with international responsibilities attached to it. ASEAN by virtue of proximity, relative importance to the Japanese economy and some strategic value, is a good candidate for Japanese developmental efforts. If such be the case, there may yet be hope for ASEAN in the Asia-Pacific in the 1990s.

NOTES

1. Many Japanese are wont to view this bilateral strain as basically a problem of restructuring the world

economy. Japan has demonstrated competitiveness in many manufacturing industries while the U.S. competitiveness in this regard is declining. On the other hand, the United States is demonstrating continued strength in services. Therefore, some basic adjustment in this could solve the present problem. Many Americans are inclined to a different view — that the United States is losing to Japan because of the absence of a "level playing field", that is, Japan is enjoying an unfair advantage. Moreover, many Americans have this probably unjustified nightmare that their "strength" in the services are those of manning hamburger stalls, sweeping Toyota factory floors and so on and are understandably not thrilled with such an adjustment.

2. "Economic Imbalances and World Politics", *Foreign Affairs* (New York), Spring 1987.
3. See the report in the *New Straits Times*, Kuala Lumpur, 7 March 1987, on the outcome of the discussions between Henry Kissinger and ASEAN leaders in a roundtable discussion organized by the Institute of Strategic and International Studies, Kuala Lumpur.
4. One of the Japanese proponents of a Japanese Marshall Plan is Saburo Okita See "Japan — Saviour of the Developing World", *Far Eastern Economic Review* (Hong Kong), 17 July 1986.
5. Saburo Okita himself is of the opinion that the Pacific community cannot proceed without ASEAN membership.

93. IMPLEMENTING AFTA, 1992–2007

SEIJI NAYA and PEARL IMADA

ASEAN is now a quarter century old. Over the past twenty-five years, it has been successful in promoting peace and stability in the region, cultural development and better personal interrelations, and, to a more limited extent, economic growth of its member states. Although the peace and stability that ASEAN cooperation brought about have had an important influence on the rapid economic growth of individual countries, ASEAN member states have not been able to internalize as a group ASEAN economic cooperation for growth.

There have been three major phases of ASEAN economic cooperation. The first stage can be considered during its first ten years of existence, from 1967 to the first Summit in 1976, wherein each country basically tried to get to know each other and lay the foundations for cooperation. The second stage spanned the subsequent fifteen years, from 1976 to the Fourth Summit of January 1992, there was active cooperation and formal though somewhat superficial agreements for economic cooperation among the member states, focussing mostly on building institutions for cooperation. The third stage, from 1992 to 2007, will be one of consolidation in building AFTA and other forms of regional cooperation, characterized by much more active and productive economic cooperation in the region.

The endorsement of the AFTA vision is a very positive development. Large benefits can accrue to member nations from the pooling of resources and sharing of markets, with dynamic effects reinforcing such benefits.

Both internal and external factors have led to the creation of AFTA. First, as mentioned earlier, internal economic conditions within ASEAN are more appropriate now for the implementation of a free trade area than they were previously.

In the past, the economic structures of the ASEAN countries were weak with most countries following inward looking economic policies. Tariff levels were relatively high in Indonesia, the Philippines and Thailand and ranged widely within each country. Malaysia, on the other hand, had relatively low levels of protection and Singapore has been virtually a free trade port since the 1960s. The recent unilateral liberalization that has been occurring has harmonized tariff structures to a considerable degree. Consequently, the disparities of tariff structures have been reduced, facilitating further regional integration efforts. Manufactures comprised only a small share of total

Reprinted in abridged form from *AFTA: The Way Ahead* (Singapore: Institute of Southeast Asian Studies, 1992), by permission of the authors and the publisher.

intra-ASEAN exports until recently, with Singapore playing a dominant role in the largely primary product and entrepot trade of the region. The rapid industrialization, which took place in the 1980s and 1990s in all of the countries, has caused the percentage of manufactured exports to rise dramatically. This rapid industrialization has given rise to a large increase in intra-industry trade in manufactured products in the region, making trade more complementary than competitive between the ASEAN nations. To realize the potential for intra-regional trade creation, it is essential to develop trade patterns based on intra-industry specialization, similar to trade between developed countries such as within the EC. Recent studies have shown that trade creation would outweigh trade diversion for AFTA.[1]

There is also increasing external pressure on ASEAN to come together economically. Developing countries in other regions are undertaking economic reforms and opening their economies to trade and investment with great success. For example, Latin American countries have recovered from the so-called "lost decade" of the 1980s; economic reforms have spurred economic growth and these countries are now beginning to attract export-oriented investment. Similar developments in Eastern Europe and South Asia accentuate the trend. Competition from these other developing areas make it critical that ASEAN's attractiveness to investors be enhanced. One way of doing so is to create a large single regional market through AFTA.

Large economic groupings taking shape in the world such as the European Community (EC) and NAFTA, present a challenge to ASEAN. The inclusion of Mexico in the U.S.-Canada Free Trade Area and possibly other developing countries, especially Chile, in the future, may divert trade and investment away from ASEAN if ASEAN does not itself create a larger internal market.

The emergence of several Asia-Pacific organizations has also pushed ASEAN to seek more cohesion to enhance its effectiveness in

Asia-Pacific Economic Cooperation (APEC) and the East Asian Economic Caucus (EAEC), etc. AFTA will be a major step in building this internal cohesion so that ASEAN's role as a single bargaining bloc will be enhanced. The ASEAN countries explicitly acknowledged this reason for promoting greater regional economic cooperation in the Singapore Declaration of 1992. It has been well understood that each member state will benefit from acting as a unit; in fact, the whole will be greater than the sum of its individual parts.

Other integration schemes have concentrated on step-by-step implementation procedures before an agreement is reached. The EC negotiated many years before a consensus was reached to form a Single Market 1992 and the U.S. and Canada took nearly two years of careful preparation, meetings, and negotiations to expand the U.S.-Canada Free Trade Area to include Mexico. GATT is on its eighth round of negotiations with countries still negotiating and its completion is yet to come. Quite differently, ASEAN countries have not worked out the details of AFTA, choosing instead to outline the vision and worry about the details later.

The commitment of the ASEAN nations to set up AFTA is impressive and should be applauded. The Singapore Declaration and the Agreements on the CEPT for AFTA do include statements on most of the issues discussed, from investment issues to non-tariff and non-border areas. However, implementation is not spelled out; the Singapore Declaration establishing AFTA remains very vague. Many of these issues—e.g., rules of origin, content requirement, rules of competition, exclusion list and safeguard measures, dispute settlement—require careful preparatory work.

Other issues such as reciprocity should also be considered. In theory, reciprocity is not necessary because comparative advantage shows that a country can get welfare gains by unilateral tariff reductions. In practice, however, trade negotiations such as GATT, EC, and NAFTA, use reciprocity as a basic guiding principle, though it is not explicitly required.

Politically, it is common to assume that tariff and other barriers would be reduced on a mutual and equivalent basis. For example, the present systems may allow low tariff countries to stall in their tariff reductions and in any case higher tariff countries may not be eligible to receive preferences for certain products if their tariffs are higher than 20 percent even if they are in the process of reducing their tariff rates.

Moreover, Singapore has virtually no tariffs to reduce and should come up with other concessions to be able to reciprocate tariff reductions being offered by other countries. Singapore can offer other concessions in the areas of services such as telecommunications links and management expertise, or provide additional support for logistical or statistical activities, possibly additional funding for the ASEAN Secretariat to maintain the free trade area. Singapore can spearhead the elimination or reduction of non-tariff barriers in ASEAN. In return, Singapore can avail the markets, labor, and raw materials of its ASEAN partners.

In conclusion, there are many technical matters requiring immediate attention, but these problems are solvable. And the ASEAN working committees have been meeting to accomplish these tasks. It is also time for an experts group to support the effort and examine the technical problems presented earlier, including government procurement issues, industrial standards and safety regulation, investment rules and regulations, rules governing competition such as anti-trust laws, subsidies and duty drawbacks, and coordination of macroeconomic and exchange rate policy among member countries, among others. It is timely and appropriate that an ASEAN Experts' Convention be held to reach consensus and adopt the necessary agreements to implement ASEAN's "Free Trade Area Plus." Given the strong political commitment to move forward, the "bold and innovative" concept of AFTA and attention to important technical issues at such an ASEAN convention, ASEAN will definitely move forward in its plans for regional integration.

Perhaps most important of all, AFTA will allow ASEAN to act more as a group in regional and international fora in pursuing mutual interests as well as in playing a leadership role. By speaking in one voice in the Asia-Pacific Economic Cooperation process, for example, the clout of ASEAN more than proportionately increases. Moreover, the most important negotiations affecting ASEAN today relate to the on-going Uruguay Round of GATT, as the stakes are very high in preserving the multilateral system of international trade. By grouping together, ASEAN can better advance its cause of freeing international markets in the face of rising protectionism and bilateralism in the West. The Heads of State have already taken initiative in this regard in the Singapore Declaration by stressing the need for a successful and effective conclusion to the Uruguay Round.

NOTE

1. Pearl Imada, Manuel Montes, and Seiji Naya, *A Free Trade Area: Implications for ASEAN*, (Singapore: Institute of Southeast Asian Studies), 1991.

ASSESSING AFTA

SREE KUMAR

The agreement to create AFTA must be seen as one of considerable political will in the wake of less successful ASEAN economic ventures in the past.[2] The initial euphoria over the agreement, however, has become less so in the months following as industries in Thailand and, more recently, in Malaysia have called for greater protection at least in the short term. This has called into sharp relief whether AFTA will actually take shape in the years to come or whether it will falter as the other ASEAN economic efforts have in the past.

More recently, the initial agreement to have a North American Free Trade Area (NAFTA) has placed ASEAN on a more cautious route. The possibility of trade diversion resulting from closure to the North American market has made ASEAN more cognizant of the need for a ballast to overcome the loss of some of the trade with North America. Similarly, growing fears about the creation of a European Economic Area (EEA) have been voiced within ASEAN. These developments in ASEAN's traditional markets must now be analysed and understood. More importantly, ASEAN has to seek alternative markets for many of its products. Market diversification has to take place in the short term to prevent significant revenue losses as the EEA and NAFTA roll out.

While the commitment to GATT and multi-laterism must be uppermost in the designs of ASEAN, it has to seek a second best solution for its own short-term survival. AFTA is seen as this possibility — the creation of a market in its own region. For AFTA to become a reality, ASEAN must now set in motion a series of policies designed to facilitate greater regional trade. These policies cannot be seen in isolation. They must be congruent with investment and industrial policies being pursued by the member countries.

The creation of AFTA seems a necessary development in the light of changes in the world economic order. The wider question which ASEAN should address is the cost at which it is willing to forge a free trade area. If the costs of AFTA far outweigh the benefits from increasing ASEAN's trade with the rest of the world through increasing investments from abroad, then ASEAN must continue acting on a common front to ensure access to its largest markets, improve the regional investment climate, and raise the overall international profile of the region through various political and economic institutions. The need for a multilateral approach to improving global and regional trade must, therefore, be uppermost in the efforts expended by ASEAN. This is

Reprinted in abridged form from *AFTA: The Way Ahead* (Singapore: Institute of Southeast Asian Studies, 1992), by permission of the authors and the publisher.

not to detract from the creation of AFTA. Until such time that AFTA can become an important element of intra-ASEAN trade relations, the urgency for multilateralism cannot be disregarded.

Nevertheless, these thrusts can change significantly if ASEAN can now overcome some of its nationalist sentiments and set about dismantling the different barriers to cross-border trade and investments. This signalling effect can have significant impact on the participants that matter — investors and consumers. There is therefore an imperative to address intra-ASEAN issues on a larger set of issues if the gains from greater economic linkages are to accrue more equitably across all the member countries.

The need for a wider approach to addressing trade issues in ASEAN has been discussed at length in previous studies (Devan, 1987; Pangestu, et al, 1991). This paper has highlighted some of the policy issues which need to be addressed if AFTA is to come into existence in the years ahead. The current proposed items on the CEPT list should be increased considerably if the scheme is to have any significant intra-ASEAN impact. This is because of the generally low levels of regional trade, in the first place, and an even lower proportion of trade when items on the CEPT are considered.

A more profound effect on intra-ASEAN trade can be achieved if non-tariff barriers to trade are dismantled concurrently with tariff cuts on a wider spectrum of goods. The present approach of a product-by-product tariff reduction may have distortionary effects on the other sectors of the economy. In order to overcome such distortions it may well be necessary to pursue a sector-by-sector approach. This also has to take into account the manner in which tariffs are reduced. A combination of radial and collapsed tariff reductions would be far more effective in minimising revenue losses while improving productive efficiencies.

A more pressing issue which has to be understood in the ASEAN context is the level of tariff redundancy. Unless tariff redundancy is reduced, the impact of tariff reduction, even when NTBs are removed, could be negated somewhat. Tariff redundancy is also closely tied to exchange rates and, hence, the need for greater co-operation on monetary policies within the region becomes salient. This brings forth the need for policy-makers to address trade issues using both commercial and exchange-rate policies.

The creation of a free trade area also entails industrial re-structuring and redistribution. As investments flow to the areas with the highest returns and the most favourable factor endowments, traditional industrial zones in the different ASEAN countries may encounter some hollowing out. This process of change has to be managed closely to prevent income and welfare losses. Thus the need for greater harmonization of investment policies and industrial selectivity amongst the ASEAN members cannot be overlooked. In the short term this calls for the trade policy discussions to take on a wider ambit in addressing the medium-term impact of trade creation and diversion on the industrial structure of the different economies within ASEAN. The formation of AFTA, therefore, has to be addressed in a larger perspective than purely looking at the trade issues.

Perhaps most pertinent to the changes being mooted within ASEAN is the level of credibility associated with the attempts at forming AFTA. If tariff cuts are seen to be permanent in the wake of dismantled NTBs, then it is unlikely that the current account would deteriorate (Engel and Kletzer, 1990; Sen and Turnovsky, 1989). This implies that for ASEAN, the commitment to AFTA must now become embedded in the political philosophy underlying the formation of the group. The private sector is awaiting signals from the bureaucracy and the political leaders on the level of commitment and the credibility of the declaration made at the ASEAN Summit in Singapore. The need for an effective institutional mechanism for addressing the issues raised by the formation of AFTA would be a first step in the creation of credibility. ASEAN must now unshackle itself from the pressures imposed by protected domestic industries if AFTA is to become fact rather than fiction.

NOTES
1. For a discussion of the theory of free trade areas, see El-Agraa and Jones (1981).
2. Langhammer (1991) gives a review of the ASEAN economic co-operation efforts of the past.

THE CONTRIBUTORS

The Contributors

FLORIAN A. ALBURO is Professor, School of Economics, University of the Philippines. He has published widely on various aspects of economic development in ASEAN, as well as on the Philippine economy. Some of his more recent publications include: *Economic Stabilization Policies in ASEAN Countries*, co-editor with Pradumna B. Rana (1987); *TNCs and Structural Change in the Philippines* (1988); and *Philippines Trade Policy Options*, with Erlina Medalla and Filologo Pante, Jr. (1989).

MUTHIAH ALAGAPPA is a Research Associate with the International Relations Programe in the East-West Center, Hawaii. His research interest is international relations and security in the Asia-Pacific region with emphasis on Southeast Asia. His recent publications include: "The Dynamics of International Security in Southeast Asia: Change and Continuity", *Australian Journal of International Affairs* 45, no. (May 1991); "Regional Arrangements and International Security in Southeast Asia: Going Beyond ZOPFAN", *Contemporary Southeast Asia* 12, no. 2, (March 1991); and "Soviet Policy in Southeast Asia: Towards Constructive Engagement", *Pacific Affairs* 63, no. 3 (Fall 1990).

ALI ALATAS was appointed Foreign Minister of the Republic of Indonesia in March 1988. He became the nation's first professional diplomat to be made Foreign Minister, capping a distinguished diplomatic career spanning more than thirty years. Mr Alatas has distinguished himself at the United Nations, the Non-Aligned Movement and other world forums. He played a critical role in negotiating a diplomatic solution to the conflict in Cambodia, as Co-Chairman of the Paris International Conference on Cambodia.

MICHAEL ANTOLIK is Associate Professor of Government and Politics, Manhattan College. He has written numerous articles on ASEAN and his research interest centres on the politics of the ASEAN states and diplomacy of Southeast Asian states. He is currently studying the role of ritual in interstate relations.

MOHAMED ARIFF is Dean and Professor of Analytical Economics at the Faculty of Economics and Administration, University of Malaya, Malaysia. Among his publications are *The Malaysian Economy: Pacific Connections* (1991); *Islamic Banking in Southeast Asia*, editor (1988); *The Islamic Voluntary Sector in Southeast Asia*, editor (1991); and *The Muslim Private Sector in Southeast Asia*, editor (1991).

MUKUL ASHER is Associate Professor and Deputy Head, Department of Economics and Statistics, and a Senior Fellow, Masters in Public Policy Programme, Centre for Advanced Studies at the National University of Singapore. He specializes in public finance of Asian countries.

He is the author of several books, and articles. His most recent work is entitled *Fiscal Incentives and Economic Management in Indonesia, Malaysia and Singapore* (1992). Other publications include *Indirect Taxation in ASEAN* with Anne Booth (1983); *Fiscal Systems and Practices in the ASEAN Countries*, editor (1989).

A. AZIZ is Royal Professor at the University of Malaysia, Kuala Lumpur, Malaysia. He was formerly Vice-Chancellor of the University of Malaya. Professor Ungku A. Aziz serves on the board of directors of a number of Malaysian companies. He has published widely on various aspects of the Malaysian economy, particularly with reference to rural development.

JOHN BASTIN is Reader Emeritus in the Modern History of South-East Asia at the University of London. He was Foundation Professor of History at the University of Malaya. His current research interests include Western art of Indonesia, Singapore and Malaysia; history of Modern Singapore; Sir Stamford Raffles; South-East Asian bibliography.

The late HARRY J. BENDA was Professor of History at Yale University at the time of his death in 1971. He is remembered for his many contributions to Southeast Asian history, some of which are *The Crescent and the Rising Sun; Indonesian Islam under the Japanese Occupation, 1942–1945* (1958); *A History of Modern Southeast Asia, Colonialism, and Nationalism, and Decolonization*, with John Bastin (1968); *Southeast Asian Transitions; Approaches through Social History*, editor Ruth McVey (1978).

LESZEK BUSZYNSKI is a Senior Research Fellow at the Strategic and Defence Studies Centre, Canberra, Australia. Prior to this he was a Senior Lecturer in the Department of Political Science at the National University of Singapore. His books include *SEATO: The Failure of an Alliance Strategy* (1983), *The Soviet Union and Southeast Asia* (1986) and *Gorbachev and Southeast Asia* (1992). His research interests are Russia and the Asia-Pacific as well as Southeast Asian security issues.

L.S. CABANILLA is Chairman and Associate Professor, Department of Economics, Philippines. He has written numerous articles on the environment, farming, irrigation, and other aspects of rural development. One of his publications is *Economic Incentives and Comparative Advantage in the Livestock Industry* (1983).

CHAI-ANAN SAMUDAVANIJA is Chairman, Chaiyong Limthongkul Foundation, Thailand. He is also President of the Social Science Association of Thailand and Director of the Institute of Public Policy Studies, Thailand. Among this many publications are *The Young Turks* (1982) and *Leadership Perceptions and National Security: The Southeast Asian Experience*, co-editor with Mohammed Ayoob (1989).

CHAIWAT KHAMCHOO is Assistant Professor and Chairman of the Department of International Relations, Chulalongkorn University, Thailand. He has written articles on Japan's role in Southeast Asian security. His interests are Japanese politics and foreign policy as well as Japan's role in the Asia-Pacific region.

CHAN HENG CHEE is Director of the Singapore International Foundation. Prior to this she was Singapore's Permanent Representative to the United Nations as well as Singapore's High Commissioner to Canada and Ambassador to Mexico (1989–91), and Director, Institute of Policy Studies (1988). Her publications include *Singapore: The Politics of Survival, 1965–1967* (1971); *A Sensation of Independence: A Political Biography of David Marshall* (1984); and *The Prophetic and the Political. Selected Speeches and Writings of S. Rajaratnam*, co-editor with Obaid Ul Haq (1987); *The Dynamics of One Party Dominance: The PAP at the Grassroots* (1976). Her research interests are in political and social change in new states, domestic and regional politics of Southeast Asia, ethnic politics, international organizations and the New World Order.

CHEE PENG LIM is serving as an Economics Affairs Officer in the Development Planning Division of the United Nation's Economic and Social Commission for Asia and the Pacific (ESCAP) Secretariat, Bangkok. Dr Chee served as a member on several committees in both the public and private sectors in Malaysia and was also a consultant to various local international organizations such as FOMFEIA, APDC, ESCAP, ILO and World Bank. He has written extensively on industrial development in Malaysia in general and on small industry in particular.

PAUL H. CHEUNG is the Chief Statistician of Singapore and heads the Department of Statistics. He is concurrently the Director of the Population Planning Unit, Ministry of Health, Singapore and Senior Lecturer, National University of Singapore. He has written extensively on Singapore's social and demographic changes. His latest publication is *A Guide to Singapore's Official Statistics, 1992*.

CHIA SIOW YUE is Associate Professor in Economics at the National University of Singapore. Her main research interests are the fields of international economics and development economics. She has researched and published extensively on the economies of China, Asian NIEs, ASEAN, and Singapore, focusing particularly on regional economic integration, trade, industrialization and foreign investment. Additional areas of research and publications include income distribution in Singapore, women in the labour force, and the role of institutions in economic development.

CHIN KIN WAH is Senior Lecturer at the Department of Political Science, National University of Singapore. He has published widely in the areas of regional security, and ASEAN affairs. Among his most recent publications are *Defence Spending in Southeast Asia*, editor (1987) and *Two Views on Summit Three*, with Narciso G. Reyes (1986).

CHNG MENG KNG is Deputy Director-General of the ASEAN Secretariat, Jakarta on leave from the National University of Singapore where he is Senior Lecturer and formerly Vice-Dean of the Faculty of Arts and Social Sciences. He received his degrees from Trinity College, Cambridge and has published on a wide range of economic issues, including various aspects of ASEAN economic co-operation. Among his publications are *Technology and Skills in Singapore*, with Linda Low, Tay Boon Nga and Amina Tyabji (1986).

DHIRA PHANTUMVANIT is Director, Natural Resources and Environment Program, Thailand Development Research Institute as well as a Chairman of the ASEAN Chambers of Commerce and Industry Steering Committee on Sustainable Development (ASEAN-CCI). He has written numerous research publications on environmental quality management and natural resources management. His current research interests are Thailand's strategy to phase out ozone depleting substances, natural resource management, and business and the environment.

CHRIS DIXON is Professor of Geography, City of London Polytechnic. His current research interests are in structural adjustment in the Southeast Asian economies; agri-business in Thailand; and the globalization of agricultural production. His publications include *Rural Development in the Third World (1990); South East Asia in the World Economy* (1991); *Colonisation in the Contemporary World*, with M. Heffernan (1991); and *Economic Growth in Pacific Asia*, with D. Drakikis-Smith (1992).

RUSSELL H. FIFIELD is Professor Emeritus of Political Science at the University of Michigan. He has held research appointments at Oxford, Harvard, Cornell and the Institute of Southeast Asian Studies in Singapore. His fellowships include Fulbright, Twentieth Century Fund, Council on Foreign Relations, and Guggenheim. He is a former American Foreign Service Officer, Consultant to the Department of State, and Professor of Foreign Affairs at the

National War College. He is the author of four books, one of which won the George Louis Beer Prize of the American Historical Association. His professional services include two terms as Secretary of the Association for Asian Studies.

J.L.S. GIRLING was Senior Fellow, Australian National University (retired). His major publications include: *People's War* (1969); *America and the Third World* (1980); *Thailand: Society and Politics* (1981); *Capital and Power* (1987) and *Myths and Politics in Western Society* (forthcoming).

BRUCE GRANT is well known for his writings on international affairs. In recent years he has been a consultant to the Australian Minister for Foreign Affairs, and he is currently Chairman of the Australian-Indonesian Institute. His most recent publications include: *The Australian Dilemma: A New Kind of Western Society* (1983); and *Australia's Foreign Relations in the World of the 1990s*, with Gareth Evans (1991).

YOSHIYUKI HAGIWARA is Professor of Comparative Politics, Dakgeyo University. His research interests are in comparative politics of Southeast Asia and Japan and Southeast Asian countries after World War II. *ASEAN* (1983) and *Malaysian Politics* (1989) are among some of his publications.

B.A. HAMZAH is Assistant Director-General at the Institute of Strategic and International Studies, Malaysia. His publications include *The Spratleys: What Can Be Done to Enhance Confidence* (1990); *The Malaysian Exclusive Economic Zone: Some Legal Aspects* (1988); and *ASEAN-Dialogue Relations: An Analysis* (1989).

HAL HILL is Senior Fellow in Economics, Research School of Pacific Studies, Australian National University. He is also Head of the University's Indonesia Project, and editor of the *Bulletin of Indonesian Economic Studies*. His main research interests are the economies of ASEAN, especially Indonesia; industrialization and foreign investment in developing countries; and Australia's economic relations with the Asia-Pacific region. His books include *Export-Oriented Industrialisation: The ASEAN Experience*, with Mohamed Ariff (1985); *Foreign Investment and Industrialization in Indonesia* (1988); and *Unity and Diversity: Regional Economic Development in Indonesia since 1970*, editor and contributor (1989).

RYOKICHI HIRONO is Professor of Economics at Seikei University, Tokyo. His more recent publications include: *ASEAN-Japan Industrial Co-operation: An Overview*, co-editor M.K. Chng (1984); and *Industrial Restructuring in ASEAN and Japan: An Overview*, co-editors C.Y. Ng and Narongchai Akrasanee (1987).

PEARL Y. IMADA is Research Associate at the Resource Systems Institute of the East-West Centre, Hawaii. He research interests are in trade and direct foreign investment in Asian developing countries; the role of small-scale and labour-intensive industries in employment and exports of Asian developing countries; and changing industrialization patterns and policy issues. Her publications include the PITO Economic Brief Series, co-editor with Michael Plummer (1991) and *A Free Trade Area: Implications for ASEAN*, with Manuel Montes and Seiji Naya (1992).

The late HANS H. INDORF was the President of Asian Affairs Analysts, a Washington, D.C. consultancy, and a contributing editor of *Asian Affairs*. His works include: *Impediments to Regionalism in Southeast Asia: Bilateral Constraints Among Asean Member States* (1984); and *Linkage or Bondage: US Economic Relations with the ASEAN Region*, with Patrick M. Mayerchak (1989).

VLADIMIR I. IVANOV is Advanced Research Fellow, the Program on U.S.-Japan Relations, Center for International Affairs at Harvard University as well as Head, Asia-Pacific Region Studies Department, Center for Japanese and Pacific Studies, IMEMO. His publications include

Soviet Union in the Asia-Pacific Regional Affairs in the 1990s, editor and co-author (1991); *A Pacific Oriented Economy, Development Prospects of the Soviet Far Eastern Areas and Economic Cooperation in the Asia-Pacific Region*, co-author and editor (1991); and *The Mineral and Energy Resources of the Soviet Far East*, co-editor and co-author (1989).

CHANDRAN JESHURUN is a Senior Fellow at the Institute of Southeast Asian Studies. His publications include *Malaysian Defence Policy: A Study in Parliamentary Attitudes 1963–1973* (1980); *Arms and Defence in Southeast Asia*, editor (1989); and *Governments and Rebellions in Southeast Asia* (1985).

JUWONO SUDARSONO is Professor of Political Science, Faculty of Social and Political Science at the University of Indonesia in Jakarta. He has published widely on ASEAN and Indonesian political developments and foreign relations. Two Indonesian titles are: *Politik dan Pembangunan (Politics and Development)* (1982) and *Mata-Rantai Hubongan Luar Negeri Kita* [our foreign relations linkages] (1989).

AARON KARP is Guest Scholar at the Stockholm International Peace Research Institute and a researcher for the Stiftung Wissenschaft und Politik, Ebenhausen, Germany. His work focuses on weapons proliferation, arms transfers and regional military procurement, and has appeared in numerous articles and monographs, including the *1990 Report of the United Nations Secretary-General on the Spread of Nuclear Missiles.*

KHAW GUAT HOON is an Associate Professor of Political Science at the Universiti Sains Malaysia. She has published a number of articles on the international politics of Southeast Asia, especially on the evolution of ASEAN and its external relations.

SREE KUMAR is a Fellow at the Institute of Southeast Asian Studies where he specializes in Southeast Asian economic development. He has published on industrial development in the Johor-Singapore-Riau Growth Triangle (with Lee Tsao Yuan), and on the ASEAN Free Trade Area. He is currently working on the role of government in industrialization.

MOCHTAR KUSUMA-ATMADJA is presently a lawyer in private practice based in Jakarta. In addition to a distinguished career as an academic affiliated to various law schools in Indonesia and abroad, Professor Mochtar served as Minister for Justice of the Republic of Indonesia, 1974–77, and as Minister for Foreign Affairs of the Republic of Indonesia, 1978–88. He has published widely on legal and security issues affecting the region.

JULIET LAMONT is a Ph.D. candidate at the Department of Economics, University of California at Berkeley. In the course of collecting research materials for her dissertation, she has been affiliated with the Thai Development Research Institute (TDRI), Bangkok.

ROLF J. LANGHAMMER is Chief of Research Division "Industrialization and Foreign Trade" in the Development Economics Department, Kiel Institute of World Economics, Germany. His publications include *Trade in Services Between ASEAN and EC Member States: Case Studies for West Germany, France, and the Netherlands* (1991); *ASEAN and the EC: Trade in Tropical Agricultural Products*, co-editor H.C. Rieger (1988); and numerous articles.

LAU TEIK SOON is an Associate Professor in the Department of Political Science, National University of Singapore, as well as Member of Parliament, Singapore, and Chairman of the Singapore Institute of International Affairs (SIIA). Dr Lau has edited numerous books and published articles in the areas of international politics and security issues of the Asia-Pacific region. Among his most recent publications are: *ASEAN-South Korean Relations: Problems and Prospects*, co-editor Bilveer Singh (1990); and *Moving into the Pacific Century: The Changing Regional Order in the Asia-Pacific*, co-editor Leo Suryadinata (1988).

LEE LAI TO is Associate Professor as well as Deputy Head at the Department of Political Science, National University of Singapore. His research interests are on territorial conflicts in the

South China Sea and security issues in the Asia-Pacific. His latest publication is *The Re-unification of China — PRC-Taiwan Relations in Flux* (1991).

LEE POH PING is Professor at the Faculty of Economics and Administration, University of Malaya. He has written articles, monographs and books on Japan, Southeast Asia and the Asia-Pacific. His publications include *Chinese Society in Nineteenth Century Singapore* (1978); *Japan's Decision to Establish Malayawata* (1977); and *Japanese Direct Investment in Malaysia*, with Chee Peng Lim (1980).

MICHAEL LEIFER is Professor of International Relations and Pro-Director at the London School of Economics and Political Science whose staff he joined in 1969. He serves on the editorial boards of *Pacific Affairs* and *Pacific Review* and is a member of the advisory board of the Center for South-East Asian Studies of the School of Oriental and African Studies of the University of London. He is also a member of the Royal Institute of International Affairs and the International Institute of Strategic Studies. Professor Leifer's research interests have been primarily in Southeast Asia. His more recent books include *Indonesia's Foreign Policy* (1983); *The Balance of Power in East Asia* (1986); and *ASEAN and the Security of South-East Asia* (1990).

LIKHIT DHIRAVEGIN is Professor of the Faculty of Political Science, Thammasat University, Bangkok. His fields of interest are political development and social change, scope and method of political science, and the modernization of Japan and Thailand. Some of his numerous publications include *The Maiji Restoration (1868–1912) and the Chakkri Reformation (1868–1910): A Comparative Perspective* (1984); *Thai Politics: Selected Aspects of Development and Change* (1985); and *Demi-democracy: Thai Politics in Transition* (1992).

LINDA LOW is Senior Lecturer at the Department of Business Policy, National University of Singapore. Her research interests and publications are in the areas of public sector economics, social security, public enterprise and privatization, industrial and manpower development policies. She has authored/co-authored six books and numerous articles.

C.P.F. LUHULIMA is Senior Research Specialist at the Center for Political and Regional Studies, Indonesian Institute of Sciences, Jakarta. His current research interests are ASEAN, European Communities, ASEAN-EC Relations and Science and Technology policies. Some of his most recent publications are "Two Years After Manila Summit: The Future of ASEAN", *Indonesian Quarterly* XVII, no. 1 (First Quarter 1990); "ASEAN, the South Pacific Forum and the Changing Strategic Environment", *Indonesian Quarterly* XX, no. 2 (Second Quarter 1992); "ASEAN-European Community Relations: Some Dimensions of Inter-Regional Cooperation", *Indonesian Quarterly* XX, no. 3 (Third Quarter, 1992).

PETER LYON is Academic Secretary of the Institute of Commonwealth Studies and Reader in International Relations at the University of London. He has published extensively on Southeast Asia, the Commonwealth and third world matters generally, including War and Peace in South-East Asia (1969). He has been editor of *The Round Table: The Commonwealth Journal of International Affairs* since 1983.

SHIBUSAWA MASAHIDE has had a long and distinguished academic career, which has included affiliations with numerous universities in Japan, the United States, and Europe. He was most recently a Visiting Professor, School of Business Administration, Portland State University. Among his publications are *Is Japan a Part of Asia?* (1985); and *Pacific Asia, Perils and Promises* (1991).

DONALD G. McCLOUD is Senior Associate Director and Treasurer of the Midwest Universities Consortium for International Activities, Inc. (MUCIA), a consortium of ten of the most prestigious universities in the United States. Dr McCloud is concurrently an Adjunct Associate

Professor of Political Science at the Ohio State University where he team teaches a class on Southeast Asia with Professor R. William Liddle, and advises graduate students. Dr McCloud has published extensively and is a member of the editorial boards of *Asian Affairs* and *An American Review*.

MUBARIQ AHMAD is Senior Economic Research Associate, Center for Policy and Implementation Studies (CPIS), Jakarta, as well as Lecturer, Faculty of Economics University of Indonesia. His recent publications include *The Merits of Market Instrument: A Strategy of Evaluating Instrument for Sustainability*, with Linda Duncan (1982); and *Issues, Problems, and the Role of Timber Production in the Indonesian Economy* (1992). His research interests are external debt, commercial policy, industrial development, regional studies, environmental and natural resource economics.

HERMAN MUEGGE is the Head of the Regional and Countries Studies Branch, Industrial Policy and Perspective Division, Department for Programme and Project Development, for the United Nations Industrial Development Organization (UNIDO), in Vienna, Austria.

MYA THAN is a Research Fellow at the Institute of Southeast Asian Studies in Singapore. He was formerly a staff member of the Department of Research and Management Studies, Institute of Economics, Yangon, Myanmar. He was written extensively on social and economic aspects of agricultural and rural development. His current research interests involve developmental issues of transitional economies in mainland Southeast Asia including Vietnam, Laos, Cambodia and Myanmar. His recent publications include *Myanmar's External Trade: An Overview in the Southeast Asian Context* (1992) and *Myanmar Dilemmas and Options: The Challenges of Economic Transition in the 1990s*, co-editor Joseph L.H. Tan (1990).

G. NAIDU is an Associate Professor in the Applied Economics Division of the Faculty of Economics and Administration at Universiti Malaya. He specializes in the economics of transport. He holds a BA (Hons) from Universiti Malaya and a B. Litt from Oxford University.

NARONGCHAI AKRASANEE is Chairman of the Board and Chief Executive Officer of the General Finance and Securities Co. Ltd., Bangkok, Thailand. He has served as a member on several committees in both the public and private sectors in Thailand and was also a consultant to various local international organizations such as International Bank for Reconstruction and the Ford Foundation. He is director of fourteen companies in Thailand. He was also a member of the Council of Policy Advisors to P.M. Suchinda Kraprayoon and P.M. Chatchai Choonhavan as well as a representative to P.M. Anand Punyarachoon on ASEAN Economic Affairs. He has written numerous articles on economics.

SEIJI NAYA is Professor and Chairman, Department of Economics, University of Hawaii, Honolulu, Hawaii, and also a Joint Appointee in the Institute for Economic Development and Policy, at the East-West Center. He was Chief Economist of the Asian Development Bank in Manila from 1980 to 1983. He has served as advisor and/or consultant to such organizations as the ASEAN Secretariat, UNDP, UNCTAD, USAID and the International Development Center of Japan. His research has focused on international economic problems of Asian countries and he has written many professional articles and books on the subject. His recent publications include *Asian Development: Economic Success and Policy Lessons* (1989); *ASEAN-U.S. Initiative: Assessment and Recommendations for Improved Economic Relations*, with K.S. Sandhu et al. (1989); *Towards an ASEAN Trade Area*, with Pearl Imada and Manuel Montes (1987); and *A Free Trade Area: Implications for ASEAN*, with Pearl Imada and Manual Montes (1992).

NG CHEE YUEN is Senior Fellow at the Institute of Southeast Asian Studies. He has co-ordinated projects and edited two books on privatization and marketization in ASEAN. His forthcoming book is *Privatization in the Asia-Pacific Region: A Survey of the Literature.*

RHONDDA M. NICHOLAS holds a Master of Philosophy degree from Griffith University. She has been a senior official in the Australian Department of Defence and is currently a senior official in the Australian Department of Transport and Communications.

NOORDIN SOPIEE is the Director-General, Institute of Strategic and International Studies (ISIS) Malaysia and columnist for the *New Straits Times*, Malaysia and the *Business Times*, Singapore. He was formerly group Editor-in-Chief, New Straits Times Press. In 1986–87 he was the Executive Director, The Secretariat of the Group of Fourteen on ASEAN Economic Co-operation and Integration. He has published widely on regional security and political affairs. Some of his more recent publications include: *Regional Cooperation in the Pacific Era*, editor (1989) and *The Cambodian Conflict 1978–1989* (1989).

PETER O'BRIEN has been a regular consultant with the Regional and Countries Studies Branch, Industrial Policy and Perspective Division, Department for Programme and Project Development, of the United Nations Industrial Development Organization (UNIDO), in Vienna, Austria.

JAKOB OETAMA is a publisher and journalist with the *Kompas Morning Daily* (Jakarta). He has published widely on Indonesian political and security issues, as well as international affairs. One of his most recent publications is *Menuju Masyarakat Baru Indonesia: Antisipasi terhadap Tantangan Abad XXI* [Towards a new Indonesian society: Anticipating the challenges of the 21st century] (1990).

SABURO OKITA is Chairman of the Institute for Domestic and International Policy Studies (IDIPS), Chancellor of the International University of Japan (IUJ), Chairman of the Japan World Wide Fund for Nature (WWF, Japan), and Honorary Chairman of the Japan National Committee of Pacific Economic Cooperation Conference (JANCPEC). He is the author of many articles and books in both English and Japanese, on Japan's economy, Asian economic development, and international relations. Two of his most recent publications are: *Japan in the World Economy of the 1980s* (1989); and *Approaching the 21st Century: Japan's Role* (1990).

TRINIDAD S. OSTERIA is Associate Professor of De La Salle University, Philippines. Prior to this she was Fellow at the Institute of Southeast Asian Studies where she compiled *The Poor in ASEAN Cities: Perspectives in Health Care Management* (1991) and edited *Women in Health Development: Case Studies of Selected Ethnic Groups in Rural Asia-Pacific* (1992). She has been the recipient of research grants from Ford Foundation and the International Development Research Centre to undertake studies on the health situation of the urban poor and the governments' response to the health challenges of urbanization in the ASEAN region.

NORMAN D. PALMER is Professor Emeritus of Political Science, University of Pennsylvania. He has visited Asia frequently over a career spanning more than forty years, and has taught and carried out research for several years in India, and for shorter periods in Pakistan, South Korea, and the People's Republic of China. Among his recent books are *The United States and India: The Dimensions of Influence* (1984); *Westward Watch: The United States and the Changing Western Pacific* (1987); and *The New Regionalism in Asia and the Pacific* (1991).

MARI PANGESTU is Head of the Department of Economics, Center for Strategic and International Studies (CSIS), Jakarta and Lecturer at the Faculty of Economics, University of Indonesia. Among her most recent publications are: *The Technological Challenge of the Pacific*, co-editor with Hadi Soesastro and David MacKendrick (1990); "The Political Economy of Adjustments" in *Essays in Honor of Prof. Mohammad Sadli*, edited by Mohd. Arsjad Anwar et al. (forthcoming); and *An Assessment of Financial Reform in Indonesia: 1983–90*, with John Chany(forthcoming).

J.C. PARREÑAS is Director as well as Associate Professor at the Institute of International and Strategic Studies, Center for Research and Communication, Philippines. His publications include *Restructuring for Stability: Economic, Political and Security Dimensions for Japanese-Philippine-U.S. Relations in the 1990s* (1989); *The Long Shadow of Perestroika: Implications of Gorbachev's Policies on Philippine Security* (1989); *and Germany and the Future of Europe: The Power of Culture* (1990).

PATYA SAIHOO is a Visiting Foreign Professor at the University of Tsukuba, Japan. He is also Professor Emeritus, Chulalongkorn University, Bangkok. Now that he is no longer engaged in full-time campus activities, he intends to continue observing the increasing impact of international, regional, and national economic and political developments on traditional societies and cultures of Southeast Asia.

MICHAEL PLUMMER is Research Associate, Institute for Economic Development and Policy, East-West Center as well as Associate Professor with the Monetery Institute of International Studies. He was one of the co-ordinators for the report on *The ASEAN-U.S. Initiative: Assessment and Recommendations for Improved Economic Relations* (1989). His publications include *The UNDP-ASEAN Relationship: Partnership in Progress*, with Seiji Naya and Cesar E.A. Virata (1991); *The ASEAN Industrial Joint Venture: Problems and Opportunities* (1990); and *ASEAN Economic Co-operation for the 1990s* (1992). His fields of interest are international economics and international development.

PURIFICACION V. QUISUMBING is presently the Regional Adviser for External Relations and Social Mobilization for the UNICEF East Asia and Pacific Regional Office located in Bangkok. Among her publications are: *EEC and ASEAN: Two Regional Community Experiences* (1983); and *Directory of ASEAN Legal Scholars*, with Myrna S. Feliciano (1986).

HANS CHRISTOPH RIEGER joined the South Asia Institute, Heidelberg University in 1965, where he is now a Senior Research Fellow. While on leave from 1980 to 1987 he was the representative of the Konrad Adenauer Foundation in Singapore and attached to the ASEAN Economic Research Unit (AERU) of the Institute of Southeast Asian Studies. Dr Rieger has spent many years in various countries of Asia and has published widely on various issues of development economics, including ASEAN economic co-operation. One of his latest publications is *ASEAN: A Handbook*, compiler (1992).

KERNIAL S. SANDHU is the Director of the Institute of Southeast Asian Studies. Among his most recent publications are *Management of Success: The Moulding of Modern Singapore*, co-editor Paul Wheatley (1989) and *Indian Communities in Southeast Asia*, co-editor A. Mani (1992).

SARASIN VIRAPHOL is a career foreign service officer with the Ministry of Foreign Affairs, Thailand. He has served in ambassadorial positions in major Thai missions and senior positions in the Ministry of Foreign Affairs. Amongst his scholarly publications are: *ASEAN and Cooperation in the Field of Security* (1982) and *Domestic Considerations of Thailand's Policy towards the Indochina States* (1982).

JOHAN SARAVANAMUTTU is Associate Professor at the School of Social Services, Universiti Sains Malaysia. He is also a Council Member and Co-ordinator of the Southeast Asian Caucus, Asia Pacific Peace Research Association. His publications include *The Dilemma of Independence: Two Decades of Malaysia's Foreign Policy 1957–1977* (1983); *ASEAN Non-Governmental Organizations: A Study of Their Role, Objectives and Activities*, with Sharom Ahmat (1986); and *Images of Malaysia*, co-editor Muhammad Ikmal Said (1991).

DAVID L. SCHULZE is currently senior lecturer in the Department of Economics at the University of New England, Armidale, Australia. His research interests include the financial development of ASEAN economies as well as the linkages between financial and real development. His latest publication in these areas is *Domestic Financial Institutions in Singapore: Public Sector Competition* (1990).

SHANKAR SHARMA is a Fellow at the Institute of Southeast Asian Studies. He has published six monographs (edited or authored) and more than 25 articles on energy and the economy of the Asia-Pacific region. His recent books are *Energy Markets and Policies in ASEAN*, co-editor Fereidun Fesharaki (1991) and *Global Oil Trends: The Asia-Pacific Market in the 1990s*, co-editor Joseph L.H. Tan (1991). He is also an editor of *ASEAN Economic Bulletin*, a Consultant Editor of *Hydrocarbon Asia* and a member of World Energy Council Committee of Energy Issues of Developing Countries (1990–92).

SHAROM AHMAT is currently Academic Adviser to the University of Brunei Darussalam. He has previously served at the University of Singapore as a Lecturer and Senior Lecturer in History and at the Universiti Sains Malaysia as Professor of History and Deputy Vice-Chancellor. He has written widely in the fields of education and history. Among his publications are: *Tradition and Change in a Malay State: A Study of the Economic and Political Development of Kedah, 1878–1923* (1984); and *Muslim Society, Higher Education and Development in Southeast Asia*, co-editor Sharon Siddique (1987).

SHARON SIDDIQUE is Deputy Director of the Institute of Southeast Asian Studies, Singapore. Her publications include *Singapore's Little India: past, present and future*, with Nirmala Puru Shotam (1982); *Readings in Islam in Southeast Asia*, co-compilers Ahmad Ibrahim and Yasmin Hussain (1986); and *Islam and Society in Southeast Asia*, co-editor Taufik Abdullah (1987).

SHELDON W. SIMON is Professor of Political Science and former Director of the Center for Asian Studies at Arizona State University. He is the author or editor of seven books, including *East Asian Security in the Post-Cold War Era* (forthcoming). Dr Simon has published approximately 80 scholarly articles and book chapters in such journals as *Asian Survey, Pacific Affairs, Current History, International Journal, The Pacific Review, Contemporary Southeast Asia, Third World Quarterly, Australian Quarterly*, and the *New Zealand International Review*. He is a consultant on Asian affairs to the U.S. Government and currently Vice President of the International Studies Association and a member of the Contemporary Affairs Council on Southeast Asia for The Asia Society.

HADI SOESASTRO is the Executive Director of the Centre for Strategic and International Studies (CSIS) in Jakarta, Indonesia. He is also a Lecturer in Economics at the Faculty of Social and Political Science, University of Indonesia (1979–present), and teaches policy analysis at the Postgraduate Faculty, University of Indonesia (1985-present). He has published widely on the political economy of the region, with special reference to Indonesia.

ESTRELLA D. SOLIDUM is Professor at the Department of Political Science, University of the Philippines. Her areas of research interest are Southeast Asian governments and politics, international relations, regionalism, and security. Her publications include *The Small State: Security and World Peace*, with Seah Chee Meow (1991); *Towards a Southeast Asian Community* (1974); *Bilateral Summitry in ASEAN* (1982); and *Decision-Making in an ASEAN Complementation Scheme: The Automotive Industry* (1987).

SOMSAK TAMBUNLERTCHAI is Co-ordinator, International Trade and Regional Co-operation Programme, APDC and Lecturer in the Faculty of Economics, Thammasat University, Bangkok, Thailand. He has published widely, particularly on foreign trade issues. Among his publications are: *Employment Effects of Small-Medium Scale Industries in Thailand* (1978) and *Import Substitution Export Expansion: An Analysis of the Industrialization Experience in Thailand* (1981).

RICHARD W. STUBBS is Associate Professor, Department of Political Science, McMaster University, Canada. His current research interests are leadership, the major powers and Southeast Asia. His publications are *Hearts and Minds in Guerrilla Warfare: The Malaysian Emergency 1948–60*, compiler (1989) and *Vietnam: Facing the 1990s* (1989).

JANG-WON SUH is Vice President of the Korea Institute for International Economic Policy (KIEP). He has written numerous articles and books including *Strategies for Industrial Development: Concept and Policy Issues*, editor (1989); *Northeast Asian Economic Cooperation: Perspectives and Challenges*, editor (1991); and *Cooperation in Small and Medium-scale Industries in ASEAN*, editor (1992).

SUKHUMBHAND PARIBATRA is Director, Institute of Security and International Studies, Chulalongkorn University, Thailand. He is also an Assistant Professor in International Relations, Faculty of Political Science, Chulalongkorn University. He has published widely on regional security issues. His publications include: *Common Insecurity: International Politics in the Era of Confrontation* (in Thai, 1984) and *Durable Stability in Southeast Asia*, co-editor Kusuma Snitwongse (1987).

GERALD TAN has taught economics at the University of London, Oxford University and the University of Singapore, and has worked as a research economist with the International Wool Secretariat (London) and the Applied Research Corporation (Singapore). At present, he teaches economics at Flinders University as well as at the Elton Mayo School of Management, University of South Australia. He has published numerous articles in professional journals, and is the author of *The Newly Industrializing Countries of Asia* (1991).

TAN KONG YAM is currently the Director, Research and Planning Division at the Ministry of Trade and Industry, Singapore. He is on leave of absence from his position as Senior Lecturer, Department of Business Policy, National University of Singapore.

PUSHPA THAMBIPILLAI teaches Politics and International Relations in the Department of Public Policy and Administration, University of Brunei Darussalam. Her interests are in regional co-operation in Southeast Asia and international relations in the Asia-Pacific region. One of her most recent publications is *Soviet Studies in the Asia-Pacific Region*, co-editor Charles E. Morrison (1986).

The late ROBERT O. TILMAN was professor of Political Science at North Carolina State University and has published widely on Southeast Asia. Amongst his most notable publications is *Southeast Asia and the Enemy Beyond: ASEAN Perceptions of External Threats* (1987).

TOH MUN HENG is Senior Lecturer at the Department of Business Policy, National University of Singapore. His research interests and publications are in the areas of econometric modelling, input-output analysis, international trade, population and manpower studies and transportation economics. In addition to four books, he has published numerous articles in his areas of research.

FRANCISCO ORREGO VICUÑA practises international law in Santiago. He is President of the Chilean Council on Foreign Relations and is a member of the Commission for the Settlement of Disputes between Chile and the United States. He is currently the President and Vice-president of the Chilean Delegation to the Law of the Sea Conference, and Ambassador to Great Britain. He was Professor of International Law at the School of Law and the Institute of International Studies, University of Chile and has been visiting professor at the Hague Academy of International Law, Stanford University, and the School of Law of the University of Paris (Paris II).

CHARAN D. WADHVA is currently Research Professor at the Centre for Policy Research, New Delhi. He has several books and articles in professional journals including *Some Problems of India's Economic Policy*, editor (1977); *Rural Banks for Rural Development* (1980).

NORBERT WAGNER is currently the Konrad Adenauer Foundation representative in Moscow, attached to the Institute of Europe, Academy of Sciences. He was a Visiting Fellow at ISEAS from 1987 to 1990, and representative of the Konrad Adenauer Foundation (Germany) in Singapore. He has written extensively on ASEAN and the EC. Among his publications are *ASEAN and the EC: European Investment in ASEAN* (1989); *Privatization and Deregulation in ASEAN and the EC: Making Markets More Effective*, co-editor Jacques Pelkmans (1990); and *ASEAN and the EC: The Impact of 1992*, editor (1991).

JOHN E. WALSH was a Research Associate and Project Co-ordinator at the Culture Learning Institute, East-West Center, Hawaii. He is now retired.

JUSUF WANANDI is member, Board of Directors, and Chairman, Supervisory Board, Centre for Strategic and International Studies, Jakarta. Among his publications are *Security Dimensions of the Asia-Pacific Region in the 1980s* (1979); *Economic, Political, and Security Issues in Southeast Asia in the 1980s*, co-editor Robert A. Scalapino (1982); and numerous articles.

WANG GUNGWU is at present the Vice-Chancellor of the University of Hong Kong, having formerly been Professor of History at the University of Malaya and Professor of Far Eastern History and the Director of the Research School of Pacific Studies at the Australian National University in Canberra. Professor Wang has published several books and many articles and essays in the fields of Chinese and Southeast Asian history.

O.W. WOLTERS is a member of the Cornell Southeast Asia Program, Cornell University. He has published widely on the history of Southeast Asia. His publications include *Early Indonesian Commerce: A Study of the Origins of Srivijaya* (1967); *History, Culture, and Region in Southeast Asian Perspectives* (1982); and *Two Essays on Dai-Viet in the Fourteenth Century* (1988).

ALINE K. WONG is Professor of Sociology at the National University of Singapore. She specializes in urban sociology, population and development, and women's studies. Among her publications are: *Ethnicity and Fertility in Southeast Asia: Comparative Analysis*, with Ng Shui Meng (1985); and *Housing a Nation: Twenty-five Years of Public Housing in Singapore*, co-editor Stephen Yeh (1985). During her sabbaticals he has been affiliated with the Center for Population Studies, Harvard University; St. Anthony's College, Oxford University; and the Institute of Southeast Asian Studies, Singapore. She is currently on secondment from the National University to the Ministry of Health, as the Minister of State for Health.

JOHN WONG is Director of the Institute of East Asian Political Economy (IEAPE), Singapore. The main research focus of IEAPE at present is the political and economic aspects of contemporary East Asia, particularly China. Professor Wong has previously taught Economics at the National University of Singapore (1971–90), and at the University of Hong Kong (1966–71). He has also taught at Florida State University briefly as a Fulbright Visiting Professor. He has held visiting appointments with Harvard's Fairbank Center, Yale's Economic Growth Center and Oxford's St. Anthony's College; and he has been an Academic Visitor at Toronto and Stanford. He has written 8 books and over 100 journal articles and conference papers on the economic development issues and various aspects of the Asia-Pacific economies, including China, ASEAN, and the NIEs.

STEVEN C.M. WONG is a Strategist for Zalik Securities (ZS) in Kuala Lumpur. After completing his undergraduate and post-graduate degrees at the University of Melbourne, Australia, he joined the Management Consulting Division of Arthur Young and Company, specializing in financial planning and control. In 1985, he joined the Institute of Strategic and International Studies (ISIS) Malaysia as a Researcher. He was subsequently appointed Senior Researcher and the Assistant Director-General (International Economics). He has also served as the Secretary General of the Malaysian Committee for Pacific Economic Cooperation and Executive Director of the Centre for Japan Studies.

ZAKARIA HAJI AHMAD is Associate Professor in the Strategic and Security Studies Unit of the Universiti Kebangsaan Malaysia. During 1992–93 he is on sabbatical leave at the National University of Singapore. His research interests are varied and he is currently researching on military leadership in Malaysia. His latest book, co-authored with M. Shibusawa and Brian Bridges, is *Pacific Asia in the 1990s* (1992).

DOCUMENTATION

The Asean Declaration
(Bangkok Declaration)
Bangkok, 8 August 1967

The Presidium Minister for Political Affairs/Minister for Foreign Affairs of Indonesia, the Deputy Prime Minister of Malaysia, the Secretary of Foreign Affairs of the Philippines, the Minister for Foreign Affairs of Singapore and the Minister of Foreign Affairs of Thailand:

MINDFUL of the existence of mutual interests and common problems among countries of South-East Asia and convinced of the need to strengthen further the existing bonds of regional solidarity and cooperation;

DESIRING to establish a firm foundation for common action to promote regional cooperation in South-East Asia in the spirit of equality and partnership and thereby contribute towards peace, progress and prosperity in the region;

CONSCIOUS that in an increasingly interdependent world, the cherished ideals of peace, freedom, social justice and economic well-being are best attained by fostering good understanding, good neighbourliness and meaningful cooperation among the countries of the region already bound together by ties of history and culture;

CONSIDERING that the countries of South-East Asia share a primary responsibility for strengthening the economic and social stability of the region and ensuring their peaceful and progressive national development, and that they are determined to ensure their stability and security from external interference in any form or manifestation in order to preserve their national identities in accordance with the ideals and aspirations of their peoples;

AFFIRMING that all foreign bases are temporary and remain only with the expressed concurrence of the countries concerned and are not intended to be used directly or indirectly to subvert the national independence and freedom of States in the area or prejudice the orderly processes of their national development;

DO HEREBY DECLARE:

FIRST, the establishment of an Association for Regional Cooperation among the countries of South-East Asia to be known as the Association of South-East Asian Nations (ASEAN).

SECOND, that the aims and purposes of the Association shall be:

1 To accelerate the economic growth, social progress and cultural development in the region through joint endeavours in the spirit of equality and partnership in order to strengthen the foundation for a prosperous and peaceful community of South-East Asian Nations;

2 To promote regional peace and stability through abiding respect for justice and the rule of law in the relationship among countries of the region and adherence to the principles of the United Nations Charter;

3 To promote active collaboration and mutual assistance on matters of common interest in the economic, social, cultural, technical, scientific and administrative fields;

4 To provide assistance to each other in the form of training ar d research facilities in the educational, professional, technical and administrative spheres;

5 To collaborate more effectively for the greater utilization of their agriculture and industries, the expansion of their trade, including the study of the problems of international commodity trade, the improvement of their transportation and communications facilities and the raising of the living standards of their peoples;

6 To promote South-East Asian studies;

7 To maintain close and beneficial cooperation with existing international and regional organizations with similar aims and purposes, and explore all avenues for even closer cooperation among themselves.

THIRD, that to carry out these aims and purposes, the following machinery shall be established:

1 Annual Meeting of Foreign Ministers, which shall be by rotation and referred to as ASEAN Ministerial Meeting. Special Meetings of Foreign Ministers may be convened as required.

2 A Standing Committee, under the chairmanship of the Foreign Minister of the host country or his representative and having as its members the accredited Ambassadors of the other member countries, to carry on the work of the Association in between Meetings of Foreign Ministers.

3 Ad-Hoc Committees and Permanent Committees of specialists and officials on specific subjects.

4 A National Secretariat in each member country to carry out the work of the Association on behalf of that country and to service the Annual or Special Meetings of Foreign Ministers, the Standing Committee and such other committees as may hereafter be established.

FOURTH, that the Association is open for participation to all States in the South-East Asian Region subscribing to the aforementioned aims, principles and purposes.

FIFTH, that the Association represents the collective will of the nations of South-East Asia to bind themselves together in friendship and cooperation and, through joint efforts and sacrifices, secure for their peoples and for posterity the blessings of peace, freedom and prosperity.

DONE in Bangkok on the Eighth Day of August in the Year One Thousand Nine Hundred and Sixty-Seven.

FOR THE REPUBLIC OF INDONESIA: FOR THE REPUBLIC OF THE PHILIPPINES: FOR THE REPUBLIC OF SINGAPORE:

ADAM MALIK
Presidium Minister for
Political Affairs
Minister for Foreign Affairs

NARCISO RAMOS
Secretary of Foreign Affairs

S. RAJARATNAM
Minister of Foreign Affairs

FOR MALAYSIA:

FOR THE KINGDOM OF THAILAND:

TUN ABDUL RAZAK
Minister of Defence and
Minister of National Development

THANAT KHOMAN
Minister of Foreign Affairs

Zone of Peace, Freedom and Neutrality Declaration

(Kuala Lumpur Declaration)

27 November 1971

We the Foreign Ministers of Indonesia, Malaysia, the Philippines, Singapore and the Special Envoy of the National Executive Council of Thailand:

FIRMLY believing in the merits of regional cooperation which has drawn our countries to cooperate together in the economic, social and cultural fields in the Association of South East Asian Nations;

DESIROUS of bringing about a relaxation of international tension and of achieving a lasting peace in South East Asia;

INSPIRED by the worthy aims and objectives of the United Nations, in particular by the principles of respect for the sovereignty and territorial integrity of all states, abstention from threat or use of force, peaceful settlement of international disputes, equal rights and self-determination and non-interference in the affairs of States;

BELIEVING in the continuing validity of the "Declaration of the Promotion of World Peace and Co-operation" of the Bandung Conference of 1955 which, among others, enunciates the principles by which States may coexist peacefully;

RECOGNIZING the right of every state, large or small, to lead its national existence free from outside interference in its internal affairs as this interference will adversely affect its freedom, independence and integrity;

DEDICATED to the maintenance of peace, freedom and independence unimpaired;

BELIEVING in the need to meet present challenges and new developments by cooperating with all peace and freedom loving nations, both within and outside the region, in the furtherance of world peace, stability and harmony;

COGNIZANT of the significant trend towards establishing nuclear-free zones, as in the "Treaty for Prohibition of Nuclear Weapons in Latin America" and the Lusaka Declaration proclaiming Africa a nuclear-free zone, for the purpose of promoting world peace and security by reducing the areas of international conflicts and tensions;

REITERATING our commitment to the principle in the Bangkok Declaration which established ASEAN in 1967, "that the countries of South-East Asia share a primary responsibility for strengthening the economic and social stability of the region and ensuring their peaceful and progressive national development, and that they are determined to ensure their stability and security from external interference in any form or manifestation in order to preserve their national identities in accordance with the ideals and aspirations of their peoples";

AGREEING that the neutralization of South East Asia is a desirable objective and that we should explore ways and means of bringing about its realization; and

CONVINCED that the time is propitious for joint action to give effective expression to the deeply felt desire of the peoples of South East Asia to ensure the conditions of peace and stability indispensable to their independence and their economic and social well-being,

DO HEREBY STATE:

1 That Indonesia, Malaysia, the Philippines, Singapore and Thailand are determined to exert initially necessary efforts to secure the recognition of, and respect for, South-East Asia as a Zone of Peace, Freedom and Neutrality, free from any form or manner of interference by outside Powers;

2 That South-East Asian countries should make concerted efforts to broaden the areas of cooperation which would contribute to their strength, solidarity and closer relationship.

DONE at Kuala Lumpur on Saturday, the 27th of November 1971.

LIST OF ABBREVIATIONS

List of Abbreviations

AARB	ASEAN Agriculture Research Co-ordinating Board.
ABC	ASEAN Brussels Committee.
ACCRRIS	ASEAN Co-ordinating Committee for the Reconstruction and Rehabilitation of Indochina States.
ACEID	ASEAN Centre for Education and Innovation for Development.
ADB	Asian Development Bank.
AECF	ASEAN Education Co-operation Fund.
AEEM	ASEAN-EC Economic Ministers.
AEGE	ASEAN Expert Group on the Environment.
AEM	ASEAN Economic Ministers.
AEMM	ASEAN Economic Ministers Meeting.
AFC	ASEAN Finance Corporation.
AFTA	ASEAN Free Trade Area.
AGTC	ASEAN General Trading Corporation.
AHRA	ASEAN Hotels and Restaurants Association.
AIC	ASEAN Industrial Complementation scheme.
AIDC	Asian Industrial Development Council.
AIEDP	Asian Institute for Economic Development and Planning.
AIEPA	Asian Institute for Economic Development and Planning.
AIJV	ASEAN Industrial Joint Venture scheme.
AIM	Asian Institute of Management.
AIP	ASEAN Industrial Projects.
AIPO	ASEAN Inter-Parliamentary Organization.

AIT	Asian Institute of Technology.
AMM	ASEAN Ministerial Meeting.
ANCOM	Andean Common Market.
APEC	Asia-Pacific Economic Co-operation.
APEID	Asia and the Pacific Programme of Educational Innovation for Development.
APO	Asian Productivity Organization.
ASA	Association of Southeast Asia.
ASAIHL	Association of Southeast Asian Institutions of Higher Learning.
ASCOJA	ASEAN Council of Japan Alumni.
ASCOPE	ASEAN Council on Petroleum.
ASEAN	Association of Southeast Asian Nations.
ASEAN PMC	ASEAN Post-Ministerial Conferences.
ASEAN-CCI	ASEAN Chambers of Commerce and Industry.
ASEP	ASEAN Environment Programme.
ASIC	ASEAN Small and Medium Industries Centre.
ASMI	ASEAN Small and Medium Industries.
ASOD	ASEAN Senior officials on Drug Matters.
ASOEAN	ASEAN Senior Officials on the Environment.
ASPAC	Asian and Pacific Council.
ATDC	ASEAN Technology Development Centre.
BIOTROP	Regional Centre for Tropical Biology.
CADEX	Council of ASEAN Directors of Extension.
CCOP	Committee for Co-ordination of Joint Prospecting for Minerals in Asian Offshore Areas.
CEPAL Review	Economic Commission for Latin America Review.
CEPT	Common Effective Preferential Tariff.
COCI	Committee of Culture and Information.
COFAB	Committee on Finance and Banking.
COFAF	Committee on Food, Agriculture, and Forestry.
COIME	Committee on Industry, Minerals, and Energy.
COSD	Committee of Social Development.
COSD	Committee on Social Development.

COST	Committee of Science and Technology.
COTAC	Committee on Transport and Communications.
COTT	Committee on Trade and Tourism.
CPSC	Colombo Plan Staff College.
CSCE	Conference on Security and Co-operation in Europe.
EAEC	East Asian Economic Caucus.
EC	European Community.
ECAFE	Economic Commission for Asia and the Far East.
EEC	European Economic Community.
FASA	Federation of ASEAN Shipowners Association.
FASC	Federation of ASEAN Shippers Council.
FASMI	Federation of ASEAN Small and Medium Industries.
FATA	Federation of ASEAN Travel Agents.
GATT	General Agreement on Tariffs and Trade.
GSP	Generalized System of Preferences.
IAII	Intra-ASEAN Industrial Investment.
IBSRAM	International Board for Soil Research and Management.
ICLARM	International Centre for Living Aquatic Resources Management.
IGOs	Inter-governmental Organizations.
INNOTEC	Regional Centre for Educational Innovation and Technology.
IWPTC	Integrated Work Programme in Transportation and Communications.
JICA	Japan International Co-operation Agency.
LAFTA	Latin American Free Trade Association.
LAIA	Latin American Integration Association.
MAPHILINDO	Malaysia, Philippines, Indonesia.
MCEDSEA	Ministerial Conference for Economic Development in Southeast Asia.
MINEDAP	Ministers of Education and those responsible for Economic Planning in Asia and the Pacific.
MOFERT	Ministry of Foreign Economic Relations and Trade.
MOP	Margin of Preference.
NAFTA	North American Free Trade Area.
NFCs	National Flag Carriers.

NGOs	Non-Governmental Organizations.
NIEs	Newly Industrialized Economies.
NTBs	Non-tariff barriers.
NTOs	National Tourism Organization.
NWFZ	Nuclear Weapons Free Zone.
OAM	Other ASEAN Ministers.
OECD	Organization for Economic Co-operation and Development.
OPIL	Overseas Private Investment Corporation.
PBEC	Pacific Business Economic Council.
PECC	Pacific Economic Co-operation Conference.
PNOC	Philippines National Oil Corporation.
PTA	Preferential Trading Arrangements.
RECSAM	Regional Centre for Education in Science and Mathematics.
RELC	Regional Language Centre.
RIC	Regional Industry Club.
RIHED	Regional Institute of Higher Education and Development.
SCCAN	Special Coordinating Committee of ASEAN Nations.
SCONTE	Society for the Conservation of National Treasures and the Environment.
SCOT	Sub-committee on Tourism.
SEACEN	Southeast Asian Central Banks.
SEAMEO	Southeast Asian Ministers of Education Organization.
SEARCA	Centre for Graduate Studies and Research in Agriculture.
SEATO	Southeast Asia Treaty Organization.
SEOM	Senior Economic Officials' Meeting.
SOM	Senior Officials Meeting.
SPAFA	Project in Archaeology and Fine Arts.
TROPMED	Tropical Medicine and Public Health Project.
UNDP	United Nations Development Programme.
UNESCO	United Nations Educational, Scientific, and Cultural Organization.
UP-ISSI	University of Philippines — Institute of Small-scale Industries in the Philippines.
WGIC	Working Group on Industrial Co-operation.
ZOPFAN	Zone of Peace, Freedom, and Neutrality.

BIBLIOGRAPHY

Bibliography

"A Few Facts About Privatization in the Philippines". *IPP Bulletin* 1, no. 2 (February 1987).

Abe, Kiyoshi. "Economic Co-operation among the ASEAN Countries and Japan". In *Security in the ASEAN Region: Proceedings and Papers of an International Symposium*. Tokyo: Takushoku University, 1983.

Acharya, Amitav. "Arms Proliferation Issues in ASEAN: Towards a More 'Conventional' Defence Posture?" *Contemporary Southeast Asia* 10, no. 3 (December 1988).

AERU. *ASEAN: The Tasks Ahead*. Singapore: Institute of Southeast Asian Studies, 1987.

"Air Force of Kampuchea Liberation Army". *International Air Forces and Military Aircraft Directory*. Stapleford, Essex: Aviation Advisory Services, 1988.

Akrasanee, N. and Koomsup P. "Economic Development of Thailand and ASEAN Economic Co-operation with Special Reference to Commodity Problems". In *Asean in a Changing Pacific and World Economy*. 10th Pacific Trade and Development Conference, Australian National University, 1979.

_____ et al. *ASEAN and the Pacific Community*. Jakarta: Centre for Strategic and International Studies, May 1981.

_____, ed. *ASEAN-Japan Relations: Trade and Development*. Singapore: Institute of Southeast Asian Studies, 1983.

_____ and Somsak Tambunlertchai. "Enhancing Cooperation between the Government and the Private Sector within the Framework of ASEAN Industrial Cooperation". *Development and South-South Cooperation* 5, no. 9 (December 1989).

_____ and Likhit Dhiravegin. "Trade and Development in Thai-Japanese Relations". In Akrasanee, ed., *ASEAN-Japan Relations*.

_____ and Hans Christoph Rieger, eds. *ASEAN-EEC Economic Relations*. Singapore: Institute of Southeast Asian Studies, 1982.

_____. *Thailand and ASEAN Economic Co-operation*. Singapore: Institute of Southeast Asian Studies, 1981.

Alagappa, Muthiah. "Asean Institutional Framework and Modus Operandi: Recommendations for Change". In *ASEAN at the Crossroads: Obstacles, Options and Opportunities in Economic Co-operation*, edited by Noordin Sopiee, Chew Lay See, and Lim Siang Jin. Kuala Lumpur: Institute of Strategic and International Studies, 1987.

_____. "A Nuclear Weapons Free Zone in Southeast Asia: Problems and Prospects". *Australian Outlook*, December 1987.

_____. "U.S.-ASEAN Security Relations: Challenges and Prospects". *Contemporary Southeast Asia* 11, no. 1 (June 1989).

Alatas, Ali. "North-South Issues and Their Relevance to ASEAN". In *ASEAN Security and Economic Development*, edited by Karl D. Jackson and M. Hadi Soesastro. Berkeley, California: Institute of East Asian Studies, University of California, 1984.

Alburo, Florian A. "The ASEAN Summit and ASEAN Economic Cooperation". In *Economic Development in East and Southeast Asia: Essays in Honor of Professor Shinichi Ichimura*, edited by Seiji Naya and Akira Takayama. Singapore: Institute of Southeast Asian Studies, and Honolulu: East-West Center, 1990.

Allen, Thomas W. *The ASEAN Report*, Vol. 1. Hong Kong: Dow Jones Publishing Co., 1979.

Ang, B.W. "ASEAN Energy Demand: Current Trends and Future Outlook". *Energy* 14, no. 12 (December 1989).

Ang, Beng Wah. "ASEAN Energy Use and its Relation to Economic Growth". *ASEAN Economic Bulletin* 2, no. 1 (July 1985).

_____. "Oil Substitution in ASEAN: Problems and Prospects". *Contemporary Southeast Asia* 7, no. 2 (September 1985).

Anon. "1933–1983: 50 Years of the Malaysian Army". *Sorotan Darat* (The House Journal of the Malaysian Army), no. 1 (March 1983).

Antolik, Michael. "ASEAN and SAARC Revisited: More Lessons". *Contemporary Southeast Asia* 9, no. 3 (December 1987).

_____. "The Pattern of ASEAN Summitry". *Contemporary Southeast Asia* 10, no. 4 (March 1989).

_____. *ASEAN and the Diplomacy of Accommodation*. Armonk, N.Y.: M.E. Sharpe Inc., 1990.

_____. "ASEAN's Singapore Rendezvous: Just Another Summit?" *Contemporary Southeast Asia* 14, no. 2 (September 1992).

Ariff, Mohamed. *Malaysia and ASEAN Economic Co-operation*. Singapore: Institute of Southeast Asian Studies, 1981.

_____. "Economic Relations Between ASEAN and Australia". *Economic Review* 63 (March 1987).

_____. [Review of] *ASEAN-South Asia Economic Relations* by Charan D. Wadhva and Mukul G. Asher. *Asia Pacific Journal of Management* 4, no. 3 (May 1987).

_____. "The Changing Role of ASEAN in the Coming Decades: Post-Manila-Summit Perspectives". In *Global Adjustment and the Future of Asian-Pacific Economy*, edited by Miyohei Shinohara and Fu-chen Lo. Tokyo: Institute of Developing Economies, and Kuala Lumpur: Asian and Pacific Development Centre, 1989.

_____ and Hal Hill. "ASEAN Manufactured Exports: Performance and Revealed Comparative Advantage". *ASEAN Economic Bulletin* 2, no. 1 (July 1985).

_____ and Hal Hill. *Export-Oriented Industrialization: The ASEAN Experience*. London: Allen and Unwin, 1985.

_____; R. Garnaut; and Hal Hill. "ASEAN-Australia Economic Relations: Recent Developments and Future Prospects". Canberra: ASEAN-Australia Joint Research Project, 1986.

_____; H. Hill; R. Garnaut; and Fong P.E. "Economic-Relations between ASEAN and Australia". *Economic Record* 63, no. 180 (1987).

_____ and Tan Loong-Hoe, eds. *The Uruguay Round: ASEAN Trade Policy Options*. Singapore: Institute of Southeast Asian Studies, 1988.

Armas, A. *Philippines Intra-Asean Trade Liberalisation*. IEDR Discussion Paper, no. 78–13. University of Philippines School of Economics, 1978.

Arrow, Kenneth, J. *Social Choice and Individual Values*. New York: Wiley, 1951.

Arunachalam, S. and K.C. Garg. "Science on the Periphery: A Scientometric Analysis of Science in the ASEAN Countries". *Journal of Information Science* 12, no. 3 (1986).

"ASEAN and China: Ideological Ire Cools as Trade Heats Up". *Business China* 13, no. 24 (21 December 1987).

ASEAN Chambers of Commerce and Industry (ASEAN-CCI). *Review of ASEAN Development.* A Report of the Special Committee of the ASEAN-CCI, 1 November 1981.

"ASEAN Countries Sharing the Gains of Higher Productivity". *Productivity Digest*, May 1988.

ASEAN Documentation Series. *Treaty of Amity and Co-operation in Southeast Asia*, Bali, 24 February 1976.

ASEAN Institutes of Strategic and International Studies. *A Time for Initiative: Proposals for the Consideration of the Fourth ASEAN Summit.* Jakarta: CSIS, June 1991.

ASEAN Secretariat Paper. *Brief Review of Transport and Communication Cooperation Efforts in ASEAN*, Annex R. Report of the Meeting of Issues Committee (VI) COTAC, June 1987.

ASEAN, The Way Forward: The Report of the Group of Fourteen on Asean Economic Co-operation and Integration. Malaysia: Institute of Strategic and International Studies (ISIS), 1987.

Asher, Mukul G. "Recent Tax Changes in ASEAN and Their Implications". *Contemporary Southeast Asia* 6, no. 4 (March 1985).

_____. "The Role of Revenue System in Economic Development, with Particular Reference to ASEAN". *Asian Pacific Tax and Investment Bulletin* 3, no. 5 (May 1985).

_____ and Charan D. Wadhva. "An Overview: ASEAN-South Economic Relations". In *ASEAN-South Asia Economic Relations*, edited by Charan D. Wadhva and Mukul G. Asher. Singapore: Institute of Southeast Asian Studies, in collaboration with the Indian Council for Research on International Economic Relations and the Marga Institute, 1985.

_____. "ASEAN Tax Systems: Salient Features, Recent Developments and Implications for Investment Flows". *Journal of Regional Policy* 8 (July/September 1988).

_____, editor. *Fiscal Systems and Practices in ASEAN: Trends, Impact and Evaluation.* Singapore: Institute of Southeast Asian Studies, 1989.

Asia Club. Agenda for Asia Club Meeting, held at the Nomura International Center, Tokyo, Japan, on 9 April 1990.

Asian Defence Journal 3 (March 1988).

Asian Development Bank. *Key Indicators of Member Developing Countries of ADB* XV, April 1984.

Aslie, Mohd Reduan Hj. and Mohd. Radzuan Hj. Ibrahim. *Polis Diraja Malaysia: Sejarah, Peranan dan Cabaran* [Royal Malaysia Police: history, role and challenge]. Kuala Lumpur: Kumpulan Karangkraf, 1984.

Atan, H.B. and P. Havardwilliams. "Library-Education in the ASEAN Countries". *International Library Review* 19, no. 2 (1987).

Atarashi, K. "Japan's Economic Cooperation Policy Towards the ASEAN Countries". *International Affairs* 61, no. 1 (1985).

Ayoob, Mohammed, ed. *Regional Security in the Third World: Case Studies from Southeast Asia and the Middle East.* London: Croom Helm, 1986.

Aziz, Ungku A. "Co-operation on Education in Asean". In *ASEAN at the Crossroads: Obstacles, Options and Opportunities in Economic Co-operation*, edited by Noordin Sopiee, Chew Lay See, and Lim Siang Jin. Kuala Lumpur: Institute of Strategic and International Studies, 1987.

Baker, Richard W. *Asian-Pacific Regionalism: New Structures, Old Impulses.* Honolulu: East-West Center, 1985.

Barrett, Charles A. "Business Links with ASEAN: ASEAN at 20". *Canadian Business Review* 15 (Autumn 1988).

Barth, A. and A. Bergaigne. *Inscriptions sancrites du Cambodge et Champa (ISCC)*. Paris, 1885.

Bastin, John and Harry J. Benda. *A History of Modern Southeast Asia: Colonialism, Nationalism, and Decolonization*. New Jersey: Prentice-Hall, Inc., 1968.

Bautista, Romeo M. *Development Policy in East Asia: Economic Growth and Poverty Alleviation*. Singapore: Institute of Southeast Asian Studies, 1992.

Bayard, Donn. "The Roots of Indochinese Civilisation". *Pacific Affairs* 51, no. 1 (1980).

Bedlington, Stanley S. "Ethnicity in the Armed Forces in Singapore". In *Ethnicity and the Military in Asia*, edited by DeWitt C. Wllinwood and Cynthia H. Enloe. New Brunswick, N.J.: Transaction Books, 1981.

Bell, Coral. In *The Asian Balance of Power: A Comparison with European Precedents*. Adelphi Papers no. 44. London: IISS, 1968.

Bensman, Joseph. "Max Weber's Concept of Legitimacy: An Evaluation". In *Conflict and Control: Challenge to Legitimacy of Modern Governments*, edited by Arthur J. Vidich and Ronald M. Glassman. Beverly Hills, Ca.: Sage Publications, 1979.

Bhalla, Praveen. "Regional Groupings in Asia: Should SAARC Follow the ASEAN Model?" *Journal of International Development* 2 (July 1990).

Bista, Nirmal K. *PTA in Intra-ASEAN Trade: Issues of Relevance to SAARC*. Singapore: Institute of Southeast Asian Studies, 1991.

Black, Joan S. "Opinion Leaders: Is Anyone Following?" *Public Opinion Quarterly* 46 (Fall 1982).

Boeki Kai, Nichietsu. *1983 nen nichietsu boeki nempyo* [A chronological table of 1983 Japan-Vietnam trade]. Tokyo: Nichietsu Boekikai, 1983.

Boon, James A. *The Anthropological Romance of Bali 1597–1972*. Cambridge University Press, 1977.

Boseman, Adda B. *Politics and Culture in International History*. Princeton, N.J.: Princeton University Press, 1960.

Boyce, Peter J. "The Machinery of Southeast Asian Regional Diplomacy". In *New Directions in the International Relations of Southeast Asia: The Great Powers and Southeast Asia*, edited by Lau Teik Soon. Singapore: Singapore University Press, 1973.

Broinowski, Alison, ed. *ASEAN into the 1990s*. London: Macmillan, 1990.

Bronson, Bennet. "Exchange at the Upstream and Downstream Ends: Notes Toward a Functional Model of the Coastal State in Southeast Asia". In *Economic and Social Interaction in Southeast Asia: Perspectives from Prehistory, History and Ethnology*, edited by Hutterer. Karl L. Michigan Papers on South and Southeast Asia no. 13, 1977.

_____ and Jan Wisseman. "Palembang as Srivijaya: The Lateness of Early Cities in Southern Southeast Asia". *Asian Perspectives* 19, no. 2 (1978).

_____. "The Late Prehistory and Early History of Central Thailand with special reference to Chansen". In *Early South East Asia. Essays in Archaeology, History and Historical Geography*, edited by R.B. Smith and W. Watson. Oxford: Oxford University Press, 1979.

Brooks, Mary R. *Fleet Development and the Control of Shipping in Southeast Asia*. Singapore: Institute of Southeast Asian Studies, 1985.

_____, ed. *Seafarers in the ASEAN Region*. Singapore: Institute of Southeast Asian Studies, 1989.

Brzoska, Michael and Thomas Ohlson. *Arms Transfers in the Third World, 1971–85*. Oxford; New York: Oxford University Press, 1987.

Buchholz, Hanns J. *Law of the Sea Zones in the Pacific Ocean*. Singapore: Institute of Southeast Asian Studies, 1987.

Bulatao, Rodolfo. "Reducing Fertility in Developing Countries: A Review of Determinants and Policy Levers". World Bank Staff Working Papers no. 680. Washington, D.C.: World Bank, 1984.

Bull, Hedley. "Human Rights and World Politics". In *Moral Claims in World Affairs*, edited by Ralph Pettman. London: Croom Helm, 1979.

Bunbongkarn, Suchit. *The Military in Thai Politics, 1981–86*. Singapore: Institute of Southeast Asian Studies, 1987.

Burton, B. "Brunei Darussalam in 1989: Coming of Age Within ASEAN". *Asian Survey* 30, no. 2 (1990).

"Business Links with ASEAN: Special Report". *Canadian Business Review* 15 (Autumn 1988).

Buszynski, L. "ASEAN: A Changing Regional Role". *Asian Survey* 27, no. 7 (1987).

––––––. "Declining Superpowers: The Impact on ASEAN". *The Pacific Review* 3, no. 3 (1990).

Cabanilla, L.S. "Economic Incentives and Comparative Advantage in Livestock Production". Ph.D thesis, University of the Philippines at Los Banoa, 1983.

––––––. "ASEAN Cooperation in Food, Agriculture and Forestry: Past and Future Directions". In *ASEAN Economic Cooperation: A New Perspective*, edited by Hendra Esmara. Singapore: Chopmen Publishers for Federation of ASEAN Economic Associations and Ikatan Sarjana Ekonomi Indonesia, 1988.

Cantor, Louis J. and Steven L. Spiegel. *The International Politics of Regions*. Englewood Cliffs, N.J.: Prentice Hall, 1970.

Castells, Manuel. "Transnational Corporations, Industrialization, and Social Restructuring in the ASEAN Region". *Regional Development Dialogue* 12 (Spring 1991).

Chan, Heng Chee. "The Interests and Role of ASEAN in the Indochina Conflict". In *Indochina and Problems of Security and Stability in Southeast Asia*, edited by Khien Theeravit and MacAlister Brown. Bangkok: Chulalongkorn University Press, 1981.

––––––. "Singapore". In *Military-Civilian Relations in Southeast Asia*, edited by Zakaria Haji Ahmad and Harold Crouch. Kuala Lumpur: Oxford University Press, 1985.

––––––. "ASEAN: Subregional Resilience". In *Security Interdependence in the Asia Pacific Region*, edited by James W. Morley. Lexington, Mass.: D.C. Heath and Company, 1986.

Chandra, M. and Chhaya Satpute. "Electronics Industry and the ASEAN". *Asian Profile* 14 (October 1986).

––––––. "ASEAN Industrialization". *Journal of Scientific and Industrial Research* 46, no. 5 (1987).

Chang P.M. "The Sino-Vietnamese Conflict and Its Implications for ASEAN". *Pacific Affairs* 60, no. 4 (1988).

Chatterji, B.R. "A Current Tradition Among the Kamboja or North India Relating to the Khmers of Cambodia". *Artibus Asiae* 24 (1961).

Chee, Peng Lim. "The Role of Small Industry in the Malaysian Economy". Ph.D. dissertation, University of Malaya, 1975.

––––––. "Policies for Assisting the Development of Small Enterprises in Malaysia". Paper presented at the Policy Conference on Small Enterprises in Asia organized by IDRC-ADIPA, Bangkok, 7–9 November 1979.

––––––. "Small Enterprises in ASEAN: Need for Regional Co-operation". *ASEAN Economic Bulletin* 1, no. 2 (November 1984).

––––––. "Trade and Investment Opportunities in Southeast Asia: Potential and Problems". In *Growth Market Southeast Asia: Opportunities for and Risks of Business Corporations*, edited by H. Laumar. Munich: IFO, Institute of Economic Research, 1984.

_____ and Jang-Won Suh, eds. *ASEAN Industrial Co-operation: Future Perspectives and an Alternative Scheme*. Kuala Lumpur: Asian and Pacific Development Centre, 1988.

_____ and Jang-Won Suh. The Executive Summary in *ASEAN Industrial Co-operation: Future Perspectives and an Alternative Scheme*, edited by Chee Peng Lim and Jang-Won Suh. Kuala Lumpur: Asian and Pacific Development Centre, 1988.

Chee, Stephen. "Southeast Asia in 1988: Portents for the Future". *Southeast Asian Affairs 1989*. Singapore: Institute of Southeast Asian Studies, 1989.

Cheng, Bifan and Zhang Nan-sheng. "Institutional Factors in China-ASEAN Economic Relations". In *ASEAN-China Economic Relations: Trends and Patterns*, edited by Chia Siow-Yue and Cheng Bifan. Singapore: Institute of Southeast Asian Studies and Beijing: Institute of World Economics and Politics, 1987.

Chew, Soon Beng and P. Thambipillai. "Japan and Southeast Asia". In *Japan 1980/81: Politics and Economy*. Hong Kong: Maruzen Asia, 1981.

Chhabra, B.Ch. *Expansion of Indo-Aryan Culture*. Delhi, 1955.

Chia, Siow Yue. "Survey of ASEAN Economic Co-operation: Development and Issues". In Chia Siow Yue, ed., *ASEAN Economic Co-operation*.

_____, ed. *ASEAN Economic Co-operation*. Singapore: Institute of Southeast Asian Studies, 1980.

_____. "China's Economic Relations with ASEAN Countries". In *ASEAN and China: An Evolving Relationship*, edited by Joyce K. Kallgren, Noordin Sopiee, and Soedjati Djiwandono. Berkeley: Institute of East Asian Studies, University of California, 1988.

_____ and Cheng Bifan, eds. *ASEAN-China Economic Relations: Trends and Patterns*. Singapore: ISEAS and Beijing: Institute of World Economics and Politics, 1987.

_____ and Cheng Bifan, eds. *ASEAN-China Economic Relations: Developments in ASEAN and China*. Singapore: Institute of Southeast Asian Studies and Beijing: Institute of World Economics and Politics, 1989.

Chiang, Hai Ding. "ASEAN-EC Relations: An ASEAN View". *Euro-Asia Business Review* 5, no. 3 (July 1986).

Chin, Kin Wah. "The Great Powers and Southeast Asia: A Year of Diplomatic Effervescence". *Southeast Asian Afairs 1979*. Singapore: Institute of Southeast Asian Studies, 1979.

_____. "The Question of a Third Summit: Pros and Cons, Approaches and Recommendations". Paper presented at the Conference on Regional Development and Security: The Ties That Bind, Kuala Lumpur, 12–16 January 1986.

_____. "The Institutional Structure of ASEAN: Governmental and Private Sectors". In *ASEAN: A Bibliography 1981–85*. Singapore: Institute of Southeast Asian Studies, 1988.

_____. "Changing Global Trends and Their Effects on the Asia-Pacific". *Contemporary Southeast Asia* 13, Number 1 (June 1991).

Chng, Meng Kng. "ASEAN Economic Co-operation: The Current Status". *Southeast Asian Affairs 1985*. Singapore: Institute of Southeast Asian Studies, 1985.

_____. "ASEAN's Institutional Structure and Economic Co-operation". *ASEAN Economic Bulletin* 6, no. 3 (March 1990).

_____ and R. Hirono, editors. *ASEAN-Japan Industrial Co-operation: An Overview*. Singapore: Institute of Southeast Asian Studies, in collaboration with the ASEAN Secretariat and the Japan Institute of International Affairs, 1984.

Chowdhury, Anisuzzaman. "Textiles and Electronics Industries in ASEAN". *ASEAN Economic Bulletin* 4, no. 3 (March 1988).

_____ and C.H. Kirkpatrick. "Human-Resources, Factor Intensity and Comparative Advantage of ASEAN". *Journal of Economic Studies* 17, no. 6 (1990).

Clapham, Ronald. *Small and Medium Entrepreneurs in Southeast Asia*. Singapore: Institute of Southeast Asian Studies, 1985.

Clark, Allen L. "ASEAN Non-renewable Mineral and Energy Resources: Present Status and Future Development". *ASEAN Economic Bulletin* 7, no. 2 (November 1990).

Cloughley, Brian. "Singapore Fortifies Defence Stance". *Jane's Defence Weekly*, 27 August 1988.

Clutterbuck, Richard. *Conflict and Violence in Singapore and Malaysia, 1945–1983*. Singapore: Times International, 1984.

Coedes, George. *Les Etats Hindouises d'Indochine et d'Indonesia* (Paris: E. de Boccard, 1948) or the English translation entitled *The Indianized States of Southeast Asia*. Honolulu: East-West Center Press, 1968.

Crawford, Sir John, ed. *Pacific Economic Cooperation*. Singapore: Heinemann Educational Books, 1981.

Crone, Donald. "ASEAN's Third Decade: Building Greater Equity". *Contemporary Southeast Asia* 9, no. 1 (June 1987).

_____. "The ASEAN Summit of 1987: Searching for New Dynamism". *Southeast Asian Affairs 1988*. Singapore: Institute of Southeast Asian Studies, 1988.

Crouch, Harold. *Domestic Political Structures and Regional Economic Co-operation*. Singapore: Institute of Southeast Asian Studies, 1984.

_____. "Indonesia". In Zakaria and Crouch, eds., *Military-Civilian Relations*.

Cultural Planning in Asia. Tehran: Asian Cultural Documentation Centre for Unesco, 1977.

Daim Zainuddin. *ASEAN Economic Co-operation: Agenda for the 1990s*. Singapore: Institute of Southeast Asian Studies, 1990.

David, C.C. "Economic Structure and Changes in Agricultural Protection in ASEAN". Canberra: ASEAN-Australia Joint Research Project, 1986.

Davidson, Jeremy H.C.S. "Archaeology in Northern Viet-Nam since 1954". In *Early South East Asia. Essays in Archaeology, History and Historical Geography*, edited by R.B. Smith and W. Watson. Oxford: Oxford University Press, 1979.

Davis, Derek. "From the Littoral of Pragmatism". *Far Eastern Economic Review*, 10 December 1982.

de Casparis, J.G. *Indonesia Palaeography. A History of Writing in Indonesia from the Beginning to c. A.D. 1500*. Leiden, 1975.

DeRosa, Dean A. "ASEAN-U.S. Trade Relations: An Overview". *ASEAN Economic Bulletin* 3, no. 2 (November 1986).

_____. "The Economic Determinants of ASEAN-U.S. Trade Relations: An Econometric Analysis". *ASEAN Economic Bulletin* 4, no. 2 (November 1987).

Desomogyi, Joseph. *History of Oriental Trade*. Hildesheim, FRG: Georg Olms Verlagsbuchhandlung, 1968.

Devan, Janamitra. "The ASEAN Preferential Trading Arrangements: Some Problems, Ex Ante Results, and a Multipronged Approach to Future Intra-ASEAN Trade Development". *ASEAN Economic Bulletin* 4, no. 2 (1987).

Dhiravegin, Likhit. "Karn Patiroop Lae Karn Patiwat" [Reform and revolution]. *Journal of Political Science* 8, no. 1 (January–April 1982).

_____. "ASEAN and the Major Powers: Today and Tomorrow". In *Internal and External Security*

Issues in Asia, edited by Robert A. Scalapino, Seizaburo Sato and Jusuf Wanandi. Berkeley, California: Institute of East Asian Studies, University of California, 1986.

Dicken, Peter and Colin Kirkpatrick. "Services-led Development in ASEAN: Transnational Regional Headquarters in Singapore". *Pacific Review* 4, no. 2 (1991).

Dicker, R.J.L. "HDW's FS 1500: The Bargain Basement Frigate". *International Defence Review* 11 (November 1984).

Dixon, Chris. *South East Asia in the World-Economy*. Cambridge: Cambridge University Press, 1991.

Dixon, John A. "Environment and Economic Growth: The Political Economy of Resource Management in ASEAN". *ASEAN Economic Bulletin* 7, no. 2 (November 1990).

Djiwandono, J. Soedjati and Yong Mun Cheong, eds. *Soldiers and Stability in Southeast Asia*. Singapore: Institute of Southeast Asian Studies, 1988.

Djiwandono, J. Soedradjad and Hendra Esmara, eds. *International Financial Instability and ASEAN Financial Cooperation*. Singapore: Chopmen Publishers, 1985.

Driscoll, Robert et al. *The ASEAN Industrial Joint Venture: Problems and Opportunities*. Washington, D.C.: U.S.-ASEAN Council for Business and Technology Inc., 1990.

Drummond, Stuart. "National Policies, Regional Cooperation and the Cohesion of ASEAN". *Southeast Asian Journal of Social Science* 14, no. 1 (1986).

Easter, K. William; John A. Dixon; and Maynard Hufschmidt, eds. *Watershed Resources Management: Studies from Asia and the Pacific*. Singapore: Institute of Southeast Asian Studies, 1991.

"Economic Imbalances and World Politics". *Foreign Affairs* (New York), Spring 1987.

Eiji, Sakuta; Katsuhiro Yokoto; and Shozu Hochi. "ASEAN's Industrialisation". *Journal of Japanese Trade and Industry* 5, no. 5 (September/October 1986).

EIU. "The ASEAN Motor Industry: Problems and Prospects". Automotive special report, no. 2, 1985.

———. Hobohm, S. "ASEAN in the 1990s: Growing Together". Special reports, no. 1131, 1989.

El-Agraa, A.M. and A.J. Jones. *Theory of Customs Unions*. New York: St Martin's Press, 1981.

Emmerson, Donald K. "Southeast Asia: What's in a Name?" *Journal of Southeast Asian Studies* 15 (March 1984).

———. "ASEAN as an International Regime". *Journal of International Affairs* 41 (Summer/Fall 1987).

Engel, Charles and Kenneth Ketzler. "Tariffs and Savings in Model with New Generations". *Journal of International Economics* 28 (1990).

Entrepreneurship and Small Enterprise Development: The Philippine Experience. Quezon City: Institute for Small-Scale Industries, University of the Philippines, 1979.

Erdmann, Georg and Bruno Fritsch. *ASEAN and the EC: Cost of Capital in Major EC Countries and Their Effects on the Production Structure*. Singapore: Institute of Southeast Asian Studies, 1989.

Erlanger, Steven. "Aid to Cambodian Non-Communists is Detailed". *New York Times*, 16 November 1989.

Esman, M.J. *Administration and Development in Malaysia*. Ithaca: Cornell University Press, 1972.

Estanislao, Jesus. *ASEAN: A Profile of Development*. Manila: Center for Research and Communication, 1983.

———. "ASEAN Economies in the Mid-1980s". *ASEAN Economic Bulletin* 3, no. 1 (July 1986).

Evans, Bryan. "Arms Procurement Policies in ASEAN: How Much is Enough?" *Contemporary Southeast Asia* 10, no. 3 (December 1988).

Evans, Paul M. "Vietnam in the Changing System of Economic and Security Relations in Eastern Asia". *Vietnam: Facing the 1990s*, compiled by Richard Stubbs. Toronto: Joint Centre for Asia Pacific Studies, 1989.

Evers, Hans-Dieter. "Group Conflict and Class Formation in Southeast Asia". In *Modernization in South-East Asia*, edited by H.D. Evers. Singapore: Oxford University Press, 1973.

Fajnzylber, Fernando. "Some Reflections on South-East Asian Export Industrialization". *CEPAL Review* (Economic Commission for Latin American Review), December 1981.

Falk, Eugene. "Small Business Prospects and Opportunities in the ASEAN Countries". Paper presented at the 10th International Small Business Congress, Singapore, 12–15 September 1983.

FBIS [*Foreign Broadcasting Information Service*], 3 March 1980, p. 02.

Federspiel, H.M. "Islam and Development in the Nations of ASEAN". *Asian Survey* 25, no. 8 (1985).

Fesharaki, F. and L. Totto, "Economic Fate Hinges on Energy Balance". *Oil and Gas News*, 4–10 September 1989.

Fifield, Russell H. "The Concept of Southeast Asia: Origins, Development, and Evaluation". *South-East Asian SPECTRUM* 4, no. 1 (October 1975).

_____. *National and Regional Interests in ASEAN: Competition and Co-operation in International Politics.* Occasional Paper, no. 57. Singapore: Institute of Southeast Asian Studies, 1979.

Fisher, Charles Alfred. *South-East Asia: A Social, Economic and Political Geography.* London: Methuen, 1966.

Fitzgerald, Bruce. "Countertrade Reconsidered". *Finance and Development*, June 1987.

"Five ASEAN Countries Planning to Set Up a Pump Manufacturing Plant in Indonesia". *Indonesian Commercial Newsletter*, no. 23 (13 March 1989).

Floyd, Robert H.; Clive S. Gray; and R.P. Short. *Public Enterprise in Mixed Economies — Some Macroecomic Aspects.* Washington, D.C.: IMF, March 1986.

Fong, C.O. "ASEAN Industrial Cooperation: The Case of Multi-Product Capacity Expansion". *European Journal of Operational Research* 23, no. 2 (1986).

_____. "ASEAN Industrialization: Structural Changes and Adjustments". *Research in International Business and Finance*, pt. B (1987).

Foreign Relations of the United States: The Conference of Berlin [The Potsdam Conference], 1945, 2 vols. Washington, D.C.: Government Printing Office, 1960.

Foreign Relations of the United States, 1944, Vol. V; *The Near East, South East, and Africa: The Far East.* Washington, D.C.: Government Printing Office, 1965.

Foreign Relations of the United States, 1945, Vol. VI; *The British Commonwealth: The Far East.* Washington, D.C. Government Printing Office, 1969.

Fratianni, Michele and John Pattison. "The Economics of International Organizations". *Kyklos* 35 (1982).

_____. *International Institutions and the Market for Information.* Discussion Paper, no. 36, Indiana Center for Global Business. Bloomington: The School of Business, Indiana University, 1990.

Frey, Bruno S. *International Political Economics.* Oxford: Blackwell, 1984.

_____ and Beat Gygi. "The Political Economy of International Organisations". *Aussenwirtschaft*
    45, no. III (1990).
Fukuyama, Francis. "The End of History?". *The National Interest*, summer 1989.

Gaimusho. *Waga gaiko no kinkyo* [The recent state of Japanese diplomacy]. Tokyo: Okurasho
    Insatsukyoku, various years.
"Gen Wanchai Says 'Arms Dealers' Behind Criticism of Stingray Purchase". *Asian Defence Journal*
    1 (January 1989).
Ghazally Ismail. "Potential Role of Biotechnology in Food and Health Problems of ASEAN
    Countries". *ASEAN Journal on Science and Technology for Development* 2, no. 1 (1985).
Girling, J.L.S. "Regional Security in Southeast Asia". *Journal of Southeast Asian Studies* II, no. 1
    (March 1971).
_____. *The Bureaucratic Polity in Modernizing Societies*. Occasional Paper, no. 64. Singapore:
    Institute of Southeast Asian Studies, 1981.
Golomb, Louis. *Brokers of Morality: Thai Ethnic Adaptation in a Rural Malaysian Setting*. Hono-
    lulu: University of Hawaii Press, 1978.
Gordon, Bernard. *The Dimensions of Conflict in Southeast Asia*. New Jersey: Prentice-Hall, 1966.
Government of Malaysia. *Guidelines on Privatization*. Kuala Lumpur: Economic Planning Unit,
    Prime Minister's Department, 1985.
Government of Singapore. *Report of the Public Sector Divestment Committee*. February 1987.
Grant, Bruce. *The Security of South-East Asia*, Adelphi Papers, no. 142. London: International
    Institute for Strategic Studies, 1978.
Grazebrook, A.Z. "Indonesia Builds for Its Needs". *Pacific Defence Reporter*, October 1986.
Grinter, Lawrence E. *The Philippine Bases: Continuing Utility in a Changing Strategic Context*.
    Washington, D.C.: National Defense University, 1980.
Group of Fourteen on ASEAN Economic Co-operation and Integration. *ASEAN: The Way Forward*.
    Kuala Lumpur: Institute of Strategic and International Studies, 1987.
Grubel, Herbert. *Multinational Banking*. Singapore: Institute of Southeast Asian Studies, 1985.
Gunasekaran, S. "Highlights of the Third ASEAN Summit". *Economic Bulletin*, January 1988.
_____. [Review of] *Socio-economic Development of ASEAN: An International Perspective* by
    Habibullah Khan. *ASEAN Economic Bulletin* 5, no. 2 (November 1988).
Guoxing, Ji. "ASEAN Countries in Political and Economic Perspectives". *Asian Affairs* 18 (June
    1987).
Gupta, Bhabani Sen, ed. *SAARC-ASEAN: Prospects and Problems of Inter-Regional Cooperation*.
    New Delhi: South Asian Publishers, 1988.
Gupta, K.L. *Finance and Economic Growth in Developing Countries*. London: Croom Helm,
    1984.

Ha Van Tan. "Nouvelles recherches prehistoriques et protohistoriques au Vietnam". *Bulletin
    de l'Ecole Française d'Extrême-Orient* 68 (1980).
Haas, Michael. "Alliance". In *World Encyclopedia of Peace*, edited by Ervin Laszlo and Jong
    Youl Yoo. Oxford: Pergamon Press, 1986.
Habibie, B.J. "Sharing Responsibility over the Less Fortunate". *Jakarta Post*, 16, 17, 18 November
    1987.
Hagiwara, Y. "Political Culture and Communism in West Malaysia". *Developing Economies* 10,
    no. 3 (September 1972).

_____. "Formation and Development of the Association of Southeast Asian Nations". *Developing Economies* XI, no. 4 (December 1973).

Hahn, Bradley. "South-East Asia's Miniature Naval Arms Race". *Pacific Defence Reporter*, Septtember 1985.

Hall, D.G.E. *A History of South-East Asia*. London: MacMillan, 1966.

_____. "The Integrity of Southeast Asian History". *Journal of Southeast Asian Studies* 4 (September 1973).

Hamilton, C.A.; P.R. Gibson; and D.L. Manifold; et al. "The Pros and Cons of Entering into Negotiations on Free Trade Area Agreements with Taiwan, the Republic of Korea, and ASEAN or the Pacific Rim Region in General; Report to the Senate Committee on Finance on Investigation no. TA-332-259 under Section 332 of the Tariff Act of 1980". Washington, D.C.: United States International Trade Commission (USITC), 1982.

Hamzah, B.A. *Asean Relations with Dialogue Partners*. Petaling Jaya: Pelanduk Publications (M) Sdn Bhd, 1989.

Hann, P. "Why ASEAN Businessmen Are Cosying Up to China". *International Management* 40, no. 10 (October 1985).

Harris, G. "The Determinants of Defense Expenditure in the ASEAN Region". *Journal of Peace Research* 23, no. 1 (1986).

Harrison, G.W. *Economic Interdependence between ASEAN and Australia: A General Equilibrium Approach*. Canberra: ASEAN-Australia Joint Research Project, 1987.

Hatch, Martin F. "Lagu, Laras, Layang. Rethinking Melody in Javanese Music". Ph.D. thesis, Cornell University, 1980.

Hayashi, N. "Nihon gunkokushugi fukkatsu no keizai-teki kiso" [The economic basis for the revival of Japanese militarism]. *Gendai to shisō*, October 1970.

Hay Kaj. "ASEAN and the Shifting Tides of Economic Power at the End of the 1980s". *International Journal* 44, no. 3 (1989).

Henderson, J.W. "The New International Division of Labour and American Semiconductor Production in South East Asia". In *Multinational Corporations and the Third World*, edited by C.J. Dixon, D. Drakakis-Smith, and H.D. Watts. London: Croom Helm, 1986.

Herrin, Alejandro; H. Pardoko; L. Lim; and C. Hongladarom. "Demographic Development in ASEAN: A Comparative Overview". *Philippine Review of Economics and Business* 18 (1981).

Herschede, F. "Trade between China and ASEAN: The Impact of the Pacific Rim Era". *Pacific Affairs* 64, no. 2 (1991).

Hewison, K.; A. Smith; and N. Badu. "Papua-New-Guinea and Membership of ASEAN". *Australian Outlook* 39, no. 3 (1985).

Hiemenz, U. "Foreign Direct-Investment and Industrialization in ASEAN Countries". *Weltwirtschaftliches Archiv* 123, no. 1 (1987).

_____. "Expansion of ASEAN-EC Trade in Manufactures: Pertinent Issues and Recent Developments". *Developing Economies* 26, no. 4 (1988).

Hiemenz, Ulrich and Rolf J. Langhammer. *ASEAN and the EC: Institutions and Structural Change in the European Community*. Singapore: Institute of Southeast Asian Studies, 1988.

Hill, Hal. "Challenges in ASEAN Economic Co-operation: An Outsider's Perspective". In *ASEAN at the Crossroads: Obstacles, Options and Opportunities in Economic Co-operation*, edited by Noordin Sopiee, Chew Lay See, and Lim Siang Jin. Kuala Lumpur: Institute of Strategic and International Studies, 1977.

_____. "LDC Manufactured Exports: Do Definitions Matter? Some Examples from ASEAN". *ASEAN Economic Bulletin* 3, no. 2 (November 1986).

_____. *Indonesia's Textile and Garment Industries: Development in an Asian Perspective*. Singapore: Institute of Southeast Asian Studies, 1992.

Hirono, R. "Private Foreign Investment — Issues and Policies". In *Southeast Asian Economy in the 1970s*, edited by Asian Development Bank. London: Longman Ltd., 1971.

_____. *The Association of Southeast Asian Nations and Economic Policy towards Australia and Japan*. Canberra: Australian National University, 1978.

Hisashi, Yoshikawa. "Economic Developments in ASEAN Countries and Cooperation Among Asia-Pacific Regions". *Digest of Japanese Industry and Technology*, no. 255 (28 February 1990).

Holdridge, John P. "Indonesia Has Neither Disposition Nor Resources to Act in Aggressive Manner". *Pacific Defence Reporter*, June 1986.

Holmes, Sir Frank. "ANZCERTA, Trade in Services, and ASEAN". *ASEAN Economic Bulletin* 7, no. 1 (July 1990).

Hosami, Takashi. "Economic Aid and Japan's Security". Roundtable Reports, no. 6. New York: East Asian Institute, Columbia University, 1983.

Hough, G.V. "ASEAN's Energy Options". *Petroleum Economist* 54, no. 4 (April 1987).

Hozumi, Toshihiko. "SLOC Security Problems in Southeast Asian and the Southeast Pacific". In *Pacific Sealane Security: Tokyo Conference, 1983*, edited by Tunhewa Ko and Yuming Shaw. Asia and World Monograph Series, no. 34. Taipei, ROC: Asia and World Institute, 1985.

Hukill, M.A. and M. Jussawalla. "Telecommunications Policies and Markets in the ASEAN Countries". *Columbia Journal of World Business* 24, no. 1 (1989).

Hull, Cordell. *The Memoirs of Cordell Hull*, Vol. II. New York: The Macmillan Company, 1948.

Hull, Terrence; V. Hull; and M. Singarimbun. "Indonesia's Family Planning Story: Success and Challenge". *Population Bulletin* 32, no. 6. Washington, D.C.: Population Reference Bureau, 1977.

Hussey, A. "Regional-Development and Cooperation Through ASEAN". *Geographical Review* 81, no. 1 (1991).

Hutterer, Karl L. "Prehistoric Trade and the Evolution of Philippine Societies: A Reconsideration". *Economic and Social Interaction in Southeast Asia: Perspectives from Prehistory, History and Ethnology*, edited by Karl L. Hutterer. Michigan Papers on South and Southeast Asia, no. 13 (1977).

Huxley, T. "ASEAN and Cambodia: The Hazards of Stalemate". *Asia Pacific Community*, no. 30 (1985).

_____. "ASEAN's Prospective Security Role: Moving Beyond the Indochina Fixation". *Contemporary Southeast Asia* 9, no. 3 (December 1987).

Imada, Pearl. "Evaluating Economic Integration in Developing Countries: An Application for the ASEAN Preferential Trading Arrangement". Ph.D. dissertation, Department of Economics, University of Hawaii, Manoa, 1990.

_____; Manuel Montes; and Seiji Naya. *A Free Trade Area: Implications for ASEAN*. Singapore: Institute of Southeast Asian Studies, 1991.

Imagawa, E. and H. Hama. *Bunka-daikakumei to Betonamu sensō* [Great cultural revolution and the Vietnam war]. Tokyo: Institute of Developing Economies, 1968.

Imagawa, Takeshi. "ASEAN-Japan Relations". *Civilisations* 39, nos. 1/2 (1989).

Indochina 3, (1988). London: EIU, 1988.

Indorf, Hans H. *ASEAN: Problems and Prospects*. Occasional Paper, no. 38. Singapore: Institute of Southeast Asian Studies, 1975.

_____. "Some Speculation on a Second Blueprint for ASEAN". *Contemporary Southeast Asia* 3, no. 2 (September 1981).

_____. "U.S.-ASEAN Relations". In *Thai-American Relations in Contemporary Affairs*, edited by Hans H. Indorf. Singapore: Executive Publications Ltd, 1982.

_____. "Political Dimensions of Intra-Regional Co-operation: The Case of ASEAN and the EEC". Asia-Pacific Community, no. 19 (Winter 1983).

_____. *Impediments to Regionalism in Southeast Asia: Bilateral Constraints among ASEAN Member States*. Singapore: Institute of Southeast Asian Studies, 1984.

_____. "The U.S.-ASEAN Dialogue: A Search for Procedural Improvements". *Contemporary Southeast Asia* 8, no. 3 (December 1986).

_____. "ASEAN in Extra-regional Perspective". *Contemporary Southeast Asia* 9, no. 2 (September 1987).

Institute of Policy Studies and Institute of Southeast Asian Studies. Resume of Major Themes of Discussion at the Joint IPS-ISEAS ASEAN Roundtable on ASEAN Economic Co-operation in the 1990s, held in Singapore, 27–28 June 1991.

Institute of Southeast Asian Studies. *ASEAN: The Tasks Ahead*. Singapore: Institute of Southeast Asian Studies, 1987.

International Labour Organization. "Privatisation: Its Impact on Labour Relations in ASEAN", 1987.

_____. Report and Technical Papers from the ASEAN Tripartite Symposium on the Prevention and Settlement of Labour Disputes, Denpasar, Indonesia, 23–26 February 1988.

_____. "Labour Relations and Development". Proceedings and lectures from the ASEAN Tripartite Course on Labour Relations and Development, Manila and Cebu City, Philippines, 12–20 May 1988.

_____. "The Administration and Enforcement of Collective Agreements: A Survey of the Current Situation in ASEAN", 1988.

Irvine, Roger. "The Formative Years of ASEAN: 1967–1975". In *Understanding ASEAN*, edited by Alison Broinowski. London: MacMillan Press Ltd, 1982.

Ishigami, E. "Japanese Business in ASEAN Countries: New Industrialization or Japanization". *IDS Bulletin* 22, no. 2 (1991).

Ivanov, Vladimir I. "From the USSR to Russia on the Pacific". *Southeast Asian Affairs 1992*. Singapore: Institute of Southeast Asian Studies, 1992.

Jackson, Karl D.; Sukhumbhand Paribatra; and J. Soedjati Djiwandono. *ASEAN in Regional and Global Context*. Berkeley, Calif.: Institute of East Asian Studies, University of California, Berkeley, 1986.

Jackson, Tom. "The 'game' of ASEAN Trade Preferences: Alternatives for the Future of Trade Liberalization". *ASEAN Economic Bulletin* 3, no. 2 (November 1986).

Jacob, Philip E. and James V. Toscano, eds. *The Integration of Political Communities*. New York: J.B. Lippincott, 1964.

Jacques, Claude. "'Funan'. 'Zhenla'. The Reality Concealed by These Chinese Views of Indochina". In *Early South East Asia. Essays in Archaeology, History and Historical Geography*, edited by R.B. Smith and W. Watson. Oxford: Oxford University Press, 1979.

James, Kenneth. "Fiscal and Financial Factors Affecting Small and Medium Business Improvement in the ASEAN Region". *ASEAN Economic Bulletin* 2, no. 3 (March 1986).

_____ and Narongchai Akrasanee, eds. *Small and Medium Business Improvement in the ASEAN Region: Financial Factors*. Singapore: Institute of Southeast Asian Studies, 1986.

_____ and Narongchai Akrasanee, eds. *Small and Medium Business Improvement in the ASEAN Region: Production Management*. Singapore: Institute of Southeast Asian Studies, 1988.

_____ and Narongchai Akrasanee, eds. *Small and Medium Business Improvement in the ASEAN Region: Marketing Factors*. Singapore: Institute of Southeast Asian Studies, 1988.

Jane's Defence Weekly, 7 April 1984.

Japan Defense Agency. *Defense of Japan 1985*. Tokyo: The Japan Times, Ltd., 1985.

_____. *Defense of Japan 1980*. Tokyo: The Japan Times, Ltd., 1981.

Japan Economic Journal, 15 March 1980.

Jayasankaran, S. "Towards an ASEAN Common Market". *Malaysian Business*, 16 November 1986.

Jenkins, R. "Divisions over the International Division of Labour". *Capital and Class* 22 (1984).

Jeshurun, Chandran. "Development and Civil-Military Relations in Malaysia: The Evolution of the Officer Corps". In Djiwandono and Yong, eds., *Soldiers and Stability*.

_____. "Civil-Military Relations and National Security in ASEAN". *Pacific Focus* IV, no. 2 (Fall 1989).

Jorgensen-Dahl, Arnfinn. *Regional Organization and Order in South-East Asia*. London: Macmillan, 1982.

Joshua, Wynfred and Stephen P. Gibert. *Arms for the Third World: Soviet Military Aid Diplomacy*. Baltimore: Johns Hopkins Press, 1969.

Kadir, A. "Electric Power in ASEAN Countries: A Shifting Fuel Mix". *Energy* 10, no. 12 (December 1985).

Kaiser, Manfred and Heinz Werner. *ASEAN and the EC: Labour Costs and Structural Change in the European Community*. Singapore: Institute of Southeast Asian Studies, 1989.

Kallgren, Joyce K.; Noordin Sopiee; and Soedjati Djiwandono, eds. *ASEAN and China: An Evolving Relationship*. Berkeley, California: Institute of East Asian Studies, University of California, 1988.

Kamal Salih. *ASEAN Economic Relations with Japan*. Kuala Lumpur: Malaysian Institute of Economic Research, 1987.

Kaosa-ard, Mingsarn Santikarn. "U.S. Contractual Arrangements in Some ASEAN Countries: Selected Case Studies in Thailand". *ASEAN Economic Bulletin* 3, no. 2 (November 1986).

Kaplan, Morton. *System and Process in International Relations*. New York: John Wiley & Sons, 1957.

Karim, Hassan Abdul. "BMF — The People's Black Paper". In *Mahathir's Economic Policy*, edited by Jomo K.S. Kuala Lumpur: Institute of Social Analysis, 1988.

Karniol, Robert. "Rebuilding the Philippines' Forces". *Jane's Defence Weekly*, 7 October 1989.

Karp, Aaron. "Military Procurement and Regional Security in Southeast Asia". *Contemporary Southeast Asia* 11, no. 4 (March 1990).

Kazuo Aichi, Parliamentary Vice-Minister for Foreign Affairs, at the preparatory meeting on on ASEAN Human Resources Development Project, 31 March 1981.

Keesing, Roger M. *Kin Groups and Social Structure*. New York: Holt, Rinehart and Winston, Inc., 1975.

Kelleher, Catherine McArdle. *The Changing Currency of Power: Paper 1 — The Future Nature of US Influence in Western Europe and North-East Asia*. Adelphi Papers, no. 256. London: IISS, Winter 1990/91.

Kesavan, K.V. "Japan, Vietnam and ASEAN". *Southeast Asian Affairs 1985*. Singapore: Institute of Southeast Asian Studies, 1985.

Kessler, Richard J. "'Development Diplomacy': The Role of the MFA in the Philippines". *Philippine Journal of Public Administration* 24, no. 1 (January 1980).

_____. "Development and the Military: Role of the Philippine Military in Development". In Djiwandono and Yong, eds., *Soldiers and Stability*.

Khamchoo, Chaiwat. "Japan's Role in Southeast Asian Security: 'Plus ca change . . .'". *Pacific Affairs* 64, no. 1 (Spring 1991).

Khaw, Guat Hoon. "ASEAN in International Politics". In *Politics in the ASEAN States*, edited by Diane K. Mauzy. Kuala Lumpur: Marican & Sons [Malaysia] Sdn Bhd, 1984.

Khong, Kim Hoong. "Security Co-operation in ASEAN". *Contemporary Southeast Asia* 9, no. 2 (September 1987).

Khwaja Sarmad and Riaz Mahmood. "Prospects for Expanding Trade Between SAARC and ASEAN Countries". *Pakistan Development Review* 27, no. 2 (Summer 1988).

Kihl, Y.W. "Intra-Regional Conflict and the ASEAN Peace Process". *International Journal* 44, no. 3 (1989).

Kimura, T. "Indochina Economy". In *The Challenge of Asian Developing Countries*, edited by S. Ichimura. Tokyo: Asian Productivity Organization, Tokyo, 1986.

Kintanar, Agustin. "Long-term Perspectives of ASEAN". *ASEAN Economic Bulletin* 2, no. 1 (July 1985).

_____ and Tan Loong-Hoe. *ASEAN-U.S. Economic Relations: An Overview*. Singapore: Institute of Southeast Asian Studies, 1986.

Kitagawa, Takafumi. "Japan's Technical Cooperation to ASEAN Countries Facing New Phases". *Digest of Japanese Industry and Technology*, no. 238 (1987).

Knodel, John; N. Havanon; and A. Pramualratana. "Fertility Transition in Thailand: A Qualitative Analysis". *Population and Development Review* 10 (1984).

Kojima, Kiyoshi. *Direct Foreign Investment: A Japanese Model of Multinational Business Operations*. London: Croom Helm, 1978.

_____. *Japanese Direct Foreign Investment*. Tokyo: Charles E. Tuttle Co., 1978.

Kumar, Sree et al. *ASEAN Free Trade Area: The Way Ahead*. Singapore: Institute of Southeast Asian Studies, 1992.

Kunstadter, P., ed. *Southeast Asian Tribes, Minorities, and Nations*. Princeton: Princeton University Press, 1967.

Kuntjoro-Jakti, Dorodjatun. "ASEAN's Eternal Trade Relations in 1987: Entering a Growing Environmental Turbulence". *Contemporary Southeast Asia* 9, no. 2 (September 1987).

_____ and T.A.M. Simatupang. "The Indonesian Experience in Facing Non-Armed and Armed Movements: Lessons from the Past and Glimpses of the Future". In Snitwongse and Paribatra, eds., *Durable Stability in Southeast Asia*.

Kusuma-Atmadja, Mochtar. "Some Thoughts on ASEAN Security Co-operation: An Indonesian Perspective". *Contemporary Southeast Asia* 12, no. 3 (December 1990).

Lai, Fung-wai Frances. *Without a Vision: Japan's Relations with ASEAN*. Singapore: Chopmen, 1981.

Lai, Yew Wah and Tan Siew Ee. "Internal Migration and Economic Development in Malaysia". In *Urbanization and Migration in ASEAN Development*, edited by P. Hauser, D. Suits, and N. Ogawa. Hawaii: University of Hawaii Press, 1985.

Langhammer, Rolf J. "The Economic Rationale of Trade Policy Co-operation between ASEAN and the EC: Has Co-operation Benefitted ASEAN?" *ASEAN Economic Bulletin* 2, no. 2 (November 1985).

———. "Declining Competitiveness of EC Suppliers in ASEAN Markets: Singular Case or Symptom". *Journal of Common Market Studies* 24, no. 2 (1985).

———. "ASEAN-EC Economic Relations on a Side-Track?". *Euro-Asia Business Review* 5, no. 4 (October 1986).

———. *Trade in Services Between ASEAN and EC Member States: Case Studies for West Germany, France, and the Netherlands*. Singapore: Institute of Southeast Asian Studies, 1991.

———. "ASEAN Economic Co-operation: A Stock-Taking from a Political Economy Point of View". *ASEAN Economic Bulletin* 8, no. 2 (November 1991).

——— and Hans Christoph Rieger, eds. *ASEAN and the EC: Trade in Tropical Agricultural Products*. Singapore: Institute of Southeast Asian Studies, 1988.

Lans, C.S. "Environmental Control of Palm Oil Industry: An Economic Analysis". Thesis submitted to Asian Institute of Technology, Bangkok, Thailand, April 1980.

"Laos: Air Force of the People's Liberation Army". *Flight International*, 29 November–5 December 1989.

Larsen, Randall J. "The Modernization of the Royal Thai Air Force". *Asian Defence Journal* 5 (May 1987).

Lau, Teik Soon. "Cultural Co-operation between the ASEAN States". In *Cultures in Encounter: Germany and the Southeast Asian Nations, A Documentation of the ASEAN Cultural Week, Tuebingen, Summer 1977*. Tubingen: Horst Erdmann Verlag, 1978.

———. "The Challenge to ASEAN Political Co-operation". *Contemporary Southeast Asia* 9, no. 2 (September 1987).

———. "ASEAN Diplomacy: National Interest and Regionalism". *Journal of Asian and African Studies* 25, nos. 1–2 (1990).

———. "Asean and Global Issues". *Asean-ISIS Monitor*, no. 1 (July 1991).

Laumig, Romulo B. "Modern Management and Small Business". Paper presented at the 10th International Small Business Congress, Singapore, 12-15 September 1983.

Lebow, Richard N. *Between Peace and War*. Baltimore: Johns Hopkins University Press, 1981.

Lee, Kum Tatt and Tan Boon Wan. "Development and Growth of the Small Industry Sector in Singapore". Paper presented at the Asian Regional Meeting of Donor Agencies on Small Scale Enterprise Development organized by the National Development Bank of Sri Lanka, Colombo and World Bank, Washington, D.C., 8–11 December 1981.

Lee, Lai To. "Deng Xiaoping's ASEAN Tour: A Perspective on Sino-Southeast Asian Relations". *Contemporary Southeast Asia* 3, no. 1 (June 1981).

Lee, Poh Ping. "Private Sector's View of the Way Forward". *Economic Bulletin*, August 1987.

———. "ASEAN and the Asia-Pacific in the 1990s". *Contemporary Southeast Asia* 9, no. 2 (September 1987).

Lee, S.Y. "The Role of Singapore as a Financial Centre". In J. Soedradjad Djiwandono and Hendra Esmara, eds., *International Financial Stability*.

Lehmann, Jean-Pierre. "Problems in ASEAN-EC Relations". In *ASEAN-EC Economic and Political Relations*, edited by R.H. Taylor and P.C.I. Ayre. Papers from the Third FCO/SOAS South East Asia Seminar, December 1985, External Services Division, School of Oriental and African Studies, University of London, 1986.

Leifer, Michael. "Trends in Regional Association in Southeast Asia". *Asian Studies* 2 (August 1964).

_____. "The ASEAN States and the Progress of Regional Cooperation in South-East Asia". In *Politics, Society And Economy In The ASEAN States*, edited by Bernhard Dahm & Werner Draguhn. Wiesbaden: Otto Harrassowitz, 1975.

_____. "The Paradox of ASEAN: A Security Organisation without the Structure of an Alliance". *The Round Table*, no. 271 (July 1978).

_____. *ASEAN and the Security of South-East Asia*. London: Routledge, 1989.

Lightbourne, Robert and A. MacDonald. *Family Size Preferences*. London: World Fertility Survey, 1982.

Lindsey, Charles W. "Transfer of Technology to the ASEAN Region by U.S. Transnational Corporations". *ASEAN Economic Bulletin* 3, no. 2 (November 1986).

Lipsey, Robert G. "The Theory of Customs Union: A General Survey". *Economic Journal* 70, no. 279 (September 1960).

Liu, W.H. "Ethnic Conflicts and the Chineseness Factor in ASEAN". *Issues and Studies* 25, no. 2 (1989).

Lombard, Frank. "Thai Army Chief Denies Tank Buy 'Irregularities'". *Jane's Defence Weekly*, 28 November 1987.

_____. "Royal Thai Army: Politics of Reform". *Jane's Defence Review*, 7 January 1989.

Lorenz, Detlef. "International Division of Labour or Closer Co-operation? A Look at ASEAN-EC Economic Relations". *ASEAN Economic Bulletin* 2, no. 3 (March 1986).

Luhulima, C.P.F. "Human Resources of the ASEAN Development and the ASEAN Countries". In *Regional Cooperation in the Pacific Era*, edited by Dalchoong Kim and Noordin Sopiee. Seoul: Institute of East and West Studies, 1988.

_____. "The Third ASEAN Summit and Beyond". *Indonesian Quarterly* XVII, no. 1 (First Quarter 1989).

Lyon, Peter. *War and Peace in Southeast Asia*. London: Oxford University Press for the Royal Institute of International Affairs, 1969.

_____. "ASEAN and the Future of Regionalism". In *New Directions in the International Relations of Southeast Asia: The Great Powers and Southeast Asia*, edited by Lau Teik Soon. Singapore: Singapore University Press, 1973.

Mabbett, I.W. "The 'Indianization' of Southeast Asia: Reflections on Prehistoric Sources". *Journal of Southeast Asian Studies* 8, no. 1 (1977).

MacIntyre, Andrew. "Don't Worry About Those Indonesian F-16s". *Pacific Defence Reporter*, August 1986.

Magenda, Bruhan. "Political and Security Dimensions in ASEAN-Japan Relations: Perspective from Indonesia". Unpublished paper presented at Asia Dialogue Workshop, Bangkok, 23–24 January 1984.

Mahapatra, Chintamani. *American Role in the Origin & Growth of ASEAN*. New Delhi: ABC Pub. House, 1990.

Mak, J.N. *Directions for Greater Defence Cooperation*. Kuala Lumpur: Institute of Strategic and International Studies, 1986.

_____ and Brian Wanstall. "Improving ASEAN Air Force Links". *Interavia* 7 (July 1989).

Mak, William Kam Hoong. "Should Singapore Play a More Active Role in Pursuing Greater ASEAN Economic Cooperation?" *Suara Ekonomi 1987*.

"Malaysia: Preparing for Change". *Jane's Defence Weekly*, 29 July 1989.

"Malaysia's Hand-Me-Down Air Strategy". *Newsweek* (International Edition), 27 May 1985.

Maligaspe, Ranjit. *ASEAN-South Asia Trade: Primary Commodities as a Component in South-South Co-operation*. Singapore: Institute of Southeast Asian Studies, 1991.

Mani, A. *Determinants of Educational Aspirations among Indonesian Youth*. Singapore: Maruzen Asia, 1983.

Martin, Linda G. "The Aging of Asia". Unpublished paper, East-West Population Institute, Honolulu, Hawaii, 1985.

Masako Kurihara. "Structural Change in ASEAN Trade Patterns: Development of Intra-horizontal Relationships". *Tokyo Financial Review* 15, no. 3 (March 1990).

Matheson, Virginia. "Concepts of State in the *Tuhfat al-Nafis* (The Precious Gift)". In *Pre-Colonial State Systems in Southeast Asia*, edited by Anthony Reid and Lance Castles. Monographs of the Malaysian Branch of the Royal Asiatic Society, no. 6, 1975.

McCawley, Peter. "Australia's Misconceptions of ASEAN". Paper presented at the Conference on Australia's External Relations, Australian National University, 1–4 September 1982.

McCloud, Donald G. *System and Process in Southeast Asia: The Evolution of a Region*. Boulder, Colorado: Westview Press, 1986.

McDivitt, James. "Mineral Development in the ASEAN Region — An Overview". *Petromin*, January 1989.

McDorman, Ted L. "Implementation of the LOS Convention: Options, Impediments, and the ASEAN States". *Ocean Development and International Law* 18, no. 3 (1987).

McDowell, M.A. "Development and the Environment in ASEAN". *Pacific Affairs* 62, no. 3 (1989).

McGuire, Martin C. *Coping with Foreign Dependence: The Simple Analytics of Stockpiling versus Protection*. Singapore: Institute of Southeast Asian Studies, 1990.

Mills, J.V. "Arabic and Chinese Navigators in Malaysian Waters in About A.D. 1500". *Journal of the Malaysian Branch of the Royal Asiatic Society* 47 (December 1974).

Milne, R.S. "Technocrats and Politics in the ASEAN Countries". *Pacific Affairs* 55, no. 3 (Fall 1982).

———. "The Politics of Privatization in the ASEAN States". *ASEAN Economic Bulletin* 7, no. 3 (March 1991).

Millione, Pauline. "Contemporary Urbanization in Indonesia". In *Changing Southeast Asian Cities: Readings in Urbanization*, edited by Y.M. Yeung and C.P. Lo. Kuala Lumpur: Oxford University Press, 1976.

Miyata, Mitsuru. "Energy Demand and Supply Forecast for the Pan-Pacific Region in Year 2000 and Tasks for Energy Co-operation". Paper presented at the Fourth Symposium on Pacific Energy Cooperation, Tokyo, 29–30 January 1990.

Mohd. Ismail Ahmad. *Foreign Manufacturing Investments in Resource-based Industries: Comparisons between Malaysia and Thailand*. Singapore: Institute of Southeast Asian Studies, 1991.

Moore, John, ed. "Vietnam". *Jane's Fighting Ships, 1987–88*. Coulsdon, Surrey: Jane's Publishing, 1987.

Mormillo, Frank B. "No More Crusaders". Proceedings of the U.S. Naval Institute, August 1987.

Morrison, Charles E. *Japan, The United States and a Changing Southeast Asia*. Lanham, Md.: University Press of America, 1985.

Mutalib, H. "Islamic Revivalism in ASEAN States: Political Implications". *Asian Survey* 30, no. 9 (1990).

Mya Than. "Trends in Burma-ASEAN Trade Relations". *Asian Economic Bulletin* 5, no. 1 (July 1988).

_____. "ASEAN, Indo-China and Myanmar: Towards Economic Co-operation?". *ASEAN Economic Bulletin* 8, no. 2 (November 1991).

_____. *Myanmar's External Trade: An Overview in the Southeast Asian Context*. Singapore: Institute of Southeast Asian Studies, 1992.

_____ and Joseph L.H. Tan, eds. *Myanmar Dilemmas and Options: The Challenge of Economic Transition in the 1990s*. Singapore: Institute of Southeast Asian Studies, 1990.

Nagi, R. *ASEAN (Association of South-East Asian Nations), 20 years: A Comprehensive Documentation*. 1st ed. New Delhi, India: Lancers Books, 1989.

Naidu, G. "ASEAN Cooperation in Transport". In *ASEAN Economic Cooperation: A New Perspective*, edited by Hendra Esmara. Singapore: Chopmen Publishers for Federation of ASEAN Economic Associations and Ikatan Sarjana Ekonomi Indonesia, 1988.

Nair, Kannan K. *Words and Bayonets: ASEAN and Indochina*. Rev. ed. Kuala Lumpur: Federal Publications, 1986.

Nasution, Anwar. "Economic Cooperation in the Asia-Pacific Region". *Journal of Japanese Trade and Industry*, no. 4 (1986).

Natarajan, S. and Tan Juay Miang. *The Impact of MNC Investments in Malaysia, Singapore and Thailand*. Singapore: Institute of Southeast Asian Studies, 1992.

Nathan, K.S. "United-States-Thai Relations and ASEAN Security". *Australian Outlook* 39, no. 2 (1985).

"National Security". In *Malaysia, A Country Study*, edited by Frederica M. Bunge. Washington, D.C.: U.S. Government, 1985.

"Natural Rubber and ASEAN: Cooperation or Competition?" *Rubber Trends*, no. 120 (December 1988).

Naya, S. "Asean Trade and Development Co-operation: Preferential Trading Arrangements and Trade Liberalisation". UNDP, UNCAP Project RAS/77/015/A/40, 1980.

_____. "Towards the Establishment of an ASEAN Trade Area". Report prepared for the ASEAN Secretariat and the Committee on Trade and Tourism. Honolulu, HI: East-West Center, 1987.

_____ et al. *ASEAN Free Trade Area: The Way Ahead*. Singapore: Institute of Southeast Asian Studies, 1992.

_____ and Ulrich Hiemenz, "Changing Trade Patterns and Policy Issues: Prospects for ASEAN and the Asian NICs". *ASEAN Economic Bulletin* 2, no. 2 (November 1985).

_____ and Michael G. Plummer. "ASEAN Economic Co-operation in the New International Economic Environment". *ASEAN Economic Bulletin* 7, no. 3 (March 1991).

_____; Kernial S. Sandhu; Michael Plummer; and Narongchai Akrasanee, co-ordinators. *ASEAN-U.S. Initiative: Assessment and Recommendations for Improved Economic Relations. Joint Final Report*. Singapore: Institute of Southeast Asian Studies and Honolulu: East-West Center, 1989.

_____ and Akira Takayama, eds. *Economic Development in East and Southeast Asia: Essays in Honor of Professor Shiichi Ichimura*. Singapore: Institute of Southeast Asian Studies, 1990.

Nayaratnam, R.V. "ASEAN Cooperation in Transportation: Looking Back/Looking Forward". First ASEAN Economic Congress, Kuala Lumpur, March 1987.

Nehen, I. Ketut. "Insurance Industry and Employment in ASEAN". *ASEAN Economic Bulletin* 6, no. 1 (July 1989).

New Straits Times (NST). "TDC, S'pore Propose Joint Promotion Drive", 26 July 1985.

Ng, Chee Yuen [Review of] *Export-oriented Industrialization: The ASEAN Experience* by Mohamed Ariff and Hal Hill. *ASEAN Economic Bulletin* 3, no. 3 (March 1987).

———; R. Hirono; and Robert Y. Siy, Jr. *Technology and Skills in ASEAN: An Overview.* Singapore: Institute of Southeast Asian Studies, 1986.

———; R. Hirono; and Narongchai Akrasanee, eds. *Industrial Restructuring in ASEAN and Japan: An Overview.* Singapore: Institute of Southeast Asian Studies, 1987.

——— and Norbert Wagner. "Privatization and Deregulation in ASEAN: An Overview". *ASEAN Economic Bulletin* 5, no. 3 (March 1989).

——— and Norbert Wagner, eds. *Marketization in ASEAN.* Singapore: Institute of Southeast Asian Studies, 1991.

Nguyen Phuc Long. "Le nouvelles recherches archéologiques au Vietnam . . .". *Arts Asiatiques*, Numéro special, 31 (1975).

Nicholas, Rhondda M. "Misperception and Muddled Thinking in Australia-ASEAN Relations". *Contemporary Southeast Asia* 5, no. 2 (September 1983).

Nishihara, Masashi. *East Asian Security and the Trilateral Countries.* A Report to the Trilateral Commission, no. 30. New York and London: New York University Press, 1985.

Nishikawa, Jun. *ASEAN and the United Nations System.* New York: UNITAR, 1983.

Nontapanthawat, Nimit. "Financial Cooperation in ASEAN". In J. Soedradjad Djiwandono and Hendra Esmara, eds., *International Financial Stability.*

Noordin Sopiee. "ASEAN and Regional Security". In *Regional Security in the Third World: Case Studies from Southeast Asia and the Middle East*, edited by Mohammed Ayoob. London: Croom Helm Ltd, 1986.

———; Chew Lay See; and Lim Siang Jin, eds. *ASEAN at the Crossroads: Obstacles, Options and Opportunities in Economic Co-operation.* Kuala Lumpur: ISIS, 1987.

Nor Laily Aziz. "Malaysia: Population and Development". Mimeographed. Malaysia: National Family Planning Board, 1981.

Nye, Joseph S. Jr., ed. *International Regionalism.* Boston: Little, Brown, 1968.

O'Brien, Peter and Herman Muegge. "Prospects for Intra-ASEAN Investment". *ASEAN Economic Bulletin* 4, no. 2 (November 1987).

Oei, Ann. "A Comparative Analysis of Tax Incentives in ASEAN Countries". *Malaya Law Review* 27, no. 1 (July 1985).

Oetama, Jakob. "The Present and Future Role of the Press in ASEAN Countries". In *Cultures in Encounter: Germany and the Southeast Asian Nations, A Documentation of the ASEAN Cultural Week, Tuebingen, Summer 1977* (Tubingen: Horst Erdmann Verlag, 1978).

Ogawa, N. "Urbanization and Internal Migration in Selected ASEAN Countries. Trends and Prospects". In *Urbanization and Migration in ASEAN Development*, edited by P. Hauser, D. Suits, and N. Ogawa. Hawaii: University of Hawaii Press, 1985.

Okita, Saburo. "Perspectives for the Asia-Pacific Region in the 21st Century". *ASIEN*, no. 42 (1992).

Olsen, Edward. *U.S.-Japan Strategic Reciprocity: A Neo-Internationalist View.* Stanford: Hoover Institution Press, 1985.

Olson, Mancur and Richard Zeckhauser. "An Economic Theory of Alliances". *Review of Economics and Statistics* 48 (1966).

Olson, Theodore. "Thinking Independently about Strategy in Southeast Asia". *Contemporary Southeast Asia* 11, no. 3 (December 1989).

Ooi, Guat Tin. *ASEAN Preferential Trading Arrangements (PTA): An Analysis of Potential Effects* on *Intra-Asean Trade*. Research Notes and Discussions Paper, no. 26. Singapore: Institute of Southeast Asian Studies, 1981.

Opening Statement by S. Dhanabalan, Minister of Foreign Affairs of Singapore, at the Fifteenth ASEAN Ministerial Meeting, Singapore, 14 June 1982.

Oriyama, Mitsutoshi. "Recent Trends in Japan-ASEAN Trade Relations". *Digest of Japanese Industry and Technology*, no. 238 (1987).

Orr, Robert M. "The Rising Sun: Japan's Foreign Aid to ASEAN, the Pacific Basin and the Republic of Korea". *Journal of International Affairs* 41 (Summer/Fall 1987).

Osborne, Susan, ed. *ASEAN External Economic Relations*. Singapore: Chopman Publishers, 1982.

Oshima, H.T. "The Construction Boom of the 1970s: The End of High Growth in the NICs and ASEAN?", *The Developing Economies* 24, no. 3 (September 1986).

Osteria, Trinidad S. "Recent Trends in Urbanization in the ASEAN Region: Implications for Health Programmes". *Southeast Asian Affairs 1987*. Singapore: Institute of Southeast Asian Studies, 1988.

Pacific Economic Cooperation Conference (PECC). Standing Committee Meeting, Singapore, 4 May 1990.

Packenham, Robert A. *Liberal America and the Third World*. Princeton, N.J.: Princeton University Press, 1973.

Palloni, Alberto. "Mortality in Latin America: Emerging Patterns". *Population and Development Review* 7 (1981).

Palmer, Norman D. *The New Regionalism in Asia and the Pacific*. Massachusetts: Lexington Books, 1991.

_____ and Howard C. Perkins. *International Relations: The World Community in Transition*. 3d ed. Boston: Houghton Mifflin, 1969.

Palmer, Ronald D. and Thomas J. Reckford. *Building ASEAN: 20 Years of Southeast Asian Cooperation*. New York; London: Praeger Publication, 1987.

Pangestu, Mari. "The Pattern of Direct Foreign Investment in ASEAN: The United States vs Japan". *ASEAN Economic Bulletin* 3, no. 3 (March 1987).

_____; Hadi Soesastro; and Mubariq Ahmad. "A New Look at Intra-ASEAN Economic Cooperation". *ASEAN Economic Bulletin* 8, no. 3 (March 1992).

Panit, Thakur. "Regional Integration Attempts in Southeast Asia: A Study of ASEAN's Problems and Progress". Ph.D. dissertation, Pennsylvania State University, 1980.

Paribatra, Sukhumbhand. "Political and Security Dimensions in ASEAN-Japan Relations: Thailand's Perspectives". Unpublished paper presented at Asia Dialogue Workshop, Bangkok, 23–24 January 1984.

Paribatra, M.R.S. "Can ASEAN Break the Stalemate?". *World Policy Journal* 3, no. 1 (1986).

Paribatra, Sukhumbhand. "The Challenge of Co-existence: ASEAN's Relations with Vietnam in the 1990s". *Contemporary Southeast Asia* 9, no. 2 (September 1987).

_____ and Chai-Anan Samudavanija. "Factors behind Armed Separatism: A Framework for Analysis". In *Armed Separatism in Southeast Asia*, edited by Lim Joo Jock with S. Vani. Singapore: Institute of Southeast Asian Studies, 1984.

_____ and Chai-Anan Samudavanija. "Internal Dimensions of Regional Security in Southeast Asia". In *Regional Security in the Third World: Case Studies from Southeast Asia and the Middle East*, edited by Mohammed Ayoob. London: Croom Helm, 1986.

Parreñas, J.C. "China and Japan in ASEAN's Strategic Perceptions". *Contemporary Southeast Asia* 12, no. 3 (December 1990).

Patrick, H.T. "Financial Development and Economic Growth in Underdeveloped Countries". *Economic Development and Cultural Change*, no. 14 (January 1966).

Pelkmans, Jacques and Norbert Wagner, eds. *Privatization and Deregulation in ASEAN and the EC: Making Markets More Effective*. Singapore: Institute of Southeast Asian Studies, 1990.

———— and Peter Sutherland. "Unfinished Business: The Credibility of 1992". In *Governing Europe: 1989 Annual Conference Proceedings, Vol. 1, The Single Market and Economic and Monetary Union*. CEPS Paper, no. 44. Brussels: Centre for European Policy Studies, 1990.

Pendakur, V. Setty. *Urban Transport in ASEAN*. Singapore: Institute of Southeast Asian Studies, 1984.

Pernia, E. *Urbanization, Population Growth and Economic Development in the Philippines*. Westport, Connecticut and London: Greenwood Press Inc., 1977.

Phantumvanit, Dhira and Juliet Lamont. *Regional Network on Sustainable Development*. Bangkok: Thailand Development Research Institute, 1990.

Phongpaichit, Pasuk. "Decision-making on Overseas Direct Investment by Japanese Small and Medium Industries in ASEAN and the Asian NICs". *ASEAN Economic Bulletin* 4, no. 3 (March 1988).

————. *The New Wave of Japanese Investments in ASEAN: Determinants and Prospects*. Singapore: Institute of Southeast Asian Studies, 1990.

Pike, Douglas. *PAVN: People's Army of Vietnam*. London: Brassey's, 1986.

Pillai, M.G.G. "ASEAN-EC Meeting: Evading the Issues". *Economic and Political Weekly* 25, no. 12 (1990).

Praet, P. and C. Stevens. "EEC ASEAN: Is the Door Half-open, or Half-closed?", *Euro-Asia Business Review* 6, no. 3 (July 1987).

Prakash, Sanjiv. "ASEAN Acquires New Teeth, New Worlds". *Defense and Foreign Affairs* 18 (November 1990).

Priebjrivat, Vuthiphong. *Financial Picture of the Thai Public Sector*. Thailand Development Research Institute Foundation, May 1987.

Pyle, Kenneth B. "Japan, the World, and the Twenty-First Century". In *The Political Economy of Japan*, edited by Takashi Inoguchi and Daniel I. Okimoto, vol. 2, *The Changing International Context*. Paulo Alto, Calif.: Stanford University Press, 1988.

Quah, Jon S.T. "Public Bureaucracy and Policy Implementation in Asia: An Introduction". *Southeast Asian Journal of Social Science* 15, no. 2 (1987).

Quisumbing, Purificacion V. "Problems and Prospects of ASEAN Law: Towards a Legal Framework for Regional Dispute Settlement". In *ASEAN Identity, Development and Culture*, edited by R.P. Anand and Purificacion V. Quisumbing. Honolulu: East-West Center, 1981.

Ramos-de Leon, Lilia, ed. *The Other Side of the Summit*. Manila: Foreign Service Institute, 1988.

Rana, Pradumna B. *ASEAN Exchange Rates: Policies and Trade Effects*. Singapore: Institute of Southeast Asian Studies, 1981.

———— and Florian A. Alburo, eds. *Economic Stabilization Policies in ASEAN Countries*. Singapore: Institute of Southeast Asian Studies, 1987.

Rasmussen, Eric. "The Competitiveness of U.S. Exports to ASEAN: A Business Economist's View". *ASEAN Economic Bulletin* 3, no. 3 (March 1987).

————. "Region Heads Towards New Phase of Economic Cooperation". *Economic Bulletin*, August 1987.

Rau, Robert L. "The Role of the Armed Forces and Police in Malaysia". In *The Armed Forces in Contemporary Asian Societies*, edited by Edward A. Olsen and Stephen Jurika, Jr. Boulder, Col.: Westview Press, 1986.

Reichel, H.C. "The European-Community and ASEAN". *Aussen Politik* 36, no. 2 (1985).

Report of the Public Sector Divestment Committee. Singapore: Ministry for Finance, 21 February 1987.

Richardson, Michael. "Thailand's Bargain Buy, But Indonesians Wonder Why". *Pacific Defence Reporter*, August 1987.

Richardson, Michael. "Singapore's A-4 Update". *Pacific Defence Reporter*, March 1988.

_____. "Huge Malay Arms Deal Signals Determination to Upgrade Defenses". *International Herald Tribune*, 4 October 1988.

_____. "U.S. is Relocating Forces as End of Manila Pact Nears". *International Herald Tribune*, 19 September 1989.

Richburg, Keith. "Cambodian Pullout: The Implications". *International Herald Tribune*, 19 September 1989.

Rieger, Hans Christoph. "ASEAN Economic Cooperation: Running in Circles or New Directions?" *Southeast Asian Affairs 1987*. Singapore: Institute of Southeast Asian Studies, 1987.

_____. *ASEAN Co-operation and Intra-ASEAN Trade*. Singapore: Institute of Southeast Asian Studies, 1985.

_____, compiler. *ASEAN Economic Co-operation: A Handbook*. Singapore: Institute of Southeast Asian Studies, 1991.

_____. "ASEAN-EC Cooperation: Some Concluding Remarks". In *Experiences in Regional Cooperation*, edited by Rita Beuter and Panos Tsakaloyannis. Maastricht: European Institute of Public Administration, 1987.

Rigg, Jonathan. *Southeast Asia: A Region in Transition; A Thematic Human Geography of the ASEAN Region*. London: Unwin Hyman, 1991.

Robison, R. *Indonesia: The Rise of Capital*. Canberra: Asian Studies Association of Australia, 1986.

Robison, Richard. "After the Gold-rush: The Politics of Economic Restructuring in Indonesia in the 1980s". In *South East Asia in the 1980s: The Politics of Economic Crisis*, edited by R. Robison, K. Hewison, and R. Higgott. Boston: Allen and Unwin, 1987.

Rose, Leo E. "India and ASEAN: Much Ado About Not Much". In *Economic, Political, and Security Issues in Southeast Asia in the 1980s*, edited by Robert A. Scalapino and Jusuf Wanandi. Berkeley: Institute of East Asian Studies, 1982.

Roth, Stanley. "Issues in Future US Policy: Negotiations over Military Base Rights". The United States-Philippines Relationship in the New Administration and Beyond. Report prepared for the use of the Committee on Foreign Relations, United States Senate. Washington, D.C.: Congressional Research Service, Library of Congress, 1988.

Royama, Michio. *The Asian Balance of Power: A Japanese View*. Adelphi Papers, no. 42. London: IISS, 1967.

Saaid, M. Shuhud. "The Singapore Army". *Asia Defence Journal* 6 (June 1987).

_____. "The Royal Brunei Armed Forces". *Asian Defence Journal* 1 (January 1988).

Sabloff, Jeremy A. and C.C. Lamber-Karlovsky. *Ancient Civilisation in the Indian Ocean: An Economic History from the Rise of Islam to 1750*. Cambridge: Cambridge University Press, 1985.

Saeng, Sanguanruang; Nisa Yuto; Preeyanuch Seangpasson; and Chucheep Piputsitee. "Development of Small and Medium Manufacturing Enterprises in Thailand". ADIPA Research Project, Vol. I: Main Report. Mimeographed. December 1979.

Saihoo, Patya. "Problems in ASEAN-Japan Cultural Exchange". *Asia Pacific Community*, no. 5 (1979).

_____. "Problems in Cultural Development in ASEAN". In *ASEAN Identity, Development and Culture*, edited by R.P. Anand and Purificacion V. Quisumbing. Diliman, Q.C.: University of the Philippines Law Center and East-West Center Culture Learning Institute, 1981.

Saksena, K.P. *Cooperation in Development: Problems and Prospects for India and ASEAN*. New Delhi: Sage Publications, 1986.

Samudavanija, Chai-Anan and Sukhumbhand Paribatra. "In Search of Balance: Prospects for Stability in Thailand during the Post-CPT Era". In *Durable Stability in Southeast Asia*, edited by Kusuma Snitvongse and Sukhumbhand Paribatra. Singapore: Institute of Southeast Asian Studies, 1987.

Sanchez, Aurora. "Non-tariff Barriers and Trade in ASEAN". *ASEAN Economic Bulletin* 4, no. 1 (July 1987).

Sandhu, K.S. "The ASEAN Equation". *Intersect* 1, no. 4 (April 1985).

Sandler, Todd, ed. *The Theory and Structures of International Political Economy*. Boulder, Colorado: Westview Press, 1980.

Saravanamuttu, J. "Malaysia's Look East Policy and Its Implications for Self-Sustaining Growth". Paper presented at the Seventh Malaysian Economic Convention, Kuala Lumpur, 1983.

_____. "Imperialism, Dependent Development and ASEAN Regionalism". *Journal of Contemporary Asia* 16, no. 2 (1986).

_____. "Japanese Economic Penetration in ASEAN in the Context of the International Division of Labor". *Journal of Contemporary Asia* 18, no. 2 (1988).

_____ and Sharom Ahmat. *ASEAN Non-Governmental Organizations: A Study of their Role, Objectives and Activities*. Penang: Universiti Sains Malaysia, 1986.

Sassheen, R.S. "The Singapore Armed Forces". *Asian Defence Journal* 4 (April 1989).

Satjipanon, Chaiyong. *Economic and Political Integration of the Southeast Asian Nations (ASEAN): The Path toward Regional Co-operation in Southeast Asia*. Ann Arbor, Mich.: University Microfilms International, 1988.

Saw, Swee-Hock. *The ASEAN Economies in Transition*. Singapore: Singapore University Press, 1980.

_____. "Growth and Structure of the ASEAN Labour Force". *Southeast Asian Journal of Social Science* 14, no. 2 (1986).

_____ and N.L. Sirisena. "Economic Framework of ASEAN Countries". In *Economic Problems and Prospects in ASEAN Countries*, edited by Saw Swee Hock and Lee Soo Ann. Singapore: Singapore University Press, 1979.

Schmitt-Rink, Gerhard. "Old and New Patterns of International Specialization: The Shares of Inter- and Intra-Industry Transactions in ASEAN-EC Trade, 1974–1982". *ASEAN Economic Bulletin* 2, no. 1 (July 1985).

Schulze, David L. "The ASEAN Finance Corporation". *ASEAN Economic Bulletin* 5, no. 1 (July 1988).

_____. "Monetization in ASEAN: 1970–1984". *Singapore Economic Review* 31, no. 2 (October 1986).

_____. "ASEAN Cooperation in Banking and Finance". In *ASEAN Economic Cooperation: A New Perspective*, edited by Hendra Esmara. Singapore: Chopmen Publishers for Federation of ASEAN Economic Associations and Ikatan Sarjana Ekonomi Indonesia, 1988.

Sekiguchi, Sueo, ed. *ASEAN-Japan Relations: Investment.* Singapore: Institute of Southeast Asian Studies, 1983.

_____. "Japanese Direct Foreign Investment and ASEAN Economies: A Japanese Perspective". In *ASEAN-Japan Relations: Investment*, edited by Sueo Sekiguchi. Singapore: Institute of Southeast Asian Studies, 1983.

Selmer, Jan and Tan Loong-Hoe, eds. *Economic Relations between Scandinavia and ASEAN: Issues on Trade, Investment, Technology Transfer and Business Culture.* Singapore: Institute of Southeast Asian Studies, 1986.

Selvaratnam, V. "Malaysia in 1981: A Year of Political Transition". *Southeast Asian Affairs 1982.* Singapore: Institute of Southeast Asian Studies, 1982.

Sen, Partha and Stephen J. Turnovsky. "Tariffs, Capital Accumulation and the Current Account". *International Economic Review* 30 (1989).

Senkuttuvan, Arun, ed. *MNCs and ASEAN Development in the 1980s.* Singapore: Institute of Southeast Asian Studies, 1981.

Septy Ruzui. *A Survey of Relations Between Indonesian, Malay and Some Philippine Languages.* Kuala Lumpur: Dewan Bahasa dan Pustaka, 1968.

Sharma, Basu. *Aspects of Industrial Relations in ASEAN.* Singapore: Institute of Southeast Asian Studies, 1985.

_____. "Changing Industrial Relations Patterns in ASEAN". *Business Review* 5, no. 2 (April 1986).

_____. "Regionalism and ASEAN Industrial Relations". *ASEAN Economic Bulletin* 3, no. 2 (November 1986).

Sharma, S.V.S. *Small Entrepreneurial Development in South Asian Countries: A Comparative Study.* New Delhi: Light & Life, 1979.

Sharma, Shankar. "ASEAN Oil Movements and Factors Affecting Intra-ASEAN Oil Trade". *Contemporary Southeast Asia* 10, no. 1 (June 1988).

_____. "Structural Change and Energy Policy in ASEAN". In *Energy Market and Policies in ASEAN*, edited by Shankar Sharma and Fereidun Fesharaki. Singapore: Institute of Southeast Asian Studies, 1991.

_____ and Fereidun Fesharaki. "The Asia-Pacific Gas Market: Implications for the ASEAN Gas Industry". *ASEAN Economic Bulletin* 6, no. 2 (November 1989).

_____ and Fereidun Fesharaki, eds. *Energy Market and Policies in ASEAN.* Singapore: Institute of Southeast Asian Studies, 1991.

_____ and Joseph L.H. Tan, eds. *Global Oil Trends: The Asia-Pacific Market in the 1990s.* Singapore: Institute of Southeast Asian Studies, 1991.

Shassheed, R.S. "Thai Armed Forces: Modernisation to Meet New Challenges". *Asia Defence Journal* 12 (December 1988).

Shee, Poon-Kim. "A Decade of ASEAN, 1967–1977". *Asian Survey* 17, no. 8 (1977).

Shenoy, George T.L. "The Emergence of a Legal Framework for Economic Policy in ASEAN". *Malayan Law Review* 29, no. 1 (July 1987).

Shibusawa, Masahide. *Japan and the Asian Pacific Region: Profile of Change.* London: Croom Helm for the Royal Institute of International Affairs, 1984.

Shimura, Akira and Takafumi Kitagawa. "Trend in Trade Relations Between Japan and ASEAN Countries". *Digest of Japanese Industry and Technology*, no. 228 (1987).

Shome, P. "Is the Corporate-Tax Shifted: Empirical-Evidence from ASEAN". *Public Finance Quarterly* 13, no. 1 (1985).

Siddayao, Corazon Morales. "Energy Policy Issues in Developing Countries: Lessons from ASEAN's Experience". *Energy Policy* 16, no. 6 (December 1988).

Sharon Siddique. "Contemporary Islamic Developments in ASEAN". In *Southeast Asian Affairs 1980*. Singapore: Heinemann Asia Pte Ltd., 1980.

―――. "Cultural Development in ASEAN: The Need for an Historical Perspective". In *ASEAN Identity, Development and Culture*, edited by R.P. Anand and Purificacion V. Quisumbing. Diliman, Q.C.: University of the Philippines Law Center and East-West Center Culture Learning Institute, 1981.

Simkin, C.G.F. *The Traditional Trade of Asia*. London: Oxford University Press, 1968.

Simon, Sheldon W. "China, Vietnam, and ASEAN: The Politics of Polarization". *Asian Survey* 19, no. 12 (1979).

―――. "ASEAN Security Prospects". *Journal of International Affairs* 41, no. 1 (1987).

―――. "ASEAN Strategies Situation in the 1980s". *Pacific Affairs* 60, no. 1 (1987).

―――. "ASEAN Security in the 1990s". *Asian Survey 1989* 29, no. 6 (1989).

―――. "United States Security Policy and ASEAN". *Current History* 89, no. 545 (March 1990).

Sinaga, Edward Janner. "ASEAN: Economic, Political and Defense Problems: Progress and Prospects in Regional Cooperation with Reference to the Role of Major Powers in Southeast Asia". Ph.D. dissertation, Graduate School of Arts and Sciences, George Washington University, 1974.

Singh, B. "Moscow New Cold-War Against ASEAN". *Asia Pacific Community*, no. 31 (1986).

Singh, Bilveer. "ASEAN's Arms Industries: Potential and Limits". *Comparative Strategy* 8, no. 2 (1989).

―――. *Soviet Relations with ASEAN, 1967–88*. Singapore: Singapore University Press, 1989.

Singh, L.P. *The Politics of Economic Cooperation in Asia: A Study of Asian International Organizations*. Columbia: University of Missouri Press, 1966.

Skully, Michael. *ASEAN Financial Cooperation: Development in Banking, Finance and Insurance*. London: Macmillan, 1985.

Smith, Herbert and Paul P.L. Cheung. "Trends in the Effects of Family Background on Educational Attainment in the Philippines". *American Journal of Sociology* 91 (1986).

Smith, Peter and Paul P.L. Cheung. "Social Origins and Sex-Differential Schooling in the Philippines". *Comparative Education Review* 25 (1981).

Smith, R.B. and W. Watson, eds. *Early South East Asia. Essays in Archaeology, History and Historical Geography*. Oxford: Oxford University Press, 1979.

Snitvongse, Kusuma. "Thai Government Responses to Armed Communist and Separatist Movements". In *Governments and Rebellions in Southeast Asia*, edited by Chandran Jeshurun. Singapore: Institute of Southeast Asian Studies, 1985.

Snitvongse, Kusuma and Sukhumbhand Paribrata, eds. *Durable Stability in Southeast Asia*. Singapore: Institute of Southeast Asian Studies, 1987.

Snooks, G.D.; A.J.S. Reid; and J.J. Pincus, eds. *Exploring Southeast Asia's Economic Past*. Melbourne: OUP, ANU and ISEAS, 1991.

Snow, Marcellus S. "Facilitating ASEAN-U.S. Trade and Direct Foreign Investment in Information Services: Alternative Policies and Their Effects". *ASEAN Economic Bulletin* 6, no. 1 (July 1989).

―――. "Facilitating ASEAN-U.S. Trade and Direct Foreign Investment in Information Services: Alternative Policies and Their Effects". *ASEAN Economic Bulletin* 6, no. 1 (July 1989).

Soedjatmoko. "Peace, Security and Human Dignity". Background Paper prepared for the Asian Conference on Religion and Peace. Singapore, 25 November 1976.

Soejono, R.P. "The Significance of the Excavation at Gilimanuk (Bali)". In *Early South East Asia. Essays in Archaeology, History and Historical Geography*, edited by R.B. Smith and W. Watson. Oxford: Oxford University Press, 1979.

Solidum, Estrella D. *Towards a Southeast Asian Community*. Quezon City: University of the Philippines Press, 1974.

_____. *Bilateral Summitry in ASEAN*. Manila: Foreign Service Institute, 1982.

_____ and Seah Chee Meow. *Decision-Making in an ASEAN Complementation Scheme: The Automotive Industry*. Singapore: Institute of Southeast Asian Studies, 1987.

Sornarajah, M. "The New International Economic Order, Investment Treaties and Foreign Investment Laws in ASEAN". *Malayan Law Review* 27 (December 1985).

Speech by Prime Minister Lee Kuan Yew at the opening of the Fifteenth ASEAN Ministerial Meeting, 14 June 1982, Singapore.

Sricharatchanya, Paisal. "The Chinese Firecracker". *Far Eastern Economic Review*, 8 December 1988.

"State Enterprise and Privatization". *Indonesia Business Digest* 1, no. 5 (June 1987).

Steiger, Jurgen. *Renewable Energy Resources in ASEAN*. Singapore: Institute of Southeast Asian Studies, 1988.

Sterling, John. "ASEAN: The Anti-Domino Factor". *Asian Affairs* 7, no. 5 (May/June 1980).

Steven, R. "Japanese Foreign Direct-Investment in Southeast Asia: From ASEAN to JASEAN". *Bulletin of Concerned Asian Scholars* 20, no. 4 (1988).

Stevens, Christopher. "The Implications of the EC's Development Policy for ASEAN". *ASEAN Economic Bulletin* 1, no. 3 (March 1985).

Stockholm International Peace Research Institute (SIPRI). *SIPRI Yearbook*. Oxford: Oxford University Press, annual.

Stubbs, Richard. *Hearts and Minds in Guerilla Warfare: The Malayan Emergency, 1948–60*. Kuala Lumpur: Oxford University Press, 1989.

_____. "Canada Relations with Malaysia: Picking Partners in ASEAN". *Pacific Affairs* 63, no. 3 (1990).

_____. "Subregional Security Cooperation in ASEAN: Military and Economic Imperatives and Political Obstacles". *Asian Survey* XXXII, no. 5 (May 1992).

Sudarsono, Juwono. "Security in Southeast Asia: The Circle of Conflict". In *Economic, Political, and Security Issues in Southeast Asia in the 1980s*, edited by Robert A. Scalapino and Jusuf Wanandi. Berkeley, California: Institute of East Asian Studies, University of California, 1982.

Sudo, Sueo. "From Fukuda to Takeshita: A Decade of Japan-ASEAN Relations". *Contemporary Southeast Asia* 10, no. 2 (September 1988).

Sueo, Sekiguchi, ed. *ASEAN-Japan Relations: Investment*. Singapore: Institute of Southeast Asian Studies, 1983.

Suh, Jang-Won. "New Forms of Industrial Cooperation". Report prepared for the ASEAN Committee on Industry Numerals and Energy. Kuala Lumpur: Asian and Pacific Development Centre, 1987.

Sukrasep, Vinita. *ASEAN in International Relations*. Bangkok: Institute of Security and International Studies, Chulalongkorn University, 1989.

Supachai, Panitchpakdi. "Investment in Finance in ASEAN: Problems and Relevant Issues". In Chia Siow Yue, ed., *ASEAN Economic Co-operation*.

Suriyamongkol, M.L. "The Role of U.S. Foreign Investment in ASEAN Industrial Co-operation". *ASEAN Economic Bulletin* 4, no. 2 (November 1987).

"Survey of ASEAN Port Development Projects". *Dredging and Port Construction* 13, no. 4 (April 1986).

Suryadinata, Leo. *China and the ASEAN States: The Ethnic Chinese Dimension.* Singapore: Singapore University Press, 1985.

Suwidjana, Njoman. *Jakarta Dollar Market: A Case of Financial Development in ASEAN.* Occasional Paper, no. 76. Singapore: Institute of Southeast Asian Studies, 1984.

Syed Naguib al-Attas. *Preliminary Statement on a General Theory of the Islamization of the Malay–Indonesian Archipelago.* Kuala Lumpur: Dewan Bahasa dan Pustaka, 1969.

Tadae, Takubo. "Senryaku naki kaigai enjo no kyoko" [Fallacy of foreign aid without strategy]. *Voice*, November 1981.

Tai, Ming Cheung. "Enemy Spotting: Malaysia buys Military Muscle at Last to Defend Itself". *Far Eastern Economic Review*, 24 November 1988.

_____. *Growth of Chinese Naval Power: Priorities, Goals, Missions, and Regional Implications.* Singapore: Institute of Southeast Asian Studies, 1990.

Takeo, Tsuchiya. *Nihon no keizai 'enjo' shin dai toa kyoeiken enjo kiso tsukuir"* [Japan's foreign "aid" paves the way for a new Greater East Asia Co-Prosperity Sphere]. *Sekai kara* 18, Special Edition (Winter 1984).

Takubo, Tade. "First Round of Nakasone's Diplomacy". *Asia Pacific Community* 2 (Summer 1983).

Talisayon, Serafin D. *Designing for Consensus: The ASEAN Grid.* Singapore: Institute of Southeast Asian Studies, 1989.

Tambunlertchai, Somsak and Umphon Panachet. "Foreign Direct Investment in ASEAN". Paper prepared for the 13th Federation of ASEAN Economic Associations on Foreign Investment in ASEAN: Strategies and Policies, held in Penang, Malaysia, on 17–19 November 1988.

Tan, Gerald. *Trade Liberalization in ASEAN: An Empirical Study of the Preferential Trading Arrangements.* Singapore: Institute of Southeast Asian Studies, 1982.

_____. "Asean Preferential Trading Arrangements: An Overview". In *ASEAN at the Crossroads: Obstacles, Options and Opportunities in Economic Co-operation*, edited by Noordin Sopiee, Chew Lay See, and Lim Siang Jin. Kuala Lumpur: Institute of Strategic and International Studies, 1987.

Tan, Joseph L.H. and Narongchai Akrasanee, eds. *ASEAN-U.S. Economic Relations: Private Enterprise as a Means for Economic Development and Co-operation.* Singapore: Institute of Southeast Asian Studies, 1991.

Tan, Kong Yam; Toh Mun Heng; and Linda Low. "ASEAN and Pacific Economic Co-operation". *ASEAN Economic Bulletin* 8, no. 3 (March 1992).

Tan, Loong-Hoe and Narongchai Akrasanee, eds. *ASEAN-U.S. Economic Relations: Changes in the Economic Environment and Opportunities.* Singapore: Institute of Southeast Asian Studies, 1988.

_____ and Chia Siow-Yue, eds. *Trade, Protectionism, and Industrial Adjustment in Consumer Electronics: Asian Responses to North America.* Singapore: Institute of Southeast Asian Studies, 1989.

Tan, Loong-Hoe Joseph and Shankar Sharma, eds. *Trade, Protectionism, and Industrial Adjustment in Vegetable Oils: Asian Responses to North America.* Singapore: Institute of Southeast Asian Studies, 1989.

Tanaka, Tsuneo. "Trade Between Japan and ASEAN". *Digest of Japanese Industry and Technology*, no. 217 (1986).

Tasker, Rodney. "Purchasing Power". *Far Eastern Economic Review*, 23 March 1989.

_____. "Diplomatic Dog Fight". *Far Eastern Economic Review*, 25 October 1984.

Tate, Muzaffar D.J. *The Making of South-East Asia*, vol. 1.

Tatsumi, Okabe, ed. *Twenty Years of ASEAN: Its Survival and Development*. Tokyo: Japan Institute of International Affairs, 1988.

_____. "Hachijunedai ni okeru Nihon no Tonan Ajia seiksaku" [Japan's Southeast Asian policy in the 1980s]. *Nihon Kokusai Mondai Kenkyusho*, 1980.

Taylor, Keith. "Madagascar in the Ancient Malayo-Polynesian Myths". In *Explorations in Early Southeast Asian History: The Origins of Southeast Asian Statecraft*, edited by Kenneth R. Hall and John K. Whitmore. Ann Arbor: Michigan Papers on South and Southeast Asia, 1976.

Taylor, Paul. "Intergovernmentalism in the European Communities in the 1970s; Patterns and Prospectives". *International Organization* 36, no. 4 (Autumn 1982).

Taylor, R.H. and P.C.I. Ayre. *ASEAN-EC Economic and Political Relations*. London: School of Oriental and African Studies, University of London, 1986.

Teo, Eric. "ASEAN-EEC Diplomatic Consultations on the Eve of An Extended Kuala Lumpur Agreement". *Contemporary Southeast Asia* 7, no. 2 (September 1985).

Testimony Before U.S. Senate Foreign Relations East Asian Subcommittee. Washington, D.C., 8–10 June 1982.

"Thailand: Chinese Fighter Interest". *Milavnews*, no. 328 (February 1989).

Thakur, Ramesh. "Liberalism, Democracy and Development: Philosophical Dilemmas in Third World Politics". *Political Studies* 30, no. 3 (September 1982).

Thambipillai, Pushpa. "Prospects for South Asian Regional Cooperation: Lessons from ASEAN". *Contemporary Southeast Asia* 8, no. 4 (March 1987).

_____ and J. Saravanamuttu. *ASEAN Negotiations: Two Insights*. Singapore: Institute of Southeast Asian Studies, 1985.

Thanat Khoman. "Reminiscences". *Contemporary Southeast Asia* 10, no. 1 (June 1988).

The Group of Fourteen. *ASEAN: The Way Forward*. Kuala Lumpur: Institute of Strategic and International Studies, 1987.

The Importance of Being ASEAN. Kuala Lumpur: Institute of Strategic and International Studies, Malaysia, 1987.

The Jakarta Resolution, adopted at the Third ASEAN Ministerial Meeting on the Environment, Jakarta, Indonesia, on 29–30 October 1987.

The Machine Tool Industry in the ASEAN Region. 2 vols. Vienna: UNIDO, 1986.

The Military Balance, 1989–1990. London: International Institute for Strategic Studies, 1989.

"The Morbidity and Mortality Differentials: ASEAN Population Programme Phase III: Thailand and Country Study Report". Bangkok: Institute for Population and Social Research, Mahidol University, 1988.

The Pentagon Papers. New York: Bantam, 1971.

"The Philippine Air Force". *International Air Forces*. London: International Institute for Strategic Studies.

The Senator Gravel Edition. *The Pentagon Papers: The Defense Department History of United States Decisionmaking on Vietnam*, 4 vols. Boston: Beacon Press, 1971.

The Value of Children: A Cross-National Study. 7 vols. Hawaii: East West Population Institute, 1975–1979.

Thorn, Richard S. *The Rising Yen: The Impact of Japanese Financial Liberalization on World Capital Markets*. Singapore: Institute of Southeast Asian Studies, 1987.

Thornton, John. "The Nature of Japan's Trading Relationship with ASEAN Countries, Hong Kong, and South Korea". *ASEAN Economic Bulletin* 3, no. 3 (March 1987).

Thrift, N. "The geography of international disorder". In *A World in Crisis: Geographical Perspectives*, edited by R. Johnston and P.J. Taylor. London: Blackwell, 1986.

Tibbetts, G.R. *Arab Navigation in the Indian Ocean Before the Coming of the Portuguese*. London: Royal Asiatic Society of Great Britain and Ireland, 1971.

———. *A Study of the Arabic Texts Containing Materials on South-East Asia*. Leiden, 1979.

Tilman, Robert O. "Mutual Predictability of Elite Behaviour: The Probable Contributions of the ASEAN Framework". Paper presented at a symposium on The Malay World in Transition, Ohio University, May 1979.

———. "Asia, ASEAN and America in the Eighties: The Agonies of Maturing Relationships". *Contemporary Southeast Asia* 2, no. 4 (March 1981).

Tin Maung Maung Than. "Burma's National Security and Defence Posture". *Contemporary Southeast Asia* 11, no. 1 (June 1989).

Tinker, Hugh. "The Search for the History of Southeast Asia". *Journal of Southeast Asian Studies* 11 (September 1980).

Tironi, Ernesto. "Trade Relations between Latin America and the Asian Advanced Developing Countries". Eleventh Pacific Trade and Development Conference, Seoul, 1–4 September 1980.

Toh, Kin Woon. "The Market Economies of Southeast Asia in 1987: Let Down by Agriculture". *Southeast Asian Affairs 1988*. Singapore: Institute of Southeast Asian Studies, 1988.

Toh, Mun Heng and Linda Low. *Economic Impact of the Withdrawal of the GSP on Singapore*. Singapore: Institute of Southeast Asian Studies, 1991.

———. "Singapore's Service Sector Development in the ASEAN Context". *ASEAN Economic Bulletin* 6, no. 1 (July 1989).

Tolentino, A.S. "Legislative Response to Marine Threats in the ASEAN Subregion". *Ambio* 17, no. 3 (1986).

Tyabji, Amina. "Monetary Policies and Financial Structures in ASEAN". *Contemporary Southeast Asia* 7, no. 3 (December 1985).

———. "Social Security Systems in *ASEAN*". *ASEAN Economic Bulletin* 3, no. 1 (July 1986).

Tyers, Rodney et al. "ASEAN and China Exports of Labour-Intensive Manufactures: Performance and Prospects". *ASEAN Economic Bulletin* 3, no. 3 (March 1987).

U Tun Wai. *Role of Foreign Capital in Southeast Asian Countries*. Singapore: Institute of Southeast Asian Studies, 1989.

———. "ASEAN Finance and Banking Trends in 1988". *Southeast Asian Affairs 1989*. Singapore: Institute of Southeast Asian Studies, 1989.

U.S. Arms Control and Disarmament Agency. *World Military Expenditures and Arms Transfers*. Washington, D.C.: U.S. Government Printing Office, various issues.

"U.S.-ASEAN Dialogue Held in Washington". *State Department Bulletin*, April 1988.

United Nations Centre on Transnational Corporations. "Transnational Corporations and the Electronics Industries of ASEAN Economies". UNCTC Current Studies Ser. A, no. 5, 1987.

United Nations. "Economic Co-operation among Member Countries of ASEAN". *Journal of Development Planning*, no. 7 (1974).

———. *Migration, Urbanization, and Development in Indonesia*. New York: United Nations, 1981.

_____. *Migration, Urbanization, and Development in Thailand.* New York: United Nations, 1981.

_____. *World Population Prospects: Estimates and Projections as Assessed in 1982.* New York: United Nations, 1985.

United States Department of Commerce. "U.S. Trade with East Asian Countries". Typescript, dated 30 January 1980.

United States: Vietnam Relations, 1945–1967, 12 vols. Washington, D.C.: Government Printing Office, 1971.

"Unsuitably Equipped". *Far Eastern Economic Review,* 26 November 1987.

Urban, Mark. "Brunei to Buy Arms for £250m from UK". *The Independent,* 21 October 1989.

van der Kroef, Justus M. *Communism in Southeast Asia.* London: Macmillan, 1981.

van der Meulen, W.J. "Suvaradvipa and the Chryse Chersonesos". *Indonesia,* no. 18 (October 1974).

van Leur, J.C. *Indonesian Trade and Society.* The Hague: W. van Hoeve, 1955.

van Naerssen, F.H. *The Economic and Administrative History of Early Indonesia.* Leiden, 1977.

Vaubel, Roland. "A Public Choice Approach to International Organization". *Public Choice* 51 (1986).

Vicuña, Francisco Orrego. "Prospects of Co-operation between Latin America and the ASEAN Countries". *Contemporary Southeast Asia* 4, no. 1 (June 1982).

_____ and Juan Reutter. "Economic Co-operation and Conflict in the Pacific Basin: A South American View". Pacific Forum Symposium, Bangkok, 14–15 November 1981.

Villegas, Bernado, M. "The Challenge to ASEAN Economic Co-operation". *Contemporary Southeast Asia* 9, no. 2 (September 1987).

Viner, Jacob. *The Customs Union Issues.* New York, NY: Carnegie Endowment, 1950.

Viraphol, Sarasin. "The People's Republic of China and Southeast Asia: A Security Consideration for the 1980s". In *Economic, Political and Security Issues in Southeast Asia in the 1980s,* edited by Robert A. Scalapino and Jusuf Wanandi. Berkeley, California: Institute of East Asian Studies, University of California, 1982.

Vo Nhan Tri. *Vietnam's Economic Policy Since 1975.* Singapore: Institute of Southeast Asian Studies, 1990.

Vorys, Karl von. *Democracy without Consensus: Communalism and Political Stability in Malaysia.* Princeton: Princeton University Press, 1975.

Wadhva, Charan D. and Mukul G. Asher, eds. *ASEAN-South Asia Economic Relations.* Singapore: Institute of Southeast Asian Studies, 1985.

Waelbroeck, Jean; Peter Praet; and Hans Christoph Rieger. *ASEAN- EEC Trade in Services.* Singapore: Institute of Southeast Asian Studies, 1985.

Wagner, Norbert, ed. *ASEAN and the EC: The Impact of 1992.* Singapore: Institute of Southeast Asian Studies, 1991.

_____. *ASEAN and the EC: European Investment in ASEAN.* Singapore: Institute of Southeast Asian Studies, 1989.

Wallerstein, Immanuel. *The Modern World System: Capitalist Agriculture and the Origins of the European World Economy in the Sixteen Century.* New York: Academic Press, 1974.

Walsh, John E. "Cultural Components of the Search for Social Justice in ASEAN: A Westerner's View". In *ASEAN Identity, Development and Culture,* edited by R.P. Anand and Purificacion V. Quisumbing. Diliman, Q.C.: University of the Philippines Law Center and East-West Center Culture Learning Institute, 1981.

Wanandi, Jusuf. "A View from ASEAN on the Interest and Role of the United States in South-east Asia". In *Regional Security Developments and Stability in Southeast Asia*. Singapore: Institute of Southeast Asian Studies, 1980.

_____. *ASEAN and Security Cooperation in Southeast Asia*. Jakarta: Centre for Strategic and International Studies, 1990.

_____. "Global Changes and Its Impact on the Asia-Pacific Region: An ASEAN View". Jakarta: Centre for Strategic and International Studies, M52/91.

_____. "Politico-Security Dimensions of Southeast Asia". *Asian Survey* 17, no. 8 (1977).

Wang, Bee-Lan. "Sex and Ethnic Differences in Educational Investment in Malaysia: The Effect of Reward Structures". *Comparative Education Review* 24 (1980).

Wang, Gungwu. "Ethnicity and Religion in Social Development". In *The ASEAN Success Story: Social, Economic and Political Dimensions*, edited by Linda G. Martin. Hawaii: East-West Center, 1987.

_____. "China and South-East Asia, 1402–1424". In *Studies in the Social History of China and South-East Asia: Essays in Memory of Victor Purcell*, edited by Jerome Ch'en and Nicolas Tarling. Cambridge: Cambridge University Press, 1970.

Wang, Ting Min. "Growth of ASEAN Trade and Tourism". In *ASEAN Economies In Transition*, edited by Saw. Singapore: Singapore University Press, 1980.

Warr, Peter G. "Trade Versus Aid in ASEAN-Australian Economic Relations". *ASEAN Economic Bulletin* 1, no. 3 (March 1985).

Watanabe, Koji. "Japan and Southeast Asia, 1980". *Asia Pacific Community* 10 (Fall 1980).

Weatherbee, D.E. "The Philippines and ASEAN: Options for Aquino". *Asian Survey* 21, no. 12 (1987).

_____. *ASEAN and Pacific Regionalism*. Bangkok: Institute of Security and International Studies, Chulalongkorn University, 1989.

_____. *ASEAN after Cambodia: Reordering Southeast Asia*. New York: Asia Society, 1989.

Weinstein, Franklin B. *Indonesian Foreign Policy and the Dilemma of Dependence, From Sukarno to Soeharto*. Ithaca: Cornell University Press, 1976.

Wells, Mike. "Brunei's Armed Forces Set for $400m Boost". *Jane's Defence Weekly*, 4 November 1989.

White, David. "UK, Malaysia Sign £1bn Arms Deal". *Financial Times*, 28 September 1988.

Wiboonchutikula, Paitoon. *ASEAN and the EC: Technological Trends and Their Impaact on ASEAN Industries*. Singapore: Institute of Southeast Asian Studies, 1990.

Wightman, David R. *Toward Economic Cooperation in Asia: The United Nations Economic Commission for Asia and the Far East*. New Haven: Yale University Press, 1963.

Wilson, Dick. *The Neutralization of Southeast Asia*. New York: Praeger Publishers, 1975.

_____. "European attractions: East Asian manufacturers set up factories in Britain". *Far Eastern Economic Review*, 25 August 1988.

Wing, Thye Woo. "The Impact of U.S. Policy Mix on the ASEAN Economies, 1980–84: The Neglected European-Japanese Connection". *ASEAN Economic Bulletin* 3, no. 2 (November 1986).

Wolters, O.W. "Northwestern Cambodia in the Seventh Century". *Bulletin of the School of Oriental and African Studies* 37, no. 2 (1974).

_____. "Khmer 'Hinduism' in the Seventh Century". In *Early South East Asia. Essays in Archaeology History and Historical Geography*, edited by R.B. Smith and W. Watson. Oxford: Oxford University Press, 1979.

_____. *History, Culture, and Region in Southeast Asian Perspectives.* Singapore: Institute of Southeast Asian Studies, 1982.

Wong, Aline K. and Paul P.L. Cheung. "Demographic and Social Development: Taking Stock for the Morrow". In *The ASEAN Success Story: Social, Economic and Political Dimensions*, edited by Linda G. Martin. Hawaii: East-West Center, 1987.

Wong, Anny. *Japan's Comprehensive National Security Strategy and Its Economic Cooperation with the Asean Countries.* Hong Kong: Hong Kong Institute of Asia-Pacific Studies, Chinese University of Hong Kong, 1991.

_____. "Japan's National Security and Cultivation of ASEAN Elites". *Contemporary Southeast Asia* 12, no. 4 (March 1991).

Wong, James. *ASEAN Economies in Perspective.* Philadelphia: Institute for the Study of Human Issues, 1979.

Wong, John. *ASEAN Economies in Perspective: A Comparative Study of Indonesia, Malaysia, The Philippines, Singapore and Thailand.* Hongkong: The Macmillan Press Ltd., 1979.

_____. *Regional Industrial Cooperation. Experiences and Perspective of ASEAN and the Andean Pact.* Vienna: United Nations Industrial Development Organisation, 1986.

_____. "The ASEAN Model of Regional Cooperation". In *Lessons in Development: A Comparative Study of Asia and Latin America*, edited by S. Naya, M. Urrutia, S. Mark and A. Fuentes. San Francisco: International Center for Economic Growth, 1989.

_____. "ASEAN Economic Cooperation Facing New Challenges". *Singapore Stock Exchange Journal* 17, no. 7 (July 1989).

_____ and A. Wong. "Equity Performance: Some Social Implications of Development in ASEAN". In *Aspects of ASEAN*, edited by M. Suh. Munich: Weltforum Verlag, 1984.

Wong, Steven C.M. "Asean Co-operation in Tourism: Looking Back and Looking Forward". In *ASEAN at the Crossroads: Obstacles. Options and Opportunities in Economic Co-operation*, edited by Noordin Sopiee, Chew Lay See, and Lim Siang Jin. Kuala Lumpur: Institute of Strategic and International Studies, 1987.

Wong, Steven. *A Case for a Malaysian Travel Tax.* Malaysia: Institute of Strategic and International Studies, 1987.

Wood, Perry and Jimmy W. Wheeler. *ASEAN in the 1990s: New Challenges, New Directions.* Indianapolis, Ind.: Hudson Institute, 1990.

World Bank. "Indonesian Cottage and Small Industry in the National Economy". Washington, D.C., 9 November 1979.

_____. "Malaysia: Development Issues and Prospects of Small Enterprises". Washington, D.C., 26 April 1982.

Yamada, T. "Foreign Investment in the ASEAN Region". In *ASEAN as a Positive Strategy for Foreign Investment*, edited by L. R. Vasey. Honolulu: Pacific Forum, 1978.

Yano, Toru. "Toward a Reorientation of Asian Policy: The Fukuda Doctrine and Japanese-U.S. Cooperation". In *Encounter at Shimoda: Search for a New Pacific Partner*, edited by Herbert Passin and Akira Iriye. Boulder, Colorado: Westview Press, 1979.

_____. Special lecture given at the Faculty of Political Science, Thammasat University, 13 January 1984.

Yasutomo, Dennis. *The Manner of Giving: Strategic Aid and Japan's Foreign Policy.* Lexington: D.C. Heath, 1986.

Yenko, Aleth L. "Monetary Base Management and BOP Movements: The ASEAN Countries". *ASEAN Economic Bulletin* 1, no. 3 (March 1985).

Yenko, Aleth. *Exchange Rate Regimes of ASEAN Countries: A Critical Evaluation*. Singapore: Institute of Southeast Asian Studies, 1982.

Yeung, Y.M. and C.P. Lo, eds. *Changing Asian Cities: Readings in Urbanization*. Kuala Lumpur: Oxford University Press, 1976.

Yoshihara, Kunio. *Japanese Investment in Southeast Asia*. Japan: Center for Southeast Asian Studies, 1978.

_____. *The Rise of Ersatz Capitalism in Southeast Asia*. Singapore: Oxford University Press, 1988.

Young, E. "Development co-operation in Asean: Balancing free trade and regional planning". Unpublished Ph.D. dissertation, University of Michigan, 1981.

_____. "The Foreign-Capital Issue in the ASEAN Chambers of Commerce and Industry". *Asian Survey* 26, no. 6 (1986).

Yu, Insun. "Law and Family in Seventeenth and Eighteenth Century Vietnam". Ph.D. thesis, University of Michigan, Ann Arbor, 1978.

Yu, Peter Kien-Hong. "Singapore Faces Training Dilemma". *Jane's Defence Weekly*, 30 September 1989.

Zakaria Haji Ahmad. "Political and Security Dimensions in ASEAN-Japan Relations: A Malaysian Perspective". Unpublished paper presented at Asia Dialogue Workshop, Bangkok, 23–24 January 1984.

_____. "ASEAN and Pan-Pacific Cooperation: The Long Way Ahead". *Asia Pacific Community*, no. 30 (1985).

_____. "The World of ASEAN Decision-Makers: A Study of Bureaucratic Elite Perceptions in Malaysia, the Philippines and Singapore". *Contemporary Southeast Asia* 8, no. 3 (December 1986).

_____. "Configurative and Comparative Aspects of Military-Civilian Relations". In Zakaria and Crouch, eds. *Military-Civilian Relations*.

_____. "The World of ASEAN Decision-Makers: A Study of Bureaucratic Elite Perceptions in Malaysia, the Philippines and Singapore". *Contemporary Southeast Asia* 8, no. 3 (December 1986).

_____. "The Military and Development in Malaysia and Brunei, with a short survey on Singapore". In Djiwandono and Yong, eds., *Soldiers and Stability*.

_____ and Harold Crouch, eds. *Military-Civilian Relations in Southeast Asia*. Kuala Lumpur: Oxford University Press, 1985.

Zarkovic, M. "The Revival of ASEAN". *Review of International Affairs*, 5 October 1977.

THE COMPILERS (designation and affiliation updated for Second Reprint Edition 2003)

K.S. Sandhu, Ph.D., deceased, was Director of the Institute of Southeast Asian Studies, Singapore.

Sharon Siddique, Ph.D., formerly Deputy Director of the Institute of Southeast Asian Studies, Singapore, is now a partner in a regional research consulting firm.

Chandran Jeshurun, Ph.D. was formerly Senior Fellow at the Institute of Southeast Asian Studies, Singapore.

Ananda Rajah, Ph.D., formerly with the Institute of Southeast Asian Studies, Singapore, is now Associate Professor at the Department of Sociology, National University of Singapore.

Joseph L.H. Tan, Ph.D., was formerly Senior Fellow at the Institute of Southeast Asian Studies, Singapore.

Pushpa Thambipillai, Ph.D., formerly with the Institute of Southeast Asian Studies, Singapore, is now Senior Lecturer at the Department of Public Policy, Faculty of Business, Economics and Policy Studies, University of Brunei Darussalam.

MYANMAR

CHINA

L
A
O
S

V
I
E
T
N
A
M

THAILAND

■Bangkok

CAMBODIA

SOU
CH
SE

BRUNE
DARUSSA
Bandar Seri Beg

MALAYSIA
(Peninsular Malaysia)

■Kuala Lumpur

SINGAPORE

(East
Malaysi

I N D O N E S I

INDIAN
OCEAN

Jakarta
■

Members of ASEAN
Brunei Darussalam, Indonesia, Malaysia, Philippines, S